Second Canadian E

COGNITIVE
PSYCHOLOGY
In and Out of the Laboratory

UNIVERSITY OF
WATERLOO

Jennifer Stolz

Jonathan Fugelsang

Myra Fernandes

Kendall Hunt
publishing company

Cover image © Shutterstock.com

Source: Any uncredited interior images are from *Cognitive Psychology: In and Out of the Laboratory*, 4e, by Kathleen M. Galotti, published by Thomson Wadsworth, Copyright 2008, 2004, by Thomson Wadsworth.

Kendall Hunt
publishing company

www.kendallhunt.com
Send all inquiries to:
4050 Westmark Drive
Dubuque, IA 52004-1840

ISBN 978-1-5249-7997-9

Published in the United States of America

About the Authors

Jennifer A. Stolz holds a B.S. in psychology from Union College and a Ph.D. in psychology from the University at Albany, State University of New York. She is a full professor of psychology at the University of Waterloo, and was previously the associate chair for undergraduate studies in psychology at the University of Waterloo. She teaches courses in cognitive psychology, memory, attention, and evolutionary psychology.

Dr. Stolz has published numerous papers on reading and spatial attention and has served as consulting editor of premier journals in psychology, including the *Journal of Experimental Psychology: Learning, Memory, and Cognition*, the *Journal of Experimental Psychology: Human Perception and Performance, Memory & Cognition,* and the *Canadian Journal of Experimental Psychology.* She was awarded a *Young Investigator Award in Experimental Psychology* by Division 3 of the American Psychological Association, and the *Premier's Research Excellence Award* by the Province of Ontario. Her work has been continually funded by the Natural Sciences and Engineering Research Council of Canada.

Dr. Stolz is the parent of two boys, Zachary and Jacob. Her spare time is devoted to ultrarunning and hiking.

Jonathan Fugelsang holds a B.A. in psychology from Lakehead University as well as an M.A. and Ph.D. from the University of Saskatchewan. He is a Professor in the cognitive area of the psychology department at the University of Waterloo, and is an affiliated faculty member of the Centre for Theoretical Neuroscience. He teaches courses in cognitive psychology, reasoning, decision making, and statistics.

Dr. Fugelsang's research spans several areas in cognitive psychology and cognitive neuroscience. Recently, his work has predominantly focused on the interplay between intuitive and analytic processes supporting complex reasoning and decision making. These decisions may involve analogical, deductive, or probabilistic information. His lab has also extended their lines of inquiry to look at the role of intuitive and analytic processes in real world domains, such as creativity, moral judgments, religious beliefs, and technology use. His research is funded by the Natural Sciences and Engineering Research Council of Canada.

In his spare time, Dr. Fugelsang enjoys running, cycling, and fishing. Together with his wife Natalie, and his two children, Aiden and Ava, he also enjoys travelling to warmer climates on occasion to escape the Canadian winters.

Myra Fernandes holds a B.Sc. (1995) in Psychology & Biology, University of Waterloo, and MA (1996) and PhD (2001) in Cognitive Neuropsychology, University of Toronto. She is a Professor in Cognitive Neuroscience at the University of Waterloo. Her research aims to identify cognitive processes and key brain structures supporting memory, using a variety of methodologies such as fMRI and behavioural testing in young adults, in aging individuals, and in those with a past head injury or concussion.

Dr. Fernandes has been recognized with numerous honours and distinctions, including the Canadian Psychological Association's President's New Researcher Award, and the Ontario Ministry of Research & Innovation's Research Excellence Award. She was also an associate editor for the journal 'Memory & Cognition', and past associate editor for the 'Journal of Gerontology'. Dr. Fernandes is a Fellow of the Association for Psychological Science and the Canadian Society for Brain Behaviour and Cognitive Science. She served on the Natural Sciences and Engineering Research Council of Canada's panel, and the Canadian Institutes of Health Research panel, reviewing grants from Canadian researchers. Dr. Fernandes is the first recipient of the Women in Cognitive Science Canada Mentorship Award. She has published numerous peer-reviewed articles, multiple book chapters, as well as books. Dr. Fernandes has two children, Martinique and Misha, who are both inspirations and constant reminders of what is truly important in life. Together with her husband Marek, she enjoys travelling and hiking from the east coast in Newfoundland, to the streets of Montreal, and through to the Rocky Mountains in Alberta.

Contents

Preface

Undergraduate students studying psychology have different reactions to the field of cognitive psychology. Some find it exciting and elegant, covering topics essential to understanding the human mind. Cognitive psychology after all, raises questions about how the mind works—how we perceive people, events, and things; how and what we remember; how we mentally organize information; how we call on our mental information and resources to make important decisions. Other students find the field of cognitive psychology technical and "geeky"—filled with complicated models of phenomena far removed from everyday life. Our goal in writing this book was to try to bridge that gap—to reach out to students who are in the latter camp and show them what this field offers to be excited about. We wanted to strengthen the link between controlled experiments conducted in the laboratory and our everyday life experiences. Too often, cognition texts focus exclusively on the lab research, without showing students how that work bears on important, real-world issues of consequence. We hope that when students finish this book, they will see why cognitive psychologists are so passionate about their topic and their research, and how this work broadens our understanding of how our cognition operates in the real world.

PEDAGOGICAL PHILOSOPHY: ENCOURAGING INSTRUCTOR CUSTOMIZATION

A textbook author can choose either to be comprehensive and strive for encyclopedic coverage or to be selective and omit many worthwhile topics and studies. We hope we've struck a balance between these extremes. While it is impossible to expect to cover all that cognitive psychology has to offer in one textbook and course, we have tried to include all of the key features and basic findings from the field of cognitive psychology. Chapters are relatively short, in the hope instructors will supplement the text with other readings. The relative brevity of the text is intended to encourage instructors to supplement and customize it with added coverage on topics they find especially interesting.

THE ROLE OF CONTEXT: WHAT SHAPES AND CONSTRAINS COGNITION

Our goal is to encourage instructors and students alike to consider cognitive phenomena as having contexts that both foster and constrain their occurrence. Universals assumed or generalized from the laboratory do not always translate to every person in every situation. Too often, topics in cognitive psychology are presented as absolute, unchanging aspects of everyone's experience. Recent work in developmental psychology, aging, and individual differences strongly suggests that this presentation is, at best, oversimplification and, at worst, fiction.

ORGANIZATION OF THIS BOOK

This book is intended for a one-semester or one-term course for students who have already completed an introductory psychology course. It is organized into four parts. The first, containing the introductory chapter, locates the field historically, theoretically, and methodologically. In this chapter we introduce the major schools of thought that underlie the field of cognitive psychology and review the major methodological designs typically used by researchers in the field. A second chapter reviews the major structures of the brain and major neuroscientific methods of study.

Part II is a review of topics that would generally be regarded as core aspects of cognition: perception, attention, and memory. The emphasis in these chapters is to review both the "classic" studies that define the field and the newer approaches that challenge long-standing assumptions. The focus of Part III is on knowledge representation and organization. These chapters centre on questions of how we mentally represent and store the vast amounts of information we acquire throughout our lives. Part IV covers topics such as reasoning and decision making, as well as individual differences, effects of normal aging on cognition, and the ever-popular topic of gender differences. These chapters are meant to highlight how basic cognitive functions can be—and are—influenced by several factors. In these chapters especially, we have tried to draw several connections between laboratory-based models and real-world problems and situations.

NEW TO THE CANADIAN EDITION

In creating this Canadian edition, we have tried, wherever possible, to highlight research conducted in Canadian universities, by Canadian researchers. We felt that by providing information about researchers and studies conducted "in your own backyard" we could make the topic more approachable. Creation of such a textbook was encouraged in feedback from students and faculty who have used and reviewed the earlier U.S. editions of this book.

We have "Canadian Research Highlight" boxes to allow the interested student to follow up on topics and researchers they find particularly interesting and might think of contacting for graduate school studies. As well, we have added "In the Real World" boxes that serve to highlight cognitive phenomena, or interesting side stories relating to the topic being discussed.

The Canadian edition includes changes to a number of chapters compared to the US edition. Most importantly, we've decreased the number of chapters in this edition to make the book easier to use in a one-semester course. We've made the book more contemporary in look by changing some of the photos based on reviewer response. Additionally,

- Chapter 1 has been updated to include new Canadian research, including work on ecological approaches using eye-tracking methodologies. In addition, new to this edition is a discussion of the significance of James Baldwin setting up the first laboratory for experimental psychology at the University of Toronto in 1889.
- Chapter 2 features prominent Canadian researchers in the field of neuroscience, includes web links to Canadian Historical Moments videos, and provides detailed explanations of how neuroimaging studies are used to infer brain functions.
- Chapter 3 expands upon the excellent treatment of the basics of perception offered in the U.S. edition to include hot new Canadian research. Specifically, this chapter explores a difficulty that some individuals have in naming items from specific categories, known as category-specific agnosia. Students will also be interested to learn about a peculiar perceptual phenomenon called synaesthesia, in which individuals experience a mingling of the senses. Both topics are grounded in basic perceptual theory.
- Chapter 4 has been greatly expanded to include an experimental paradigm that has been central to the study of attention for nearly 30 years, the spatial cueing paradigm. In addition, cutting-edge Canadian research that challenges the long-held view of automatic processing of words in the Stroop paradigm is presented here.
- Chapters 5 and 6 have been reorganized. Photos and examples have been updated and added, and a discussion of the neurological basis of memory highlighted. While Chapter 5 focuses mainly on the structures and systems involved in memory, Chapter 6 examines how we use memory structures to recreate the past. We discuss models of the organization of memory, and ways of assessing or testing their validity. Here we make extensive use of real-world examples of what happens when memory processes and structures fail, by describing the everyday life of an amnesic injured—and subsequently studied by researchers—in Ontario.
- Chapter 7 now highlights the work of Canadian researchers looking at categorization strategies in medical diagnoses. We've also included a section looking at the neuroanatomical foundations of category induction in the brain.
- Chapter 8 includes a new section on spatial cognition that features work by Canadian researchers on "blind-walking."
- In Chapter 9 we've included a section on visual word recognition with Canadian content. In addition, the section on the neuropsychology of language processing has been expanded to cover seminal Canadian research on brain lateralization.

- In Chapter 10, we've highlighted work conducted by Canadian researchers looking at the way scientists and politicians use analogies in the real world. We've also expanded the section on neuroanatomical foundations of reasoning.
- Chapter 11 now includes two updated sections on research in real-world decision making being conducted by Canadian researchers. We have also included a section outlining research in neuroeconomics ("Decision Making, Emotions, and the Brain").
- Chapter 12 has been re-organized to focus on three major areas: individual differences, aging, and gender effects in cognition. The addition of a section on bilingualism reflects the importance of this factor in today's multicultural world, and is of particular relevance to Canada given the makeup of our population. The section on aging reflects the fact that the number of senior citizens in Canada, and the world, is growing at an unprecedented rate—understanding the cognitive changes associated with old age is fast becoming a major area of research.

Throughout the book we have included new references and photographs, and make a special effort to point the student to relevant work in cognitive neuroscience.

Acknowledgments

We would like to acknowledge our greatest support system: our families. Their love, support, and constant encouragement will never be forgotten. This Second Canadian Edition is dedicated to our parents, our spouses, our children, and our students.

We would also to give special thanks to the reviewers whose feedback was critical in writing the First Canadian Edition. Your feedback and expertise has been invaluable to us. We thank,

Thomas Allaway, *Algoma University College*
Sheryl M. Green, Ph.D., C.Psych, *McMaster University*
Bob Heller, *Athabasca University*
Valerie Lloyd, *Langara College*
Laura Melnyk, *King's University College at the University of Western Ontario*
Dr. William Owen, *University of Northern British Columbia*
Darren Piercey *University of British Columbia*
Richard Rinaldo, *Georgian College*
Daniel Smilek, *University of Waterloo*
Jennifer Tomes, *Mount Allison University*

Jennifer Stolz
Jonathan Fugelsang
Myra Fernandes

Overview

PART

I

Cognitive Psychology: History, Methods, and Paradigms

CHAPTER 1

This book is about cognitive psychology— that branch of psychology concerned with how people acquire, store, transform, use, and communicate information (Neisser, 1967). Put differently, cognitive psychology deals with our mental life: what goes on inside our heads when we perceive, attend, remember, think, categorize, reason, decide, and so forth.

To get a better feel for the domain of cognitive psychology, let's consider a few examples of cognitive activity.

You're walking along a dark, unfamiliar city street. It's raining and foggy, and you are cold and a bit apprehensive. As you walk past a small alley, you catch some movement out of the corner of your eye. You turn to look down the alley and start to make out a shape coming toward you. As the shape draws nearer, you are able to make out more and more features, and you suddenly realize that it's . . .

What cognitive processes are going on in this admittedly melodramatic example? In general, this example illustrates the initial acquisition and processing of information.

In particular, the cognitive processes depicted include **attention,** mentally focusing on some stimulus (the mysterious shape); **perception,** interpreting sensory information to yield meaningful information; and **pattern recognition,** classifying a stimulus into a known category. In recognizing the shape as something familiar, you no doubt called on **memory,** the storage facilities and retrieval processes of cognition. All this processing occurred rapidly, probably within a few seconds or less. Most of the cognitive processing in this example appears so effortless and automatic that we usually take it for granted. Here's another example:

You're in a crowded public place, such as a shopping mall during the holiday season. Throngs of people push past you, and you're hot and tired. You head for a nearby bench, aiming to combine some rest with some people watching. As you make your way, a young woman about your age jostles up against you. You both offer polite apologies ("Oh, excuse me!" "Sorry!"), glancing at each other as you do. She immediately exclaims, "Oh, it's you! How are you? I never thought I'd run into anyone I know here—can you believe it?" You immediately paste a friendly but vague smile on your face to cover your frantic mental search: Who is this woman? She looks familiar, but why? Is she a former classmate? Did you and she attend camp together? Is she saying anything that you can use as a clue to place her?

This example illustrates your use of memory processes, including **recognition** (you see the woman as familiar) and **recall** (you try to determine where you know her from). Other cognitive processes are involved here too, although they play a lesser role. For instance, you perceive the entity talking to you as a person, specifically a woman, more specifically a vaguely familiar woman. You pay attention to her. You may be using various strategies or techniques of **reasoning** and **problem solving** to try to figure out who she is. Your success or failure at this task may also depend on your mental organization of the knowledge you have accumulated in your lifetime—your **knowledge representation.** To communicate with her, you use **language** as well as nonverbal cues or signals. Eventually, you'll have to use **decision making** to determine how to deal with the situation: Will you admit your forgetfulness, or will you try to cover it up?

As these two examples demonstrate, our everyday lives involve a great deal of cognition. Furthermore, this everyday cognition is complex, often involving several cognitive processes. We tend to remain unaware of this complexity, however, because much of our cognitive processing occurs so often, so rapidly, and with so little effort that we do not even know it is taking place.

In both of the preceding examples, several cognitive processes were occurring either simultaneously or very closely in time. In fact, it is nearly impossible to specify, in either of these examples, exactly how many cognitive processes occurred or in what sequence. This uncertainty typifies everyday situations: So much is going on so quickly that we can't be sure of even what information is being received or used. How, then, can cognition be studied with any precision?

This kind of problem is one all scientists face: how to study a naturally occurring phenomenon with sufficient experimental rigour to draw firm conclusions. The answer, for many, is to try to isolate the phenomenon and bring it (or some stripped-down version of it) into the laboratory. The challenge, then, is to decide what is essential and what is inessential about the phenomenon under study.

For example, in studying how memory works, psychologists have often used experiments in which people are presented with lists of words or nonsense syllables. The experimenters then control or systematically vary variables such as the complexity, length, frequency, meaningfulness, relatedness, and rate of presentation of items on the list, along with the state of alertness, expertise, practice, and interest of the research participants. The experimenters assume factors that increase or decrease performance in the laboratory will also increase or decrease performance under less controlled conditions. Further, the researchers assume that although in everyday life people do not encounter material to be remembered in this manner, the processes of memory work in essentially the same ways in laboratory experiments as in everyday life. So, if increasing the number of items to be remembered decreases memory performance in a laboratory, then we can also expect having to remember more information in an everyday situation would be more difficult than remembering less under the same circumstances.

The key challenge for all scientists, however, is to make sure the laboratory tasks they develop really do preserve the essential workings of the processes under study. The most rigorously controlled experiment is of at best limited value if the phenomenon being studied does not occur or occurs in significantly different ways outside the laboratory. Unfortunately, there is no simple or guaranteed way to ensure that laboratory tasks model everyday tasks. Therefore, students and other "consumers" of science must take a critical stance when considering how experimental situations apply to everyday ones. Throughout this book, we will be looking at how laboratory models do or do not accurately describe, explain, and predict cognitive processing in real life (i.e., outside the laboratory). We will cover studies that attempt to measure cognitive processes while people are behaving naturally in the real world. We will also consider how situational and personal factors, such as people's level of development, degree of expertise, gender, and cultural background, affect cognitive processing.

An ordinary activity, such as reading a map, involves a great deal of cognitive processing.

Before we discuss specific cognitive processes, however, an overview of the field of cognitive psychology will provide a useful framework within which to consider specific topics, experiments, and findings in the field. We will first examine the historical roots of cognitive psychology to see how the field has developed. Next, we'll look at traditional and common research methods used in cognitive psychology. Finally, we'll consider four paradigms, or schools of thought, that represent the current streams of thought in the field.

INFLUENCES ON THE STUDY OF COGNITION

A complete treatise on how modern cognitive psychology has evolved over the course of human history could fill several volumes and would obviously be beyond our scope. Worth noting, however, is that several ideas about certain mental abilities date back to at least the Greek philosophers Aristotle and Plato (Murray, 1988). For example, both these philosophers wrote extensively on the nature of memory. Plato, for instance, likened storing something in memory to writing on a wax tablet. In other writings, he compared the mind to an aviary in which many birds are flying, and memory retrieval to trying to catch a specific bird: Sometimes you can, but at other times you can grab only a nearby bird.

Other historians of psychology trace the field's roots to the philosophers of the 17th to 19th centuries, including John Locke, David Hume, John Stuart Mill, René Descartes, George Berkeley, and Immanuel Kant. These philosophers also debated the nature of mind and knowledge, with Locke, Hume, Berkeley, and Mill following Aristotle and a more empiricist position, and Descartes and Kant aligning with Plato and a nativist position.

Briefly, **empiricism** rests on the tenet that knowledge comes from an individual's own experience—that is, from the empirical information that people collect from their senses and experiences. Empiricists recognize individual differences in genetics but emphasize human nature's malleable, or changeable, aspects. Empiricists believe people are the way they are, and have the capabilities they have, largely because of previous learning. One mechanism by which such learning is thought to take place is through the mental **association** of two ideas. Locke (1690/1964) argued that two distinct ideas or experiences, having nothing to do with each other, could become joined in the mind simply because they happened to occur or to be presented to the individual at the same time. Empiricists accordingly believe the environment plays a powerful role in determining one's intellectual (and other) abilities.

Nativism, by contrast, emphasizes the role of constitutional factors—of native ability—over the role of learning in the acquisition of abilities and tendencies. Nativists attribute differences in individuals' abilities less to differences in learning than to differences in original, biologically endowed capacities and abilities. Nativism is an important idea in cognitive psychology, as we will see. Nativists often suggest that some cognitive functions come built in, as part of our legacy as human beings. "Hard-wired" functions such as short-term memory, for example, are attributed to innate structures of the human mind that are present, in at least a rudimentary form, at birth and are not learned, formed, or created as a result of experience.

Interestingly, only in the last 120 years have central cognitive issues such as the nature of mind and the nature of information in the mind been seen as amenable to scientific psychological investigation. Indeed, until the 1870s no one really thought to ask whether actual data could help resolve any of these questions. When people began doing so, experimental psychology was born. However, the nativist–empiricist debate is still a controversial one in the 21st century (Pinker, 2002, p. 10). We will look next at different schools of experimental psychology that laid the foundations for cognitive psychology today.

Structuralism

Many students are surprised to find out that psychology as a formal discipline has been around for little more than a century. Historians often date the "founding" of the actual field of psychology back to 1879, when Wilhelm Wundt converted a laboratory into the first institute for research in experimental psychology (Fancher, 1979). Wundt wanted to establish a "science of mind," to discover the laws and principles that explained our immediate conscious experience. In particular, Wundt wanted to identify the simplest essential units of the mind. In essence, he wanted to create a table of "mental elements," much like a chemist's periodic chart. Once the set of elements was identified, Wundt believed, psychologists could determine how these units combine to produce complex mental phenomena. Wundt foresaw an entire field devoted to the study of how systematically varying stimuli would affect or produce different mental states; he described this field in a volume titled *Principles of Physiological Psychology* (Fancher, 1979).

Shortly after Wundt set up his laboratory in Germany, an influential North American scientist, James Baldwin (after studying with Wundt during 1884 and 1885), set up an experimental laboratory at the University of Toronto in 1889. Although he stayed at Toronto for only four years, he was instrumental in creating the first experimental psychological laboratory in Canada (and all of North America, for that matter). He is most well known for his work on mental development in children (Baldwin, 1895), and was a major influence in the

James Baldwin (1861–1934) came to the University of Toronto in 1989, and founded the first experimental psychological laboratory in North America there in that year.

JHU Sheridan Libraries/Gado/Contributor/Getty

work of Jean Piaget. In fact, he was the first person to conduct controlled experiments with children (namely his own daughter Elizabeth).

Wundt and his students carried out hundreds of studies, many involving a technique of investigation called **introspection.** Although this term today connotes "soul searching," Wundt's technique was much more focused. It consisted of presenting highly trained observers (usually graduate students) with various stimuli and asking them to describe their conscious experiences. Wundt assumed that the raw materials of consciousness were sensory and thus "below" the level of meaning. In particular, Wundt thought any conscious thought or idea resulted from a combination of sensations that could be defined in terms of exactly four properties: mode (for example, visual, auditory, tactile, olfactory), quality (such as colour, shape, texture), intensity, and duration.

Wundt's goal was to "cut through the learned categories and concepts that define our everyday experience of the world" (Fancher, 1979, p. 140). Wundt believed strongly that with proper training, people could detect and report the workings of their own minds. A student of Wundt, Edward B. Titchener, applied the term **structuralism** to his own endeavours as well as to Wundt's (Hillner, 1984). The term was meant to convey Wundt's focus on what the elemental components of the mind are rather than on the question of why the mind works as it does.

Functionalism

While Wundt was working in Leipzig, William James was working to establish the new discipline of psychology in the United States. In many ways, Wundt and James were opposites. A prolific researcher who personally carried out or supervised hundreds of rigorous experiments, Wundt was not known for his interpersonal style. James (the brother of the writer Henry James), in contrast, carried out little original research but wrote eloquently about psychological findings and their relevance to everyday life (Fancher, 1979). His textbook *The Principles of Psychology* (1890/1983) is still highly regarded and widely cited today.

James regarded psychology's mission to be the explanation of our experience. Like Wundt, James was interested in conscious experience. Unlike Wundt, however, James was not interested in the elementary units of consciousness. Instead, he asked why the mind works the way it does. He assumed that the way the mind works has a great deal to do with its function—the purposes of its various operations. Hence, the term **functionalism** was applied to his approach.

James's writings, which introduced psychological questions to many academics, still offer food for thought to students and teachers of psychology, perhaps because they so directly address everyday life. Consider one of the best-known chapters in his textbook, on "habit." James saw habit as the "flywheel of society" (1890/1983, vol. 1, p. 125), a mechanism basic to keeping our behaviour within bounds. He saw habits as inevitable and powerful and drew from this a practical conclusion:

> *Every smallest stroke of virtue or of vice leaves its ever so little scar. The drunken Rip Van Winkle, in Jefferson's play, excuses himself for every fresh dereliction by saying, "I won't count this time!" Well! he may not count it, and a kind Heaven may not count it; but it is being counted none the less. Down among his nerve-cells and fibres the molecules are counting it, registering and storing it up to be used against him when the next temptation comes. (James, 1890/1983, vol. 1, p. 131)*

James's point, of course, is that people should take great care to avoid bad habits and establish good ones. He offered advice about how to do so, urging people to never allow an exception when trying to establish a good habit, to seize opportunities to act on resolutions, and to engage in a "little gratuitous effort" every day to keep the "faculty of effort" alive (James, 1890/1983, vol. 1, p. 130).

Functionalists drew heavily on Darwinian evolutionary theory and tried to extend biological conceptions of adaptation to psychological phenomena (Hillner, 1984). Structuralists and functionalists differed in their methods as well as their focus. The structuralists were convinced the proper setting for experimental psychology was the laboratory, where experimental stimuli could be stripped of their everyday meanings to determine the true nature of mind. Functionalists disagreed sharply with this approach, attempting instead to study mental phenomena in real-life situations. Their basic belief was that psychologists should study whole organisms in whole, real-life tasks (Hillner, 1984).

Behaviourism

You probably learned the terms *classical conditioning* and *instrumental conditioning* in your introductory psychology class. The Russian psychologist Ivan Pavlov used the first, and psychologists such as Edward Thorndike used the second, to explain psychological phenomena strictly in terms of observable stimuli and responses.

In the United States, a school of psychology known as **behaviourism** took root in the 1930s, dominating academic psychology until well into the 1960s. Many regard it as a branch of functionalism (Amsel, 1989). One of the general doctrines of behaviourism is that references to unobservable, subjective mental states (such as consciousness), as well as to unobservable, subjective processes (such as expecting, believing, understanding, remembering, hoping for, deciding, and perceiving), were to be banished from psychology proper, which behaviourists took to be the scientific study of behaviour.

Behaviourists rejected such techniques of study as introspection, which they found in principle to be untestable. In an article published in 1913, John Watson most directly described his view of what psychology is and isn't:

> *Psychology as the behaviorist views it is a purely objective natural science. Its theoretical goal is the prediction and control of behavior. Introspection forms no essential part of its methods, nor is the scientific value of its data dependent upon the readiness with which they lend themselves to interpretation in terms of consciousness. The behaviorist, in his efforts to get a unitary scheme of animal response, recognizes no dividing line between man and brute. The behavior of man, with all of its refinement and complexity, forms only a part of the behaviorist's total scheme of investigation. (p. 158)*

Why did behaviourists so disdain the technique of introspection? Mainly because of its obviously subjective nature and its inability to resolve disagreements about theory. Suppose two observers are presented with the same stimulus, and one reports an experience of "greenness" and the other an experience of "green-yellowness." Which one is correct? Is one misrepresenting or misinterpreting his or her experience? If no physiological cause (for example, colour blindness) explains the different reports, then the scientist is left with an unresolvable dispute. Titchener restricted his research participants to graduate students trained to introspect "properly" (advising those who couldn't learn to do this to find another career). This, however, created more problems than it solved. The reasoning was circular: How do we know that a particular sensation is a true building block of cognition? Because trained observers report it to be so. How do we know the observers are trained? Because they consistently report that certain sensations and not others are the true elements of consciousness.

Watson, in fact, regarded all "mental" phenomena as reducible to behavioural and physiologic responses. Such things as "images" and "thoughts," he believed, resulted from low-level activity of the glands or small muscles. In his first textbook, Watson cited evidence showing that when people report they are "thinking," muscles in the tongue and larynx are actually moving slightly. Thought, for Watson, simply amounted to perception of these muscle movements (Fancher, 1979).

Watson's contribution to cognitive psychology—banishing all "mental language" from use—was largely negative, insofar as he believed the scientific study of mental phenomena was simply not possible. Watson and his followers did, however, encourage psychologists to think in terms of measures and research methods that moved beyond subjective introspection, thereby challenging later psychologists to develop more rigorous and more testable hypotheses and theories, as well as stricter research protocols.

B. F. Skinner (1984), psychology's best-known behaviourist, took a different tack with regard to mental events and the issue of mental representations. Skinner argued that such "mentalistic" entities as images, sensations, and thoughts should not be excluded simply because they are difficult to study. Skinner believed in the existence of images, thoughts, and the like and agreed they were proper objects of study but objected to treating mental events and activities as fundamentally different from behavioural events and activities. In particular, he objected to hypothesizing the existence of **mental representations** (internal depictions of information), which he took to be internal copies of external stimuli. Skinner believed images and thoughts were likely to be no more or less than verbal labels for bodily processes. But even if mental events were real and separate entities, Skinner believed, they were triggered by external environmental stimuli and gave rise to behaviours. Therefore, he held, a simple functional analysis of the relationship between the stimuli and behaviours would avoid the well-known problems of studying mental events (Hergenhahn, 1986).

Other behaviourists were more accepting of the idea of mental representations. Edward Tolman, for example, believed even rats have some goals and expectations. As he explained it, a rat learning to run a maze must have the goal of attaining food and must acquire an internal representation—some cognitive map or other means of depicting information "in the head" about the maze—to locate the food at the maze's end. Tolman's work centred on demonstrating that animals had both expectations and internal representations that guided their behaviour.

Gestalt Psychology

The school of **Gestalt psychology** began in 1911 in Frankfurt, Germany, at a meeting of three psychologists: Max Wertheimer, Kurt Koffka, and Wolfgang Köhler (Murray, 1988). As the name *Gestalt* (a German word that loosely translates to "configuration" or "shape") suggests, these psychologists' central assumption was that psychological phenomena could not be reduced to simple elements but rather had to be analyzed and studied in their entirety. Gestalt psychologists, who studied mainly perception and problem solving, believed an observer did not construct a coherent perception from simple, elementary sensory aspects of an experience but instead apprehended the total structure of an experience as a whole.

As a concrete example, consider Figure 1-1. Notice that (A), (B), and (C) contain the same elements—namely, eight equal line segments. However, most people experience the three arrays quite differently, seeing (A) as four pairs of line segments, (B) as eight line segments haphazardly arranged, and (C) as a circle, or more precisely, an octagon, made up of eight line segments. The arrangement of lines—that is, the relationships among the elements as a whole—plays an important role in determining our experience.

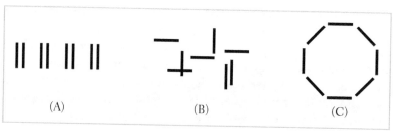

FIGURE 1-1 Examples of Gestalt figures. Although (A), (B), and (C) all contain eight equal lines, most people experience them differently, seeing (A) as four pairs of lines, (B) as eight unrelated lines, and (C) as a circle made up of eight line segments.

The Gestalt psychologists thus rejected structuralism, functionalism, and behaviourism as offering incomplete accounts of psychological and, in particular, cognitive experiences. They chose to study people's subjective experience of stimuli and to focus on how people use or impose structure and order on their experiences. They believed that the mind imposes its own structure and organization on stimuli and, in particular, organizes perceptions into wholes rather than discrete parts. These wholes tend to simplify stimuli. Thus, when we hear a melody, we experience not a collection of individual sounds but larger, more organized units: melodic lines.

The Study of Individual Differences

Yet another strand of the history of psychology is important to mention here, even though no particular "school" is associated with it: the investigations into **individual differences** in human cognitive abilities by Sir Francis Galton and his followers. Galton trained in medicine and mathematics at Cambridge University, England. Like many of his fellow students (and many of today's university students), Galton felt a great deal of academic pressure and competitiveness and "was constantly preoccupied with his standing relative to his fellow students" (Fancher, 1979, p. 257). This strong preoccupation developed into a lifelong interest in measuring intellectual ability.

Galton's interest in intellectual differences among people stemmed in part from his reading of Charles Darwin's writings on evolution. Darwin believed animals (including humans) evolved through a process of natural selection, by which certain inherited traits are perpetuated because individuals possessing those traits are more likely to survive and reproduce. Galton wondered whether intellectual talents could also be inherited. Galton noticed "intelligence" or "smartness" or "eminence" seemed to run in families; that is, smart parents appeared to produce smart children. Of course, this could be explained in terms of either genetics or environment (for example, intelligent parents may have greater resources to spend on their children's education and/or greater interest or motivation to do so). Thus, Galton's question of how large a role genetics plays in intelligence was difficult to answer. To address it, Galton put his mathematical training to use in analyzing data (usually family trees of "eminent" men) and, later, inventing statistical tests, some of which are still used today.

Galton (1883/1907) studied a variety of cognitive abilities, in each case focusing on ways of measuring the ability and then noting its variation among different individuals. Among the abilities he studied (in both laboratory and "naturalistic" settings) was mental imagery. He developed a questionnaire instructing respondents to "think of some definite object—suppose it is your breakfast-table as you sat down this morning—and consider carefully the picture that rises before your mind's eye" (p. 58). He then asked, Is the image dim or clear? Are all of the objects in the image well defined? Does part of the image seem to be better defined? Are the colours of the objects in the image distinct and natural? Galton was surprised to discover much variability in this capacity: Some respondents reported almost no imagery; others experienced images so vividly they could hardly tell they were images!

Galton left a large legacy to psychology, and to cognitive psychology in particular. His invention of tests and questionnaires to assess mental abilities inspired later cognitive psychologists to develop similar measures. His statistical analyses, later refined by other statisticians, allowed hypotheses to be rigorously tested. His work on mental imagery is still cited by current investigators. Most broadly, Galton's work challenged psychologists, both those who believed in the importance of genetic influences and those strongly opposed to the idea, to think about the nature of mental—that is, cognitive— abilities and capacities.

The "Cognitive Revolution"

Despite the early attempts to define and study mental life, psychology came to embrace the behaviourist tradition in the first five decades of the 1900s. A number of historical trends, both within and outside academia, came together in the years during and following World War II to produce what many psychologists think of as a "revolution" in the field of cognitive psychology. This **cognitive revolution,** a new series of psychological investigations, was mainly a rejection of the behaviourist assumption that mental events and states were beyond the realm of scientific study or that mental representations did not exist. In particular, the "revolutionaries" came to believe no complete explanation of a person's functioning could exist that did not refer to the person's mental representations of the world. This directly challenged the fundamental tenet of radical behaviourism, that concepts such as "mental representation" were not needed to explain behaviour.

One of the first of these historical trends was a product of the war itself: the establishment of the field of **human factors engineering.** During the war, military personnel had to be trained to operate complicated pieces of equipment. Engineers quickly found they needed to design equipment (such as instrument operating panels, radar screens, and communication devices) to suit the capacities of the people operating it. Lachman, Lachman, and Butterfield (1979) offered an anecdote about why such problems were important to solve:

> *One type of plane often crashed while landing. It turned out that the lever that the pilot had to use for braking was near the lever that retracted the landing gear. During landing, the pilot could not take his eyes off the runway: He had to work by touch alone. Sometimes pilots retracted their landing gear instead of putting on their brakes; they touched the ground with the belly of the plane at top speed. The best way to keep them from crashing was not to exhort them to be careful; they were already highly motivated to avoid crashing and getting klled. Improving training procedures was also an ineffi-cient approach; pilots with many safe landings behind them committed this error as well as rookie pilots. The most reasonable approach was to redesign the craft's controls so that completely different arm movements were required for braking and for retracting the landing gear. (p. 57)*

Psychologists and engineers thus developed the concept of the man-machine system, now more accurately referred to as the **person–machine system:** the idea that machinery operated by a person must be designed to interact with the operator's physical, cognitive, and motivational capacities and limitations.

Psychologists in World War II also borrowed concepts, terminology, and analogies from communications engineering. Engineers concerned with the design of such things as telephones and telegraph systems talked about the exchange of information through various "channels" (such as telegraph wires and telephone lines). Types of channels differ in how much information they can transmit per unit of time and how accurately.

Psychologists learning of this work started to describe human beings as "communication channels," examining their capacities for receiving, sending, and processing information and the circumstances under which they distort the information they receive. Humans were quickly seen to share properties with better known, inanimate communications channels and came to be described as **limited-capacity processors** of information.

What is a limited-capacity processor? As the name suggests, it means that people can do only so many things at once. For example, you probably find it difficult to simultaneously type on essay on your computer while following a television show. Although you can do some tasks at the same time (e.g., folding laundry while watching television), the number and kinds of things you can do at the same time are limited. Many landmark studies of cognitive psy-chology—those that cognitive psychologists regard as "classics"—date from just after World War II and clearly focus on exploring the nature of our capacity limitations.

For instance, George Miller, in his now classic 1956 paper "The Magical Number Seven, Plus or Minus Two," observed that (a) the number of unrelated things we can perceive dis-tinctly without counting, (b) the number of unrelated things on a list we can immediately remember, and (c) the number of stimuli we can make absolute discriminations among is between five and nine for most normal adults. Miller's work thus exemplified how the limits of people's cognitive capacities could be measured and tested.

At about the same time, developments in the field of **linguistics,** the study of language, made clear that people routinely process enormously complex information. Work by linguist Noam Chomsky revolutionized the field of linguistics, and both linguists and psychologists began to see the central importance of studying how people acquire, understand, and produce language.

In addition, Chomsky's early work (1957, 1959, 1965) showed that behaviourism could not adequately explain language. Consider the question of how language is acquired. A behaviourist might explain language acquisition as a result of parents' reinforcing a child's grammatical utterances and punishing (or at least not reinforcing) ungrammatical utterances. However, both linguists and psychologists soon realized such an account had to be wrong. For one thing, psychologists and linguists who observed young children with their parents found that parents typically respond to the content rather than to the form of the child's language utterances (Brown & Hanlon, 1970). For another, even when parents (or teachers) explicitly tried to correct children's grammar, they could not. Children seemed simply not to "hear" the problems, as is evident in the following dialogue (McNeill, 1966, p. 69):

> Child: Nobody don't like me.
> Mother: No, say, "Nobody likes me." [eight repetitions of this dialogue]
> Mother: No, now listen carefully; say, "Nobody likes me."
> Child: Oh! Nobody don't likes me.

Chomsky's work thus posed a fundamental challenge to psychologists: Here were human beings, already shown to be limited-capacity processors, quickly acquiring what seemed an enormously complicated body of knowledge—language—and using it easily. How could this be?

Reversing engineers' arguments that machines must be designed to fit people's capabilities, many linguists tried to describe structures complex enough to process language. Chomsky (1957, 1965) argued that underlying people's language abilities is an implicit system of rules, collectively known as a *generative grammar.* These rules allow speakers to construct, and listeners to understand, sentences that are "legal" in the language. For example, "Did you eat all the oat bran cereal?" is a legal, well-formed sentence, but "Bran the did all oat eat you cereal?" is not. Our generative grammar, a mentally represented system of rules, tells us so, because it can produce (generate) the first sentence but not the second.

Chomsky (1957, 1965) did not believe all the rules of a language are consciously accessible to speakers of that language. Instead, he believed the rules operate implicitly: We don't necessarily know exactly what all the rules are, but we use them rather easily to produce understandable sentences and to avoid producing gobbledygook.

Another strand of the cognitive revolution came from developments in neuroscience, the study of the brain-based underpinnings of psychological and behavioural functions. A major debate in the neuroscience community had been going on for centuries, all the way back to Descartes, over the issue of **localization of function.** To say a function is "localized" in a particular region is, roughly, to claim that the neural structures supporting that function reside in a specific brain area. In a major work published in 1929, a very influential neuroscientist, Karl Lashley had claimed there was no reason to believe that major functions (such as language and memory) are localized (Gardner, 1985).

However, research in the late 1940s and 1950s accumulated to challenge that view. Work by Donald Hebb, a world renowned professor at McGill University suggested that some kinds of functions, such as visual perceptions, were constructed over time by the building of *cell assemblies*—connections among sets of cells in the brain. In the 1950s and 1960s, Nobel Prize–winning neurophysiologists David Hubel (from Windsor, Ontario) and Torsten Wiesel discovered that specific cells in the visual cortex of cats were in fact specialized to respond to specific kinds of stimuli (orientation of lines, particular shapes). Equally important, Hubel and Wiesel demonstrated the importance of early experience in nervous system development. Kittens who were experimentally restricted to an environment with only horizontal lines would fail to develop the ability to perceive vertical lines. This work suggested that at least some functions are localized in the brain (Gardner, 1985).

There is yet one more thread to the cognitive revolution, also dating from about World War II: the development of computers and artificially intelligent systems. In 1936, a mathematician named Alan Turing wrote a paper describing universal machines: mathematical entities that were simple in nature but capable in principle of solving logical or mathematical problems. This paper ultimately led to what some psychologists and computer scientists call the **computer metaphor:** the comparison of people's cognitive activities to an operating computer. Just as computers have to be fed data, people have to acquire information.

Both computers and people often store information and must therefore have structures and processes that allow such storage. People and computers often need to recode information—that is, to change the way it is recorded or presented. People and computers must also manipulate information in other ways—transform it, for example, by rearranging it, adding to or subtracting from it, deducing from it, and so on. Computer scientists working on the problem of **artificial intelligence** now study how to program computers to solve the same kinds of problems humans can and whether computers can use the same methods that people apparently use to solve such problems.

Current Trends in the Study of Cognition

During the 1970s, researchers in different fields started to notice they were investigating common questions: the nature of mind and of cognition; how information is acquired, processed, stored, and transmitted; and how knowledge is represented. Scholars from fields such as cognitive psychology, computer science, philosophy, linguistics, neuroscience, and anthropology, recognizing their mutual interests, came together to found an interdisciplinary field known as **cognitive science.** Gardner (1985) even gave this field a birth date— September 11, 1956—when several founders of the field attended a symposium on information theory at the Massachusetts Institute of Technology (MIT).

Gardner (1985) pointed out that the field of cognitive science rests on certain common assumptions. Most important among these is the assumption that cognition must be analyzed at what is called the *level of representation*. This means cognitive scientists agree that cognitive theories incorporate such constructs as symbols, rules, images, or ideas—in Gardner's words, "the stuff . . . found between input and output" (p. 38). Thus, cognitive scientists focus on representations of information rather than on how nerve cells in the brain work or on historical or cultural influences.

Another approach to studying cognitive issues comes from clinical work. Practitioners of **cognitive neuropsychology** (Ellis & Young, 1988; Milner & Goodale, 1995; Streimer & Danckert, 2007) study cognitive deficits in certain brain-damaged individuals. Milner and Goodale described patient DF, who could accurately make visually guided motor movements but was severely impaired in tasks testing her spatial vision. These findings were taken to support the hypothesis that vision for action and vision for perception are based on different neural substrates, and thus can function somewhat independently. Similarly, Ellis and Young described PH., a 19-year-old who lost his right arm in a motorcycle accident and sustained a severe head injury that left him in a coma for almost two weeks. Four years after his accident, P.H. appeared to have normal language abilities, including reading, and he tested normal in many short- and long-term memory tests. His IQ (91) also seemed normal. His head injury seemed to have caused at least one cognitive deficit, however:

> One of P.H. s problems was most resistant to rehabilitation; he could not recognize people's faces. As soon as a familiar person spoke he would know who it was but, to P.H., all faces seemed unfamiliar. He could tell if a face belonged to a man or a woman, an old or a young person, and he could describe the general appearance and facial features reasonably accurately. But P.H. had no sense of recognizing people who had previously been very familiar to him. In neuropsychological terms, his accident had left P.H. prosopagnosic—able to see, but unable to recognize once familiar faces. (Ellis & Young, 1988, pp. 1–2)

Cognitive neuropsychologists proceed by identifying people with certain patterns of brain damage and examining their cognitive performance. What cognitive processes can these individuals no longer perform? What cognitive activities have been spared? By finding answers to such questions, cognitive neuropsychologists not only develop a better understanding of how everyone's cognitive processes operate, but also gain new insights that might help people who have brain damage. For example, Streimer and Danckert (2007) examined how special glasses designed to shift one's visual attention (i.e., prism adaptation) alleviate some of the symptoms of patients who cannot attend to portions of their visual field. In later chapters of the book, we'll be returning to examples from cognitive neuropsychology.

General Points

Each school of psychology described so far has left a visible legacy to modern cognitive psychology. Structuralism asked the question, What are the elementary units and processes of the mind? Functionalists reminded psychologists to focus on the larger purposes and contexts that cognitive processes serve. Behaviourists challenged psychologists to develop testable hypotheses and to avoid unresolvable debates. The Gestalt psychologists pointed out that an understanding of individual units would not automatically lead to an understanding of whole processes and systems, and Galton demonstrated that individuals can differ in their cognitive processing. Developments in engineering, computer science, linguistics, and neuroscience have uncovered processes by which information can be efficiently represented, stored, and transformed, providing analogies and metaphors for cognitive psychologists to use in constructing and testing models of cognition. As we take up particular topics in this book, we will see more of how cognitive psychology's different roots have shaped the field.

Keep in mind that cognitive psychology shares in the discoveries made in other fields, just as other fields share in the discoveries made by cognitive psychology. This sharing and borrowing of research methods, terminology and analyses gives many investigators a sense of common purpose. It also all but requires cognitive psychologists to keep abreast of new developments in fields related to cognition.

RESEARCH METHODS IN COGNITIVE PSYCHOLOGY

Throughout this book, we will be reviewing different empirical studies of cognition. Before we plunge into those studies, however, we will look at some of the different kinds of studies that cognitive psychologists conduct. The following descriptions do not exhaust all the studies a cognitive psychologist could conduct but should acquaint you with the major methodological approaches to cognitive psychology.

Naturalistic Observation

As the name suggests, **naturalistic observation** consists of an observer watching people in familiar, everyday contexts going about their cognitive business. For example, an investigator might watch as people try to figure out how to work a new automated check-in kiosk at an airport. Ideally, the observer remains as unobtrusive as possible, so as to disrupt or alter the behaviours being observed as little as possible. In this example, for instance, the investigator might stand nearby and surreptitiously note what people who use the automated kiosk do and say. Being unobtrusive is much harder than it might sound. The observer needs to make sure the people being observed are comfortable and do not feel as though they are "under a microscope." At the same time, the observer wants to avoid causing the people being observed to "perform" for the observer. In any case, the observer can hardly fully assess his or her own effects on the observation: After all, how can one know what people would have done had they not been observed?

Naturalistic observational studies have the advantage that the things studied really do occur in the real world and not just in an experimental laboratory. Psychologists call this property **ecological validity.** Furthermore, the observer has a chance to see just how cognitive processes work in natural settings: how flexible they are, how they are affected by environmental changes, how rich and complex actual behaviour is. Naturalistic observation is relatively easy to do, doesn't typically require a lot of resources to carry out, and does not require other people to formally volunteer for study.

The disadvantage of naturalistic observation is a lack of **experimental control.** The observer has no means of isolating the causes of different behaviours or reactions. All he can do is collect observations and try to infer relationships among them. However plausible different hypotheses may seem, the observer has no way of verifying them. Some psychologists believe that naturalistic observation is most appropriately used to identify problems, issues, or phenomena of interest to be investigated with other research methods that have more experimental control down the road.

A second problem, which all scientists face, is that an observer's recordings are only as good as her initial plan for what is important to record. The settings and people she chooses to observe, the behaviours and reactions she chooses to record, the manner of recording, and the duration and frequency of observation all influence the results and conclusions she can later draw. Moreover, whatever biases the observer brings to the study limit and possibly distort the recordings made.

Introspection

We have already seen one special kind of observation, dating back to the laboratory of Wilhelm Wundt. In the technique of introspection, the observer observes his or her own mental processes. For example, participants might be asked to solve complicated arithmetic problems without paper or pencil and to "think aloud" as they do so.

Introspection has all the benefits and drawbacks of other observational studies, plus a few more. One additional benefit is that observing one's own reactions and behaviour may give one better insight into an experience and the factors that influenced it, yielding a richer, more complete picture than an outsider could observe. But observing yourself is a double-edged sword. Although perhaps a better observer in some ways than an outsider, you may also be more biased in regard to your own cognition. People observing their own mental processes may be more concerned with their level of performance and may be motivated to subtly and unconsciously distort their observations. They may try to make their mental processes appear more organized, logical, thorough, and so forth, than they actually are. They may be unwilling to admit when their cognitive processes seem flawed or random. Moreover, with some cognitive tasks (especially demanding ones), observers may have few resources left with which to observe and record.

Experiments and Quasi-Experiments

The major distinction between experiments and observational methods is the investigator's degree of experimental control. Having experimental control means the experimenter can assign participants to different experimental conditions so as to minimize preexisting differences between them. Ideally, the experimenter can control all variables that might affect the performance of research participants other than the variables on which the study is focusing. A true **experiment** is one in which the experimenter manipulates one or more independent variables (the experimental conditions) and observes how the recorded measures (dependent variables) change as a result. The vast majority of research conducted by cognitive psychologists is of this type.

For example, an experiment in cognitive psychology might proceed as follows: An experimenter recruits a number of people for a study of memory, randomly assigns them to one of two groups, and presents each group with exactly the same stimuli, using exactly the same procedures and settings and varying only the instructions (the independent variable) for the two groups of participants. The experimenter then observes the overall performance of the participants on a later memory test (the dependent variable).

This example illustrates a **between-subjects design,** wherein different experimental participants are assigned to different experimental conditions and the researcher looks for differences in performance between the two groups. In contrast, a **within-subjects design** exposes the same experimental participants to more than one condition. For example, participants might perform several memory tasks but receive a different set of instructions for each task. The investigator then compares the performance of the participants in the first condition to the performance of the *same* participants in another condition.

Some independent variables preclude random assignment (that is, having the experimenter assign a research participant to a particular condition in an experiment). For example, experimenters cannot reassign participants to a different sex, ethnicity, age, or educational background. Studies that appear in other ways to be experiments but that have one or more of these factors as independent variables (or fail to become true experiments in other ways) are called **quasi-experiments** (Campbell & Stanley, 1963).

Scientists value experiments and quasi-experiments because they enable researchers to isolate causal factors and make better-supported claims about causality than is possible using observational methods alone. However, many experiments fail to fully capture real-world phenomena in the experimental task or research design. The laboratory setting or the artificiality or formality of the task may prevent research participants from behaving normally for example. Further, the kinds of tasks amenable to experimental study may not be those most important or most common in everyday life. As a result, experimenters risk studying phenomena that relate only weakly to people's real-world experience.

The general point to draw here is that the various research methods are all ways of investigating questions. Ultimately, cognitive psychologists hope that the findings from different studies will converge on similar explanations.

Investigations of Neural Underpinnings

Much work in cognitive neuropsychology involves examining the neural underpinnings of various cognitive faculties. Before the second half of the 20th century, this kind of examination could be conducted only after a patient died, during an autopsy. However, since the 1970s various techniques of **brain imaging,** the construction of pictures of the anatomy and functioning of intact brains, have been developed. We will discuss many of these techniques in Chapter 2.

General Points

This brief outline of different research designs barely scratches the surface of all the important things we could look at. There are a few general points to note, however. First, cognitive psychologists use a variety of approaches to study cognitive phenomena. In part, these approaches reflect philosophic differences among psychologists over what is important to study and how tradeoffs should be made between certain drawbacks and benefits. In part, they reflect the intellectual framework in which researchers find themselves working. They may also reflect how amenable different areas of cognition are to different research approaches.

Second, no research design is perfect. Each has certain potential benefits and limitations that researchers must weigh in designing studies. Students, professors, and other researchers must also examine the design of studies, both critically and appreciatively, thinking carefully about how well the research design answers the research question posed. We hope you'll keep these thoughts in mind as you read in the rest of the book examples of the wide variety of research studies that cognitive psychologists have carried out.

Table 1-1 presents a summary (oversimplified) of the different traditions within cognitive psychology and/or cognitive neuropsychology. For each tradition, it lists one of the major researchers associated with the tradition, the central question posed by the tradition, and the research methods typically used.

Table 1-1 Antecedents of Cognitive Psychology

Tradition	Name	Question	Method
Individual differences	Galton	How do people differ?	Tests, statistical analysis
Physiology	Hebb	What kinds of disruptions accompany specific kinds of brain damage?	Tests, observations, autopsy
Structuralism	Titchener	What are the basic building blocks of consciousness?	Introspection under controlled conditions
Functionalism	James	Why does the mind have the operations it has?	Introspection under naturalistic conditions
Gestalt psychology	Koffka	What organization does the mind impose on different configurations of simple stimuli?	Introspection under controlled conditions
Behaviourism	Skinner	How is behaviour affected by context?	Observation under controlled conditions
Human factors engineering	Broadbent	What leads to maximally efficient use of a machine by a person?	Observation under controlled conditions

PARADIGMS OF COGNITIVE PSYCHOLOGY

Having looked at cognitive psychology's historical roots and research methods, we can now focus on cognitive psychology today. In this section, we will examine the four major paradigms that cognitive psychologists use in planning and executing their research.

First of all, what is a **paradigm?** The word has several related meanings, but you can think of it as a body of knowledge structured according to what its proponents consider important and what they do not. Paradigms include the assumptions investigators make in studying a phenomenon. Paradigms also specify what kinds of experimental methods and measures are appropriate for an investigation. Paradigms are thus intellectual frameworks that guide investigators in studying and understanding phenomena.

In this section, well review four paradigms used by cognitive psychologists today. In learning about each one, ask yourself the following questions: What assumptions underlie the paradigm? What questions or issues does the paradigm emphasize? What analogies (such as the analogy between the computer and the mind) does the paradigm use? What research methods and measures does the paradigm favour?

The Information-Processing Approach

The **information-processing approach** dominated cognitive psychology in the 1960s and 1970s and remains strong and influential today (Atkinson & Shiffrin, 1968). As its name implies, the information-processing approach draws an analogy between human cognition and computerized processing of information. Central to the information-processing approach is the idea that cognition can be thought of as information (what we see, hear, read about, think about) passing through a system (us or, more specifically, our minds).

Researchers following an information-processing approach often assume that information is processed (received, stored, recoded, transformed, retrieved, and transmitted) in stages and that it is stored in specific places while being processed. One goal within this framework, then, is to determine what these stages and storage places are and how they work.

Other assumptions underlie the information-processing approach as well. One is that people's cognitive abilities can be thought of as "systems" of interrelated capacities. We know different individuals have different cognitive capacities—different attention spans, memory capacities, and language skills, to name a few. Information-processing theorists try to find the relationships between these capacities, to explain how individuals go about performing specific cognitive tasks.

In accordance with the computer metaphor, information-processing theorists assume that people, like computers, are general-purpose symbol manipulators. In other words, people, like computers, can perform astonishing cognitive feats by applying only a few mental operations to symbols (such as letters, numbers, propositions, or scenes). Information is then stored symbolically, and the way it is coded and stored greatly affects how easy it is to use it later (as when we want to recall information or manipulate it in some way).

A general-purpose information-processing system is shown in Figure 1-2. Note the various memory stores where information is held for possible later use and the different processes that operate on the information at different points or that transfer it from store to store. Certain processes, such as detection and recognition, are used at the beginning of information processing; others, such as recoding or retrieval, have to do with memory storage; still others, such as reasoning or concept formation, have to do with putting information together in new ways. In this model, boxes represent stores, and arrows represent processes (leading some to refer to information-processing models as "boxes-and-arrows" models of cognition). The model is depicted best by something computer scientists call flowcharts, which illustrate the sequential flow of information through a system.

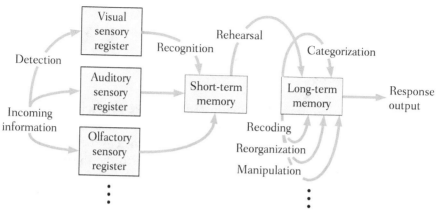

FIGURE 1-2 A typical information-processing model.

The information-processing tradition is rooted in structuralism, in that its followers attempt to identify the basic capacities and processes we use in cognition. The computer metaphor used in this approach also shows an indebtedness to the fields of engineering and communications. Psychologists working in the information-processing tradition are interested in relating individual and developmental differences to differences in basic capacities and processes. Typically, information-processing psychologists use experimental and quasi-experimental techniques in their investigations.

The Connectionist Approach

Early in the 1980s, researchers from a variety of disciplines began to explore alternatives to the information-processing approach that could explain cognition. The framework they established is known as **connectionism** (sometimes also called parallel-distributed processing, or PDP). Its name is derived from models depicting cognition as a network of connections among simple (and usually numerous) processing units (McClelland, 1988). Because these units are sometimes compared to neurons, the cells that transmit electrical impulses and underlie all sensation and muscle movement, connectionist models are sometimes called **neural networks** (technically speaking, there are distinctions between connectionist and neural network models, but we will not review them here).

Each unit is connected to other units in a large network. Each unit has some level of activation at any particular moment in time. The exact level of activation depends on the input to that unit from both the environment and other units to which it is connected. Connections between two units have weights, which can be positive or negative. A positively weighted connection causes one unit to excite, or raise the level of activation of, units to which it is connected; a negatively weighted connection has the opposite effect, inhibiting or lowering the activation of connected units.

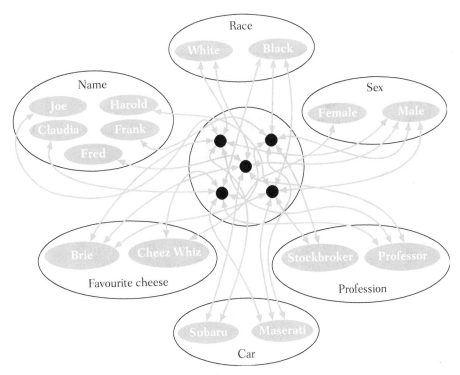

FIGURE 1-3 A typical connectionist model.

Republished with permission of Brooks/Cole Publishing, from Cognitive Psychology: A Neural-Network Approach, Colin Martindale, © 1991; permission conveyed through Copyright Clearance Center, Inc.

Figure 1-3 depicts a connectionist network, showing both units and their connections. In this example, the units are the black circles at the centre of the figure, with all the arrows pointing to them. Each of these units (sometimes called nodes) represents a particular individual. Each unit is connected to other units (shown as small ellipses) that depict certain information about individuals—for example, their names, cars, or professions. The arrows between units depict excitatory, or positively weighted, connections. When any unit reaches a certain level of activation, it activates all the other units to which it has positively weighted connections. In this example, all units within the same larger ellipse have negatively weighted, or inhibitory, connections. Thus, if the node for "Joe" is activated, it inhibits activation of the nodes "Claudia," "Fred," "Frank," and "Harold." At the same time, the "Joe" node activates the top left-hand node in the centre circle, and activates the nodes "male," "professor," "Subaru," and "brie." The activation of these nodes inhibits, or lowers, the activation of all other nodes in their respective ellipses.

One major difference between the information-processing and the connectionist approaches is the manner in which cognitive processes are assumed to occur. In information-processing models, cognition is typically assumed to occur *serially*—that is, in discrete stages (first one process occurs, feeding information into the next process, which feeds information into the next process, and so on). In contrast, most (but not all) connectionist models assume that cognitive processes occur in *parallel,* many at the same time.

The connectionist framework allows for a wide variety of models that can vary in the number of units hypothesized, number and pattern of connections among units, and connection of units to the environment. All connectionist models share the assumption, however, that there is no need to hypothesize a central processor that directs the flow of information from one process or storage area to another. Instead, different patterns of activation account for the various cognitive processes (Dawson, 1998). Knowledge is not stored in various storehouses but within connections between units. Learning occurs when new connective patterns are established that change the weights of connections between units.

Feldman and Ballard (1982), in an early description of connectionism, argued that this approach is more consistent with the way the brain functions than an information-processing approach. The brain, they argued, is made up of many neurons connected to one another in various complex ways. The authors asserted that "the fundamental premise of connectionism is that individual neurons *do not transmit large amounts of symbolic information.* Instead they compute by being *appropriately connected* to large numbers of similar units. This is in sharp contrast to the conventional computer model of intelligence prevalent in computer science and cognitive psychology" (p. 208). Rumelhart (1989, p. 134) puts the issue more simply: "Connectionism seeks to replace the computer metaphor of the information-processing framework with a brain metaphor."

Like the information-processing approach, connectionism draws from structuralism an interest in the elements of cognitive functioning. However, whereas information processors look to computer science, connectionists look to cognitive neuropsychology and cognitive neuroscience for information to help them construct their theories and models. Information-processing accounts of cognition try to provide explanations at a more abstract, symbolic level than do connectionist accounts. Connectionist models are more concerned with the "sub-symbolic" level: how cognitive processes actually could be carried out by a brain. Most connectionist work seeks to replicate the findings of experimental and quasi-experimental research using computer programs based on a neural-network model.

The Evolutionary Approach

Some of our most remarkable cognitive abilities and achievements are ones we typically take for granted. Two that come immediately to mind are the ability to perceive three-dimensional objects correctly and the ability to understand and produce language. These abilities may seem rather trivial and mundane—after all, a 3-year-old can do quite a bit of both. However, researchers in the field of artificial intelligence quickly found that it is not so easy to program computers to carry out even rudimentary versions of these tasks (Winston, 1992).

So why can young children do these tasks? How can a wide range of people carry them out seemingly with little effort, even people who don't seem particularly gifted intellectually? Some psychologists search for an answer in evolutionary theory (Cosmides & Tooby 2002; Krebs, 2007). The argument goes something like this: Like other animal minds, the human mind is a biological system, one that has evolved over generations. Like other animal minds, it too is subject to the laws of natural selection. Therefore, the human mind has responded to evolutionary pressures to adapt in certain ways rather than others in response to the environments encountered by our predecessors. Evolutionary psychologist Leda Cosmides (1989) notes that the environments our ancestors experienced were not simply physical, but ecological and social as well.

The idea here is that humans have specialized areas of competence produced by our evolutionary heritage. Cosmides and Tooby (2002) argue that people have "a large and heterogeneous set of evolved, reliably developing, dedicated problem-solving programs, each of which is specialized to solve a particular domain or class of adaptive problems (e.g., grammar acquisition, mate acquisition, food aversion, way finding)" (p. 147). In other words, people have special-purpose mechanisms (including cognitive mechanisms) specific to a certain context or class of problems.

Cosmides and Tooby (2000, 2002) believe that some of the most significant issues our ancestors faced involved social issues, such as creating and enforcing social contracts. To do this, people must be especially good at reasoning about costs and benefits, and be able to detect cheating in a social exchange. Therefore, evolutionary psychologists predict that people's reasoning will be especially enhanced when they are reasoning about cheating, a topic we examine in much greater detail in Chapter 10.

In general, evolutionary psychologists believe we understand a system best if we understand the evolutionary pressures on our ancestors. Explaining how a system of reasoning works, they believe, is much easier if we understand how evolutionary forces shaped the system in certain directions rather than other, equally plausible ones.

The Ecological Approach

A fourth major approach to the study of cognition comes from both psychologists and anthropologists, and overlaps much more with the evolutionary approach than it does with either the information-processing or connectionist approach. The central tenet of this approach is that cognition does not occur in isolation from larger cultural contexts; all cognitive activities are shaped by the culture and by the context in which they occur.

Jean Lave, a current theorist in this tradition, has conducted some fascinating work that illustrates the **ecological approach.** Lave (1988) described the results of the Adult Math Project as "an observational and experimental investigation of everyday arithmetic practices"

(p. 1). Lave, Murtaugh, and de la Rocha (1984) studied how people used arithmetic in their everyday lives. In one study, they followed people on grocery-shopping trips to analyze how and when people calculate "best buys." They found that people's methods of calculation varied with the context. This was somewhat surprising, because students in our culture are taught to use the same specified formulas on all problems of a given type to yield one definite numerical answer. To illustrate, compare a typical third-grade arithmetic problem presented by teachers to students—"Brandi had eight seashells. Nikki had five more. How many seashells did the two of them have together?"—with the following problem, posed and solved by one of the grocery shoppers, regarding the number of apples she should purchase for her family for the week:

There's only about three or four [apples] at home, and I have four kids, so you figure at least two apiece in the next three days. These are the kinds of things I have to resupply. I only have a certain amount of storage space in the refrigerator, so I can't load it up totally. . . . Now that I'm home in the summertime, this is a good snack food. And I like an apple sometimes at lunchtime when I come home. (Murtaugh, 1985, p. 188)

Lave (1988) pointed out a number of contrasts between this arithmetic problem solving and the kind used in solving school problems. First, the second example has many possible answers (for example, 5, 6, 9), unlike the first problem, which has one (13). Second, the first problem is given to the problem solver to solve; the second is constructed by the problem solver herself. Third, the first problem is somewhat disconnected from personal experience, goals, and interests, whereas the second comes out of practical daily living.

Although there has been much recent interest in the ecological approach, the idea of studying cognition in everyday contexts actually arose several years earlier. A major proponent of this viewpoint was J. J. Gibson, whose work on perception we will discuss at length in Chapter 3. Ulric Neisser, a friend and colleague of Gibson, wrote a book in 1976 aimed at redirecting the field of psychology toward studying more "realistic" cognitive phenomena.

Following this tradition, Daniel Smilek at the University of Waterloo, and Alan Kingstone at the University of British Columbia, have been focusing on understanding how attention operates in everyday situations by examining eye movements in real-world displays (Kingstone, Smilek, & Ristic, 2003; Smilek, Birmingham, Cameron, Bischof, & Kingstone, 2007). For example, in one of their studies they presented participants with pictures of art and sports scenes, and monitored their eye movements while they described the pictures aloud. They found that, regardless of the type of image participants were viewing, most eye fixations were committed to the eyes and faces of the people in the scene. They argued that eye gaze, head position, body position, and situational context are important cues that people use to understand not only the basic gist of scenes, but also the intentional state of others.

We can see the influences of both the functionalist and the Gestalt schools on the ecological approach. The functionalists focused on the purposes served by cognitive processes, certainly an ecological question. Gestalt psychology's emphasis on the context surrounding any experience is likewise compatible with the ecological approach. The ecological approach would deny the usefulness (and perhaps even the possibility) of studying cognitive phenomena in artificial circumstances divorced from larger contexts. Thus, this tradition relies less on laboratory experiments or computer simulations and more on naturalistic observation and field studies to explore cognition.

General Points

Each of these four paradigms makes an important contribution to cognitive psychology, and in some ways the four offer complementary perspectives on how the underlying principles of cognition ought to be investigated and understood. The information-processing paradigm, for example, focuses researchers on the functional aspects of cognition—what kinds of processes are used toward what ends. The connectionist approach, in contrast, focuses on the underlying "hardware"—how the global cognitive processes described by an information-processing model are implemented in the human brain. The evolutionary approach centres on questions of how a cognitive system or function has evolved over generations. The ecological approach stresses the need to consider the context of any cognitive process to understand more completely how that process functions in the real world.

Not all cognitive research fits neatly into one of these three paradigms. Some research incorporates parts of different paradigms; some fits no paradigm neatly. However, we hope these four paradigms will provide a useful backdrop against which to consider individual studies.

This framework offers a sense of where we're headed in the rest of the book, as we take up specific cognitive topics in more detail. Throughout, you should examine how the research studies discussed bear on cognitive activities in your everyday life. Are the questions posed, and the research approaches used to answer them, appropriate? How do the theoretical assumptions shape the way the questions are posed? What do the research findings mean, and what new questions do they raise?

SUMMARY

1. Cognition plays a large role in our everyday existence. We take much of our cognitive experience for granted because the ways in which we function cognitively are so routine we simply don't pay attention to them. Nonetheless, on closer inspection we see that many cognitive activities are astonishingly complex.

2. We've examined different traditions in the study of cognition, tracing the history of study back at least as far as Wundt's Leipzig laboratory. We've seen how different major schools of thought—structuralism, functionalism, behaviourism, and Gestalt approaches—have framed cognitive questions.

3. Structuralism, a school of psychology associated with Wilhelm Wundt, sought to discover the laws and principles that explain our immediate conscious experience. In particular, structuralists wanted to identify the simplest essential units of the mind and to determine how these units combine to produce complex mental phenomena.

4. Functionalism, a school of psychology associated with William James, took as the basic aim of psychology understanding the function of the mind—the ways in which mental functions let individuals adapt to their environment.

5. Behaviourism, regarded by some as a branch of functionalism, took as the central aim of psychology the scientific study of behaviour, an observable consequence of psychological experience. Radical behaviourists insisted that references to unobservable, subjective, mental states (such as consciousness) as well as to unobservable, subjective processes (such as expecting, believing, understanding, remembering, hoping for, deciding, perceiving) should be banished from psychology proper.

6. The school of Gestalt psychology held as its central assumption that psychological phenomena cannot be reduced to simple elements but must be analyzed and studied in their entirety. Gestalt psychologists believed observers do not construct a coherent perception from simple, elementary sensory aspects of an experience but instead apprehend the total structure of an experience as a whole.

7. Work by Francis Galton emphasized the idea that individuals differ, even as adults, in their cognitive capacities, abilities, and preferences.

8. We've also seen how the present study of cognitive psychology grows out of, and contributes to, innovations in other fields, such as computer science, communications, engineering, linguistics, evolution, and anthropology.

9. Cognitive psychology draws upon many different research methods, including experiments, quasi-experiments, introspection, and naturalistic observation.

10. Finally, we've reviewed four major approaches to the modern study of cognitive phenomena: the information-processing, connectionist, evolutionary, and ecological paradigms. We've seen that the information-processing approach emphasizes stage-like processing of information and specific storage of that information during processing. The connectionist approach instead depicts cognitive processing as a pattern of excitation and inhibition in a network of connections among simple (and usually numerous) processing units that operate in parallel. The evolutionary paradigm examines how a cognitive process has been shaped by environmental pressure over long periods of time. The ecological paradigm stresses the ways in which the environment and the context shape the way cognitive processing occurs.

REVIEW QUESTIONS

1. How has cognitive theory of research been used outside the laboratory?

2. What roles do laboratory experiments and naturalistic observation play in cognitive research?

3. What similarities and differences exist among the following three "schools" of psychology: structuralism, functionalism, behaviourism?
4. What is a mental representation, and how is this concept viewed by Gestalt psychologists, information-processing psychologists, behaviourist psychologists, and connectionists?
5. Describe how research on individual differences might bear on cognitive psychology.
6. What was the "cognitive revolution"? What resulted from it?
7. Describe and critique the major research methods of cognitive psychology.
8. Compare and contrast the four major paradigms of cognitive psychology reviewed in this chapter (information processing, connectionism, the evolutionary approach, the ecological approach).

KEY TERMS

artificial intelligence
association
attention
behaviourism
between-subjects design
brain imaging
clinical interview
cognitive neuropsychology
cognitive revolution
cognitive science
computer metaphor
connectionism
controlled observation
decision making
ecological approach
ecological validity

empiricism
experiment
experimental control
functionalism
Gestalt psychology
human factors engineering
individual differences
information-processing
  approach
introspection
knowledge representation
language
limited-capacity processor
linguistics
localization of function
memory

mental representation
nativism
naturalistic observation
neural network
paradigm
pattern recognition
perception
person-machine system
problem solving
quasi-experiment
reasoning
recall
recognition
structuralism
within-subjects design

The Brain: An Overview of Structure and Function

When the field of cognitive psychology first began (in the 1950s and '60s), cognitive psychologists found the workings of the brain to be quite interesting, but not necessarily relevant to their understanding of how cognitive processes worked. The idea was that description of cognitive processes and structures was best done at a level of abstraction above the neural level, which was thought to be too inordinately complicated. Many feared that a description of how each neuron in the brain worked would not yield a comprehensible explanation of a cognitive process, such as, for example, how you learn to conjugate French verb endings, or how you remember where you parked your car at the mall. There is still strong argument among psychologists, biologists, philosophers, and computer scientists over which level of explanation is most useful for different kinds of understanding. However, increasing numbers of cognitive psychologists have become interested in the functioning of the brain as an underpinning for cognitive activity. Although the question of which level provides the most useful explanation remains, many cognitive psychologists feel they cannot investigate cognition without a working knowledge of how the brain develops and functions. One of the ongoing challenges for cognitive psychologists is developing and applying methods of inquiry that can conclusively link cognitive processes to underlying neural activity. A full understanding of how cognitive operations arise from the activity of individual neurons, or of distributed brain systems, as well as the functional interaction of various brain regions is the main goal in the growing field of cognitive neuroscience. A related goal is to determine how cognitive functions are affected by damage to certain brain structures, and whether it is possible to recover cognitive functions following brain injury due to strokes, disease, and accidents (Kolb & Gibb, 2007).

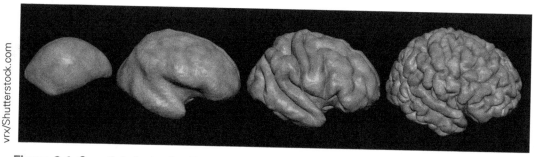

vrx/Shutterstock.com

Figure 2-1 Growth in brain size. The brain of a baby shown in an x-ray graphic 3D rendering.

Of course, the topic of brain functioning and its relationship to cognition is itself a vast and complex one, and only brief highlights are given here. The interested student is referred to other, in-depth treatments of the topic (e.g., Stephen, 2016; Gazzaniga, 2004; Johnson, Munakata, & Gilmore, 2002).

First, some growth statistics: The brain grows from 0 to 350 grams (about three-quarters of a pound) during the prenatal period, but this growth doesn't stop at birth.

The maximum brain weight of 1350 grams (about three pounds) is achieved when the individual is about 20 years old (Nowakowski & Hayes, 2002). Most post-birth growth takes place before the child's fourth birthday, but some changes continue through adulthood. But keep in mind that in the human adult brain, bigger is not always better!

Box 2-1 Canadian Research Highlight

Dr. Bryan Kolb is a professor of psychology at the University of Lethbridge (https://www.uleth. ca/artsci/neuroscience/dr-bryan-e-kolb) holds the Board of Governors Research Chair in Neuroscience, is a founding researcher with the Canadian Centre for Behavioural Neuroscience, and is one of the world's most influential neuroscientists. He was the first to show how the growth of new brain cells following injury can restore cognitive and behavioural function. His work investigating factors that influence brain development in infancy has led to the development of new treatments and strategies for improving behaviour following early brain injury and offers new insights into recovery of function in victims of stroke, Alzheimer disease, and drug abuse.

STRUCTURE OF THE BRAIN

Many different structures make up the human brain. These are easiest to learn about if we group structure in some way. We'll begin with a phylogenetic division. The adult brain is made up of several structures that can grouped based on when and how each develops: the hind-brain, midbrain, and forebrain. In our brief discussion, we will focus specifically on the cerebral cortex, a part of the forebrain. However, it is worth talking briefly about the hindbrain and midbrain first.

The Hindbrain and Midbrain

The **hindbrain** develops originally as one of three bulges in the embryo's neural tube. Evolutionarily structures within the hindbrain are the most primitive (Zillmer & Spiers, 2001). The brain stem (a structure consisting of the medulla and pons in the hindbrain, as well as the midbrain and certain structures of the forebrain), shown in Figure 2-2, comprises about 4.4% of the total weight of an adult brain; the cerebellum accounts for an additional 10.5%.

The hindbrain contains three major structures. The **medulla oblongata** (sometimes referred to simply as the medulla) transmits information from the spinal cord to the brain and regulates life support functions such as respiration, blood pressure, coughing, sneezing, vomiting, and heart rate (Pritchard & Alloway 1999). The **pons** (the name derives from the Latin word for bridge) also acts as a neural relay centre, facilitating the "crossover" of

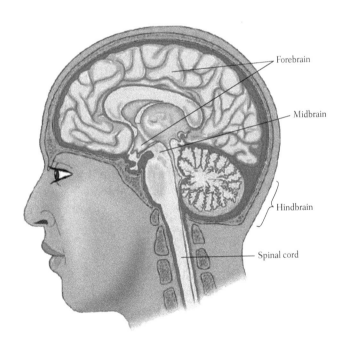

FIGURE 2-2 Major structures in the brain.

Source: From *Biological Foundations of Human Behavior* by Josephine F. Wilson. Copyright © 2002 by Josephine F. Wilson. Reprinted by permission.

information between the left side of the body and the right side of the brain and vice versa. It is also involved in balance and in the processing of both visual and auditory information.

The **cerebellum** contains neurons that coordinate muscular activity (Pritchard & Alloway, 1999). It is one of the most primitive brain structures. It also governs balance and is involved in general motor behaviour and coordination.

Brain lesions in the cerebellum can cause irregular and jerky movements, tremors, and impairment of balance and of gait. It has also been implicated in people's ability to shift attention between visual and auditory stimuli, and in dealing with temporal stimuli such as rhythm (Akshoomoff & Courchesne, 1994).

The **midbrain** is located (unsurprisingly) in the middle of the brain. Many of the structures contained in the midbrain (such as the tectum and tegmentum) are involved in relaying information between other brain regions, such as the cerebellum and forebrain. Another midbrain structure, the reticular formation, helps keep us awake and alert and is involved in the sudden arousal we may need to respond to a threatening or attention-grabbing stimulus (Pritchard & Alloway 1999).

The Forebrain

Because of our interest in cognitive issues, we will focus the remainder of our discussion of the brain on the **forebrain.** Some of the structures of the forebrain are presented in Figure 2-3. The **thalamus,** for example, is yet another structure for relaying information, especially to the cerebral cortex (Pritchard & Alloway 1999), which we will talk about shortly. The **hypothalamus** controls the pituitary gland by releasing hormones, specialized chemicals that help to regulate other glands in the body. The hypothalamus also controls so-called homeostatic behaviours, such as eating, drinking, temperature control, sleeping, sexual behaviours, and emotional reactions. Other structures, such as the **hippocampus,** involved in the formation of long-term memories, and the **amygdala,** which modulates the strength of emotional memories and is involved in emotional learning (LeDoux, 1996), are also located in the forebrain, as are the basal ganglia, which are involved in the production of motor behaviour.

Subcortical structures of the brain:

- **Thalamus**: Switching station for sensory information; also involved in memory
- **Hypothalamus**: Regulates basic biological functions, including hunger, thirst, temperature, and sexual arousal; also involved in emotions
- **Hippocampus**: Involved in learning, memory and emotions
- **Amygdala**: Involved in memory, emotion, and aggression
- **Cerebellum**: Controls coordinated movement; also involved in language and thinking
- **Medulla**: Controls vital functions such as breathing and heart rate
- **Spinal Cord**: Transmits signals between brain and rest of the body

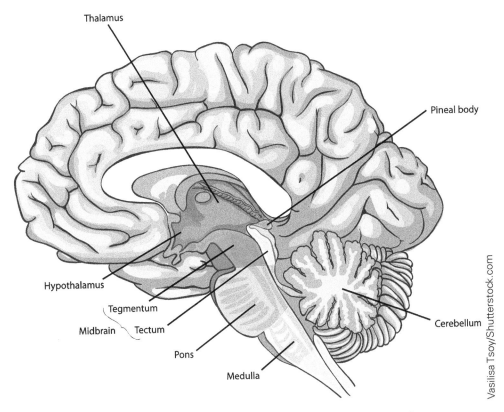

Thalamus

Pineal body

Hypothalamus

Tegmentum

Midbrain   Tectum

Pons

Medulla

Cerebellum

Vasilisa Tsoy/Shutterstock.com

FIGURE 2-3 Brainstem structure shown on the medial surface of the brain.

We will discuss many of these structures, including the hippocampus and amygdala, in the chapters to come. For the present, we will focus on the cerebrum (from the Latin word for brain), the largest structure in the brain. It consists of a layer called the **cerebral cortex,** consisting of about a half-dozen layers of neurons with white matter beneath, which carries information between the cortex and the thalamus or between different parts of the cortex.

Figure 2-4 presents a more detailed diagram of the cerebral cortex, which neurologists divide into four lobes: **frontal** (underneath the forehead), **parietal** (underneath the top rear part of the skull), **occipital** (at the back of the head), and **temporal** (on the side of the head) (Pritchard & Alloway, 1999). The left and right hemispheres are connected by the corpus callosum (in the case of the frontal, parietal, and occipital lobes) and the anterior commisure (in the case of the temporal lobes). A structure known as the central sulcus (a prominent shallow groove on the surface of the brain) divides the frontal and parietal lobes; another sulcus, the lateral sulcus, helps define the temporal lobe. Actually, since our heads have two sides, right

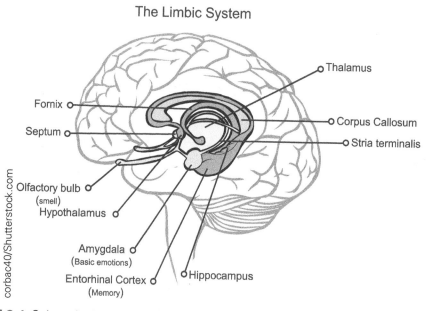

FIGURE 2-4 Subcortical structures of the brain.

and left, we have two lobes of each kind—the right frontal, left frontal, right parietal, left parietal, and so forth.

The parietal lobes contain the somatosensory cortex, which is contained in the postcentral gyrus (a gyrus is a convolution or ridge of the brain), the area just behind the central sulcus. It is involved in the processing of sensory information from the body—for example, sensations of pain, pressure, touch, or temperature (Kolb & Whishaw, 2003). The occipital lobes process visual information, and the temporal lobes auditory information, as well the ability to recognize certain stimuli such as faces. Because the temporal lobes are right above structures such as the amygdala and hippocampus, both involved in memory, damage to the temporal lobes can result in memory disruption as well (Kolb & Whishaw, 2003).

The frontal lobes have three separate regions. The **motor cortex** (located in the precentral gyrus) directs fine motor movement; the premotor cortex seems to be involved in planning such movements. The **prefrontal cortex** or lobe is involved with what neuroscientists call **executive functioning**—planning, making decisions, implementing strategies, inhibiting inappropriate behaviours, and using working memory to process information (Stuss, 1992). Damage to certain parts of the prefrontal cortex can also result in marked changes in personality, mood, affect, and the ability to control inappropriate behaviour (Pritchard & Alloway 1999).

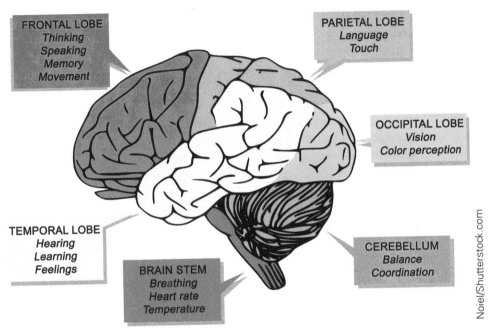

FRONTAL LOBE
Thinking
Speaking
Memory
Movement

PARIETAL LOBE
Language
Touch

OCCIPITAL LOBE
Vision
Color perception

TEMPORAL LOBE
Hearing
Learning
Feelings

BRAIN STEM
Breathing
Heart rate
Temperature

CEREBELLUM
Balance
Coordination

Noiel/Shutterstock.com

FIGURE 2-5 Regions and functions of the human brain

The prefrontal cortex shows the longest period of maturation; it appears to be one of the last brain regions to mature (Casey, Giedd, & Thomas, 2000). Interestingly, this region may also be one of the "first to go" in aging effects seen toward the end of life (see Chapter 12 for more details). It has been hypothesized that brain regions that show the most plasticity over the longest periods may be the most sensitive to environmental toxins or stressors.

LOCALIZATION OF FUNCTION

When we describe a particular brain region or structure as having a particular role to play (as in memory or attention), you may wonder what the basis of such a claim is. That is, how do neuroscientists *know* what brain region does what? The answer lies in studies of **localization of function,** a means of mapping the brain.

The original idea of localization of function traces back to an Austrian anatomist named Franz Gall (1758–1828), who proposed an early localization theory. Gall believed in something called **faculty psychology.** Faculty psychology was the theory that different mental abilities, such as reading or computation, were independent and autonomous functions, carried out in different parts of the brain (Fodor, 1983). Gall believed that different locations in the brain were associated with such faculties as parental love, combativeness, acquisitiveness, and secretiveness, to name a few. Later, Gall's student Johan Spurzheim carried on Gall's teachings, developing the study of **phrenology** (see Figure 2-6), a now discredited idea that psychological strengths and weaknesses could be precisely correlated to the relative sizes of different brain areas.

The major problem with phrenology was not the assumption that different parts of the brain controlled different functions, but rather with two subsidiary assumptions: (1) that the size of a portion of the brain corresponded to its relative power, and (2) that different faculties were absolutely independent. We now know that different mental activities—for example, perception and attention—are not wholly distinct and independent, but rather interact in many different ways. We also know that the overall size of a brain or brain area is not indicative of the functioning of that area. Therefore, having a different configuration of bumps and indentations in a brain does not determine or even predict how an individual will function cognitively or socially.

More modern approaches to localizing function in the brain date back to Paul Broca (1824–1880), who in the early 1860s presented findings at a medical conference that brain injury to a particular part of the left frontal lobe (the posterior, inferior region shown in Figure 2-7)

FIGURE 2-6 Phrenology machine (about 1905) was intended to measure "bumps" on the skull and correlate those with specific human attributes.

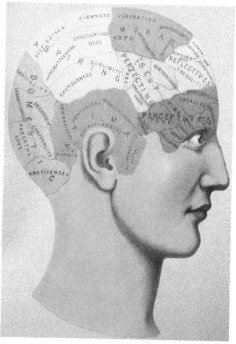

FIGURE 2-7 Phrenology head. Specific locations on the skull were thought to correspond to specific abilities.

Source: http://www.vintagemedstock.com

resulted in a particular kind of **aphasia,** or disruption of expressive language (Springer & Deutsch, 1998). This brain region has become known as Broca's area; injury to this area leads to a kind of aphasia known as Broca's or nonfluent aphasia, in which the person is unable to produce many words or to speak very fluently.

A decade after Broca's discovery, Carl Wernicke (1848–1904) announced the discovery of a second "language centre" in the brain, this one thought to control language understanding (as opposed to language production). This region, which has come to be known as Wernicke's area, is located in the superior posterior region of the temporal lobe, also typically in the left hemisphere, and is also shown in Figure 2-8. Patients with so-called Wernicke's aphasia (also called fluent aphasia) are able to produce speech with seemingly fluent contours of pitch and rhythm. However, the speech often makes no sense and contains gibberish. Moreover, these patients show impairments in their ability to understand speech (Pritchard & Alloway 1999).

Work by other neuropsychologists began to establish connections between lesions in particular brain regions and loss of specific motor control or sensory reception. Using research performed either on animals or as part of neurosurgical procedures intended to address problems such as epilepsy, scientists began to "map out" the portion of the frontal lobe known as the motor cortex as shown in Figure 2-9.

In addition, neuropsychologists have mapped out a second area of the brain, located in the parietal lobe just behind the motor cortex, known as the **primary somatosensory cortex** (see Figure 2-10). Like the motor cortex, the primary somatosensory cortex is organized such

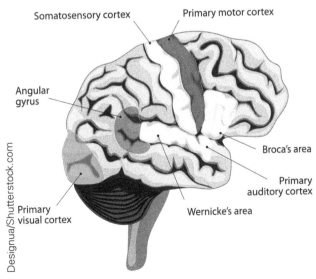

FIGURE 2-8 Classic speech centres.

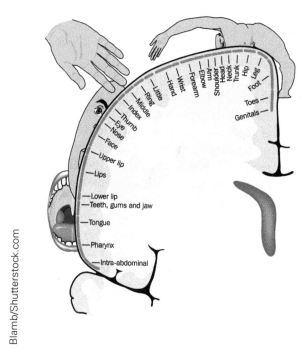

Blamb/Shutterstock.com

FIGURE 2-9 Penfield cortical body map, showing body parts mapped to specific areas of the cerebral cortex.

that each part of it receives information from a specific part of the body. As with the motor cortex, the total amount of "brain real estate" devoted to a particular part of the body is not proportional to the size of that body part. In other words, a large region of the body, such as a leg, corresponds to only a small portion of the primary somatosensory cortex. A more sensitive body part, such as the fingers or lips, has a correspondingly larger amount of cortex devoted to it.

A famous Canadian researcher, Wilder Penfield, took this work a step further. Penfield was a groundbreaking researcher and highly original surgeon working at the Montreal Neurological Institute in the 1930s. Before operating on his patients, who were undergoing surgery for treatment of severe epilepsy, he stimulated the brain with electrical probes while the patients were conscious on the operating table (under only local anesthesia), and observed their responses. In this way he targeted the areas of the brain involved in certain cognitive functions such as smelling, motor control, and speaking, among others (see www.histori.ca/minutes/minute.do?id=10211 for a web clip featuring Penfield's work). Using this technique he created maps of the sensory and motor cortices of the brain. These maps are still used today.

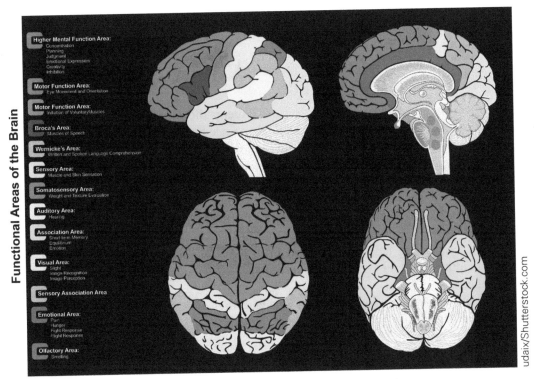

Functional Areas of the Brain

Higher Mental Function Area:
Concentration
Planning
Judgment
Emotional Expression
Creativity
Inhibition

Motor Function Area:
Eye Movement and Orientation

Motor Function Area:
Initiation of Voluntary Muscles

Broca's Area:
Muscles of Speech

Wernicke's Area:
Written and Spoken Language Comprehension

Sensory Area:
Muscle and Skin Sensation

Somatosensory Area:
Weight and Texture Evaluation

Auditory Area:
Hearing

Association Area:
Short-term Memory
Equilibrium
Emotion

Visual Area:
Sight
Image Recognition
Image Perception

Sensory Association Area

Emotional Area:
Pain
Hunger
Fight Response
Flight Response

Olfactory Area:
Smelling

udaix/Shutterstock.com

FIGURE 2-10 Modern localization of functions within the human brain

This same principle, of linking cognitive behaviours to underlying brain regions, has been used over the many decades since Penfield's work. Figure 2.10 depicts examples of our current understanding of these relationships for several different cognitive functions.

Many neuroscientists subscribe to the principle that higher-order cognitive processes are too complicated and interconnected to be localized to any one region (Pritchard & Alloway 1999). This view drew support from the work of Karl Lashley (1890–1958), who performed several landmark studies in neuroscience, studying the effects of brain **ablation** (removal of parts of the brain) on the maze-running ability of rats. Lashley (1929) reported that impairment in maze running was related to the total amount of cortex removed, and not to which specific area was removed. Thus mapping cognitive functions to underlying brain regions is a complicated matter as the brain is dynamic. While basic cognitive functions seem to rely on particular brain regions, some more complex cognitive functions likely rely on a combination of regions that must interact to produce function.

Complicating this already involved picture of brain organization is the notion of the **plasticity** of the brain (Black, 2004; Kolb, 1995). Some brain regions can adapt to "take over" functions of damaged regions, depending on the injury and the function involved. In general, the younger the patient and the less extensive the injury, the better is the chance of regaining function.

LATERALIZATION OF FUNCTION

Paul Broca's report of a language centre in his patients did more than argue for localization of function. Broca and many neuropsychologists since have been able to show that the two cerebral hemispheres seem to play different roles when it comes to some cognitive functions, especially language. We call this phenomenon **lateralization.**

Most individuals (around 95%) show a specialization for language in the left hemisphere. In these individuals, the left hemisphere is likely to be larger in size, especially in the areas where language is localized (Springer & Deutsch, 1998). We say that these individuals have a left-hemisphere dominance in language. A small percentage or people do not show such specialization, having language function in both hemispheres (these are called *bilateralized* individuals), and an even smaller percentage have language centres located in the right hemisphere.

If the left hemisphere is dominant for language, then what role does the right hemisphere play? Structurally, the right hemisphere often has larger parietal and temporal areas, and it is speculated that this leads to better integration of visual and auditory information and better spatial processing by the right than the left hemisphere. The right hemisphere is associated with working on geometric puzzles, navigation around familiar spaces, and even musical ability (Springer & Deutsch, 1998).

Some describe the difference in function between the two hemispheres by labelling the left hemisphere as the analytical one and the right hemisphere as the synthetic one (Wang, Buckner, & Liu, 2014; Carlson, 2004). The idea here is that the left hemisphere is particularly good at processing information serially—that is, information with events occurring one after another. If you think about processing a sentence, the events would be the individual words that are spoken or read in sequence. By contrast, the right hemisphere is thought to be more synthetic, putting individual elements together to make up a whole. Cognitive processes here might include constructing maps or other spatial structures, drawing sketches, and navigating through mazes.

Popular press articles have made much of the difference between the two cerebral hemispheres, going so far in some cases as to classify people as either right-brained or left-brained. It's very important to remember that this is a gross oversimplification. The vast majority of individuals have two quite functional cerebral hemispheres that continually interact to process information and carry out cognitive functions. The odds that only one hemisphere would be active in any everyday task are remote. Moreover, the two hemispheres are connected by a large neural structure known as the **corpus callosum,** which sends information from one hemisphere to the other very quickly.

BRAIN IMAGING TECHNIQUES

In Broca's day, neurologists had to wait until a patient died to really investigate the structural features of his or her brain. In the early part of the 20th century, more information came from studies performed as patients underwent brain surgery—to remove a tumour or stop the spread of epilepsy, most commonly. Fortunately for people but unfortunately for science, ethical considerations precluded doing brain surgery on healthy people, which limited our understanding of how "normal" brains functioned.

However, in the last four decades, technology has advanced to the point where neurologists and neuropsychologists can examine the functioning of normal brains using noninvasive means. We will briefly review some of these methods, known collectively as **brain imaging techniques.**

Some of these methods give us information about neuroanatomy—the structures of the brain. One of the earliest such brain-imaging techniques, developed in the 1970s, was X-ray computed tomography—also called X-ray CT, **computerized axial tomography,** or **CAT** scan—a technique in which a highly focused beam of X-rays is passed through the body from many different angles. Differing densities of body organs (including the brain) deflect the X-rays differently, allowing visualization of the organ. Figure 2-11 depicts a person undergoing a CAT scan.

Typically, CAT scans of a person's brain result in 9 to 12 different "slices" of the brain, each one taken at a different level of depth. CAT scans depend on the fact that structures of different density show up differently. Bone, for example, is denser than blood, which is denser than brain tissue, which is in turn denser than cerebrospinal fluid (Banich, 2004). Recent brain hemorrhages are typically indicated by the presence of blood; older brain damage, by areas of cerebrospinal fluid. Thus clinicians and researchers can use CAT scans to pinpoint areas of brain damage and also to make inferences about the relative "age" of the injury.

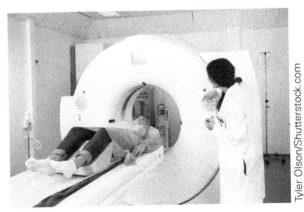

FIGURE 2-11 CT scanner. A person's head is placed into the device and then a rapidly rotating source sends X-rays through the head while detectors on the opposite side make photographs.

Another "window on the brain" can be obtained through electrical recording methods. You may already know that when neurons in the brain (or anywhere else, for that matter) fire, they generate electrical activity. Some animal research has involved placing electrodes in individual neurons to detect when and how often those single cells fire. Such work is not done with humans. Instead, the sum total of electrical activity generated by a large number of neurons comprises the information gathered (Banich, 2004).

Electroencephalography (EEG) can be used to detect different states of consciousness. Metal electrodes are positioned all over the scalp. The waveforms record changes in predictable ways when the person being recorded is awake and alert, drowsy, asleep, or in a coma. EEGs provide the clinician or researcher with a continuous measure of brain activity (Banich, 1997). Figure 2-12 shows the equipment being used to measure brain waves in a child.

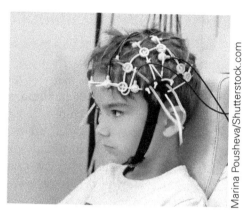

FIGURE 2-12 Equipment to measure brain waves.

A newer technique, magnetoencephalography or MEG, measures changes in magnetic fields generated by electrical activities of neurons. It has been called the "magnetic equivalent" of EEG (Springer & Deutsch, 1998). MEG gives a more precise localization of brain region activity than does EEG.

Another electrical recording technique, called **event-related potential**, or **ERP**, measures an area of the brain's response to a specific event. Participants in an ERP study have electrodes attached to their scalp and are then presented with various external stimuli, such as sights or sounds. The recording measures brain activity from the time before the stimulus is presented until some time afterward. The brain waves recorded also have predictable parts, or components. That is, the shape of the waveform can vary depending on whether the participant expects the stimulus to occur or is attending to the location in which the stimulus appears, and whether the stimulus is physically different from other recent stimuli.

Yet another functional brain-imaging technique, which dates back to the 1970s, is called **positron emission tomography**, or **PET**. This technique involves injecting a radioactively labelled compound (radioisotopes of carbon, nitrogen, oxygen, or fluorine subatomic particles that rapidly emit gamma radiation, which can be detected by devices outside the head). PET scans measure the blood flow to different regions of the brain, allowing an electronic reconstruction of a picture of a brain, showing which areas are most active at a particular time (Posner & Raichle, 1994). A variation of the PET procedure involves measuring local metabolic changes instead of blood flow, using an injection of fluorodeoxyglucose, a radioisotope structurally similar to glucose.

PET scans rely on the fact that when an area of the brain is active more blood flows to it, and its cells take up more glucose from the blood vessels that penetrate it (Frith & Friston, 1997; Kung, 1993). People undergoing a PET brain scan sit with their head in a ring of photocells.

A radioactive tracer, typically $^{15}O2$ (oxygen with one electron removed), is injected into a vein as water (that is, as $H2^{15}O$). Within 30 seconds, the tracer starts to reach the brain. The tracer ^{15}O accumulates in the brain in direct proportion to the amount of blood flowing to that brain region (Banich, 2004). Within the roughly two minutes before the radioactive tracer decays to its half-life several scans can be made, showing the amount of blood flowing to that region (Frith & Friston, 1997). Another technique to measure cerebral blood flow is known as single-photon emission computed tomography, or SPECT for short. The basic technique is similar to a PET scan, but does not require some of the expensive equipment a PET scan does; thus it is sometimes known as a "poor person's PET." Like CAT scans, however, PET and SPECT scans use radiation.

Although an important diagnostic tool in neuropsychology CAT (PET and SPECT) scans are used less often than a newer brain-imaging technique, **magnetic resonance imaging,** or **MRI.** Like CAT scans, MRI provides information about neuroanatomy. Unlike CAT scans, however, MRI requires no exposure to radiation and often permits clearer pictures, which shows an MRI scan of a brain.

Someone undergoing an MRI typically lies inside a tunnel-like structure that surrounds the person with a strong magnetic field. Radio waves are directed at the head (or whatever body structure is being scanned), causing the centres of hydrogen atoms in those structures to align themselves in predictable ways. Computers collate information about how the atoms are aligning and produce a composite three-dimensional image from which any desired cross-section can be examined further.

MRI scans are often the technique of choice, as they now produce "textbook-quality anatomy pictures" of a brain (Carlson, 2004, p. 192). However, not everyone can undergo an MRI scan. The magnetic fields generated in an MRI scan interfere with electrical fields, so people with pacemakers are not candidates for an MRI (pacemakers generate electric signals). Nor are people with metal in their bodies, such as a surgical clip on an artery or a metal shaving in the eye. The magnetic field could dislodge the metal in the body, causing trauma. Metal anchored to hard surfaces, such as dental fillings, is not a problem. Because MRIs require people to lie very still in a tunnel-like machine that often leaves little room for arm movements, people with claustrophobia are also not good candidates for this technique.

While CAT and MRI scans provide pictures of brain structures, and investigators can use these pictures to pinpoint areas of damage or other abnormality, they provide only static pictures of the parts of a brain. No information is gleaned about *how* a brain functions— that is, what areas of the brain show activity when people perform different cognitive tasks. To answer such questions, different brain-imaging techniques are needed. Fortunately, recent developments have created techniques that fit the bill.

A newer technique may offer a way out of these difficulties. **Functional magnetic resonance imaging,** or **fMRI,** relies on the fact that blood has magnetic properties. As blood is carried from the heart, it is maximally magnetic. As it passes through capillaries, it becomes less magnetic. Brain regions that are active show a change in the ratio of oxygenated to deoxygenated blood (Banich, 2004). Such fMRI scans use existing MRI equipment but provide clinicians and investigators with a noninvasive, nonradioactive means of assessing blood flow to various brain regions.

These techniques for studying the way the brain functions make possible new connections and new questions in cognitive psychology. Before the availability of these techniques, cognitive theories did not refer to the biological mechanisms that implement various cognitive processes. Now cognitive neuroscientists offer us findings from studies based on a new assumption: "The mapping between physical activity in the brain and its functional state is such that when two experimental conditions are associated with different patterns of neural activity it can be assumed that they have engaged distinct cognitive functions" (Rugg, 1997, p. 5). For example, Ravi Menon and his colleagues at the Robarts Institute at the University of Western Ontario have been instrumental in using fMRI techniques to allow a clear delineation of the human primary visual cortex in the occipital lobe (Menon et al., 1993). As well, a review of 275 PET and fMRI studies (Cabeza & Nyberg, 2000) summarizes how different areas of the brain are active for different cognitive functions such as attention, perception, imagery, language, and memory.

The strategy used to produce a functional map of the brain is based on a concept introduced by Dutch physiologist Franciscus Donders in 1868/1969. He suggested a general method for measuring a cognitive process. This logic has been adapted to develop functional maps of cognitive processes in the brain. He measured the time it took a person to respond (by making a keypress) to a light and subtracted this from the time needed to respond to a particular colour of light. His experiment revealed that discriminating colour requires about 50 msec of cognitive processing. In neuroimaging studies the same logic, termed **subtraction technique,** has been applied to isolate the brain region(s) contributing to a given cognitive process. That is, the relative amount of activation in a particular brain region needed for a given cognitive task can be measured by subtracting a control state (responding to a light) from a task state (discriminating colour). Figure 2-13 shows examples of how this logic has been applied to isolate brain region contributing to various cognitive functions.

In 2000, Daniel Bub at the University of Victoria wrote a review of subtractive logic and other issues relating to fMRI, and proposed other methods of data analysis. Borowsky and colleagues (2005) at the University of Saskatchewan have applied a different statistical approach than subtractive logic to understanding how the brain processes information. As well, researchers at the Rotman Research Institute in Toronto have pioneered a new approach to understanding brain activation that does not involve subtraction logic; rather than focus on single regions of the brain active for a given cognitive task, a network analysis of brain region whose activity co-varies across different tasks is conducted using multivariate statistics (McIntosh et al., 1996). Using these new methods of analysis of fMRI data, researchers

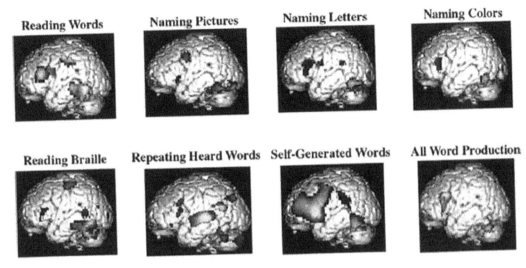

FIGURE 2-13 Areas of brain activation revealed by subtracting viewing letter strings with reading words (silently) (Price et al., 1996), by subtracting viewing nonsense figures from naming visual pictures (Price et al., 1997), and by subtracting self-generated words from repeating heard words (Frith et al., 1991a).

Source: Cabeza, Roberto & Alan Kingstone (eds.), *Handbook of Functional Neuroimaging of Cognition*, figure 7.11, © 2001 Massachusetts Institute of Technology, by permission of The MIT Press.

are able to paint a clearer picture of how the human brain achieves cognitive processing—and capture just how dynamic the human brain really is, coordinating functions across different brain regions depending on the given environment, task constraints, and motivations at the time of processing information.

Brain imaging and recording techniques certainly include a lot of acronyms! How can the novice keep them all straight? One way to do so is to categorize the techniques according to the kind of information they provide. CAT and MRI scans yield neuroanatomical information. PET, SPECT, and fMRI provide dynamic information about how blood flows during various cognitive activities. MEG, EEG, and ERPs all measure electrical activity during cognitive activities. In the chapters to come, we will see examples of studies that have made use of each of these techniques to investigate the neural underpinnings of different cognitive activities.

We have covered a lot of ground in this chapter, and yet we have still only begun to grapple with the complexities of the human brain. The interested student should refer to a text on neuropsychology, physiology, or biological psychology for more detail on any of the topics introduced here (see, for example, Ward, 2015; Banich, 2004, and Zillmer & Spiers, 2001).

What is important to remember is that cognitive processes are implemented in human brains. Some researchers make an analogy between human minds and computers; in this view, the brain is the "hardware" ("wetware") and the cognitive processes the software. Although the two aspects of functioning can be distinguished, to really understand either we must have some familiarity with both, and with how they interact. We'll return to this idea throughout the upcoming chapters.

SUMMARY

1. The hindbrain, containing some of the most evolutionarily primitive structures, is responsible for transmitting information from the spinal cord to the brain, regulating life support functions, and helping to maintain balance.

2. The midbrain contains many "relay" centres to transfer information between different brain regions.

3. The forebrain contains the thalamus, hypothalamus, hippocampus, amygdala, and the cerebral cortex, structures that are most directly implicated in cognitive processes such as memory, language, planning, and reasoning.

4. The cerebral cortex has four lobes: frontal (involved with movement and planning), parietal (involving reception and integration of sensory information), occipital (processing visual information), and temporal (processing auditory information as well as information about taste and smell).

5. Although some specific brain areas have specific functions localized to them (for example, the motor cortex or the primary somatosensory cortex), most higher-order cognitive processes do not map to one specific neural area.

6. Aphasia, a disorder of language, has been traced to two different areas of the brain, Broca's area and Wernicke's area, although other brain areas are likely involved as well.

7. Cerebral hemispheres have been shown to be lateralized in many individuals, with the left hemisphere usually processing analytical information and the right hemisphere synthesizing information. In normal operation, however, the two hemispheres communicate extensively.

8. A variety of modern techniques have been developed to measure the functioning of the brain during cognitive processing. Among the major techniques are CAT scans, MRI, PET scans, fMRI, EEG recordings, and ERP recordings.

9. The subtraction technique provides a means of isolating brain regions whose activity varies in a task state compared to a control state.

REVIEW QUESTIONS

1. Predict which brain areas are likely to be most involved with the cognitive processes of perception, attention, memory, language, and problem solving. Provide a rationale for your predictions.
2. Describe the functions of the four lobes of the cerebral cortex.
3. Explain how modern-day localization of brain function differs from phrenology.
4. What does it mean to say that the cerebral hemispheres show lateralization? What is the typical pattern of lateralization?
5. Compare and contrast the various brain imaging and brain recording techniques.

KEY TERMS

ablationa

mygdala

aphasia

brain imaging techniques

CAT (computerized axial tomography)

cerebellum

cerebral cortex

corpus callosum

EEG (electroencephalography)

ERP (event-related potential)

executive functioning

faculty psychology

fMRI (functional MRI)

forebrain

frontal lobe

hindbrain

hippocampus

hypothalamus

lateralization

localization of function

medulla oblongata

midbrain

motor cortex

MRI (magnetic resonance imaging)

occipital lobe

parietal lobe

PET (positron emission tomography)

Phrenology

Plasticity

pons

prefrontal cortex

primary somatosensory cortex

subtraction technique

temporal lobe

thalamus

Basic Cognitive Processes

PART

II

Perceiving Objects and Recognizing Patterns

Look across the room right now, and notice the objects you see. Maybe, if you are looking out a window, you see some trees or bushes, perhaps a bicycle or car, maybe a person walking or a group of children playing.

What you've just done, cognitively speaking, is an amazing achievement: You've taken sensory input and interpreted it meaningfully, in a process known as **perception**. In other words, you have perceived patterns, objects, people, and possibly events in your world. You may not consider this achievement at all remarkable—after all, it's something you do every day. However, computer scientists trying to create artificially intelligent systems have discovered the many complexities involved in the process of perception. Neuroscientists have estimated that the areas of our brain responsible for visual processing occupy up to half of the total cortex space (Tarr, 2000).

The central problem of perception is explaining how we attach meaning to the sensory information we receive. In the example just given, you received and somehow interpreted a great deal of sensory information: You "saw" certain objects as trees, people, and so forth. You recognized certain objects—that is, saw them as things you had seen before. The question for cognitive psychologists is how we manage to accomplish these feats so rapidly and (usually) without error.

The vast topic of perception can be subdivided into visual perception, auditory perception (the two most studied forms), olfactory perception, haptic (touch) perception, and gustatory (taste) perception. For the purposes of this chapter, we will concentrate on visual perception—in part to keep our discussion manageable and in part because visual perception is the kind psychologists study most. From time to time, we will also look at examples of other kinds of perception to illustrate different points.

Notice that when you look at an object, you acquire specific bits of information about it, including its location, shape, texture, size, and (for familiar objects) name. Some psychologists—namely, those working in the tradition of James Gibson (1979)—would argue that you also immediately acquire information about the object's function. Cognitive psychologists seek to describe how people acquire such information and what they then do to process it.

Several related questions immediately arise. How much of the information we acquire through perception draws on past learning? How much of our perception do we infer, and how much do we receive directly? What specific cognitive processes enable us to perceive objects (and events, and states, and so on)? Where can the line be drawn between perception and sensation, the initial reception of information in a specific sensory modality—vision, hearing, olfaction? Where can the line be drawn between perception and other kinds of cognition, such as reasoning or categorization? Clearly, even defining perception so as to answer these questions is a challenge.

For the present, we will adopt what might be called the "classic" approach to defining perception. Figure 3-1 illustrates this approach for visual perception.

Out in the real world are objects and events—things to be perceived—a book or, as in our earlier example, trees and shrubs. Each such object is a **distal stimulus**. For a living

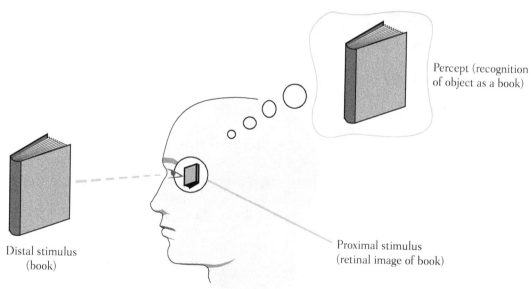

Percept (recognition of object as a book)

Distal stimulus (book)

Proximal stimulus (retinal image of book)

FIGURE 3-1 Distal stimuli, proximal stimuli, and percepts.

organism to process information about these stimuli, it must first receive the information through one or more sensory systems—in this example, the visual system. The reception of information and its registration by a sense organ make up the **proximal stimulus**. In our earlier example, light waves reflect from the trees and cars to your eyes, in particular to a surface at the back of each eye known as the **retina**. There, an image of the trees and cars, called the **retinal image**, is formed. This image is two-dimensional, and its size depends on your distance from the window and the objects beyond (the closer you are, the larger the image). In addition, the image is upside down and is reversed with respect to left and right.

The meaningful interpretation of the proximal stimulus is the **percept**—your interpretation that the stimuli are trees, cars, people, and so forth. From the upside-down, backward, two-dimensional image, you quickly (almost instantaneously) "see" a set of objects you recognize. You also "recognize" that, say, the giant oak tree is closer to you than are the lilac shrubs, which appear to recede in depth away from you. This information is not part of the proximal stimulus. Somehow, you must interpret the proximal stimulus to know it.

Although researchers studying perception disagree about much, they do agree that percepts are not the same things as proximal stimuli. Consider a simple demonstration of **size constancy**. Extend your arm away from your body, and look at the back of your hand. Now, keeping the back of your hand facing you, slowly bring it toward you a few inches, then away from you. Does your hand seem to be changing size as it moves? Probably not, although the size of the hand in the retinal image is most certainly changing. The point here is that perception involves something different from the formation of retinal images.

Related to perception is a process called **pattern recognition**. This is the recognition of a particular object, event, and so on, as belonging to a class of objects, events, and so on. Your recognition of the object you are viewing as belonging to the class of things called "shrubs" is an instance of pattern recognition. Because the formation of most percepts involves some classification and recognition, most, if not all, instances of perception involve pattern recognition.

We will begin by considering proposals from the Gestalt school of psychology that perception involves the segmentation, or "parsing," of visual stimuli into objects and backgrounds (and just how complicated this seemingly easy process is). We will then turn to examine some (mostly) bottom-up models of perception. Then we will examine phenomena that have led many cognitive psychologists to argue that some top-down processes must occur in perception in interaction with bottom-up processing. We will examine some neurological findings pertaining to object perception and will also consider a connectionist model of word perception.

We will then review a very different view: work inspired by J. J. Gibson (1979) on "direct perception." Gibson's view departs from most other theories of perception in that he claims perceivers actually do little "processing" of information, either bottom-up or top-down. Instead, he believes the information available in the world is sufficiently rich that all the perceiver needs to do is detect or "pick up on" that information. We will conclude by looking at some neuropsychological work on patients who have an inability to perceive (but have intact visual abilities) to help illustrate just what the process of perception is all about.

GESTALT APPROACHES TO PERCEPTION

One of the most important aspects of visual perception has to do with how we interpret stimulus arrays as consisting of objects and backgrounds. Consider, for instance, Figure 3-2. This stimulus pattern can be seen in two distinct ways: as a white vase against a black background or as two silhouetted faces against a white background. This segregation of the whole display into objects (also called the figure) and the background (also called the ground) is an important process known to cognitive psychologists as **form perception**.

Reversible figures aren't just for perceptual psychologists, either! The artist Salvador Dali exploits the existence of reversible figures in his work *The Slave Market with Disappearing Bust of Voltaire*, shown in the top half of Figure 3-3. Psychologist Robert Solso, who has written on the intersection of cognitive psychology and the visual arts, presents a "blowup" of the hidden "bust of Voltaire" in the bottom half of the figure.

The segregation of figure from ground has many consequences. The part of the display seen as figure is seen as having a definite shape, as being some sort of "thing," and is better remembered than the part of the display interpreted as ground, which is seen as more shapeless, less formed, and farther away in space (Brown & Deffenbacher, 1979). Form perception is a cognitive task most of us perform quickly and easily and thus take for granted. We assume, intuitively, that we perceive objects and backgrounds because there really *are* objects and backgrounds and all we do is see them.

But consider Figure 3-4. Almost everyone sees this figure as consisting of two triangles, overlaid so as to form a six-pointed star. The corners of the top triangle are typically seen as resting on three coloured circles. Now look closely at the figure, in particular at the top triangle. Recall that a triangle is defined as a

imagewriter/Shutterstock.com

FIGURE 3-2 Goblet/silhouetted faces.

closed geometric figure that has three sides. Notice that in the figure itself there are *no* sides. There is only white space that you, the viewer, interpret as a triangle. You, the viewer, are somehow adding the three sides or contours.

Gregory (1972), who studied this phenomenon (called illusory contours or **subjective contours**), believed that this relatively complex display is subject to a simplifying interpretation the perceiver makes without even being aware of making it: A triangle is lying on top of other parts of the figure and blocking them from view. The point here is that this perception is not completely determined by the stimulus display; it requires the perceiver's active participation.

Click this link to view image:

https://www.dalipaintings.com/slave-market-with-the-disappearing-bust-of-voltaire.jsp

FIGURE 3-3 Salvador Dali, The Slave Market with Disappearing Bust of Voltaire. The two nuns standing in the archway at left-centre reverse to form a bust of Voltaire. The painting exploits the reversible figures phenomenon.

A number of individuals in the early part of the 20th century—among them, Max Wertheimer, Kurt Koffka, and Wolfgang Köhler—were deeply interested in how perceivers come to recognize objects or forms. As we saw in Chapter 1, these researchers, who formed the Gestalt school of psychology, were particularly concerned with how people apprehended *whole* objects, concepts, or units. The Gestalt psychologists believed that perceivers follow certain laws or principles of organization in coming to their interpretations. They first asserted that the whole, or *Gestalt*, is not the same as the sum of its parts. To put it another way, Gestalt psychologists rejected the claim that we recognize objects by identifying individual features or parts; instead, we see and recognize each object or unit as a whole.

What are the **Gestalt principles of perceptual organization** that allow us to see these wholes? The complete list is too long to describe (see Koffka, 1935), so we will examine only five major principles. The first is the *principle of proximity*, or nearness. Look at Figure 3-5(A). Notice that you tend to perceive this as a set of rows, rather than as a set of columns. This is because the elements within rows are closer than the elements within columns. Following the principle of proximity, we group together things that are nearer to each other.

Yuriy Vlasenko/Shutterstock.com

FIGURE 3-4 Subjective, or illusory, contours.

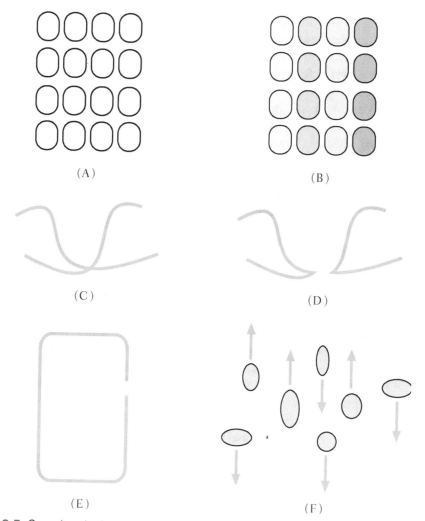

FIGURE 3-5 Gestalt principles of perceptual organization: (A) the principle of proximity; (B) the principle of similarity; (C) and (D) the principle of good continuation; (E) the principle of closure; and (F) the principle of common fate.

Figure 3-5(B) illustrates the *principle of similarity*. Notice that you perceive this display as formed in columns (rather than rows), grouping together those elements that are similar. A third principle, the *principle of good continuation*, depicted in Figure 3-5(C), states that we group together objects whose contours form a continuous straight or curved line. Thus we typically perceive Figure 3-5(C) as two intersecting curved lines and not as other logically possible elements, such as Figure 3-5(D).

We encountered the fourth principle, the *principle of closure*, when we looked at subjective contours. Figure 3-5(E) illustrates this principle more exactly. Note that we perceive this display as a rectangle, mentally filling in the gap to see a closed, complete, whole figure. The fifth principle, the *principle of common fate*, is difficult to illustrate in a static drawing. The idea is that elements that move together will be grouped together, as depicted in Figure 3-5(F). You can construct a better demonstration of this principle yourself (Matlin, 1988). Take two pieces of transparent plastic (such as report covers cut in half). Glue some scraps of paper on each. Lay one sheet upside down on top of the other, and you will have a hard time telling which sheet of plastic any particular scrap is on. Now move one sheet, holding the other still. You will suddenly see two distinct groups of scraps, or the phenomenon of grouping via movement. Canadian researchers Allison Sekuler and Patrick Bennett have shown that the principle of common fate extends beyond grouping by movement, however, and includes grouping by luminance change. You can learn more about their work in the Canadian Research Highlight box.

Box 3-1 Canadian Research Highlight

Allison Sekuler of the Rotman Research Institute (https://www.baycrest.org/Baycrest/Research-Innovation/People/Researchers/Scientists) and Patrick Bennett of McMaster University http://pnb.mcmaster.ca/bennett/ have demonstrated that, in addition to using common movement to group objects together, observers also make use of concurrent changes in luminance (Sekuler & Bennett, 2001). In their study, observers were presented with a 10×10 checkerboard of squares of varying luminance. Six adjacent squares (organized in a 2×3 or 3×2 format) were selected to be the target. On a given trial, each of the 100 squares in the checkerboard would increase and decrease in luminance in a cyclical fashion. The six adjacent target squares were made to vacillate in common (i.e., all would increase or decrease at the same time), and the observer's task was to determine whether the target was horizontal (i.e., a 2×3 configuration) or vertical (i.e., a 3×2 configuration). Sekuler and Bennett found that despite the fact that the target squares were not identical in luminance, when they became brighter or darker together, and 180 degrees out of phase with the luminance change of the background squares, observers could readily identify them as the target and indicate whether they were organized horizontally or vertically. Sekuler and Bennett both maintain active research labs at McMaster, studying basic perceptual phenomena such as orientation discrimination and face recognition, and also perception in special populations—such as the effects of aging on motion and direction identification and facial feature discrimination in autism.

Most of the Gestalt principles are subsumed under a more general law, the *law of Prägnanz* (Koffka, 1935). This law states that of all the possible ways of interpreting a display, we will tend to select the organization that yields the simplest and most stable shape or form. Thus simple and symmetric forms are seen more easily than more complicated and asymmetric forms. This law may help to explain our experience of Figure 3-4 with subjective contours. Because the phantom "triangle" forms a simple, symmetric form, we "prefer" to interpret the pattern as if the triangle were there.

Many researchers of visual perception consider the Gestalt principles fundamental (Tarr, 2000), and researchers are beginning to demonstrate the use of some Gestalt principles by infants as young as three to six months (Quinn, Bhatt, Brush, Grimes, & Sharpnack, 2002). Some work on formalizing the Gestalt law of Prägnanz has been undertaken in a theory called *minimal model theory* (Feldman, 1999, 2003).

Despite its intuitive appeal, the Gestalt approach to form perception leaves a number of questions unanswered (Pomerantz & Kubovy, 1981). We don't know, for instance, just how these principles are translated into cognitive or physiological processes. Moreover, without further specification the law of Prägnanz can be seen as circular. (Why do we see two triangles in Figure 3-4? Because this interpretation makes for a simple, stable figure. How do we know this figure is simple and stable? Because we so readily see it.)

Many cognitive psychologists studying perception acknowledge their debt to the Gestalt psychologists. The challenge for current researchers is to blend the rich observations of Gestalt psychology with research techniques designed to tell us just how the processes used to form perception operate.

BOTTOM-UP PROCESSES

Psychologists studying perception distinguish between **bottom-up** and **top-down processes**. The term *bottom-up* (or *data-driven*) essentially means that the perceiver starts with small bits of information from the environment that she combines in various ways to form a percept. A bottom-up model of perception and pattern recognition might describe your seeing edges, rectangular and other shapes, and certain lighted regions and putting this information together to "conclude" you are seeing doors and a hallway. That is, you would form a perception from only the information in the distal stimulus.

In *top-down* (also called *theory-driven* or *conceptually driven)* processing, the perceiver's expectations, theories, or concepts guide the selection and combination of the information in the pattern recognition process. For example, a "top-down" description of the door-and-hallway example might go something like this: You knew you were in your dorm room and knew from past experience approximately how close to the window the various trees, shrubs, and other objects were. When you looked in that direction, you expected to see trees, shrubs, walkways with people on them, a street with cars passing by, and so on. These expectations guided where you looked, what you looked at, and how you put the information together.

In this section, we will focus on bottom-up models. The idea here is that the system works in one direction, starting from the input and proceeding to a final interpretation. Whatever happens at a given point is unaffected by later processing; the system has no way of going back to an earlier point to make adjustments.

When psychologists speak of bottom-up perceptual processes, they typically have in mind something that takes information about a stimulus (by definition a "lower" level of processing) as input. Bottom-up processes are relatively uninfluenced by expectations or previous learning (the so-called higher-level processes). Posner and Raichle (1994) argued that bottom-up processes involve automatic, reflexive processing that occurs even when the perceiver is passively regarding the information. In this section we will consider three distinct examples of bottom-up models of perception: template matching, featural analysis, and prototype matching.

Template Matching

Figure 3-6 shows a copy of a Quick Response Code, or QR code. You've undoubtedly seen these begin to appear on everything from products, to posters, to even t-shirts. The basic premise underlying a QR code is that the patterns of black and white contained within the code area provide a unique link to some form of information. By using your cell phone, or any QR code reader, you can scan the QR code and access the associated information, such as a restaurant menu, product information, or tour dates for your favourite band. Essentially, a machine has been built to scan and "read" these patterns of black boxes and white spaces and compare them to previously stored patterns, called **templates**. The machines (i.e., your cellphone or QR code reader) "decide" which pattern is represented by comparing the pattern to these templates.

You can think of a template as a kind of stencil—one of the art supplies you probably owned as a child. Recall that those stencils let you trace as many copies as you wanted of the same thing. Templates work like stencils in reverse. An unknown incoming pattern is compared to all of the templates (stencils) on hand and identified by the template that best matches it.

As a model of perception, template matching works this way: Every object, event, or other stimulus that we encounter and want to derive meaning from is compared to some previously stored pattern, or template. The process of perception thus involves comparing incoming information to the templates we have stored, and looking for a match. If a number of templates match or come close, we need to engage in further processing to sort out which template is most appropriate. Notice that this model implies that somewhere in our knowledge base we've stored millions of different templates—one for every distinct object or pattern we can recognize.

FIGURE 3-6 An illustration of how information is encoded in a Quick Response Code.

As may already be apparent to you, template-matching models cannot completely explain how perception works. First, for such a model to provide a complete explanation, we would need to have stored an impossibly large number of templates. Second, as technology develops and our experiences change, we become capable of recognizing new objects—thumb drives, laptop computers, cellular phones, wireless ear buds. Template-matching models thus have to explain how and when templates are created and how we keep track of an ever-growing number of templates.

A third problem is that people recognize many patterns as more or less the same thing, even when the stimulus patterns differ greatly. Figure 3-7 illustrates this point. We constructed this figure by having nine people write the sentence "I like cog. psych." in their own handwriting. You should be able to read each sentence despite the wide variation in the size, shape, orientation, and spacing of letters.

How can a template-matching model explain your recognition that all nine people have written the "same" sentence? In everyday life, much of the stimulus information we perceive is far from regular, whether because of deliberate alteration, degradation, or an unfamiliar orientation (compare an overturned cup or bicycle with one that is right side up). Is a separate template needed for each variation? And how is the perceiver to know whether an object should be rotated or otherwise adjusted before she tries to match it to a template? Remember, matching information to templates is supposed to tell the perceiver the object's identity. The perceiver can't know ahead of time whether an input pattern should be adjusted before he tries to match it to different templates, because presumably the perceiver does not yet know what the object is!

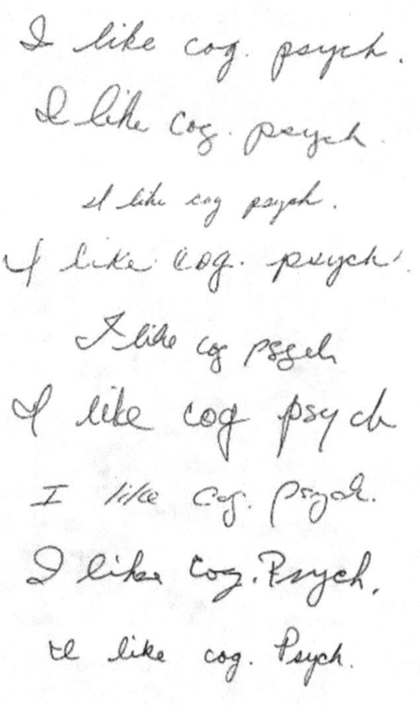

So although there are real technological examples of template matching, we probably don't rely heavily on such a process in our everyday perception. (We will consider a possible exception to this generalization when we talk about experiments involving mental rotation of line drawings in Chapter 8.) Template matching works only with relatively clean stimuli, for which we know ahead of time what templates may be relevant. It does not adequately explain how we perceive as effectively as we typically do the "noisy" patterns and objects—blurred or faint letters, partially blocked objects, sounds against a background of other sounds—that we encounter every day.

FIGURE 3-7 Handwriting samples.

Try staring at the object you perceive to be your classroom door. As you do, you're able to recognize not only the whole door but also certain parts of it: the narrow edge facing you, the inside and outside doorknobs, the latch, the metal plate on the bottom of the outside of the door to protect it from scuffing. Some psychologists believe such analysis of a whole into its parts underlies the basic processes used in perception. Instead of processing stimuli as whole units, we might instead break them down into their components, using our recognition of those parts to infer what the whole represents. The parts searched for and recognized are called **features**. Recognition of a whole object, in this model, thus depends on recognition of its features.

Such a model of perception—called *featural analysis*—fits nicely with some neurophysiologic evidence. Some studies of the retinas of frogs (Lettvin, Maturana, McCullogh, & Pitts, 1959) involved implanting microelectrodes in individual cells of the retina. Lettvin and colleagues found that specific kinds of stimuli could cause these cells to fire more frequently. Certain cells responded strongly to borders between light and dark and were called "edge detectors"— "edge" because they fired when stimulated by a visual boundary between light and dark, "detectors" because they indicated the presence of a certain type of visual stimulus. Others responded selectively to moving edges, and others, jokingly called "bug detectors," responded most vigorously when a small, dark dot (much like an insect) moved across the field of vision. Hubel and Wiesel (1962, 1968) later discovered fields in the visual cortexes of cats and monkeys that responded selectively to moving edges or contours in the visual field that had a particular orientation. In other words, they found evidence of separate "horizontal-line detectors" and "vertical-line detectors," as well as other distinct detectors.

How does this evidence support featural analysis? Certain detectors appear to scan input patterns, looking for a particular feature. If that feature is present, the detectors respond rapidly. If that feature is not present, the detectors do not respond as strongly. Each detector, then, appears designed to detect the presence of just one kind of feature in an input pattern. That such detectors exist, in the form of either retinal or cortical cells, confirms the applicability of the featural analysis model.

Behavioural research, conducted on intact human observers, has provided additional evidence of featural processing in perception. For example, flashing letters on a computer screen for very brief intervals of time typically results in certain predictable errors. For example, people are much more likely to confuse a *G* with a *C* than with an *F*. Presumably this is because the letters *C* and *G* share many features: a curved line, an opening to the right. Eleanor Gibson (1969) has tabulated the features of capital letters for the Roman alphabet we use.

Studies by Neisser (1963) confirmed that people use features to recognize letters. Neisser had participants perform a **visual search task** in which researchers presented them with arrays of letters, such as those shown in Figure 3-8. The researchers asked them to respond

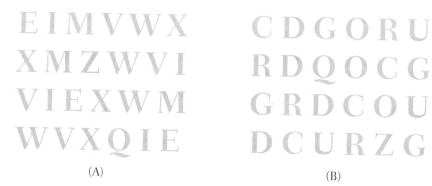

(A)   (B)

FIGURE 3-8 Visual search stimuli. Notice how long it takes to find a *Z* or a *Q* in (A) and (B).

if they detected the presence of a particular target, such as the letter *Q* or the letter *Z*. Shown an array such as Figure 3-8(A), participants took much longer to find a *Z* than they did to find a *Q*; the reverse was true for arrays similar to Figure 3-8(B). The nontarget letters in array (A) all share features like straight and angular lines, whereas those in array (B) share features such as roundness. Similarity between the target letter (*Z* or *Q)* and the nontarget letters can make the search much harder.

Similar findings have been reported for auditory perception of syllables that share many articulatory features. For example, *da* and *ta* are more likely to be confused than are two syllables that share fewer similarities, such as *da* and *sa* (Miller & Nicely, 1955). Examples of articulatory features (for consonants) include voicing, or vibration of the vocal cords (*b* is voiced, for example, but *p* is not); nasality, whether the air is directed into the nasal passages (*n*) or not (*l*); duration, how long the (consonant) sound lasts (compare *s* with *t)*; and place of articulation, where in the mouth the sound is formed (compare *p* and *b*, formed in the front; *t* and *d*, formed in the middle; and *k* and *g*, formed in the back).

Selfridge (1959) developed a model for the perception of letters that was based on featural analysis. The model was called **Pandemonium**, for reasons that will soon become clear. It consists of a number of different kinds of "demons," which function basically as feature detectors. Demons at the bottom (first) level of processing scan the input, and demons at higher levels scan the output from lower-level demons. In response to what they find, the demons scream. The first type of demons is image demons, which convert the proximal stimulus into representations, or internal depictions of information, that higher-level demons can assess. Each representation is scanned by several feature demons, each looking for a different particular feature (such as a curved or a vertical line). If a demon finds such a feature, that demon screams.

Feature demons communicate their level of confidence that the feature is present by screaming more softly or loudly. Letter demons cannot look at the stimulus itself but can only listen to the feature demons. The letter demons pay particular attention to the demons associated with their particular letter. The *A* demon, for instance, listens especially hard to the feature demons for "slanted line" and "vertical line." Letter demons scream when the output from the feature demons convinces them their letter is in the representation—again, more loudly or softly, depending on the level of confidence. A single decision demon listens to all this screaming and decides what letter is being presented.

The Pandemonium model, named with a sense of humour, illustrates a number of important aspects of featural analysis. First, demons can scream more loudly or softly depending on the clarity and quality of the input. This allows for the fact that real-life stimuli are often degraded or incomplete, yet objects and patterns can still be recognized. Second, feature demons can be linked to letter demons in such a way that more important features carry greater weight. This takes into account that some features matter more than others in pattern recognition.

Take the case of the letter *A*. In writing this letter, some people are sloppy about their slanted vertical lines (sometimes the lines are almost parallel), yet the *A* is still often recognizable. Without the horizontal line, however, the pattern seems to stop being an *A*. In the Pandemonium model, then, the letter demon for *A* would be more tightly connected to the horizontal-line feature demon than it would be to the slanted-line demons. Last, the weights of the various features can be changed over time, allowing for learning. Thus a demon model could learn to recognize your professor's handwritten *A*'s, even though she makes her capital *A*'s with no slanted lines, only two very curved lines. With practice, this model could learn to read even your doctor's handwriting— something even his nurses have trouble with! It is worth noting that even though Selfridge published his model nearly 40 years ago, the general principles he laid out are still relevant today. That is, the idea of processing being distributed across many areas of the brain or model is still central to many models of pattern recognition today, such as Plaut, McClelland, Seidenberg, and Patterson's (1996) model of word reading.

Featural analysis models are not without problems, however. To begin with, there are at present no good definitions of what can be a feature and what cannot, except in very restricted domains, such as the perception of letters or the perception of line drawings of familiar objects. Consider the perception of a face. Are there general features for eyes, nose, mouth? Are there specific features for right nostril, left eyebrow, lower lip? Just how many features can there be? Do different kinds of objects have different sets of features? Consider a vertical line. Although this feature is no doubt important for perceiving the letter *A*, how does it relate to perceiving a real human face? A beach ball? A wave crashing on shore? If there are different sets of features for different objects, how does the perceiver know which ones to use to perceive an object (remember, this must be decided *before* the perceiver knows what the object is). If the same set of features applies to all objects, the list of possible features would appear huge. How does the perceiver perceive objects so fast, then?

By the way, we will encounter featural models again when we talk about concepts in Chapter 7. All the questions and concerns about featural models will appear there as well.

Prototype Matching

Another kind of perceptual model, one that attempts to correct some of the shortcomings of both template-matching and featural analysis models, is known as *prototype matching*. Such models explain perception in terms of matching an input to a stored representation of information, as do template models. In this case, however, the stored representation, instead of being a whole pattern that must be matched exactly or closely (as in template-matching models), is a **prototype**, an idealized representation of some class of objects or events—the letter *M*, a cup, a pair of ear buds, a collie, and so forth.

You can think of a prototype as an idealization of the thing it represents. The prototypical dog, for instance, would be a depiction of a very, very typical dog— the "doggiest" dog you could think of or imagine. There may or may not be in existence any particular dog that looks exactly like the prototype. Figure 3-9 shows variations of the letter *M*. If your intuitions agree with those of most people we've shown this figure to, you'll judge the letters toward the centre of the figure to be more prototypical.

Prototype-matching models describe perceptual processes as follows. When a sensory device registers a new stimulus, the device compares it with previously stored prototypes. An exact match is not required; in fact, only an approximate match is expected. Prototype-matching models thus allow for discrepancies between the input and the prototype, giving prototype models a lot more flexibility than template models. An object is "perceived" when a match is found.

Prototype models differ from template and featural analysis models in that they do not require that an object contain any one specific feature or set of features to be recognized. Instead, the more features a particular object shares with a prototype, the higher the probability of a match. Moreover, prototype models take into account not only an object's features or parts but also the relationships among them.

Where, though, do prototypes come from? Cabeza, Bruce, Kato, and Oda (1999) demonstrated that people can form prototypes surprisingly quickly. These researchers took photographs of real individuals (the prototype photographs) and modified them

FIGURE 3-9 Examples of the letter *M*.

by displacing certain features (e.g., mouth, eyebrows, etc.) by 8 or 12 pixels (see Figure 3-10). Participants were shown some of the photographs as part of an incidental learning exercise. That is, they were not told that their memories for the faces would be tested at a later time, but were instead asked to rate the "masculinity/femininity" of each face. Over

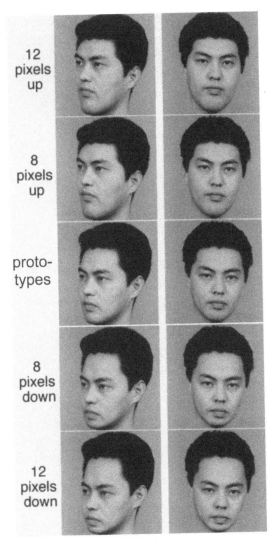

FIGURE 3-10 Stimuli used in the studies by Cabeza et al. (1999, p. 141).

Source: Reprinted with permission of Psychonomic Society, Inc., Springer Nature, from "The Prototype Effect in Face Recognition: Extension and Limits" Cabeza, R., Bruce, V., Kato, T. et al., 27, 139 (1999); permission conveyed through Copyright Clearance Center, Inc.

a series of experiments, Cabeza and colleagues found that observers had learned these face prototypes, as they were likely to call a face they had not seen before "old" if it was similar to one that had been viewed before (either with displaced features or rotated in position).

We will encounter the idea of prototypes again in Chapter 7, when we talk about concepts and categorization. The challenge, then, is to figure out when and how we form and use prototypes, what kind of processing is involved in matching, and how we know what prototypes to try to match inputs with. Note that many of these issues, including the number and origins of the stored representations, also arose for template-matching models.

TOP-DOWN PROCESSES

All bottom-up models share a number of problems in explaining how viewers "make meaning" of the stimuli they perceive. Two of the biggest problems are **context effects** and expectation effects.

Context effects have been demonstrated with perceivers looking to identify objects in real-world scenes: Both accuracy and the length of time needed to recognize objects vary with the context (Biederman, Glass, & Stacy, 1973; Palmer, 1975). For example, people recognize objects such as food or utensils faster in a scene depicting a kitchen than they do in the same scene jumbled up (see photos on the next page). These effects have led many psychologists to argue that any model of perception must incorporate context and expectations. We will look next at further demonstrations of the need to include top-down processes in theories and models of perception and pattern recognition.

Top-down, or conceptually driven, processes are those directed by expectations derived from context or past learning or both. If someone were to tell you a fly is in the room you are in right now, where would you look? This looking would change if you were to look for a spider or a cockroach. Your past experience with such creatures guides where you look first—whether to the walls, the floor, or the ceiling. You can think of the processing you do when you look for different insects as being top-down, in that your expectations and knowledge guide where you look.

Top-down processes have to interact with bottom-up processes, of course. Otherwise, you would never be able to perceive anything you were not expecting, and you would always perceive what you expected to perceive—clearly not true. A well-known example of a largely perceptual model incorporating both bottom-up and top-down processes is that of David Marr (1982). Marr's model is quite technical and mathematically elegant, and the interested reader is referred to his full description of it. For our purposes here, we offer a very brief sketch.

FIGURE 3-11 An example of context effects in perception.

Source: Igor Sinkov/Shutterstock.com. Adapted by Kendall Hunt Publishing Company.

The context surrounding an object can make perceiving it easy or hard. If we were to measure reaction time, we might find that it took people longer to recognize the toaster in the photo above than to recognize the same toaster in the photo below. The coherent kitchen scene sets up a context that aids perception of objects we expect to see in kitchens. The jumbled version of the scene destroys this context.

Marr proposed that perception proceeds in terms of several different, special-purpose computational mechanisms, such as a module to analyze colour, another to analyze motion, and so on. Each operates autonomously, without regard to the input from or output to any other module, and without regard to real-world knowledge. Thus they are bottom-up processes.

Marr believed that visual perception proceeds by constructing three different mental representations, or sketches. The first, called a *primal sketch*, depicts areas of relative brightness and darkness in a two-dimensional image as well as localized geometric structure. This allows the viewer to detect boundaries between areas but not to "know" what the visual information "means." According to Gardner (1985),

The primal sketch consists of a set of blobs oriented in various directions; these are reminiscent of the sorts of features discerned by Hubel and Wiesel's detectors— contrasts, spatial extent, general orientation at a local level. All these reductions and

simplifications are conceived of as mental representations or symbolic depictions of the "raw information" transmitted by the light: Perception consists of a series of such simplified sketches en route to a more veridical view of the world. (p. 302)

Once a primal sketch is created, the viewer uses it to create a more complex representation, called a 2 1/2-D (two-and-a-half-dimensional) sketch. Using cues such as shading, texture, edges, and others, the viewer derives information about what the surfaces are and how they are positioned in depth relative to the viewer's own vantage point at that moment.

Marr believed that both the primal sketch and the 2 /2-D sketch rely almost exclusively on bottom-up processes. Information from real-world knowledge or specific expectations (that is, top-down knowledge) is incorporated when the viewer constructs the final, 3-D sketch of the visual scene. This sketch involves both recognition of what the objects are and understanding of the "meaning" of the visual scene.

Marr's theory is not the only one to incorporate top-down processes. Other perceptual phenomena in which these processes seem to operate are perceptual learning, change blindness, and the word superiority effect, each of which we will cover in turn.

But first, here's another connection between the psychology of perception and the world of fine art: a look at the technique of impressionist painting, as depicted in Figure 3-12. The artist, Paul Signac, created a painting using small dabs of paint in a style known as *pointillism*.

FIGURE 3-12 Paul Signac, *The Dining Room*. This painting is an example of top-down processing in viewing fine art.

Source: Study for The Dining Room, c.1886 (oil on canvas), Signac, Paul (1863–1935) / Private Collection / Bridgeman Images.

If you were to examine these dabs up close, they would not be very meaningful. However, when you view the whole painting from a reasonable distance, the little dabs somehow cohere into a meaningful interpretation: two patrons having coffee. Top-down processing allows this meaningful interpretation to emerge as we gaze at the painting!

Change Blindness

A recent area of research in visual perception that provides a startling demonstration of the role of top-down processes in perception concerns a phenomenon known as **change blindness** (Rensink, 2002). One of the first demonstrations of change blindness, the inability to detect changes to an object or scene especially when given different views of that object or scene, came from the lab of University of British Columbia psychologist Ronald Rensink.

This phenomenon occurs outside the laboratory very frequently during the viewing of movies. Simons and Levin (1997) give the following examples: In the movie *Ace Ventura: When Nature Calls*, the pieces on a chessboard disappear completely from one shot to the next. In *Goodfellas*, a child is playing with blocks that appear and disappear across shots. One inevitable consequence of film production is the need to shoot scenes out of order, and often to shoot components of the same scene at different times. As a result, unintentionally, many details within a scene may change from one view to the next. Although filmmakers go to considerable effort to eliminate such errors, almost every movie—in fact, almost every cut—has some continuity mistake. Yet, most of the time, people are blind to the changes (p. 264).

Simons and Levin (1997) provided a laboratory demonstration of this phenomenon. They showed undergraduate participants a short film clip depicting a young man sitting at a desk, then rising from the desk and answering a phone (see photos on next page). There was a camera cut during this sequence. Even when viewers were warned ahead of time there would be "continuity errors," they could not easily detect a fairly significant change: The actor first shown at the desk (photo A) is replaced by another actor, wearing different clothes (photo C)! One explanation for these findings is that the visual representations people make of a scene encode the "gist" of the scene (the basic meaning) but usually not the specific details. Thus changes to the scene that don't interrupt the "meaning" of the sequence don't call attention to themselves.

This implies that our visual percepts are not precise copies of our visual world. But is this simply a function of viewing motion pictures? Simons and Levin (1997), in a very clever study, conducted a "real-world" version of the laboratory study. They describe it as follows:

Imagine that a person approaches you and asks for directions. Kindly, you oblige and begin describing the route. While you are talking, two people interrupt you rudely by carrying a door right between you and the person you were talking to. Surely you would notice if the person you were talking to was then replaced by a completely different person. (p. 266)

But, in fact, only about 50% of their "participants" did. (The replacement was achieved by having the second "interviewer" carry the back half of the door up to the first interviewer and the participant; the first "interviewer" then changed places with him, in a scene reminiscent of a *Candid Camera* segment.) The change in person went undetected even though the two interviewers were of different heights and builds, had noticeably different voices, had different haircuts, and wore different clothing!

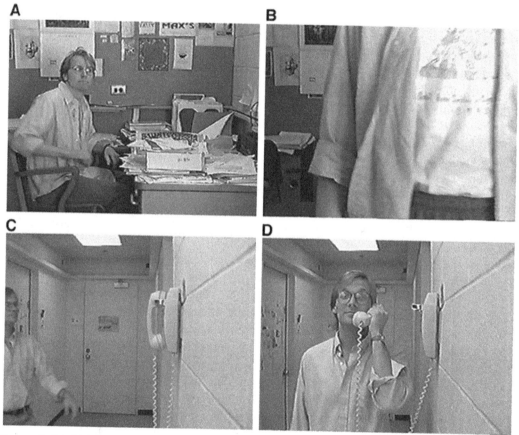

Figure 3.13 Although viewers shown this film clip in an experiment were told in advance that it would contain continuity errors, they failed to notice that the actor in (A) is replaced in (C) by another actor, wearing different clothes.

Source: Reprinted by permission from Psychonomic Society, Inc., Springer Nature, *Psychonomic Bulletin & Review*, Levin, D.T. & Simons, D.J. Psychonomic Bulletin & Review (1997) 4: 501. https://doi.org/10.3758/BF03214339, Failure to Detect Changes to Attended Objects in Motion Pictures, Daniel T. Levin, Daniel J. Simons © 1997.

Interestingly, student participants were more likely to notice the change than were older participants. But when the two interviewers donned construction worker clothing, fewer than half the *students* noticed the change. Simons and Levin (1997) speculated that participants encoded the status (including age or profession) of the interviewer only for gist; students would pay more attention to the interviewers when they looked like other students, but less when the interviewers looked like construction workers.

The change blindness paradigm reinforces the idea that perception does seem driven by expectations about meaning. Instead of keeping track of every visual detail, we seem to represent the overall meaning of the scene. This may help prevent our perceptual system from being overwhelmed by the sheer amount of information available in any one glance or view.

Rensink (2002) has argued that to detect change, viewers must be focusing on the stimulus. Aginsky and Tarr (2002) further argue that some aspects of scene perception, such as presence and position of objects, automatically attract attention, whereas other aspects of a scene, such as colour of objects, do not. We will turn to the topic of focused attention and a phenomenon known as inattentional blindness (Mack, 2003)—the inability to see what is directly in front of us unless we are paying attention—in Chapter 4.

The Word Superiority Effect

A study by Reicher (1969) illustrates another top-down phenomenon—the effects of context on perception in practised perceivers. The basic task was simple: Participants were asked to identify which of two letters (for instance, *D* or *K*) was briefly presented on a screen. Later, they were presented with two alternatives for what the letter might have been, displayed directly above the letter's original position. Figure 3-14 depicts the experimental procedure.

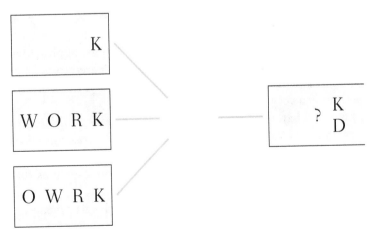

FIGURE 3-14 Stimulus displays and procedures used by Reicher (1969).

The experiment contained an interesting twist, however. Sometimes a single letter was presented. At other times the letter appeared in the context of a word (such as *WORD* or *WORK*; notice that either *D* or *K* forms a common English word in combination with the same three letters). At still other times, the letter was presented with three other letters in a combination that did not form a word (*OWRD* or *OWRK*, for instance). In each case, the stimuli were then masked, and the participant was asked merely to say which letter, *D* or *K*, had been presented.

Surprisingly, participants could much more accurately identify letters presented in the context of words than the same letters presented alone or in the context of nonwords. This result, called the **word superiority effect** or the *word advantage*, has been replicated several times (Massaro, 1979). Letters are apparently easier to perceive in a familiar context (a word) than in an unfamiliar context or in no context at all. Theoretical explanations of this effect have been debated (Massaro, 1979; Papp, Newsome, McDonald, & Schvaneveldt, 1982). Not clear, for instance, is whether people detect more features in the letter when it occurs in a word or whether people make inferences about—guess at— the letter that would best complete the word. The point for our present purposes is that, once again, context and perceptual experience (for instance, at reading words) influence even as straightforward a task as perceiving a single letter. This insight has led to detailed models of letter perception that incorporate context-guided—that is, top-down—processes with bottom-up processes such as feature detection (McClelland & Rumelhart, 1981; Rumelhart & McClelland, 1982).

Recent research using event-related potentials has provided evidence consistent with models of letter perception that include both top-down and bottom-up processes. For instance, Martin, Nazir, Thierry, Pauliganan, and Démonet (2006) studied the identification of letters that were displayed as part of briefly presented words or non-pronounceable nonwords. The observers were asked to choose which of two letters were displayed, and while this decision was made, the researchers measured event-related potentials (ERPs; an electrical measure of brain processing). The researchers showed that within 200 ms of presentation of the crucial stimuli, the ERP measure was different for word as compared to nonword stimuli. The authors argued, then, that whether the stimulus was a word or a nonword was able to affect perception of the letter at a very early stage of processing.

Interestingly, however, letter detection seems to operate very differently in a different context. When readers are asked to read a written text and cross out all the occurrences of a certain letter (say, *f*'s), they are very likely to miss the *f* in words like *of* or *for*, but to catch the *f*'s in words like *function or future*, a phenomenon known as the missing letter effect (Greenberg, Healy Koriat, & Kreiner, 2004). Presumably, as readers read connected text, they quickly divide the words into content words (which carry meaning) and function words (which structure the content words); they focus their attention more on the moderately familiar content words and thus are likely to miss the letters in the highly familiar function words. We will explore this idea more fully in Chapter 10 when we discuss text processing. The point for now is that the ability to detect letters is enhanced by word familiarity when words appear in isolation, but inhibited by increased familiarity or role when a word appears in real text.

A Connectionist Model of Word Perception

One of the detailed models is a connectionist model of letter and word perception, presented by McClelland and Rumelhart (1981). Figure 3-15 illustrates some of the processing levels the model assumes. Note that the model assumes that input—whether written (visual), spoken (acoustic), or of a higher level, such as arising from the context or the observer's expectations—is processed at several different levels, whether in terms of features, letters, **phonemes** (sounds), or words. Notice, too, the many arrows in the diagram, indicating the assumption that the different levels of processing feed into one another. Each level of processing is assumed to form a representation of the information at a different level of abstraction, with features considered less abstract than letters, and letters less abstract than words.

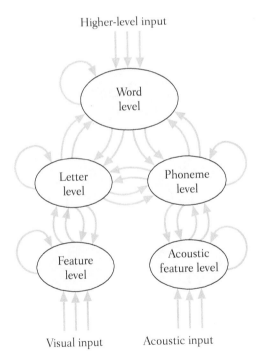

FIGURE 3-15 McClelland and Rumelhart's (1981) model of letter perception.

Source: From *Psychological Review, 88* by James L. McClelland and David E. Rumelhart. Copyright © 1981 by James L. McClelland and David E. Rumelhart. Reprinted by permission.

The model is presented in more detail in Figure 3-16. Each circle and oval in this figure depicts a node of processing in the model. The model assumes a different node for each distinct word, letter, and feature. Nodes have a certain level of activity at any given point in time. When a node reaches a given level of activity, we can say that its associated feature, letter, or word is perceived.

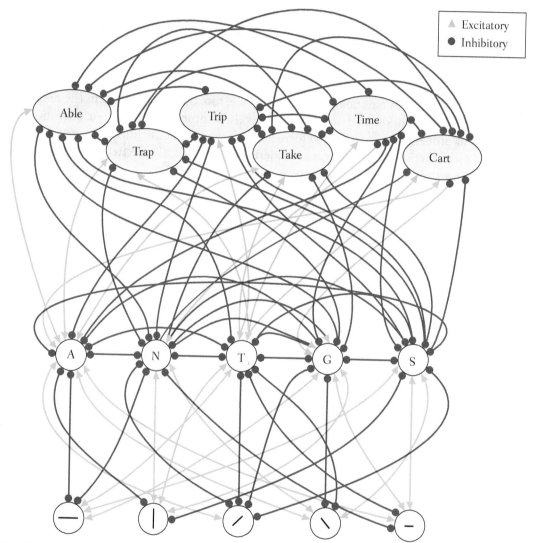

FIGURE 3-16 Nodes and connections in McClelland and Rumelhart's (1981) model of word perception.

Source: From *Psychological Review*, 88 by James L. McClelland and David E. Rumelhart. Copyright © 1981 by James L. McClelland and David E. Rumelhart. Reprinted by permission.

Note all the lines between nodes. These represent connections, which can be either excitatory or inhibitory. When an excitatory connection links two nodes, the two nodes suggest each other. Consider the nodes for the word

TRAP and the letter T, for example. Imagine seeing a stimulus such as __RAP in a crossword puzzle in a family newspaper: four blanks, the last three of which are filled in with R, A, and P. Wouldn't this suggest the word TRAP to you? If so, a connectionist would say your node for TRAP had been activated.

Once a node is activated, that activation spreads along that node's excitatory connections to other nodes. If the TRAP node has an excitatory connection to the T node, then the T node will become more active when the TRAP node becomes more active, and vice versa. Excitatory connections are represented in Figure 3-16 by arrows ending with points. The lines ending in dots in Figure 3-16 indicate inhibitory connections, as in the line between the TRAP node and the ABLE node. Thus if the TRAP node is active, the ABLE node becomes less active. If you perceive the word TRAP, you are less likely to perceive the word ABLE at the same instant. The assumption is that you can perceive only one word at any given instant.

More could be said about this model, but our focus here is on how a connectionist model can be used to explain the word superiority effect. Why might a letter be easier to perceive in the context of a word? According to this model, perception of a word—that is, activation of the relevant node for the word—also activates the nodes corresponding to all the letters within the word, thereby facilitating their perception. Without the word context, the node for the individual letter is less active, so perception of the letter takes longer.

A Neuroscientific Perspective on Word Perception

A very interesting study making use of PET technology also bears on the perception of words. Petersen, Fox, Snyder, and Raichle (1990) presented eight adults with four different kinds of stimuli: true English words; pseudowords, which follow the pronunciation rules of English but happen not to be real words; letter strings that contain no vowels and hence are not pronounceable; and *false fonts* that use the features of letters of the alphabet, but never in the usual combinations.

Words and pseudowords produced different PET scans from those produced when participants saw letter strings or false fonts. That is, different brain areas were active when the different types of stimuli were shown. With all four types of stimuli, the PET scan showed activity in the visual cortexes of both hemispheres. With both pseudowords and real words, however, the PET scans showed greater activity in the left than the right hemisphere and in regions outside the primary visual cortex (see Figure 3-17). The authors argued that this part of the brain is the part involved in semantic processing—that is, processing of stimuli for meaning. This study lays the groundwork for further work in creating a detailed "map" of the brain to understand further how various cognitive processes are realized neurologically

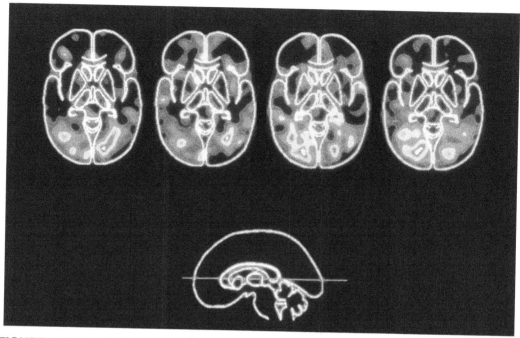

FIGURE 3-17 Results from the PET scan study of processing words. See text for explanation.

Source: From *Science*, 31 Aug 1990, Vol. 249, Issue 4972, pp. 1041–1044, DOI: 10.1126/science.2396097. Reprinted with permission from AAAS.

DIRECT PERCEPTION

The models of perception we have looked at so far all share a common assumption. Recall that, as shown in Figure 3-1, the perceiver must acquire information about a distal stimulus, presumably by interpreting the proximal stimuli (retinal images, in the case of visual perception). The common assumption underlying the models of perception we have examined (especially the top-down models) is that the perceiver does something to the proximal stimulus. Presumably, because the proximal stimulus doesn't contain all the information we need to identify the object (for instance, because retinal images are two-dimensional instead of three-dimensional or because objects might be blurred or blocked by other objects), we, as observers, must use our knowledge to fill in gaps.

To put it more simply, these models describe the act of perception as the construction of mental representations of objects. From the information we are perceiving, we somehow construct a depiction that may or may not physically resemble the object or event being perceived but that our cognitive and physiological processes can recognize as corresponding to the information perceived. We use both the information in the proximal stimulus and information from our long-term memory to construct these mental representations.

This idea is called the **constructivist approach to perception** (Hochberg, 1978), for obvious reasons. It describes people as adding to and distorting the information in the proximal stimulus to obtain a percept, a meaningful interpretation of incoming information. People are not seen as passively taking in all the available information; instead, they are seen as active selectors, integrators, and constructors of information.

James Gibson and his followers (J. Gibson, 1979; Michaels & Carello, 1981) adopted an opposite stance. Gibson rejected the idea that perceivers construct mental representations from memories of past encounters with similar objects and events. Instead, Gibson believed that the perceiver does very little work, mainly because the world offers so much information, leaving little need to construct representations and draw inferences. He proposed that perception consists of the direct acquisition of information from the environment.

According to this view, called **direct perception**, the light hitting the retina contains highly organized information that requires little or no interpretation. In the world we live in, certain aspects of stimuli remain invariant (or unchanging) despite changes over time or in our physical relationship to them. You may already be familiar with the idea of invariance. For example, consider a melody played on a piano in the key of C. Now, imagine that same melody transposed to the key of G. Although all the individual notes in the melody have been changed, the melody is still easily recognized. If sufficient time lapses between renditions, many listeners may not even recognize the key change. The elements (notes) have changed, but the relationships between the notes have remained constant, or invariant.

A visual example of perceptual invariance was demonstrated in a study by Johansson (1973). Researchers attached lightbulbs to the shoulders, elbows, wrists, hips, knees, and ankles of a model who wore black clothing and was photographed in the dark so only the lights could be seen (see Figure 3-18). Participants who were shown a still photograph of the model reported seeing only a random group of lights. Participants who saw a videotape of the model engaged in familiar activities—walking, dancing, climbing, and so forth—immediately recognized a person carrying out a particular activity. Later work (Koslowski & Cutting, 1977) even showed that observers could distinguish between a male and a female model, just by the movement of the lights! Apparently, the motion of the lightbulbs relative to one another gave an observer enough information to perceive a human being in motion. Note that in this example the observer did not see the person's shape or any individual features such as hair, eyes, hands, or feet. If a human form can be quickly recognized under these limited viewing conditions, imagine how much more information is available under normal circumstances.

J. J. Gibson (1950) became convinced that patterns of motion provide a great deal of information to the perceiver. His work with selecting and training pilots in World War II led him to thinking about the information available to pilots as they landed their planes. He developed the idea of optic flow, as the visual array presented to a pilot approaching a runway for landing. The arrows represent perceived movement—that is, the apparent movement of the ground, clouds, and other objects relative to the pilot. There is a texture to this motion: Nearer things appear to move faster than things farther away, and the direction in which an

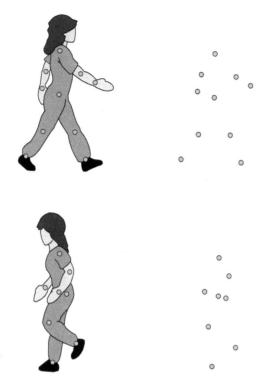

FIGURE 3-18 A depiction of Johansson's (1973) experimental stimuli.

Source: Reprinted with permission of Psychonomic Society, Inc., Springer Nature, from "Visual Perception of Biological Motion and a Model for its Analysis" Johansson, G., 14, 2 (1973); permission conveyed through Copyright Clearance Center, Inc.

object seems to move depends on the angle of the plane's movement in relation to it. The pilot can use all this information to navigate the plane to the runway.

Turvey Shaw, Reed, and Mace (1981) argued that whereas non-Gibsonian models of perception try to explain how people come to perceptual beliefs and judgments, Gibson tried to explain how people "adjust," physically and otherwise, to the environment. For Gibson, the central question of perception is not how we look at and interpret a stimulus array, but rather how we see and navigate among real things in the world. Why don't we normally walk into walls, for instance, or flinch from a perceived impending collision with walls?

An important idea in Gibson's theory is that the information available to an organism exists not merely in the environment but in an animal–environment ecosystem (Michaels & Carello, 1981). As animals move about, they continuously experience their environments. Different biological organisms have different perceptual experiences because (among other things) different organisms have different environments, different relationships to their environments, or both. Organisms directly perceive not only shapes and whole objects but also each object's **affordances**—the "acts or behaviors permitted by objects, places, and events" (Michaels & Carello, 1981, p. 42)—in other words, the things offered by the environment to the organism. Thus for human beings, chairs afford sitting, a handle or knob affords grasping, a glass window affords looking through. J. J. Gibson (1979) claimed that affordances of an object are also directly perceived; that is, we "see" that a chair is for sitting just as easily as we "see" that a chair is one metre away or made of wood.

According to Gibson, then, we avoid crashing into walls and closed doors because such surfaces do *not* afford passing through, and we perceive this as we move toward them. We sit on chairs or tables or floors but not on top of bodies of water, because the former afford sitting, whereas the latter do not. By virtue of our activity with and around different objects, we pick up on these affordances and act accordingly. Perception and action, for Gibson, are intimately bound.

Gibsonian theory has been both staunchly admired and sharply criticized. Fodor and Pylyshyn (1981), for example, argued that Gibson's proposals, while intriguing, are not well defined. Without sharp definitions of what an affordance is, they argued, the theory is not helpful in explaining perception. They charged that Gibson failed to specify just what kinds of things are invariant and what kinds are not. Without this specification, the following kinds of circular explanations can result: How do people perceive that something is a shoe? There is a certain (invariant) property that all and only shoes have—namely, the property of being a shoe. Perceiving that something is a shoe consists in the pickup of this property (Fodor & Pylyshyn, 1981, p. 142).

How much of a challenge do Gibsonian views pose to constructivist views of perception? Put another way, can constructivist and direct perception views be reconciled? Cognitive psychologists have not yet resolved the issue. One proposal tried to incorporate aspects of both approaches. Neisser (1976) described what he called the *perceptual cycle*, depicted in Figure 3-19. In this model, cognitive structures called *schemata* (singular: **schema**), derived from the knowledge base and containing expectations derived from context, guide the perceiver to explore the environment in particular ways. The environment, in turn, supplies certain information that confirms some expectations but not others. This helps the perceiver modify her expectations and, perhaps, bring other schemata to bear in the next cycle of perception. We will discuss the idea of schemata in much greater depth in Chapter 7. For the present, note that Neisser's model again assumes an active perceiver.

However the debate between supporters and critics of Gibson is resolved, he has reminded everyone in cognitive psychology of the need to pay attention to the way cognition operates outside the laboratory and of the relationship between the way information is processed and the goals and needs of the organism doing the processing. We will return to these themes throughout the book.

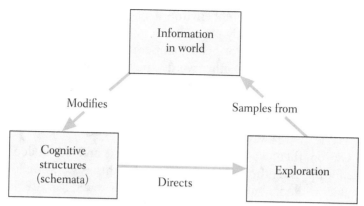

FIGURE 3-19 Neisser's (1976) perceptual cycle.

Source: Neisser, U. (1976). *Cognition and Reality: Principles and Implications of Cognitive Psychology*, page 21. © 1976 by W.H. Freeman and Company.

DISRUPTIONS OF PERCEPTION: VISUAL AGNOSIAS

Earlier, we said that perception is a process by which we attach meaning to sensory information we receive. That definition distinguishes between sensation (for example, vision, hearing, olfaction), or the receiving of sensory information, and another process, perception, which makes sense of that sensory information.

One of the best illustrations that sensation and perception are distinct processes comes from cognitive neuropsychological work on **visual agnosias**, impairments in the ability to *interpret* (although seeing) visual information (Banich, 1997). For example, consider Figure 3-20, from a case study reported by Rubens and Benson (1971). This figure shows drawings shown to a patient and his reproduction of them. As you can see, this patient saw the drawings clearly, and his renditions of each drawing reproduce several details. But this same patient could not correctly name *any* of the objects he saw and drew, saying of the pig that it "could be a dog or any other animal," and of the bird that it "could be a beech stump" (p. 310). Patients suffering from visual agnosia do not simply have a language problem, because they are similarly unable to use nonverbal means of recognizing familiar objects (such as pantomiming their usual uses). Nor do they have a memory problem, because they can tell you what a pig or a key is. Instead, the problem seems to lie in understanding what the visual pattern or object presented to them is (Farah, 1990). The deficit seems modality specific: Patients with visual agnosia can't recognize objects by sight but may be able to recognize them by sound, or touch, or smell. Put in our earlier terms, the problem seems to lie in creating a percept from the proximal stimulus.

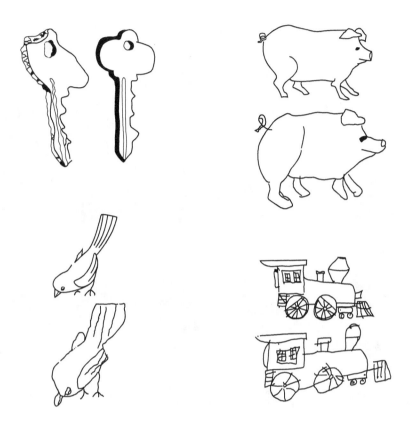

FIGURE 3-20 Four drawings and the copies made by the associative agnosic patient studied by Rubens and Benson (1971). Despite being able to see the drawings well enough to copy them, the patient was unable to recognize them.

Source: Reproduced with permission from JAMA Neurology, 1971, Vol. 24(4): 305–316. Copyright © 1971 American Medical Association. All rights reserved.

Researchers classify visual agnosias into different types. The first is called *apperceptive agnosia*. Patients with this disorder seem able to process a very limited amount of visual information. They can see the *contours*, or outlines, of a drawing or object but have a very difficult time matching one object to another or categorizing objects. Some cannot name objects at all, and at least one has been reported to be unable to distinguish printed *X*'s from *O*'s (Banich, 1997). Other patients can do this much processing but have trouble recognizing line drawings when some parts of the outlines are missing, such as the drawing of a chair shown in Figure 3-21(A), or recognizing objects shown in an unusual orientation, as in the drawing of the chair as viewed from the top in Figure 3-21(B).

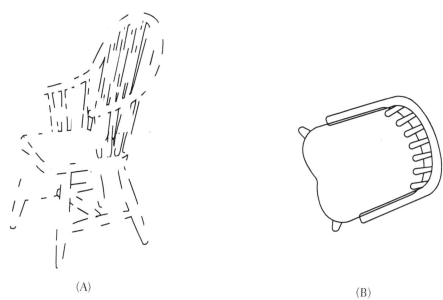

(A)

(B)

FIGURE 3-21 Examples of how contour information influences recognition in persons with apperceptive agnosia. (A) Patients with apperceptive agnosia have difficulty recognizing this object as a chair because they cannot interpolate the missing contours. (B) Patients with apperceptive agnosia would have difficulty recognizing the chair when it is viewed from this unusual angle.

A second kind of agnosia is called *associative agnosia.* Patients with this deficit *can* match objects or drawings and copy drawings, but they tend to do so very slowly and very, very carefully, almost point by point (Banich, 1997), instead of using the more typical technique of drawing the big features first and then filling in details. Associative agnosic patients may also become distracted by small details, such as an extra dot or stray line on a drawing. Associative agnosic patients cannot readily name the objects they have seen and drawn.

The two different types of visual agnosia seem associated with injury to two different areas of the brain. Apperceptive agnosia is typically associated with one hemisphere, or one side of the brain, the right. Associative agnosia is correlated with *bilateral* damage to a particular region of the brain (that is, in both cerebral hemispheres).

Adding to the mysteries associated with visual agnosia is a form in which affected individuals have difficulty identifying items of a particular category (say animate objects), whereas their ability to identify other types of objects (say inanimate objects) is unaffected (Warrington & Shallice, 1984). University of Waterloo psychologist Mike Dixon offered a major advance in the study of category-specific agnosia when he and his colleagues noted that certain affected categories appeared to include clusters of objects that are both highly visually and semantically similar (e.g., Dixon, Bub, & Arguin, 1997). By developing a novel paradigm in which they were able to tease apart the effects of physical and semantic similarity, Dixon and colleagues showed that both affect object identification (Dixon, 2000).

Yet another kind of visual agnosia, called **prosopagnosia**, is a very specific visual agnosia for faces (Farah, 1990). Prosopagnosic patients, who typically suffer from damage to a particular region in the right hemisphere (possibly with some left hemisphere involvement as well), may have intact object recognition abilities but may be unable to recognize faces of their family members or political leaders or even photographs of their own faces. They can see details—a nose, an eyebrow, a mole—but can't seem to put the visual details together into a coherent percept. A book by Oliver Sacks (1985) gives vivid details of cases of prosopagnosia.

Visual agnosias are not the only kind of neurological deficit relevant to the cognitive processes of perception and pattern recognition. Another well-known impairment, known as *unilateral neglect* (sometimes also called hemineglect), comes about as a result of damage to the parietal cortex and causes the patient to virtually ignore stimuli on the opposite side (Mozer, 2002). For example, patients with right-hemisphere parietal damage may fail to wash the left side of their body, comb the hair on the left side of their face, or respond to stimuli that originate on the left side of the body.

This very brief review of neurological deficits in perception shows there is more to perception than simply receiving information. Seeing, whether or not it is believing, is certainly not perceiving! An additional example of that, a case in which people perceive stimuli differently from how they are presented, is discussed in Box 3-2.

Box 3-2 Canadian Research Highlight

Synaesthesia is a condition in which ordinary stimuli lead to experiences that are anything but ordinary. The most common form of synaesthesia, digit-colour synaesthesia, exists for individuals who experience a specific colour whenever they see, hear, or even think about a specific number. For instance, the digit "9" may be "experienced" as the colour red. The University of Waterloo has established a Synaesthesia Research Group to study this amazing phenomenon. One of their most intriguing reports is that there appears to be a group of synaesthetes for whom a colour is "projected" out onto a digit, whereas a second group of synaesthetes experience the link of colour and digit as "associated" in the "mind's eye" (Dixon, Smilek, & Merikle, 2004).

SUMMARY

Researchers have proposed a number of distinct approaches to the study of perception. Despite differences in the theoretical assumptions made and the experimental methods used in each approach, researchers agree on at least two general principles, shown as points 1 and 2 in the following list.

1. Perception is more than the sum of static, individual sensory inputs. Perception clearly involves some integration and, perhaps, some interpretation of the sensations we receive. Perception is *not* a matter of simply taking in information from the world and creating from it a duplicate internal representation.

2. Perception sometimes involves "seeing" things that are not there (as in the case of subjective contours or synaesthesia) or distorting things that are (as in the case of other context effects). Perception involves both bottom-up processes, which combine small bits of information obtained from the environment into larger pieces, and top-down processes, which are guided by the perceivers expectations and theories about what the stimulus is.

3. One important perceptual task is the segregation of the figure from the background. Gestalt psychologists offered many principles of how we accomplish this task, including the principles of proximity, similarity, good continuation, closure, and common fate. All of them follow the law of Prägnanz, which states that of all the possible interpretations a perceiver could make of a stimulus, he or she will select the one that yields the simplest, most stable form.

4. Various bottom-up models of perception include template matching, which holds that patterns are recognized when perceivers match them to stored mental representations; prototype matching, which posits that the stored mental representations are not exact copies of stimuli but rather idealizations; and featural analysis, which holds that we first recognize features or components of patterns and objects and then put information about those components together to form an integrated interpretation.

5. Top-down models of perception incorporate perceivers' expectations into the model of how we interpret sensory information. Recent work on change blindness suggests that people process everyday visual information only to the level of gist, glossing over many details. Research on the word superiority effect demonstrates that context changes our perception of stimuli.

6. The connectionist model of letter perception illustrates just how complex the task of recognizing single letters (all typewritten in a single, simple font) can be.

7. Perception involves a great deal of activity on the part of the perceiver. We do more than simply record the visual world around us; we are not cameras. In both the constructivist and the direct-perception approaches to perception, perception is assumed to be the

result of activity, either mental or physical. We navigate the world, gathering information as we go, seeking more information about objects of interest as a matter of course. Any theory of perception must ultimately take into account our own activity in our everyday perception.

8. Disruptions of perception (as in visual agnosias, including prosopagnosia) involve not understanding or recognizing what is seen. Apperceptive agnosias involve intact recognition of contours but an inability to recognize what the object is. Associative agnosics can (sometimes, slowly) recognize the identity of objects but focus intently on small details. Prosopagnosia is an inability to recognize faces, either of relatives, famous people, or even one's own reflection or photograph.

The topic of perception is fundamental to the study of cognition and relates to many topics discussed later in this book. Perception relates directly to attention, for example—the subject of Chapter 4—in that often our level of attention affects whether or not we perceive and remember something. When we talk about imagery, in Chapter 8, we will look again at how people process visual information. Moreover, what is perceived often constrains what else the perceiver can do with the information, in terms of recording and storing it, thinking about it, and drawing inferences from it. We will thus continue to encounter perceptual issues in the chapters ahead.

REVIEW QUESTIONS

1. Describe the differences in assumptions about perception made by researchers working in (a) the traditional information-processing paradigm, (b) the connectionist paradigm, and (c) the Gibsonian ecological paradigm.
2. Describe two of the Gestalt laws of perceptual organization, illustrating each with a specific example.
3. Distinguish between bottom-up and top-down perceptual processes.
4. In what ways are featural analysis and prototype-matching models an improvement over template-matching models? In what ways are they not?
5. Describe some real-life examples of context effects in perception.
6. Consider McClelland and Rumelhart's connectionist model of letter perception. How might a Gestalt psychologist regard this model, and what would he or she see as the model's strengths and weaknesses? How might a cognitive neuropsychologist regard this model, and what would he or she see as its strengths and weaknesses?
7. Discuss the following: "Part of the reason why J. J. Gibson's supporters and detractors have such spirited debates is that they are talking past each other. Gibson doesn't just present a different model of perception—he redefines what the task of perception is."

8. What do the different visual agnosias tell us about perception? (*Hard:* What are the limitations, both theoretical and empirical, of using case studies of braindamaged individuals to inform theories of "normal" cognitive functions?)

KEY TERMS

affordance
bottom-up process
change blindness
constructivist approach
   to perception
context effects
direct perception
distal stimulus
feature
form perception

Gestalt principles of
   perceptual organization
Pandemonium model
pattern recognition
percept
perception
phoneme
prosopagnosia
prototype
proximal stimulus

retina
retinal image
schema
size constancy
subjective contours
template
top-down process
visual agnosia
visual search task
word superiority effect

Paying Attention

Even before opening this chapter, you probably had a good idea what the word "attention" meant. Having progressed this far in your education, there were likely numerous times when you felt that you needed to force yourself to "pay attention" when reading a challenging chapter for an exam because your mind kept wandering to thoughts of the after-exam party. You may have even heard a friend, parent, or teacher tell you to stop daydreaming or put down your phone and pay attention, like the employee shown in the cartoon below. When your goal was to pay attention, or when you were encouraged by others to pay attention, what exactly was expected of you? In short, what does it mean to pay attention?

The central goal of this chapter is to explore the question: What does it mean to pay attention? In doing so, we'll see that this seemingly simple question is actually quite complex. This is because, in part, the term attention has been used to talk about several different types of mental activities. For instance, we'll examine research that has investigated attention as

"Yoo hoo, the meeting's over here."

Paying attention involves selecting relevant information and ignoring irrelevant information.

cognitive resources that can be allocated to various tasks. Right now you might be devoting most of your attentional resources to what you are reading in this chapter, but perhaps some of your resources are being used to think about what you might snack on when your study session is over. The term *selective attention* refers to the fact that we usually focus our attention on one or a few tasks or events at any given time.

We'll also examine the relation between how well-practiced an individual is with a certain task, and how many attentional resources the task requires. For many tasks, extensive practice can result in the tasks becoming so easy and effortless that performing them requires no attention. When this happens, performance is said to be *automatic*. This can mean, among other things, that attention is freed up for a person to do another task simultaneously with the automatic one. This topic, known as *divided attention*, has captured the interest of cognitive psychologists, and we will examine some recent proposals about the relation between attention and automatic processing.

In addition, we will discuss how *we focus attention* on various events and objects that occur in our external environment. For example, when you need to find your keys on your desk, how does attention aid in your search for them? The term *spatial attention* refers to the fact that attention can be focused on objects and events of interest in our environment in order to aid in our ability to recognize them amongst other objects and events.

When we discuss both selective attention and spatial attention we will see that researchers are interested in not only how we process attended information, but also the fate of information that has not been attended. That is, do we process *unattended information?* If so, does this unattended information have consequences for our behaviour?

Finally, we will take a look at what some recent work in *cognitive neuropsychology* tells us about brain mechanisms involved when people "pay attention." We will see that particular areas of the brain seem to become active when we pay attention or refocus our attention, and that attended information elicits different responses in the brain from those elicited by unattended information.

Interestingly, each of the topics introduced briefly above can be found in the short passage by William James below. Like many topics in psychology, attention captured the interest of William James in the late 1800s. James (1890/1983) anticipated the writings of current investigators studying attention when he argued that only one system or process of conception can go on at a time very easily; to do two or more things at once, he believed, required that the processes be habitual. James's (1890/1983) description of attention, as clear today as it was a hundred years ago, ably sums up the phenomenon psychologists study when they investigate attention:

Everyone knows what attention is. It is the taking possession by the mind, in clear and vivid form, of one out of what seem several simultaneously possible objects or trains of thought. Focalization, concentration, of consciousness are of its essence. It implies withdrawal from some things in order to deal effectively with others, and is a condition which has a real opposite in the confused, dazed, scatterbrained state which in French is called distraction *and* Zerstreutheit *in German. (pp. 381–382)*

SELECTIVE ATTENTION

The term **selective attention** refers to the fact that we usually focus our attention on one or a few tasks or events rather than on many. To say we mentally focus our resources implies that we shut out (or at least process less information from) other competing tasks. As attention researcher Hal Pashler (1998) puts it, "At any given moment, [people's] awareness encompasses only a tiny proportion of the stimuli impinging on their sensory systems" (p. 2).

Do your intuitions agree? Try this experiment. Stop and reflect: Can you hear noises in your environment? Probably some or all of those noises were there just a second ago, when you read the preceding paragraph. But you weren't paying attention to those noises—they weren't "getting through." Ditto for other stimuli—can you feel your clothes or perhaps some jewellery against your skin when you direct your attention to them? Probably, although you weren't aware of them a second ago. Presumably we process information differently depending on whether or not we have been actively focusing on a stimulus.

How do cognitive psychologists study what information people process about things to which they are not paying attention? If you think about it, this is a tough challenge: How do you present people with information while making sure they do *not* pay attention to it? Simply instructing them to not pay attention is almost guaranteed to have the opposite effect. (Try this: For the next 25 seconds, pay no attention to the feelings in your fingers.)

It turns out that a solution is well known to cognitive psychologists. Depicted in Figure 4-1, it is known as the **dichotic listening task**. It works like this: A person listens to an recorded message over a set of headphones. On the recording are different messages, recorded so as to be heard simultaneously in opposite ears. Participants in a dichotic listening task typically are played two or more different messages (often texts borrowed from literature, newspaper stories, or speeches) and asked to "shadow"—that is, to repeat aloud—one of them. Information is presented at a rapid rate (150 words per minute, or so), so the shadowing task is demanding. At the end of the task, participants are asked what information they remember

FIGURE 4-1 Depiction of a dichotic listening task. The listener hears two messages and is asked to repeat ("shadow") one of them.

from either message—the attended message or the unattended message. (Sometimes the tapes are recorded so that both messages are heard in both ears—called *binaural presentation*—and some researchers have used it in addition to dichotic listening tasks.)

The logic of this experimental setup is as follows: The person must concentrate on the message to be shadowed. Because the rate of presentation of information is so fast, the shadowing task is difficult and requires a great deal of mental resources. Therefore, fewer resources are available to process information from the non-shadowed, unattended message.

Cherry (1953) demonstrated in a classic study that people can, with few errors, shadow a message spoken at a normal to rapid rate. When researchers later questioned these participants about the material in the unattended message, they could nearly always report accurately whether the message contained speech or noise, and, if speech, whether the voice was that of a man or a woman. When the unattended message consisted of speech played backward, some participants reported noticing that some aspect of the message, which they assumed to be normal speech, was vaguely odd.

Participants could not recall the content of the unattended message or the language in which it was spoken. In one variation of the procedure, the language of the unattended message was changed from English to German, but participants apparently did not notice the switch. Participants in an by experiment Moray (1959) heard prose in the attended message and a short list of simple words in the unattended message. They failed to recognize the occurrence of most words in the unattended message, even though the list had been repeated 35 times!

Filter Theory

To explain these findings, Broadbent (1958) proposed a **filter theory** of attention, which states that there are limits on how much information a person can attend to at any given time. The person uses an attentional filter to let some information through and to block the rest. The filter (see Figure 4-2) is based on some physical (in this particular example, basic acoustic) aspect of the attended message: the location of its source or its typical pitch or loudness, for instance. Only material that gets past the filter can be analyzed later for meaning. In other words, the filter *selects* information for later processing.

This theory explains why so little of the meaning of the unattended message can be recalled: The meaning from an unattended message is simply not processed. Put another way, Broadbent's filter theory maintains that the attentional filter is set to make a selection of what message to process *early*, typically before the meaning of the message is identified (Pashler, 1998). In other

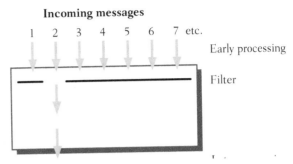

Incoming messages

FIGURE 4-2 Depiction of a filter model of attention. Different incoming messages, shown as arrows, all arrive at the same time. The filter (black line) blocks all but message 2, which has been selected to receive more cognitive processing.

words, according to Broadbent's model, it should not be possible to recall *any* of the meaning of an unattended message.

Does this mean that people can never pay attention to two messages at once? Broadbent (1958) thought not, believing instead that what is limited is the amount of information we can process at any given time. Two messages that contain little information, or that present information slowly, can be processed simultaneously. For example, a participant may be able to attend simultaneously to more than one message if one repeats the same word over and over again, because it would contain little information. In contrast, messages that present a great deal of information quickly overcome the filter; fewer of them can be attended to at once. The filter thus protects us from "information overload" by shutting out messages when we hear too much information to process all at once.

Other investigators subsequently reported results that contradicted filter theory. Moray (1959) discovered one of the most famous, called the "cocktail party effect": Shadowing performance is disrupted when one's own name is embedded in either the attended or the unattended message. Moreover, the person hears and remembers hearing her name. You may have had a similar experience at a party: While engaged in conversation with one or more people, you hear someone behind you say your name. Until your name was spoken, you "heard" nothing that speaker was saying, but the sound of your name seemed to reach out and grab your attention.

Why does the cocktail party effect pose a problem for filter theory? Filter theory predicts that *all* unattended messages will be filtered out—that is, not processed for recognition or meaning—which is why participants in dichotic listening tasks can recall little information about such messages. The cocktail party effect shows something completely different: People sometimes *do* hear their own name in an unattended message or conversation, and hearing their name will cause them to switch their attention to the previously unattended message.

Moray (1959) concluded that only "important" material can penetrate the filter set up to block unattended messages. Presumably, messages such as those containing a person's name are important enough to get through the filter and be analyzed for meaning. Left unexplained, then, is how the filter "knows" which messages are important enough to let pass.

Note that participants did not *always* hear their name in the unattended channel: When not cued in advance to be vigilant, only 33% of the participants ever noticed their names (Pashler, 1998). Thus an alternative explanation for the name recognition finding is that the shadowing task does not always take 100% of one's attention. Therefore, attention occasionally lapses and shifts to the unattended message. During these lapses, name recognition occurs.

Treisman (1960) discovered a phenomenon that argues against this alternative interpretation of the cocktail party effect. She played participants two distinct messages, one to the right ear and one to the left, and asked the participants to shadow one of them, for example, the right. At a certain point in the middle of the messages, the content of the first message and the second message was switched so that the second continued the story-line of the first and vice versa (see Figure 4-3). Immediately after the two messages "switched ears," many participants repeated one or two words from the "unattended ear." In the example shown, for instance, a participant shadowing message 1 might say, "At long last they came to a fork in the road but did not know which way to go. The trees on the left *side of* refers to the relationships…," with the italicized words following the meaning of the first part of message 1 but coming from the unattended channel (because they come after the switch point). If participants processed the unattended message only when their attentional filter "lapsed," it would be very difficult to explain why these lapses always occurred at the point when the messages switched ears.

At long last they came to a fork in the road but did not know which way to go. The trees on the left /term refers to the relationships among the logical subject and object; the latter to what is called "meaning."

Many linguists make a distinction between the logical form of a sentence and its deep structure. The former / side of the road seemed to be filled with singing birds; the path itself looked smooth and inviting.

FIGURE 4-3 Depiction of Treisman's (1960) experimental paradigm. The two messages "switch ears" at the point indicated by the slash mark.

To explain this result, Treisman reasoned that participants must base their selection of which message to attend to at least in part on the meaning of the message—a possibility not consistent with filter theory. Interestingly, most participants had no idea that the passages had been switched or that they had repeated words from the "wrong ear." Again, this poses a problem for filter theory, which predicts that information from the unattended channel should be shut out.

The issue of whether information from the unattended channel can be recognized was taken up by Wood and Cowan (1995). In one experiment, they had 168 undergraduate participants perform a dichotic listening task. Two of the groups shadowed an excerpt from *The Grapes of Wrath* (read very quickly, at a rate of 175 words per minute) in the attended channel (always presented to the right ear) and were also presented with an excerpt from *2001: A Space Odyssey* in the unattended channel, always presented to the left ear. Five minutes into the task, the speech in the unattended channel switched to backward speech for 30 seconds. Previous experiments had established that under these conditions, roughly half of the participants would notice the switch and half would not. The two groups differed only in how long the "normal" speech was presented after the backward speech: two and a half minutes for one group; one and a half minutes for the other. A third, control group of participants heard an unattended message with no backward speech.

Wood and Cowan (1995) first asked whether the people who noticed the backward speech in the unattended message showed a disruption in their shadowing of the attended message. In other words, if they processed information in the unattended message, did this processing have a cost to their performance on the main task? The answer was a clear yes. Wood and Cowan counted the percentage of errors made in shadowing and noted that the percentage rose to a peak during the 30 seconds of the backward-speech presentation. The effect was especially dramatic for those people who reported noticing the backward speech. Control participants, who were never presented with backward speech, showed no rise in their shadowing errors, nor did most of the participants who did not report noticing the backward speech.

What caused the shift in attention to the backward speech? Did the participants (or even some of them) switch their attention back and forth between the two messages periodically? Or did the backward speech cause the attentional filter to be reset automatically (that is, without awareness, intention, or effort)? To address these questions, Wood and Cowan (1995) analyzed shadowing errors by 5-second intervals for the 30 seconds preceding, during, and following, the backward-speech segment (for the groups who were presented with backward speech). These findings, presented in Figure 4-4, show that control participants and participants who did not notice the backward speech made no more errors over the time studied. However, participants who did report hearing backward speech made noticeably more errors, which peaked 10 to 20 seconds after the backward speech began.

Wood and Cowan (1995) concluded that the attentional shift to the unattended message was unintentional and completed without awareness. They based this conclusion on the facts

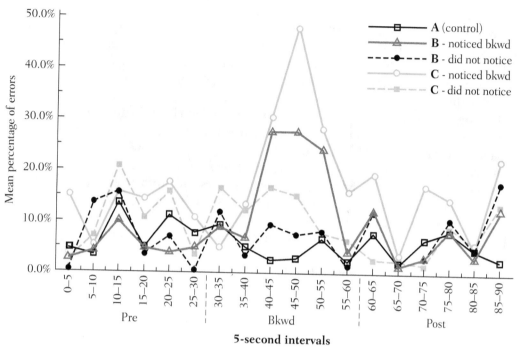

FIGURE 4-4 Mean percentage of errors in shadowing for each 5-second interval within the 30-second periods immediately before, during, and after backward speech, shown separately for participants who did and did not notice the backward speech. A = control condition; B = backward speech during the first half of the 6th minute; C = same as B but ending after 6 minutes rather than 8.5 minutes. BKWD = backward.

that detection of the backward speech interrupted and interfered with shadowing and that error rates peaked in a uniform time for all participants who noticed the backward speech. Put another way, Wood and Cowan believed that the participants who noticed the backward speech had their attention "captured" by the backward speech, which led to poorer performance on the main shadowing task.

Indeed, Conway Cowan, and Bunting (2001) showed that research participants who detect their name in the unattended message are those who have a lower working-memory span. (We'll talk about working memory in the next chapter. For now, you can think of it as the memory "space" or capacity a person has for keeping things in immediate mind.) In fact, 20% of participants with high working-memory spans detected their names in the unattended channel, compared with 65% of participants with low working-memory spans. The authors interpreted this finding as follows: A lower working-memory capacity means less ability to actively block the unattended message. In other words, people with low working-memory spans are less able to focus attention.

Attenuation Theory

Given her research findings, psychologist Anne Treisman (1960) proposed a modified filter theory, one she called **attenuation theory**. Instead of considering unattended messages completely blocked before they could be processed for meaning (as in filter theory), Treisman argued that their "volume" was "turned down." In other words, some meaningful information in unattended messages might still be available, even if hard to recover. She explained this idea as follows.

Incoming messages are subjected to three kinds of analysis. In the first, the message's physical properties, such as pitch or loudness, are analyzed. The second analysis is linguistic, a process of parsing the message into syllables and words. The third kind of analysis is semantic, processing the meaning of the message.

Some meaningful units (such as words or phrases) tend to be processed quite easily. Words that have subjective importance (such as your name) or that signal danger ("Fire!" "Watch out!") have permanently lowered thresholds; that is, they are recognizable even at low volumes. You might have noticed yourself that it is hard to hear something whispered behind you, although you might recognize your name in whatever is being whispered. Words or phrases with permanently lowered thresholds require little mental effort by the listener to be recognized. Thus, according to Treisman's theory, the participants in Moray's experiments heard their names because recognizing their names required little mental effort.

Only a few words have permanently lowered thresholds. However, the context of a word in a message can temporarily lower its threshold. If a person hears "The dog chased the…," the word *cat* is **primed**—that is, especially ready to be recognized (we'll talk more about priming in Chapter 9). Even if the word *cat* were to occur in the unattended channel, little effort would be needed to hear and process it, because of this priming. This explains why people in Treisman's experiment "switched ears": Hearing the previous words in a sentence primed the participants to detect and recognize the words that followed, even when those words occurred in the unattended message.

According to Treisman (1964), people process only as much as is necessary to separate the attended from the unattended message. If the two messages differ in physical characteristics, then we process both messages only to this level and easily reject the unattended message. If the two messages differ only semantically we process both through the level of meaning and select the to-be-attended message based on this analysis. Processing for meaning takes more effort, however, so we do this kind of analysis only when necessary. Messages not attended to are not completely blocked but rather weakened in much the way that turning down the volume weakens an audio signal from a stereo. Parts of the message with permanently lowered thresholds ("significant" stimuli) can still be recovered, even from an unattended message.

Note the contrasts here between attenuation theory and filter theory: Attenuation theory allows for many different kinds of analyses of all messages, whereas filter theory allows for only one. Attenuation theory; filter theory holds that unattended messages, once processed for physical characteristics, are discarded and fully blocked.

Late-Selection Theory

Broadbent's (1958) filter theory holds that no information about the meaning of an unattended message gets through the filter to be retained for future use. Treisman's (1964) attenuation theory allows for some information about meaning to get through to conscious awareness. Deutsch and Deutsch (1963) proposed a theory, called the **late-selection theory**, which goes even further. Later elaborated and extended by Norman (1968), and sometimes referred to as the Deutsch-Norman model of attention, this theory holds that *all* messages are routinely processed for at least some aspects of meaning. Attentional selection occurs *after* this routine processing, very late relative to the two earlier models. How much processing occurs? According to Pashler's (1988) interpretation of late-selection theory, at a minimum, the recognition of familiar objects of stimuli would be achieved:

> *Recognition of familiar objects proceeds unselectively and without any capacity limitations. One cannot voluntarily choose to identify or recognize something, according to these theorists. Whether there is just one sensory input or many does not affect the extent to which stimuli are analyzed or the timing of such analyses. (p. 17)*

Note that filter theory hypothesizes a *bottleneck*—a point at which the processes a person can bring to bear on information are greatly limited—at the filter. Late-selection theory also describes a bottleneck but locates it later in the processing, after certain aspects of the meaning have been extracted. All material is processed up to this point, and information judged to be most "important" is elaborated more fully. This elaborated material is more likely to be retained; unelaborated material is forgotten.

A message's "importance" depends on many factors, including its context and the personal significance of certain kinds of content (such as your name). Also relevant is the observer's level of alertness: At low levels of alertness (such as when we are asleep), only very important messages (such as the sound of our newborn's cry) capture attention. At higher levels of alertness, less important messages (such as the sound of a television program) can be processed. Generally, the attentional system functions to determine which of the incoming messages is the most important; this message is the one to which the observer will respond.

How well does the evidence for late-selection theory measure up? Different theorists take different positions on this issue. Pashler (1998) argues that the bulk of the evidence suggests it is undeniably true that information in the unattended channel sometimes receives some processing for meaning. At the same time, it appears true that most results thought to demonstrate late selection could be explained in terms of either attentional lapses (to the attended message) or special cases of particularly salient or important stimuli grabbing attention. In any event, it seems unlikely that unattended messages are processed for meaning to the same degree as are attended messages.

Attention, Capacity, and Mental Effort

Broadbent (1958) originally described attention as a bottleneck that allowed limited amounts of information to pass through for processing. To understand the analogy, think about the shape of a bottle. The smaller diameter of the bottle's neck relative to the diameter of the bottle's bottom reduces the rate at which liquid can pass through. The wider the neck, the faster the contents can pass through. Applying this analogy to cognitive processes, the wider the bottleneck, the more information can "spill through" to be processed. Although Treisman's (1960) attenuation theory and the late-selection models posed by Deutsch and Deutsch (1963) and Norman (1968) differed from Broadbent's in terms of the extent to which extraneous information passed through the bottleneck, these models also adopted the structural (i.e., filter or bottleneck) metaphor.

Daniel Kahneman (1973) proposed a different metaphor to represent attention. He viewed attention as a set of cognitive processes for categorizing and recognizing stimuli. The more complex the stimulus, the harder the processing, and therefore the more attentional resources were required. People have some control over where they direct their mental resources, however: They can often choose what to focus on and where to allocate their attentional resources.

Kahneman's (1973) model of attention depicts the allocation of mental resources to various cognitive tasks. An analogy could be made to a student managing a monthly budget. The student needs to decide how much money can be spent on food, entertainment, and perhaps a gym membership, in order to have enough left over to pay rent, tuition, and to buy books. In the case of Kahneman's model, the individual "spends" mental capacity on one or more of several different tasks. Many factors influence this allocation of capacity, which itself depends on the extent and type of mental resources available. The availability of mental resources, in turn, is affected by the overall level of *arousal*, or state of alertness.

Kahneman (1973) argued that one effect of being aroused is that more cognitive resources are available to devote to various tasks. Paradoxically, however, the level of arousal also depends on a task's difficulty. This means we are less aroused while performing easy tasks, such as adding 2 and 2, than we are when performing more difficult tasks, such as multiplying a social insurance number by pi. We therefore bring fewer cognitive resources to easy tasks, which, fortunately, require fewer resources to complete.

Arousal thus affects our capacity (the sum total of our mental resources) for tasks. But the model still needs to specify how we allocate our resources to all the cognitive tasks that confront us. The "allocation policy" is affected by an individual's enduring dispositions (for example, you generally prefer the work in your Psych courses to the work in other courses), momentary intentions (your vow to finish your English paper right now, before doing anything else!), and evaluation of the demands on one's capacity (the knowledge that a task you need to do right now will require a certain amount of your attention).

Essentially, this model predicts that we pay more attention to things we are interested in, are in the mood for, or have judged important. For example, opera lovers listen carefully during an operatic performance, concentrating on nuances of the performance, whereas people less interested in opera may sometimes have a hard time even staying awake. In Kahneman's (1973) view, attention is part of what the layperson would call "mental effort." The more effort expended, the more attention we are using.

Effort is only one factor that influences performance on a task, however. Greater effort or concentration results in better performance on some tasks— those that require resource-limited processing, performance of which is constrained by the mental resources or capacity allocated to it (Norman & Bobrow, 1975). Taking a midterm is one such task. On some other tasks, one cannot do better no matter how hard one tries. An example is trying to detect a dim light or a soft sound in a bright and noisy room. Even if you concentrate as hard as you can on such a task, your vigilance still may not help you detect the stimulus. Performance on this task is said to be *data limited*, meaning that it depends entirely on the quality of the incoming data, not on mental effort or concentration. Norman and Bobrow pointed out that both kinds of limitations affect our ability to perform any cognitive task.

AUTOMATICITY AND THE EFFECTS OF PRACTICE

As we become well-practiced doing something, that act takes less of our attention to perform. Driving is a good example. Remember back to when you first started driving. Your initial experience was probably one of feeling overwhelmed. Even when driving in a parking lot, driving requires many physical skills—steering, braking, hitting the turn signal, and being able to coordinate the clutch and shift if you are driving a manual transmission. Now add to that the complexities associated with your first attempt at driving on a road, such as scanning the road and the surrounding area and also periodically checking your mirrors and your speedometer, and you quickly find that there are a lot of demands on what feels like a very small attentional pool. It is therefore very unlikely that you spent any time during that first on-road drive singing along with (or even listening to) the radio or deep in conversation with a passenger.

Compare that initial driving experience with your current sense of your behaviour behind the wheel. Chances are you are much more relaxed now, and you probably don't spend any time consciously thinking about when or how to change gears, hit the accelerator or the brake, or begin a turn. You may even find that now you not only spend time singing along with the radio or talking with friends, but also may even do things like drink a coffee, get a piece of gum from your backpack, change your music, or talk on your cell (we'll discuss whether talking on one's cell while driving is ever a good idea later in the chapter). Compared to when you first started driving, you are able to "spend" far fewer of your attentional resources now than you could then. More formally said, an important variable that governs the number of things we can do simultaneously (like "driving" versus "driving, singing with the radio, and drinking a pop") is the capacity a given task consumes.

What affects the capacity a task requires? One factor is obviously the difficulty of the task. In the case of driving, however, it doesn't make sense to argue that the act of driving itself has become easier since you first started. People learning to drive today find it as challenging as you did when you began. Another important issue that affects the capacity a task requires is the individual's familiarity with the task. Practice is thought to decrease the amount of mental effort a task requires. Put simply, you are now a far more practised driver than you were at age 16, thus driving now consumes fewer of your attentional resources than it did when you began.

The Stroop Effect

A famous demonstration of the effects of practice on the performance of cognitive tasks was given by John Ridley Stroop (1935). Stroop presented participants with a series of colour bars (red, blue, green, brown, purple) or colour words *(red, blue, green, brown, purple)* printed in conflicting colours (the word *red*, for example, might be printed in green ink).

Participants were asked to name, as quickly as possible, the ink colour of each item in the series. When shown bars, they did so quickly, with few errors and apparently little effort. Things changed dramatically, however, when the items consisted of words that named colours other than that of the ink in which the item was printed. Participants stumbled through these lists, finding it difficult not to read the word formed by the letters.

According to Stroop (1935), the difficulty stems from the following: Adult, literate participants have had so much practice reading that the task requires little attention and is performed rapidly. In fact, according to Stroop, literate adults read so quickly and effortlessly that *not* reading words is hard. Thus when confronted with items consisting of words, participants couldn't help reading them. We describe this kind of response—one that requires no attention and cannot be inhibited—as *automatic*. Indeed, the most common theoretical account of the Stroop effect is that for literate adults reading is automatic and its products, which conflict with the ink colour on a Stroop trial, interfere with a participant's ability to name the ink colour (see MacLeod's [1991] review). More recently, however, this view has been challenged, as you'll see in Box 4-1.

Automatic versus Attentional (Controlled) Processing

What exactly does it mean to perform a task "automatically"? We often talk about being "on autopilot" when we do something without being aware of it— but what is actually going on cognitively? Posner and Snyder (1975) offered three criteria for cognitive processing to be called **automatic processing:** (1) it must occur without intention; (2) it must occur without involving conscious awareness; and (3) it must not interfere with other mental activity.

Consider our driving example once again. A practised driver driving a familiar route under normal, nonstressful conditions may well be operating the car automatically. Driving home, for example, you may have found yourself in the middle of making a turn without actually intending to: Your hand seems to hit the turn signal and your arms turn the steering wheel without your consciously deciding to do so. Indeed, you may follow your usual route home even when you've previously intended to go a different way. For example, you may intend to go to the dry

---

Box 4-1 Is Reading an Automatic Process?

As we discussed above, the dominant view in the literature has been that the Stroop effect occurs because word reading is automatic in highly skilled readers (MacLeod, 1991). That is, when trying to identify the ink colour of a coloured word, the observer can't prevent herself from reading the irrelevant word. Research by Derek Besner, Jennifer Stolz, and their colleagues at the University of Waterloo has challenged this view, however (Besner & Stolz, 1999; Risko, Stolz, & Besner, 2005). These researchers have shown that by manipulating the manner in which a participant attends to the Stroop stimulus it is possible to reduce, and even eliminate, the Stroop effect. This indicates that rather than being automatic and not requiring attention, word reading *depends on* attention.

Also consistent with this finding is recent work by Amir Raz (currently at McGill University and the Jewish General Hospital in Montreal) and his colleagues. They have shown that the Stroop effect can be eliminated by use of a post-hypnotic suggestion telling observers that they are unable to read (Raz, Shapiro, Fan, & Posner, 2002).

---

cleaners but start thinking of something else and then, to your surprise and embarrassment, find yourself in your own driveway, simply because you forgot to change your automatic routine!

Schneider and Shiffrin (1977) examined automatic processing of information under well-controlled laboratory conditions. They asked participants to search for certain targets, either letters or numbers, in different arrays of letters or numbers called *frames*. For example, a participant might be asked to search for the target *J* in an array of four letters: *B M K T.* (*Note*: This trial is "negative," in the sense that the target is not present in the frame.)

Previous work had suggested that when people search for targets of one type (such as numbers) in an array of a different type (such as letters), the task is easy. Numbers against a background of letters seem to "pop out" automatically. In fact, the number of nontarget characters in an array, called distractors, makes little difference *if* the distractors are of a different type from the targets. So finding a *J* among the stimuli *1, 6, 3, J, 2* should be about as easy as finding a *J* among the stimuli *1, J, 3.* Finding a specific letter against a background of other letters seems much harder. So searching for *J* among the stimuli *R J T* is easier than searching for the *J* among the stimuli *G K J L T*, both of which are more difficult than finding a *J* amongst digits. In other words, when the target and the distractors are of the same type, the number of distractors does make a difference.

Schneider and Shiffrin (1977) had two conditions in their experiment. In the varied-mapping condition, the set of target letters or numbers, called the *memory set*, consisted of one or more letters or numbers, and the stimuli in each frame were also letters or numbers. Targets in one trial could become distractors in subsequent trials. So a participant might search for a *J* on one trial, then search for an *M* on the second trial, with a *J* distractor included. In this condition, the task was expected to be hard and to require concentration and effort.

In the consistent-mapping condition, the target memory set consisted of numbers and the frame consisted of letters, or vice versa. Stimuli that were targets in one trial were never distractors in other trials. The task in this condition was expected to require less capacity.

In addition, Schneider and Shiffrin (1977) varied three other factors to manipulate the attentional demands of the task. The first was *frame size*—that is, the number of letters and numbers presented in each display. This number was always between 1 and 4. Slots not occupied by a letter or number contained a random dot pattern. Second was the *frame time*—that is, the length of time each array was displayed. This varied from approximately 20 milliseconds to 800 milliseconds. The last variable manipulated was the *memory set*—that is, the number of targets the participant was asked to look for in each trial (for example, find a *J* versus find a *J, M, T,* or *R).*

Figure 4-5 presents the results of the Schneider and Shiffrin (1977) study. The graphs are a little hard to follow, but try to do so in conjunction with what you read in the next few paragraphs. In the consistent-mapping condition, thought to require only automatic processing

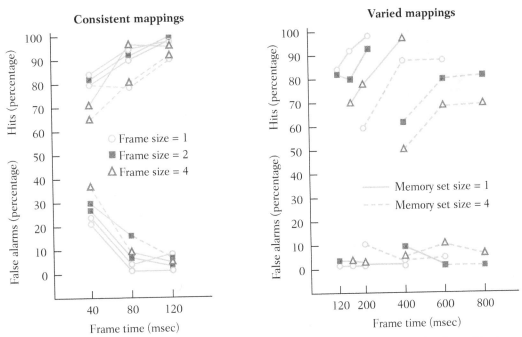

FIGURE 4-5 Results of Schneider and Shiffrin's (1977) experiments. Notice that for subjects in the consistent-mapping condition, only the variable of frame time affects reaction time. Subjects in the varied-mapping condition are also affected by frame size and memory set size.

Source: From *Psychological Review* by Walter Schneider and Richard M. Shiffrin. Copyright © 1977 by American Psychological Association. Reprinted by permission.

(because the targets and distractors were not the same type of stimuli), participants' performance varied only with the frame time, not with the number of targets searched for (memory set) or the number of distractors present (frame size). This means participants were just as accurate in searching for one as for four targets and in searching among one, two, or four items in a frame. Accuracy depended *only* on the length of time the frames were displayed.

In the varied-mapping condition, thought to require more than automatic processing (because the targets and distractors could both be letters, or both numbers, and because targets on one trial could become distractors on another), participants' performance in detecting the target depended on all three variables: memory set size (number of targets searched for), frame size (number of distractors present), and frame time. You can see this in the second panel of Figure 4-5, where all the lines are separated, indicating that participants responded differently on trials with different memory set sizes and/or different frame sizes.

Schneider and Shiffrin (1977) explained these results by distinguishing between two kinds of processing. Automatic processing, they asserted, is used for easy tasks and with familiar items. It operates in parallel (meaning it can operate simultaneously with other processes) and does not strain capacity limitations. This kind of processing is done in the consistent-mapping condition: Because the targets "popped out" from the background, little effort or concentration was required. That searching for four targets was as easy as searching for one illustrates the parallel nature of this kind of processing: Several searches can be conducted simultaneously.

Schneider and Shiffrin (1977) dubbed the second kind **controlled processing**. Controlled processing is used for difficult tasks and ones that involve unfamiliar processes. It usually operates serially (with one set of information processed at a time), requires attention, is capacity limited, and is under conscious control. Controlled processing occurred in the varied-mapping condition (where targets and distractors could alternate across different trials). More generally, controlled processing is what we use with nonroutine or unfamiliar tasks.

DIVIDED ATTENTION

If attention is a flexible system for allocating resources, and if tasks differ in the amount of attention they require, then people should be able to learn to perform two tasks at once (known as **divided attention**). Parents of teenagers, for example, often marvel over how their children seem able to listen to music, talk on the phone to their friends, and study all at the same time. How difficult is doing two or more tasks at once, and on what factors does this ability depend?

Dual-Task Performance

Spelke, Hirst, and Neisser (1976) examined this question in a clever and demanding laboratory study. Two Cornell University students were recruited as participants. Five days a week, for 17 weeks, working in 1-hour sessions, these students learned to write words dictated while they read short stories. Their reading comprehension was periodically

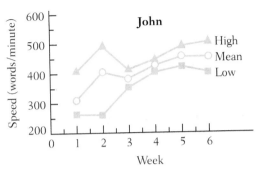
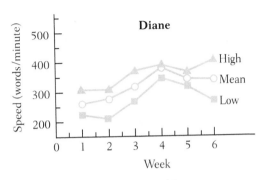

FIGURE 4-6 Reading speeds during practice phase of learning to do two things at once. Weekly means and interquartile ranges of reading speeds, plotted for each week of practice, for two subjects, John and Diane.

Source: Reprinted with permission of SAGE Publications, Inc., from "Our Eyes Do Not Always Go Where We Want Them to Go," Jan Theeuwes, Arthur F. Kramer, Sowon Hahn, et al, 9, 5 (1998); permission conveyed through Copyright Clearance Center, Inc.

tested. After 6 weeks of practice, their reading rates (shown in Figure 4-6) approached their normal speeds. Also by the end of 6 weeks, their scores on the reading comprehension tests were comparable whether they were only reading stories (and thus presumably giving the reading task their full attention) or reading stories while writing down dictated words. Further investigation revealed that participants could also categorize the dictated words by meaning and could discover relations among the words without sacrificing reading speed or comprehension.

Many psychologists were surprised that the participants in this study could process information about meaning without conscious attention, and some offered alternative explanations for the findings. One hypothesis is that participants alternated their attention between the two tasks, attending first to the story, then to the dictation, then back to the story, and so on. Although this possibility was not directly tested, the authors argued that the fact the participants' reading speeds were comparable whether or not they were taking dictation suggests that if they were alternating their attention, they were doing so without any measurable lag.

Hirst, Spelke, Reaves, Caharack, and Neisser (1980) found evidence against this alternation hypothesis. Their participants were trained in ways similar to those used by Spelke et al. (1976). All participants copied dictated words while reading. Some participants read short stories, presumably containing some redundant material and therefore requiring relatively little attention. Other participants read encyclopedia articles, thought to contain less redundant material and thus to require more concentration. After they reached normal reading speeds and reading comprehension during dictation, the participants' tasks were switched:

Those who had been reading short stories were now given encyclopedia articles, and those trained using encyclopedia articles now read short stories. Six of the seven participants performed comparably with the new reading material, indicating that the participants were probably not alternating their attention between the two tasks. If they were, then learning to take dictation while reading short stories should not have transfered well to doing so while reading encyclopedia articles.

A second possible explanation for participants' ability to learn to do two tasks at once is that one of the two tasks (for example, the dictation task) was being performed automatically. According to one of Posner and Snyder's (1975) criteria for automaticity—that processing not interfere with other mental activity—taking dictation in this study might be considered automatic. However, participants were clearly aware that words were being dictated, and they typically recognized about 80% of the dictated words on tests immediately following trials. Moreover, participants clearly intended to copy the dictated words. Therefore, taking dictation does not meet Posner and Snyder's last two criteria: lack of intention and lack of conscious awareness.

Hirst and colleagues (1980) also offered evidence against the possibility that one task becomes automatized. Participants trained to copy complete sentences while reading were able to comprehend and recall those sentences, suggesting that the participants had processed the dictation task for meaning. This in turn suggests they paid at least some attention to the dictation task, given that most psychologists believe automatic processing occurs without comprehension.

A third explanation for how participants were able to perform two tasks at once, which Hirst and colleagues (1980) favoured, is that the participants learned to combine two separate tasks: reading and taking dictation. That is, practice with these two specific tasks caused the participants to perform the tasks differently from the way they did them at first. This implies that if either one of these tasks were combined with a third (such as shadowing prose), additional practice would be needed before the two tasks could be done together efficiently.

Practice thus appears to play an enormous role in performance and is one important determinant of how much attention any task requires. Studies such as those by Hirst and colleagues are not without critics (see Shiffrin, 1988). However, this work and related studies are beginning to change our understanding of the role that practice plays in cognitive tasks (see Pashler et al., 2001, for a more detailed discussion).

The Psychological Refractory Period (PRP)

Even with lots of practice, however, some sets of tasks are hard to do together at the same time. The old child's hand play of rubbing your stomach while simultaneously patting your head comes to mind. However, it's fairly easy (if absurd-looking) to pat your own head while carrying on a conversation or singing a song.

Pashler (1993) reported on studies from his and others' laboratories that examined the issue of doing two things at once in greater depth. The participant is asked to work on two tasks. The first is a tone choice response task, in which on each trial the participant is presented with either a low- or a high-pitched tone and is instructed to respond "low" or "high" as quickly as possible. Response times are recorded, and the participant is often given feedback regarding speed and accuracy. The second task involves visual presentation of a letter, and the participant is instructed to press one of several response keys that correspond to the letter presented.

The interval between the presentation of the tone (S1 in the diagram) and the letter (S2 in the diagram) is systematically varied. At long intervals, participants show no interference and appear to perform the two tasks successively, finishing their response to the first task before beginning to work on the second. However, as the interval between the presentation of S1 and S2 gets shorter and shorter, the time to complete the second task gets longer and longer. The hypothesized explanation is that while the participant is working on the first task, he cannot devote any attention to make progress on the second (Johnston, McCann, & Remington, 1995).

Let's pause here to consider an analogy modified from Pashler (1993). Imagine a kiosk with one bank machine (ATM) and two customers. The amount of time that customer 2 has to wait for the ATM depends on the interval between her arrival and that of customer 1. If customer 2 arrives any time after customer 1 has completed her transactions with the ATM, then there is no waiting time—the bank machine is fully available to customer 2. However, if customer 2 arrives while customer 1 is still using the ATM, then customer 2 will have to wait until customer 1 is finished. Customer 2 cannot insert her bank card until Customer 1's transactions have been completed and his card has been returned. This waiting time is analogous to the slowed response time to the second stimulus, S2, at short intervals between the presentation of S1 and S2, called the **psychological refractory period**, or **PRP**.

In the ATM example above the bank machine functions as a bottleneck—the limiting factor in the speed with which the second task (customer) gets processed. Coming back to the issue of cognitive processing of two tasks, where is this bottleneck? Pashler considered three distinct possibilities: at the stage of perception of the stimulus (A), at the stage of making a response (C), or at the stage in which a response is selected or chosen (B). In fact, the work of Pashler (1993) and his colleagues supports the theory of Welford (1952), who argued for this last possibility (B) and who coined the term *psychological refractory period*. Pashler (1993) also found evidence that retrieving information from memory caused a bottleneck and disrupted attention to the second task.

Canadian researchers Mike Tombu and Pierre Jolicœur have offered an alternative to the bottleneck account of the psychological refractory period, however (Tombu & Jolicœur, 2003). Rather than posit that attention must be divided in an all-or-none fashion between two tasks, Tombu and Jolicœur argued that it can be shared in a more flexible manner. That is, while performing an attention-demanding phase of task 1, people can choose to allocate some attention to a demanding phase of a second task. Tombu and Jolicœur's account predicts that when people choose to share some attention between the two tasks performance on the first task will be impaired relative to when all attention is devoted to it. Research from their lab supports this capacity-sharing model (Tombu & Jolicœur, 2005).

The Attention Hypothesis of Automatization

Work by Gordon Logan and Joseph Etherton (Logan & Etherton, 1994; Logan, Taylor, & Etherton, 1996) has sought to tie together many concepts we have talked about in this chapter. These researchers propose what they call the **attention hypothesis of automatization**, which states that attention is needed during the practice phase of a task and determines what gets learned during practice. Attention also determines what will be remembered from the practice. Logan and colleagues (1996) put it this way: "Learning is a side effect of attending: People will learn about the things they attend to and they will not learn much about the things they do not attend to" (p. 620). Specifically, Logan and colleagues argued that attention affects what information gets encoded into a memory and what information is later retrieved (topics we will take up in detail in Chapters 5 and 6).

In a series of experiments, Logan and Etherton (1994) presented university student participants with a series of two-word displays and asked them to detect particular target words (for example, words that named metals) as fast as possible. For some participants, the word pairs remained constant over trials; for example, if the words *steel* and *Canada* were paired on one trial, then neither word ever appeared with any other word on subsequent trials. Other participants saw word pairs that varied from trial to trial, such as *steel* with *Canada* on one trial and *steel* with *broccoli* on another. The question was: Would participants in the first condition gain an advantage in performance because the words were consistently paired?

The answer was yes, but only when the specifics of the target detection task forced the participants to pay attention to both words in the display. If, for example, the experimenters coloured one of the two words green and asked participants only to decide whether the green word in a stimulus display was a target word on each trial, then participants did not gain an advantage from consistent pairings of words and indeed later recalled fewer of the distractor words. Apparently the colour cue made it easy for participants to ignore the second word in the display. To ignore something means not to pay attention to it, and thus apparently little gets learned about it. Even with extensive practice (five sessions), participants in the consistent pairing condition were unlikely to learn which words had been paired if they had no reason to pay attention to the distractor word.

Divided Attention Outside the Laboratory: Cell Phone Usage While Driving

Let's see if we can apply some of the theoretical concepts just reviewed to an actual instance of **dual-task performance** in the real world. In-car electronics such as cell phones, Multi-media centers and navigation systems are becoming commonplace.

As they become more common, however, it is clear that the public is becoming more concerned about their use. A discussion paper by Transport Canada (2003) states that driver distraction contributes to approximately 20% to 50% of all collisions. In particular, distraction tied to cell phone use has been associated with a 38% to 400% increase in the risk of an accident. It is no surprise, then, that 37% of Canadians state that distracted drivers are a "serious or extremely serious problem" (Beirness, Simpson, & Desmond [2002]), and that 64% of those polled believe that cell phones, in particular, are a serious problem. Recently, several provinces have enacted or have considered enacting legislation to prohibit drivers from talking on cell phones while behind the wheel. The argument against driving while using a cell phone is that talking on a cell phone distracts the driver's

Driving while talking on a cell phone is often a real-world example of dangerous dual-task performance.

attention from what should be the primary task, navigating the vehicle on the road.

In a clever simulation, Strayer and Johnston (2001) investigated this interference. In their first experiment, they had research participants perform a pursuit-tracking task: They used a joystick to move a cursor on a computer to keep it positioned over a moving target. At various intervals the target flashed either red or green, a signal to the "driver" to push a "brake" button on the joystick (red) or ignore the flash (green). Participants first performed the tracking ("driving") task by itself, then performed the dual-task portion of the study: either listening to a radio broadcast or talking on a cell phone with a confederate of the experimenters. The confederate, who was in a different location, talked with the participants, either about the then-current Clinton presidential impeachment issue or about the Salt Lake City Olympic Committee bribery scandal, and tried to ensure that the participant talked and listened approximately equally. Listening to the radio broadcast did not cause people to miss red lights or to react to them more slowly than they had when they performed the pursuit task by itself (the single-task condition). However, talking on the cell phone did cause both problems, as shown in Figure 4-7.

In a second experiment, the authors had participants talk on a cell phone, either "shadowing" lists of words the confederate read to them or else performing a word-generation task. In the latter task, the participant listened to the word the confederate read (let's say the word was *cream*) and then had to generate a new word that began with the last letter of the word read (in our example, participants had to say a word beginning with the letter *m*). For some participants the pursuit task was easy, with few unpredictable changes, whereas for others it was more difficult, with many such changes. Shadowing words did not lead to reliable decrements in performance. However, generating words did, and the decrement

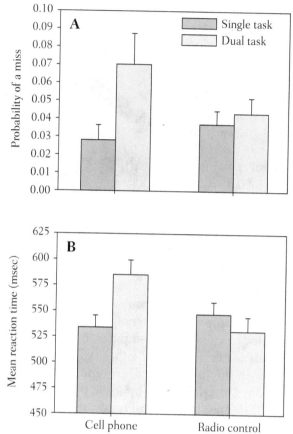

FIGURE 4-7 Results from the Strayer and Johnston (2001) study.

Source: David L. Strayer and William A. Johnston, *Psychological Science*, vol. 12, issue 6, pp. 462–466, copyright © 2001 by SAGE Publications. Reprinted by Permission of SAGE Publications, Inc.

was especially pronounced when the task was difficult. Strayer and Johnston (2001) offered these additional observations:

> *It is also interesting to consider the potential differences between cell-phone conversations, and in-person conversations with other occupants of the vehicle . . . there is evidence that in-person conversations are modulated by driving difficulty, so that as the demands of driving increase, participation by all participants in a conversation decreases . . . . By contrast, at least one of the participants in a cellular phone conversation is unaware of the current driving conditions (and may even be unaware that the cell-phone user is driving). (p. 466)*

In summary, research on divided attention suggests that there are serious limits on the number of things we can actually do at once. It may seem that we can do things simultaneously in the real world, when in many cases we do both tasks by rapidly switching our attention back and forth between the two. Of course, when those individual tasks become more demanding, it becomes harder and harder to do them simultaneously.

SPATIAL ATTENTION

We've talked quite a bit about attention as a limited resource that can be concentrated on an object or a mental event to govern processing. Researchers have also spent considerable time studying how we orient attention in visual space. Imagine the following scenario: You've just returned from a summer back-packing trip to Europe and have landed at Pearson airport. You're looking forward to seeing your family and friends, and expect your mother, father, and best friend to be at the terminal to greet you. You exit the luggage claim area and immediately begin scanning the crowd for a familiar face (i.e., a "target") amongst a large number of unfamiliar people (i.e., distractors). Attention plays a large role in how efficient you are in your **visual search**, and in the types of things that aid and impair your performance, as we'll see.

Now imagine that as you're searching for your target you are suddenly distracted by a bright flash of light off to your right. Without thinking about it, you immediately turn your attention to the area of the flash and find that it is a fellow traveller being photographed by some happy family members. Although it was not your intent to look over there—your goal was to find your family— your attention was summoned by the flash coming from the cellphone being used to take the picture. As we will see below, the flash acted much like a **spatial cue** in directing attention to a particular area in space. We will now talk about spatial attention—both in the context of a spatial cueing paradigm, and in the context of visual search.

Spatial Cueing

Posner and colleagues (e.g., Posner, Nissen, & Ogden, 1978; Posner, Snyder, & Davidson, 1980) devised an ingenious way to study spatial attention. They asked observers to fixate on a plus sign in the centre of the screen. An arrow cue then appeared above the fixation, and it pointed either to the right, to the left, or had two heads (one pointing left and one pointing right). Observers were told to move attention, but not their eyes, in the direction indicated by the one-headed arrow cue. In the case of a two-headed cue, they were told to leave attention (and their eyes) at the fixation sign. A simple target (a square) then appeared on the screen, and observers were asked to hit a key when they detected the target. On 80% of trials with a one-headed cue, the target appeared in the same location indicated by the cue; this was called a *valid trial*. On 20% of trials with a one-headed cue, the target appeared in the location opposite to that indicated by the cue; this was called an *invalid trial*. Finally, in the case of two-headed cues, targets were equally likely to appear on either side. This was called a *neutral trial*.

Posner and colleagues measured the time it took observers to detect targets in the valid, invalid, and neutral trial conditions. The results indicated that observers were fastest in the validly cued condition and slowest in the invalidly cued condition. Posner and colleagues interpreted these results as showing that performance was *facilitated* on valid trials (relative to neutral trials), presumably because observers shifted attention to the location of the target prior to its appearance. Likewise, there was an important *cost* (relative to a neutral trial) to having shifted attention to the wrong location on an invalid trial. From results like these, Posner and colleagues (1980) developed a spotlight metaphor of attention and suggested that, "attention can be likened to a spotlight that enhances the efficiency of detection of events within its beam" (p. 172). The spotlight metaphor is therefore an important way to characterize *input attention* (e.g., Johnston, McCann, & Remington, 1995), as it affects the ease with which stimuli can be brought into the system for processing.

Under what circumstances might a spotlight be useful? Recall the initial example of searching for your family and friend at Pearson airport. A spotlight that enhances the efficiency of detection during such a search would certainly prove useful. In fact, this type of input attention has been studied extensively in visual search tasks, in addition to the type of spatial cueing task discussed above.

Visual Search

Look at Figure 4-8. In Panel A, search for the blue letter " Z." As you do so, take mental note of the difficulty involved in finding the letter. Once you have located the blue Z, perform

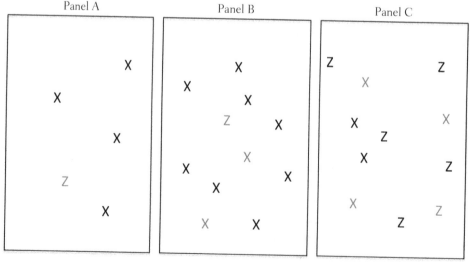

FIGURE 4-8 Visual search.

the same search (i.e., find a blue "Z") in Panel B, again being sure to take mental note of the difficulty of the search. Finally, search once again for the blue Z, this time in Panel C. You no doubt noticed that the search in Panel A was by far the simplest. Indeed, the letter Z probably seemed to "pop out" at you. The remaining two searches probably seemed more difficult, however, with Panel C posing the greatest challenge.

This demonstration was modelled after experiments done by Anne Treisman and her colleagues (e.g., Treisman & Gelade, 1980). In one experiment, Treisman and Gelade (1980) presented participants with a series of simple objects (such as letters) that differed in several features (such as colour or shape). Participants were asked to search for a particular object— for example, a blue letter "Z". If the item being searched for differed from the background items in the critical feature (such as a blue item amongst all black items, as in panel A), the target item seemed to pop out of the display, and the number of background items did not affect participants' response times. Treisman and Gelade interpreted this pattern of results as evidence that the detection of individual features is automatic—that is, it does not require attention and can be performed in parallel across the entire display. In other words, all items in the display can be searched at once under these conditions.

Box 4-2 Canadian Research Highlight

Ray Klein at Dalhousie University (https://www.dal.ca/faculty/science/psychology_neuroscience/faculty-staff/our-faculty/raymond-klein.html) is a world-renowned attention researcher. One of his most interesting works is his seminal paper, published in *Nature*, that examines two visual attention phenomena: spatial cueing and visual search (Klein, 1988). As discussed above, observers are typically faster to detect a target when it appears in a validly cued location than when it appears in an uncued location. Posner and Cohen (1984) showed, however, that this is not always the case. Specifically, if the appearance of the target is delayed by a short period of time observers are actually slower to detect a target at the validly cued location. This finding is known as *inhibition of return*. Klein cleverly speculated that inhibition of return might function as an adaptive process to enhance search. That is, it may act as an "inhibitory tagging system" (1988, p. 431), or, in other words, a way for the observer to keep track of locations that have already been searched. According to Klein's view, the cue summons the observer's attention to its location, but with the longer delay between the cue and the appearance of the target the observer finds that the target is not there and moves attention elsewhere. When the target finally does appear at the cued location, the observer is now slower to move attention back to that location because it is marked as "already searched." This is the kind of process that prevents you from continually searching for your keys on the kitchen table once you have discovered they are not there.

In another condition, participants were asked to search for an object with a combination of features. For example, in panel C you were asked once again to search for the blue *Z*, but in this case the blue *Z* was hidden amongst other items that included both other blue letters (that were not *Z*s) and other *Z*s (that were not blue). In this condition, search was much more difficult and participants' response times varied with the number of background items. That is, locating the target item took longer the more dis-tractor items were in the display. Treisman and Gelade (1980) argued that search in this case was difficult because the observer not only had to find the features "*Z*" and "colour blue," but also had to make sure both of those features were on the same object. In other words, in panel C participants were asked to perform a *conjunction search*. Treisman and Gelade (1980) argued that in order to perform a conjunction search, observers require controlled, nonautomatic processing. This can be likened to moving the attentional spotlight that we discussed above across the search display in a serial (i.e., one-item-at-a-time) manner.

This led Treisman to propose what has come to be called **feature integration theory**. Her general idea is that we perceive objects in two distinct stages. In the first stage, which is preattentive, or automatic, we register features of objects, such as their colour or shape. This allows us to detect or recognize all objects that can be identified on the basis of a single feature, like the blue *Z* in panel A, without the use of attention. In the second stage, attention allows us to "glue" the features together into a unified object (Tsal, 1989a). This stage is necessary in order to identify complex objects, or to detect objects that share features with other background objects, such as the blue *Z* in Panel C.

Interestingly, in a later study Treisman and Schmidt (1982) showed that when attention is diverted or "overloaded," participants make "gluing" errors, resulting in what Treisman called *illusory conjunctions*. Consider the example of glancing quickly and without much attention out the window at a red Honda Civic and a blue Toyota Prius. Later, when asked to report what you saw, you might say, "A blue Honda Civic." Such combining of two stimuli is erroneous; the conjunction reported is illusory.

In the experimental demonstration of this phenomenon (Treisman & Schmidt, 1982), participants saw two black digits displayed on either side of a row of three larger coloured letters, presented briefly (for 200 milliseconds). They were asked to pay attention to and recite the black digits, with the experimenter emphasizing the importance of accuracy. Participants were also asked, *after* they had reported the digits, to report the positions (left, right, or middle), colours, and names of any letters they had seen. They were asked to report only information about which they were highly confident. Participants were able to provide correct information on letters 52% of the time, but in 39% of the trials they reported illusory conjunctions (such as a red *X* instead of either a blue *X* or a red *T*). In other words, when mentally taxed, people mistakenly combined features in illusory conjunctions.

Putting these ideas together, Treisman argued that individual features can be recognized automatically, with little mental effort. What apparently requires mental capacity is the integration of features, the putting together of pieces of information to recognize more complicated objects. Thus, according to Treisman, perceiving individual features takes little effort or attention, whereas "gluing" features together into coherent objects requires more. Many researchers (Briand & Klein, 1989; Quinlan, 2003; Tsal, 1989a, 1989b) have tested the theory's predictions and offered refinements and critiques. Further evidence that attention is a necessary prerequisite in order to achieve perception of a stimulus can be found in the phenomenon of *inattentional blindness*.

Inattentional Blindness

Recall that in Chapter 3 we discussed the phenomenon of *change blindness*, the inability to notice large changes to scenes when the scene is somehow disrupted (Simons, Nevarez, & Boot, 2005). Change blindness has been linked to another phenomenon known as **inattentional blindness**, the phenomenon of not perceiving a stimulus that might be literally right in front of you, unless you are paying attention to it (Mack, 2003; Simons & Ambinder, 2005). Mack gives the following everyday example of inattentional blindness:

> *Imagine an experienced pilot attempting to land an airplane on a busy runway. He pays close attention to his display console, carefully watching the airspeed indicator on his windshield to make sure he does not stall, yet he never sees that another airplane is blocking his runway! (p. 180)*

You may be skeptical that such a phenomenon really does happen. After all, how can a (nonpsychotic) person look at an object and not really see it? One dramatic (and humorous) demonstration comes from the laboratory of Daniel Simons. Figure 4-9 depicts four experimental conditions (each research participant was assigned to only one condition). Participants were asked to follow either the "white team" or the "black team" and to count the number of times the team they were watching passed a basketball (Easy condition) or to keep track separately of both the number of bounce passes and the number of aerial passes made by the target team (Hard condition). At a little under a minute into the presentation, an unexpected event occurred:

> *After 44–48 s of this action, either of two unexpected events occurred: in the Umbrella-Woman condition, a tall woman holding an open umbrella walked from off camera on one side of the action to the other, left to right. The actions of the players, and this unexpected event, were designed to mimic the stimuli used by Neisser and colleagues. In the Gorilla condition, a shorter woman wearing a gorilla costume that fully covered her body walked through the action in the same way In either case, the unexpected event lasted 5 s, and the players continued their actions during and after the event. (Simons & Chabris, 1999, p. 1066)*

After viewing the entire videotape, students first wrote down their counts and then were asked to describe anything unusual they had seen on the video. Questions became increasingly specific, beginning with "While you were doing the counting, did you notice anything unusual on the video?" and ending with "Did you see a gorilla (or a woman carrying an umbrella) walk across the screen?"

FIGURE 4-9 Single frames from each of the display tapes used. (These tapes were in colour.) The transparent conditions (top row) were created by superimposing three separately filmed events by means of digital video editing. The opaque conditions (bottom row) were filmed as a single action sequence with all seven actors. This figure shows the display for each condition halfway through the unexpected event, which lasted for 5 seconds of the 75-second-long video.

Source: Daniel J. Simons, Perception, vol. 28, issue 9, pp. 1059–1074, copyright © 1999 by SAGE Publications. Reprinted by Permission of SAGE Publications, Ltd.

Overall, 46% of participants failed to notice either the umbrella woman or the gorilla. Only 44% of participants ever reported seeing a gorilla, although this number was much greater for the subjects watching the Black team, who presumably shared more visual features with the gorilla (dark colour) than did the White team (see Table 4-1 for a full presentation of results). Simons and Chabris (1999) concluded that unexpected events can be overlooked. Presumably, we perceive only those events to which we attend, especially if the unexpected event is dissimilar to the focus of our attention, and if our attention is tightly focused somewhere else.

Table 4-1 Percentage of subjects noticing the unexpected event in each condition. Each row corresponds to one of the four video display types. Columns are grouped by monitoring task and attended team (White or Black). In the Easy task, subjects counted the total number of passes made by the attended team. In the Hard task, subjects maintained separate simultaneous counts of the aerial and bounce passes made by the attended team.

	Easy task		Hard task	
	White team	**Black team**	**White team**	**Black team**
Transparent				
Umbrella Woman	58	92	33	42
Gorilla	8	67	8	25
Opaque				
Umbrella Woman	100	58	83	58
Gorilla	42	83	50	58

Source: Simons, D. J., & Chabris, C. F. (1999). Gorillas in our midst: Sustained inattentional blindess for dynamic events. *Perception, 28*, 1059–1074. Figure provided by Daniel Simons.

This discussion has hopefully shed some light on the role of the attentional spotlight in visual search. Returning to our example of your search for your family and friends at Pearson airport, it should now be clear the detection of your "targets" will require your focused attention (as people are multi-featured, complex stimuli) to be moved across the crowd in a serial manner (meaning that the time to find your companions will be longer the more people are in the crowd). Canadian researcher Ray Klein from Dalhousie University speculated about another very interesting role of attention in visual search. To learn more about this, see the Canadian Research Highlight box.

NEUROSCIENTIFIC STUDIES OF ATTENTION

So far, we've focused our discussion on experimental investigations of attention. There are also researchers who are interested in linking attention as a behaviour to brain function. Cognitive neuroscientists are interested in examining which areas of the human brain are active when a person is attending to a stimulus or event. Researchers have long suspected the parietal lobe of the brain is one such location.

Clinical neurologists have documented the phenomenon of sensory neglect (sometimes called hemineglect) in patients who have parietal lobe damage. (You may recall some discussion of hemineglect in Chapter 3.) These patients often ignore or neglect sensory information located in the visual field opposite the damaged hemisphere. Thus if an area of the right parietal lobe is the damage site (as it often is), the patient overlooks information in the left visual field. This neglect may include, for example, neglecting to wash one side of the face or body, neglecting to brush the teeth on one side of the mouth, or eating from only one side of the plate.

In clinical studies, patients showing hemi-neglect have been studied in more detail. Typically, they are presented with stimuli and asked to copy them. Examples of stimuli such as a clock and house were presented to a patient with right parietal lobe damage and the was asked to draw them. Note that in both cases the left part of the drawing was missing, something the patient did not appear to notice.

Clinical work has established that hemi-neglect is attentional, rather than sensory (Banich, 1997). Were it simply a sensory deficit, we would expect patients to turn their gaze to the part of the visual field they were missing—in other words, to be aware their visual information is incomplete. Indeed, some patients have just this type of deficit, and they do compensate by just such strategies. In contrast, patients with hemi-neglect seem unaware of one side of their body and disinclined to try to attend to information from that side. In extreme cases, patients with hemi-neglect even deny that some of their own limbs belong to them. In one case study, a patient thought hospital staff had cruelly placed a severed leg in his bed; he tried to throw it to the floor, but the rest of his body followed the leg (Banich, 1997).

Although the parietal lobe is one brain region known to be associated with attention, it is not the only one. Areas of the frontal lobe as well play a role in people's ability to select motor responses and develop plans (Milham, Banich, Webb, Barad, Cohen, Wszalek, & Kramer, 2001). But how do the various brain regions communicate with each other to produce attentional performance? This question is clearly significant, and we will provide only a short, focused answer, by looking specifically at one kind of attention.

Networks of Visual Attention

Much work on brain processes of attention has centred on visual attention. Researchers have identified more than 32 areas of the brain that become active during visual processing of an attended stimulus (LaBerge, 1995). We obviously don't have the time or room to perform a detailed review of each. Instead, we will focus on three "networks" or systems of visual attention proposed by Posner and Raichle (1994).

In a series of studies, Posner and his colleagues used the following cueing task, which is quite similar to the one we discussed earlier. A participant is seated in front of a visual display, fixating on a central point. On either side of the point are two boxes. On each trial, one box brightens or an arrow appears, indicating on which side of the screen the participant should expect to see the next stimulus. The purpose of this cue is to encourage the participant to focus his or her attention at a particular location. The participant's task is to respond as fast as possible when he detects the stimulus. Sometimes no cue is given, and at other times an invalid cue is given, to assess the benefit of having attention focused in either the valid or invalid location (Posner & Raichle, 1994).

Posner and Raichle (1994) argued that to perform this task a person needs to execute three distinct mental operations. She first must *disengage* her attention from wherever it was previously directed. Brain activity in the posterior parietal lobe is heightened during this process. Once disengaged, attention must be refocused on the spatial location of the new to-be-attended stimulus. Posner and Raichle called this the *move* operation. They reported that patients with brain damage in the superior colliculus, a major structure of the midbrain, have difficulty moving their attention from one location to another. Finally, according to Posner and Raichle, when attention is redirected, neural processing of the new location is *enhanced*; stimulus information presented at the to-be-attended location is emphasized, and the brain circuitry underlying this operation (the pulvinar, located in the thalamus) becomes more active. As you might expect, patients with damage to the pulvinar do not show the enhanced processing of which other people are capable when attending to a stimulus in a particular location.

The idea that attention consists of several different processes that operate independently has received some support from clinical psychological studies of children and adults with ADHD, attention-deficit/hyperactivity disorder (Barkley 1998; Rubia & Smith, 2001; Woods & Ploof, 1997). An estimated 3% to 5% of the general school-age population has some form of ADHD (Casat, Pearson, & Casat, 2001), with the disorder approximately three times more common in boys than girls. Barkley's (1998) classic work suggests that ADHD clients suffer not so much from an inability to be alert or to devote mental resources to a task (Posner and Raichle's disengage and move operations) as from an inability to sustain vigilance on dull, boring, repetitive tasks, such as "independent schoolwork, homework, or chore performance" (Barkley, 1998, p. 57). Logan, Schachar, and Tannock (2000) suggest that in fact the major deficit in ADHD children is an inability to inhibit an ongoing response (for example, talking or playing a game when asked to do homework), an inability that may be a part of Posner and Raichle's enhance operation.

Posner and Raichle's (1994) description of attentional networks postulated that distinct areas of the brain underlie distinct cognitive processes. Posner more recently has described three different attentional networks that recruit individual cognitive processes (such as moving or disengaging). These are the alerting network, responsible for achieving and maintaining an alert state; the orienting network, which selects information from sensory input; and the executive control network, which resolves conflicts among different responses (Fan, McCandliss, Sommer, Raz, & Posner, 2002; Posner & Fan, 2001). Posner believes that the alerting network is associated with the frontal and parietal regions of the right hemisphere; the orienting network with areas of both the parietal and frontal areas; and the executive control network with the frontal lobes, especially the prefrontal cortex.

Event-Related Potentials and Selective Attention

Cognitive neuropsychologists have reported some fairly dramatic findings suggesting that information is processed very differently in attended versus unattended channels. Some of this work relies on measures such as a series of electrical potential recordings (electroencephalogram, or EEG) taken from the scalp of a participant. For technical reasons, researchers often average EEG records over many trials to reduce noise, ending up with the average electrical potential recorded 1 millisecond after presentation of a stimulus, 2 milliseconds after a stimulus, and so forth. This procedure results in a measure, already introduced briefly in Chapter 2, called an **event-related potential (ERP)**.

Banich (1997) has described the methodology of a typical study. Participants are asked to listen to one channel and to count long-duration tones. Short-duration tones and long-duration tones are both presented in each channel, attended and unattended. Researchers keep track of the ERPs to each stimulus. Results from many studies show that ERPs differ as a function of whether a stimulus was attended to (Pashler, 1998). In examples of some typical results, the amplitude of the waveforms (that is, how much the waveform deviates from the horizontal) is usually much larger for the attended than for the unattended stimulus. This difference usually begins 80 milliseconds after presentation of the stimulus, which is enough time for information to travel from the sensory receptors in the ears to the cerebral hemispheres, suggesting that the effect occurs in the brain, not in the ears (Banich, 1997).

SUMMARY

The different theoretical approaches to attention surveyed here suggest that psychologists are far from agreeing on how to explain attentional phenomena. Nonetheless, some general themes have emerged.

1. Attention has been shown to be a flexible aspect of cognition. We see that attention, rather than being rigidly and mechanically limited, as first described, is instead a more flexible system, affected by things such as practice, the kinds of tasks being performed, and the person's intention.

2. The idea that there are limits on the number of things we can pay attention to at once is known as *selective attention*. Anecdotal, laboratory, and even neuroscientific evidence seems to suggest that we process information to which we are actively paying attention differently from the way we process information to which we are not attending.

3. Whereas once attention was compared to a bottleneck, today people tend to liken attention more to a pool of resources that can be allocated in a fairly flexible manner.

4. The most common metaphor to describe spatial attention seems to be a spotlight (although some disagree over how far that metaphor extends). The idea here is that attention can vary in effectiveness, just as a spotlight, aimed at one spot, more or less lights surrounding areas, depending on its size and intensity.

5. Cognitive neuropsychologists have identified three different neural (brain) networks of attention, which they have localized in specific regions of the brain. They have also demonstrated a different pattern of event-related potentials for attended and unattended information.

6. Practice with a physical or cognitive task seems to change the amount of attention we need to perform that task. Tasks that require little mental capacity to perform are said to be *automatic*.

7. Some criteria offered to call a task or process "automatic" include the following: (a) it occurs without intention; (b) it occurs without conscious awareness; and (c) it does not interfere with other mental activity. Recently, however, these criteria have been the subject of criticism.

8. It appears that tasks can be performed simultaneously so long as operations such as memory retrieval or response selection are performed serially.

9. A real-world example of the relevance of laboratory research on attention comes from work on conversing via cell phone while driving a car.

REVIEW QUESTIONS

1. Cognitive psychologists have offered several different definitions of the term *attention*. Which one seems to you the most useful? Describe and defend your criteria.

2. Describe the dichotic listening task, and explain why cognitive psychologists find it a useful way to study attention.

3. Describe the differences and similarities among filter theory, attenuation theory, and late-selection theory.

4. Discuss the similarities between change blindness (Chapter 3) and inattentional blindness.

5. Describe and evaluate Kahneman's capacity model of attention. What, if any, real-world phenomena does it predict or explain?

6. What questions are answered by the work on the neurological underpinnings of attention? What questions are raised?

7. Evaluate Posner and Snyder's criteria for what makes a cognitive process automatic. Which criterion is the strongest, and why?

8. Consider the studies on divided attention. Can these findings be used in training workers who need to process a great deal of information from different sources simultaneously? Why or why not?

KEY TERMS

attention hypothesis of
    automatization
attenuation theory
automatic processing
controlled processing
dichotic listening task
divided attention

dual-task performance
event-related potential
  (ERP)
feature integration theory
filter theory
inattentional blindness
late-selection theory

priming
psychological refractory
    period (PRP)
selective attention
spatial cue
Stroop effect
visual search

Memory Structures

The ability of humans to revisit and reflect on events in the past is often thought of as one of the most basic, and important, cognitive process humans possess. We rely on memory whenever we think back to a personal event—when we remember, for example, our first day of school, our 10th birthday party, or a trip to the zoo, or when we reminisce the feeling we had the time our hockey team made it to the playoffs, or when we went camping for the first time. Memory is also obviously involved when we remember information about historical events, such as the the 9/11 attacks, or the sudden death of Diana, Princess of Wales. Memory is also essential to remember a new telephone number, or directions to a new restaurant. All these cases illustrate memory, in its different forms, and involve **encoding**, acquiring information, and **retrieval**, the calling to mind of previously experienced information. The ways in which we do so are the focus of this chapter.

In one way or another, memory is implicated in almost every cognitive activity. Clearly, activities such as taking an exam or remembering the name of your Grade 3 teacher require memory. But other activities, such as balancing a chequebook or comprehending a sentence, also involve some aspect of memory. While doing the calculations necessary to balance a chequebook, we have to keep some numbers in mind, at least for a moment. Similarly, when we hear or read a sentence, we have to keep the beginning of the sentence in mind while we process its middle and end. We use memory so frequently that, as with other cognitive processes, we tend to take it for granted.

Try, for example, to recall your first day at university. What do you remember about that day? Now ask yourself how you are able to recall any of these memories (if in fact you can). If you drew a total blank, why? What exactly goes on when you try to recall? What makes some information memorable and other information hard to recall? For example, can you describe what your cognitive psychology professor wore two lectures ago?

Sometimes we fail to notice how extraordinary a particular ability is until we encounter someone who lacks it. Baddeley (1990) has described the tragic case of Clive Wearing, a musician and broadcaster who, because of brain damage caused by encephalitis, has been left with severe amnesia. Although many people suffer from amnesia, Wearing's case is one of the most devastating on record. As Baddeley described it:

> *His amnesia was so dense that he could remember nothing from more than a few minutes before, a state that he attributed to having just recovered consciousness. Left to his own devices, he would often be found writing down a time, for example, 3:10, and the note, "I have just recovered consciousness," only to cross out the 3:10 and add 3:15, followed by 3:20, etc. If his wife left the room for a few minutes, when she returned he would greet her with great joy, declaring that he had not seen her for months and asking how long he had been unconscious. Experienced once, such an event could be intriguing and touching, but when it happens repeatedly, day in, day out, it rapidly loses its charm. (pp. 4–5)*

Interestingly, a few of Wearing's memory abilities seem to have been spared. He continues to be able to conduct a choir through a complex piece of music and can still play the harpsichord and piano. These abilities are the exception rather than the rule, however. Wearing cannot go out alone because he would quickly become lost and unable to find his way back. He cannot recognize much in photographs of familiar places, and his memories of his own life are quite sketchy.

In this chapter and the next, we will try to explain these phenomena. To do so, we will look in detail at the processes people use to form, store, and retrieve information. We will examine theoretical approaches to the study of memory, considering memory that lasts only briefly as well as memory that endures for hours, weeks, and even years. Much of the research described in this chapter comes from the laboratory, where experiment participants, often university student volunteers, are presented with lists or series of words, syllables, or pictures under highly controlled conditions. In the next chapter we will consider how well laboratory-based models apply to memory phenomena outside the laboratory, most often to memories for episodes from people's own life stories.

A brief review of terminology is in order before we begin. We say that **encoding** occurs when information is first translated into a form that other cognitive processes can use. It is held in **storage** in one form or another for later retrieval. We say that **forgetting** occurs when we cannot retrieve information.

TYPES OF MEMORY

Fascination with what memory is and how it works has a long tradition in philosophy, predating any psychological investigations. Neath and Surprenant (2003) noted that the Greek philosopher Plato wrote about memory, comparing it both to an aviary and to a wax tablet on which impressions are made. Throughout

According to Plato memory is a wax tablet on which impressions are made.

the Middle Ages and Renaissance, other analogies were made between memory and a cave, an empty cabinet, and a body in need of exercise.

In the 1950s, memory was compared to a telephone system, and later it was compared to a computer. One theoretical approach to studying memory, which dominated cognitive psychology throughout the 1960s and 1970s, distinguishes among kinds of memory according to the length of time information is stored. More recently, cognitive neuroscience is attempting to establish the brain basis of memory.

This **modal model of memory** assumes that information is received, processed, and stored differently for each kind of memory (Atkinson & Shiffrin, 1968; Waugh & Norman, 1965). Unattended information presented very quickly is stored only briefly in **sensory memory**. Attended information is held in **short-term memory (STM)** for periods of up to 20 or 30 seconds. (Synonyms for STM include *primary memory* and *short-term storage*, or *STS*). Information needed for longer periods of time—the correct spelling of the words on tomorrow's test, for example, or the name of your Grade 4 **memory (LTM)**, sometimes called *secondary memory* or *long-term storage (LTS)*.

We will discuss these hypothesized kinds of memory in this chapter, examining first sensory memory then STM and LTM. After a look at the modal model and its predictions and explanations, we will focus on a proposal from psychologist Alan Baddeley called *working memory*. We will then consider models of the organization of memory, and evidence for these. In the next chapter we'll turn our attention to processes that guide memory encoding and retrieval, and we'll examine neuropsychological evidence for multiple memory systems.

SENSORY MEMORY

Sensory "memory" is closely connected to what we call "perception" because it refers to the initial brief storage of sensory information—what you might retain, for example, if you glanced up quickly at a billboard and then glanced quickly away. Many cognitive psychologists hypothesize that separate sensory memories exist for each sensory modality. In other words, they believe there is a visual sensory memory, an auditory sensory memory, an olfactory (pertaining to smell) sensory memory, a gustatory (pertaining to taste) sensory memory, and a tactile (pertaining to touch) sensory memory. The overwhelming bulk of the research on sensory memories to date has focused on the first two types of sensory memory, called the *icon* and the *echo*, respectively.

The Icon

Imagine it is a dark stormy night, rain falling, a brewing mist apparent in the sky as you glance outside. Then, lightning strikes. The lightning seems to linger for a couple of seconds, if not more. In reality, however, the lightning bolt is only present for less than a third of a second, yet we often perceive it as lasting much longer. The same phenomenon occurs when you "write" your name with a sparkler on a dark night; here you will have the experience of briefly "seeing" your name hanging in the air, even though the sparkler leaves no physical trace. Why does this occur? The "after-image" of the lightning, or your name, is a mental experience believed to persist in our sensory memory.

It was a doctoral student at Harvard by the name of George Sperling who first conducted experiments, now considered classic, to investigate the properties of a visual, iconic, sensory memory. He presented participants with displays containing letters such as those shown in Figure 5-1, and asked them to recall all the letters they saw. The displays were presented briefly, for only 50 milliseconds. Sperling found that, on average, people could report only 4 or 5 of the 12 letters presented. Extending the display time, even to 500 milliseconds, did not improve performance. The problem wasn't perceptual; 500 milliseconds, or half a second, is plenty of time to perceive something about all the letters (Klatzky 1980). Sperling spoke to his participants afterward and many said they had seen all the stimuli quite clearly, but once they started reporting what they saw, forgot the rest. Put another way, even as participants were recalling the display, the information was fading from wherever it was being stored. This implies that information lasts only briefly in this memory system.

Armed with this information, Sperling (1960) devised a method of more accurately measuring the available content in his participant's sensory store. He used the logic of a multiple-choice test in which only a subset of the total material is tested, and the percentage correct is taken as a measure of the student's knowledge of the entire material. He created what has become known as the *partial-report technique*. Sperling informed participants that they would have to recall only a single row of the display, but they wouldn't know which row until after the display was

FIGURE 5-1 Example of the kind of stimulus display used by Sperling (1960).

shown. An auditory tone was used to cue participants as to the row they were to report. After seeing the display, participants were presented with either a low-, medium-, or high-pitched tone. A low pitch indicated they were to report only the letters in the bottom row of the display; a high pitch, those in the top row; and a medium pitch, those in the middle row. Using this method, Sperling showed that regardless of which tone sounded, participants' reports indicated they had roughly nine of the twelve letters available in sensory memory. This was true as long as the tone was presented immediately after the display. If the tone cure was delayed, however, by 1 second, their level of, recall dropped to four of the twelve letters, as in the whole-report method. These data suggest that the visual store could hold about nine items, but that it held this information only briefly, as the advantage of the partial-over whole-report method was reduced when the delay stimuli and the cue tone was 0.3 seconds (see Figure 5-2). Neisser (1967) called this brief visual memory the **icon**.

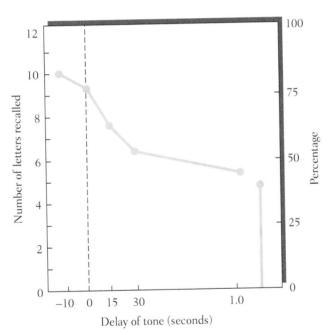

FIGURE 5-2 This figure shows the average number of letters recalled by a participant (on left axis, with percentage equivalents on right axis), as a function of the delay between the presentation of the letters and the tone signalling when to recall letters aloud. The bar in the lower right corner indicates the average number of letters recalled by participants in the whole-report procedure.

Source: Republished with permission of Thomson/Wadsworth, from *Cognitive Psychology*, Robert J. Sternberg and Jeffrey Scott Mio, 4 ed., © 2006; permission conveyed through Copyright Clearance Center, Inc.

Other researchers built on this work to define the properties of this type of memory. Averbach and Coriell (1961) showed that the icon can be "erased" by other stimuli presented immediately after the icon, a phenomenon known as *masking*. For instance, if the display with letters was followed by a display with circles, and if the participant was told to report which letters had been in the locations of the circles, the circles appeared to "erase" the memory trace of the letters originally shown.

Other work investigated how many ways participants could be cued to give partial reports (see Coltheart, 1980, for a review). Different investigators showed that such things as the colour or brightness of the letters could be used to cue partial reports. Interestingly cueing partial reports by category or phonological sound (for instance, "Report all the letters that rhyme with *B*") is all but impossible. This suggests the information available in the icon is only visual—not auditory or related to type of stimulus.

The Echo

There is also a sensory memory for auditory material, which Neisser (1967) called the **echo**. Moray, Bates, and Barnett (1965) offered a clever demonstration of the echo. Participants were given a "four-eared" listening task, similar to a dichotic listening task (refer to Chapter 4 if you've forgotten what this is). They heard, simultaneously over headphones, four channels of incoming information, each apparently coming from a different location, consisting of a string of random letters. (The four channels were created by stereophonic mixing.)

In one condition, similar to Sperling's (1960) whole-report condition, participants were asked to report all the letters they had heard. In another condition, each participant held a board with four lights on it, each light corresponding to one of the channels, cueing the participant to report only the letters from a particular channel. As did Sperling, Moray and colleagues found that participants giving partial reports could report proportionately more letters. This suggests that the echo, like the icon, stores information only briefly.

Crowder (1976), reviewing the literature on echoic memory, proposed that echoic memory has a larger capacity than iconic memory. Watkins and Watkins (1980) provide evidence that echoes can last longer than icons, perhaps even as long as 20 seconds. A good demonstration of the echo occurs regularly, when, for example someone asks you a question while you are engrossed in a TV show, or reading a book. When asked "Where did you put the car keys?" the immediate response might be "Huh? What?" but after a couple of seconds you answer, "Oh, they are over there on the table." In this case it is as if the question is still lingering (in your echoic store), allowing you to answer it even after the question has been spoken.

A demonstration called the "suffix effect" also reveals something about the nature of echoic memory. Imagine you are a research participant in a memory experiment, and a list of random digits, letters, or the like is being presented to you. If the list is presented to you auditorily (as opposed to visually), and if there is an auditory recall cue such as a spoken word or specific item, recall of the last few items on the list is seriously hindered (Crowder, 1972).

Researchers think the recall cue, called the *suffix*, functions as an auditory "mask" of sorts, because when the suffix is simply a beep or tone, or a visual stimulus, there is usually not much effect. Nor is there any effect if the items on the list are presented visually—say, on a computer screen. Finally the more auditory similarity there is between the suffix and the items on the list, the greater the suffix effect.

Neath and Surprenant (2003) argued that sensory memory research has a very practical use outside the laboratory: Having directory assistance operators say "Have a nice day" after giving a phone number should (and apparently does) disrupt recall for the phone number because their pleasant sign-off acts as a suffix!

Research on the echo suggests that telephone operators who wish callers a nice day may inadvertently be disrupting their auditory sensory memory of the phone number they've just provided.

Although research continues to refine our understanding of both the icon and the echo (Cermak, 2014, Di Lollo et al., 2000; Enns et al., 1999; Wingfield, 2016, sensory memory can currently best be described by a number of properties. First, sensory memories are *modality specific*: the visual sensory memory contains visual information; the auditory sensory memory, auditory information; and so forth. Second, sensory memory capacities appear relatively larger for visual than auditory sensory memory, but the length of time information can be stored is longer in the auditory than the visual store. Third, the information that can be stored appears relatively unprocessed, meaning that most of it has to do with physical aspects of the stimuli rather than with meaningful ones. Sensory memory is useful, in the real world, as it guarantees a minimum of time during which information presented to us (that we pay attention to) is available for processing (Baddeley 1990). In other words, by this argument sensory memory plays an important role in the everyday workings of normal memory: It ensures that we will be able to "re-inspect" incoming data, if not with our actual eyes and ears, then with the mind's eye and the mind's ear.

SHORT-TERM MEMORY

Most of the time, when people think about memory they think about holding on to information for longer than a second or two. In the rest of this chapter and the next, we'll talk about kinds of memory more familiar to non-psychologists.

Many empirical findings seem to support the idea of different memory systems. One well-known finding comes from free-recall experiments, in which people are given a list of words to remember, such as that shown in Figure 5-3(A), and are asked to recall the words in any

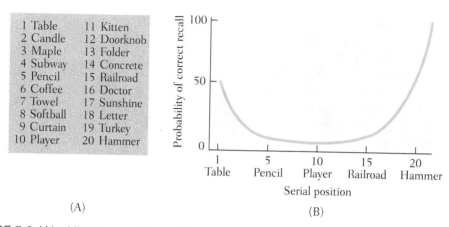

FIGURE 5-3 Word list for a serial position curve experiment (A); typical results (B).

order. Next, the experimenter, using data from all the participants, computes the probability of recall of each word as a function of the word's serial position in the original list. In our example, *table* would be in serial position 1 because it is the first word on the list; *candle* is in serial position 2; and so forth. Figure 5-3(B) shows an idealized version of typical results reported in seminal work on this topic by Ben Murdock (1962) at University of Toronto.

Notice that the two ends of the curve are higher than the middle, indicating that people recall more words at either the beginning or the end of the list than they do words in the middle. This is known as the **serial position effect**. The improved recall of words at the beginning of the list is called the **primacy effect**; that at the end of the list, the **recency effect**.

What accounts for these two effects? Participants typically report subvocalizing to themselves as follows when they first start the experiment:

Experimenter (reading list at a fixed rate): Table.

Participant (to self): Table-table-table-table.

Experimenter: Candle.

Participant (a little faster): Table-candle-table-candle.

Experimenter: Maple.

Participant (very rapidly): Table-candle-maple-table-candle.

Experimenter: Subway.

Participant (giving up on rehearsing earlier words): Subway.

We'll see later that the participant's repetition of items, or **rehearsal**, is thought to help the items enter long-term storage. In fact, if the experimenter reads the list rapidly enough to prevent the participant from having enough time to rehearse, the primacy effect disappears, although the recency effect stays intact (Murdock, 1962).

The recency effect is thought to result from participants' using either sensory memory or short-term memory. Participants often report that they can still "sort of" hear the last few words, and they often report these first and quickly. If the experimenter prevents the participant from reporting words right away, by having her first perform an unrelated counting task, the recency effect (but not the primacy effect) disappears (Postman & Phillips, 1965).

That the primacy and recency effects can be independently affected suggests they reflect two kinds of memory. Those who endorse the idea of sensory memory believe that incoming information first passes through this rapidly decaying storage system. If attended to, the information next moves to STM. To be held for longer than a minute or two, the information must be transferred again, this time to LTM.

We'll first look at STM. You use this kind of memory system when you look up a phone number, walk across a room to a telephone, and dial the number. Suppose we asked you to call one of our colleagues, whose phone number is (519) 885–1211. Suppose further that you couldn't take this book with you but had to remember the number until you could dial it on a nearby phone. How would you accomplish this task? Chances are you'd begin by rehearsing the number aloud several times as you walked across the room. You'd dial the number, but as soon as the conversation started, you'd be likely to have forgotten the number you dialed. This example illustrates one aspect of STM: it lasts only a short while. (Cognitive psychologists typically regard STM as lasting for a minute or two, if rehearsal is not prevented; however, neuropsychologists sometimes consider information in STM as lasting for up to a day, which can lead to some confusion. When we talk about STM, we'll be talking about material stored for up to about a minute.)

Does any other distinguishing characteristic separate STM from LTM, other than length of time information is stored? Psychologists who make the distinction believe there are a number of such characteristics, including how much information can be stored (capacity), the form in which the information is stored (coding), the ways in which information is retained or forgotten, and the ways in which information is retrieved. How psychologists working within the information-processing paradigm conceptualize STM has changed a great deal over the past two decades. We'll begin with a look at the traditional description of STM before looking at a newer proposal of what has been renamed *working memory* to avoid confusion.

Short-Term Store—Capacity

If you are going to store information for only a short period of time (as in the phone number example), how much room do you have in which to do so? In other words, how much information can you remember for only a brief period of time? A classic paper by George Miller (1956) begins with the following rather unusual confession addressing these questions:

> *My problem is that I have been persecuted by an integer. For seven years this number has followed me around, has intruded in my most private data, and has assaulted me from the pages of our most public journals. This number assumes a variety of disguises, being sometimes a little larger and sometimes a little smaller than usual, but never changing so much as to be unrecognizable.*

> *The persistence with which this number plagues me is far more than a random accident. There is, to quote a famous senator, a design behind it, some pattern governing its appearances. Either there really is something unusual about the number or else I am suffering from delusions of persecution. (p. 81)*

The integer plaguing Miller was 7 (plus or minus 2). Among other things, 7 (plus or minus 2, depending on the individual, the material, and other situational factors) seems to be the maximum number of independent units we can hold in STM. We call this the **capacity** of STM.

Miller (1956) reviewed evidence demonstrating that if you are presented with a string of random digits you'll be able to recall them only if the string contains about seven or fewer digits. The same is true if you are presented with random strings of any kinds of units: letters, words, abbreviations, and so on. The only way to overcome this limitation is by somehow **chunking** the individual units into larger units. For instance, consider the following string of letters: *N F L C B C F B I M T V*. This 12-letter string would normally exceed almost everyone's short-term memory capacity. But if you look closely at the letters, you'll see they really form four sets of abbreviations for well-known entities: *NFL* (the National Football League), *CBC* (the Canadian Broadcasting Corporation), *FBI* (the Federal Bureau of Investigation), and *MTV* (the music video cable television station). If you notice that the 12 letters are really four organized sets, you'll be more likely to recall the entire string. In recognizing that the three sets of letters really "go together" and in forming them into a single unit, you are said to be chunking them.

Chunking depends on knowledge. Someone not familiar with our culture might regard *MTV* as merely three randomly presented letters. Miller regarded the process of forming chunks (he called it "recoding") as a fundamental process of memory—a very powerful means of increasing the amount of information we can process at any given time, and one we use constantly in our daily lives. The process of chunking can be seen as an important strategy in overcoming the severe limitation of having only seven or so slots in which to temporarily store information.

The term **coding** refers to the way in which information is mentally represented—that is, the form in which the information is held. When you try to remember a phone number, as in the preceding example, how do you represent it? A study by R. Conrad (1964) addressed this question. He presented participants with lists of consonants for later recall. Although the letters were presented visually participants were likely to make errors that were similar in *sound* to the original stimuli. So, if a *P* had been presented, and participants later misrecalled this stimulus, they were much more likely to report a letter that *sounded* like *P* (for example, *G* or *C*) than to report a letter that *looked* like *P* (such as *F*). Remember, the original presentation was visual, but participants apparently were confused by the sound. Participants were apparently forming a mental representation of the stimuli that involved the acoustic rather than the visual properties.

Later work by Baddeley (1966a, 1966b) confirmed this effect even when the stimuli were words rather than letters: Similar-sounding words make for poor immediate recall, although similar-meaning words don't, and the reverse is true for delayed recall. Although an acoustic code is not the only one used in STM, researchers have regarded it as the dominant code used, at least by hearing adults and older children (Baddeley, 2012; Neath & Surprenant, 2003).

We regard STM as the storage of information for short periods of time. But how short is short? John Brown (1958) and Peterson and Peterson (1959), working independently, came to the same conclusion: If not rehearsed, information is lost from STM in as little as 20 seconds. That length of time is called the **retention duration** of the memory.

The Brown–Peterson task works as follows. Participants are presented with a three-consonant trigram, such as *BKG*. They are also given a number, such as 347, and asked to count backward out loud by threes, at the rate of two counts per second, in time to a metronome. The purpose of the counting task is to prevent the participant from rehearsing the trigram. The length of time a participant must count varies. If asked to count backward for only 3 seconds, roughly 80% of participants can recall the trigram. If asked to count for 18 seconds, this drops to about 7%. The authors of the study interpreted this finding as meaning that the **memory trace**—the encoded mental representation of the to-be-remembered information that is not rehearsed—**decays**, or breaks apart, within about 20 seconds. Putting this interpretation into our phone number example gives us the following: If a new friend tells you her phone number, and you fail to do something to remember it (say, by rehearsing it or writing it down), you'll be able to remember it only for a maximum of about 20 to 30 seconds. After that time, the memory trace will simply decay, and the information will be lost.

However, other cognitive psychologists soon began to challenge this decay explanation of forgetting. They proposed a different mechanism, called **interference**, that worked as follows: Some information can "displace" other information, making the former hard to retrieve. You can think of the interference explanation as being akin to finding a piece of paper on your professor's desk. At the start of each academic term, her desk is (relatively) free of clutter.

Any piece of paper placed on the desktop is trivially easy to find. However, as the term goes on and time grows short, your prof tends to allow all kinds of memos, papers, journals, and the like to accumulate. Papers placed on the desk at the beginning of the term become buried; they're there, all right, but can be very difficult to find at any given moment. The late-arriving papers have "displaced" the early papers.

Can we explain the Brown–Peterson task results in terms of interference? Think once

Piles of paper on a cluttered desk represent the idea of memorial interference.

again about the counting task. Notice that it supposedly has very little purpose other than to distract the participant from rehearsing the trigram. Yet maybe the counting task does more than prevent participants from rehearsing; it may actually interfere with their short-term storage of the trigram. As participants count aloud, they compute and announce the values. As they compute and announce the values, they put them into STM. Thus the counted values may actually be displacing the original information.

Other evidence also supported the view that interference, not decay, accounts for forgetting in STM. Keppel and Underwood (1962), for instance, found that forgetting in the Brown–Peterson task doesn't happen until after a few trials. They suggested that, over time, **proactive interference** builds up. This term refers to the fact that material learned first can disrupt retention of subsequently learned material. Keppel and Underwood showed that even one trial's worth of practice recalling a three-letter trigram was enough to hurt subsequent memory for other trigrams.

Wickens, Born, and Allen (1963) extended the idea one more step. They reasoned as follows: If STM, like LTM (as we will soon see), is subject to proactive interference, then STM (like LTM) should also be subject to a related phenomenon, *release from proactive interference*. In other words, if you learn a number of pieces of similar information, after a while any new learning becomes more difficult because the old learning interferes with the retention of new (because of proactive interference). The greater the similarity among the pieces of information, the greater the interference. This implies that if a new and very distinct piece of information were presented, the degree of interference would be sharply reduced.

Wickens and colleagues (1963) demonstrated release from proactive interference in a clever experiment. They gave participants a series of either three-digit strings (such as *179*) or three-letter strings (such as *DKQ*). There were 10 trials in all. Some participants received 10 trials of the same type (that is, all-letter strings or all-digit strings). Others saw a "switch" in the stimuli partway through the 10 trials. For example, a person might see 3 trials with letters but then be switched to seeing digits on all subsequent trials. Figure 5-4 shows the results. Participants getting a "switch" performed almost as well immediately after the switch as they did on the first trial. Their memory is said to have been released, or freed, from the clutches of proactive interference!

It may be that the question "Is it decay or is it interference?" is badly posed, because it rules out the possibility that both may be involved. That is, maybe STM loses information by more than one mechanism. Baddeley (1990) argues that some (although very little) trace decay does occur in STM along with interference. Altmann and Gray (2002) propose that decay does occur and in fact is essential to avoid catastrophic proactive interference. These authors believe that when information must be updated frequently in memory—for example, when you are driving and have to remember the speed limit on each new road you take—its current value (100 km/h on the highway) decays to prevent interference with later values (you get off the highway and the speed limit is now 60 km/h).

Short-Term Store—Retrieval of Information

We've talked about the ways in which people hold on to information for brief periods of time: how they encode it, how much they can encode, and how long they can retain it. That brings us to the question "How do we retrieve this information from STM when we need it again?"

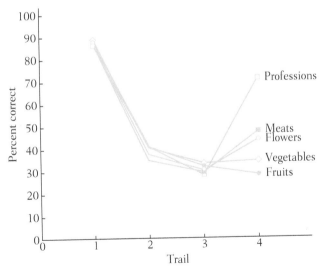

FIGURE 5-4 Results from a study by Wickens et al. (1976) examining release from proactive interference in short-term memory.

Source: Wickens DD, Dalezman RE, Eggemeier FT. Multiple encoding of word attributes in memory. Memory & Cognition. 1976;4:307–310.

Saul Sternberg (1966, 1969), in a series of experiments, found some surprising things about how we retrieve information from short-term memory. Before turning to his experiments, let's consider various possibilities of how information might be retrieved from STM.

Sternberg's first question was whether we search for information held in STM in a *parallel* or a *serial* manner. Imagine, for example, that STM is full of some (small) number of movie titles. Let's say STM holds a list of your best friend's all-time favorite movies, which he has just orally given you. Let's call the number of movie titles the *memory set size*. Now suppose that someone asks you if *Titanic* is on that list; to answer the question, you mentally search the list.

If you compare *Titanic* simultaneously to all the titles on the list, you are performing a **parallel search**. Essentially, no matter what the number of titles is, you examine them at the same time, and it takes you no more time to compare *Titanic* to 1 title than to 10 titles. Figure 5-5(A) depicts how the data would look if you used parallel search, plotting time to search against memory set size.

Suppose, instead, that you use a **serial search**. In our movie titles example, this would mean comparing *Titanic* to the first movie title on the list, then to the second title on the list, and so on until you come to the last title. The comparisons are done one at a time. In this model, the longer the list is, the longer it should take to decide if *Titanic* matches a title on that list. Successful searches are indicated by the "yes" line; unsuccessful searches (where a target is not found) by the "no" line.

We can also ask whether the search is self-terminating or exhaustive. A **self-terminating search** stops when a match is found. Suppose the list of movie titles is *The Dark Knight, Ocean's 11, Deadpool, Titanic, Dunkirk,* and *Atomic Blonde*. If you do a self-terminating search,

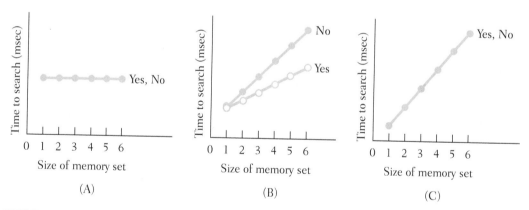

FIGURE 5-5 Theoretically predicted results from the Sternberg (1966) short-term memory-scanning experiment. "Yes" and "No" refer to whether the subject will report finding the probe letter in the memory set. (A) depicts a parallel search; (B), a serial, self-terminating search; (C), a serial, exhaustive search. The data that Sternberg reported looked most like those in (C).

you will stop after the fourth comparison because you've found a match. On average, then, successful searches take less time (because you don't continue searching after you've found the match) than unsuccessful searches (where you have to search through everything). Figure 5-5(B) depicts the results we should see if retrieval from memory uses serial, self-terminating search.

Another kind of serial search is an **exhaustive search**, meaning that even if a match is found, you continue looking through every other item in the set. In our example, this would mean that even after you find *Titanic*, you check the remaining titles on the list. With this kind of search, it takes just as long for successful as for unsuccessful searches. Figure 5-5(C) shows this possibility.

Sternberg's (1966) experimental task was the following. First, participants were presented with a set of seven or fewer letters. These were to be encoded and held in short-term memory and hence could be called the "memory set." After the participant had the set in memory, he indicated readiness for an upcoming trial. A single letter, called a probe, was presented, and the participant's task was to decide, as quickly as possible, whether the probe was in the memory set. For example, the memory set might be *B K F Q*, and probes might be *K* (yes, in the memory set) and *D* (no, not in the memory set).

As counterintuitive as it sounds, Sternberg's (1966) results argue for serial, exhaustive search as the way we retrieve information from STM. Sternberg's explanation is that the search process itself may be so rapid and have such momentum it is hard to stop once it starts. From a processing point of view, it may be more efficient just to let the search process finish and then make one decision at the end, instead of making several decisions, one after each item in the memory set. A review by Hunt (1978) found that people of all sorts (university students, senior citizens, people with exceptionally good memories, people who are developmentally delayed) showed results consistent with the idea that retrieval from STM uses serial, exhaustive search, although search rate changes with the group, being faster for people with exceptional memories and slower for senior citizens.

Let's summarize our review of the STM system so far. The general picture that emerged in the 1960s and 1970s was that STM is a short-term, limited-capacity storehouse where information is coded acoustically and maintained through rehearsal. Information can be retrieved from this storage using highspeed, serial, exhaustive search. The nature of the information in STM, however, can help change the capacity and processing of stored information.

LONG-TERM MEMORY

In the modal model, long-term memory (LTM) is thought to differ from short-term memory (STM) in many ways. LTM is described as a place for storing large amounts of information for indefinite periods of time. Note the contrast here with the modal description of STM as holding a very limited amount of information (seven, plus or minus two, pieces of unrelated information) for a very short period of time (seconds, or at most a few minutes). In other words, LTM is commonly thought to be a sort of mental "treasure chest" or "scrap-book": the material you have cognitively collected in your lifetime is stored there in some form. In this section, we will examine the capacity, coding, storage, and retrieval of information from long-term storage, as well as review evidence bearing on forgotten material.

Long-Term Memory—Capacity

What is the capacity of LTM? The question cannot be answered with a single number. Think about information you have stored in your LTM now. It would have to include your memory of all the word meanings you know (probably between 50,000 and 100,000), all the arithmetic facts, and all the historical, geographic, political, and other kinds of information you've learned. You also probably stored in LTM, at one time or another, the names and faces of all sorts of people: family members, significant teachers, neighbours, friends, enemies, and others. You also surely have stored various pieces of other information about each of them: physical attributes, birthdays, favorite colour or musical group, and so on. All your information about various ways of doing familiar things—getting a transcript from the registrar's office; checking out a book from the library; asking for, accepting, or turning down a date; finding a phone number; addressing a letter—must also be in LTM. Indeed, a complete list of all information you have at one time or another put into long-term storage would be very long. This intuition has led psychologists to estimate that the capacity of LTM is virtually unlimited.

Thomas Landauer (1986) has tried to provide a more quantitative answer to this question. He begins with two previous estimates. The first is that the size of human memory is equal to the number of synapses in the cerebral cortex of the brain. As you may remember from your introductory psychology course, a synapse is the gap between two neurons, basic cells of the body, across which neurotransmitters pass chemical messages. The cerebral cortex has 10^{13} synapses, so some believe that human memory can hold 10^{13} distinct bits of information.

Another estimate is 10^{20} bits of information, the estimated number of neural impulses, or electrical messages, transmitted within the brain during a person's lifetime. Landauer argued that both these estimates are probably too high: Not every neural impulse or synaptic connection results in a memory. Through various different analyses, in which he tried to estimate the rate at which new information is learned and the rate at which information is forgotten or lost, he came to an estimate of about 1 billion bits of information for an adult at midlife (say, about age 35).

Whatever the actual number of bits of information stored in LTM, not all that information is retrievable at any given moment. Indeed, there are many everyday examples of failures to retrieve information. You meet someone you know you know but can't place, or you think of a word but can't name it. The information probably is in your long-term storage somewhere, but you somehow can't access it. We'll return to the issues of retrieval and forgetting later.

Long-Term Memory—Coding

Many studies of recall from LTM report a common finding: Errors made while recalling information from LTM are likely to be semantic confusions. That is, words or phrases that mean things similar to the words or phrases actually presented are likely to be "recalled" in error, if errors are made. Baddeley (1966a) demonstrated this phenomenon experimentally. He presented participants with lists of words that sounded similar (such as *mad, map, man*) or that were matched to the first list but did not sound alike (such as *pen, day, rig*). Others also saw a list of words with similar meanings (such as *huge, big, great*; such words are called "semantically similar") and another list of control words that were matched to the third list but did not share meaning (such as *foul, old, deep*). Recall was tested after a 20-minute interval, during which participants worked on another task, to prevent rehearsal and to ensure the material would be drawn from long-term rather than short-term storage. The results showed that acoustic similarity produced little effect on performance but that the list of semantically similar words was harder to learn. Baddeley (1976), reviewing this and other work, concluded that the following generalization, although not absolute, is roughly true: *acoustic similarity affects STM; semantic similarity affects LTM.*

Long-Term Memory—Retention Duration

How long can information be stored in LTM? Although most laboratory experiments test recall after several hours or days, evidence is abundant that at least some information can last for decades or even a lifetime. Harry Bahrick (1983, 1984) has studied people's memory for material learned to varying degrees at varying times, including memory for the faces of college classmates 20 or 30 or even 50 years after graduation.

In one study, Bahrick (1984) tested 733 adults who had taken or were taking a high school or university course in Spanish. The participants who were not currently enrolled in a Spanish course had not studied Spanish for periods ranging from 1 to 50 years. They also varied in their original degree of learning of Spanish. Bahrick plotted "forgetting curves" for different aspects of knowledge of Spanish—for example, grammar recall and idiom recognition. Although forgetting differed slightly as a function of the measure, the pattern of results was remarkably consistent. For the first 3 to 6 years after completing Spanish study, participants' recall declined. But for the next three decades or so, the forgetting curve was flat, suggesting no further loss of information (see Figure 5-6). Retention showed a final decline after about 30 to 35 years.

Bahrick (1984) interpreted the findings as follows:

Large portions of the originally acquired information remain accessible for over 50 years in spite of the fact the information is not used or rehearsed. This portion of the information in a "permastore state" is a function of the level of original training, the grades received

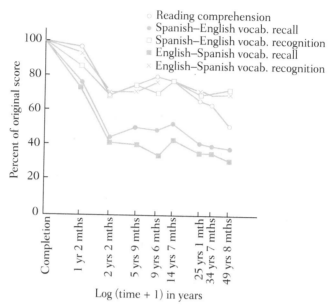

FIGURE 5-6 Forgetting curves for Spanish language tested weeks to years after initial learning.

in Spanish courses, and the method of testing (recall vs. recognition), but it appears to be unaffected by ordinary conditions of interference. (p. 1)

So you thought that after the final exam you'd forget everything about cognitive psychology? If your professor contacts you in 20 years or so, you might surprise both of you: You'll probably remember at least some of the course material!

Long-Term Memory—Forgetting

If information can last indefinitely in LTM, why does so much of it seem unavailable, even a week later? There are several familiar examples: "knowing" you know the answer to an exam question but being unable to quite remember it; meeting someone on the street who is extremely familiar but you don't know from where. What has happened to your memory in these instances? Has it been erased somehow?

Forgetting or even "misremembering" is a topic that dates back to the early days of experimental psychology. Hermann Ebbinghaus, a Prussian psychologist, pioneered the empirical study of memory under controlled conditions (Hoffman, Bamberg, Bringmann, & Klein, 1987). His master work (Ebbinghaus, 1885/1913) reported on 19 of his studies using himself as a subject.

Ebbinghaus created stimuli he thought were carefully controlled and free from any contamination from prior learning; he called them *nonsense syllables* (such as *rur, hal,* and *beis*). He carefully and precisely presented, at a controlled rate, hundreds of lists of these syllables to a single and dedicated subject: himself. Day after day, Ebbinghaus memorized, tested himself, recorded the results, and prepared new stimuli. Altogether, he spent about 830 hours memorizing 85,000 syllables in 6,600 lists (Hoffman et al., 1987). The primary questions he asked had to do with the number of repetitions needed for perfect recall, the nature of forgetting, the effects of fatigue on learning, and the effects of widely spaced versus closely spaced practice.

One of Ebbinghaus's many findings is presented in Figure 5-7. Depicting a "forgetting curve," the graph plots the amount of time it took him to relearn a list of nonsense syllables after initial learning followed by a retention interval of varying amounts of time (the retention interval is plotted on the *x* axis). Ebbinghaus assumed that the more forgetting, the more effort it would take to relearn a list; conversely, the less forgetting, the less effort to relearn. The curve suggests that forgetting is not a simple linear function of time. Instead, *forgetting is rapid at first and then levels off.* Notice how well this laboratory finding anticipates the real-world memory studies of Bahrick, reported earlier.

As with STM, many psychologists believe that interference, not decay, accounts for "forgetting" from LTM (McGeoch, 1932). They believe material that can't be retrieved successfully from LTM is there but "buried" or in some other way unavailable. Much of the literature on interference has used a task called **paired associates learning**. Participants hear lists of pairs of words such as *flag–spoon* and *drawer–switch*. After one or more presentations of a list, the experimenter then presents participants with the first word in each pair—for example, *flag*—and the participant is asked to recall the word originally paired with it, such as *spoon*.

Researchers have used this task to study interference in two ways (see Table 5-1). The first is through *proactive interference (PI)*, a phenomenon described earlier. The term *PI* refers to

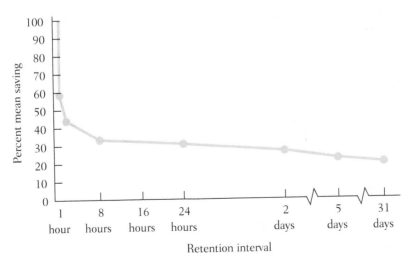

FIGURE 5-7 Ebbinghaus's (1885/1913) forgetting curve.

Table 5-1 Experimental Paradigms for Assessing Proactive and Retroactive Interference

Phase	Experimental Group	Control Group
Proactive Interference		
I	Learn List A–B	(Unrelated activity)
II	Learn List A–C	Learn List A–C
Test	List A–C	List A–C
Retroactive Interference		
I	Learn List A–B	Learn List A–B
II	Learn List A–C	(Unrelated activity)
Test	List A–B	List A–B

the fact that *previous learning can make retention of subsequent learning more difficult.* Thus if a group of participants learns a list of paired associates ("List A–B" in the table) and then learns a second list with the same set of first terms but new second ones ("List A–C" in the table), recalling information from the second list is harder.

A more familiar example of proactive interference might come from foreign-language vocabulary learning. Imagine you are taking beginning courses in French and in German at the same time and for some perverse reason you decide to study their vocabularies sequentially. You first learn a list of French words by pairing them with their English alternatives—for example, *dog–chien.* Next, you learn the German equivalents for the English words, again by pairing—for example, *dog–hund.* If we compare how well you perform on a test of German vocabulary to the performance of your roommate (who is not studying French), we'll generally find, all other things being equal, that your recall is not as good. We call the kind of interference you experience *proactive* to indicate that earlier material is interfering with subsequent material.

Underwood (1957) demonstrated the effects of proactive interference using the data from 14 studies (see Figure 5-8). These data show that the more previous experience (that is, number of experimental trials) a person has with a particular task, the worse that person's performance is on the current trial.

The other kind of interference is called **retroactive interference**. Imagine you and another friend both study a list of English words and their French equivalents. Your friend now works on a physics problem set while you work on a list of the same English words with their German equivalents. The next day, you and your friend take a quiz in French class. All other things being equal, your recall of French will be worse than your friend's, because of retroactive (or backward) interference. Presumably, your recall of French is contaminated by intrusions of your recall of German.

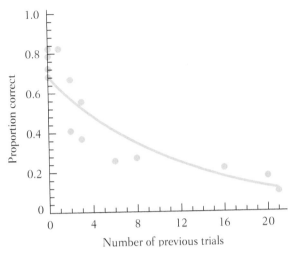

FIGURE 5-8 Proportion correct plotted as a function of the number of previous trials. Data were collected from 14 different studies.

Source: Republished with permission of Cengage Learning, from *Human Memory: An Introduction to Research, Data and Theory*, Ian Neath, © 1997; permission conveyed through Copyright Clearance Center, Inc.

Some researchers have argued that interference plays a role in most, if not all, forgetting of material from the long-term storage system (Barnes & Underwood, 1959; Briggs, 1954; Postman & Stark, 1969). Of course, it is impossible to rule out the idea that decay occurs, because it is impossible to design a task in which interference cannot occur.

How exactly does interference work? Anderson and Neely (1996) presented several possibilities. They started with the assumption diagrammed in Figure 5-9(A): that a **retrieval cue** points to, and leads to the recovery of, a target memory. However, when that retrieval cue becomes associated to other targets, during retrieval the second target "competes" with the first. Anderson and Neely offered the following example:

> *Consider, for example, the deceptively simple task of recalling where you parked your car at a local shopping center. If you have never before been to that shopping center, recalling your car's location may be fairly easy. If you park there frequently, however, you may find yourself reunited with the spot where you parked yesterday or, if you are like the present authors, standing befuddled at the lot's edge. Further, if asked where you parked on previous visits, you would almost certainly fail to recall the locations, as though your intervening parking experiences had overwritten those aspects of your past. (p. 237)*

Put in terms of Figure 5-9(B), the more times you park in a particular parking lot, the more "targets" (actual parking spots) get associated with a retrieval cue (such as the question you ask yourself as you leave the store: "Now where did I park?"). The more possible targets

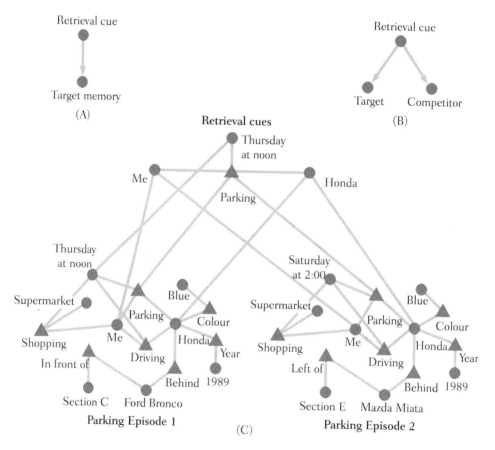

FIGURE 5-9 Illustration of the notion of competition among items sharing the same retrieval cue. (A) A retrieval cue that is associated to only one target item in memory. (B) The basic situation of interference, in which a retrieval cue becomes associated to one or more additional competitors that impede recall of the target, given presentation of the shared retrieval cue. (C) How the basic situation of interference illustrated in (B) may be applied to understand a more complex example of interference in which two episodes of having parked at the supermarket interfere because they share the retrieval cues "Me," "Honda," and "Parking" at the time of retrieval Circles and triangles in the representations of episodes 1 and 2 in (C) depict concepts and relations, respectively.

Source: Reprinted from Memory, Michael C. Anderson, James H. Neely, Chapter 8 Interference and Inhibition in *Memory Retrieval*, pp. 237–313, Copyright © 1996, with permission from Elsevier.

associated with the cue, the less the chances of finding any particular one of them. Complicating matters even further, a given retrieval cue can become associated with different targets (or other cues), leading to even more complexity, as diagrammed in Figure 5-9(C), and making it that much harder to traverse a path from the cue to the correct target.

To account for some of these results, psychologist John Anderson (1974; Anderson & Reder, 1999) described a phenomenon known as the **fan effect**. Anderson's idea is that as research participants study more facts about a particular concept, the time they need to retrieve a particular fact about that concept increases. So, for example, if you study lots of facts about forgetting, your ability to recall any individual fact about it (for example, that many psychologists think it is caused by interference) is slowed.

Anderson and Neely (1996) speculated that forgetting may not be so much a shortcoming of memory as a side effect of our ability to direct memory. In particular, they wonder whether sometimes it is beneficial to be able to forget voluntarily. Example: You are working for the summer break as a short-order cook. Servers spend their time shouting orders at you: "Egg salad on wheat, lettuce, no mayo!" It behooves you both to maintain this information in immediate memory as you construct the sandwich *and* to clear this information when you are done so it does not interfere with newer incoming orders. Laboratory work that Anderson and Neely reviewed suggests that when people lose information through "directed" (voluntary or intentional) forgetting, they experience much less proactive interference. Forgetting, then, can be a useful thing to do!

In this section, we've explored mechanisms for forgetting. It makes sense now to ask: What happens to information that is retained? Let's look now at how information from LTM is retrieved successfully.

Long-Term Memory—Retrieval of Information

Suppose you want to improve your chances of recalling information at a later date (for example, material for an upcoming midterm in cognitive psychology). What do we know about retrieval that can help? In Chapter 8 we'll discuss a number of *mnemonics*, techniques to improve memory, many of them having to do with visual imagery. For the present, we will consider a few principles of retrieval that can be used to aid recall.

The first is the principle of **categorization**. This states that material organized into categories or other units is more easily recalled than information with no apparent organization. This effect happens even when organized material is initially presented in a random order.

Early work documents this principle: Bousfield (1953) presented participants with a list of 60 words. The words came from four categories—animals, names, professions, and vegetables—but were presented in scrambled order. Nevertheless, participants tended to recall the words in clusters—for example, a number of animals together, then a group of vegetables, and so on. Memory improved depending on the extent to which organization, or semantic clustering, of the to-be-remembered information was used (Hultsch, 1975; Stuss, 1986). It turns out that even if the material doesn't have apparent organization, asking people to organize it into their own subjective categories improves recall (Mandler, 1967). Some people, senior citizens and young adults who've suffered a head injury to the front part of the brain, fail to make use of this principle and do not group similar items together during recall, and this partly explains their poor memory (Incisa della Rocchetta & Milner, 1993; Stuss, Alexander, Palumbo, Buckle, Sayer, et al., 1994; Stuss et al., 1998).

How can we apply the principle of categorization to your studying for a midterm? Simply put, the best advice is to categorize and organize your information! Make a list of types of memories (sensory, short-term, long-term), for example, and organize your notes about memory phenomena around this list. You could also colour code your notes to help impose a structural organization to the material. That way, if you are asked to write an essay about types of memory, you will likely recall more of the relevant information.

A second principle of retrieval, discovered by Thomson and Tulving (1970), is called **encoding specificity**. The idea is that memory is improved when information available at encoding is also available at retrieval. For example, the encoding specificity principle would predict that recall of information for a midterm would be better if students were tested in the same room in which they had studied, as opposed to studying in one room and being tested in a different room. The principle provides a general theoretical framework for understanding how contextual, or background, information affects memory. At the time of recall, it is a great advantage to have the same context information available, as aspects of the context can function as cues that aid retrieval.

Box 5-1 Canadian Research Highlight

Dr. Endel Tulving is professor emeritus at the University of Toronto (http://www.neuroscience.utoronto.ca/faculty/list/tulving.htm). In 1979, he was made a Fellow of the Royal Society of Canada. In 1992, he was made a Fellow of the Royal Society of London. In 2005, he won a Gairdner Foundation International Award, Canada's leading prize in biology and medicine. In 2006, he was made an Officer of the Order of Canada, Canada's highest civilian honour. In 2007, he was inducted into the Canadian Medical Hall of Fame. Tulving remains an active researcher at the Rotman Research Institute in Toronto. One of his main contributions to memory is his theory of "encoding specificity." He is also known for his seminal research on the episodic/semantic distinction. These theories have had a long-lasting impact on research in memory.

Tulving and Thomson (1973) demonstrated the encoding specificity principle as follows. Participants saw lists of words, with the to-be-remembered words printed in capital letters. Some participants saw these "target" words paired with other words printed in small letters. Both groups were told that the words in small letters were cues or hints. Cues were either highly related to the target (such as *hot–COLD*) or not very related (such as *ground–COLD*). Participants in the control condition were presented with the target words, but no cues (such as *COLD*).

At recall, memory performance for participants in the control condition (who hadn't seen any cues during the learning phase of the task) was aided if highly related cues were presented, even though these cues hadn't been seen in the learning phase. In contrast, as you might expect, the not-very-related cues were not very effective in prompting recall in the control group. However, the results were very different for participants who *had* seen cues during the learning phase. For these participants, the not-very-related cues were in fact very effective in aiding recall, even better than highly related cues that had not been presented during the learning phase. Thomson and Tulving interpreted these results to mean that even a weakly related word can act as a potent retrieval cue if it is presented at the time of encoding.

Roediger and Guynn (1996) summarized the encoding specificity hypothesis slightly differently:

A retrieval cue will be effective if and only if it reinstates the original encoding of the to-be-remembered event. When a word like black is presented without context, it is presumably encoded with regard to its dominant meaning (as associated with white). Therefore, white serves as an effective retrieval cue, and a weak associate like train does not. However, when black is encoded in the context of a weak associate like train, subjects are likely to engage in a more idiosyncratic encoding of the target word (e.g., they might imagine a black train). In this case, the weak associate could serve as an excellent retrieval cue, but now the strong associate is completely ineffective. (p. 208)

Apparently even information unrelated to the material, such as the environmental stimuli present at the time of encoding, can become a good retrieval cue. One of our favourite studies showing this effect is by Godden and Baddeley (1975), who presented lists of 40 unrelated words to 16 scuba divers, all wearing scuba gear. Divers learned some of the lists on the shore and the others 20 feet under water. They were later asked to recall the words either in the same environment where they were learned or in the other environment. Results showed that recall was best when the environment was the same as the learning environment. Lists learned underwater were best recalled underwater, and lists learned on the shore were best recalled on the shore (see Figure 5-10). This finding, that recall is best when performed in the original environment, is called a **context effect**.

Interestingly, researchers later found that recognition memory does not show the same context effect (Godden & Baddeley 1980), suggesting that recognition and recall work differently. In particular, this finding suggests that physical context affects recall but not recognition (Roediger & Guynn, 1996). Presumably, in the former task the participant must do more work to generate his or her own retrieval cues, which may include certain features of the learning environment, whereas on recognition tasks the test itself supplies some retrieval cues (in the form of the question and the possible answers).

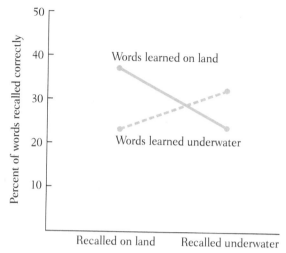

FIGURE 5-10 The effect of context on recall of word lists: words learned underwater are best recalled underwater and those learned on land are best recalled on land.

Source: Baddeley, A.D. (2002). *Human Memory,* page 195 from Psychology Press, Taylor & Francis Group.

Other studies have demonstrated similar effects (called **state-dependent learning**) with pharmacological states: Material learned while someone is chemically intoxicated (for example, by alcohol or marijuana) is usually recalled better when the person recreates that state (J. E. Eich, 1980). By the way, to ensure you don't use this scientific finding as an excuse to party, we must note that overall performance was best for those participants who learned and recalled material while sober! However, the finding of interest was that participants who learned material while in a chemically altered state showed significantly better recall if they were again chemically intoxicated at the time of recall. Later studies suggest that this **state-dependent memory** effect, like context effect, is found only with recall and not with recognition tasks (Roediger & Guynn, 1996).

WORKING MEMORY

Now that we have discussed the characteristics of short- and long-term memory, we turn to a consideration of how information is processed within each, and how information travels between these. The idea that memory consists of a number of information-processing stores was most completely described by Atkinson and Shiffrin (1968). These authors distinguished between the information being stored, calling this "memory" (for example, STM, LTM), and the structure that did the storing, which they termed a "store" (for example, STS, LTS). Their conception of STS was that it does more than merely hold on to seven or fewer pieces of information for a few seconds. In addition, they thought, information in STS somehow activates relevant information from LTS, the long-term store, and relays some of that information into STS. They equated STS with consciousness and saw it as the location of various *control processes* that govern the flow of information, such as rehearsal, coding, integration, and decision making.

Baddeley and Hitch (1974) performed a series of experiments to test this model. The general design was to have participants temporarily store a number of digits (thus absorbing some of the STS storage capacity) while simultaneously performing another task, such as reasoning or language comprehension, that was also thought to require resources from STS—specifically, the control processes mentioned earlier. Because researchers think STM has a capacity of about seven items, plus or minus two, the six-digit memory load should have essentially stopped any other cognitive activity. Baddeley and Hitch (1974) therefore argued for the existence of what they called **working memory (WM)**. They see WM as consisting of a limited-capacity "workspace" that can be divided between storage and control processing.

Let's look at one of Baddeley and Hitch's studies in detail. Participants saw a sentence, and had to reason whether it was true or false; for example, "*A* is preceded by *B*"—together with two letters in a particular order—for example, "*B A*." The task was to decide, as quickly as possible, if the sentence correctly described the two letters (the answer here is no). Participants were given from one to six digits to hold in memory while they verified the sentences. The results showed that participants were able to verify the sentences while holding one or two digits in memory about as well as they could without holding any digits in memory. However, a six-digit memory load did hurt performance: The sentence took longer to verify (see Figure 5-11).

The effect was especially pronounced if the sentence was negative and passive (for example, "*B* is not preceded by *A*"), both of which are known to be harder to process. Although performance was hurt by storing six digits, the effects were not catastrophic (Baddeley, 1990). That is, it took people much longer to reason while rehearsing six digits, but they still could perform the task. According to the predictions from Atkinson and Shiffrin's (1968) model, they should not have been able to do so at all.

Baddeley (1981, 1986, 1990, 2000) conceived of WM as consisting of three components, as depicted in Figure 5-12. The first is the **central executive**. This component directs the flow of information, choosing which information will be operated on, when, and how. Researchers assume it has a limited amount of resources and capacity to carry out its tasks. The central executive is thought to function more as an attentional system than a memory store (Baddeley, 1990), meaning that rather than dealing with the storage and retrieval of information, the central executive deals with parcelling out resources needed for cognitive tasks. The central executive is also thought to coordinate information coming from the current environment with the retrieval of information about the past, enabling people to

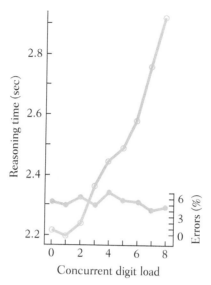

FIGURE 5-11 Speed and accuracy of reasoning increases with increasing digit load.

Source: Baddeley, A.D. (2002). *Human Memory*, page 51 from Psychology Press, Taylor & Francis Group.

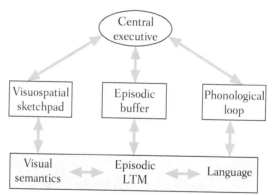

FIGURE 5-12 Baddeley's (2000) revised model of working memory.

Source: Brom Baddeley (2000, Figure 1).

use this information to select options or form strategies. Baddeley (1993a) equated this coordination with conscious awareness.

The two other components of Baddeley's model are concerned with the storage and temporary maintenance of information: the **phonological loop**, used to carry out subvocal rehearsal to maintain verbal material, and the **visuospatial sketch pad**, used to maintain visual material through visualization. Researchers think the phonological loop plays an important role in such tasks as learning to read, comprehending language, and acquiring vocabulary. The visuospatial sketch pad involves the creation and use of mental images, for example mentally rotating luggage in a trunk and visualizing how all the pieces will fit in. The phonological loop consists of two structures: a short-term phonological buffer (which holds on to verbal information for short periods of time, such as a few minutes, assuming rehearsal is not prevented), and a sub-vocal rehearsal loop used to compensate for the rapid decay of information in the phonological buffer (Demetriou, Christou, Spanoudis, & Platsidou, 2002). The idea here is that when the person initially encounters information, particularly verbal information, he/she translates it into some sort of auditory code and processes it through the phonological loop. Because the information from the phonological buffer decays rapidly the person must subvocally rehearse the information, and the faster the rehearsal process, the more information can be maintained. If the phonological buffer is "filled up"—say, by having a person repeat a syllable or count aloud—then less capacity from this system would be available to devote to other tasks.

Researchers have devised various working-memory-span tasks to measure the capacity of the phonological buffer. A very well known one, created by Daneman and Carpenter (1980), works like this: A person is given a set of sentences to read (usually aloud), but at the same time is asked to remember the last word in each sentence for later recall. For example, the participant might be presented with the following three sentences:

The leaves on the trees turn various hues in autumn.

A group of students congregated outside the front entrance of the delicatessen.

Although lying and fabrication are generally not acceptable, they are sometimes necessary.

After reading the sentences aloud, the participant is cued to recall the last word in each sentence. In this example, the correct answers are *autumn*, *delicatessen*, and *necessary*. The number of sentences a participant can process and reliably recall words from is said to be a measure of his span. This measure has been shown to correlate significantly with other cognitive measures, such as reading comprehension and other complex cognitive tasks (Miyake, 2001), and vocabulary level in children (Daneman & Hannon, 2001). Working memory capacity has also been linked to general fluid intelligence (Suess, Oberauere, Wittman, Wilhelm, & Schulze, 2002), as well as cognitive decline associated with normal aging, which will be discussed in Chapter 12.

The original model of working memory proposed by Baddeley & Hitch (1974) comprised three components: the central executive and the two "slave" systems, the phonological loop and the visuospatial sketch pad. A fourth component was added by Baddeley in 2000. He proposed the existence of another slave system, called the *episodic buffer*. This buffer is believed to be required when remembering specific events from the past. The buffer is needed to link information across domains (visual, spatial, verbal), and to allow one to sequence various events in chronological order. Such a slave system was hypothesized because of the recent finding that some amnesic patients are perfectly able to remember entire stories that are told to them, as long as recall is assessed within a short time period of hearing the story (Baddeley & Wilson, 2002). Remembering details of a story, and the ordering of events, requires more storage capacity than can be held in the phonological loop; hence the proposal of the episodic buffer.

THE SEMANTIC/EPISODIC DISTINCTION

While the concept of working memory helps us to understand how information is held and manipulated over a short duration, the next section focuses on how we hold on to information in such a way that it can be accessed days, or sometimes years, after it is stored. Consider the vast range of information everyone must have stored in permanent memory. In addition to information regarding events in your life (your sixth birthday party, the time you broke your arm, going to the circus, your first day of high school), you have also stored a great deal of knowledge: definitions of the words you know; arithmetic facts and procedures; historical, scientific, and geographic knowledge; and (we hope) even some knowledge of principles of cognitive psychology.

To start, do your memories of specific events (say, your sixth birthday party) differ in important ways from your memories of general knowledge (for example, that 2 + 2 = 4)? Endel Tulving (1972, 1983) drew a distinction between memories for events and memories for general knowledge. He argued that long-term memory consists of two separate and distinct yet interacting systems.

One system, **episodic memory**, holds memories of specific events in which you yourself somehow participated. The other system, **semantic memory**, holds information that has entered your general knowledge base: You can recall parts of that base, but the information recalled is generic—it doesn't have much to do with your personal experience. For example, your memory that Sigmund Freud was a founding practitioner of psychoanalysis is presumably in your general knowledge base but divorced from your personal memories of when you acquired this knowledge. It's probable, actually, that you can't even remember when the fact about Freud entered your memory. Contrast this situation with when information about your first date or the 9/11 attacks on the World Trade Center and Pentagon entered your memory. For those instances you may recall not only the information itself but also the circumstances surrounding your acquisition of the information (where, when, why, how, and from whom you heard, saw, or otherwise acquired it). After reviewing arguments and evidence for the episodic/semantic distinction, we'll go on to concentrate on semantic memory. Specifically, we'll look at a number of proposals for how our knowledge base or bases are organized and the implications that organization has for the ways we access information.

Tulving (1972, 1983, 1989) proposed a classification of long-term memories into two kinds: episodic and semantic. Episodic memory is memory for information about one's personal experiences. As Tulving (1989) put it, episodic memory "enables people to travel back in time, as it were, into their personal past, and to become consciously aware of having witnessed or participated in events and happenings at earlier times" (p. 362). Episodic memory has also been described as containing memories that are temporally dated; the information stored has some sort of marker for when it was originally encountered.

Any of your memories that you can trace to a single time are considered to be in episodic memory. If you recall your high school graduation, or your first meeting with your first-year roommate, or the time you first learned of an important event, you are recalling episodic memories. Even if you don't recall the exact date or even the year, you know the information was first presented at a particular time and place, and you have a memory of that presentation.

Semantic memory, in contrast, is thought to store general information about language and world knowledge. When you recall arithmetic facts (for example, "6 + 6 = 12"), historical dates ("In fourteen hundred and ninety-two, Columbus sailed the ocean blue"), or the past tense forms of various verbs (*run, ran; walk, walked; am, was*), you are calling on semantic memory.

Notice in these examples that in recalling "2 + 2 = 4," you aren't tracing back to a particular moment when you learned the fact, as you might do with the 9/11 attacks. Instead of "remembering" that 2 + 2 = 4, most people speak of "knowing" that 2 + 2 = 4. This distinction between memories of specific moments and recall from general knowledge marks the major difference between semantic and episodic memory. Why make such a distinction? Doing so captures our intuition that the recall of some things differs from the recall of others. Recalling your graduation simply has a different "feel" from recalling the sum of 2 and 2.

Tulving (1972, 1983, 1989) described episodic and semantic memory as **memory systems** that operate on different principles and hold on to different kinds of information. Tulving (1983) pointed to a number of differences in the ways episodic and semantic memory seem to work, and we'll describe a few of the major differences here.

As we have just discovered, the nature of the information thought to be held in the two memory systems is different. In episodic memory, we hold on to information about events and episodes that have happened to us directly. In semantic memory, we store knowledge: facts, concepts, and ideas. With episodic memory, the memories are encoded in terms of personal experience. Recalling memories from the episodic system takes the form of "Remember when. . . ." With semantic memory, the information is encoded as general knowledge, context effects are less pronounced, and retrieval of information consists of answering questions from our general knowledge base in the form of "Remember what. . . ." Organization of episodic memory is temporal; that is, one event will be recorded as having occurred before, after, or at the same time as another. Organization of semantic memory is arranged more on the basis of meanings and meaning relationships among different pieces of information, and will be considered in detail in the next chapter.

Memory processes ultimately are instantiated in the brain, of course. In the next section we will consider some relevant background and findings from the study of neuropsychology Previous discussion of "stores" or "components" of memory can make it seem as if memory were located in one place in the brain—a sort of neural "filing cabinet" that holds on to memory traces of information being stored.

NEUROLOGICAL STUDIES OF MEMORY

Schacter (1996) offered a number of case studies of people suffering from different kinds of amnesia that support the episodic/semantic distinction. Gene, for example, survived a motorcycle accident in 1981 (when he was 30 years old) that seriously damaged his frontal and temporal lobes, including the left hippocampus. Gene shows anterograde amnesia and retrograde amnesia. In particular, Gene cannot recall any specific past events, even with extensive, detailed cues. That is, Gene cannot recall any birthday parties, school days, or conversations. Schacter noted further that "even when detailed descriptions of dramatic events in his life are given to him—the tragic drowning of his brother, the derailment near his house, of a train carrying lethal chemicals that required 240,000 people to evacuate their homes for a week—Gene does not generate any episodic memories" (p. 149).

In contrast, Gene recalls many facts (as opposed to episodes) about his past life. He knows where he went to school; he knows where he worked. He can name former co-workers; he can define technical terms he used at the manufacturing plant where he worked before the accident. Gene's memories, Schacter argued, are akin to the knowledge we have of other people's lives. You may know, for example, about incidents in your mother's or father's lives that occurred before your birth: where they met, perhaps, or some memorable childhood incidents. You know *about* these events, although you do not have specific *recall* of them. Similarly, according to Schacter, Gene has *knowledge* of some aspects of his past (semantic memory), but no evidence of any *recall* of specific happenings (episodic memory).

Schacter (1996) also described neuropsychological case studies of people with deficits that are "mirror images" of Gene's. A case was reported, for instance, of a woman who, after a bout of encephalitis and resultant damage to the front temporal lobe,

> *no longer knew the meanings of common words, had forgotten virtually everything she once knew about historical events and famous people, and retained little knowledge of the basic attributes of animate and inanimate objects. She had difficulty indicating the color of a mouse, and had no idea where soap would ordinarily be found. . . . However, when asked about her wedding and honeymoon, her father's illness and death, or other specific past episodes, she readily produced detailed and accurate recollections. (p. 152)*

These two cases, and others like them (some described by Schacter, 1996; see also Riby Perfect, & Stollery, 2004), provide some clinical neuropsychological evidence supporting the idea that episodic memory and semantic memory operate independently. That is, the existence of people in whom one type of memory seems seriously impaired while the other appears spared gives concrete evidence for the existence of two separate systems of memory.

Tulving's (1972, 1983, 1989) proposals have provoked strong controversy within the field of cognitive psychology. McKoon, Ratcliff, and Dell (1986) presented a series of arguments centring on the usefulness of considering episodic and semantic memories to be two separate memory *systems* and on the kind of evidence needed to support the distinction. Many psychologists find it hard to draw sharp lines between knowledge that includes information about the time it was first learned and knowledge that is more "generic" in character (Baddeley 1984). However, almost everyone agrees that at the very least there seems to be two kinds of memories—semantic and episodic—even if they are stored within a single system. Indeed, studies with patients with amnesia most often show a deficit in episodic but preserved semantic memory (Tulving, Hayman, & MacDonald, 1991).

Much of the interest in "localizing" memory in the brain dates back to a famous case study. In 1953, William Beecher Stover, a neurosurgeon, performed surgery on H.M., a 27-year-old epileptic patient. Before the operation, H.M. was of normal intelligence. Stover removed many structures on the inner sector of the temporal lobes of both sides of H.M.'s brain, including most of the hippocampus, the amygdala, and some adjacent areas. This noticeably reduced H.M.'s seizures, and H.M.'s postoperative IQ actually rose about 10 points (Schacter, 1996).

Unfortunately, however, H.M. suffered another decrement: He lost his ability to transfer new episodic memories into long-term memory, and thus became one of the most famous neuropsychological case studies in the literature. H.M. could remember semantic information, and events that he had experienced several years before the operation. However, H.M. could no longer form new memories of new events. He could remember a series of seven or so digits, as long as he was not distracted, but if he turned his attention to a new task, he could not seem to store that (or much other) information. In addition to this **anterograde amnesia** (amnesia for new events), H.M. had **retrograde amnesia** (amnesia for old events) for the period of several years just before his operation.

H.M.'s case, widely publicized by Canadian psychologist Brenda Milner in the hope of preventing similar surgeries this extensive, suggested strongly that the structures removed from his brain, especially the hippocampus and surrounding rhinal cortex and underlying structures, played a major role in forming new memories (Scoville & Milner, 1957). Other researchers reported other case studies and other animal studies that seemed to provide corroborating evidence.

Findings from other brain-damaged people have implicated areas in the frontal lobe as having much to do with working memory. Damage to this brain region is often reported to disrupt attention, planning, and problem solving (that is, the central executive in Baddeley's model; see Gathercole, 1994). Shimura (1995) suggested that these problems may arise not because attention and planning are located in the frontal lobe but rather because areas of the frontal lobe inhibit activity in the posterior part of the brain. People with frontal-lobe damage seem more distractible and less able to ignore irrelevant stimuli.

How does the activity of different brain regions change as memories are formed? We are far from reaching a complete answer to this question. However, some preliminary answers are emerging. Neil Carlson (1994) described some basic physiological mechanisms for learning new information. One basic mechanism is the *Hebb rule*, named after the man who posited it, Canadian psychologist Donald Hebb. The Hebb rule states that if a synapse between two neurons is repeatedly activated *at about the same time* the postsynaptic neuron fires, the structure or chemistry of the synapse changes. A more general, and more complex, mechanism is called **long-term potentiation**. In this process, neural circuits in the hippocampus that are subjected to repeated and intense electrical stimulation develop hippocampal cells that become more sensitive to stimuli. This effect of enhanced response can last for weeks or even longer, suggesting to many that this could be a mechanism for long-term learning and retention (Baddeley 1993b). As you might suspect, disrupting the process of long-term potentiation (say, through different drugs) also disrupts learning and remembering.

Despite the intriguing results from neuropsychological studies, we are far from having a complete picture of how the brain instantiates all, or even many, memory phenomena. It is not clear which aspects of memory are localized in one place in the brain and which are distributed across different cortical regions. It is not clear what kinds of basic neural processes are involved in any one particular complex cognitive activity. Tulving (1995) made the point quite explicitly:

> *Memory is a biological abstraction. There is no place in the brain that one could point at and say, Here is memory. There is no single activity, or class of activities, of the organism that could be identified with the concept that the term denotes. There is no known molecular change that corresponds to memory, no behavioral response of a living organism that is memory. Yet the term* memory *encompasses all these changes and activities. (p. 751)*

Tulving noted further that neuroscientists today reject the idea of studying memory as though it were a single process. Instead, they are likely to look for neurological underpinnings at a more precise level—at such processes as encoding or retrieval.

SUMMARY

1. Memory is a very basic cognitive process used in almost every cognitive activity. It involves encoding information, storing it, and later retrieving it from that storage. Cognitive psychologists consider memory an active, constructive process. This means the information does not "sit still" in a storehouse, waiting to be retrieved, but instead is elaborated and sometimes distorted or constructed.

2. One approach to the study of memory, called the *modal approach*, divides memory into different types: *sensory memory*, which holds information in specific modalities for fractions of a second up to several seconds (depending on the modality); *STM*, which holds a

limited amount of information for brief periods of seconds or minutes; and *LTM*, which holds on to memories for longer periods of time.

3. The number of unrelated pieces of information that can be held in the short term (without rehearsal or recoding) seems to be seven, plus or minus two. This limit can be overcome through techniques such as *chunking*, which requires some knowledge about the pieces of information and how they relate.

4. There is controversy in the explanations proposed for why we forget information. The question is whether information in a memory store ever decays or "disintegrates," or whether all supposedly "forgotten" information is actually buried information displaced by interference from other information. Although these two possibilities are quite distinct, as a practical matter it is very difficult to design critical experiments that would rule out one of them. Perhaps both kinds of processes play some role in forgetting.

5. Saul Sternberg's work suggests that retrieval from STM is serial and exhaustive. Later work suggests that this may depend on the nature of the stimuli presented.

6. A newer conception of STM, proposed by Alan Baddeley is called *working memory (WM)*. Working memory is thought to consist of a *central executive*, concerned with coordinating and controlling incoming information; a *phonological loop*, acting as an inner "ear"; and a *visuospatial sketch pad*, used as an inner "eye." Recent work suggests that WM capacity is a powerful variable, relating to the ability to resist distraction and distortion, to reason with abstract or concrete premises, and to maintain control of attention more generally.

7. Retrieval of information is made easier when the information to be retrieved is categorized, when the retrieval cues match the cues that were available at the time of encoding (the encoding specificity principle), and when the retrieval cues are very distinctive.

8. Consistent with the encoding specificity principle, investigators have found that recall (but not recognition) is made easier when the recall context is the same as the learning context (the context effect), or when the pharmacological state of the person at recall matches his or her pharmacological state during encoding (the state-dependent learning effect).

9. Neuropsychological studies of memory provide a glimpse at some very exciting "cutting-edge" research. Investigators are examining the role of particular brain structures, such as the hippocampus and medial temporal cortex, in memory formation, as well as attempting to localize the brain regions involved in encoding and retrieval.

REVIEW QUESTIONS

1. Review the evidence that has led some psychologists to posit the existence of different memory stores or systems (such as sensory memory, short-term memory, long-term memory, episodic memory, semantic memory).

2. Discuss the importance of research on icons and echoes for understanding how people process incoming information. Consider issues of both experimental control and ecological validity.

3. Psychologists have posited two distinct mechanisms for forgetting: decay and interference. Describe each, briefly review the experimental evidence supporting each, and state the problem in distinguishing between them.

4. Describe the methods used in Sternberg's memory-scanning experiment. What do the results tell us about retrieval of information from STM?

5. How does Baddeley's conception of working memory differ from traditional descriptions of STM?

6. Describe two ways in which our knowledge of findings from research on working memory can help us design effective real-world strategies for coping with everyday tasks and problems.

7. Describe and evaluate encoding specificity as a principle of retrieval of information. How does it relate to such phenomena as state-dependent learning, and context effects on retrieval?

8. Summarize the findings of neuropsychological research on localizing memory in the brain.

KEY TERMS

anterograde amnesia
capacity
categorization
central executive (of WM)
chunking
coding
context effect
decay
echo
encoding
encoding specificity
episodic memory
exhaustive search
fan effect
forgetting
icon

interference
long-term memory (LTM)
long-term potentiation
memory systems
memory trace
modal model of memory
paired associates learning
parallel search
phonological loop (of WM)
primacy effect
proactive interference
recency effect
rehearsal
retention duration
retrieval
retrieval cue

retroactive interference
retrograde amnesia
self-terminating search
semantic memory
sensory memory
serial position effect
serial search
short-term memory (STM)
state-dependent learning
state-dependent memory
storage
visuospatial sketch pad (of WM)
working memory (WM)

Memory Processes

In this chapter we turn our attention to models of memory that focus less on the different types of memory stores and more on the way information is processed in everyday life, both at the time of encoding and at the time of retrieval. We'll look at how various cues become associated, either intentionally or unintentionally, with the information to be remembered, and then at how these cues can be used to maximize the chances of retrieving information. We will then look at the malleability of memory. In this section, we'll review research on memory for events, and how those memories can be distorted without a person's awareness. Finally, we will look in greater detail at the topic of amnesia, reviewing the types of memory loss that can occur.

THE LEVELS-OF-PROCESSING VIEW

The modal approach to memory makes a distinction between different kinds of memory—for example, sensory memory, STM, and LTM stores (refer to Chapter 5 for a detailed discussion). Researchers think these components process information differently, store information differently, and retain information for different lengths of time. The component used at any given time depends primarily on how long information is stored.

The modal approach is not universally endorsed, however. Some psychologists argue that there is only one kind of memory storage (Melton, 1963), but that different kinds of information processing take place within that store. One alternative to the modal view of memory is the **levels-of-processing theory of memory**. In this model, memory is thought to depend not on how long material is stored or on the kind of storage in which the material is held, but on the initial encoding of the information to be remembered (Craik & Lockhart, 1972). That is, the levels-of-processing approach does not suggest that there are different memory stores (such as STM and LTM) but rather focuses on the different kinds of cognitive processing that people perform when they encode, and later retrieve, information.

The fundamental assumption is that retention and coding of information depend on the kind of perceptual analysis done on the material at encoding. Some kinds of processing, done at a superficial or "shallow" level, do not lead to very good retention. Other kinds of "deeper" (more meaningful or semantic) processing improve retention. According to the levels-of-processing view, improvement in memory comes not from rehearsal and repetition but from greater depth of analysis of the material.

Craik and Tulving (1975) performed a typical levels-of-processing investigation. Participants were presented with a series of questions about particular words, and later a surprise memory test was given. During the "study" session, each word was preceded by a question, and participants were asked to respond to the questions as quickly as possible; no mention was made of the upcoming memory test, or learning of the words. Any learning that happened to occur, inadvertently, in such a situation is called **incidental learning**.

In one of their experiments, three kinds of questions were used. One kind asked the participant whether the word was printed in capital letters. Another asked if the target word rhymed with another word. The third kind asked if the word fit into a particular sentence (for example, "The girl placed the ___ on the table"). The three kinds of questions were meant to induce different kinds of processing. To answer the first kind of question, you need look only at the typeface (physical processing). To answer the second, you need to read the word and think about what it sounds like (acoustic processing). To answer the third, you need to retrieve and evaluate the word's meaning (semantic processing). Presumably, the "depth" of the processing needed is greatest for the third kind of question and least for the first kind of question.

As predicted, Craik and Tulving (1975) found that on a surprise memory test words processed semantically were remembered best, followed by words processed acoustically. However, the experiment gave rise to an alternative explanation: Participants spent more time answering questions about sentences than they did questions about capital letters. To respond to this explanation, in subsequent experiments the authors showed that even if the physical processing was slowed down (by asking participants, "Does this word follow a consonant-vowel-consonant-vowel-consonant-vowel pattern?"), memory was still best for more deeply processed information (see Figure 6-1).

Craik and Tulving (1975) initially equated depth of processing with degree of semantic processing. But Bower and Karlin (1974), studying memory for faces, found similar results

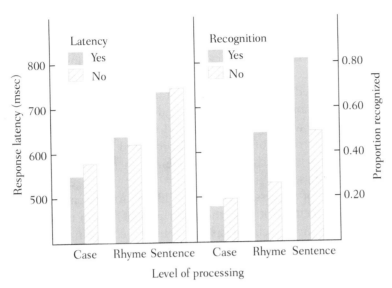

FIGURE 6-1 Effects of encoding tasks requiring different levels of processing on response latency and an incidental recall task performance. The graph shows the pattern for words given yes and no responses.

with nonverbal stimuli: Participants who rated faces for "honesty" (which requires deep semantic processing) showed better memory than participants who rated the faces according to gender (superficial processing of faces). One problem with this approach, though, was pinning down the definition of what defined a level and what made for "depth" (Baddeley, 1978).

Craik and Tulving (1975) found, for instance, that the "meaningfulness" of the initial task was not the only factor that could account for better retention. Participants who were asked to determine if words fit into sentences showed poorer recall for simple sentences (for example, "She cooked the") than they did for more complex sentences (for example, "The great bird swooped down and carried off the struggling"). Levels-of-processing theory as initially formulated would argue that both words were processed semantically so that could not account for the difference in recall. Craik and Tulving therefore extended the levels-of-processing idea, arguing that the **elaboration** of material could also aid recall. Presumably, the second, more complicated sentence calls to mind a richer idea: The sentence itself has more underlying propositions (there was a bird, the bird was very large, the bird swooped down, the bird carried something off) than the first sentence (there is a female, she is baking something). Sentences that specified more precisely the relation of the target word to the context were found especially likely to increase the probability of recalling the target word (Stein & Bransford, 1979).

Craik and Lockhart (1972) viewed memory as a continuum of processes, from the "transient products of sensory analyses to the highly durable products of semantic . . . operations" (p. 676). This view ties memory in with other cognitive systems quite neatly.

For example, recall the work on dichotic listening tasks reviewed in Chapter 4. Recall that material from the unattended channel is typically not remembered after the task is completed. The levels-of-processing approach can account for this finding, holding that material not analyzed for meaning receives only "shallow" processing, which results in poor retention.

Baddeley (1978) presented a thorough critique of the levels-of-processing approach. First, he argued that without a more precise and independent definition of "depth of processing," the usefulness of the theory was very limited. Second, he reviewed studies that showed, under certain conditions, greater recall of information processed acoustically than semantically. Finally, he described ways in which the modal view of memory could explain the typical levels-of-processing findings.

Nonetheless, the levels-of-processing approach did help to reorient the thinking of memory researchers, drawing their attention to the importance of the *way* material is encoded. The approach has helped cognitive psychologists think about the ways in which people approach learning tasks. It has reinforced the idea that the more "connections" an item has to other pieces of information (such as retrieval cues) the easier it will be to remember—a point that fits nicely with the idea of encoding specificity discussed earlier.

THE RECONSTRUCTIVE NATURE OF MEMORY

Thus far, we have concentrated on laboratory studies of memory. This tradition dates back at least to Ebbinghaus. One can't help admiring Ebbinghaus's dedication and feeling gratitude for his many insights about memory. However, a similarly common reaction is to find his efforts somewhat amusing. After all, what relevance do his heroic studies have to memory in "real life"? Does the study of memory for nonsense syllables really tell us very much about how to study for an upcoming midterm, how to remember where we left our house key, or how we recall our first day of kindergarten (if in fact we remember anything about it)?

Another pioneer in the study of memory, Frederick Bartlett, rejected the emphasis on laboratory studies of memory. Bartlett (1932) believed that in the real world (as opposed to the laboratory) memory largely uses world knowledge and **schemata**—frameworks for organizing information. According to Bartlett, at retrieval time this knowledge and organizational information is used to reconstruct the material. Bartlett tested both friends and students, first presenting them with stories such as the one in Box 6-1.

Bartlett used the method of serial reproduction, meaning participants were asked to recall the stories on more than one occasion. Participants were asked to recall the tales at varying intervals, some as long as years. Bartlett was interested in what information was remembered and what information was "misremembered"—distorted or reordered in the participants' recollections. Box 6-2 provides examples of repeated recollections of the "War of the Ghosts" story as retold by one participant. This retelling shows concretely that over time the same person's recall becomes more distorted.

Box 6-1 "The War of the Ghosts": A Story Used by Bartlett (1932) to Investigate Long-Term Memory

One night two young men from Egulac went down to the river to hunt seals, and while they were there it became foggy and calm. Then they heard war-cries, and they thought: "Maybe this is a war-party." They escaped to the shore, and hid behind a log.

Now canoes came up, and they heard the noise of paddles, and saw one canoe coming up to them. There were five men in the canoe, and they said: "What do you think? We wish to take you along. We are going up the river to make war on the people." One of the young men said: "I have no arrows." "Arrows are in the canoe," they said.

"I will not go along. I might be killed. My relatives do not know where I have gone. But you," he said, turning to the other, "may go with them." So one of the young men went, but the other returned home.

And the warriors went on up the river to a town on the other side of Kalama. The people came down to the water, and they began to fight, and many were killed. But presently the young man heard one of the warriors say: "Quick, let us go home: that Indian has been hit." Now he thought: "Oh, they are ghosts." He did not feel sick, but they said he had been shot.

So the canoes went back to Egulac, and the young man went ashore to his house, and made a fire. And he told everybody and said: "Behold I accompanied the ghosts, and we went to fight. Many of our fellows were killed, and many of those who attacked us were killed. They said I was hit, and I did not feel sick." He told it all, and then he became quiet. When the sun rose he fell down. Something black came out of his mouth. His face became contorted. The people jumped up and cried.

He was dead.

SOURCE: Bartlett (1932, p. 67).

Bartlett used examples of recall such as these as evidence to argue for a constructive view of long-term memory (LTM). He believed that participants unintentionally introduced distortions during recall to make the material more rational and more coherent from their own point of view, or schemata. A schema is thought to be a large unit of organized information used for representing concepts, situations, events, and actions in memory (Rumelhart & Norman, 1988).

Interestingly, the original story a Native American folktale, was often "misrecalled" in ways more consistent with people's cultural conventions for stories. Thus, the "foggy and calm" weather might be changed to a "dark and stormy night"—something more in keeping with a Western assumption of how weather portends bad events. Bartlett thus rejected the idea of LTM as a warehouse where material is stored unchanged until retrieval. Rather, he

---

Box 6-2 One Participant's Recall of "The War of the Ghosts"

Recalled 15 minutes after hearing story:

THE GHOSTS

There were two men on the banks of the river near Egulac. They heard the sound of paddles, and a canoe with five men in it appeared, who called to them, saying: "We are going to fight the people. Will you come with us?" One of the two men answered, saying: "Our relations do not know where we are, and we have not got any arrows." They answered: "There are arrows in the canoe." So the man went, and they fought the people, and then he heard them saying: "An Indian is killed, let us return." So he returned to Egulac, and told them he knew they were ghosts.

He spoke to the people of Egulac, and told them that he had fought with the Ghosts, and many men were killed on both sides, and that he was wounded, but felt nothing. He lay down and became calmer, and in the night he was convulsed, and something black came out of his mouth.

The people said: "He is dead."

Recalled two weeks later:

THE GHOSTS

There were two men on the banks of a river near the village of Etishu (?). They heard the sound of paddles coming from the up-stream, and shortly a canoe appeared. The men in the canoe spoke, saying: "We are going to fight the people: will you come with us?"

One of the young men answered, saying: "Our relations do not know where we are; but my companion may go with you. Besides, we have no arrows."

So the young man went with them, and they fought the people, and many were killed on both sides. And then he heard shouting: The Indian is wounded; let us return." And he heard the people say: They are the Ghosts." He did not know he was wounded, and returned to Etishu (?). The people collected round him and bathed his wounds, and he said he had fought with the Ghosts. Then he became quiet. But in the night he was convulsed, and something black came out of his mouth.

And the people cried: "He is dead."

SOURCE: Bartlett (1932, pp. 68–69).

---

saw memory as an active and often inaccurate process that encodes and retrieves information so as to "make sense."

Thus part of the reason why Bartlett's participants produced such distorted recalls of "The War of the Ghosts" is that they used their schemata for stories and "regularized" the original folktale, making it conform more to their own cultural expectations of how a story should proceed.

Autobiographical Memory

When describing our memories in everyday life, we most often are referring to events that occurred in our personal past, from our **autobiographical** memories. How do these memories differ from the types of memories described so far? Marigold Linton's (1975, 1982) work is a good example of a classic study of autobiographical memory. She was a researcher who spent six years in a true Ebbinghausian endeavour: she studied her own recall of events from her own life. Each day she would record short descriptions of that day's events, typing them onto a 4-by-6 index card, on the back of which she recorded the actual date, as well as different ratings of the event (for example, how clearly distinguishable she believed the event would be in the future, the emotionality of the event, and the importance to her life goals of the event). At the end of the month (when 60 to 90 cards had accumulated), she would gather and randomly sort them into 14 piles for testing during the following three years. Twelve of the piles were tested in the following 12 months; the remaining sets were used two and three years after the events, respectively.

Each month, after doing a brief free recall of life events as a warm-up task, Linton shuffled all the cards due for testing that month, then exposed two cards at a time while starting a stopwatch. She recorded the cards' code numbers, then tried to order the two exposed events (that is, which happened before the other). Her time to perform this ordering was recorded. Next she restarted the stopwatch, timing how long it took to recall the exact date of the left-hand card. Finally, she did the same for the right-hand card.

During the first 20 months of the study, Linton recorded 2,003 events and tested 3,006 (1,468 of these were retests of previously tested items). She had expected, before running the study, that she would quickly forget many of the items, but in fact that did not happen, perhaps because she needed only to recognize the events (not recall them) and to date them, not answer detailed questions about them. In fact, Linton's results suggested that real-world memories are much more durable than those of most laboratory experiments!

Linton also recorded protocols of herself thinking aloud as she tried to date items. She found that she often used problem-solving strategies to arrive at a date, even when she had no explicit recall of the event. You might be able to re-create this phenomenon by trying to answer the following question: Where were you on June 28, 2015, at 11:20 a.m.? Your first reaction may be to laugh and to claim you can't possibly answer the question. But think about it. No doubt you can find some "markers" that point you toward some sort of answer. For instance, you might note that June is during the summer. You might be able to figure out June 28 must have been a Tuesday, because (say) your mother's birthday is June 25, and you remember that being on a Saturday. You might remember you held a summer job at a local department store and conclude that at 11:20 on June 28, you must have been working, probably stocking shelves. Notice that what you've done is to "zero in" on the date and time by finding and using different "markers." You haven't necessarily remembered what you were doing; instead, you've reconstructed it.

Brewer (1988) took a different methodological approach to studying recall for ordinary events. He found eight very cooperative undergraduates to serve in a demanding multiweek experiment. During the data acquisition phase, participants were asked to wear beepers programmed to go off on a random schedule about once every two hours. When the beeper sounded, participants were asked to fill out a card with information about the event that had occurred when the beeper went off. Specifically, participants were asked to report the time and their location, actions, and thoughts and then to complete a number of rating scales (rating such things as how often this kind of event occurred, how pleasant the event was, and how trivial or significant). Fortunately, participants were given the option of recording the word "private" on a card instead of giving a detailed account, if the activity they were engaged in was one they preferred for any reason not to report. Brewer noted that most participants exercised this option at least occasionally, which no doubt led to some systematic undersampling of certain kinds of events, such as dating or parties.

Brewer (1988) argued that this methodology had certain advantages over the one Linton used. Obviously, it involves separating the experimenter from the participant, which methodologically has many advantages. More important, however, Brewer argued that Linton wrote down the most "memorable" events of each day, which would tend to skew the set of items to be remembered. To allow comparison between Linton's study and his, Brewer also asked his participants to list the most memorable event of each day.

Brewer (1988) later tested his participants' recall of the events they had recorded on cards. Each participant was tested three times: once at the conclusion of the data acquisition period, once about 21 months later, and once about 41 months after the end of the acquisition period. Items tested were randomly selected from all items the participants had initially described.

Brewer (1988) reported very good overall retention from his participants, who recognized more than 60% of the events. Memory was better for actions than for thoughts, and better for "memorable" events than for events randomly prompted by beepers. Consistent with some of the results Linton reported (1975, 1982), Brewer found that events that occurred in a unique or infrequent location were better remembered than occurrences in frequented locations. Similarly, rare actions were more likely to be recalled than frequent actions. Interestingly, the time period of study encompassed

Autobiographical memories include recollections of events both mundane and important. What do you remember about the first time you met your roommate at university?

the Thanksgiving break for Brewer's participants. Memories from that mini-vacation were recalled especially well. The reason for this, Brewer argued, was that these trips were taken during the participants' first trip home from college (all the participants were first-year students). Those trips, he believed, were likely to be quite distinctive, especially in comparison with the routine events of going to class and studying that preceded and followed the vacation. Brewer concluded that the more distinct the mental representation of an event, the more likely it is to be recalled, a conclusion similar to the one Linton reached.

Flashbulb Memories

Where were you when you learned of the terrorist attack on the World Trade Center on September 11, 2001? Many of us recall information not only about the tragic disaster itself but also about where we were, whom we were with, and what we were doing at the time we first heard about it. For example, one author of this text remembers she was standing in line at Second Cup, the coffee shop on campus, trying to decide on whether to order a latte or moccaccino. She was getting ready for an important meeting, and thinking about all the things she had to do that day, when a friend saw her and asked if she'd heard the news. She immediately left the coffee line and searched everywhere for more information—turning on the radio, using her computer to surf the web, and calling family to let them know what was going on. For most of the day she talked in horrified tones to friends and co-workers, the meeting all but forgotten. That evening, she huddled with friends and family in front of the TV screen watching images of the events over and over. The day seems etched permanently in her memory.

Brown and Kulick (1977) coined the term **flashbulb memory** to describe this phenomenon. Why, though, do we remember details about our own circumstances when we first heard the news? Why can you remember how you heard about September 11, 2001 so vividly, but you cannot remember where you put your eyeglasses an hour ago? Some have argued that part of the explanation involves our physiological response when we hear such news: Parts of the brain that are involved in

The 9/11 attacks were events that easily led to the formation of flashbulb memories.

Editorial credit: Ken Tannenbaum / Shutterstock.com

emotional responses, such as the amygdala, become activated and the cognitive effects of this activation result in the storage of a great deal of information, even that which is only indirectly related to the main information (Brown & Kulik, 1977). The memory-enhancing effect of emotion has been demonstrated in a large number of laboratory studies, using stimuli ranging from words to pictures to narrated slide shows (Cahill & McGaugh, 1995; Christianson, 1992; Hamann, 2001) as well as autobiographical memory studies (Conway et al., 1994).

Neisser (1982b) offered a different explanation for the origin of flashbulb memories: People are finding a way to link themselves to history. Flashbulb memories come about because the strong emotions produced by the event prompt people to retell their own stories of where they were when they heard the news. Flashbulb memories, then, result from the retellings of stories. Over time, the memories can become distorted, in much the same way that participants in Bartlett's (1932) study distorted their retellings of the "War of the Ghosts" story: People elaborate and fill in gaps in their stories, making them approximate a standard story format. Future research will help differentiate between these accounts of flashbulb memories, or determine whether both, together, account for the enhanced memories we have for flashbulb events. In line with this, recent work has suggested that these flashbulb memories are often inaccurate (Hirst et al., 2015), and that social media has a strong influence on how a memory gets re-shaped over time (Kensingner et al., 2016).

Eyewitness Memory

Imagine yourself a juror assigned to a robbery/murder case. The defendant, a young man, is alleged to have robbed and killed a convenience store clerk at gunpoint at around 11 p.m. No physical evidence (such as fingerprints or fibre samples) links the defendant to the crime. Instead, the case hinges on the sworn testimony of a convenience store patron who insists the defendant is the man she saw on the night in question. In cross-examination, the defence attorney gets the witness to agree that the lighting was poor, the robber was wearing a stocking cap over his face, she was nervous and paying more attention to the gun than to the face of the robber, and so on. Nevertheless, the witness remains convinced that the defendant is the man she saw rob and murder the store clerk that night.

How much would the eyewitness testimony convince you of the defendant's guilt? Elizabeth Loftus, a cognitive psychologist specializing in the study of **eyewitness memory**, would argue that the testimony would have a disproportionate effect on your behaviour. She stated (Loftus, 1979) that "eyewitness testimony is likely to be believed by jurors, especially when it is offered with a high level of confidence," even when the confident witness is inaccurate. Indeed, she believed that "all the evidence points rather strikingly to the conclusion that there is almost nothing more convincing than a live human being who takes the stand, points a finger at the defendant, and says 'That's the one!'" (p. 19). Several studies Loftus reviewed, however, suggest that confidence in eyewitness testimony may be far too strong. As well, relying on memory to create composite facial images of the perpetrator is also wrought with problems (Wells & Hasel, 2007).

In one study, for example, participants viewed a series of slides depicting a (simulated) automobile accident. The automobile, a red Datsun, came to either a stop sign (for half the participants) or a yield sign (for the other half) before becoming involved in an accident with a pedestrian. The experimental manipulation came in the questioning that followed the slide show. About half the participants (half of whom had seen a stop sign; the other half, a yield sign) were asked, "Did another car pass the red Datsun while it was stopped at the stop sign?" The other half of the participants were asked, "Did another car pass the red Datsun while it was stopped at the yield sign?" After answering these and other routine questions, participants worked on an unrelated activity for 20 minutes. Then they were given a recognition test of several slides. Included in the test was a critical test pair depicting a red Datsun stopped either at a stop sign or at a yield sign. Participants were to decide which of the two slides they had originally seen. Those who received a question consistent with the slide originally seen (for example, a question about the stop sign when the slide they had previously seen con-

tained a stop sign, not a yield sign) correctly recognized the slide 75% of the time. Participants who received an inconsistent question, however, had an overall accuracy rate of 41%, a dramatic decrease given that guessing alone would have produced an overall accuracy rate of 50%. Thus our ability to recognize past scenes or events can be biased by the type of questions asked after viewing.

Other studies by Loftus (1975) have demonstrated that people's memories can be altered by presenting misleading questions. For example, some participants viewed a film and were then asked, "How fast was the white sports car going when it passed the barn while travelling along the country road?" Other participants were merely asked, "How fast was the white sports car going while travelling along the country road?" Actually, no barn was presented in the film. One week later, all participants were asked whether they had seen a barn. Fewer than 3% of the participants in the second condition reported having seen a barn, whereas 17% of the participants who had been asked the misleading question reported having seen a barn. Lane, Mather, Villa, and Morita (2001) found that experimental "witnesses" who

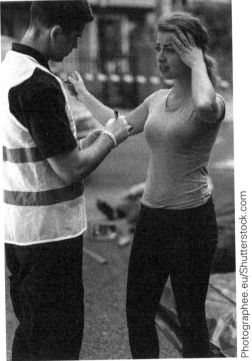

Although eyewitness testimony often has dramatic effects on jurors' decision making, research suggests it is not always accurate.

Photographee.eu/Shutterstock.com

were asked to focus on specific details of a videotaped crime were more likely to confuse what they'd actually seen with information given to them in postevent questions than were "witnesses" asked only to summarize the major aspects of the crime.

"Memory malleability" fits well with some laboratory studies of sentence recall; both support Bartlett's conception of memory as a constructive process. A classic study by Bransford and Franks (1971) illustrates this idea. They gave participants a list of sentences, all derived from four basic sentences:

"The ants were in the kitchen"

"The jelly was on the table"

"The jelly was sweet"

"The ants ate the jelly"

The sentences the participants saw included two of the preceding sentences, combinations of two of the simple sentences (for example, "The sweet jelly was on the table"), and combinations of three of the simple sentences (example, "The ants ate the sweet jelly on the table"). On a later recognition test, the participants were asked to decide, for each sentence presented, if they had seen that exact sentence before and to rate their confidence in their judgment. They were most confident in "recognizing" the sentence that combined all four of the simple sentences, "The ants in the kitchen ate the sweet jelly that was on the table," even though it had never been presented.

Bransford and Franks (1971) explained that the participants had not stored a copy of the actually presented sentences in memory Instead, they had abstracted and reorganized the information in the sentences, integrating the ideas and storing the integration. The participants later could not distinguish between the presented sentences and their own integration. One might argue this is just what Loftus's participants were doing: integrating the original memories with later questions. If the later questions were misleading, that incorrect information became integrated with the original memory to produce a distorted memory.

The Recovered/False Memory Debate

One of the biggest debates to erupt in cognitive psychology in recent years concerns issues of forgetting, retrieving, and creating false autobiographical memories. The debate has far-reaching implications well beyond the boundaries of an experimental laboratory. At stake are issues that touch, and indeed tear apart, the lives of real people. The issues concern whether victims of physical and sexual abuse can and/or do repress memories of such incidents, retrieving these so-called **recovered memories** later in therapy, or whether instead some therapists (in fact, a small minority), misinformed about the workings of memory, inadvertently prompt their clients to create **false memories** of things that never really happened.

Note that the topics of eyewitness testimony and false versus recovered memory share many similarities: Both essentially involve the alleged witnessing of an event, sometimes traumatic, often followed later by newer, distorting information. But differences between the topics should also be kept in mind. In the case of eyewitness testimony, the issue is typically focused on recall for information acquired within the past days, weeks, or months. In the case of false or recovered memories, the issue is whether one can recall information from several years to several decades earlier.

Elizabeth Loftus is again an active participant in the debate over whether such "recalls" represent recovered or false memories. Loftus examined various questions—among them, how authentic recovered memories are. The idea that memories of traumatic events can be repressed—buried in the unconscious mind for long periods of time, even forever—is a tenet of psychoanalytic forms of therapy dating back to Freud. But from a cognitive psychology perspective, the question is whether such **repressed memories** can be carefully described, documented, and explained.

Loftus and Ketchan (1994) and Lindsay and Read (1994) pointed to advice given in different self-help books, one of the best known being *The Courage to Heal* (Bass & Davis, 1988). That book encourages readers who are wondering whether they have ever been victims of childhood sexual abuse to look for the presence of various symptoms, such as having low self-esteem, depression, self-destructive or suicidal thoughts, or sexual dysfunction. The problem, Lindsay and Read (1994) noted, is that these symptoms can also occur for people who have *not* been victims of abuse; the symptoms are just not specific enough to be diagnostic. In *The Courage to Heal*, Bass and Davis (1988) make a further, very strong claim: "If you are unable to remember any specific instances [of abuse] like the ones mentioned above but still have a feeling that something abusive happened to you, it probably did" (p. 21) and "If you think you were abused and your life shows the symptoms, then you were" (p. 22). The book goes on to recommend that readers who are wondering about their past spend time exploring the possibility that they were abused. It offers techniques for recalling specific memories, such as using old family photographs and giving the imagination free rein, or using a recalled childhood event as a beginning point and then deliberately trying to remember abuse connected with that event.

We have seen earlier that there is plenty of room to doubt the absolute accuracy of people's autobiographical memories, even when people seem very sure of them. Research on eyewitness memory has shown how receptive people can be to post-event suggestions (Newman et al., 2014). But is it possible for false "memories"—of events that never happened—to be somehow implanted? Loftus and Pickrell (1995; see also Loftus & Ketcham, 1994, and Loftus, 2000) reported on a study that suggests just such a possibility.

Twenty-four people took part in the study. Experimenters first interviewed relatives of the participants (who, to be included in the study had to be familiar with the participant's early childhood) and from the interviews generated three true events that had happened to the research participant when the latter was ages 4 to 6. Relatives were instructed that these events were not to be "family folklore" or to be so traumatic that they would be effortlessly recalled. Relatives also provided details about shopping malls and favourite treats of the research participant when he or she was a 5-year-old. From the interviews with relatives, experimenters then created false accounts of an event that had never actually happened, in which the target participant had allegedly become lost in a shopping mall at age 5. Included in the accounts were details about the name of the mall that had been the closest one to the participant then, as well as names of family members who plausibly might have accompanied the target participant on the alleged trip. Here is an example of a "false memory" created for a 20-year-old Vietnamese American woman:

> *You, your mom, Tien, and Tuan all went to the Bremerton K-Mart. You must have been 5 years old at the time. Your mom gave each of you some money to get a blueberry Icee. You ran ahead to get into the line first, and somehow lost your way in the store. Tien found you crying to an elderly Chinese woman. You three then went together to get an Icee. (Loftus & Pickrell, 1995, p. 721)*

Participants were given booklets containing instructions, and four stories. Three of the stories recounted actual events, and the fourth story recounted the false event. Each event was described in about a paragraph, with room left for the participant to describe his or her own recall of the event. One to two weeks later, the participants were individually interviewed about their recollections (again being asked to recall as much as they could about the four "events"); the participants were re-interviewed about two weeks later.

As a group, research participants recalled 68% of the true events. However, when completing the booklets, 29% of the participants (7 out of the 24) "recalled" the false event of being lost in a shopping mall. One of the seven later said she did not recall the false memory at the first interview, but the rest (6, or 25%) maintained at least partial recall of the false event through both interviews. Participants' length of recall (measured in number of words they used to describe events) was higher for the true than for the false memories, and they rated the clarity of their memories as lower for the false than for the true memories, but endorsed it as true nonetheless.

Loftus and Pickrell (1995) interpreted the results as proof that false memories *can* be formed through suggestive questioning, and they offered a speculative account of the mechanism(s) responsible.

> *The development of the false memory of being lost may evolve first as the mere suggestion of being lost leaves a memory trace in the brain. Even if the information is originally tagged as*

a suggestion rather than a historic fact, that suggestion can become linked to other knowledge about being lost (stories of others), as time passes and the tag that indicates that being lost in the mall was merely a suggestion slowly deteriorates. The memory of a real event, visiting a mall, becomes confounded with the suggestion that you were once lost in a mall. Finally, when asked whether you were ever lost in a mall, your brain activates images of malls and those of being lost. The resulting memory can even be embellished with snippets from actual events, such as people once seen in a mall. Now you "remember" being lost in a mall as a child. By this mechanism, the memory errors occur because grains of experienced events or imagined events are integrated with inferences and other elaborations that go beyond direct experience. (p. 724)

Other researchers have also been able to induce "recollections" of events that never happened. Hyman, Husband, and Billings (1995), for instance, were able to induce about 25% of their undergraduate participants to falsely "recall" different childhood events: being hospitalized for an ear infection; having a fifth birthday party with pizza and a clown; spilling punch at a wedding reception; being in the grocery store when sprinklers went off; and being left in a parked car, releasing the parking brake, and having the car roll into something. Garry and Wade (2005) induced false memories with both narratives and (doctored) photographs, finding that the narratives were more effective in inducing false memories.

Not all cognitive psychologists have received the research just described on false memories with complete enthusiasm, however. Pezdek (1994), for example, has argued that just because an explanation exists for how false memories *could* be formed does not mean that false memories, especially for ones as traumatic as childhood abuse, actually *are* formed in this way. By analogy, Pezdek noted that an aeronautical engineering explanation exists for why it is impossible for bumblebees to fly (even though they obviously do). Pezdek cautioned against assuming that "memory recovery therapy" is very widespread and argued that the existing evidence for therapist-implanted memories is quite weak.

Obviously, much more work needs to be done on the issue of whether, how, and when false information can be made a part of one's memory. Loftus and Pickrell's (1995) and Hyman et al.'s (1995) work is suggestive and provocative, but the question of to what degree they can be generalized remains open. A recent fMRI study (Cabeza, Rao, Wagner, Mayer, & Schacter, 2001) showed that different areas of the brain become activated in a word recognition task for "true" than for "false" words (ones that were not presented but are semantically related to the "true" words that were), suggesting that true memories have a neural signature that false or "implanted" memories do not (see Figure 6-2). Extending these findings, from lab-based word recognition tasks to real-world narrative memory, however, may not be straightforward.

It is becoming clearer to cognitive psychologists that autobiographical memories do not function the way video cameras do, faithfully recording details and preserving them for

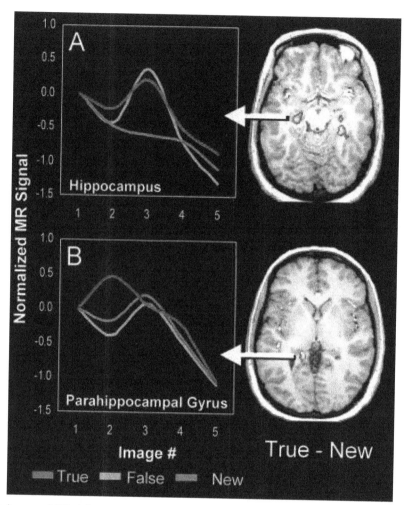

Figure 6-2 In panel (A), bilateral hippocampal regions were more activated for True and False than for New items, with no difference between True and False. In panel (B), a left posterior parahippocampal region was more activated for True than for False and New items, indicating some parts of the brain can differentiate between items that were truly presented and those that were not.

long-term storage and later review. Instead, human memories are malleable and open to "shaping" by later questioning or information. Just how often such shaping occurs, and by what mechanisms, remain open and exciting questions with important real-world implications and consequences.

AMNESIA

In the preceding sections, we discussed how memories are formed, retrieved, forgotten, or created in LTM. Here, we will take a more detailed look at cases in which people suffer profound impairments in their LTM—people suffering from memory disorders collectively known as **amnesia**. We will discuss the classic case of H.M., a patient who underwent surgery in 1953 that removed many brain structures in the medial temporal lobe region of the brain bilaterally (on both sides), including most of the **hippocampus**, the **amygdala**, and some adjacent areas. As a result, H.M. has suffered since that date from profound amnesia, both for any events after the surgery (anterograde amnesia) and for events that happened within a span of several years before the surgery (retrograde amnesia). H.M. is not the only person to suffer from amnesia, of course, and over the years neurologists and psychologists have amassed a great number of clinical cases from which to draw generalizations and principles. Amnesia can result from damage either to the hippocampal system (which includes the hippocampus and amygdala) or to the closely related midline diencephalic region. This damage can arise from oxygen deprivation, blockage of certain arteries through a stroke, the herpes simplex encephalitis virus, a closed head injury such as those typically suffered in automobile accidents, Alzheimer's disease, Korsakoff's syndrome (a disease of chronic alcoholism), certain tumours, or, in the short term, bilateral electroconvulsive shock treatments, or ECT (Cohen, 1997).

Box 6-3 Canadian Research Highlight

Dr. Brenda Milner is the Dorothy J. Killam Professor of Psychology at the Montreal Neurological Institute and Department of Neurology & Neurosurgery at McGill University (https://www.mcgill.ca/neuro/research/researchers/milner). Dr. Milner is a pioneer in the field of neuropsychology and in the study of memory and other cognitive functions in humans. She was the first to study the effects of damage to the medial temporal lobe on memory; she systematically described the deficits, and preserved abilities, in one of the most famous patients in cognitive neuroscience, H.M. In 1984, she was made an Officer of the Order of Canada and was promoted to Companion in 2004. Among her many awards, Dr. Milner was also given the prestigious Neuroscience Award from the United States National Academy of Science.

The severity of the amnesia varies from case to case, with H.M. exhibiting some of the most severe memory impairments. Some patients recover some memories over time; for example, those undergoing bilateral electroconvulsive therapy (ECT; a treatment used today for severe forms of depression) recover completely within a few months, and people who suffer a closed head injury likewise often recover some or all of their memories. Some amnesias, such as those brought on by accidents or strokes, have very sudden onsets; others, typically those originating through brain tumours or disease, appear more gradually (Cohen, 1997).

One famous case of amnesia resulting from an accident clearly illustrates that memory loss can be severe for certain types of memories, while leaving other cognitive functions and general intelligence intact. Rosenbaum, a memory researcher at York University in Toronto, and her colleagues (2001) described Kent Cochrane (known in the field as patient K.C.), a man with 16 years of formal education, born in 1951 and raised within a supportive family of two parents and four younger siblings in a suburb of Toronto. In 1981, K.C.'s life took a dramatic turn. He suffered a devastating head injury leaving him densely amnesic, when he rode his motorcycle off an exit ramp on the stretch of highway nearby his home. High-resolution MRI scans of his brain revealed widespread damage, with almost complete hippocampal loss bilaterally. As in H.M., the damage to his temporal lobes left him with anterograde and retrograde amnesia on explicit tests of episodic and autobiographical memory. What is especially notable is his extensive retrograde amnesia. All details of events he experienced before his head injury, even if particularly meaningful, such as a wedding or a death, no longer existed in his mind. This was especially striking given that he maintained many other cognitive capacities, such as perception, language, and reasoning skills. Unlike other amnesic patients (patient HM, for example), Cochrane had his semantic memory intact, but lacked episodic memory with respect to his entire past.

Rosenbaum's group went on to describe a few examples of K.C.'s behaviour (in 2005 and 2009) that illustrate how profound his amnesia was. Growing up, K.C. was inseparable from his younger brother; sadly, this brother had a tragic accident of his own, and died. Rosenbaum goes on to describe that "K.C. remembers nothing of the circumstances in which he had learned of this shocking news, including where he was at the time, who told him of the event, and how he reacted emotionally" (p. 994, 2005), which any non-head-injured person would have branded in memory. K.C. did have some memory for major events, but these tended to lack personal meaning for him. For example, his memory for events surrounding a chemical spill from a train derailment near his home that forced him and his family to evacuate their house for over a week was recalled only as a dry fact of the world; the memory holds no personal meaning, nor does it conjure up his feelings experienced during that time. Similarly, K.C. had no memory for the events surrounding a recent fall at his family's cottage that resulted in several operations to repair his shattered knee (a cast from waist to toe!), which led to him being confined to the main floor living room of his home, with crutches, for over six months. In line with these examples, K.C. had no memory for the events of September 11, and expressed the same horror and disbelief as someone hearing of the news for the very first time.

The deficits in K.C.'s episodic memory are in striking contrast to other forms of memory, which appear largely intact. For example, K.C. has retained many skills and semantic facts learned prior to his accident, and these allow him to locate without difficulty his morning cereal and spoon in the kitchen. This semantic knowledge retention also applies to recreations games. As Rosenbaum and her colleagues (2005) describe, he knows that the eight-ball is the last to sink in a game of pool, and he can explain the difference between a strike and spare in bowling, and between the front crawl and the breast stroke. When playing Bridge he expects a new "trick" after four cards are placed in the centre of the table, and when watching TV he anticipates Bob Barker on *The Price Is Right* asking contestants to "spin the wheel." Spatially, he has retained knowledge of the layout of his house and summer cottage, and the shortest route between them. Interestingly, as in others with amnesia, K.C. has shown that he is able to learn new information or skills. After his accident, K.C. got a job sorting books according to the Dewey decimal system. He carried out this work correctly and efficiently, even though he was unable to recall who taught him the system, or how he came to acquire such a skill.

As can be gleaned from the above description of K.C, his memory has qualities of both retrograde and anterograde amnesia. To better understand these different forms of amnesia in terms of the way each affects functions, we will now consider these in more detail.

Box 6-4 A day in the life of patient K.C.

Patient K.C. passed away in 2014. The following is a description of a typical day in K.C.'s life, noted in a 2005 publication by Rosenbaum and her colleagues. ". . . details of personal occurrences continue to exist only in the present, vanishing from K.C.'s reality the moment his thoughts are directed elsewhere. He remains single and without children, and continues to live with his parents in the house in which they had lived since he was 9 years old. On most days, his mother wakes him between 7:30 h and 8:00 h in the morning for breakfast. After finishing his meal, a note on the microwave door tells him to return upstairs for his daily exercise routine on a treadmill and stationary bicycle. He then dresses and grooms himself in preparation for one of his scheduled half-day excursions, which alternate between volunteering at a local library and participating in such activities as playing pool, swimming, and bowling with a small group of other head-injured people whom he again sees on Friday nights for dinner and a movie. Weekends in the summer and autumn are spent at the family cottage, as they were before his injury, and in the winter and spring at home visiting with family and friends. When nothing specific is planned, K.C. will sit down to play the organ, but he most enjoys playing card games on the computer (particularly Bridge and Solitaire) with the television on in the background (his favourite shows include "Mash" reruns and "The Price is Right"). He then eats dinner with his family, watches television, and retires on his own at 11:00 p.m." (p. 994)

SOURCE: From Rosenbaum et al., 2005.

Anterograde Amnesia

Cohen (1997) noted that the **anterograde** form of amnesia, a memory deficit extending forward in time from the initial point of memory loss, has five principal features. The first is that <u>anterograde amnesia affects LTM but not working memory</u>. We discussed this idea in Chapter 5 in our look at the H.M. case study. Cohen related an illustrative anecdote about a conversation he had with H.M.

> *One day during a lengthy car drive to MIT's Clinical Research Center to be tested, H.M. proceeded to tell me about some guns that were in his house (actually, he had them only in his youth). He told me that he had two rifles, one with a scope and certain characteristics, and the other with just an open sight.*

> *He said that he had magazines from the National Rifle Association (actually, just a memory of his earlier family life), all about rifles. But, he went on, not only did he have rifles, he also had some handguns. He had a .22, a .32, and a .44. He occasionally took them out to clean them, he said, and had taken them with him on occasion to a shooting range. But, he went on, not only did he have some handguns, he also had rifles. He had two rifles, one with a scope and the other with an open sight. He had magazines from the National Rifle Association, all about rifles, he said. But, not only did he have rifles, he also had handguns. . . . On and on this went, cycling back and forth between a description of the rifles and a description of the handguns, until finally I derailed the conversation by diverting his attention. (p. 323)*

Cohen argued that H.M.'s memory of his handguns and of his rifles were both intact because they derived from his very remote past, several years before his surgery. These items were related in his LTM, thus his discussion of one piece of knowledge called to mind features and details of the other. Once the details of one piece were retrieved from LTM, these filled up his working-memory capacity. When H.M. finished talking about one, however, he forgot that he had just finished talking about the other.

The second feature is that anterograde amnesia <u>affects memory regardless of the modality</u>—that is, regardless of whether the information is visual, auditory, kinesthetic, olfactory, gustatory, or tactile. Cohen (1997) noted that global anterograde amnesia results from bilateral damage to the medial temporal lobe or midline diencephalic structures; unilateral (one-sided) damage to these areas typically impairs only one kind of memory—for example, either verbal or spatial. Moreover, whether the mode of testing memory is free recall, cued recall, or recognition, the memory of someone with anterograde amnesia is similarly hampered.

Third, according to Cohen (1997) and as illustrated in the story about H.M. and the guns, anterograde amnesia <u>spares memory for general knowledge</u> (acquired well before the onset of amnesia) but generally impairs recall for new facts and events. H.M. can not report any personal event that had occurred after his surgery, and he performed very poorly on tasks in which he was asked to recall lists of words for any length of time beyond a few minutes.

H.M. also had difficulty retaining newly learned pairings of information, such as learning new vocabulary (*Jacuzzi, granola,* and other words that came into usage after 1953, the year of his surgery).

A fourth principal feature of anterograde amnesia is that it <u>spares skilled performance</u>. For example, it has been reported that some amnesics who were musicians previous to their disorder retain the ability to play and even to conduct a complex piece of music! Other studies have shown that amnesic patients can be taught to perform a skill, as in the case of K.C. learning the Dewey decimal system.

The fifth principal feature of anterograde amnesia is that even when amnesic patients do learn a skill, <u>they show</u> *hyperspecific* <u>memory</u>: They can express this learning only in a context extremely similar to the conditions of encoding. In a sense, this seems to be a version of the encoding specificity principle, described in the previous chapter, carried to the extreme.

Retrograde Amnesia

Loss of memory for information acquired and stored before the onset of amnesia is known as **retrograde amnesia**. Although such loss has some similarities with anterograde amnesia, important differences appear as well. Interestingly, all amnesic patients seem to show at least some retrograde amnesia, most notably for the minutes and hours just preceding a head injury; they may or may not exhibit anterograde amnesia. Cohen (1997) described four basic features of retrograde amnesia.

The first is that the <u>temporal extent</u>—the time span for which memory is lost—can vary enormously in retrograde amnesia. Patients suffering from Korsakoff's, Alzheimer's, Parkinson's, or Huntington's disease are likely to exhibit temporally extensive amnesia, with loss of memory acquired and stored for several decades. Other patients, such as those who have suffered a closed head injury or have undergone bilateral ECT, a procedure whereby an electric current is passed through the brain as a method of treating depression, show temporally limited retrograde amnesia, losing information for a span of only months or perhaps weeks. In many cases, over time the patient either fully (in the case of ECT) or partially recovers the lost memories. Damage to the hippocampal region can also cause retrograde amnesia. H.M.'s retrograde amnesia was found to cover a span of 11 years, less than for some other cases reported in the literature, such as K.C.

A second feature of retrograde amnesia is observable when scientists examine which particular memories are lost—<u>it is the episodic ones that are compromised</u>. Patients undergoing ECT treatments were asked to recall information about television shows that had aired for a single season only (that way, the experimenters knew precisely when the memories were formed; this study was conducted well before the proliferation of cable channels!). Before the ECT treatments, the patients were best at recalling facts from very recently aired shows, as you would be. After the ECT treatments, however, these same patients' data showed a temporal gradient, with the most recent memories being the most likely to be lost.

In the case of ECT patients, we would expect full recovery, in time, of the lost memories. With patients suffering from a closed head injury, the story is a little different. There, the temporal extent of the retrograde amnesia often shrinks slowly over time, with the most remote memories being the most likely to return. For example, initially the retrograde amnesia might span several years before the head trauma occurred; after a year in recovery, the total span of retrograde amnesia might be the two weeks immediately preceding the trauma.

Cohen (1997) described a third feature of retrograde amnesia: It typically spares information that was "overlearned" before the onset.

> *Despite their extensive retrograde amnesias, patients with amnesia associated with Korsakoff's disease, anoxia, or encephalitis have intact knowledge about the world; preserved language, perceptual, and social skills; and spared general intelligence. Only the extensive retrograde amnesias associated with progressive dementias, as in Alzheimer or Huntington disease, impair this kind of information, and then only later in the progression of the disease. (p. 339)*

Finally, as with anterograde amnesia, retrograde amnesia seems not to affect skill learning. Even when patients cannot remember ever having practised the skill, their performance still seems to show normal rates of improvement (Cohen, 1997).

Many neuropsychologists believe the study of amnesia supports some specific ideas about the organization of memory in general. That amnesia can disrupt long-term memory without any impairment in working memory provides some support for considering these as two distinct types of memory. That retrograde amnesia covers a defined time span and shows a temporal gradient implies that even after being formed, new memories continue to undergo neurological change for some period of time, perhaps years. That some kinds of information (personal memories, memories for events or random tidbits of information) are lost in amnesia and others are not (such as overlearned and well-practised information and skills) suggests multiple memory systems exist. Finally, there is a strong suggestion that the structure in the brain known as the hippocampus plays a very important role in both learning and retrieving information.

Studies of amnesic patients also tell us something about **memory consolidation**, a process originally proposed a century ago. According to the "standard model," storage of information initially requires the hippocampus to link different aspects (sights, smells, sounds) of an event and to retrieve these at a later time; blows to the head disrupt this process, causing newly learned information to be lost. According to the standard model, over time the need for the hippocampus to retrieve information lessens, accounting for the temporal gradient in retrograde amnesia (Squire et al., 1984). Recent evidence, however, calls this standard model into question. The "multiple memory trace" (MMT) theory (Nadel & Moscovitch, 1997) suggests that the hippocampus is always involved in storage and retrieval of episodic information, but that following multiple re-activations of the same event factual information from episodes is extracted and integrated with semantic memory stores. By this account, very remote memories that appear to be spared in patients with retrograde amnesia represent "semanticized" memories of the past, somewhat akin to "family lore" rather than personal autobiographical memoirs of the past. Neuroimaging studies support the idea that retrieval of very remote (25-year-old) memories elicits just as much activation in the hippocampus as retrieval of quite recent memories (Ryan et al., 2000). Other researchers (McGaugh, 2000) suggest an important role for other structures—such as the amygdala, involved in processing of emotion—in the memory consolidation process. Clearly there is much to learn about the organization of memory from studies of neurological patients. New ways of thinking about how memories are created, established in the brain, and subsequently remembered can be found throughout modern cognitive neuroscience (see Nadel et al., for an example). This, together with neuroimaging tools to visualize the brain, contribute to the growing field of cognitive neuroscience, which brings biology and cognitive psychology closer together.

SEMANTIC MEMORY

Throughout this chapter, we've been focusing on memory for specific events, such as hearing a particular word list in the lab, or witnessing a crime, in the real world. In addition to these episodes, throughout your life you have acquired a vast amount of general knowledge about the world: you know that the capital of Canada is Ottawa, and that the term "Maritimes" refers to the Atlantic provinces; you know how to multiply numbers, and how to divide; you also know that dogs bark and cats meow, though you won't likely recall how you came to learn such facts and general information about the world. In this next section, we will take a more detailed look at this kind of permanent memory for knowledge and information. Our vast knowledge of language and concepts also appears to have associated with it a great deal of implicit knowledge. For instance, if I asked you, "Does a Bernese mountain dog have a liver?" you would very likely answer yes (correctly). Your answer comes (we assume) not from your extensive study of Bernese mountain dogs but from your knowledge that Bernese mountain dogs are dogs, dogs are mammals, mammals have livers. In this section, we will consider models of how knowledge is represented in semantic memory such that we can make these inferences quickly and efficiently.

The Hierarchical Semantic Network Model

Because our world and language knowledge is so great, the storage space requirements to represent it are large. One way of organizing this information is to use a library analogy. This metaphor grows out of an information-processing paradigm, which sees memory as consisting of one or more distinct storage areas. If a library (storage area) contains only a handful of books, it makes little difference how they are arranged or stored; it would be an easy matter for a patron looking for a particular book simply to browse through the entire collection. As the number of books grows, however, the need for some sort of organizational system becomes pressing. One might say knowledge bases are comparable to a large library; therefore, understanding their organization is crucial for understanding how we retrieve and use information. There are several distinct ways of arranging and storing information, and each has different implications for ease of access and retrieval. Think about how books can be arranged on your bookshelf. You may have a section for textbooks, a section for nonfiction, a section for mysteries, and a section for trashy romances. Or you may have all the books arranged alphabetically by author. Or you may have tall books on one shelf, paperbacks on another. Each possibility represents a different way of organizing.

Each possibility also has different implications for how you would retrieve, or look for, a particular book and how easy it is to find. Suppose you want to find *Gone With the Wind*, but you've forgotten the author's name. If you've arranged your books alphabetically by author, you'll have a much more difficult time than if you've arranged them by title or by category. A variety of models have been proposed for how our knowledge is mentally represented and organized. Each makes different predictions about how we search for particular pieces of information, given our huge general knowledge base.

One way to conserve memory (knowledge) space would be to try to avoid storing redundant information wherever possible. Therefore, rather than storing the information "has live young" with the mental representation for a Bernese mountain dog and again with the mental representations for human, lion, tiger, and bear, it makes more sense to store it once, at the higher-level representation for mammal. This illustrates the principle of **cognitive economy**: Properties and facts are stored at the highest level possible. To recover information you use inference, much as you did to answer the earlier question about Bernese mountain dogs having livers.

A landmark study on semantic memory organization was performed by Collins and Quillian (1969). They tested the idea that semantic memory is analogous to a network of connected ideas. Each node is connected to related nodes by means of *pointers*, or links that go from one node to another. Thus the node that corresponds to a given word or concept, together with the pointers to other nodes to which the first node is connected, constitutes the semantic memory for that word or concept. The collection of nodes associated with all the words and concepts one knows about is called a **semantic network**. Figure 6-3 depicts a portion of such a network for a person who knows a good deal about Bernese mountain dogs.

Collins and Quillian (1969) also tested the principle of cognitive economy just described. They reasoned that if semantic memory is analogous to a network of nodes and pointers, and if semantic memory honours the cognitive economy principle, then the closer a fact or property is stored to a particular node the less time it should take to verify the fact and property. Collins and Quillian's reasoning led to the following prediction: If a person's knowledge of Bernese mountain dogs is organized along the lines of Figure 6-3, he or she should be able to verify the sentence "A Bernese mountain dog has an exuberant disposition" more quickly

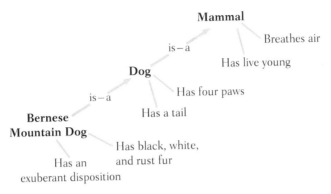

Figure 6-3 Partial semantic network representation for Bernese mountain dog.

than to verify "A Bernese mountain dog has live young." Note that the property "has an exuberant disposition" is stored right with the node for Bernese mountain dog, indicating that this property is specific to this kind of animal. The property "has live young" is not specific to Bernese mountain dogs, so it is stored a number of levels higher in the hierarchy.

In their study (see Figure 6-4), Collins and Quillian (1969) presented people with a number of similar sentences, finding, as predicted, that it took people less time to respond to sentences whose representations should span two levels (for example, "A canary is a bird") than they did to sentences whose representations should span three (for example, "A canary is an animal").

The model was called a *hierarchical semantic network model of semantic memory*, because researchers thought the nodes were organized in hierarchies.

Meyer and Schvaneveldt (1971) performed a series of experiments that elaborated the semantic network proposal. They reasoned that if related words are stored close by one another and are connected to one another in a semantic network, then whenever one node is activated or energized energy spreads to the related nodes, as in Figure 6-5. They demonstrated this relationship in a series of experiments based on **lexical decision tasks**. In this kind of experiment, participants see a series of letter strings and are asked to decide, as quickly as possible, if the letter strings form real words. Thus they respond yes to strings such as *bread* and no to strings such as *rencle*.

Meyer and Schvaneveldt (1971) discovered an interesting phenomenon. In their study, participants saw two words at a time, one above the other, and had to decide whether both strings were words or not. If one of the

Actual Bernese mountain dog.

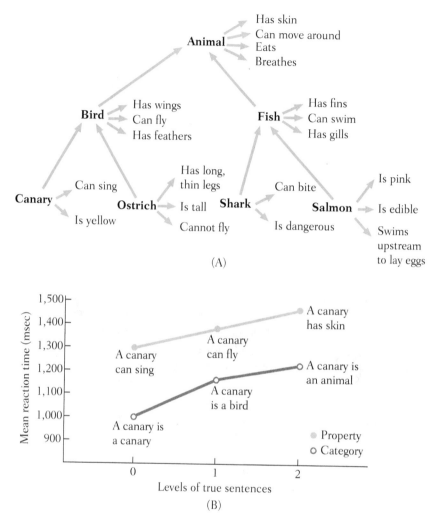

Figure 6-4 Illustration of the Collins and Quillian (1969) experiment. Panel (A) shows the hypothesized underlying semantic network, and panel (B) shows reaction times to verify sentences about information in the semantic network.

Reprinted from Journal of Verbal Learning and Verbal Behavior, Vol. 8, issue 2, Allan M. Collins and M. Ross Quillian, Retrieval Time from Semantic Memory, pp. 240-247, Copyright © 1969, with permission from Elsevier.

strings was a real word (such as *bread)*, participants were faster to respond if the other string was a semantically associated word (such as *butter)* than if it was an unrelated word (such as *chair)* or a nonword (such as *rencle)*. One interpretation of this finding invokes the concept of **spreading activation**, the idea that excitation spreads along the connections of nodes in a

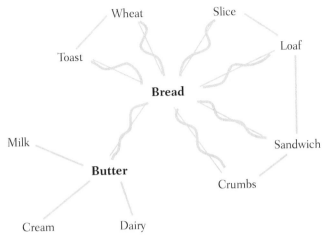

Figure 6-5 Depiction of spreading activation. Once the node for "bread" is excited, the activation travels to related nodes.

semantic network. Presumably, when the person read the word *bread*, he activated the corresponding node in semantic memory. This activity primed, or changed the activation level, of the nodes corresponding to words related to *bread*. Thus, when processing of the word *butter* began, the node corresponding to it was already excited, and processing was consequently faster. This priming effect, originally discovered by Meyer and Schvaneveldt, has been widely replicated in the years since (see Neely, 1990), and is a very important idea in understanding connectionist networks.

Connectionist Models

Earlier in the chapter we referred to the library metaphor, acting as though each piece of information stored in long-term memory existed as a particular item, stored in a particular location, much like a book in a library. This metaphor is a useful one within the information-processing framework, which assumes the existence of one or more distinct "stores" of memory.

Connectionist models make very different assumptions, and thus do not incorporate the library metaphor as easily. Let's look at a concrete example, comparing network and connectionist models of semantic memory. Figure 6-6(A) presents a semantic network model of various concepts and should look rather familiar. Figure 6-6(B) presents a connectionist model of these same concepts. The concept *robin*, depicted in Figure 6-6(A) as a particular node with several related links to other nodes, is depicted in Figure 6-6(B) as a specific set of units being activated. A unit might correspond to an ability possessed by certain living creatures (e.g., fly) or to certain aspects such as colour. Darkened units are activated units, and a

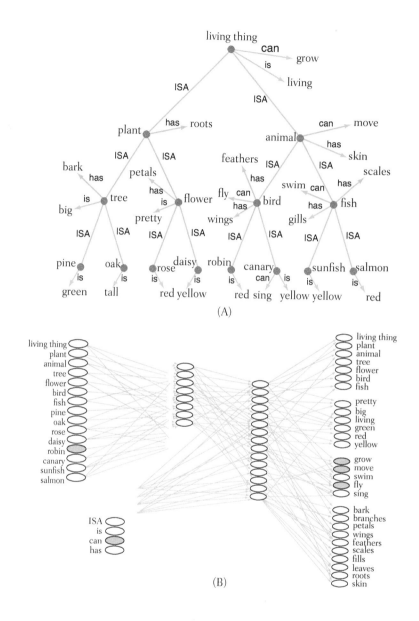

Figure 6-6 (A) A network description of "robin." (B) A connectionist network showing an alternative depiction of the same information as in part (A).

Source: Meyer, D.E., and Sylvan Kornblum, S. (Eds.), *Attention and Performance XIV: Synergies in Experimental Psychology, Artificial Intelligence, and Cognitive Neuroscience,* figure 1.8. From Massachusetts Institute of Psychology, The MIT Press.

connectionist network learns, over trials, that when the unit for "robin" becomes active, then other units should become active as well (for example, "can" and "grow," "move," and "fly" but not "swim").

How does this learning occur? Essentially, a connectionist network must be taught to develop patterns of activation through many trials with training examples. The procedure used, called "back propagation," is actually quite complicated, but we will offer a very simplified version here.

Initially, the connections between units (depicted in Figure 6-6(B) as the lines between the units) have weights that are all set at random and neutral values (such as 0.5, if the minimum and maximum values are 0 and 1). Activation weights result in the units they connect becoming active (or not). Training occurs by presenting a specific example (input pattern) to the network, which then generates a particular output. So, for example, at the beginning of training the example "robin" might be activated, and the units for "can" and "pretty" and "fly" and "branches" might then become activated. This output is compared to target (correct) output, such as "can," "grow," "move," and "fly" all being activated, and no others. The network connections are then adjusted in this direction (they take on values closer to 1), all other connections are incrementally decreased (they take on values closer to 0), and the training process repeats, with new examples.

Other models exist for how knowledge is represented in semantic memory, but like network and connectionist models they all must account for our amazing ability as humans to make inferences, interpret information, and compare it to our existing knowledge store quickly and efficiently.

IMPLICIT VERSUS EXPLICIT MEMORY

We have already seen that psychologists make a distinction between at least two types of memory: episodic and semantic. Some psychologists also distinguish between declarative and procedural memories. Many argue these kinds of memory form different systems; that is, they operate on different principles, store different kinds of information, and so on. Others disagree, declaring there is no compelling reason to believe that more than one *type* of memory exists.

Another distinction between kinds of memory has also been proposed: implicit and explicit (Roediger, 1990; Schacter, 1987). **Explicit memories** are things that are consciously recollected. For example, in recalling your last vacation you explicitly refer to a specific time (say, last summer) and a specific event or series of events. Your recall is something you are aware of and may even be something deliberate. **Implicit memory**, by contrast, is memory that is not deliberate or conscious but shows evidence of prior learning and storage. Schacter (1996) poetically described implicit memory as "a subterranean world of nonconscious memory and perception, normally concealed from the conscious mind" (pp. 164–165).

Priming

Laboratory work on implicit memory has been mainly concerned with a phenomenon known as *repetition priming*. This is different from the phenomenon of **semantic priming**, in which exposure to one word (for example, *nurse*) facilitates the recognition or other cognitive processing of a semantically related word (for example, *doctor*). **Repetition priming** is priming of a somewhat different sort: facilitation of the cognitive processing of information after a recent exposure to that same information (Schacter, 1987, p. 506). For example, participants might be given a very brief exposure (of 30 milliseconds or less) to a word (such as *button*) and soon afterward be given a new word completion task (for example, "Fill in the blanks to create the English word that comes to mind: _U _T 0_"). This task is called a *word stem completion* task. The repetition priming effect is demonstrated by an increased probability of responding "button" to the stimulus given in the word completion task, relative to the performance of participants not shown the word *button*. (Note that there are other possible ways to complete the word, such as *mutton* or *suitor*.)

Research on repetition priming has yielded several findings relevant to the topic of how we represent information. The first is that nonwords typically show no or little repetition priming relative to real words. Thus, exposing a participant to a stimulus such as *daxton* will probably not prime the participant to recognize or remember it later. Presumably, this is because *daxton* is not a word and therefore has no associated node in semantic memory that can be activated. A second finding is that priming is greater for words that share the same morphology, or roots of meaning, than for words that are visually or aurally similar. Thus a stimulus such as *sees* can prime responses to *seen* (a word that shares meaning with *sees*) but not to *seed* (a visually similar stimulus) or *seize* (a similar-sounding stimulus).

Do laboratory demonstrations of implicit memory have any real-world relevance? Investigators who study implicit memory believe so. One real-world example of implicit memory was reported by Sergei Korsakoff, who in 1889 described patients with amnesic symptoms that have come to be known as *Korsakoff's syndrome*. One patient to whom he had administered an electric shock professed not to remember the shock but, on seeing the case containing the shock generator, told Korsakoff that he feared Korsakoff had probably come to electrocute him (Schacter, 1987, pp. 503–504).

Other work with amnesic patients demonstrated findings to support the idea of a dissociation between implicit and explicit memory. For example, Warrington and Weiskrantz (1970) conducted a more controlled investigation: They presented a variety of memory tasks to four amnesic patients, as well as to eight patients without brain damage who served as a control group. In one experiment (Experiment 2), participants received two "explicit memory" tasks: a free-recall task and a recognition task.

Participants also worked on two "implicit memory" tasks. One was a word completion task, similar to the one just described. The other presented participants with words in which the letters were visually degraded; they were asked to guess the word being displayed. All four tasks involved a prior presentation of various words. In the two "explicit" tasks, participants were asked to recall consciously or recognize the words previously presented. In the two "implicit" tasks, participants were *not* reminded of the prior presentation of words but merely asked to guess the word being presented (that is, in degraded letters or partially, by a word stem).

Figure 6-7 presents the results. It shows quite clearly that amnesic participants performed more poorly than non-amnesic participants on the explicit memory tasks but quite comparably to non-amnesic participants on the implicit memory tasks. In other words, their amnesia seemed to selectively hurt performance on explicit memory tasks. These results have been replicated several times and on a variety of tasks (Shimura, 1986).

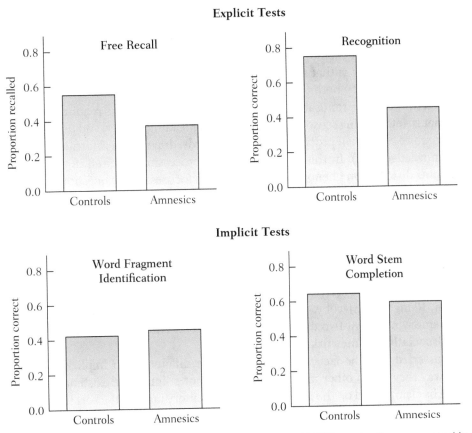

Figure 6-7 Results from the Warrington and Weiskrantz (1970) study; figure created by Roediger (1990).

Source: Reprinted with permission of Springer Nature, Nature, from "Amnesic Syndrome: Consolidation or Retrieval?," Elizabeth K. Warrington, L. Weiskrantz, 228, 5272 (1970); permission conveyed through Copyright Clearance Center, Inc.

Phenomena such as the one depicted in Figure 6-7 are sometimes called "dissociative," because performance on one task appears independent of (or dissociated from) performance on another. Dissociative phenomena do not by any means occur only with amnesic participants. Many studies (reviewed by Roediger, 1990) have demonstrated striking differences in performance on implicit and explicit memory tasks with normal participants. Schacter (1996) reported that repetition priming effects could persist as long as an entire week, even when his experimental participants denied that the primed words had been previously seen in the laboratory!

How are such dissociation phenomena best explained? Roediger (1990) presented two distinct possibilities. One is to postulate two memory *systems*, such as declarative and procedural memory, and to assert that explicit memory tasks rely on the former and implicit memory tasks rely on the latter. Schacter (1996) even speculated that different brain structures are associated with the two different memory systems. The dissociation in performance on the two tasks would then be assumed to reflect that two memory systems operating in different ways are at work.

The second possibility is that the two kinds of memory tasks require different cognitive procedures, although they both tap into a common memory system (Roediger, 1990). One idea consistent with this proposal is that most implicit memory tasks require *perceptual* processing (that is, interpreting sensory information in a meaningful way) and that explicit memory tasks require *conceptual* processing (in other words, drawing on information in memory and the knowledge base). In this view, the type of processing required in the two types of tasks explains dissociation phenomena. Much debate focuses on the question of whether the two approaches can be reconciled (Schacter, 1989; Whittlesea & Price, 2001). Essentially, this debate hinges on whether there are multiple and distinct systems of memory, each operating on different principles, or a single memory system that supports different kinds of processing.

The Process Dissociation Framework

Jacoby and his colleagues (Hay & Jacoby 1996; Jacoby 1991, 1998; Toth, Lindsay, & Jacoby, 1992; Toth, Reingold, & Jacoby, 1994) took issue with the idea that implicit memory and explicit memory represent two distinct memory systems and argued for what he called the **process dissociation framework**.

Jacoby asserted that the fact that people perform differently on implicit memory tasks from the way they do on other memory tasks does not point to the existence of an implicit memory. His claim rested on the idea that implicit memory tasks of the sort used by Schacter, Warrington, and Weiskrantz and others are not necessarily *pure* measures of any memory system. Any task relies on a combination of abilities; rarely, if ever, can any test be constructed that measures *only* the aspect it is intended to measure. As an example, consider the last midterm exam you took. Although this test was, we hope, a valid and reliable test of the subject matter (calculus, history, music, or whatever), the test also reflected some of your other abilities (for example, to read, to recall relevant information).

Jacoby (1991) preferred to think about memory tasks as calling on two different processes: intentional and automatic ones.

Performance on direct [that is, explicit] tests of memory typically requires that people intentionally recollect a past episode, whereas facilitation on indirect [implicit] tests of memory is not necessarily accompanied by either intention to remember or awareness of doing so. This difference between the two types of test can be described in terms of the contrast between consciously controlled and automatic processing. (pp. 515–516)

Jacoby (1991) argued that some memory tasks, such as one in which you try to recall a specific incident or fact, involve a great deal of conscious intention. Other tasks, such as judgments of familiarity (for example, the kind of task where you are asked if you've ever seen or heard a stimulus before), involve much more automatic processing. However, each task could draw on both intentional and automatic processing. As you try to recall a specific formula for a test, for instance, you might write down what you think it is, then see if what you've written looks familiar. Conversely, if you are a participant in an implicit memory experiment who is asked to fill in the blanks to make a word out of ___Z___LE___, you actually might briefly recall having seen the word *azalea* just a day ago in the same laboratory.

Jacoby (1991) developed a procedure in which automatic memory processes would either facilitate or hinder performance on an intentional memory task. Automatic processes are commonly described as arising when one is distracted or inattentive; controlled processes occur when one is focused, alert, and intentional about performing a particular task. Some of Jacoby's best-known work comes from what have been called his "false fame" experiments (Jacoby, Woloshyn, & Kelley 1989). Participants are shown a list of names of people, none of whom were famous (for example, Sebastian Weisdorf). Some participants are asked to study this list with full attention; others, in a divided-attention task. Later, all participants are given a new list of names, which includes names of famous people, names from the previously studied list (which they are told consisted only of nonfamous people), and names never before seen that were nonfamous, and they are asked to judge the fame of each name on this new list.

Participants in the divided-attention condition were more likely to falsely attribute fame to those names that had been previously studied. Jacoby and colleagues (1989) interpreted this as evidence for an automatic memory process. Their reasoning was as follows: Participants in the full-attention condition knew that names from the studied list were nonfamous and, moreover, had better recollection of just what names had been studied. Therefore, they consciously used that information to identify names that were nonfamous. Participants in the divided-attention condition, however, were likely unable to consciously elaborate, and learn the list of names as well; when encountering the second list, they did not have clear memories (or rich recollections) for whether a particular name was on the studied list. Instead, these participants had a sort of fuzzy familiarity with the names from the study list, but could not place where or why they felt familiar with the name (because their attention was divided during study), and thus it was incorrectly judged to be of a famous person.

When we consider the findings from these cognitive studies, work with amnesics, and models of memory representation, it becomes apparent that the human mind is complex, and that we are just beginning to understand its inner workings.

SUMMARY

1. We've seen in this chapter, as well as in Chapter 5, that cognitive psychologists approach the study of memory in a variety of ways and that this diversity dates back at least to "founding" cognitive psychologists such as Ebbinghaus and Bartlett. Some of the diversity arises in theoretical orientations: Some psychologists seek evidence for the proposition that there are different memory *stores* (for example, sensory memory, STM, LTM), whereas others focus on the kind of processing done with to-be-remembered information.

2. Work on the levels-of-processing theory has demonstrated that the more active and meaningful the original processing of information, the more memorable the information will be. This idea has obvious and practical relevance for students: If you want to improve your recall of material for later testing (in midterms and finals), organize it and think about its meaning (deep processing) rather than merely reading, underlining, or highlighting the words (shallow processing).

3. The work reported here on people's recall of their own life events dovetails in several ways with the laboratory-based investigations of memory described in this chapter and the last. Some of the findings that have emerged—for example, the constructive nature of recall—fit well with laboratory findings. However, different results are found in laboratory- and everyday-based studies. Autobiographical recall seems better than recall of laboratory stimuli, but whether different cognitive mechanisms are at work remains an open question.

4. Work on flashbulb and eyewitness memories suggests that people's recollections of moments of their past can be wrong, even when those people seem absolutely convinced of the accuracy of the memory. This suggests that our own confidence in our memories may sometimes be too high; at the very least, there are probably occasions when we are both very sure of our memories and also very wrong. Work on eyewitness testimony suggests that memory traces of a witnessed event are very malleable and subject to disruption by post-event leading questions.

5. Debates over whether memory traces can be repressed for long periods of time, then recalled, have erupted in recent years. Some studies purport to show that under repeated urgings, people can be induced to "recall" emotional events that never happened.

6. Neuropsychologists who study memory deficits recognize two different kinds of amnesia. Both seem to involve damage to either the hippocampal system or the midline diencephalic region. This damage can arise in several different ways: through closed head injury, a stroke, oxygen deprivation to the brain, bilateral electroconvulsive shock treatments, a virus such as encephalitis, or other diseases such as Alzheimer's or Korsakoff's.

7. Anterograde amnesia, which extends forward in time from the onset of amnesia, selectively affects long-term (but not working) memory, regardless of modality or type of memory test, and spares memory for general knowledge and skilled performance (although the learning of the latter will not be explicitly remembered) but can result in memories for skills that are hyperspecific to the original learning context and cannot be transferred to other, similar contexts.

8. Retrograde amnesia, the loss of memory acquired and stored before the point of onset, is almost always a component of amnesia. The temporal extent of the amnesia varies in different patients; it is worst for memories of information acquired closest to the point of onset. Some recovery of some of the lost retrograde memories is often possible. Retrograde amnesia also spares material that has been "over-learned" before the onset, including such things as language, general knowledge, and perceptual and social skills. As with anterograde amnesia, retrograde amnesia seems to spare skill learning.

9. Some theorists have proposed a distinction between *explicit* and *implicit* memory: The former refers to conscious recollections; the latter, to facilitation in performance as a function of past learning without awareness of that past learning. In this proposal, implicit memory phenomena have been seen as ways of determining how general knowledge is organized.

10. Some have argued against associating different memory *tasks* with different memory systems. Jacoby (1991) believed the best way of understanding memory processes is to distinguish between automatic and intentional memory processes.

REVIEW QUESTIONS

1. In what ways do the underlying assumptions of the levels-of-processing theory differ from the underlying assumptions of the modal model?

2. Apply the cognitive research on memory to the practical problem of giving a university student advice about how to study for an upcoming midterm. What advice would you give, and which principles would this advice draw on?

3. How do findings from the eyewitness testimony and the flashbulb memory literature fit with laboratory-based findings reported earlier? What are the differences, if any?

4. Is there a need to posit special mechanisms for flashbulb memories? Defend your view.

5. Describe the debate over "recovered" versus "false" memories of traumatic events. What are the most important issues for cognitive psychologists to address, and what issues (pragmatic, ethical, theoretical) are they likely to face in doing so?

6. Explain the concept of spreading activation, and review the evidence that leads some psychologists to maintain that it is a property of semantic memory.

7. The research on knowledge representation typically involves laboratory research with people working on somewhat artificial tasks (for example, lexical decision, sentence verification). Does such research have much bearing on cognition in real life? Defend your answer, and use specific examples to illustrate your points.

8. Review the similarities and differences between anterograde and retrograde amnesia.

9. What exactly do findings from memory studies with amnesic patients tell us about the way memory operates in non-amnesic people? (*Note:* This question is a controversial one within the field—can you see why?)

10. Describe how evidence from neuropsychological studies can be used to illuminate debates over the existence of different memory systems. What are some possible limitations of these studies?

KEY TERMS

amnesia
amygdala
anterograde amnesia
autobiographical memory
cognitive economy
elaboration
explicit memory
eyewitness memory

false memory
flashbulb memory
hippocampus
implicit memory
incidental learning
levels-of-processing theory of memory
lexical decision tasks
memory consolidation

process dissociation framework
recovered memory
repetition priming
repressed memory
retrograde amnesia
schemata
semantic priming
spreading activation

Representation and Organization of Knowledge

Concepts and Categorization

For your university degree you probably have to fulfill certain graduation requirements—among them distribution requirements, which mandate that you take a certain number of courses in several groups. For example, to obtain an arts degree at the University of Waterloo you need to take courses in four distribution groups: Group A(i) (courses in English, history, philosophy), Group A(ii) (courses in language other than English), Group A(iii) (courses in classical studies, drama, fine arts, music, religious studies, speech communication), and Group B (courses in anthropology, economics, geography, political science, psychology, sociology). The grouping of subject matter into larger groups illustrates the university's *categorization,* or assignment of courses to groupings.

Of course, not all universities have the same groups or the same assignment of courses to groups. For example, at the University of Waterloo, psychology is in the faculty of arts. At other schools (like McMaster), psychology is in the faculty of science. At many schools (like the University of Saskatchewan), arts and sciences are grouped together. It's not entirely clear how the groupings at various universities have come to be, but you can be certain the dean or committee that created them had a mental representation of this category, something that a cognitive psychologist would call a *concept.*

We have encountered the idea of mental representations several times before. We have seen that many cognitive psychologists (particularly those within the information-processing paradigm) believe that such representations guide cognitive processing and behaviour. How you regard something may often be influenced by what type of thing you believe it to be. For example, you would probably react and behave one way if told that a severe thunderstorm was taking place outside, and another way if you were told it was a hurricane. Your classification of storms into two categories suggests that you see distinctions between them. Presumably, such distinctions cause your reactions to storms to depend on classification.

A related real-life example comes from medical diagnosis. Suppose you wake up one day feeling achy, lethargic, congested, and feverish. Your symptoms could indicate nothing more serious than the flu. Or your symptoms could be the harbinger of a much more serious illness. It is your doctor's job to make the diagnosis, which essentially is to assign your pattern of symptoms to a category corresponding to known diseases or medical problems (Kulatunga-Moruzi, Brooks, & Norman, 2004). The categorization allows the physician to determine appropriate treatment and predict the time course of recovery. To make the diagnosis, your physician must have an idea of the various categories (possible medical problems) to be considered. Indeed, physicians are not the only ones who categorize illnesses, as shown by a study of laypeople's categorization of forms of mental illness (Kim & Ahn, 2002).

In this chapter, we will look at concepts and how they are formed. We will examine different theoretical descriptions of how concepts are structured and their implications for how we assume our mental representations work. We will then focus on how concepts are accessed and used in categorizing new objects, patterns, or events. Many ideas discussed in the early part of the chapter will extend and elaborate on proposals presented in Chapter 3, "Perceiving Objects and Recognizing Patterns" (pattern recognition and classification have many similarities, as we shall see), and in Chapter 6, "Memory Processes." Similarly, our examination of categorization will anticipate some later discussions about language, thinking, reasoning, and decision making (Chapters 9–11). You can probably already see that an understanding of how people form and use concepts is relevant to several other cognitive processes and abilities. Medin (1989) has in fact argued that "concepts and categories serve as building blocks for human thought and behavior" (p. 1469). Similarly, Lamberts and Shanks (1997) have argued that the issue of how things such as concepts are mentally represented is a central concern of cognitive psychology.

Box 7-1 Categorization in the Real World

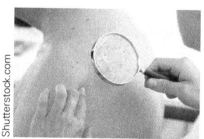

Andrey_Popov/Shutterstock.com

Researchers at McMaster University have been examining the types of categorization strategies doctors use when categorizing electrocardiograms and dermatological conditions. Based on their research, they have found evidence to support the hypothesis that doctors' categorization strategies involve the unconscious referencing of stored exemplars in memory.

What are concepts and categories, and how do they differ? The distinction turns out to be a little blurry but can still be made. Medin (1989) defined a concept as "an idea that includes all that is characteristically associated with it" (p. 1469). In other words, a **concept** is a mental representation of some object, event, or pattern that has stored in it much of the knowledge typically thought relevant to that object, event, or pattern. Most people's concept of "dog," for example, would include information to the effect that a dog is an animal, has four legs and a tail, has a reputation as "man's best friend," is a common pet, and so on.

A **category** can be defined as a class of similar things (objects or entities) that share one of two things: either an essential core (example: why all science courses are considered "science"), or some similarity in perceptual, biological, or functional properties (Lin & Murphy, 2001). When a psychologist thinks about categories, she usually thinks about several different ones, into which various things get sorted. In the game 20 Questions, a common opener is, "Is it an animal, vegetable, or mineral?" This question seeks to categorize, or sort, the to-be-guessed item into one of three things. Sometimes categories are described as existing objectively in the world, and concepts are described as mental representations of categories (Medin, 1989).

Concepts help us establish order in our knowledge base (Medin & Smith, 1984). Concepts also allow us to categorize, giving us mental "buckets" in which to sort the things we encounter, letting us treat new, never-before-encountered things in the same way we treat familiar things that we perceive to be in the same set (Neisser, 1987). Categorization also allows us to make predictions and act accordingly. If you see object in the water with a dorsal fin poking out of the water coming towards you, your classification of it as either a shark or a dolphin has implications for how you would react. Smith and Medin (1981) elaborated on the important role concepts play in our mental life:

> *Without concepts, mental life would be chaotic. If we perceived each entity as unique, we would be overwhelmed by the sheer diversity of what we experience and unable to remember more than a minute fraction of what we encounter. And if each individual entity needed a distinct name, our language would be staggeringly complex and communication virtually impossible. Fortunately, though, we do not perceive, remember, and talk about each object and event as unique, but rather as an instance of a class or concept that we already know something about. (p. 1)*

We will first examine different theoretical accounts about the nature and structure of concepts. Next, we will look at how concepts are formed or acquired. Finally, we will examine how people actually use concepts through the process of categorization. Throughout this chapter, we will be focusing on concepts of objects and nouns, because they are the most commonly studied at present in cognitive psychology. We will see, however, that the kind of concept studied may affect the concept theories that are subsequently created. It will be useful to keep in mind that psychologists have yet to explore fully the entire range of people's concepts.

CHAPTER 7

THEORETICAL DESCRIPTIONS OF THE NATURE OF CONCEPTS

In Chapter 6, we reviewed proposals for how our knowledge is represented and organized. Models of semantic memory describe the ways in which representations of different concepts are interrelated. Here we will concentrate on the representation and organization of individual concepts. We will explore five distinct proposals on how concepts are represented and structured. Each one provides a different answer to the question "What information do we have when we have a particular concept in mind?" Each proposal will therefore have different implications for the question of how concepts are formed, acquired, or learned.

The Classical View

The classical view of concepts was the dominant view in psychology up until the 1970s and dates back to Aristotle (Smith & Medin, 1981). This proposal is organized around the belief that all examples or instances of a concept share fundamental characteristics, or **features** (Medin, 1989). In particular, the **classical view of concepts** holds that the features represented are individually necessary and collectively sufficient (Medin, 1989). To say a feature is individually necessary is to say that each example must have the feature if it is to be regarded as a member of the concept. For example, "has three sides" is a necessary feature of the concept *triangle*; things that do not have three sides are automatically disqualified from being triangles. To say that a set of features is collectively sufficient is to say that anything with each feature in the set is automatically an instance of the concept. For example, the set of features "has three sides" and "closed, geometric figure" is sufficient to specify a triangle; anything that has both is a triangle. Table 7-1 presents some other examples of sets of features or of concepts that are individually necessary and collectively sufficient.

The classical view of concepts has several implications. First, it assumes that concepts mentally represent lists of features. That is, concepts are not representations of specific examples but rather abstractions containing information about properties and characteristics that all examples must have. Second, it assumes that membership in a category is clear-cut: Either something has all the necessary and sufficient features (in which case it is a member of the category), or it lacks one or more of the features (in which case it is not a member).

Table 7-1

	Bachelor	**Triangle**	**Uncle**
Concept	Male	Geometric figure	Male
Features	Adult Unmarried Human	Three-sided Planar	Sibling One or more siblings a child has

Third, it implies that all members within a category are created equal: There is no such thing as a "better" or "worse" triangle.

Work by Eleanor Rosch and colleagues (Rosch, 1973; Rosch & Mervis, 1975) confronted and severely weakened the attraction of the classical view. Rosch found that people judged different members of a category as varying in "goodness." For instance, most people in North America consider a robin and a sparrow very good examples of a bird but find other examples, such as chickens, penguins, and ostriches to be not as good. Notice the problem this result presents for the classical view of concepts. The classical view holds that membership in a category is all-or-none: Either an instance (such as robin or ostrich) belongs to a category, or it doesn't. This view has no way to explain peoples intuitions that some birds are "birdier" than others.

Peoples judgments of typicality, the "goodness" of the instance in the category, was later shown to predict several aspects of their performance on different tasks. For example, participants in a sentence verification task were faster to respond (true or false) to a sentence such as "A robin is a bird" than to a sentence such as "A chicken is a bird" (McCloskey & Glucksberg, 1978; Rosch, 1973; Smith et al., 1974). Asked to list instances of a concept, people were more likely to list typical than atypical instances (Mervis, Catlin, & Rosch, 1976). In semantic priming studies (see Chapter 6 for a review), highly typical instances often led to better priming (Rosch & Mervis, 1975; Rosch, Simpson, & Miller, 1976).

All these results are not easily explained within a classical framework. In addition, other studies cast doubt on the idea that people typically store and refer to a list of necessary features when judging category membership. McCloskey and Glucksberg (1978) gave participants a list of items and asked them to judge whether the items belonged to certain categories (for example, "Does 'chair' belong to the category 'furniture'?"). The classical view would predict very strong agreement across people, but McCloskey and Glucksberg's participants in fact disagreed considerably on atypical instances (for example, "Do 'bookends' belong to the category 'furniture'?"). Participants were often inconsistent in their own responses in different sessions. This result argued especially strongly against the classical assumption that categories have clearly defined boundaries. Instead, it was proposed that category membership is "graded" and boundaries between categories "fuzzy." Finally, even when given specific instructions to do so, most people cannot generate lists of features that are individually necessary and collectively sufficient to specify membership in a category (Ashcraft, 1978; Rosch & Mervis, 1975).

The Prototype View

A second theoretical view of the nature of concepts, known as the *prototype view,* was proposed in the 1970s stemming from the work of Eleanor Rosch and colleagues. The **prototype view of concepts** denies the existence of necessary-and-sufficient feature lists (except for a limited number of concepts such as mathematical ones), instead regarding concepts as a different sort of abstraction (Medin & Smith, 1984). Like perceptual researchers (see Chapter 3), conceptual researchers believe in the existence of mental **prototypes,** idealized representations of some class of objects or events. Specifically, researchers studying the prototype view of concepts hold that prototypes of concepts include features or aspects that are *characteristic*—that is, typical—of members of the category rather than necessary and sufficient. No individual feature or aspect (except very trivial ones, such as "is an object") need be present in the instance for it to count as a member of the category but the more characteristic features or aspects an instance has, the more likely it is to be regarded as a member of the category

The prototype view of concepts and categories often refers to the **family resemblance structure of concepts** (Wittgenstein, 1953), a structure in which each member has a number of features, sharing different features with different members. Few, if any, features are shared by every single member of the category; however, the more features a member possesses, the more typical it is. Figure 7-1 provides an example of family resemblance. Note

FIGURE 7-1 An example of family resemblance.

Source: Reprinted from *Cognition*, Vol. 13, issue 3, Sharon Lee Armstrong, Lila R. Gleitman, Henry Gleitman, What Some Concepts Might Not Be, pp. 263–308, Copyright © 1983, with permission from Elsevier.

that the Smith brothers (modelled after the men on Smith Bros. cough drop boxes) have several shared features: light hair, bushy mustache, large ears, and eyeglasses. Not every Smith brother has every feature, but the brother in the middle, having them all, would likely be judged by Smith friends to be the most typical Smith of the bunch. Note that he shares big ears, eyeglasses, and light hair with the brother in the "ten o'clock" position and a mustache and big ears with the "seven o'clock" brother. Indeed, different pairs of brothers share different features.

The prototype view of concepts explains typicality effects by reference to family resemblance. The idea is that the more characteristic features an instance of a concept has, the stronger the family resemblance between that instance and other instances, and therefore the more typical an instance it is. Presumably, then, a robin is thought of as a more typical bird than a penguin because the robin possesses more characteristic bird features, such as "is small," "flies," "eats worms," and "lives in a tree." Even with well-defined concepts such as *bachelor,* some examples seem more bachelorlike than others.

For example, is a 16-year-old unmarried man a good example of a bachelor? He is male and unmarried. And, probably, he's a better example of a bachelor today than he was 10 years ago. What about the pope? The point here is that both people may meet the technical definition of a bachelor (there's some disagreement over whether the definition includes "adult"), but neither is as good an example as might be someone such as, say, Leonardo DiCaprio.

In one set of studies, Rosch and Mervis (1975) presented their undergraduate participants with terms (such as *chair, car, orange, shirt, gun, peas*) from six different superordinate categories (such as "furniture," "vehicle," "fruit," "clothing," "weapon," "vegetable") and asked them to list attributes "common to and characteristic of those objects. So, for example, for the word *chair* a participant might list "has four legs; used to sit in; sometimes has arms; used in homes and offices." Then Rosch and Mervis tallied a list of all the attributes any participant listed for all basic-level terms belonging to a superordinate category (for example, all the attributes listed for *chair, sofa, table, dresser, desk, bed, clock, closet, vase, telephone*). Next, they computed, for each item, the number of attributes commonly listed for it. They found that items such as chair and sofa—ones that seem more prototypical of the superordinate category "furniture"—had many more of the "furniture" attributes listed than did items such as clock or telephone, which are both not at all prototypical examples of furniture. However, very few (0 or 1) attributes in any of the six superordinate categories were true of all 20 items for the category (for example, attributes true of all fruits).

A prototype, then, is some sort of abstraction that includes all the characteristic features of a category. The prototype may or may not be an actual instance of the category. Prototypes are often thought of as mental "summaries" or "averages" of all the instances, although there are some problems with this view (Barsalou, 1985). The general idea of the prototype view, then, is that concepts have one or more "core" representations, based on a family resemblance structure, but have no rigid boundaries.

Rosch and her colleagues (Rosch, Mervis, Gray, Johnson, & Boyes-Braem, 1976) made another important discovery about concepts. Although concepts exist at many different levels of a hierarchy (for example, "Bernese mountain dog," "dog," "canine," "mammal," "animal"), one level of abstraction appears psychologically fundamental. They called this the "basic" level and distinguished it from both higher-level (superordinate) and lower-level (subordinate) concepts.

To understand the distinctions between the **basic level of categorization** and other levels, consider the purpose of categorization. On the one hand, we want to group together similar objects, events, people, ideas, and so on. On the other hand, we want our categorization to distinguish among objects, events, people, and ideas that differ in important ways. There must be some compromise between these two goals. Rosch and colleagues consider the basic level to be the best compromise.

"Piano" and "guitar" are examples of two basic-level categories. Such categories include members that are maximally similar to one another, unlike **superordinate levels of categories** (such as "musical instruments"), which contain members (such as pianos and guitars) that are dissimilar in several respects. At the same time, basic-level categories are most differentiated from one another, especially relative to subordinate categories. "Grand piano" and "upright piano" are two categories at the **subordinate level of categories;** these categories are less distinct than are two basic-level categories, such as "piano" and "guitar." The list in Table 7-2 presents examples of basic-level categories, along with related superordinate and subordinate categories.

The prototype view does a very good job at explaining why certain members of a category are seen as more typical than others. It also explains why people have a hard time providing strict definitions of their concepts: Strict definitions likely do not exist for many categories. Finally, the prototype view can explain why some classifications are especially easy to make and others are unclear. Take tomatoes, which some people classify as a vegetable and others classify as a fruit. Tomatoes are often eaten with other vegetables instead of with other fruits, and they share some similarities with other vegetables. However, to a biologist, tomatoes are a fruit because they develop from the flower of the plant (technically, the pistil). Vegetables, in contrast, are any nonreproductive parts of a plant, such as the stem or root. The prototype view explains the ambiguity of tomatoes: They share features both with vegetables (leading to classification as a vegetable) and with fruits (leading to classification as a fruit).

The prototype view is not totally free of problems. For one thing, it fails to capture people's knowledge about the limits of conceptual boundaries. To illustrate, even though a Pomeranian seems in many ways more similar to a Siamese cat than to a Great Dane, the Pomeranian and Great Dane are classified together as dogs (Komatsu, 1992). The prototype view has a hard time telling us why. Unlike the classical view, which sets constraints or boundaries around which things can and can't belong to a category, the prototype view does not specify clear constraints.

Table 7-2 Basic-Level Categories with Related Superordinate and Subordinate Categories

Superordinate	Basic Level	Subordinate
Musical Instrument	Guitar	Classical guitar
		Folk guitar
	Piano	Grand piano
		Upright piano
	Drum	Bass drum
		Kettle drum
Fruit	Apple	Delicious apple
		McIntosh apple
	Peach	Cling peach
		Freestone peach
	Grapes	Concord grapes
		Green seedless grapes
Tool	Hammer	Claw hammer
		Ball-peen hammer
	Saw	Hack handsaw
		Cross-cutting handsaw
	Screwdriver	Phillips screwdriver
		Regular screwdriver
Clothing	Pants	Levis
		Double-knit pants
	Socks	Knee socks
		Ankle socks
	Shirt	Dress shirt
		Knit shirt
Furniture	Table	Kitchen table
		Dining room table

(continued)

Table 7-2 (continued)

Superordinate	Basic Level	Subordinate
	Lamp	Floor lamp
		Desk lamp
	Chair	Kitchen chair
		Living room chair
Vehicle	Car	Sports car
		Four-door sedan
	Bus	City bus
		Cross-country bus
	Truck	Pickup truck
		Tractor-trailer truck

Source: Reprinted from *Cognitive Psychology*, Vol. 8, issue 3, Eleanor Rosch, Carolyn B. Mervis, Wayne D. Gray, David M. Johnson, Penny Boyes Braem, Basic Objects in Natural Categories, pp. 382–439, Copyright © 1976, with permission from Elsevier.

A Great Dane, a Pomeranian, and a Siamese cat: Even though the overall similarity may be greater between the latter two, the former two are classified together in the category "dogs."

Source: Great dane: Vivienstock/Shutterstock.com; Pomeranian: Csanad Kiss/Shutterstock.com; Cat: Axel Bueckert/Shutterstock.com.

Rosch and colleagues (Rosch, 1973; Rosch & Mervis, 1975; Rosch, Mervis, et al., 1976) have argued that some constraints around different categories come from the environment itself. Having wings and being able to fly, for example, tend to co-occur, often in those things we call *birds* (but also in airplanes, butterflies, and insects). Boundaries between categories, then, come not just from us as cognitive processors of information but from the way the world works: Certain patterns of attributes or features occur in the world, and others don't (Komatsu, 1992; Neisser, 1987). People's main job in categorizing, then, is to pick up information about the world's regularities, not to impose arbitrary groupings, as the classical view might imply. (The idea of "picking up information" about the world might remind the alert student of Gibsonian theories of perception, discussed in Chapter 3.)

A second problem for the prototype view has to do with typicality ratings. Barsalou (1985, 1987) and Roth and Shoben (1983) showed that the typicality of an instance depends to some extent on context. So, although a robin may be seen as a typical bird in the context of birds you see in the neighbourhood, it is atypical of birds you see in a barnyard. These findings contrast with the idea that a member of a category has a certain level of typicality Instead, typicality apparently varies with the way the concept itself is being thought about.

Studies by Armstrong, Gleitman, and Gleitman (1983) demonstrated additional problems with typicality ratings. In these studies, the investigators asked participants to rate the typicality of instances of both natural concepts (such as "vehicle" or "fruit") previously studied by Rosch and her colleagues and of well-defined concepts (such as "even number," "female," "geometric figure"). Armstrong and colleagues found that participants happily rated the typicality of members of well-defined categories, generally agreeing that 3 is a more typical odd number than 57, for example. The same participants also agreed, however, that the category "odd number" was well defined and that it makes little sense to talk about degree of membership in the category: Numbers either are or are not odd. The investigators concluded that the typicality ratings task is flawed, at least for discovering the underlying representation of concepts.

The Exemplar View

The previous two views of concepts both hold that concepts are some sort of mental abstraction or summary. In other words, individual instances are not specifically stored or mentally represented but instead are averaged into some sort of composite representation. The **exemplar view of concepts** makes just the opposite assumption: It asserts that concepts include representations of at least some actual individual instances. The exemplar approach assumes that people categorize new instances by comparing them to representations of previously stored instances, called *exemplars*. That is, people store representations of actual instances (Fido, the golden retriever with the long ears; Rover, the black and white sheltie who's missing a tail due to an unfortunate encounter with a raccoon; Precious, the Yorkshire terrier who always has painted toenails and a bow in his hair).

Like the prototype view, it thus explains people's inability to state necessary and defining features: There are none to be stated. It also explains why people may have difficulty categorizing unclear, atypical instances: Such instances are similar to exemplars from different categories (for example, tomato is similar both to fruit exemplars, such as oranges or apples, and to vegetable exemplars, such as beets or squash) or are not similar enough to any known exemplars (Medin & Smith, 1984). Typical instances are thought to be more likely to be stored than less typical ones (Mervis, 1980) or to be more similar to stored exemplars, or both. This explains why people are faster to process information about typical instances. So, in trying to retrieve information about a typical instance, it is faster to find very similar stored exemplars. Atypical instances, in contrast, being rather dissimilar from stored exemplars, take longer to process.

Allen and Brooks (1991) conducted a clever experiment that demonstrated how specific prior examples influence categorization over and above the use of simple defining features. Figure 7-2 presents some example stimuli from their experiment. Participants were trained on a series of pictures that contained fictional creatures called "builders" and "diggers." Builders were creatures that lived in shelters that they built from materials available in their environment, and diggers lived in holes that they dug. Participants were also given a verbal rule that could be used to classify them: If a creature has at least two of the following three features (long legs, angular body, and spots), it is a builder. The authors were interested in a number of hypotheses. The one we will focus on is the degree to which item categorization of specific creatures was influenced by stored exemplars from training. To do this, the experimenters introduced stimuli at the test that were slightly different to those during training. Specifically, they presented stimuli that were either a "positive match" or a "negative match." The positive match stimuli were categorically (based on the rule) *and* visually similar to the training instances (see top right panel of Figure 7-2). Notice how the builder in this case has two of the characteristics of the known builder (long legs and angular body), plus looks similar to the known builder as it is imbedded in the environment of the known builder. The negative match stimuli, on the other hand, were categorically a builder based on the rule, but visually similar to a digger (see bottom right panel of Figure 7-2). Notice how the builder in this case has two of the characteristics of the known builder (long legs and spots), but looks more similar to the digger and is imbedded in the environment of the known digger. They found that participants took longer to classify, and made many more errors in categorizing, the negative matches than the other items. They interpreted these data to support the hypothesis that the physical similarity to previous exemplars stored in memory influenced the categorization despite participants having a simple and sufficient categorization rule to follow.

The biggest problem with the exemplar view is that, like the prototype view, it is too unconstrained. It fails to specify, for example, which instances will eventually be stored as exemplars and which will not. It also does not explain how different exemplars are "called to mind" at the time of categorization. In addition, several researchers (including Mark Blair from Simon Fraser University and John Paul Minda from the University of Western Ontario) have found

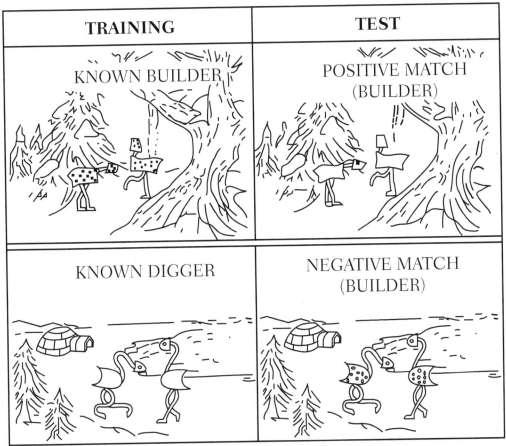

FIGURE 7-2 An example of the stimuli used by Allen and Brooks (1991). According to the rule "If a creature has at least two of the following three features (long legs, angular body, and spots), it is a builder," the training items shown are a builder [top left; long legs, angular body, spots] and a digger [bottom left; long legs only]. The positive match appears only in test and, according to the rule, is in the same category as the most similar training item. The negative match is similar to one of the training items but, according to the rule, is in the opposite category to that item (spots in addition to long legs makes it a builder).

Source: Allen, S. & Brooks, L. (1991), *Journal of Experimental Psychology: General*, 120, page 4.

that that the exemplar model has difficulty accommodating data from large and complex categories (e.g., Blair & Homa, 2001; Minda & Smith, 2001). However, many psychologists believe people often store information about some specific category members in their conceptual representations, as we will see later.

The Schemata View

We have already touched on the concept of a schema, or organized framework for representing knowledge, in talking about Bartlett's (1932) work on people's memories for stories (see Chapters 5 and 6), so our coverage here will be brief. Be sure you have understood the material from those chapters on schemata as you read what is here.

The schemata view of concepts is that concepts are schemata—frameworks of knowledge that have roles, slots, variables, and so on. Schemata can embed themselves in one another hierarchically. Thus, any schema can have sub-schemata and/or superschemata. The "meeting a university roommate for the first time" schema can be a subschema of an "orientation to university" schema, which may be embedded in an "attending university" schema, and so on. Similarly, the "meeting a university roommate for the first time" schema may contain subschemata of "residence room," "meeting new person," and "roommate" embedded within it. The schema for "dog" may be a part of the schemata for "mammal," "pet," "animal," and "living thing"; it may contain subschemata such as "fur," "paws," and "wagging tail." The notion of schemata as underlying organizational units of memory has had significant impact on cognitive psychologists' thinking about how memory is organized and concepts represented. Some (e.g., Komatsu, 1992) have seen the **schemata/scripts view of concepts** as sharing features with both the prototype view (in that both schemata and prototypes store information that is abstracted across instances) and the exemplar view (in that both schemata and exemplars store information about actual instances).

The schemata view shares some of the problems facing the prototype and exemplar views. It does not specify clear enough boundaries among individual schemata. Moreover, some psychologists argue that in its current state the schema framework is not sufficiently delineated to be empirically testable (Horton & Mills, 1984). Answers to the following questions are still needed: What kinds of experiences lead to the formation of new schemata? How are schemata modified with experience? How do people know which schemata to call up in different situations—that is, what sorts of environmental cues are used?

The Knowledge-Based View

A number of cognitive psychologists (e.g., Keil, 1989; Lin & Murphy, 2001; Murphy & Medin, 1985) have argued that concepts have much more to do with people's knowledge and worldviews than previously recognized. Murphy and Medin (1985) suggested that the relationship between a concept and examples of the concept is analogous to the relationship between a theory and data supporting that theory. The idea of the **knowledge-based view of concepts** is that a person classifying objects and events doesn't just compare features or physical aspects of the objects and events to features or aspects of stored representations. Instead, the person uses his or her knowledge of how the concept is organized to justify the classification and to explain why certain instances happen to go together in the same category. The knowledge-based view helps explain how an apparently disparate collection of objects can form a coherent category in particular circumstances.

To take an example from Barsalou (1983), consider the category comprising children, pets, and family heirlooms. On the face of it, these things don't seem to go together very well, but in the context of a scenario in which a fire is about to engulf a house, these things fall neatly into the category "things to save." We know that each object mentioned is precious to its owner or parents and also irreplaceable. Notice, however, that the category becomes coherent only when we know its purpose.

Recall that the prototype, exemplar, and schemata/scripts approaches to concepts and categories fail to offer much of an answer to the question of how things in the same category go together. The knowledge-based view proposes that people's theories or mental explanations about the world are intertwined with their concepts and provide the basis for categorization (Heit, 1997). This view lets people explain to themselves and to others the instances that go together and why, the features or aspects of instances that are important and why, and the features or aspects that are irrelevant and why.

The five approaches to conceptual structure just reviewed have been themselves categorized into two major types: similarity-based and explanation-based (Komatsu, 1992). The similarity-based category consists of the classical, prototype, and exemplar views (and some parts of the schemata/scripts view). It includes approaches in which categorization is assumed to be based on the similarity of an instance to some abstract specification of the category (such as a definition or a prototype) or to one or more stored exemplars.

However, to say that objects are categorized on the basis of similarity raises some problems, some of which Goodman (1972) pointed out. Consider two objects, a fork and a spoon. We say they are similar, probably because they share many properties: Both are made of metal, both are less than a foot long, and both are used as eating utensils. Now consider two other objects, a plum and a lawnmower. Are these similar? Well, they share several properties: Both weigh less than 100 kilos (and in fact, both weigh less than 101 kilos, 102 kilos, and so forth). In fact, these two apparently dissimilar items share an infinite number of properties (Hahn & Chater, 1997). But the property of weighing less than 100 kilos seems somehow beside the point when you are evaluating the similarity between a plum and a lawnmower. The key point is that similarity is meaningful only in certain respects. But Goodman concluded that the term *similarity* is pretty empty without some specification of what the relevant respects are.

Komatsu (1992) defined a different type of approach to concepts, which he called the *explanation-based category*, comprising some of the schemata/scripts view and some of the knowledge-based view. In this approach to the study of concepts, people are seen as basing classifications on meaningful relationships among instances and categories. The contrast between the similarity-based and the explanation-based approaches has to do with the degree to which people focus on superficial, perceptual information about a particular object versus the degree to which they focus on deeper, knowledge-derived information about an object's function or role.

The five approaches to concepts differ on several dimensions. The first dimension is the cognitive economy of the mental representation. Recall our discussion of cognitive economy from Chapter 6. The idea is to save on mental resources (such as storage space, processing time) by limiting the amount of information we must store. If we treated every single object or event as completely unique, thereby forming a unique mental representation for each, we would not be using our cognitive resources very economically.

In contrast, if we categorized all objects into one category (called "things"), the category wouldn't be very informative. So, any theory of concepts and categorization must strike a balance between cognitive economy and informative-ness (Komatsu, 1992). At the same time, any theory of concepts must explain a concept or category's coherence—what holds the class of things together into a natural grouping. Some approaches, such as the classical approach, do this very directly; others have fuzzier boundaries around and between concepts.

Thus far, we have looked at different proposals for what concepts are— their nature and structure. In the next section, we will examine empirical studies looking at how concepts are actually formed and used. Presumably, understanding something about the ways in which people classify new instances can shed light on the nature of concepts. The studies we'll review next will help us think more carefully about the five approaches just discussed.

FORMING NEW CONCEPTS AND CLASSIFYING NEW INSTANCES

To have a concept of something is to group similar things together; to treat in more or less similar ways members of the category that the concept includes. To form a concept, people must have some basis for generalization, for grouping certain things but not others together. When you think about it, forming a concept is a remarkable cognitive achievement. It requires that we figure out which attributes or features of things are relevant and which should be ignored. Often we must carry out the task with very little feedback. In this section, we'll explore some investigations of how people manage this complex undertaking. Throughout, we'll see that psychologists' assumptions about how concepts are mentally represented have influenced their views on how people acquire or form new concepts.

Concept Attainment Strategies

Bruner, Goodnow, and Austin (1956) conducted some of the earliest work on how people form (or, in their terminology, "attain") concepts. They saw several components in the process: acquiring the information necessary to isolate and learn a concept, retaining the information for later use, and transforming the information to make it usable when testing ideas about new possible instances. Bruner and colleagues (1956) studied the ways people attained concepts, using cards depicting differing geometric figures, as shown in Figure 7-3. Note that each card has one of three shapes (circle, square, or cross), one of three colours (here, black, white, or striped), different numbers of shapes (one, two, or three), and different numbers of borders around the shapes (one, two, or three). The experimenter first placed before each participant all the cards appearing in Figure 7-3. Participants were told the experimenter had in mind a certain concept, such as "black circles" or "all cards

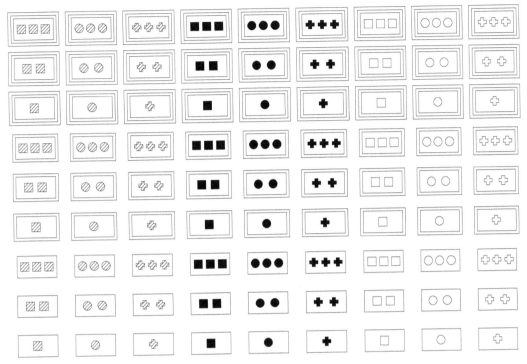

FIGURE 7-3 Stimuli used by Bruner et al. (1956).

Source: Republished with permission of Taylor and Francis Group LLC, from *A Study of Thinking*, Jerome Bruner, Jacqueline Goodnow, George Austin, © 1986; permission conveyed through Copyright Clearance Center, Inc.

containing two borders and striped figures." Participants were then shown one card that illustrated the concept—in other words, a positive instance. Their subsequent task was to test the other cards, one at a time, for inclusion in the category. The experimenter provided feedback after each card was considered. Each person was asked to determine the nature of the concept as efficiently as possible, choosing cards in any order and offering hypotheses whenever he felt comfortable doing so.

From the participants' choices, the researchers tried to determine the strategies used. Bruner and colleagues (1956) described distinct strategies that could be used to perform the task. They called one strategy *simultaneous scanning*. People who pursued this strategy used each card to test and rule out multiple hypotheses. The strategy required participants to figure out ahead of time the hypothesis to which each card was relevant and to consider carefully how to eliminate the maximum number of hypotheses by choosing the optimal card at each point in the process. As you might expect, this strategy is difficult to use and makes heavy demands on working memory.

A second strategy, *successive scanning,* appeared more manageable. Here, a participant tested one hypothesis at a time. For example, he first tried to see, by choosing appropriate cards, if the concept was "black figures"; if he became convinced this was the wrong concept, he or she tested another idea, and so on, until amassing enough evidence that the correct concept had been attained. The contrast between simultaneous and successive scanning is that the former involves testing a number of ideas at the same time; the latter involves testing ideas one at a time. Successive scanning is therefore less efficient but more cognitively manageable.

A third strategy was called *conservative focusing.* It consisted of finding a card that illustrated the concept (called the "focus" card), then choosing to test other cards that varied from it in only one aspect. For instance, if the focus card had two black crosses and one border, the participant might next select one of the following cards: a card with two black circles and one border; a card with one black cross and one border; a card with two black crosses and two borders; or a card with two white crosses and one border. If any of these cards was also a member of the category, then the participant could logically eliminate the changed attribute as being relevant to the concept. For example, if the card with two white crosses and one border was also a member of the category, then the participant knew colour did not define the concept. This strategy is interesting because it is both efficient and relatively easy, but unless the cards are laid out in an orderly fashion so a particular one can be easily located, it may be difficult to carry out.

Bruner and colleagues (1956) found that the effectiveness of each of these strategies depended to some extent on the task conditions. For instance, when participants had to do the problem "in their heads," without the cards being displayed, those using scanning strategies had more trouble than did participants who could lay out the cards on a table to refer to as they worked. The strategy participants adopted also depended to some extent on the task, such as whether the cards were initially arranged in an orderly or random way.

Aficionados of the game Mastermind might recognize that it has many basic similarities to the Bruner and colleagues (1956) concept attainment task. Laughlin, Lange, and Adamopoulos (1982) studied college students playing a simplified version of the game and found that the two dominant strategies that emerged were similar to Bruner and colleagues' conservative focusing and simultaneous scanning. Participants who used these strategies had more success at playing the game than did those who did not, with the conservative focusing strategy being the most successful.

Will Thomass/Shutterstock.com

The game of Mastermind is a real-life example of the concept attainment task used by Bruner et al. (1956).

Notice the kind of concept being learned in these tasks. In all the tasks, valid instances of the category share necessary and sufficient features. In fact, the concepts involved in these experiments were what philosophers and psychologists might call *nominal:* concepts that have precise definitions (Schwartz, 1980). The results of the Bruner and colleagues (1956) studies suggest that when concepts are defined with necessary and sufficient features, people form representations that include necessary and sufficient features. We will see later that when people acquire other kinds of concepts, especially those that do not have clear-cut definitions, their acquisition strategies vary.

Acquiring Prototypes

Recall that in Chapter 3 we reviewed experiments by Cabeza, Bruce, Kato, and Oda (1999), where participants learned to classify faces that were slight modifications from prototypes. In their experiment, prototype faces were modified by displacing certain facial features to create multiple exemplars that were slight deviations from the prototypes. Undergraduates learned to classify the exemplar faces even without seeing the original prototypes. These results suggest that people do form and use prototypes, even when given distorted instances during the learning phase.

The results obtained by Cabeza and colleagues appear very different from those of Bruner and colleagues (1956) discussed previously. What might account for this difference? Two important differences are apparent: the type of stimuli being used and the type of concepts being acquired. Notice that the task used by Bruner and colleagues involved concepts with clear-cut definitions; the Cabeza and colleagues task did not. This latter task involved learning concepts that were defined by similarity to previous examples. When categories are defined in this way people apparently learn to classify by forming and using mental representations of prototypes. Taken as a whole, the results from these studies reinforce the idea that the way people form and learn concepts depends critically on the instances and the categories they must work with.

Acquiring Concepts in the Brain

How does the brain change when acquiring prototypes? To answer this question, Seger, Poldrack, Prabhakaran, Zhao, Glover, and Gabrieli (2000) presented participants with a categorization task where they were required to sort abstract drawings by two fictional painters (Smith and Jones) into two groups, according to their two unseen, but strongly related, prototypes. The basic methodology is very similar to the experiment conducted by Cabeza and colleagues. As illustrated in Figure 7-4(A), each prototype was a pattern of red and blue boxes in a 10 by 10 checkerboard grid. A group of participants were presented with 48 exemplars (24 Smith and 24 Jones), which were created by changing the colour of each square of the prototype with a 7% probability. This ensured that each exemplar was very similar to the unseen prototype of one painter, and dissimilar to the other. Sample exemplars are also depicted in Figure 7-4(B). Note that each of the exemplars looks very similar to the prototype. Importantly, participants were never shown the prototype and were simply instructed to try to learn to distinguish between the paintings of two artists. They were given feedback after each trial. As is evident in Figure 7-4(B), brain activations were limited to frontal and parietal regions in the right hemisphere during the early trials. Presumably, this could be due to the idea that early classification mainly involves the processing of the visual patterns of the stimuli without the application of any rules. As learning progresses, however, regions in left hemisphere begin to be recruited, specifically in the left parietal lobe and left dorsolateral prefrontal cortex. Why would this be the case? The authors claim that the shift to left hemisphere processing may be the result of the formulation, and application of abstract rules. Reasoning from abstract rules, similar to inferential language processes, and logical processes like those in other forms of reasoning, is generally thought to be the realm of the left hemisphere.

It is important to note that the frontal and parietal cortices are not the only regions that are involved in categorization. Several researchers have also highlighted the important role of the *basal ganglia* (e.g., Seger, 2008). Here, the basal ganglia, a major relay centre in the brain, is thought to be involved in the further processing of visual stimuli, selecting appropriate actions based on visual stimuli, and the processing of feedback in order to promote learning. As such, categorization tasks typically involve a complex interplay between cortical and subcortical regions of the brain.

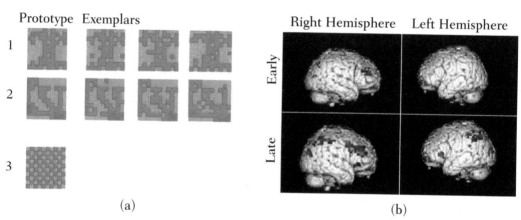

(a)   (b)

FIGURE 7-4 (A) Concept prototype and sample stimuli for the two concepts used in the study. Stimuli were formed by randomly reversing the colour of 7% of the square elements. (B) Areas of activation for trials occurring early versus late in the sequence.

Source: Reprinted from *Neuropsychologia*, Vol. 38, issue 9, Carol A. Carol A Seger, Russell A Poldrack, Vivek Prabhakaran, Margaret Zhao, Gary H Glover, John D.E Gabrieli, Hemispheric Asymmetries and Individual Differences in Visual Concept Learning as Measured by Functional MRI, pp. 1316-1324, Copyright © 2000, with permission from Elsevier.

Implicit Concept Learning

The results just described imply that people can and do form and use prototypes, at least under certain conditions and with certain stimuli. This raises the question of whether participants ever retain and make use of information about specific exemplars. Arthur Reber (1967, 1976) conducted a series of studies bearing on this issue. In his experiments, participants were given strings of letters to learn, such as the ones shown in Figure 7-5(A). Unknown to people in some of the experimental groups, the letters were not randomly chosen but were generated by a structure sharing similarities with certain kinds of language grammars.

Figure 7-5(B) depicts one such grammar. To generate a "legal" letter string—that is, in accord with the grammar—imagine yourself starting at the path marked "In" and moving to the path marked "Out," following the directional arrows as you go. As you take each path, you add the letter of that path to your string. So, the first letter of a "legal" string is always either a T or a V. Notice two loops in the grammar, one labelled P and one X. These loops can be followed any number of times (each time adding either a P or an X to the letter string), allowing letter strings that are infinitely long.

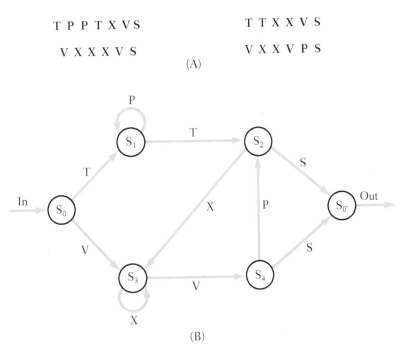

T P P T X V S   T T X X V S

V X X X V S   V X X V P S

(A)

(B)

FIGURE 7-5 Possible stimuli (A) and their underlying "grammar" (B) used by Reber (1967).

Source: Reprinted from *Journal of Verbal Learning and Verbal Behavior*, Vol. 6, issue 6, Arthur S. Reber, Implicit Learning of Artificial Grammars, pp. 855–863, Copyright © 1967, with permission from Elsevier.

Box 7-2 *Canadian Research Highlight*

Dr. Lee Brooks (https://www.science.mcmaster.ca/pnb/86-people-sp-716/199-dr-lee-brooks.html#academic-history) was a professor of psychology at McMaster University. He has made many influential discoveries throughout his career. His main area of research throughout his career was in concept learning–specifically how people acquire concepts about complex structures. He studies this in a variety of domains, ranging from artificial grammars to real world medical diagnosis (see also Chapter 11 for more examples of his work). He has been at the forefront of examining how people continually learn the structure of the world around them (e.g., learn the category structure of basic concepts) without being consciously aware of it. Here, he has demonstrated that much of the learning associated with concepts and categories is implicit in nature, operating below the level of consciousness. He also made significant advances in determining the conditions under which people would classify based on rules, prototypes, or priori instances.

Reber (1967, 1976) found, first, that participants learning letter strings that followed the grammar made fewer errors than did control participants learning random letter strings. More surprising, participants who were told ahead of time that letter strings followed certain complex rules remembered strings less well than participants who were simply asked to memorize particular letter strings but were not told anything about the strings' following a structure. Reber concluded that when complex underlying structures exist (such as his grammar), people are better off memorizing exemplars than trying to figure out what the structure is, primarily because participants who try to guess the structure often induce or invent incorrect rules or structures. They argued that people implicitly *abstract* the rule and apply this rule to new instances. Others have argued against this view (e.g. Brooks & Vokey 1991), suggesting instead that learning is based on the abstract similarity between new stimuli and specific training stimuli.

Brooks (1978, 1987) believed that the processes Reber (1967) discovered are at work much of the time in ordinary cognition. Brooks called these processes **nonanalytic concept formation,** in contrast to analytic (logical, scientific, focused) concept formation such as exhibited by research participants in the Bruner and colleagues (1956) study Nonanalytic concept formation, also sometimes called **implicit learning,** requires that people pay attention to individual exemplars, storing information about and representations of them in memory. Later classification is done by comparing new instances to the representations, drawing analogies between new and old.

In one study, Brooks (1978) had participants perform a paired-associates learning task, learning to associate hieroglyphic symbol strings with English words. Figure 7-6(A) presents examples of his stimuli. Each symbol in the string had a certain meaning, as shown in Figure 7-6(B), but participants were not alerted to this fact. Later they were unexpectedly given new strings, such as those in Figure 7-6(C), and were asked four questions: Does it fly? Is it big? Is it alive? Does it attack? Most of the participants reported they answered the questions by thinking of a previous example that looked similar. However, they generally couldn't point to any particular symbol in the string as a basis for their response.

Brooks's results pose a puzzle for cognitive psychologists. Apparently, participants sometimes explicitly test specific hypotheses when forming concepts (as in the Bruner et al., 1956 experiments), sometimes they form prototypes (as in the Cabeza et al., 1999, experiments), and sometimes they memorize exemplars (as in the Reber, 1967, 1976, and Brooks, 1978 experiments). The question is, when and why do people adopt such different approaches?

Brooks (1978) believed the answer had to do with the concept formation task itself. Some simple laboratory tasks, such as the one used by Bruner and colleagues (1956), seem to lead

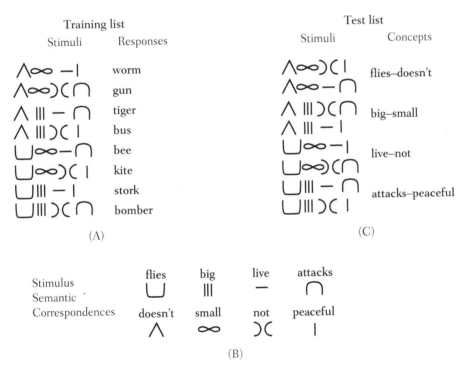

FIGURE 7-6 Stimuli from Brooks's (1978) experiments.

Source: Reprinted from *Journal of Verbal Learning and Verbal Behavior*, Vol. 23, issue 6, Deborah G. Kemler Nelson, The Effect of Intention on What Concepts are Acquired, pp. 734–759, Copyright © 1984, with permission from Elsevier.

participants to adopt an analytical, hypothesis-testing framework. Other, more complex stimuli lead people to abandon this approach for another. Brooks went on to describe five factors that encourage people to store information about individual exemplars.

The first factor involves task requirements to learn information that distinguishes among individual instances. Brooks (1978) reminded us that in natural situations, different items in the same category must sometimes be treated differently. It is all very well to recognize that Rover, the lovable family dog, and Killer, the attack dog for the company down the street, are both dogs, but the child or adult who treats them as interchangeable could be in for a painful surprise.

A second factor involves the original learning situation. In many real-life situations, instances are not presented one at a time in rapid succession (as in many laboratory experiments). Instead, the same instance (Rover, the family dog) may appear repeatedly (especially at mealtimes!), affording the person a chance to get to know certain instances very well.

Third, some stimuli lend themselves to hypothesis testing better than others do. Notice that in the Bruner and colleagues (1956) stimuli, instances varied on only four dimensions. In real life, things vary in many complicated ways. Often, the relevant dimensions of variation are not apparent to the novice, an idea we discussed in the section on perceptual learning. A fourth factor is that in real-life concept learning, instances may belong to a number of categories all at the same time. Rover might belong to any of the following categories: "dog," "family pet," "partner to take to obedience classes," "source of mud on rainy days," or even "incurrer of large food bills." Finally, Brooks pointed out that in natural settings, we learn about instances without knowing how we will be called on to use the information later.

Kemler Nelson (1984) also argued that much of our real-life conceptual knowledge is acquired nonanalytically rather than analytically. Her research has shown that children are especially likely to use this mode of concept learning, as are adults when they are not allowed to devote many cognitive resources to the task—for example, when they are forced to process information more rapidly than they might otherwise do (Smith & Kemler, 1984).

Furthermore, Kemler Nelson (1984) believed that nonanalytic concept formation is especially likely with materials that have strong family resemblance structures. Participants in one of her experiments were presented with artificial faces, such as those in Figure 7-7. The faces varied on four attributes—curliness of hair, length of nose, size of ears, and breadth of mustache—with each attribute having three values (such as slightly curly mustache, medium curly mustache, and very curly mustache). Participants learned which faces belonged to the category "doctors" and which to the category "policemen." Faces presented during the learning phase were carefully chosen, such that one attribute distinguished between the two categories (in this example, length of nose: Doctors have long noses; policemen, short ones). At the same time, the two categories differed in their family resemblance structure, although the difference was not absolute. In this example, doctors tend to have slightly curly mustaches, large ears, and broad mustaches, and policemen, very curly mustaches, small ears, and thinner mustaches, although not every instance shared all these features.

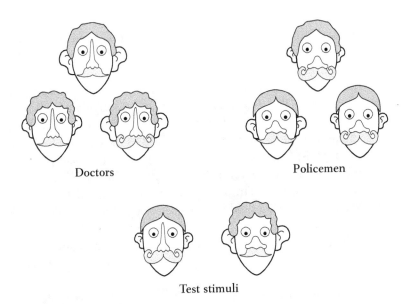

Doctors

Policemen

Test stimuli

FIGURE 7-7 Stimuli used by Kemler Nelson (1984).

Source: Kemler Nelson, D.G. (1984). The effect of intention on what concepts are acquired. *Journal of Verbal Learning and Verbal Behavior*, 23, 6 page 742. Copyright 1984, with permission from Elsevier.

In the subsequent test phase, participants were presented with a number of test faces, including two "critical" test faces, and were asked to classify each one. These faces pitted the criterion feature (such as length of nose) against the family resemblance structure. The way people classified these faces revealed the basis of their classification: If they used a criterion feature, they classified the faces one way; if they used family resemblance structure, they were more likely to make a different classification. In this example (see Figure 7-7 again), note that the left test face has a long nose, suggesting it belongs to the "doctor" category, but that it has more overall similarity to faces in the "policemen" category; the reverse is true for the right face.

Some of Kemler Nelson's (1984) participants were explicitly told to search for a means of distinguishing between doctors and policemen; others were simply asked to learn to recognize the pictures. Kemler Nelson found the latter group was especially likely to use family resemblance structure as a basis for classification; approximately 60% did so. Of those in the former group, only 46% used that approach. She concluded that both the kinds of concepts being learned and the instructions about the task influence the concept acquisition strategy that people adopt. In addition, it is likely there were large individual differences in how people form categories for complex stimuli.

Using and Forming Scripts

In Chapter 6 we discussed the concept of scripts, schemata for routine events. If you and each of your classmates listed your knowledge of what happens when you purchase a meal at Tim Hortons, all the lists would likely show a very high level of agreement in terms of what events and actions you mention, the order in which you mention them, and the level of description you use. Your "Tim Hortons script" may be roughly as follows: You enter; walk to the counter; wait in line; order coffee and food; pay the counterperson; wait while your order is assembled; carry the tray of coffee and food to the counter that holds napkins, straws; gather those supplies; find a table; sit and eat; gather the trash onto the tray; take the tray to the trash bin; dump the contents of the tray into the trash bin; leave. There may be some personal variations to your Tim Hortons script, but for the most part your script probably overlaps with the one presented here a great deal. Notice we don't specify details at the level of how many steps you need to walk to the counter or whether you need to turn right or left—these details vary at different Tim Hortons locations and don't much affect the script. The point is, the presented Tim Hortons script would work at pretty much any Tim Hortons.

Bower, Black, and Turner (1979) investigated how much people typically use scripts. They first asked participants to write their scripts for a number of specific events: going to a restaurant, attending a lecture, getting up in the morning, grocery shopping, visiting a doctor. They compared the notes generated by all the participants and found a high degree of overlap in what people mentioned. The participants generally agreed about which characters to describe, which props and actions to mention, and the order in which different actions would occur.

The investigators also found a high degree of agreement in description level. Thus, most people would mention "eating the food" instead of "picking up a spoon, dipping it into soup, raising the spoon to lips, and sipping." In another study, Bower and colleagues (1979) showed that if information from a story was presented in scrambled order, people tended to recall it in the scripted order. In a further experiment, the investigators presented stories that mentioned only some of the events in a typical script. They found that in a later recall task, people often "recalled" information that wasn't in the story but was in the relevant script. Rizzella and O'Brien (2002) found that when people were given a narrative text to read and remember, central concepts relevant to the script (such as, in a restaurant script, being served a meal) were typically better remembered than concepts of less importance to the script (such as giving one's name to a hostess).

Psychological Essentialism

A proposal by Medin (1989), drawing on work by the philosopher Hilary Putnam (1975), has examined people's reliance on underlying nature as a basis for many concepts. Medin proposed a framework he called **psychological essentialism** and described several assumptions. The first is that people generally act as if objects, people, or events have certain essences or underlying natures that make them what they are. Presumably, for instance, a human being is a human being by virtue of having a certain molecular structure. That essence constrains or limits the kinds of variation that different instances of a category can show. So, for instance, people can vary in height, weight, hair colour, eye colour, bone structure, and the like, but they must have certain other properties in common by virtue of the underlying essence they share. People's theories about the essences of various categories help them connect deeper properties (such as the structure of DNA) to more superficial properties (such as eye colour or hair colour). For example, Medin pointed out that although most of us believe the categories "male" and "female" are genetically determined, most of us look at characteristics such as hair length, facial hair, and so on rather than conducting genetic tests when classifying a new person as a woman or a man. We may make errors in using superficial characteristics, but we probably won't often be led astray.

People's knowledge of the essence of a category varies by level of expertise. Biologists, in general, know a lot more about the genetic structure of a human being than do laypeople. For this reason, experts can generally be expected to make different and more accurate classifications, especially if the criteria for the classifications are subtle. Medin's (1989) idea is that classifying on the basis of perceptual or other superficial similarity may be a strategy that can be pretty effective much of the time. Still, when the situation calls for it and if the expertise is possessed, people classify on the basis of deeper principles. (Note how this is a similar idea to the discussions of the effects of expertise on Perception in chapter 3. We also discuss how expertise effects Problem Solving in Chapters 10 and 12). This suggestion implies, then, that people's classification of instances will change as they become more experienced and knowledgeable— an idea that fits well with our discussion of perceptual learning, as well as with the currently available data.

The way people acquire and mentally represent concepts may also vary as a function of what the concepts are (Murphy, 2005). Some psychologists have adopted the perspective of philosophers in distinguishing among kinds of concepts. **Nominal-kind concepts** include concepts that have clear definitions. **Natural-kind concepts,** such as "gold" or "tiger," are of things naturally occurring in some environment (Putnam, 1975). A third kind of concept is **artifact concepts,** things constructed to serve some function or accomplish some task (see Keil, 1989; Schwartz, 1978, 1979, 1980). Different information may be represented in different kinds of concepts.

For instance, nominal-kind concepts (such as the ones Bruner taught participants in his studies) may include information about necessary and sufficient features, because these things exist as part of the concept definition. Natural-kind concepts may include more information about definitional or essential features, especially about molecular or chromosomal structure. Natural-kind concepts may also be more likely to have a family resemblance structure but can be equally well explained within a knowledge-based approach.

Artifact concepts, in contrast, may highlight information about the object's purpose or function and may be adequately described only within the knowledge-based approach. In one study, Barton and Komatsu (1989) presented participants with five natural-kind concepts (such as *goat, water, gold)* and five artifacts (such as *TV, pencil, mirror).* With each concept, they asked the participants to imagine different transformations. Some transformations were phrased in terms of function or purpose (for example, a female goat that did not give milk or a TV with no visible picture); others were in terms of physical features (for example, gold that was red in colour or a pencil that was not cylindrical). A third type of change was molecular (for example, water that did not consist of the formula H2O, or a mirror not made out of glass). The investigators found that with natural-kind terms participants were most sensitive to molecular transformations, whereas with artifact terms they were most sensitive to functional changes. Apparently, then, all concepts are not treated equally, and, under at least some conditions, people use their knowledge about why instances of a category should be grouped together in their representation of the related concept (Medin, Lynch, & Solomon, 2000).

As is evident form the preceding sections, concept formation and categorization is a complex cognitive phenomenon likely involving both conscious and unconscious processes. In addition, the type of strategy adopted by individuals likely depends on many aspects of the stimuli (category size, structure, and complexity), situation, and goals of the individual. These goals may involve the initiation of specific behaviours relevant to the categories. In addition, as categorization involves attention, perception, learning, and memory, it is important to think of categorization in light of these cognitive processes.

SUMMARY

1. Categories are classes of similar objects, events, or patterns. Concepts are mental representations of those categories. Concepts are thought to help us order our knowledge and to relate new objects or patterns to previously encountered ones.
2. There are five distinct approaches to the study of concepts. These have been themselves categorized into two major types: similarity-based and explanation-based (Komatsu, 1992).
3. The similarity-based category, comprising the classical, prototype, and exemplar views (and some parts of the schemata view), includes the approaches in which categorization is assumed to be based on the similarity of an instance to some abstract specification of the category (for example, a definition or a prototype) or to one or more stored exemplars.
4. The explanation-based category, comprising aspects of the schemata/scripts view and aspects of the knowledge-based view, instead sees people as classifying instances based on meaningful relationships among instances and categories.

5. The classical approach to concepts posits that each concept is defined by a set of necessary and sufficient features.
6. The prototype approach to concepts holds that we categorize objects by comparing them to mental abstractions, called prototypes, which are idealized representations of some class of objects or events.
7. Some researchers have found that the acquisition of concepts results in a shift from right- to left-hemisphere processing in the brain.
8. The exemplar approach to concepts assumes we store specific individual instances and use these stored representations to categorize.
9. The schemata/scripts view regards concepts as schemata, packets of information with specific parts that fill in default values for aspects of the situation.
10. Proponents of the knowledge-based view of concepts hold that people use their own theories to guide their classification of objects.
11. When people are explicitly asked to form concepts and to search for underlying rules or features, they seem to acquire and use different kinds of information from what they use when left to their own exploration. This raises the question of applicability of very traditional laboratory-based investigations of concept formation to the processes people use outside the laboratory. What gets learned depends, apparently, on the original learning materials, the task instructions, and the learner's anticipation of how the learned information will be used in the future. As in other areas of cognition, then, the way people process information is flexible and varies with the situation and the purpose of the task.

REVIEW QUESTIONS

1. Describe the distinction many cognitive psychologists make between concepts and categories. What are the cognitive benefits of having concepts? Explain.
2. Contrast the classical, prototype, and exemplar proposals for how concepts are mentally represented. What kinds of arguments and/or empirical findings support each? What kinds of arguments and/or empirical data are troublesome for each?
3. Describe what a family resemblance structure is and how it relates to the prototype approach to concepts.
4. Compare and contrast the schemata view and the knowledge-based view of concepts. Are the two compatible? How or how not?
5. Briefly review Reber's work on implicit learning and its implications for concept formation.
6. Give some new examples of scripts, and justify your examples.
7. Discuss this statement: "Any approach to concepts must strike some balance between cognitive economy and informativeness."

KEY TERMS

artifact concept
basic level of categorization
category
classical view of concepts
concept
exemplar view of concepts
family resemblance structure
   of concepts
features

implicit learning
knowledge-based view of
   concepts
natural-kind concept
nominal-kind concept
nonanalytic concept
   formation
prototype
prototype view of concepts

psychological essentialism
schemata/scripts view
   of concepts
subordinate level
   of categories
superordinate level
   of categories

Visual Imagery and Spatial Cognition

CHAPTER

8

Think of the house or apartment you consider your permanent residence. In particular, think about its kitchen. How many cabinet doors does it have? Obviously, this question draws on your memory. Most people can answer it after some mental work. What sort of work is required? In the process one author of this text used, she first recognized that she didn't have the information needed already stored; that is, she didn't know the answer "off the top of her head." So she had to determine the answer in another way. She mentally pictured her kitchen by drawing on memory. Then, starting at one end of the room, she scanned her mental picture, counting cabinet doors. Her procedure is neither difficult nor original (Shepard, 1966), but seems to be the one commonly used.

The nature of these "mental pictures," or **visual images,** is the focus of this chapter. We will look at the role of images in memory and at how images are used in techniques called *mnemonics,* which are designed to aid or improve memory. We will also consider experiments investigating the ways in which people construct and use visual images and what these findings suggest about cognition. Finally, we will turn to the nature of visual images, considering the kinds of mental representations used to create and store them.

Throughout the chapter, we will confine ourselves to discussion of visual images. Recognize, however, that other kinds of mental images exist. Examples include auditory images (such as the imagined sound of your favourite song), olfactory images (such as the imagined smell of your grandmother's chocolate-chip cookies), and cutaneous images (such as the imagined feeling of your toe being stubbed into the wall). Visual images, like visual perception, have received the most attention within cognitive psychology. Thus, as we did in examining perception (Chapter 3), where we focused on visual perception, in this chapter we will focus on visual imagery.

The study of visual imagery has had a controversial history within psychology (Paivio, 1971). Although occasional references to imagery were made at the turn of the 20th century, the rise of behaviourism essentially dictated that even the mere concept of an image be rejected. Visual images are problematic as objects of scientific inquiry. After all, the experience of a visual image is just about as private an experience as one can have. If our author asserts that she is forming a visual image of her kitchen, no one but she can tell if she really has the image or is just pretending. Visual images, unlike behaviours, cannot be seen, counted, or controlled by other people. Because visual images can be reported only by the person who asserts she is experiencing them, that person can distort or bias them, either consciously or inadvertently. Behaviourists argue that imagery is not the sort of topic that can be investigated with sufficient scientific rigor or control.

Nonetheless, interest in visual imagery never completely vanished (Paivio, 1971), and in fact became stronger after the popularity of behaviourism waned in the 1960s. It is difficult to explain how people perform certain cognitive tasks, such as the one described earlier, without talking about visual images. Moreover, research on memory suggests that people who report using imagery are better able to recall information than people who do not.

Sports psychologists, too, have a strong interest in the use of visual imagery. An athlete who before competing spends time mentally imagining a smoothly executed, well-timed, elegant performance has been shown to perform better a bit later when engaging in her or his sport (Martin, Moritz, & Hall, 1999; Munroe-Chandler & Guerrero, 2017). Recent research suggests further that imagery can be used to help people cope with negative emotional events, such as remembering a real incident of being rejected, abandoned, or excluded. Research participants asked to visualize so-called "cool" aspects of the experience—for example, where they were standing or sitting in relation to other people during the incident—were better able to reduce their hostile feelings than were participants asked to image their visceral reactions during the incident, or participants not asked to form any images (Ayduk, Mischel, & Downey, 2002).

Psychologists now recognize that to eliminate imagery as a subject of discussion and investigation is to overlook a potentially fundamental aspect of cognition. Hence visual imagery has regained credibility as a worthwhile topic among most cognitive psychologists.

MNEMONICS AND MEMORY CODES

If you want to increase your chances of remembering (and especially recalling) information, you can make use of several techniques, collectively called **mnemonics.** We will see that many (although not all) involve the construction of mental pictures or images. We'll begin by looking at a number of the best-known mnemonics, examining two theoretical explanations for why they work.

Mnemonics

Around 500 B.C., the Greek poet Simonides was called out from entertaining diners at a banquet. While he was out of the hall, the roof caved in, crushing the guests so badly that they could not be identified by members of their families. Simonides, by recalling where each guest sat, was able to help relatives find the remains of their family members (Paivio, 1971). Thus was invented one of the first mnemonic techniques, often called the **method of loci.**

The method of loci, as the name might suggest, requires the learner to imagine a series of places (locations) that have some sort of order to them. For example, you might use a series of landmarks you pass on your way from your dorm room or apartment to the gym. You would then divide the material you wanted to remember, mentally picturing the different pieces at the different landmarks.

Suppose your professor needed to remember to bring certain things to a meeting—for example, her tablet, a pen, certain computer printouts, a book, and a coffee (to get her through the meeting). She could use the method of loci to remember these materials in the following way. First, she would imagine herself walking through her office doorway (first locus) and propping the first object (her tablet) against the door as a doorstop. Next she would see herself walking by a table in her office vestibule, leaving her pen teetering on top of all the student essays that are piled high on the table. Then she would see herself walking into the hall and down the nearby stairwell, draping the printouts over the railing at the top of the stairs. She would mentally exit the building, pass a big oak tree to her left, and place the book on one of its branches. Finally, as she entered the building where the meeting was to take place, she would picture the coffee rushing at her like a river as she opened the door. When she needed to remember these five items, all she would need to do would be to mentally "take a walk" over the same route, noticing the objects she passed. Essentially, she would take the same path again, this time looking around in her image as she did so.

Bower (1970a) provided a list of principles that improve the workings of the method-of-loci technique (see Box 8-1). Ross and Lawrence (1968) showed that college students trained in using the method of loci could recall up to 38 of 40 words after one presentation; by any standard, this level of performance is exceptional.

Another technique for improving memory could be called the technique of *interacting images.* A study reported in 1894 anticipated the usefulness of this technique. The results indicated that recall of concrete nouns on a list improved when participants were told to form images of the words, in comparison to when they were not given such instructions (Kirkpatrick, 1894). Bower (1970b) found similar results in experiments of paired-associates learning (review Chapter 5 if you've forgotten what this is). In other words, if participants were given pairs of words such as *goat–pipe,* participants who formed images of, say, a goat smoking a pipe recalled almost twice as many paired associates as control participants who were not instructed to use imagery These figures may underestimate the effect, because some control participants may have spontaneously used imagery

Bower's (1970b) research showed in particular that for images to be maximally effective in paired associates, participants should try to form images that interact—for example, a goat *smoking* a pipe rather than simply a picture of a goat next to a picture of a pipe, with the two pictures separated in space. The principle of interactive imagery applies equally to the method-of-loci technique: The images should depict the to-be-remembered items interacting in some way with items at the various loci (see Principle 6 in Box 8-1).

A third mnemonic technique, one that also involves imagery, is called the *pegword method.* Like the method of loci, it involves picturing the items with another set of ordered "cues"— pegging them to the cue. In this case, the cues are not locations but rather nouns that come from a memorized rhyming list: "One is a bun, two is a shoe, three is a tree, four is a door, five is a hive, six is sticks, seven is heaven, eight is a gate, nine is wine, and ten is a hen." The method calls for the participant to picture the first item interacting with a bun, the second with a shoe, the third with a tree, and so forth (notice that the method works for lists of only 10 items or fewer). Bugelski, Kidd, and Segmen (1968) showed that the method also improves

---

Box 8-1 Principles of Use of the Method of Loci

1. Use a list of cues that you know well. You can't retrieve any associations if the cue images aren't available at both presentation and recall.
2. The cues must be memory images of geographic locations.
3. Associations must be formed between the items to be remembered and the cue locations at the time you originally encounter the items.
4. The associations between cue locations and the items must be one to one.
5. Use imagery especially visual imagery to form associative links.
6. Use interactive images to link the item and its cue location.
7. If you study the items more than once, the same cue location should be used for a given memory item.
8. During recall, cue your own memory by using the list of locations.
9. Use the same recall cues (locations) that you used during study.

Source: Adapted from Bower (1970a).

recall in paired-associates tasks as long as participants are given 4 seconds or more per item to form the images.

Not all mnemonic techniques have to do with imagery. One set of techniques that does not involve visual imagery per se involves *recoding* the material to be recalled, adding extra words or sentences to *mediate,* or go between, your memory and the material. One example, familiar to most schoolchildren, involves taking the first letter of each word you want to remember and forming a word or sentence from these letters. This technique can be used to recall the names of the Great Lakes (*HOMES:* Huron, Ontario, Michigan, Erie, Superior) or to recall the names of the notes on the lines of a musical staff ("Every good boy deserves fudge"). Research investigating the usefulness of this technique reports mixed results, although the technique is popular (Carlson, Zimmer, & Glover, 1981). Notice, by the way, that the words and sentences serve functions similar to those of the images in the techniques described previously. Both are *mediators:* internal codes that connect the items to be remembered and your (later) overt responses (Klatzky 1980).

Box 8-2 Does Imagery Affect Memory for Autobiographical Events?

We've seen how the use of imagery can improve memory for things like grocery lists, new languages, and the like. But what impact, if any, does imagery have on memory for autobiographical events? Katherine Arbuthnott at the University of Regina has asked this very question. In a paper published in *Applied Cognitive Psychology* (2005), she had participants repeatedly image both autobiographical events from earlier in life (e.g., a family vacation) and a "made-up" memory (e.g., a canoeing trip that could plausibly have happened, but did not). Over multiple sessions, Arbuthnott had her participants rehearse these memories (both real and "made-up") using guided imagery techniques. In a fourth session, some three weeks following the beginning of the experiment, Arbuthnott asked her participants to recall as much as they could from the autobiographical memories they had reviewed in earlier weeks. This allowed her to assess whether people could accurately distinguish their real memories from their imagined ones. Following that test, Arbuthnott administered a memory test in which people were asked to distinguish between statements they had made about their memories and those they had not. Finally, they were asked to rate the phenomenological characteristics (how real does this seem?) of each of the memories (real and made-up). Arbuthnott's results indicated that repetition increased the similarity of the phenomenology ratings of the real and imagined events, but also made people more accurate in identifying statements they had actually made. Arbuthnott concluded that because of the increase in phenomenology ratings for imagined events (i.e., they *feel* real), psychotherapists should take caution when using guided imagery with clients who have legally relevant issues. For other work on this issue, see Arbuthnott, Arbuthnott, and Rossiter (2001), and Arbuthnott, Geelen, and Kealy (2002).

Finally, as mentioned in Chapter 6, various types of categorization and organization of material also improve recall. Arranging material into categories helps organize the material, and this in turn raises its probability of recall. As discussed in Chapter 6, organization presumably adds to the number of "hooks" attached to the material to be remembered, and the greater the number of hooks, the greater the probability of recall.

Why do so many mnemonic techniques use visual imagery? How do imagery-based mnemonics function differently from non–imagery-based mnemonics? Does something about visual images per se make them especially memorable? We will consider two opposing views on this matter.

The Dual-Coding Hypothesis

Allan Paivio (1969, 1971, 1983), from the University of Western Ontario, originated the **dual-coding hypothesis** of memory to explain the workings of various mnemonics. According to Paivio, long-term memory contains two distinct coding systems (or codes) for representing information to be stored. One is verbal, containing information about an item's abstract, linguistic meaning. The other involves imagery: mental pictures of some sort that represent what the item looks like. Items to remember can be coded by either verbal labels or visual images and in some cases both. Paivio's idea is that pictures and concrete words give rise to both verbal labels and visual images; that is, they have two possible internal codes or mental representations. Abstract words, in contrast, typically have only one kind of code or representation: a verbal label.

One study by Paivio (1965) provided evidence to support this hypothesis. Participants were asked to learn one of four lists of noun pairs. The first list (CC) included pairs in which both referred to concrete objects (for example, *book–table*). The second list (CA) included pairs in which the first noun was concrete and the second abstract (such as *chair–justice*). The third list (AC) was the converse of the second (such as *freedom–dress*). The fourth (AA) contained pairs of abstract nouns (for example, *beauty–truth*). Of a possible 16 correct responses, participants averaged 11.41, 10.01, 7.36, and 6.05 correct responses for the CC, CA, AC, and AA lists, respectively.

Paivio (1965) explained the results as follows. Whenever possible, participants spontaneously formed visual images of the noun pairs. The formation was easiest with concrete nouns. Paivio (1969) assumed that visual imagery, unlike verbal labelling, increases as a function of concreteness: the more concrete the noun, the richer the image and the more elaborated the internal code. This helps explain why pictures (very concrete) are often remembered better than words (see, for example, Kirkpatrick, 1894; Shepard, 1967). When items are coded by both images and verbal labels (as concrete nouns can be), the chances of the learner's retrieving them are obviously better. If the learner forgets the verbal label, he or she might still access the visual image, or vice versa. Items coded only by verbal labels are disadvantaged; if the verbal label is forgotten or "misplaced," the learner has less to go on.

Further, Paivio (1969) believed that the first noun in a pair (called the "stimulus" noun) serves as a *conceptual peg* on which the second ("response") noun is hooked. In this sense, the stimulus noun serves as a "mental anchor," a place to which the representation of the response noun can be attached. Thus, the imaginability of the first noun is particularly important in improving memorability, explaining why recall in the CA condition was significantly higher than in the AC condition.

The Relational-Organizational Hypothesis

Bower (1970b) proposed an alternative to the dual-coding hypothesis that he called the **relational-organizational hypothesis.** He believed that imagery improved memory not because images are necessarily richer than verbal labels, but because imagery produces more associations between the items to be recalled. Forming an image (say, between two words in a pair, or between a word and a location, as in the method of loci) typically requires the person to create a number of links or hooks between the information to be remembered and other information. Recall from Chapter 6 that the more "hooks" a piece of information in memory has to other information, the greater are the chances of recalling it. Bower's argument, then, is that imagery works by facilitating the creation of a greater number of hooks that link the two to-be-remembered pieces of information.

Bower (1970b) performed an experiment to distinguish between the dual-coding and the relational-organizational hypotheses. Participants were divided into three groups, each given different instructions for a paired-associates learning task. One group was told to use "overt rote repetition" (that is, to rehearse aloud); the second, to construct two images that did not interact and were "separated in imaginal space"; the third, to construct an interactive scene of the two words in a pair (p. 530). Results showed that all participants recognized about 85% of the previously seen words. However, recall of those words differed greatly. Those who used rote memorization recalled about 30% of the paired associates; those using noninteractive imagery, 27%; and those who formed interacting images, about 53%.

If imagery simply led to more elaborated coding of the paired associates, as the dual-coding hypothesis predicts, then participants in the two conditions that involved instructions to form two images ought to have performed similarly. In fact, only those who formed interacting images showed an improvement over the rote memorizers. Apparently, it is not imagery per se that helps memory but rather the way in which imagery is used. Interacting images presumably create or suggest more links between the target information and other information, making the target information easier to retrieve.

Although the dual-coding hypothesis continues to attract proponents (see Yuille, 1983), still unresolved are how well it explains the workings of imagery mnemonics and what kind of explanations it provides for nonimagery mnemonics. However imagery mnemonics work, there is at least little doubt that many do aid memory. To understand how these mnemonics work, it will be necessary to explore further what imagery is and how it works, topics we turn to next.

EMPIRICAL INVESTIGATIONS OF IMAGERY

A series of studies by McMaster University's Lee Brooks (1968) is widely regarded as yielding some of the best evidence that images are distinct from verbal materials or at least use different processes from those used by verbal materials. Figure 8-1 depicts different conditions of Brooks's primary experiment. In one condition, participants were asked to imagine a letter, such as the outlined capital F in Figure 8-1(A), and then to move clockwise mentally from a particular corner (marked in Figure 8-1 with an asterisk) and to indicate, for each corner, whether it was at the extreme top or extreme bottom of the letter. In this example, the correct responses are "yes, yes, yes, no, no, no, no, no, no, yes."

Participants indicated their responses in different ways. One mode of response was verbal: Participants said "yes" or "no," as noted. Another response mode was spatial. Participants were given a response sheet on which the letters *Y* and *N* were printed in an irregular pattern and were told to point to either a *Y* or an *N* in each row to indicate their responses. Brooks (1968) found that participants took almost two and a half times longer when they responded by pointing than they did by responding verbally.

On a second task, Figure 8-1(B), participants were asked to remember a sentence, such as "A bird in the hand is not in the bush," and, for each word, to indicate whether it was a concrete noun. In this example, the correct responses are "no, yes, no, no, yes, no, no, no, no, yes." As with the previous task, sometimes participants responded verbally, and other times they pointed to *Y* or *N* on a response sheet. With this task, however, people were faster to respond by pointing than they were to respond verbally (although the difference in response times was not as great).

A BIRD IN THE HAND IS NOT IN THE BUSH.

Start at the corner marked with an asterisk, and indicate whether or not each corner is at the extreme top or bottom.

(A)

For each word in the sentence above, indicate whether or not each word is a noun.

(B)

FIGURE 8-1 Stimuli from the Brooks (1968) study.

Source: Copyright 1968, Canadian Psychological Association.

One explanation for these results is as follows. The first task requires the formation of a visual image of an *F*. The visual image probably has at least some picture-like qualities (spatial or visual), so a spatial or visually guided response (pointing) would be interfered with to a greater extent than would a verbal response. In other words, the visual image is more disruptive of, and disrupted by, another spatial or visual type of task (pointing) than by a verbal kind of task (talking). The converse is also true: Holding a sentence in memory (a verbal task) is easier to do with a concurrent visual/spatial task (such as pointing) than with another verbal task. Notice that pointing or talking do not differ in difficulty overall but vary in difficulty as a function of the task with which they are being performed. Brooks's (1968) work supports the idea that images and words use different kinds of internal codes (as the dual-coding hypothesis suggests).

Brooks's (1968) task is not the only one that apparently requires people to form visual images. Here is another. Answer the following question: Which is larger, a pineapple or a coconut? (Finke, 1989). To answer the question, you most likely constructed a visual image of a coconut next to a pineapple and "read" the answer from your image.

Moyer (1973) asked similar questions and found that people were faster to respond when the two objects (in his study, animals) differed greatly. This effect, called the *symbolic-distance effect*, works as follows. Other things being equal, you'd be faster to answer the question "Which is bigger, a whale or a cockroach?" than the question "Which is bigger, a hog or a cat?" Interestingly, the same pattern of response times is also obtained when people look at actual objects (Paivio, 1975). In other words, you'd be faster to answer the first question even if, instead of consulting visual images, you looked at the actual animals or at photographs of the animals. This result suggests that images seem to function, at least in some ways, like pictures. If people merely retrieved verbal information (for example, from a semantic network such as those described in Chapter 7), it would be difficult to explain this pattern of results.

Mental Rotation of Images

The preceding studies suggest that people create and use visual images to answer certain questions and perform certain tasks. They also suggest that the images created are in some ways picturelike (although this conclusion has been energetically debated, as we'll see). At the same time that these findings were reported, other studies showed that people could do more than simply create images; they could also, apparently, mentally transform them.

One of the most famous studies of this type was performed by Shepard and Metzler (1971). They showed participants perspective line drawings of three-dimensional objects (Figure 8-2 presents examples). On each trial, participants would see two drawings. In some cases, the two drawings depicted the same object but with one rotated by some degree. In the other cases, the drawings depicted mirror-image reversals; in other words, the objects were similar but not identical. The mirror images were also sometimes rotated. The kinds of rotations

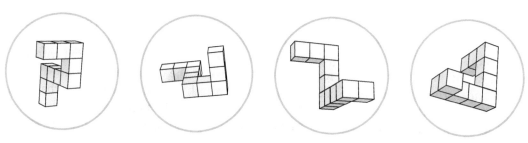

FIGURE 8-2 Stimuli from the Shepard and Metzler (1971) study.

Source: From *Science*, 19 Feb 1971, Vol. 171, Issue 3972, pp. 701–703, DOI: 10.1126/science.171.3972.701. Reprinted with permission from AAAS.

used were either in the picture plane (that is, as if the drawing were rotated on the page) or in depth (that is, as if the object were going toward or away from the viewer). Shepard and Metzler (1971) found that the amount of time it took participants to decide if the two drawings depicted the same object or a mirror-image reversal was directly proportional to the angle of rotation between the drawings.

Figure 8-3 shows their results. This close correspondence between the angle of rotation of the two drawings and the participants' response times strongly suggests that they performed the task by **mental rotation** of one drawing. Moreover, the time it took participants to come to a decision was the same for rotations in the picture plane and in depth. This suggests they were mentally rotating three-dimensional images, not just the two-dimensional drawings. Had participants been rotating only the latter, their performance would have differed as a function of whether the rotation was in the picture plane or in depth.

Later studies by Cooper and Shepard (1973, 1975) showed that participants also mentally rotated more recognizable stimuli, such as alphabet letters or drawings of hands. In one study (Cooper & Shepard, 1973), participants were sometimes given a drawing of the letter to be used on a trial, followed by a cue showing the orientation to which the test stimulus would be rotated, before the test stimulus appeared. If these two cues were presented early enough (for example, 1,000 milliseconds before the test stimulus appeared), then the participants' performances were the same for all angles of rotation. Figure 8-4 depicts the experimental conditions, and Figure 8-5 shows the results.

Note the shape of the curves in Figure 8-5, which suggests that participants were able to mentally rotate their images either clockwise or counterclockwise, depending on which direction led to a lesser angle. These results differ from those of Shepard and Metzler (as a comparison of Figures 8-4 and 8-5 shows), presumably because alphanumeric characters have a known "upright" position, whereas Shepard and Metzler's line drawings do not. By the way, one reason for the "peaks" in reaction times at 180 degrees might be that participants were uncertain about which direction to rotate the figure, so that the uncertainty contributed to some hesitance.

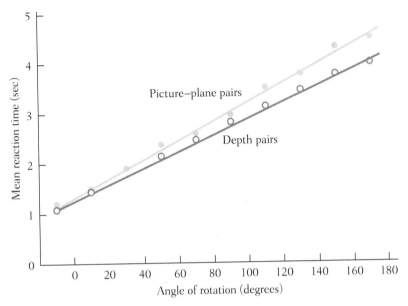

FIGURE 8-3 Results from the Shepard and Metzler (1971) study.

Source: From *Science*, 19 Feb 1971, Vol. 171, Issue 3972, pp. 701–703, DOI: 10.1126/science.171.3972.701. Reprinted with permission from AAAS.

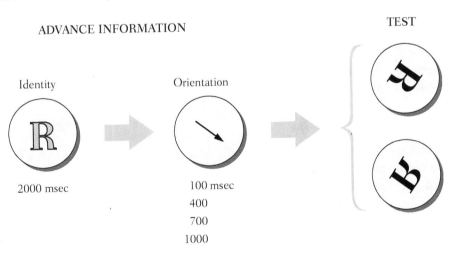

FIGURE 8-4 Cooper and Shepard's (1973) experimental design.

Source: Reprinted with permission of Psychonomic Society, Inc., Springer Nature, from "The Time Required Prepare for a Rotated Stimulus" Cooperau, L.A. & Shepard, R.N., 1, 3 (1973); permission conveyed through Copyright Clearance Center, Inc.

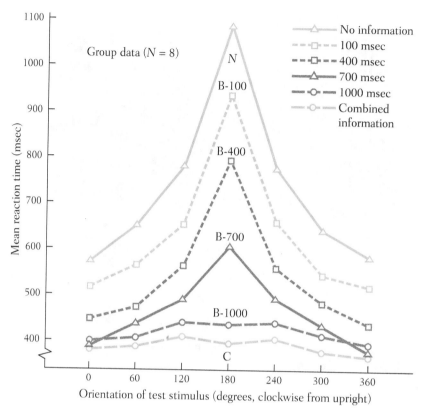

FIGURE 8-5 Results from the Cooper and Shepard (1973) study.

Source: Reprinted with permission of Psychonomic Society, Inc., Springer Nature, from "The Time Required Prepare for a Rotated Stimulus" Cooperau, L.A. & Shepard, R.N., 1, 3 (1973); permission conveyed through Copyright Clearance Center, Inc.

Are participants in these experiments mentally rotating the whole stimulus, or are they looking only at certain parts? To answer this question, Lynn Cooper (1975) performed studies that presented participants with irregular polygons, such as those shown in Figure 8-6. The polygons were formed by connecting a randomly scattered number of points, with more complex polygons resulting from a greater number of points. Participants were first trained to discriminate between original and mirror-image reflections of the polygons. Next, they were shown either the original polygons or the reflections at different angles of rotation and were asked to determine whether the object depicted was the original or a reflection of the original.

Cooper (1975) found that the reaction times once again increased linearly with the angle of rotation and that the rate of rotation was the same for all the polygons, regardless of their complexity. If participants were attending only to parts of the polygons, then performance ought to have differed as a function of the polygon complexity. Instead, it appears that participants mentally rotated entire polygons, treating the very simple polygons in exactly the same manner as they did the very complex ones.

In another study, Cooper (1976) showed that mental rotations, like physical rotations, are continuous in nature. Her demonstration worked as follows. She determined, for each person, his or her rate of mental rotation. To do this, she showed participants a polygon at a particular orientation. The polygon was removed, and participants were asked to start mentally rotating it in a clockwise direction. As they were doing this, a test shape (the polygon or its mirror

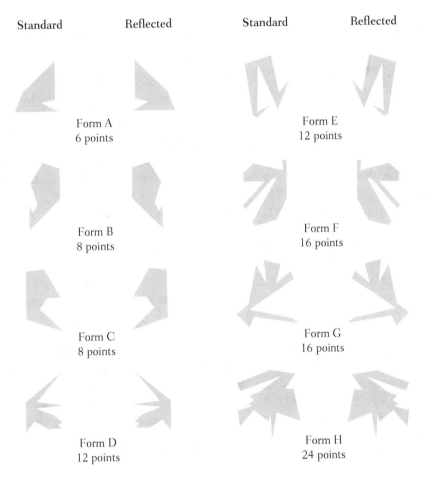

Standard   Reflected   Standard   Reflected

Form A
6 points

Form E
12 points

Form B
8 points

Form F
16 points

Form C
8 points

Form G
16 points

Form D
12 points

Form H
24 points

FIGURE 8-6 Stimuli from the Cooper (1975) study.

Source: Reprinted from *Cognitive Psychology*, vol. 7, issue 1, Lynn A. Cooper, Mental Rotation of Random Two-Dimensional Shapes, pp. 20–43, Copyright © 1975, with permission from Elsevier.

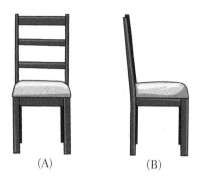

(A)   (B)

FIGURE 8-7 Two views of a chair. The pose depicted in (A) is a 90-degree clockwise rotation of the pose depicted in (B).

Source: Adapted from Biederman and Gerhardstein (1993, p. 1163). © Kendall Hunt Publishing Company.

image reflection) was presented in some orientation. If the test shape was presented at the orientation corresponding to the orientation at which the participants' visual images would be expected to be, their reaction times were always fast. As the disparity between the actual orientation of the test shape and the expected orientation of the visual image grew, the reaction times to respond grew longer.

These results in particular suggest that mental rotation works like physical rotation. If you draw a shape on a piece of paper and slowly rotate the paper 180 degrees, the drawing will pass through intermediate orientations: 10 degrees, 20 degrees, and so on. Similarly, it appears from Cooper's (1976) work that rotating images pass through intermediate angles of orientation.

Since Cooper's landmark studies, other cognitive psychologists have studied whether and how people use mental rotation in recognizing objects presented at unusual angles. Consider, for example, the object(s) depicted in Figure 8-7(A) and (B). How do you recognize (A) as depicting the same object as (B)? One possibility is that you mentally rotate an image of (A) until it reaches some canonical, or standard, orientation of depiction, such as shown in (B). Tarr and Pinker (1989) and Gauthier and Tarr (1997a, 1997b) provided evidence of mental rotation in recognizing two-dimensional shapes drawn to resemble asymmetric characters. Biederman and Gerhardstein (1993), in contrast, argued that when people view three-dimensional objects (or line drawings of them), as long as the distinctive geons (the basic geometric components) of the object remain visible people can recognize the object without performing mental rotation. This debate is very much ongoing. However, notice that both sides of the debate employ concepts and models used to explain perceptual phenomena.

Scanning Images

The research reviewed so far suggests that people can construct and transform their visual images. This evidence also seems to suggest that images are in many ways like pictures: They contain visual information, and the kinds of transformations performed on them seem to correspond to similar transformations on pictures. Another series of studies, carried out by Stephen Kosslyn, investigated the spatial properties of images. The series typically required participants first to form a visual image and then to scan it, moving from one location to another in their image, a process known as **imaginal scanning.** The idea is that the time people take to scan reveals something about the ways images represent spatial properties such as location and distance (Finke, 1989).

In one study, Kosslyn (1973) had participants study drawings of objects such as those shown in Figure 8-8. Notice that these drawings are elongated either vertically or horizontally and that each has three easily describable parts: two ends and the middle. After the initial learning phase, participants were told to form an image of one of the drawings and then to "look for" a particular part (for example, the petals of the flower). Some participants were told to focus first on one part of the image (for example, the top or the left) and then to scan, looking for the designated part. Kosslyn's results showed that the longer the distance from the designated end to the location of the part, the longer it took people to say whether the part they were looking for was in the drawing. So, for example, participants told to form an image of the flower and to start scanning at the bottom took longer to "find" the petals (at the top of the drawing) than they did to "find" the leaves (in the middle of the drawing). Presumably, this is because the visual image formed preserves many of the spatial characteristics of the drawings: Parts of the drawings that are separated in space are also separated in the image.

The results of the study were not entirely clear, however. Lea (1975), for instance, argued that perhaps the response times increased not because of increased distance in the image, but because of the number of items in the image that had to be scanned. Notice, in the flower example, that if

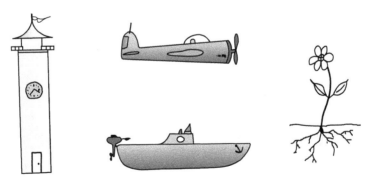

FIGURE 8-8 Stimuli from the Kosslyn (1973) study.

Source: Reprinted with permission of Psychonomic Society, Inc., Springer Nature, from "Scanning Visual Images: Some Structural Implications" Kosslyn, S.M., 14, 90 (1973); permission conveyed through Copyright Clearance Center, Inc.

one started from the bottom one would scan over the roots and the leaves on the way to the petals, but only over the roots to get to the leaves. Lea reported results supporting this interpretation.

In reply, Kosslyn, Ball, and Reiser (1978) performed another series of studies of image scanning. In one, they first created a map of a fictional island and had participants memorize the locations of seven objects shown on the map, reproduced in Figure 8-9. Notice that the seven objects allow for the construction of 21 distinct paths—for example, from the tree to the lake and from the tree to the hut. The paths vary in length, from 2 cm to 19 cm, and none contains any intervening objects.

Participants were instructed to focus mentally on one object. A few seconds later, the experimenter named another object on the island, and participants were then asked to imagine scanning to this second object by imagining a small black speck moving across the map in a straight line. They were instructed to push a button when they "arrived" at the second object, and their reaction times were recorded. The reaction times to scan between objects were correlated with the distance between objects (Kosslyn et al., 1978); that is, participants took more time to scan between two distant objects than they did to scan between two nearby ones. This reinforced the idea that images preserve spatial relations. Related studies by Pinker (1980) showed similar results when the stimulus was a three-dimensional array of objects (toys suspended inside an open box).

FIGURE 8-9 Stimuli from the Kosslyn et al. (1978) study.

Kosslyn's work suggests that people's scanning of their visual images is in some ways similar to their scanning of actual pictures: The greater the distance between two parts, the longer it takes to scan between them. Images apparently depict at least some spatial information, and people can retrieve this information from their images. These conclusions have strengthened the metaphor of images as kinds of "mental pictures" (Kosslyn, 1980).

Adding some interesting wrinkles to Kosslyn's conclusions, however, is work by Barbara Tversky (1981) on people's systematic errors in memory for maps. Before reading further, close this book, draw a map of Canada, and put in it the following cities: Vancouver, BC; Cranbrook, BC; Edmonton, Alberta; Grande Prairie, Alberta; Saskatoon, Saskatchewan; Winnipeg, Manitoba; Toronto, Ontario; Ottawa, Ontario; Montreal, QC; Quebec City, QC; Saint John, NB; Halifax, NS; and St. John's, NF. Presumably, to carry out this task you are drawing on a previously stored mental image of a map of Canada, formed perhaps in your Grade 4 geography class or maybe even from staring at a vinyl placemat showing the country.

Now, referring to your image, answer the following questions: (a) Which city is farther north, Quebec City or Vancouver? (b) Which city is farther west, Halifax or Ottawa? (c) Which city is farther east, Cranbrook or Grande Prairie? Now look at Figure 8-10, which shows the actual locations of these cities. If you are like Tversky's Stanford University participants, you made errors on questions (a) and (c). Tversky (1981) argued that people's maps are systematically distorted, because people use different **heuristics,** or rules of thumb, in orienting and anchoring oddly shaped units such as continents or provinces. Using principles of perceptual organization, such as those discussed in Chapter 3, people try to "line up" things to make them more orderly. Thus South America is "remembered" in an image as being directly south of North America, instead of southeast of North America, as it actually is.

A similar principle applies to your location of the various cities on your map. You probably know that the province of British Columbia is west of Alberta, a fact largely true. However, *parts* of Alberta are west of *parts* of British Columbia. In fact, Cranbrook, BC is *east* of Grande Prairie, AB, not west. And Vancouver is significantly *north* of Quebec City. But your knowledge of the provinces' relative locations, combined with your propensity to make your mental image of the map more aligned, contributes to systematic distortions. These distortions are one way in which mental images are *not* like mental pictures.

Another way is found in the work of Chambers and Reisberg (1992). They first asked their research participants to form an image of the creature shown in Figure 8-11(A). You might recognize the creature as the ambiguous "duck/ rabbit" shown in many introductory psychology textbooks. Sometimes experimenters told participants that the creature was a duck; other times, they said it was a rabbit. They presented the actual drawing for only about 5 seconds (enough time to form an image of the figure but not enough time to "reverse" the figure).

When participants had formed an image, they were then presented with a pair of duck/rabbits, either (A) and (B) or (A) and (C), and were asked to choose which had actually been

FIGURE 8-10 Map of Canada with selected cities.

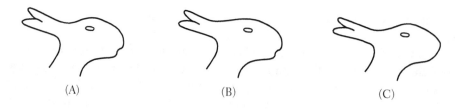

FIGURE 8-11 Test stimuli for Chambers and Reisberg's experiments: (A) unmodified figure, (B) modification on the duck's bill, (C) modification on the rabbit's nose.

Source: Reprinted from *Cognitive Psychology*, Vol. 24, issue 2, Deborah Chambers, Daniel Reisberg, What an Image Depicts Depends on What an Image Means, pp. 145–174, Copyright © 1992, with permission from Elsevier

presented. You'll notice that the distinctions between any pair are very subtle and hard to detect. Chambers and Reisberg (1992) found that when participants thought they were imaging a *duck,* they were well above chance at detecting the difference between (A) and (B) [the alteration in (B) is to the duck's bill] but could not clearly distinguish between (A) and (C) [the alteration in (C) is to the rabbit's nose]. Exactly the opposite pattern emerged for those who had formed an initial image of a rabbit. Chambers and Reisberg believed the reason for this effect is that people paid more attention to the region they took to be the creature's "face" and less to the back of the creature's head. In any case, the result shows that people who form images of the same physical stimulus, but who give different construals or meanings to the stimulus, actually form different images. In fact, Chambers and Reisberg reported from their previous work that even with hints and prompts, few participants spontaneously reversed their image of the duck/rabbit, although almost everyone looking at the picture of the duck/rabbit did.

This review sounds so far as if it were always beneficial to be able to construct and use mental images. But a recent study by Knauff and Johnson-Laird (2002) provides a counterexample. They studied people reasoning with what are called *three-term series problems,* such as

Tandy is furrier than Bussey.

Eskie is less furry than Bussey.

Which dog is furriest?

The authors varied the kinds of terms used in the problems. Some were easy to envisage both visually and spatially such as *above–below or front–back.* In other words, it's easy to mentally image one person in front of or behind another, *and* it is easy to mentally depict the three terms. Let's say, for example, that the premises state

Tandy is in back of Bussey.

Bussey is in back of Eskie.

Then it is easy to spatially depict the relative positions of the three dogs without forming a visual image of them, as in this "map":

(front) Eskie Bussey Tandy *(back)*

Notice that this representation doesn't show visual details of any of the dogs. Knauff and Johnson-Laird (2002) created other problems with different content, which were easy to form mental images of but not quite as easy to form spatial representations of—for example, *cleaner–dirtier, fatter–thinner.* If you form a representation of "Tandy is dirtier than Bussey," for instance, you probably do it by constructing a visual image of one dog more covered in mud than another one. There were also control problems, which were not easy to form any kind of image or spatial representation of (for example, *better–worse, smarter–dumber).*

Results showed that visual relations (for example, *cleaner–dirtier)* slowed down performance relative to either control problems (for example, *better–worse)* or visuospatial problems *(in back of–in front of).* Plausibly, the mental effort devoted to constructing the visual images used up mental capacity that could have been solely focused on drawing a logical conclusion. Thus, imagery is not always a boon to cognitive performance—a lot depends on the nature of the task at hand.

THE NATURE OF MENTAL IMAGERY

All the results reviewed so far suggest that images share some properties with pictures. People typically report their experience of images as looking at mental pictures, and the kinds of mental transformations done on images seem very similar to transformations done on pictures. This leads directly to the questions: Just what are images? What kinds of properties do images have? and How are these like and unlike the properties that real pictures have?

Presumably, answers to such questions have implications for the way information is stored, retrieved, and used. Research on visual imagery, then, can potentially tell us a great deal about how information is mentally represented and organized. Our coverage of knowledge representation (Chapter 6) and concepts (Chapter 7) focused primarily on verbal information. Research on visual imagery suggests there may be another kind of information that is stored and used.

Debate over the nature of visual images has been intense in cognitive psychology. We will review highlights of the debate here, taking a close look at the image-as-mental-picture metaphor. To organize this discussion, we will first review Ronald Finke's (1989) principles of visual imagery. Then we will examine critiques of this research and of the image–mental picture metaphor.

Principles of Visual Imagery

Finke's (1989) principles of visual imagery, taken together, are meant to describe the fundamental nature and properties of visual images. There are five principles, and each covers a different aspect or characteristic of imagery.

Implicit Encoding

Finke's first principle of visual imagery states that "mental imagery is instrumental in retrieving information about the physical properties of objects, or about physical relationships among objects, that was not explicitly encoded at any previous time" (Finke, 1989, p. 7). This principle implies that images are places from which some information can be obtained, even if that information was never intentionally stored. Imagery can thus be used to answer questions for which you probably don't have a directly stored answer. The task at the beginning of this chapter—you were asked about the number of cabinet doors in the kitchen of your permanent residence—is a case in point. My guess is that if you are like most people, you've never had much reason to count kitchen cabinet doors. So this information was probably not represented directly in long-term memory. However, the information was **implicitly encoded,** meaning it was stored unintentionally along with other information that allows you to construct a visual image of your kitchen. To answer the question, then, all you need to do is form the visual image, scan it, and count cabinets.

Brooks's (1968) task in which people had to answer questions about an outlined capital *F* provides another illustration. Presumably, most people have never bothered to check whether each corner of an outlined capital *F* is at the top or bottom of the letter. Yet people are able to perform this task, presumably because the required information has been implicitly encoded together with the information that allows them to form a visual image of an *F.*

Perceptual Equivalence

Finke's second principle of visual imagery has to do with the similarities between the construction of visual images and the perception of real objects and events. It states that "imagery is functionally equivalent to perception to the extent that similar mechanisms in the visual system are activated when objects or events are imagined as when the same objects or events are actually perceived" (Finke, 1989, p. 41). In other words, many of the same kinds of internal processes used in mental visualization are used in visual perception as well.

An early study by Perky (1910) bears on this principle. Perky had participants imagine that they were looking at an object (such as a tomato, a banana, an orange, a leaf) while staring at a blank screen. After they reported having formed the image, they were briefly distracted by one experimenter while another two experimenters operated an apparatus that projected faint pictures of the objects the participants were imagining. Perky found that many of the participants were unable to distinguish between their own images and the faint pictures. Presumably, this is because images share many similarities with faint pictures.

A related group of studies, including many more experimental controls, was reported by Martha Farah (1985). Participants were asked to form an image of a certain letter—for example, an *H* or a *T.* Very soon after, they were sometimes presented with one of these letters, but at a low level of contrast, making the letters very difficult to see. Those who imagined a letter first were more accurate at detecting the actual presented letter than they were at detecting another letter. These results suggest that imagery can "prime" the visual pathway used in detecting an actual stimulus (Finke, 1989). Some authors even regard visual imagery as perceptual "anticipation": the visual system "getting ready" to actually see something (Neisser, 1976).

Spatial Equivalence

Finke's third principle of visual imagery has to do with the way that spatial information, such as location, distance, and size, is represented in visual imagery. The principle states that "the spatial arrangement of the elements of a mental image corresponds to the way objects or their parts are arranged on actual physical surfaces or in an actual physical space" (Finke, 1989, p. 61).

Much of the evidence for this principle comes from the scanning studies by Kosslyn and associates, reviewed above. The general finding is that the amount of time it takes people to scan from one element of a visual image to another corresponds to the distance between the elements in a physical representation. Thus the spatial relationships among elements of a drawing or object (for example, relative locations, distances, sizes) all seem to be preserved in the visual image of the drawing or object.

Separating the visual characteristics from the spatial characteristics of an image (or object or drawing) is quite difficult. But an ingenious series of studies by Nancy Kerr (1983) has apparently succeeded at this task. Hers was a map-scanning study, very similar to that of Kosslyn and colleagues (1978) described earlier. However, in this case some of the participants were congenitally blind and learned the "map" by feeling objects (each of which had a distinct shape) placed on a flat surface. Once participants had learned the locations, they heard the experimenter name a pair of objects and were asked to focus mentally on one and to imagine moving a raised dot from that object to the second. Kerr found that the greater the distance between objects, the longer it took both blind and sighted participants to scan.

Results of this study echoed those of Kosslyn and colleagues (1978), suggesting that visual imagery has spatial properties. The spatial properties are similar to visual representations but need not be visual, because congenitally blind people—without vision—apparently are able to make use of spatial images.

Transformational Equivalence

Finke's fourth principle of visual imagery has to do with the way that images are mentally transformed. It states that "imagined transformations and physical transformations exhibit corresponding dynamic characteristics and are governed by the same laws of motion" (Finke, 1989, p. 93).

The best evidence for this principle comes from the studies of mental rotation. Recall that the findings from those studies suggest that mental rotation apparently works in the same way physical rotation does: It is continuous, with rotating objects moving through intermediate orientations on their way to their final orientation. The time it takes to perform mental rotation depends on how much rotation is to be done, as with physical rotation. And, as with physical rotation of an object, the whole object, and not just parts of it, is rotated. The principle of transformation equivalence extends beyond mental rotation, however, in asserting that other kinds of transformations will work with images in much the same way they work with real objects.

Structural Equivalence

Finke's fifth principle of visual imagery has to do with the ways that images are organized and assembled. It states that "the structure of mental images corresponds to that of actual perceived objects, in the sense that the structure is coherent, well organized, and can be reorganized and reinterpreted" (Finke, 1989, p. 120).

Imagine that you need to draw a picture of an object or (if your artistic skills and inclinations are less than stellar) that you need to look carefully at an object. How would you do this, and what properties of the object would influence the difficulty of your task? Generally speaking, the larger the object, the more time it would take to look over or to draw. Also, the more complicated the object— that is, the more different parts the object had—the harder it would be (and the longer it would take) to look at carefully or to draw. Apparently, the construction of visual images works the same way. Visual images are formed not all at once, but in pieces that are assembled into a final rendition (Finke, 1989).

Kosslyn, Reiser, Farah, and Fliegel (1983) studied image generation as it relates to the complexity of the object to be imagined. Participants were asked to form images of pictures that differed in amount of detail, such as those in Figure 8-12(A). It took participants about one and a third times as long to form an image of the detailed pictures as it did other participants to form images of outline drawings. In a related study, the authors used geometric forms such as those shown in Figure 8-12(B) as stimuli, all of which allowed for different descriptions. For instance, Figure 8-12(B) could be described either as "five squares in the shape of a cross" or as "two overlapping rectangles." Participants first read a description, then saw the corresponding figure, then covered it up and formed a visual image of the figure. Kosslyn and colleagues found that people given the first description took longer to form the image than did people given the second description, even though the physical pattern was the same. Notice, by the way, that it would probably be faster to draw or look over Figure 8-12(B) if you conceived of it as two rectangles rather than as five squares. With images, apparently, the greater the complexity of the *conceived* structure of the object, the longer it takes to assemble an image of it.

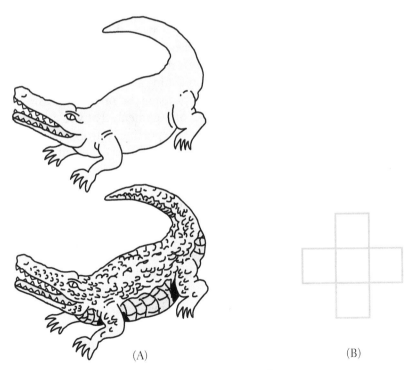

(A)   (B)

FIGURE 8-12 Stimuli from the Kosslyn et al. (1983) study.

Critiques of Mental Imagery Research and Theory

In the introduction to this chapter, we noted that the study of imagery has been controversial in psychology; it is time now to examine the controversy. Although almost every imagery study has been subject to some debate (Finke, 1989 provides several examples), we will focus on three general and interrelated themes. The first concerns criticism of imagery research. In particular, the criticism is that the experiments themselves give enough "hints," either explicitly or implicitly, for people to perform by relying on their beliefs and knowledge rather than relying strictly on visual imagery. A second critique questions the metaphor of images as pictures. A third kind of criticism is more theoretical, questioning the need to talk about imagery as a distinct kind of internal code. We will consider each critique in turn.

Tacit Knowledge and Demand Characteristics

Zenon Pylyshyn (1981), while on faculty at the University of Western Ontario, argued that the results from many imagery studies reflect participants' underlying and implicit **tacit knowledge** and beliefs about the task rather than their construction and manipulation of visual images. He paid special attention to image-scanning experiments. Participants' scanning time is proportional to distance scanned, Pylyshyn asserted, because they know that the amount of time it takes to physically scan between two points in a visual display depends on distance *and* because they expect the experiment to demand this kind of performance.

Finke (1989) explained how this knowledge and expectation could distort results. Imagine you want to move an object (say, your coffee cup) from one location (the right side of your desk) to another (the left side of your desk). You could (à la movie scenes in western bars) try to slide the cup across the desk, but it would probably be safer to pick up your cup and place it in the new location. Imagine, for the sake of argument, that you could move the cup instantaneously, regardless of the distance (maybe "teleporting" it from one set of coordinates to the other, à la *Star Trek*). Suppose, however, you believed or expected that the amount of time it took to move the coffee cup to the new location should depend on the total distance from the old to the new location. You could adjust your time by pausing and holding the cup over the new location for some amount of time before you placed it down on the desk. Then your reaction time in moving the cup would be proportional to the distance the cup moved, although the time would depend arbitrarily on the time you chose to pause.

Pylyshyn's (1981) argument was that people may be "mentally pausing" in image-scanning experiments because of their beliefs and expectations about what the experimenters want them to do. Tasks that are affected by people's beliefs and expectations are termed by Pylyshyn to be *cognitively penetrable*. Some tasks make it obvious to participants how they ought to perform. The instructions, the tasks themselves, or something else about the situation cues the person on how to behave. Such a task is said to have **demand characteristics** (Orne, 1962). In other words, the task "demands" somehow that the person behave in a certain way.

Typically, participants in psychology experiments try to please and may behave artificially just to perform in ways they believe will satisfy the experimenter.

Moreover, sometimes experimenters unconsciously give subtle cues to participants. Intons-Peterson (1983) has argued that these **experimenter expectancy effects** have influenced at least some of the imagery investigations. In various studies, she had undergraduate experimenters conduct a number of imagery studies. Some of the experimenters were led to believe that the results would turn out one way; the other experimenters were led to believe the opposite. In all the studies, participants performed as the experimenters expected them to.

In one study, Intons-Peterson (1983) used four undergraduate experimenters, all known "for their intelligence, dependability, good judgment, and maturity" (p. 396). None was familiar with the imagery literature. Each experimenter was assigned to supervise a total of 18 participants in three different conditions in a mental rotation study. Some participants were "primed" by either seeing or imagining a stimulus before each trial; participants in a control condition received no primes. Two of the four experimenters were told to expect that imaginal primes (primes that participants were asked to imagine) would be more effective than perceptual primes (primes actually presented to participants). The other two experimenters were told the opposite: Perceptual primes would be more effective than imaginal primes. Although all stimuli were presented by microcomputer, and although experimenters were not in the same room with the participants, except initially when they read instructions, the results mirrored the experimenters' beliefs. Participants supervised by experimenters who believed imaginal primes would be more effective than perceptual primes produced data to support that belief; participants supervised by the other experimenters produced data that resulted in the opposite findings.

Intons-Peterson (1983) found similar results in imaginal scanning experiments. She concluded that participants in imagery experiments were sensitive to subtle, unintentional cues given by experimenters, including slight differences in intonation or pauses when reading instructions. Intons-Peterson further argued that imagery research, by virtue of the subjective nature of the phenomenon, may be especially vulnerable to demand characteristics and experimenter expectations. Although she did *not* assert that results from all visual imagery experiments are the result of experimenter effects and demand characteristics, she did warn that visual imagery researchers must take special care to minimize these effects.

The Picture Metaphor

Much of the discussion so far has suggested an analogy between pictures and images. Some psychologists speak casually of visual images as "mental pictures." The question is, How far does the analogy go? As Pylyshyn (1973) pointed out, pictures and images differ in several ways. Perhaps the most important difference is that you can physically look at a picture without first knowing what it's a picture of (say, if someone wordlessly hands you a photograph, and you ask, "What's this?"), but you cannot "look" at an image unless you first know what it is. After all, images are internal constructions formed with some intention in mind. You don't just spontaneously create random images; rather, you form images of particular things.

Second, pictures and images are disrupted, and disruptable, in different ways. You can cut a photograph in half, with the result that arbitrary parts of the objects depicted disappear. Images are organized more meaningfully, and when they fade, only the meaningful parts disappear (Finke, 1989).

Last, images seem more easily distorted by the viewer's interpretations than are pictures or photographs. Remember Bartlett's (1932) work on story recall? (See Chapter 6 if you need to review.) We saw how people's memory for stories changed over time and often depended on their initial or subsequent interpretations. So also with images. Carmichael, Hogan, and Walter (1932) presented participants with patterns such as those in Figure 8-13, with one of two labels (different participants were given different labels). Participants' later reproductions of the patterns (presumably based on imagery) were distorted in accordance with the label initially provided, as shown in the figure.

Similarly, Nickerson and Adams (1979) have shown that people make many errors when trying to reproduce their images of familiar objects. Try drawing a picture of a loonie without looking at one, and then compare it to a real loonie. Is the Queen facing the right way? Is her name in the right place? Where is the date? Is it perfectly round? Notice in this case that your image probably has far less information in it than would a clear picture or photograph of a loonie.

What's the significance of finding differences between images and pictures? Visual images are thought to be one means of internal coding and representation of information. Although many cognitive psychologists believe that visual imagery exists as a distinct mental code, and although they believe the code has many visual and/or spatial qualities, the evidence to date suggests that the visual image-as-picture analogy works only roughly.

Propositional Theory

A broader criticism of work on imagery is theoretical and is aimed at the very premise behind the field. Proponents *of propositional theory* reject the idea that images serve as a distinct mental code for representing information. Instead, propositional theorists believe there is a single code, neither visual nor verbal but propositional in nature (Anderson & Bower, 1973), which is used to store and mentally represent all information. As we saw in Chapter 7, propositions are a means of specifying relationships between different concepts.

For example, the idea that Ottawa is a city located to the west of Montreal might be represented by the following propositions: CITY (Ottawa); WESTOF (Montreal, Halifax). Propositions can be linked together in networks, with two closely related ideas joined by sharing a number of propositions.

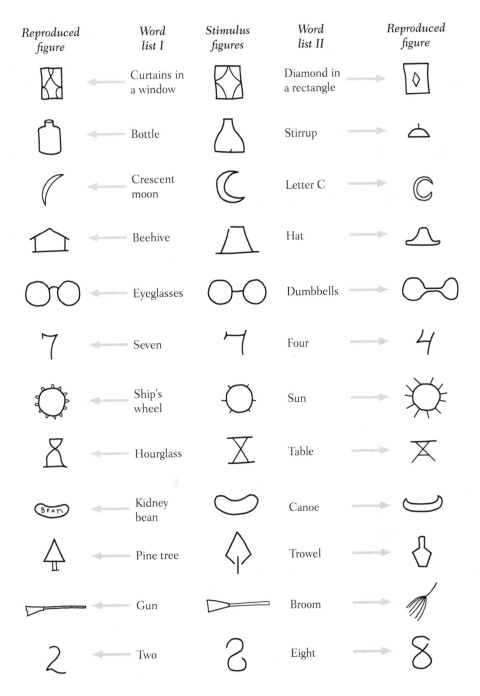

FIGURE 8-13 Materials from the Carmichael et al. (1932) study.

Pylyshyn (1973) asserted that propositional theory could explain the results of imagery experiments. His idea was that all information is mentally represented and stored by propositions. Participants in visual imagery experiments might *look* as if they were consulting or manipulating internal visual representations, but they would actually be using internal propositional representations, the same kind of representations that underlie their processing of verbal material, such as sentences or stories.

Two studies by Kosslyn (1976) attempted to test this assertion. Kosslyn first tested the *association strength* between animals and their physical attributes. For instance, for most people "claws" are more strongly associated with "cat" than is "head," although cats, of course, have both. Kosslyn found that when people did *not* use imagery, they were faster to verify that cats had claws (high association value, small visual part of a cat) than that cats had heads (low association value, large visual part of a cat). Propositional theory would predict that the higher the association value, the more propositions relating the two items, and thus the faster the verification time (Finke, 1989). However, when participants reported having used imagery to do the task, their reaction times went in the opposite direction. Here, they were faster to verify visually larger parts with low association values than visually smaller parts with higher association values. Apparently, using imagery results in performance that propositional theory does not predict.

What does it matter in the real world whether people use imagery as a means of coding information? Understanding how and under what circumstances people mentally represent information is crucial to explaining how they carry out a variety of cognitive tasks. If they use different codes for different tasks, and we can make good predictions about when they use which code, we can perhaps predict when they are likely to be able to do things easily, and when they are not.

NEUROPSYCHOLOGICAL FINDINGS

Farah (1988) reported on the work of a number of investigators examining neuropsychological aspects of visual imagery. Some work has examined the pattern of blood flow in the brain. Cerebral blood flow is thought to provide a fairly precise measure of brain activity in a particular region. Roland and Friberg (1985) asked people to perform three cognitive tasks while their cerebral blood flows were being monitored. The tasks were mental arithmetic, memory scanning of an auditory stimulus, and visual imagery (visualizing a walk through a familiar neighbourhood). The experimenters made sure the tasks were approximately equal in difficulty. They found that each person tested showed massive activation in the parts of the brain important for visual processing of information (mostly in the occipital lobe and other posterior regions) during the imagery task. During the other two tasks, however, there were no such increases in cerebral blood flow to those parts. Farah and her colleagues have replicated these results using other neuropsychological measures, such as event-related potentials (ERPs) measuring electrical activity in the brain (Farah, Péronnet, Gonon, & Giard, 1988).

Other investigators report a wealth of studies showing that the creation of visual images activates those areas of the brain involved in visual processing (Kosslyn & Ochsner, 1994; Miyashita, 1995). These regions are often locatedin the occipital lobe, that region of the cerebral cortex devoted to visual processing. In one study, for example, Kosslyn, Thompson, Kim, and Alpert (1995) tested 12 volunteers asked to form images of previously memorized line drawings of common objects. They were also asked (in different parts of the testing session) to form their images at different sizes. During the tasks, the cerebral blood flow of the volunteers was monitored using PET scans. Results indicated that all the imagery tasks produced activation in the visual cortex, replicating many previous findings, such as those just described. Of greater interest was the fact that the specific area of the occipital lobe showing maximal activation differed depending on whether the image created was small, medium, or large.

Montreal Neurological Institute researchers Zatorre, Halpern, Perry, Meyer, and Evans (1996) conducted a study similar in spirit, during which the cerebral blood flow of 12 participants was measured while the participants either (a) saw two words and judged which was longer, (b)saw two words from a song while hearing the song and judged whether a pitch change occurred in the song between the two words, or (c)again saw the two words from the song *without* hearing the song but were still asked to judge whether a pitch change occurred in the song. Tasks (b) and (c) led to similar patterns of cerebral blood flow changes with respect to the control condition, (a). During both task (b) and task (c), there was noticeable activity in both hemispheres in the secondary auditory cortex, in the temporal lobes. Imagining the songs led to somewhat weaker activation than did actually hearing the songs.

O'Craven and Kanwisher (2000) showed additionally in an fMRI study that when people form a mental image of faces, a different area of the brain becomes activated than when they imagine a place. When participants formed images of faces, the *fusiform face area* of the brain was activated—the same area that becomes activated when subjects view photographs of faces. (The fusiform face area is located in the occipital-temporal areas.) Conversely, when participants formed a mental image of a place, the *parohippocampal place area* of the brain (located in the ventromedial area) was active—just as it is when people view photographs of complex scenes.

How can neuropsychological findings bear on the controversies in the literature on visual imagery? Neuropsychological work by Farah (1985) is particularly effective in addressing the issues of demand characteristics. Farah argued that the data from her laboratory showing that visual imagery involves activation of the same parts of the brain used in vision are not susceptible to a demand characteristics explanation unless certain questionable assumptions are made:

A tacit knowledge account of the electrophysiological and blood flow data, implicating the use of cortical visual areas during visual imagery activity, would need to include the following two assumptions: (a) that subjects know what parts of their brains are normally active during vision and (b) that subjects can voluntarily alter their brain electrical activity, or modulate or increase regional blood flow to specific areas of their brains. (Farah, 1985, p. 314)

Kosslyn and colleagues (1995) argued that their data also argue against the propositional account of visual images. The fact that visual processing areas become active when visual images are formed makes a strong case for the proposal that images are processed visually and/or spatially and that the findings from purely cognitive tasks are not simply produced by people's tacit theories of how imaginal processing ought to function.

SPATIAL COGNITION

The study of visual imagery can be construed as part of a broader picture: **spatial cognition,** or how people represent and navigate in and through space (Montello, 2005). That is, how do we acquire, store, and use mental representations of spatial entities, and use them to get from point A to point B? One example of a spatial entity might be a "cognitive map"—a mental depiction of some part of our environment, presumably showing major landmarks and spatial relationships among them.

For example, right where you are sitting (or standing, or lying down), point in the direction of the building in which your cognitive psychology class is held. To do this, presumably you call upon some stored knowledge of the relationship between your current location and the specified location. Opinions vary as to how maplike a cognitive map really is. (You might note a similarity here to the debate over how picturelike a visual image is.) In any case, most agree that cognitive maps are mental constructs people use to navigate spatially through an environment, especially one that is too large to be immediately perceived (Kitchin, 1994).

Barbara Tversky (2005) notes that in the realm of spatial cognition, there are really a number of different kinds of spaces to be distinguished. The way people think about space depends on which kind of space is under consideration. Each kind of space seems to have different attributes and organization.

The first kind of space is the **space of the body.** This space includes knowledge of where the different parts of one's body are located at any given moment (such as knowing that your right foot currently rests flat against the floor but your left foot is wrapped around the bottom of your desk chair); knowing what other objects different body parts are interacting with (your fingers with the keyboard; your derriere with the seat of the chair); as well as internal sensations (your hungry belly, the chill you're feeling from your chronically underheated room). You use your knowledge of the space of the body to direct different parts of your body spatially—as you reach for something, duck to avoid something, walk or run toward something.

The second kind of space is the **space around the body.** This space refers to the area immediately around you: the room you are in, say, or the region in which you can easily perceive and act on objects. Tversky's work suggests that people localize objects in this space along three axes that are extensions of the body. One axis is the front–back axis; another is the up–down axis, and the third is the left–right axis. Studies by Tversky and colleagues had people imagine being in a particular space and then locating an imaginary object in that space; people heard narratives describing them standing, say, in a hotel lobby or a museum, with objects on all six sides of their body (front, back, at the head, at the feet, to the right, to the left). Next they were asked to imagine themselves facing a different direction, and then to locate objects while facing this new direction. Times to "retrieve" objects at the head and feet were consistently fastest; times along the left–right axis were consistently slowest (Tversky, 2005).

These hikers are immersed in what Tversky calls the "space of navigation" as they explore this canyon.

Dudarev Mikhail/Shutterstock.com

The **space of navigation** refers to larger spaces—ones we walk through, explore, and travel to and through. In Tversky's words:

> *Constituents of the space of navigation include places, which may be buildings or parks or piazzas or rivers or mountains, as well as countries or planets or stars, on yet larger scales. Places are interrelated in terms of paths or directions in a reference frame. The space of navigation is too large to perceive from one place so it must be integrated from different pieces of information that are not immediately comparable. Like the space around the body it can be acquired from descriptions and from diagrams, notably maps, as well as from direct experience. One remarkable feature of the human mind is the ability to conceive of spaces that are too large to be perceived from one place as integral wholes. In order to conceive of spaces of navigation as wholes, we need to paste, link, join, superimpose, or otherwise integrate separate pieces of information. (p. 9)*

When we give directions to someone, we are dealing with the space of navigation. Whether we adopt a "route" perspective and give those directions in terms of landmarks ("go straight two blocks till you come to the gas station, then take a right and go until you see a Tim Hortons, then turn left") or a "survey" perspective and give directions in terms of a bird's-eye view ("Wilfrid Laurier University is two blocks east of the University of Waterloo entrance, and one block northwest of the Quizno's sub shop"), we communicate some spatial information. However, the representations we form within the space of navigation aren't always accurate or complete (see the Canadian Research Highlight box for more detail). Thus, Tversky (2005) prefers the term "cognitive collage" to the term "cognitive map." Cognitive collages are subject to systematic errors and distortions, as we saw earlier with people's inappropriate beliefs about whether Vancouver or Quebec City is farther north.

Further, Montello (2005) has argued that navigation consists of two major components: locomotion (moving the body over terrain) and wayfinding (planning and making decisions about where to go and how to get there). The investigation of how people (and animals) navigate shows integration of a number of cognitive processes we have previously encountered, including perception, attention, memory, and knowledge representation, as well as some topics (planning, reasoning, decision making) yet to come.

Box 8-3 Canadian Research Highlight

Colin Ellard of the University of Waterloo

Imagine yourself waking up in your apartment on a pitch-black Saturday night. You're starved, but remember you've left some cookies on the kitchen table. Not wanting to wake anyone up by turning on the lights, you opt to use your visual memory of the layout of your apartment and the distance to the kitchen table to go find the cookies. Will you be successful? Research by Colin Ellard (https://uwaterloo.ca/psychology/people-profiles/colin-ellard) and his colleagues at the University of Waterloo says yes, you will. Ellard and Shaughnessy (2003) have shown that people are very accurate when "blind-walking" to a previously viewed target. Imagine, though, that you had never seen the distance between the bed and the *Colin Ellard of the University of Waterloo* kitchen table before, you were staying in a friend's apartment, and you had arrived after dark. You had been previously led, again "blind," from the bed to the kitchen table for cookies. Now that your friend is asleep, could you recreate the trip from the bed to the cookies without having seen the route before, only having walked it? Again, the answer is yes, you could. People can navigate quite well using only the locomotor information they've gathered from their previous trip to the target (cookies). Most interesting, however, was performance under conditions in which Ellard and Shaughnessy gave their participants conflicting visual and locomotor information. In these conditions participants were shown the location of the target and "blind-walked" to the target (in various orders), only Ellard and Shaughnessy used visual and locomotor targets that were of different distances. When later made to make the test walk to the target, the distance walked by participants appeared to be a weighting of the two distances they had experienced. This occurred despite the fact that most participants failed to notice any discrepancy between the visual and locomotor cues. Ellard and Shaughnessy therefore concluded that people's use of locomotor target information is carried out largely in the absence of awareness, because even very large discrepancies between visual and locomotor target locations are not noticed but still affect behaviour.

SUMMARY

1. Visual images are mental representations of perceptual experiences. There are also auditory, olfactory, cutaneous, and other images, each thought to be a mental representation of a perceptual experience.

2. Visual images are often used in mnemonics, techniques that improve the chances of recalling information. Some examples include the method of loci and the method of interacting images.

3. The dual-coding hypothesis of memory states that when information can be coded both by a verbal label and by a visual image, the memorability of that information is enhanced relative to information that can be coded only by a verbal label.

4. Not all psychologists believe in the existence of these two distinct codes. However, despite the theoretical possibility that only one propositional code is used to perform the visual imagery tasks described, many cognitive psychologists are persuaded by the evidence of the existence of some sort of a distinct visual-spatial code.

5. Research on visual imagery has suggested that images function in some ways like internal pictures, undergoing certain kinds of mental operations and transformations. These mental operations and transformations appear to function in ways similar to corresponding physical operations and transformations.

6. However, other researchers and theoreticians have pointed out limitations in the image-as-picture metaphor. There are a number of ways in which images work differently from pictures. Some investigators, such as Farah (1988), have therefore concluded that "imagery is not *visual* in the sense of necessarily representing information acquired through visual sensory channels. Rather, it is visual in the sense of using some of the same neural representational machinery as vision" (p. 315).

7. Finke (1989) has proposed five principles of visual imagery: (a) implicit encoding, (b) perceptual equivalence, (c) spatial equivalence, (d) transformational equivalence, and (e) structural equivalence.

8. Neuropsychological findings, taken in conjunction with the older studies, can help distinguish among different proposals. The studies that show activation of the visual cortex when forming imagery provide convincing evidence that the processing of visual images and the processing of visual perceptual information share a neural substrate.

9. Images are necessarily a private mental experience. It is all the more exciting, then, when results from cognitive psychology and neuropsychology converge. Many consider the empirical investigations of imagery a major victory in the larger task of understanding how cognition, a collection of private mental experiences, functions.

10. Visual imagery can be seen as part of a broader topic of spatial cognition. Spatial cognition encompasses the ways in which people acquire, store, and use information about spatial properties to navigate.

REVIEW QUESTIONS

1. Describe four mnemonics, two that rely on visual imagery and two that don't, and contrast the underlying mechanisms thought to account for their effectiveness.
2. Describe and contrast the dual-coding hypothesis and the relational-organizational hypothesis, and describe experimental means of distinguishing between them.
3. What interpretations have cognitive psychologists performing mental rotation studies (for example, Shepard, Metzler, and Cooper) drawn from their findings? In what ways are such interpretations consistent with those drawn by Kosslyn from his image-scanning experiments?
4. Describe and discuss Finke s five principles of imagery.
5. Pylyshyn asserted that many of the results from visual imagery experiments are attributable to tacit knowledge and demand characteristics. Describe and critique his arguments.
6. What objections did Intons-Peterson raise to some of the findings from visual imagery experiments? In your view, how strong are such objections? Defend your view.
7. In what ways are visual images like pictures? In what ways are they different?
8. Some researchers have used neuropsychological findings to try to resolve some of the controversies in the imagery field. How decisive are such findings? Explain.
9. Describe Tversky's proposal for different "spaces" of which people have knowledge. Why is it important to distinguish among them?

KEY TERMS

demand characteristic
dual-coding hypothesis
experimenter expectancy
    effect
heuristic
imaginal scanning

implicit encoding
mental rotation
method of loci
mnemonics
relational-organizational
    hypothesis

space around the body
space of navigation
space of the body
spatial cognition
tacit knowledge
visual image

COGLAB DEMONSTRATIONS

To check your knowledge of the key concepts in this chapter, take the chapter quiz at www.cognitivepsychology1Ce.nelson.com. Also explore the links that provide more information.

WEB RESOURCES

Visit our website. Go to www.cognitivepsychology1Ce.nelson.com where you will find online resources directly linked to your book, including quizzes, flash-cards, crossword puzzles, and glossaries. You will also find practice questions organized and integrated by chapter.

As its name suggests, the **Mental Rotation** demonstration gives a recreation (with some slight variation of stimuli) of the famous Shepard and Metzler mental rotation task.

CHAPTER 9

Language

Right now, as you read this sentence, you are engaged in the process of language comprehension. As the author of this chapter writes this sentence, she is engaged in language production. Probably neither of us finds this behaviour remarkable. We comprehend and produce language all day long—when we read or speak, when we listen to dialogue or conversations, when we struggle to write a term paper (or a textbook chapter), or even when we compose the most mundane pieces of prose ("Gone to the library—meet me at 5 at the car"). In short, we take our language abilities for granted.

Evidence is abundant, however, that language use and abilities are not so straightforward. Researchers studying artificial intelligence have found it extremely difficult to build computer systems that can understand language (spoken or written) as easily as a 4-year-old child can. Parents of toddlers can attest that although language acquisition is rapid, a person takes several years to become proficient. Many high school and university students come to appreciate fully the complexities of language only when they try to master a second one.

Language use is intimately connected to cognition. Much of the information we receive comes from spoken or written language; we use language to ask questions, explain conclusions, clarify problems, and so on. Like perception or memory, then, language seems to be a crucial cognitive ability so easily used that we typically overlook its complexity.

265

In this chapter, we will first look at the structural elements of a language: the pieces or aspects that go into the elaborated, rule-governed, and creative communication systems we recognize as different human languages. We will then examine models of language comprehension and production: how we understand and create spoken discourse and written material. Finally, we will consider the relation between language and other cognitive processes.

Continuing themes from earlier chapters, we will see that some language processes are bottom-up, or driven by incoming data, whereas others are top-down, or driven by the listener or speaker's expectations. Some language processing appears automatic, carried out without awareness or intention. Other language processing, of course, is performed intentionally and with effort. Thus, processing language is very clearly constrained by other cognitive processes we have studied—perception, attention, and memory, in particular. At the same time, language is used in cognitive processes described in later chapters—thinking, planning, reasoning, and making decisions.

It is important to define language precisely and, in particular, to distinguish between *language* and *communication*. Although language is often used as a communication system, there are other communication systems that do not form true languages. Many bees, for example, use elaborate dances to tell other bees about a newfound source of food. Although this dance communicates where the food is, it can *only* communicate that kind of message—the dance can't inform the bees about an interesting sight to see along the way to the food source. Birds have songs and calls to broadcast territorial boundaries or to attract mates (Demers, 1988). But, again, these communication systems can send only very specific messages. How do these systems of communication differ from language? To decide, we must first define a language.

A natural language has two necessary characteristics: It is *regular* (governed by a system of rules, called a **grammar**), and it is *productive*, meaning that infinite combinations of things can be expressed in it. Other characteristics of human languages include *arbitrariness* (the lack of a necessary resemblance between a word or sentence and what it refers to) and *discreteness* (the system can be subdivided into recognizable parts—for example, sentences into words, words into sounds; see Demers, 1988, or Hockett, 1960).

Using these criteria, we can conclude that bees do not have a language, because the physical motions in the dance carry information about the nectar source (lack of arbitrariness). For instance, the direction of the food source is indicated quite literally by the direction of the bee's dance, and the distance is indicated in the dance by the rate at which the bee wiggles (Harley 1995). Further, the dances are restricted to communicating about food sources, thus failing on the grounds of productivity. Bird songs and calls also cannot be classified as languages, primarily on the grounds of productivity, because the songs and calls communicate only about certain topics (mostly mates, predators, and territories; see Demers, 1988). These illustrations help clarify the relation between language and communication systems: All human languages are communication systems, but not all communication systems have the prerequisites to be classified as natural languages.

Investigators have studied animal communication during various endeavours, such as play or tool use (Bekoff & Allen, 2002; Hauser, 2000), and many others have attempted specifically to teach various language and communication systems to chimpanzees (Gardner & Gardner, 1971; Premack, 1976; Savage-Rumbaugh, McDonald, Sevcik, Hopkins, & Rubert, 1986; Terrace, 1979). Some investigators have taught their participants to use sign language; others have relied on systems of plastic tokens or geometric symbols. Most agree chimpanzees can be taught to use symbols or signs to make requests or label objects (for example, "Kanzi chase Sue," "Me more eat," or "Orange juice"). A study by Sue Savage-Rumbaugh and colleagues (1986) suggests that pygmy chimpanzees can even learn to spontaneously use symbols to communicate, learn to use symbols simply by watching others (people or chimpanzees) use them, and learn to understand spoken English words.

Although these animals are clearly communicating, there is little evidence that their communication system forms a true language.

Despite these impressive findings, most researchers in this field would agree there are substantial differences between the language that even the brightest and most linguistically sophisticated chimpanzees have acquired to date and the language of most 3-year-old children. Most would agree, too, that although chimpanzees can acquire many vocabulary items and some rudimentary language structure, their communication system still falls far short of any known human language. To understand why, we need to review the structure of human language in detail.

THE STRUCTURE OF LANGUAGE

As with any complex ability, language comprises a number of systems working together. We will illustrate some of the ways in which the systems work together through the example of conversation. We use the example of a conversation because it is considered a basic setting for language, one common to all people, even the estimated one-sixth of the world's population who lack literacy necessary for reading and writing (Clark & Van Der Wege, 2002).

When you have a conversation, you first have to listen to and perceive the sounds the speaker directs at you. Different languages have different sounds (called **phonemes**). The study of the ways in which phonemes can be combined in any given language constitutes the study of *phonology*. Next, you have to put the sounds together in some coherent way, identifying the meaningful units of language, an aspect known as *morphology*. Word endings, prefixes, tense markers, and the like are critical parts of each sentence. Some of the **morphemes** (smallest meaningful units of language) are words, and you also need to identify these and to determine the role each word plays in a sentence.

To do so, you need to determine the **syntax**, or structure, of each sentence. Figure 9-1 illustrates the different "levels" of language a simple sentence can be broken into. We will come back to the topic of sentence structure very shortly. A syntactically correct sentence does not by itself make for a good conversation. The sentence must also mean something to the listener. **Semantics** is the branch of linguistics and psycholinguistics devoted to the study of meaning. Finally, for the conversation to work there must be some flow or give-and-take. Listeners must pay attention and make certain assumptions, and speakers must craft their contributions in ways that will make the listener's job feasible. This aspect of language, **pragmatics**, will conclude our discussion of the structure of language. Keep in mind throughout that although the various aspects of language will be discussed separately, in actual conversation they must work together.

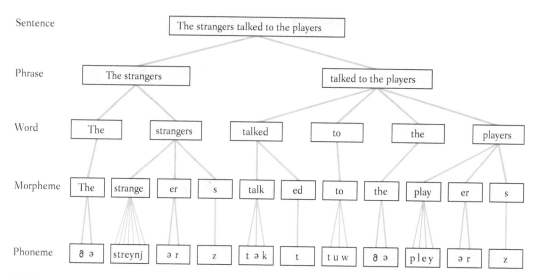

FIGURE 9-1 An analysis of a simple English sentence. As this example shows, verbal language has a hierarchical structure. At the base of the hierarchy are the phonemes, which are units of vocal sound that do not, in themselves, have meaning. The smallest units of meaning in a language are morphemes, which include not only root words but such meaning-carrying units as the past tense suffixed and the plural -s. Complex rules of syntax govern how the words constructed from morphemes may be combined into phrases, and phrases into meaningful statements, or sentences.

We will repeatedly encounter the idea of different linguistic rules (such as phonological rules or syntactic rules) in this section. These rules make up the *grammar* of the language and, taken together, define the way a language works. It is important that linguists and psychologists use the term *grammar* in a very restricted sense here, meaning "the set of rules for a language." In particular, *grammatical* in this context has nothing to do with the "rules" of "good English" such as "Don't use *ain't*" or "Use end punctuation at the end of a complete statement." To a linguist or a psycholinguist, the sentence "I ain't going to happily do it" is perfectly meaningful and "legal"—that is, it follows the "rules" of English that native speakers observe—and is therefore grammatical. (You understand it perfectly well, right?) Here *grammar* refers not to polite ways of speaking but to ways of speaking that form intelligible phrases or utterances recognizable as examples of language that a native speaker of the language might produce.

Linguists and psychologists distinguish between people's explicit and implicit knowledge of linguistic rules. It is doubtful, for instance, that most of us could state with precision or accuracy just what the rules for English syntax are. (If it were easy, many linguists would be out of a job!) Still, most of us can easily and almost immediately detect violations of the rules—for example, syntactically ill-formed sentences such as "Ran the dog street down cat after yellow the very the." Moreover, not only would we recognize the example as ungrammatical, but we would never produce such gross violations (although we frequently produce sentences with minor grammatical violations). Our knowledge of the rules is therefore not explicit (we cannot articulate what all the rules are, nor are we consciously aware of all of them) but implicit (whatever the rules are, we somehow follow them). We can often articulate the so-called prescriptive rules (such as "Don't say *ain't*"), which tell us how we *should* talk or write, even though we may violate them (for instance, whenever we actually say *ain't*). In contrast, we find it hard to articulate the descriptive rules of English, which characterize which sentences are legal and which are not.

Linguists and psychologists also distinguish **linguistic competence** from **linguistic performance**. The term *competence* refers to the underlying linguistic knowledge that lets people produce and comprehend their language. Competence is not always fully evident in actual use or performance of language. Lapses of attention or memory, nervousness or tiredness, environmental changes, shifts in interest, and random error can all interfere with our use of language, causing us to produce ungrammatical sentences or to comprehend a sentence incorrectly. Linguistic performance would reflect linguistic competence only under completely ideal conditions (Chomsky, 1965). In real life, such ideal conditions are never achieved. So if you overhear an ungrammatical utterance, it is probably not that the speaker's linguistic knowledge (competence) is faulty (especially if he is speaking in his native language) but rather that various other factors and pressures in his life at the time he spoke (performance) caused the error or errors.

Phonology

To some, French sounds musical and German sounds harsh. No doubt, you too would describe various languages with various adjectives. Part of what distinguishes languages is their idiosyncratic sounds. Here we will consider the sounds of language (in our case, English) and how they are combined. We will draw on findings from two disciplines: **phonetics**, the study of speech sounds and how they are produced, and **phonology**, the study of the systematic ways in which speech sounds are combined and altered in language.

The English language has about 40 phonetic segments (sometimes called *phones*). Although a language may have a large number of phones, only certain ones are "meaningful" to it. Linguists use the term *phoneme* to refer to the smallest unit of sound that makes a meaningful difference in a given language. So if one phoneme in a word is exchanged for another, the word itself is changed. Thus, if the phoneme \d\ is replaced with the phoneme \t\ the word *duck* becomes *tuck*. In English, we distinguish between the \l\ and the \r\ sound; other languages, such as the Cantonese dialect of Chinese, do not. Some of the dialect jokes about a Chinese speaker's saying "flied lice" instead of "fried rice" are based on the fact that a native speaker of Cantonese dialect simply wouldn't hear the difference (Fromkin & Rodman, 1974). Of course, other languages make sound distinctions that English doesn't, and native English speakers learning those languages can make errors that are just as ridiculed by the native speakers. Table 9-1 presents a list of English phonemes.

Linguists and phoneticians distinguish between consonants and vowels. Vowels work without obstructing the airflow, simply depending on the shape and position of the tongue and lips (Halle, 1990). Try articulating vowel sounds, and observe how your mouth changes configurations as you do.

Consonants are more complicated. In general, they are phonemes made by closing, or at least almost closing, part of the mouth. They differ first in what linguists call "place of articulation," meaning where the obstruction of the airflow occurs. For example, the \b\ and \p\ sounds are made by closing the lips, and the \s\ and \z\ sounds are made by placing the tongue against the hard palate of the roof of the mouth, just behind the ridge of gums. Consonants differ also in "manner of articulation," the mechanics of how the airflow is obstructed. The \m\ sound, for example, is made by closing the mouth while opening the nasal cavity; the \f\ sound is made through an obstruction of the airflow, producing a hissing sound. A third distinction between groups of consonants is known as *voicing*. Compare the \s\ in the syllable "sa" with the \z\ in "za." The \s\ does not require the vocal cords to be vibrated as the \z\ does; therefore, the \z\ is said to be voiced and the \s\ unvoiced.

Features of phonemes, such as those just reviewed, are involved in certain *phonological rules* that govern the ways in which phonemes can be combined. For example, if two "true"

Table 9-1 Examples of Some English-Language Phonemes

Symbol	Examples
p	**p**at, a**pp**le
b	**b**at, am**b**le
d	**d**ip, love**d**
g	**g**uard, o**g**re
f	**f**at, **ph**ilosophy
s	**s**ap, pa**ss**, pea**c**e
z	**z**ip, pad**s**, **x**ylophone
y	**y**ou, ba**y**, f**eu**d
w	**w**itch, q**u**een
l	**l**eaf, pa**l**ace
ē	b**ee**t, b**ea**t, bel**ie**ve
e	**a**te, b**ai**t, **eigh**t
	b**i**t, **i**njury
u	b**oo**t, tw**o**, thr**ou**gh
U	p**u**t, f**oo**t, c**ou**ld
oy	b**oy**, d**oi**ly
ay	b**i**te, s**igh**t, **i**sland
š	**sh**oe, mu**sh**, dedu**c**tion

consonants (that is, all the consonants except \h\, \w\, \y\, \r\, or \l\ plus certain other sounds, such as the \th\ in *thy*, the \th\ in *thigh*, and the \ch\ in *chip)* are at the beginning of an English word, then the first must be an \s\ (Clark & Clark, 1977). This rule prevents word strings such as *dtop* or *mkeech* from being "legal" words in our language (although they may be so in other languages), whereas *stop* and *speech* are.

These phonological rules also explain how to pronounce new words and how to pronounce prefixes and suffixes to words, such as plural or past-tense endings. To illustrate, the way to form a plural for an English word depends on the phoneme with which the singular form of the word ends. From work in phonetics, we can state the following rule (after Halle, 1990):

If the Word Ends With	Of the Word Is	The Plural Ending Examples
\s z c j\	\z\	places, porches, cabbages
\p t k f \	\s\	lips, lists, telegraphs
Anything else	\z\	clubs, herds, phonemes

Different languages have different phonological rules; hence there are two answers to the question, Why do different languages sound different? One answer is that they contain different sounds (phonemes). A second answer is that they have different rules for combining those sounds (phonology).

Syntax

The term *syntax* refers to the arrangement of words within sentences or, more broadly, to the *structure* of sentences—their parts and the way the parts are put together. Syntactic rules, similar to phonological rules, govern the ways in which different words or larger phrases can be combined to form "legal" sentences in the language. Thus sentences such as "The book fell off the table" are clearly acceptable to English speakers, and examples such as "Chair the on sits man" are not. Syntactic rules should meet two requirements: They should be able to describe every "legal" sentence, and they should never be able to describe an "illegal" sentence (Chomsky, 1957).

What does it mean to say that sentences have structure? Consider the following sentence:

(1) *The poodle will chase the red ball.*

If you were to try to divide the words of this sentence into groups (linguists call these *constituents*), you might proceed as follows. Certainly the word *poodle* goes with the word *the*. Similarly, *red* appears to modify *ball*, and *the* forms another constituent with *red ball*. *Chase* could also form a constituent with *the red ball*, and *will* seems to modify this larger grouping. Notice that there are various levels of groupings or constituents, as depicted in Figure 9-2(A).

This kind of diagram is called a *tree diagram*, and the small grey circles, called *nodes*, depict the various constituents of the sentence. Notice also that each word is a constituent by itself, but that there are higher-level constituents as well, made out of different word groupings. Thus, the word *ball* is a member of four constituents: [ball]; [the red ball]; [chase the red ball]; and [The poodle will chase the red ball].

Figure 9-2(B) shows a similar diagram of the sentence, but here labels that tell the type, or category, of each constituent have replaced the grey dots. At the very bottom level in the tree, you'll see labels for familiar terms: V for verb, N for noun, Adj for adjective, and so forth.

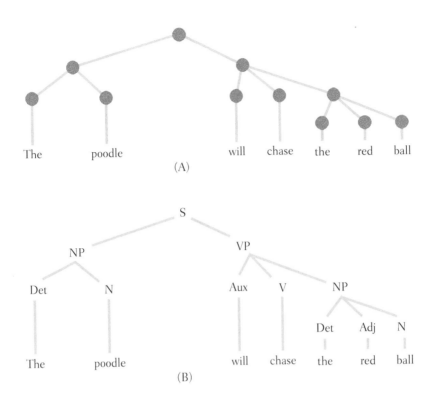

FIGURE 9-2 Tree diagrams of Sentence 1.

The labels give us some idea of the role that each word plays in the sentence and allow us to see that, generally speaking, if we replace a noun with another noun we will still have a syntactically grammatical sentence. So, substituting *shoe* for *ball* gives us "The poodle will chase the red shoe." Higher up in the tree, other labels categorize the larger constituents. Thus the constituents "the poodle" and "the red ball" are both noun phrases (NP). The labelling is meant to capture our intuition that these constituents are similar to other constituents, such as "the angry fireman," "her grandfather's birthday," or "my first tooth." Figure 9-2(B) is called a *labelled tree diagram*, and it depicts what is called the *categorical constituent structure* of the sentence.

Notice that one noun phrase (NP) can be substituted for another in a sentence, yielding a sentence that is semantically anomalous (its meaning, if any, is hard to determine) but syntactically grammatical. So we could substitute the NP "my first tooth" for "the poodle" in Sentence 1 and get "My first tooth chased the red ball," an odd but certainly "legal" sentence.

What's the point of such diagrams? For one thing, they help explain why certain kinds of changes can be made in a sentence and others can't. One illustration comes from a change called *preposing*—taking a certain part of a sentence and moving it to the front, usually for emphasis (Radford, 1988). In the following examples, the italicized material has been preposed:

(2) *My naughty dog*, I'm mad at.
(3) *That inflated price*, I will not pay.
(4) *Up the mountain*, the hikers climbed furiously.

Preposing works (results in a grammatical or legal sentence) only when certain kinds of whole phrases or constituents are moved to the front. Thus it isn't legal to say, "Naughty dog, I'm mad at my," "Price, I will not pay that inflated," or "Mountain, the hikers climbed furiously up the." Tree diagrams such as the ones in Figure 9-2 provide answers to which parts of the sentence form constituents and are therefore candidates for preposing.

It is interesting that this kind of analysis of sentences explains an apparent paradox. The following four sentences are all "legal":

(5) Susan rang up Jodie.
(6) Martha stood up her blind date.
(7) Adrian looked up the number.
(8) Aristophanes ran up the mountain.

Preposing the phrase "up the mountain" can result in a legal sentence:

(8a) Up the mountain, Aristophanes ran.

But none of the other sentences can undergo preposing in this way, as the following illegal sentences (marked with asterisks) show:

(5a) *Up Jodie, Susan rang.
(6a) *Up her blind date, Martha stood.
(7a) *Up the number, Adrian looked.

Figure 9-3 provides tree diagrams of Sentences 5 through 8 and shows that in Sentences 5 through 7 the word *up* is part of the constituent involving the verb and hence must stay with the verb in the sentence. However, in Sentence 8 the word *up* is a part of the constituent "up the mountain," so it is perfectly acceptable to prepose it as long as the entire constituent gets moved.

How can we concisely summarize this discussion of what can and can't be legally preposed? Linguists do so by formulating constraints on syntactic rules like this: Only constituents labelled as being whole phrases—for example, nodes marked as NP or VP (verb phrase)—can undergo movement from one position in a sentence to another. Such rules describe the ways in which parts of sentences are formed and work together.

Various linguists have proposed a variety of syntactic rules, as well as a variety of *kinds* of syntactic rules. For example, Chomsky (1965) proposed one set of rules, called *phrase*

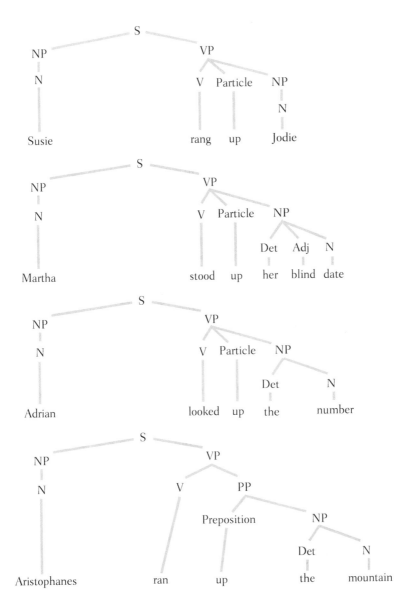

FIGURE 9-3 Tree diagram of Sentences 5 through 8.

structure rules, that functions to generate the structures depicted in tree diagrams such as Figures 9-2 and 9-3. These rules, sometimes called *rewrite rules*, describe the ways in which certain symbols can be rewritten as other symbols. The rule S → NP VP says that a symbol S (which stands for "sentence") consists of different constituents and can be rewritten as the symbol NP (the symbol for the constituent "noun phrase") followed by the symbol VP (the symbol for the constituent "verb phrase"). The point is that phrase structure rules allow certain symbols to be rewritten as other symbols. To rewrite a symbol with an actual word in the English language (for example, N → poodle) requires a different type of syntactic rule, a *lexical-insertion rule*, which allows the insertion of words (linguists call these *lexical items*) into the structures generated by the phrase structure rules.

Another type of syntactic rule is a *transformational rule*. Transformational rules turn structures such as those depicted in tree diagrams into other structures. Preposing phrasal constituents, for example, might be allowed through a transformational rule. Even a brief explanation of these or other syntactic rules, or other proposals for what the rules could be, would take us far afield (interested readers are referred to an introductory linguistics course or to Cowper, 1992). The point here is to show that just as the sounds of a language are organized and rule-governed in the way they are combined, so too are phrases and sentences.

Again, rules of syntax, like rules of phonology, are probably not rules you are consciously aware of. However, the evidence accumulated by linguists and psycholinguists strongly suggests that you have some access to these rules, because your language behaviour indicates a great deal of compliance with them and your judgments of grammaticality (under reasonable conditions) are remarkably consistent.

Semantics

Semantics, the study of meaning, also plays an important role in our language use. After all, the sounds we produce are meant to communicate ideas, and for communication to take place the listener (or audience) must somehow receive the speaker's (or sender's) meaning. The task of creating a complete theory of meaning is daunting and currently unfinished. Many of these topics relate to ones we covered in Chapters 7 and 8, so what we will cover here will be theories of meaning narrowly defined.

Theories of meaning have to explain several things, at a minimum (Bierwisch, 1970):

- *Anomaly* (Why can't one say things like "Coffee ice cream can take dictation"?)
- *Self-contradiction* (Why is it contradictory to say, "My dog is not an animal"?)
- *Ambiguity* (Why isn't it clear where I intend to go in "I need to go to the bank"—to a financial institution or to the side of a river?)
- *Synonymy* (Why does "The rabbit is not old enough" mean the same thing as "The rabbit is too young"?)
- *Entailment* (Why does "Pat is my uncle" mean that Pat is male?)

Such theories should also explain how we use word meanings to process whole sentences and discourses. Much of cognitive psychologists' interest in semantics has to do with how knowledge is organized and stored and theories of how people form concepts and categorize things accordingly topics we discussed in Chapter 7.

Let's examine how semantics enters into our understanding of a sentence. Consider the sentence "Sara exchanged a dress for a suit." Generally we interpret this to mean that Sara took her dress somewhere (most likely to the store where she had bought it) and gave it to someone (probably a salesperson), and in return that person gave Sara a suit. Exchanging thus seems to have something to do with two people, each giving something to the other, although *mutual giving* and *exchanging* are not defined as precisely the same thing (Miller & Johnson-Laird, 1976). What exactly does *exchanging* mean? Miller and Johnson-Laird (p. 577) offered the following definition: Someone, *X*, "exchanges" something, *w*, for something, *z*, with someone, *Y*, if two conditions are met: (1) *X* gives *w* to *Y* and (2) this obligates *Y* to give *z* to *X*. Notice that this analysis explains why exchanging and mutual giving are similar but not identical: Exchanging creates an *obligation* for *Y* to give something back to *X*, although *Y* might renege on the deal; in mutual giving, *X* and *Y* must give something to each other.

For listeners to figure out the meaning of a sentence, they need to pay attention to more than just the meanings of individual words. Syntax also gives clues as to what a sentence means. Were this not the case, the following two sentences, because they make use of the same words, would mean exactly the same thing:

(9) The professor failed the student.
(10) The student failed the professor.

Clearly, the meaning of *failed* in the two sentences is not identical. Something in the way words are arranged, then, must cue the listener or reader about who the actor of the sentence is, what the action is, and to whom or what the action is done.

The study of semantics also involves the study of *truth conditions* of sentences and of the relations between sentences. As the term itself suggests, truth conditions are simply the circumstances that make something true. Refer to our earlier example sentence, "Sara exchanged a dress for a suit." Under what circumstances would this sentence be true? First of all, Sara has to be the person either actually carrying out the exchange or causing the exchange to happen (perhaps she sends Jane, her personal assistant, to the store). Second, Sara must, at the beginning of the transaction, have a dress to give and must give it to someone who gives her back a suit. If Sara gets back a hat instead of a suit, or gives a skirt rather than a dress, then the sentence is false. The point here is that our understanding of the meaning of this sentence requires (a) an understanding of the meaning of each word in the sentence, (b) an understanding of the syntax of the sentence, and (c) an understanding of the truth conditions of the sentence.

Pragmatics

To communicate verbally with another speaker of the English language, you must produce utterances that follow rules of phonology, syntax, and semantics. In addition, a fourth set of rules must be honoured if you want to communicate successfully. Known as *pragmatics*, these rules are the social rules of language; they include certain etiquette conventions, such as not interrupting another speaker and beginning conversations with certain conventional greetings (such as "Hi. How are you?").

Searle (1979) pointed out that in listening to another person, we must understand not only the sounds, words, and structure of the utterances but also the kinds of utterances. Different kinds of utterances demand different responses from us. For instance, in *assertives* the speaker asserts her or his belief in some proposition—for example, "It's hot in here" or "I'm a Raptors fan." These require little overt response from the listener, who is assumed to add the information asserted by the speaker into her or his own model of the world. *Directives*, another kind of speech act, are instructions from the speaker to the listener—for example, "Close the door" or "Don't believe everything you hear." *Commissives* are utterances that commit the speaker to some later action—for example, "I promise to clean my room" or "I guarantee this will work." *Expressives* describe psychological states of the speaker—for example, "I apologize for eating the last piece of pie" or "I thank you for the favour you did for me." Finally, *declarations* are speech acts in which the utterance is itself the action. Examples include "I now pronounce you husband and wife" or "You're fired." According to Searle's *speech act theory*, part of our job as listeners is to figure out which of the five types a particular utterance is and to respond appropriately.

Moreover, there are usually a number of distinct ways of stating or asking something. Imagine, for instance, that you are sitting in a room and a cold breeze is blowing through an open window. You want the window closed, but for one reason or another you do not wish to close it yourself. What could you say to someone else to get him or her to close the window? Here are a few possibilities (all of which would be classified as directives in Searle's, 1979, classification): (a) "Close the window"; (b) "Could you close the window, please?"; (c) "Hey, would you mind if we closed the window?"; (d) "I'm getting cold"; or (e) "Gee, there's quite a breeze today, isn't there?" How are you to choose among these (or other) options?

Note that in this example, how you choose to make your request will no doubt depend on whom you are talking to and where the conversation takes place (say, to your roommate in your dorm room versus to your host in his house). Option (e), for instance, might be too subtle to communicate your intention if you were speaking to a preschooler (who might take it as a general and rather uninteresting comment on the weather). However, (a) might communicate clearly but mark you as an overbearing and rude guest if you were to say this to your host while dining at his house.

Pragmatic understanding is something often exploited by advertising as well. Consider a television commercial for a new product, Eradicold cold pills. The video shows athletic, healthy looking people vigorously skiing, sledding, skating, and generally wending their way through a snow-covered winter wonderland. The voice-over says, "Aren't you tired of sniffles and runny noses all winter? Tired of always feeling less than your best? Get through a whole winter without a cold. Take Eradicold pills as directed." Odds are, you would draw the inference that taking Eradicold as directed would cause you to evade colds all winter. But the ad doesn't directly say that. Advertisers rely on the fact that the way they word ads implies causal relationships that may or may not be true. Harris (1977), who studied comprehension of such ads, showed that people are not very good at distinguishing between what an ad directly states and what it only implies.

So far, we've seen that our language is structured and rule-governed at several different but interacting levels. Although much more can be said about each of these levels (each of which gives rise to several linguistics courses), we need to turn our attention to how the structure of language directs and is influenced by other kinds of cognitive processing. We'll look first at how speakers of a language process incoming utterances or written sentences to comprehend their meaning.

LANGUAGE COMPREHENSION AND PRODUCTION

Like other information, language must be transformed from raw input into meaningful representations. One of the first stages of this transformation is perceptual. In this section, we'll examine the perception of speech, noticing the special ways in which speech input is initially processed. We will then turn to further stages of processing—in particular, comprehension and the processing of discourse, such as conversations. Finally, we will examine the processing of written language through reading.

Speech Perception

One way we encounter and use language is in the form of speech. Understanding the speech of someone talking to you is usually quite easy unless it is in a foreign language or the speaker has a very marked speech impediment. We can almost always understand the speech of children, adults, fluent speakers, and those with strong foreign or regional accents. As we will see, this ability is pretty remarkable.

It might seem reasonable to suppose we perceive speech in the way (we think) we perceive written text: one sound at a time, using the pauses between sounds (like the white space between letters) to identify letters and the pauses between words to identify when one word ends and another begins. Unfortunately, this tidy explanation doesn't work. (Actually, evidence suggests we really don't process written text letter by letter, either.)

George Miller (1990) described two fundamental problems in speech perception. First, speech is continuous. Rarely are there pauses around each sound; different sounds from the same word blend into each other. This is shown most clearly in Figure 9-4, which displays a spectrogram of a spoken sentence. A spectrogram is a graphic representation of speech, showing the frequencies of sound, in hertz (cycles per second), along the y axis, plotted against time on the x axis. Darker regions in the figure indicate the intensity of each sound at each frequency. Note that the boundaries (white spaces) do not correspond to word or syllable boundaries. Indeed, nothing in the physical stimulus itself indicates where these

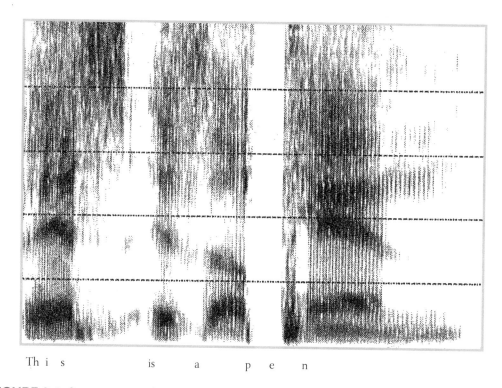

Th i s   is   a   p   e   n

FIGURE 9-4 Spectrogram of a person pronouncing the indicated sentence.

boundaries are. In other words, when you listen to someone talk, it sounds as if there were pauses between syllables and words, but many of those pauses are illusory!

A second problem in speech perception is that a single phoneme sounds different, depending on context. Although it casually appears as if *baby, boondoggle,* and *bunny* all began with the same identical sound, this is not the case. Figure 9-5 presents a spectrogram of a person pronouncing these three words, and examination of the spectrogram reveals few if any properties present for all three words. Moreover, men and women generally speak with different pitches (women's voices generally having higher pitch, or frequencies), different people have different accents, and speakers talk differently when shouting, coaxing, whispering, or lecturing. Thus you can realize just how complicated it is to ascertain which phoneme is being produced simply from the physical properties of the acoustic stimulus.

Given these problems, how do most of us manage to perceive speech rather easily? In part, the answer is that we seem to come specially equipped to perceive speech in efficient ways. Although the actual acoustic stimulus can vary infinitely in its phonetic properties, our perception of speech sounds is *categorical:* In processing speech sounds, we automatically, without awareness or intention, force the sounds into discrete categories.

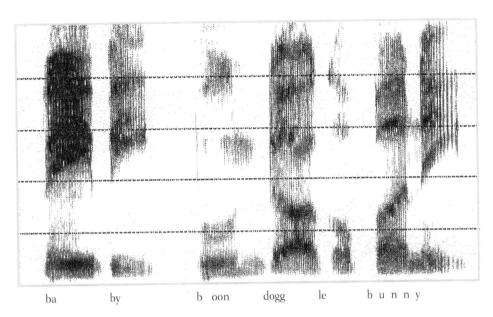

ba   by   b oon   dogg   le   b u n n y

FIGURE 9-5 Spectrogram of the words baby, boondoggle, and bunny.

Lisker and Abramson (1970) demonstrated the categorical perception of speech sounds. They used a computer to generate artificial speech sounds consisting of a bilabial stop consonant (which sounds like either a \b\ or a \p\ sound) followed by an "ah" sound. The \b\ and \p\ sounds have the same consonantal features and differ only in voice onset time. (Voice onset time, or VOT, has to do with how quickly after the consonant sound is released the vocal folds begin to vibrate; negative values of VOT indicate the vocal cords begin to vibrate *before* the sound is released.) Lisker and Abramson varied the VOT, by computer, from 20.15 second to 10.15 second, generating 31 syllables.

When they presented the syllables to listeners, the listeners "heard" only two sounds: a "ba" and a "pa." Any syllable with a VOT of 10.03 second or less was heard as a "ba," and any syllable with a VOT of more than 10.03 second was heard as a "pa." Participants did not report differences in the sounds of the syllables that were on the same side of the boundary. To them, a syllable with a VOT of 20.10 second was indistinguishable from a syllable with a VOT of 20.05 second. However, two syllables that were just as close in VOTs but fell on opposite sides of the boundary (such as 0.00 and 10.05) were identified by 100% of the participants as being different sounds: a "ba" sound and a "pa" sound, respectively.

Apparently, then, we pay attention to certain acoustic properties of speech (those that make a meaningful difference in our language) but ignore others. This might explain why we can understand the speech of a stranger (who speaks our language) quickly and effortlessly: We ignore the differences in his or her speech (pitch of voice, accent) that are not meaningful.

Incidentally, categorical perception has also been demonstrated for some nonspeech sounds, such as tones, buzzes, and musical notes played on different instruments (Harnad, 1987). Moreover, studies of infants have shown that although very young infants can discriminate many, if not all, of the sound distinctions used in all the world's languages, that ability begins to narrow to just the phonemes in the infant's primary language when the infant is about 6 months of age (Eimas, 1985).

Although we clearly pay careful attention to critical sound distinctions in our language, it isn't just sounds that influence us. A clever study by Massaro and Cohen (1983) demonstrated that we also make use of visual information in the perception of speech. These investigators examined the categorical perception of the stop consonants \b\ and \d\, two sounds that differ only in the place of articulation. Participants heard nine computer-synthesized syllables that ranged in their acoustic properties from a clear "ba" sound to a clear "da" sound. In the "neutral" condition, participants heard the syllables with no visual information. In two other conditions, participants heard the syllables while watching a silent but synchronized videotape of a speaker who was pronouncing either "ba" or "da." One question was whether participants would notice a discrepancy when the auditory information presented was "ba" but the videotaped speaker was saying "da." The participants did not. It is interesting, however, that what the speaker appeared to be saying influenced what was heard: Syllables in the middle of the "ba"–"da" continuum were perceived slightly differently as a function of what the speaker appeared to be saying relative to the perception reported in the neutral condition.

Apparently, then, visual cues affect how sounds are perceived. One might describe this as a kind of *context effect*, first described in Chapter 3. A number of other studies have demonstrated that speech perception is subject to a number of other context effects. Studies by Warren and his collaborators (Warren, 1970; Warren & Obusek, 1971) have demonstrated that in some cases people "hear" phonemes that are not there! In the 1970 study, Warren presented participants with a recording of the sentence "The state governors met with their respective legi*latures convening in the capital city," in which a 120-millisecond portion had been replaced with a coughing sound (indicated by the asterisk). Only 1 of 20 listeners reported detecting a missing sound covered by a cough, and the one who did misreported its location. The other 19 demonstrated *phoneme restoration effect*, so called because listeners apparently "restore" the missing phonemes predicted by other linguistic information during the course of perception.

Other studies also suggest that people use context to help them perceive speech. One study, by Marslen-Wilson and Welsh (1978), required participants to "shadow" speech—that is, to repeat it aloud. (We encountered shadowing tasks in Chapter 4, as you may recall.) The investigators introduced some distortions into the speech presented to participants (for example, the pseudoword *cigaresh*). They found participants were often likely to restore the distortion to the proper pronunciation *(cigarette)*, especially if the word was highly predictable from the preceding context (for example, "Still, he wanted to smoke a _____"). This result suggests that readers and listeners typically use the context of the previous words in a sentence to predict the next word and can even "mishear" or "misread" that word if it is presented in a distorted fashion. You might note here a parallel to context effects in visual perception, a topic reviewed in Chapter 3.

In the last decade, many companies (e.g., airline, credit cards, Internet service providers) have installed voice recognition systems. So, for example, you can call a toll-free number and check your credit card balance, or receive flight departure and arrival information, simply by speaking the numbers of the card or flight clearly into the phone. If speech recognition is so complicated, you might wonder, how can a computer do it?

The answer parallels that for handwriting recognition systems, as we discussed in Chapter 3. Simply put, the incoming stimuli are limited to a number of discrete categories. The voice recognition systems really only recognize names of different digits. They don't have to figure out which language you are speaking in (they only work in one or two languages, and you specify that at the beginning of the call), and they expect only certain responses "one" or "two" or "three" but not "zebra" or "toque" or "hurricane."

Speech Errors in Production

So far, we have examined the ways in which we perceive language, specifically spoken sounds, but this is only part of the story regarding the ways in which we process speech. As native speakers of a language, we do more than comprehend and process it—we also produce speech for others to comprehend and process. One kind of study of speech production focuses on *speech errors*, defined as instances in which what the speaker intended to say is quite clear, but the speaker makes some substitution or reorders the elements. Some examples of speech errors are the following (adapted from Garrett, 1990):

(15) Sue keeps food in her *v*esk. (Substitution of "v" for "d")
(16) Keep your greedy hands off my *w*eet *s*peas. (Shift of "s")
(17) . . . got a lot of *p*ons and pa*t*s to wash. (Exchange of sounds)
(18) We'll sit around the *song* and sing *fires*. (Exchange of words and morphemes)

Much of the data from speech error studies is observational rather than experimental, for the simple reason that it seems to be difficult to control experimentally the ways in which people produce speech. Because of the observational nature of the studies, assertions about causation are problematic. However, one can look at the relative frequency of occurrence of different kinds of errors and make inferences regarding the underlying mechanisms. Garrett (1990) advocated this approach.

In studying one kind of speech error, word substitution, Garrett (1988) found two broad classes: errors that showed meaning relations (for example, using *finger* in place of *toe*, or *walk* instead of *run*) and errors that showed form relations (for example, *guest* instead of *goat*, *mushroom* for *mustache*). Garrett argued that the two kinds of errors were very distinct: Those that showed similarities of meaning rarely involved similarities of form, and vice versa. Although such errors are possible (such as *head* for *hair*, *lobster* for *oyster*), they seldom occur.

According to Garrett (1990), the relative infrequency of word substitution errors showing *both* meaning and form similarities indicates the language production system processes information about meaning and information about form at different points in sentence construction. His reasoning: If meaning and form processes operate simultaneously, then sentences in which both kinds of similarity are present ought to produce the most errors because there is greater opportunity for error to come about. This doesn't happen, suggesting that the two kinds of processing are separate and operate at different points.

Retrieving Meaning—Single Words

How do people understand or recover the meaning from text? As the previous discussion has indicated, this is a very complicated task. One approach researchers have taken has been to study how we retrieve meaning from single words. A technique that has been used to do this, the lexical decision task, was mentioned in Chapter 6. In the lexical decision task observers are presented with target letter strings and are asked to decide, as quickly as possible, whether the target letter strings constitute properly spelled words. As noted earlier, Meyer and Schvaneveldt (1971) found that observers are faster and more accurate in making a lexical decision when a target word is preceded by another word, called a prime, that is associated in meaning. This has been termed the semantic priming effect, and is considered to reveal information about the structure and processing of memory.

In a seminal paper, Neely (1977) identified the operation of two types of processes that could be responsible for semantic priming: a fast-acting automatic spread of activation, and a slower expectancy-driven process. In his experiments, Neely included prime-target pairs, such as *BIRD-sparrow*, that were related in meaning. These items produced priming, as expected. He also added a clever twist, however. Neely instructed participants in his experiments that whenever they saw the prime word BUILDING, they should expect it to be followed by a target word that named a part of the body, such as *foot*. Likewise, whenever they saw the prime word BODY, they were told to expect it to be followed by a target word that named a part of a building, such as *door*. These were known as switch instructions. On most trials in his experiment, Neely held true to his instructions. Thus, when the prime word BUILDING appeared, it was often followed by a target word like *foot*, *nose*, or *arm*. When the prime word BODY appeared, it was often followed by a target word like *window*, *door*, or *roof*. Sometimes, however, Neely violated the switch instructions he gave to participants, and paired the primes and targets in the "regular" related manner. For instance, BUILDING appeared before *roof* and BODY appeared before *foot*.

Neely found the following: When the target word was presented very shortly after the prime word, say within 250 ms, Neely's instructions to the participants did not matter. That is, semantic priming was still observed for pairs like BODY-*foot*, even though they violated the participants' expectations. In contrast, no priming was observed for pairs like *BODY-window*, even though they were consistent with participants' switch expectation. Neely interpreted this as evidence for automatic spreading activation. In other words, when the prime word BODY was read by the participant, the concept BODY was activated in memory. Activation then spread immediately and automatically to related concepts, such as *foot, arm*, and *nose*, despite the fact the participant was expecting to see some other target word appear.

Interestingly, when Neely increased the amount of time that separated the presentation of the prime and target, to around, say, 700 ms, something completely different happened. In that case, Neely observed priming for expected pairs, such as *BODY-window* and BUILD-ING-*foot*, and found that participants were actually slower to respond to items that were really related, such as *BODY-nose* and BUILDING-*door*, than they were to respond to items that were completely unrelated, such as BIRD-*arm*! He attributed these complex findings to the operation of a slow-acting expectancy process. Neely argued that because of his instructions, participants began to expect certain types of targets to follow specific primes and activated those targets in memory. This, according to Neely requires participants awareness of the relation between the primes and targets, their willingness to use this strategy, and the time to do it. From the time of Neely's (1977) classic paper, it is generally accepted that there are at least two processes involved in producing priming when observers retrieve meaning from memory. More recent work, however, has challenged the idea that a word's meaning is automatically activated in memory any time a word is encountered. Starting with the innovative work of Smith (1979), there has been a great deal of work showing that semantic priming does not automatically occur when related pairs are presented (e.g., Smith, Besner, & Miyoshi, 1994; Stolz & Besner, 1996, 1998).

Sentence Comprehension

Our understanding of how we retrieve meaning from individually presented words can be thought of as a building block to help us begin to understand how we understand full sentences. Sentence comprehension is a complicated task and, as we have seen, requires us to retrieve not only the meaning of individual words but also syntactic structure. Moreover, comprehending a sentence often involves resolving its possible ambiguities. Box 9-1 offers examples of phonetic, lexical (that is, word-level), and syntactic

---

Box 9-1 Examples of Ambiguous Sentences

Phonetic ambiguity

Remember, a spoken sentence often contains many words not intended to be heard.

Ream ember us poke can cent tense off in contains men knee words knot in ten did tube bee herd.

Lexical ambiguity

I've got to go to the bank this morning.

I've got to go to TD Canada Trust this morning.

or

I've got to go to the river's edge this morning.

Syntactic ambiguity

Have the missionaries eaten.

(Spoken by the bishop as a question or spoken by a cannibal chief as an order)

Source: Garrett (1990).

---

ambiguities present in different sentences. The interesting thing about the sentences is that we would ordinarily not notice the ambiguities; our processing would result in one unambiguous representation.

Only rarely, and with certain kinds of sentences, do we even notice ambiguities. Consider the following sentences (Garrett, 1990, p. 137):

(21) Fatty weighed 350 pounds of grapes.
(22) The cotton shirts are made from comes from Arizona.
(23) The horse raced past the barn fell.

These sentences are sometimes called *garden path sentences* because they lead the listener or reader down one path, to one interpretation, until somewhere in the middle or the end of processing, he or she realizes the interpretation is incorrect and the sentence must be reprocessed. Normal sentence processing somehow goes astray with these examples.

The three preceding sentences have initial fragments (such as "The cotton shirts are made from") that are *syntactically ambiguous:* They are consistent with at least two different parses. In this sentence, the word *cotton* could be treated as an adjective, modifying *shirts* (as in "The cotton shirts are made from dyed fibres"), or as a noun (as in "The cotton shirts are made from comes from Arizona"). Some have argued that we have a preference for parsing the fragment in certain ways. According to this line of thinking, we come to the second interpretation only when forced to because the first parse does not work. We notice that the first parse does not work only when we get to the fragment "comes from Arizona" and don't know what to do with it (Altmann, 1987).

A sentence processor encounters other ambiguities as well. One type is called **lexical ambiguity**. It occurs with words that have two meanings, such as *bank*, which can refer to either a financial institution or the edge of a river. How are lexical ambiguities normally resolved? A study by Swinney (1979) offers some insights.

Swinney (1979) presented people with spoken passages. Some of these contained ambiguous words; other, similar passages (heard by different experimental participants) did not. In each case, the unambiguous version included a word synonymous with one of the meanings of the ambiguous word. Here is an example of such a passage (with the ambiguous/unambiguous words italicized):

> (24) Rumour had it that, for years, the government building had been plagued with problems. The man was not surprised when he found several roaches, spiders, and other *(bugs/insects)* ‡ in the corner of his room. (Swinney, 1979, p. 650)

Simultaneously, people participated in a visual lexical decision task (we discussed such tasks in Chapter 6) in which they were presented with a string of letters and asked to decide, as quickly as possible, whether the string formed an English word. The letter strings were presented at the point marked with a double dagger ‡ in the preceding example. Previous work by Swinney and others had demonstrated the existence of priming across the modalities (that is, a spoken word can prime a visually presented word). Swinney's question here was, Would all the meanings (such as "insect," "recording device") of an ambiguous word (such as *bug*) be subject to priming, or would priming occur only for the meaning activated by the context?

Swinney's (1979) results suggested that even in highly biased contexts such as the preceding one, both meanings of an ambiguous word (in this case, *bug*) were able to prime performance in the lexical decision task if the visual presentation happened immediately after the auditory presentation of the ambiguous word. So, for example, Passage 24 primed both "spy" and "ant," which are semantically related to different meanings of the word *bug*, when they were presented immediately after the participants heard *bug*. If the visual presentation of letter strings was delayed for even as few as four syllables after the auditory presentation of the ambiguous word, however, priming occurred only for the contextually appropriate meaning of the ambiguous word. So, with a delayed presentation of words visually, the spoken word *bug* would prime "ant" but not "spy" in the context of Passage 24. Subsequent research by Gernsbacher (1993) supports Swinney's findings. Gernsbacher and her colleagues have shown that good readers suppress the inappropriate meaning of a word ("spy"), and use the appropriate meaning ("ant"), more efficiently and readily than do poor readers.

These results have several implications. First, when we process ambiguous sentences, all the meanings of an ambiguous word are temporarily available through what looks to be an automatic, bottom-up process or set of processes. So however context effects operate, they do not operate immediately to restrict the listener or reader to the most appropriate "reading" of the words. Instead, for a period of time all meanings are accessible; however, the period is very short.

Three syllables after presentation of the ambiguous word (for most people, about 750 to 1,000 milliseconds) only one meaning remains active, suggesting that people resolve sentence ambiguity fairly quickly. Garrett (1990), reviewing these and other results, concluded that sentence comprehension normally occurs with left-to-right processing (each word in the sentence is processed sequentially), with each word normally processed once and normally one interpretation assigned. Sentence processing results in each sentence's being assigned a "logical structure" so that the reader knows the role of each word in the sentence and how the sentence fits with preceding sentences. Garden path sentences, however, demonstrate that normal processing can sometimes fail. Still, the rarity of garden path sentences suggests that most of the time we process sentences very rapidly and efficiently.

Comprehending Text Passages

We've just examined some evidence concerning how we process individual sentences. One question we can now ask is how processing of individual sentences works when they are bundled together into connected passages, such as paragraphs or stories. Much of the time, when we encounter text passages, they are in written form. Thus, to examine text processing, we will first need to review briefly some findings on how people read.

Mangostar/Shutterstock.com

The language comprehension processes used in reading are complex but are often taken for granted.

Just and Carpenter (1987) conducted a number of studies on how people read. They often use computer-driven instruments to measure and record *eye fixations* on parts of the written text. Fixations are brief pauses that everyone makes as their eyes scan text. Reading consists of a series of fixations and jumps, known as *saccades*, between fixations. The average fixation lasts about 250 milliseconds (about a quarter of a second); the average saccade lasts 10 to 20 milliseconds (Just & Carpenter, 1987).

Just and Carpenter's model of reading assumes that as soon as readers encounter a new word, they try to

Box 9-2 Gaze Durations of a Typical Reader

Eye fixations of a college student reading a scientific passage. Gazes within each sentence are sequentially numbered above the fixated words with the durations (in msec) indicated below the sequence number.

1	2	3	4	5	6	7	8	91			
1566	267	400	83	267	617	767	450	450	400		
Flywheels	are	one	of the	oldest mechanical	devices	known	to	man.	Every		
2	3	5	4	6	7	8	9	10			
616	517	684	250	317	617	1116	367	467			
Internal	combustion	engine	contains	a small	flywheel	that	converts	the	jerky		
11	12	13	14	15	16	17	18	19	20	21	
483	450	383	284	383	317	283	533	50	366	566	
motion of the	pistons	into	the	smooth	flow	of	energy that	powers	the	drive	shaft.

interpret it and assign it a role. The authors called this the *immediacy assumption*. In addition, Just and Carpenter (1987) proposed what they called the *eye–mind hypothesis*, which holds that the interpretation of each word occurs during the time it is fixated. Therefore, the time spent on each fixation provides information about ease of interpretation. (Rayner and Sereno, 1994, gave reasons against both these assumptions, or hypotheses, although these probably do not undermine the results reported next. Tanenhaus, Magnuson, Dahan, and Chambers, 2000, present a similar model of eye movements that they believe indicate access of stored words from memory during spoken language comprehension.) Just and Carpenter argued that among the factors that increase fixation duration, and thus ease of interpretation, are word length, word infrequency and syntactically or semantically anomalous words.

The researchers (Carpenter & Just, 1983; Just & Carpenter, 1980) presented college students with passages from magazines such as *Newsweek* and *Time* describing scientific inventions, technical innovations, or biological mechanisms. Box 9-2 shows sample results for one student. Numbers above each word indicate the fixation time (measured in milliseconds) for that word. Note that content words, such as *flywheels*, *devices*, or *engine*, almost always receive longer fixations than function words, such as *the*, *on*, or *a*, which often are not fixated at all. Although not every word is fixated, the content words almost always are. These results suggest that more time is spent on the meaningful or semantically rich parts of the text, as would be expected given the reader's goal of understanding meaning.

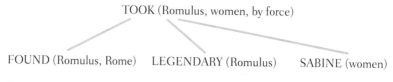

"Romulus, the legendary founder of Rome, took the women of the Sabine by force."

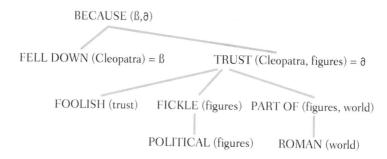

"Cleopatra's downfall lay in her foolish trust in the fickle political figures
of the Roman world."

FIGURE 9-6 Propositional structure of two sentences.

Source: Reprinted from *Cognitive Psychology*, vol. 5, issue 3, Walter Kintsch, Janice Keenan,
Reading Rate and Retention as a Function of the Number of Propositions in the Base
Structure of Sentences, pp. 257–274, Copyright © 1973, with permission from Elsevier.

Other research on reading also suggests that semantic factors influence the reading task.
Kintsch and Keenan (1973) showed that two sentences of equal length might be differentially
difficult to process. The source of the difficulty, they suggested, lies in the **propositional complexity** of the sentences, the number of basic ideas conveyed. The two sentences in Figure 9-6
are approximately equal in length, although they differ greatly in the number of underlying
propositions, or basic ideas. This model predicts that the second sentence, having the same
number of words but more propositions than the first, will be more difficult to process, and
indeed this is what Kintsch and Keenan found.

Participants were asked to press a button after reading a sentence (or passage) silently and
then to immediately recall as much of the sentence as they could. The more propositions a
sentence contained, the longer it took for the participants to read and comprehend it. Further, they were much more likely to recall the more "central" propositions, those critical to
the meaning of the sentence, than the more peripheral ones that merely elaborated on the
central ideas. This result suggests that propositions are mentally represented in some sort of
hierarchy with more central propositions at the top of the hierarchy as shown in Figure 9-6.

The peripheral, lower-level propositions apparently serve the function of elaborating the more central propositions and so are less important to remember.

Another factor influencing the processing of text has to do with the relations among sentences. How do people integrate related ideas that may come from different sentences? Haviland and Clark (1974) described what they called the *given–new* strategy a pragmatic approach to processing sentences whereby listeners and readers divide sentences into two parts: the given and the new. The given part of a sentence contains information that is (or should be) familiar from the context, the preceding information (including other sentences just presented), or background knowledge. The new part, as the term implies, contains unfamiliar information. Listeners first search memory for information corresponding to the given information and then update memory by incorporating the new information, often as an elaboration of the given.

The given–new strategy can work only if the information in the given part of the sentence corresponds to some information in the listener's memory called the *antecedent*. One way to help the listener make this connection is to use the same description in the given part of the sentence as in memory. However, as a practical matter, it is often easier to use slightly different ways of referring to things and to expect the listener to make some connections—the obvious ones—on his or her own. These connections, called *bridging inferences*, bolster text coherence by linking ideas of concepts across sentences (e.g., Singer & Remillard, 2004), although they will naturally take some time to make.

In one experiment, Haviland and Clark (1974) presented people with passages consisting of context followed by target sentences. Sometimes (as in Passage 25) the target sentence had given information that exactly matched the antecedent information (from the context); other times, participants had to draw a bridging inference (as in Passage 26).

(25) We got some beer out of the car. The beer was warm.
(26) We checked the picnic supplies. The beer was warm.

As predicted, it took participants longer to read and comprehend the target sentence in Passage 26 than it did participants who read the same target sentence in Passage 25, presumably because those participants reading Passage 25 had to draw the bridging inference "The picnic supplies included beer."

Readers must sometimes also make inferences between sentences that are far apart in a text. Think about a mystery story, for example. To understand how the clues of a mystery fit together to create a solution, readers must infer how the central propositions from each clue connect to the essential ideas of another clue. These connections need to occur even though the clues may appear at different times in the story. Readers vary in the number of such inferences they can create at any one time, and the inferences themselves vary in how strongly they connect one piece of information to another. Researchers have consistently shown that the number of inferences readers make and the strength of the inferences created

---

Box 9-3 An Ambiguous Story

If the balloons popped, the sound wouldn't be able to carry since everything would be too far away from the correct floor. A closed window would also prevent the sound from carrying, since most buildings tend to be well insulated. Since the whole operation depends on a steady flow of electricity, a break in the middle of the wire would also cause problems. Of course, the fellow could shout, but the human voice is not loud enough to carry that far. An additional problem is that the string could break on the instrument. Then there could be no accompaniment to the message. It is clear that the best situation would involve less distance. Then there would be fewer potential problems. With face-to-face contact, the least number of things could go wrong.

Source: Bransford, J.D., & Johnson, M.K. (1972). Contextual prerequisites for understanding: Some investigations of comprehension and recall. *Journal of Verbal Learning and Verbal Behavior,* 11, page 718. Copyright © 1972. Reprinted with permission from Elsevier.

---

affect how well readers remember and understand what they read (Goldman & Varnhagen, 1986; Graesser & Clark, 1985; Trabasso, Secco, & van den Broek, 1984; Trabasso & van den Broek, 1985). In short, inferences of all types, including bridging inferences between sentences or inferences that tie more distant parts of a text together, are crucial to how well you or I understand what we read.

The role of context in processing language has been extensively documented by John Bransford and Marcia Johnson. Read the passage in Box 9-3, then cover it and try to recall as much as you can. If you are like Bransford and Johnson's (1972) participants, you may find the task very difficult, and your recall may include only a few of the ideas. However, if you were first provided with a context for the passage, such as the one depicted in Figure 9-7, your recall would be much more complete. Bransford and Johnson showed that with the context provided before the passage, participants recalled an average of 8.0 out of 14.0 distinct ideas. Without any context, or even with the context provided after the passage, participants only recalled about 3.6 ideas.

Van den Broek and Gustafson (1999) offer three conclusions from research on reading texts. The first is that "the mental representation is a construction by the reader that differs from, and goes beyond, the information in the text itself (p. 17), meaning that people recruit their own background knowledge to draw inferences to comprehend text. Second, "a good representation is coherent" (p. 18), implying that structures such as schemata or story grammars are used to make the information in a text fit together. A third principle, which we have seen evidence for in earlier chapters, is that a reader's attentional resources are limited. Therefore, to cut down on their workload, readers do not draw every logically possible inference

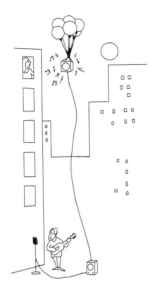

FIGURE 9-7 Context for story in Box 9-3.

Source: Reprinted from *Journal of Verbal Learning and Verbal Behavior*, vol. 11, issue 6, John D. Bransford, Marcia K. Johnson, Contextual Prerequisites for Understanding: Some Investigations of Comprehension and Recall, pp. 717–726, Copyright © 1972, with permission from Elsevier.

they could from a text (the number of inferences drawn would be overwhelming). Instead, van den Broek and Gustafson posit, inferences are created only when they are needed to create coherence.

Gricean Maxims of Conversation

Not all the connected information people must process occurs in written form. We can think of ordinary conversations as examples of connected spoken text. Conversations are interesting to study because they occur so frequently and because (unlike written texts) they normally involve the production of a great deal of language with little time for planning and revision. Indeed, Clark and Van Der Wege (2002) argue,

> *the essence of language use is found in face-to-face talk. It is here that speaking and listening arise in their natural, universal states. It is here that researchers can study why speakers say the things they say and how listeners interpret these things—ultimately, as a way of coordinating joint activities. . . .*

The problem is that too little is known about spontaneous language and how it differs from reciting, reading aloud, listening to idealized speech, and other such forms. Understanding language in its natural habitat is a major challenge for the second century of psycholinguistics. (p. 250)

We've already seen a number of examples of linguistic rules that people follow in producing or comprehending language. Some of these have to do with ways of combining sounds to produce words, combining words to produce sentences, or even combining ideas to produce meanings. Many researchers believe, however, that yet another set of rules is necessary for people to use language appropriately or effectively, especially in conversations: pragmatic rules.

Here we will examine some pragmatic rules specific to conversations called the **Gricean maxims of cooperative conversation** (Grice, 1975). Grice believed that for people to converse, they must do more than produce utterances that are phonologically, syntactically, and semantically appropriate. Consider the following "conversation."

Sally: I just heard that Joe won an NSERC undergrad scholarship. Isn't that great?
Jane: Kelowna is located in British Columbia.
Mike: No, Charles Darwin is the father of evolutionary theory.
Sally: What's the square root of 34?
Jane: Chocolate ice cream is tasty.

What is wrong with this conversation? Notice that all the sentences are "legal." Each obeys the phonological rules of English. Each is syntactically well formed. Each is meaningful. Yet, all together, they don't add up to a conversation. Put simply, there is a lack of connection between what one speaker says and anything else the other speakers say. Normally in conversation, each of a person's contributions or utterances bears some relation to what others have already said or to what the speaker plans to say later. In this sense, speakers can be said to provide a context for one another's contributions.

Grice (1975) argued that for a conversation to take place, all the speakers must cooperate with

Rawpixel.com/Shutterstock.com

Grice proposed four maxims, or rules, that people must follow to have a successful conversation.

one another. Although speakers in a conversation have many choices to make concerning what they will say, as well as when and how they will say it, they must still obey constraints, or general rules (Miller & Glucksberg, 1988). Grice described speakers in a conversation as all following a general "cooperative principle." Speakers do this, Grice believed, by following four specific conversational *maxims* or rules (Grice, 1975):

1. *Maxim of quantity.* Make your contribution as informative as required. Do not make your contribution more informative than is required.
2. *Maxim of quality.* Try to make your contribution one that is true. Do not say what you believe to be false. Do not say that for which you have no evidence.
3. *Maxim of relation.* Be relevant.
4. *Maxim of manner.* Be clear. Avoid obscurity of expression. Avoid ambiguity. Be brief. Be orderly

Violations of the maxims produce conversations that are noticeably odd. For instance, if someone asks, "Do you have a watch?" and you respond, "Yes, I do," you are violating the first maxim of quantity: You are being less informative than is required. Your conversation partner is not, in all likelihood, taking a census for Timex or Rolex; he or she probably wants to know the time. As a member of the language community that you live in, you are expected to know that the question asked is really a request for the time and to respond appropriately.

It is also possible to violate the first maxim by being *too* informative. For example, imagine you were to invite your professor to have coffee with you after lecture. When you arrange to get together, you will probably ask something like "Where should we meet?" Your prof's response is generally "How about at Tim's in five?" rather than something much more detailed like "Please come to the Tim Hortons kiosk in the Arts Lecture Hall in approximately five minutes, and I will be standing nearby." The latter is bizarre, presumably because it's too specific.

The second maxim has to do with truthfulness. Generally, conversation partners assume the other is telling the truth, or at least what the speaker believes to be the truth. On some occasions, it is permissible to violate this maxim—for example, to be ironic. Imagine that a friend who's missed a lecture in a class in which you are both enrolled asks, "How was class today?" You can respond, "Utterly fascinating!" even if it really was dry as toast, *if* you somehow signal your answer isn't to be taken literally. Rolled eyes, exaggerated intonation, winks, and the like, help to communicate that your violation of the maxim of quality is itself meant to communicate something—in this case, ironic humour. If you simply utter an untruthful response without letting your listener know you aren't being candid, then your conversation will not be successful, and your conversation partner could legitimately complain about your conversation skills. (See the Canadian Research Highlight in Box 9-4 for more on processing verbal irony.)

Box 9-4 Canadian Research Highlight

Your ability to communicate your disappointment over an exam mark by telling a friend, "Gee, I totally nailed that midterm" depends on both of you being able to process nonliteral language that illuminates the discrepancy between reality and what is expected. Penny Pexman (https://psyc.ucalgary.ca/profiles/penny-pexman) and her colleagues at the University of Calgary have argued that our ability to do this depends on multiple cues, such as tone of voice, incongruity, and our understanding that the person with whom we are speaking is capable of picking up on these cues. In addition, these cues need to be processed rapidly and in parallel with the literal content of the message (e.g., Pexman, in press; Pexman, Ferretti, & Katz, 2000). More recently, Pexman has begun to investigate nonliteral language comprehension in populations that have difficulty understanding irony, for instance very young children (e.g., Pexman, Glenwright, Hala, Kowbel, & Jungen, 2006). Her work has demonstrated that by the age of 5 or 6 children can begin to appreciate that an ironic speaker is sharing a message different from the overt message being stated, and that this ability continues to develop into adolescence. In addition to using cues like the speaker's tone of voice to make their interpretation, children are also influenced by what they know about the speaker's personality. Pexman states that by studying young children, and others who have difficulty in understanding irony such as individuals with brain injury and autism spectrum disorder, we can learn much about the complexities involved in this process.

Someone who consistently violates the maxims of quantity or quality may well be perceived as uncooperative or obnoxious and, after a while, may find it difficult to attract conversation partners. Someone who consistently violates the third maxim of relation by responding with irrelevant utterances will have a bigger problem: He or she will simply be regarded as, at best, very bizarre. To illustrate, imagine a conversation between Tom and Joe, two university roommates.

Tom *(looking around):* Hey, Joe, have you seen my sweater?

Joe *(looking at Tom, and smiling):* Lo, a flaming squirrel!

If Joe persists in violating the maxim of relation, he will likely find himself at a complete loss for conversation partners, if not roommates and friends.

The fourth maxim, the maxim of manner, generally governs the way you choose to construct your conversation contributions. The general idea is that you should speak as clearly as possible, using language appropriate to your listener and the context. Among other things, this maxim forbids you to answer your professors in pig Latin or your younger siblings in "academese." It also prevents you from holding a filibuster (unless you are a member of Parliament) and requires that you at least *attempt* to organize what you say before you begin speaking.

Gricean maxims are not always obeyed, but the assumption is that people try to obey them most of the time. When the maxims are violated, the speaker apparently wishes to end the conversation, wishes to avoid the conversation, or expects the listener to understand that the violation is occurring and why (Levinson, 2000; Miller & Glucksberg, 1988). Again, though, it is doubtful the average person is consciously aware of the rules. As with most linguistic rules, maxims are implicitly understood even if they can't be precisely stated.

LANGUAGE AND COGNITION

Language is used in ways other than social conversation. Lecturers use language to get ideas across to students, authors to readers, newscasters to audiences, and so on. It should be evident by now that language is used in a number of cognitive processes. When we perceive a familiar object and name it (either aloud or to ourselves), we use language; when we follow one conversation rather than another, we are processing language; when we repeat information aloud or take notes to organize it, we are using language. Similarly, when we reason, make plans, or brainstorm new ideas, we rely heavily on language, as we will see in the next chapters.

Our use of language in a wide variety of cognitive tasks raises the following important question: What influences does language have over other cognitive processes? Two extreme positions exist: (a) language and other cognitive processes operate completely independently, and (b) language and other cognitive processes are completely related, with one determining the other. Between the extremes is a broad middle ground, where language and other cognitive processes are seen as related in some ways but independent in others.

The relation between language and thought has been heavily debated. In the early days of American psychology, John B. Watson (1930) asserted that thought was language and nothing more. In particular, he rejected the idea that thought (internal mental representation or other cognitive activity) could occur without some sort of conditioned language responses occurring. Watson believed that all apparent instances of thinking (such as mentally computing sums, daydreaming about a vacation, weighing the pros and cons of a plan) were really the results of subvocal speech. Thinking was equated with talking to yourself, even if so quietly and covertly that no one (including you) knew you were using language.

Smith, Brown, Toman, and Goodman (1947) conducted a heroic experiment to test Watson's theory. Smith served as the subject and allowed himself to be injected with a curare derivative, which paralyzed all his muscles, necessitating the use of an artificial respirator for the duration of the experiment. Because he could not move any muscles, he could not engage in subvocal speech. The question was, Would this also prevent him from other kinds of cognitive activity? The answer was a decisive *no*. Smith reported remembering and thinking about events that took place while under curare. Apparently, then, subvocal speech and thought are not equivalent.

The Modularity Hypothesis

A proposal from the philosopher Jerry Fodor (1983, 1985) made a quite different argument about the relationship of language to other aspects of cognition. Fodor argued that some cognitive processes—in particular, perception and language—are *modular*. What does it mean for a process to be a module? First, it means the process is *domain-specific:* It operates specifically with certain kinds of input and not others. With regard to language, for example, Fodor argued that sentence parsing involves processes that are specific to the division of phrases and words into constituents. Such processes are meant only for parsing and are of little use in other cognitive tasks.

Modularity of a process also implies that it is an **informationally encapsulated process:** It operates independently of the beliefs and the other information available to the processor. Another way of explaining this is to say that an informationally encapsulated process operates relatively independently of other processes. Fodor (1983) compared informationally encapsulated processes to reflexes:

> *Suppose that you and I have known each other for many a long year . . . and you have come fully to appreciate the excellence of my character. In particular, you have come to know perfectly well that under no conceivable circumstances would I stick my finger in your eye. Suppose that this belief of yours is both explicit and deeply felt. You would, in fact, go to the wall for it. Still, if I jab my finger near enough to your eyes, and fast enough, you'll blink. . . .*
>
> *[The blink reflex] has no access to what you know about my character or, for that matter, to any other of your beliefs, utilities, and expectations. For this reason the blink reflex is often produced when sober reflection would show it to be uncalled for. (p. 71)*

The **modularity hypothesis**, then, argues that certain perceptual and language processes are modules. (In the case of language, one such process is that which parses input utterances.) These processes are thought to be set apart from other cognitive processes, such as memory, attention, thinking, and problem solving, which are thought to be nonmodular. Modular processes operate automatically and independently (at least at the first stages of processing) of other cognitive processes, such as thought. Modular processes are domain specific, which means that they are specialized to work with only certain kinds of input. The syntactic parsing aspects of language are not used in other kinds of cognitive processing. In this sense, then, language really is a special and very independent cognitive process.

Is there evidence for the modularity hypothesis? The experiment by Swinney (1979) on lexical ambiguity resolution offers findings that are consistent with the modularity hypothesis. Recall that Swinney found that when people are presented with an ambiguous word (even in a context that should disambiguate the meaning of the word) all possible meanings are triggered for a fraction of a second. This triggering appears to be automatic and reflexive, and completely independent of whatever other cognitive processes might be operating at the time. That all the meanings are activated, independent of the context, demonstrates some informational encapsulation.

The Whorfian Hypothesis

The modularity hypothesis can be taken as a proposal for treating language (or at least certain aspects of language) as quite independent of any other cognitive process. Other investigators have argued for a different proposal: Strong relations exist between language and other cognitive processes. One hypothesis, called the **Whorfian hypothesis of linguistic relativity**, was originated by Benjamin Whorf, a chemical engineer whose hobby was studying Native American languages of North America. It states that language both directs and constrains thought and perception. Whorf (1956) stated the hypothesis as follows:

> We dissect nature along lines laid down by our native languages. The categories and types that we isolate from the world of phenomena we do not find there because they stare every observer in the face; on the contrary, the world is presented in a kaleidoscopic flux of impressions which has to be organized by our minds—and this means largely by the linguistic systems in our minds. We cut nature up, organize it into concepts, and ascribe significance as we do, largely because we are parties to an agreement to organize it in this way—an agreement that holds through our speech community and is codified in the patterns of our language. The agreement is, of course, an unstated one, but its terms are absolutely obligatory. (pp. 213–214)

Whorf believed that the language (or languages) one grows up learning and speaking thus determines the way one perceives the world, organizes information about the world, and thinks. Whorf (1956) based his hypothesis on the observation that each language differs in how it emphasizes various aspects of the world. For example, he observed that the Eskimo language has several words for snow, whereas English has one. (In a very amusing essay, Pullum, 1991, offered evidence and arguments to refute this belief about Eskimos and snow.) English has a number of words to describe basic colours, but the language of the Dani, an Indonesian agricultural group, has only two: *mill* for dark or black and *mola* for white or light (Heider, 1972). Whorf's hypothesis predicts that these language differences could limit the information available to speakers of different languages: As English speakers, we might fail to make distinctions between kinds of snow that Eskimos are thought to make routinely. Similarly, the Dani might process information about colours in very different ways from us because of differences in language about colour terms.

Eleanor Rosch (formerly Heider) conducted a series of studies that directly tested the Whorfian hypothesis. If Whorf were correct, then the Dani should have great difficulty perceiving or remembering colours not named in their language (such as green versus yellow), relative to speakers of English, whose language names each colour. Dani-speaking and English-speaking participants were shown various colour chips. Some depicted basic *or focal* colours—chips considered to be the best examples of basic colour terms (say, a very green green, as opposed to a blue green). Others depicted nonfocal colours, those that English speakers would describe as a combination of focal colours or as a shade of a focal colour (such as light pink, scarlet, olive green, aquamarine).

Heider (1972) presented participants with a chip of either a focal or a non-focal colour, typically for 5 seconds. Thirty seconds later, they were shown 160 colour chips and asked to point to which one matched the chip they had just seen. Like English speakers, and contrary to Whorf's hypothesis, Dani speakers performed much better if the initial chip showed a focal rather than a nonfocal colour. In another experiment, Rosch (1973) asked participants to learn new, arbitrary names for colours. Once again, Rosch found that Dani speakers, like English speakers, performed better when the colours shown were focal rather than nonfocal.

A more recent controversy regarding linguistic relativity comes from a proposal of Alfred Bloom (1981), who proposed to study a weaker form of the Whorfian hypothesis: The presence of certain linguistic markers makes some kinds of comprehension and thinking easier or more natural. Specifically, Bloom noticed that the Chinese language lacks a structure equivalent to those in Indo-European languages that marks a *counterfactual inference*, such as "If your grandmother had been elected president, there would be no taxation." Counterfactuals require inferences to be drawn on the basis of a premise known to be false. By using the past tense of the verb, or by the phrase "were to" in the first clause, English marks the fact that the premise is false. In contrast, Chinese has no direct marker of a counterfactual, although there are various indirect ways of getting the idea across.

On the basis of anecdotal evidence from Chinese-speaking associates, Bloom (1981) hypothesized that Chinese speakers would have a more difficult time drawing counterfactual inferences than would speakers of English, especially when text passages containing counterfactual inferences were difficult. In a series of studies, Bloom gave both Chinese-speaking and English-speaking participants different stories to read in their native languages. He reported that only 7% of the Chinese-speaking participants offered counterfactual interpretations of the story, whereas 98% of the English-speaking participants did so. At first blush, these findings offered nearly perfect confirmation of Bloom's predictions (which, recall, were predictions derived from the Whorf hypothesis).

Later investigations by native Chinese speakers, however, disputed Bloom's findings. They maintained that various *artifacts*, or unrelated aspects of the way he conducted the studies, accounted for his results. Au (1983, 1984), for instance, argued that Bloom's Chinese versions of his story were unidiomatic— that is, awkwardly phrased. When she provided new and more idiomatic stories to her Chinese-speaking participants, they showed very little difficulty responding idiomatically. Liu (1985) replicated Au's findings on counterfactual interpretations with Chinese-speaking participants who had minimal or no exposure to the English language. Recently, a spirited debate has emerged between Li and Gleitman (2002) and Levinson, Kita, Huan, and Rasch (2002) over whether speakers of different languages encode spatial directions differently, constructing fundamentally different structures of space.

Apparently, then, little evidence suggests that language constrains either perception (as demonstrated in the colour-naming studies) or higher-level forms of thinking (as demonstrated in the counterfactual reasoning studies). This is not to say that language has no effects on people's thinking, only that empirical evidence causes us to reject the original, strong form of Whorf's hypothesis. Bates, Devescovi, and Wulfeck (2001) summarize the ideas as follows:

> *We are not suggesting that some languages are inherently harder to learn, process, or retain under brain damage than others. All languages must have achieved a roughly comparable degree of learnability and processability across the course of history, or they would not still be around. However, overall processability is the product of cost–benefit tradeoffs, a constraint satisfaction problem that must be solved across multiple dimensions of the language system. As a result, we may obtain powerful differences between languages in the relative difficulty of specific language structures, with differential effects on performance be children, aphasic patients, and healthy normal adults. (p. 374)*

Nonetheless, it is true that language at least reflects thought in many instances. For example, although most of us have only a single word for snow, those interested in the white stuff (such as skiers) have developed a more extensive vocabulary, presumably to communicate better about conditions on the slope. In general, experts or connoisseurs in given areas do tend to develop their own specialized vocabularies that reflect distinctions and differences that novices might have difficulty (at first) seeing or labelling. Presumably, this is because the experts need to communicate about the subtle differences and so develop the enabling vocabulary. Novices, who have little need to discuss the differences, don't develop the vocabulary (nor, by the way, do they develop the perceptual differentiation skills, as we saw in Chapter 3).

Neuropsychological Views and Evidence

That we process complex language information with amazing speed is an understatement. Caplan (1994) reported, for example, that people typically recognize spoken words after about 125 milliseconds (about one eighth of a second!)—that is, while the word is still being spoken. Normal word production, estimated over a number of studies, requires us to search through a mental "dictionary" of about 20,000 items, and we do so at the rate of three words per second.

Obviously, the brain architecture to support this rapid and complex cognitive processing must be sophisticated indeed. Neuropsychologists have been trying to understand what the underlying brain structures involved with language are, where they are located, and how they operate. In this section, we will take a brief look at some of the major findings.

Interest in *localizing* language function in the brain dates back at least to the 1800s, when a French physician with interests in anthropology and ethnography, Pierre Paul Broca, read a

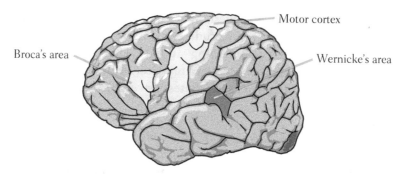

FIGURE 9-8 Some underlying brain structures involved with language.

paper in 1861 at the meeting of the Société d'Anthropologie in Paris. The paper reported on a patient, nicknamed "Tan" because he had lost the ability to speak any words save for *tan*. Shortly after the patient died, his brain was examined and found to have a lesion in the left frontal lobe. The very next day, Broca reported this exciting (for science, not for the patient or his family, probably) finding (Posner & Raichle, 1994). The area of the brain, henceforth known as *Broca's area*, is shown in Figure 9-8. Subsequently, several other patients were reported who had similar difficulties in speaking and who were found to have lesions in the same brain region.

About 13 years later, German neurologist Carl Wernicke identified another brain area that, if damaged by a small lesion (often the result of a stroke), left patients with extreme difficulty *comprehending* (but not producing) spoken language (Posner & Raichle, 1994). (Not surprisingly, this area has come to be called *Wernicke's area*, and it is also shown in Figure 9-8.)

Both these language disorders were termed **aphasia**, although the first was called **expressive aphasia** (or **Broca's aphasia**) and the second **receptive aphasia** (or **Wernicke's aphasia**). Broca's aphasia appeared to leave language reception and processing undisturbed; Wernicke's, to spare fluent production of words and sentences (although the language was often gibberish). More recent evidence provides qualifications to these statements, suggesting, for example, that patients with Broca's aphasia do have some difficulties in understanding spoken language. Thus our understanding of different kinds of aphasia is becoming more elaborated. Other kinds of aphasia have also been reported and correlated with brain damage in specific brain regions, often ones adjacent to Broca's or Wernicke's areas (Banich, 1997).

Researchers studying aphasia also noticed an interesting generalization about aphasic patients: Usually the area of damage to the brain was in the left and not the right hemisphere. This led to the idea that the two cerebral hemispheres of the brain play different roles and have different functions. The term for this specialization of function between the two hemispheres is **lateralization**.

Briefly, it appears that in most people the left cerebral hemisphere is associated with the ability to produce and comprehend language, and the right hemisphere with the ability to process complex spatial relationships (Springer & Deutsch, 1998). Evidence for this lateralization began with the clinical observation (beginning with Broca) of aphasic patients. Some of the earliest experimental evidence for lateralization comes from work done at the Montreal Neurologic Institute by Doreen Kimura (1961, 1963). Kimura (1963) further showed that this left hemisphere specialization for language processing arises as early as 4 years of age for both boys and girls, although boys tend to lag behind girls in the development of speech perception overall.

Not all people have language in the left hemisphere, however. About 96% of right-handers do, with the other 4% showing a mirror-image pattern: language in the right hemisphere. Left-handers show a different pattern: Seventy percent of them still show language in the left hemisphere, 15% show language in the right hemisphere, and the remaining 15% show language in both hemispheres (Banich, 1997).

Technologies such as CAT and PET scans have also been used to study language functioning in both aphasic and nonaphasic people. Kempler and colleagues (1990) studied three patients with an aphasia known as *slowly progressive aphasia*, noting either normal or mild atrophy of the left language regions (shown by CAT scans) and hypometabolism (that is, less use of glucose) by the left hemispheres of the three patients.

A now classic study conducted by Petersen, Fox, Posner, Mintun, and Raichle (1988) examined the processing of single words using PET scans. Participants were presented with single words, either in writing or auditorily, and were asked either to make no response, to read written stimuli, or to generate a word related to the presented word. Results showed that different areas of the brain were activated for different tasks. Simply viewing visually presented words led to activation of the inner left hemisphere, in the occipital lobes (the part of the brain known to be specialized for visual information). When the task was simply to listen to words, participants showed elevated cortical activity in the temporal lobes (known to be the area of the brain having to do with auditory processing, which includes Wernicke's area) of both hemispheres.

One important finding from the study is that the areas activated did *not* overlap. In other words, the area of the brain activated in written-word recognition is separate from that area activated when words are heard. When presented with a visual word and asked to pronounce it, participants showed activation in both hemispheres, but this time in the motor cortex, the part of the brain that directs motor behaviours. Interestingly, the PET scans did not show elevated levels of activity in either Wernicke's or Broca's areas (Posner & Raichle, 1994). However, when participants were asked to generate another word in response to the one presented, many areas of the brain previously quiet became active, including Broca's area. Many of the findings reported by Petersen and colleagues (1988) have been replicated using functional magnetic resonance imaging (fMRI), a newer noninvasive technique (Cuenod et al., 1995).

Other research, however, has clouded this neat picture. Not all patients with lesions in Broca's area, for example, develop Broca's aphasia, and not all patients with Broca's aphasia have damage in Broca's area. Moreover, not all Broca's aphasia patients show the same degree of impairment; many of them show an inability to process subtle nuances of language. The story is similarly complicated with Wernicke's aphasia.

Caplan (1994) concluded that the localization of specific language processing in particular brain regions is not straightforward. One possible idea entertained by Caplan is that language processes do not necessarily have a specific location in the brain. Instead, they may be distributed across a region of the brain in a neural network configuration similar to the connectionist models presented in Chapters 1 and 6 (see Christiansen and Chater, 2001, for a description of some such models). The exact location differs from individual to individual, but probably lies somewhere on a pathway connecting the frontal, parietal, and temporal lobes (Catani, Jones, & Ffytche, 2005). Small lesions in any one area are unlikely to "knock out" an entire language process, but larger lesions might.

Obviously, much work is needed with the newer neuroimaging techniques to test many of these intriguing ideas (Gernsbacher & Kaschak, 2004). However, at present it looks as if Fodor's modularity idea is gaining some support from the neurolinguistic and neuropsychological data reported to date. How well this proposal will withstand further tests is an open question.

SUMMARY

1. To be a language, a system must exhibit regularity (that is, be governed by a system of rules, called *a grammar)* and productivity (be able to express an infinite number of ideas).

2. When researchers say that people "follow" the rules of a language, they distinguish between conscious awareness of a rule (which neither psychologists nor linguists believe is the way people apply most linguistic rules) and implicit access to a rule (such that a person follows a rule, though perhaps unaware of its existence and unable to articulate just what the rule is).

3. Language is structured on several levels: the phonological (sound), syntactic (ordering and structuring of words and phrases in sentences), semantic (meaning), and pragmatic (the ways in which language is actually used), to name a few. Each of these levels has a different set of rules associated with it.

4. People use different linguistic rules both when they produce and when they comprehend language. The ways in which a number of our perceptual systems are set up help people master the very complicated task of processing language relatively easily. Despite ambiguity in many of the utterances we encounter, we can use the context of the utterance as well as other strategies to settle on the most likely intended meaning.

5. Perceptual context effects exist at many levels. Context can affect even the perception of individual sounds. The phoneme restoration effect demonstrates that people effortlessly "fill in" experimentally created gaps in a stream of speech. Context affects the ways in which individual words are interpreted, although Swinney's (1979) study suggests that context effects operate not instantaneously but after a brief (fraction of a second) period.

6. People seem to parse sentences into syntactic constituents as they construct the sentence's meaning. They appear to discard the exact wording of a sentence and to retain only its gist when they finish the processing. Many sentences involve some sort of ambiguity, which people seem to resolve very quickly.

7. In processing text passages, listeners and readers seem to be affected by the difficulty of the individual words and the syntactic complexity, as well as by the propositional complexity, the relationships among sentences, and the context in which the passage is presented.

8. Conversations, spoken versions of texts, also seem governed by a system of implicit rules known as the *Gricean maxims of cooperative conversation*. Speakers who consistently violate the maxims are doing so for humorous or ironic effect, trying to end or avoid a conversation, being inattentive or inappropriate, or showing a gross disregard for the expectations of their conversation partners.

9. Two distinct proposals regarding the relation of language to other cognitive processes are the modularity hypothesis and the Whorfian hypothesis of linguistic relativity. The modularity hypothesis proposes that some aspects of language, especially syntactic processes, function autonomously, independen of any other cognitive process. This proposal, being relatively recent, awaits rigorous empirical testing, although some evidence is consistent with it. The strong version of the Whorfian hypothesis of linguistic relativity, despite its intriguing nature, has so far failed to receive strong or lasting empirical support.

10. The development of various neuroimaging techniques has allowed researchers to construct detailed "brain maps" that localize different functions. There is some ongoing disagreement over just how localized any one language process is.

REVIEW QUESTIONS

1. Describe and evaluate the criteria that linguists and psychologists use to distinguish between (human) languages and communication systems.

2. What does the term *grammar* mean to linguists and psychologists? How does their understanding of the term differ from that of a layperson?

3. Explain the competence/performance distinction and the arguments linguists and psychologists give for making it.

4. What does it mean to say that our knowledge of linguistic rules is implicit rather than explicit? Discuss the implications of this statement.

5. Contrast the Gricean maxims of conversation with syntactic and phonological rules.
6. Describe the modularity hypothesis and its implications for the study of language as part of cognitive psychology.
7. What is the Whorfian hypothesis of linguistic relativity? Evaluate the empirical evidence bearing on it.
8. In what ways do (and don't) neuropsychological findings support Fodor's modularity hypothesis?

KEY TERMS

aphasia
Broca's aphasia
expressive aphasia
grammar
Gricean maxims of
    cooperative conversation
informationally encapsulated
    process
lateralization

lexical ambiguity
linguistic competence
linguistic performance
modularity hypothesis
morpheme
phoneme
phonetics
phonology
pragmatics

propositional complexity
receptive aphasia
semantics
syntax
Wernicke's aphasia
Whorfian hypothesis
    of linguistic relativity

Using and Manipulating Information

PART
IV

Thinking, Problem Solving, and Reasoning

This chapter is about different kinds of thinking, **problem solving**, and reasoning— the kind of mental work you do in each of the following tasks:

1. Imagine your favourite restaurant. What is its name? Where is it? What are its best dishes? What makes it your favourite?
2. Solve this problem: If 10 apples cost $2, how much do 3 apples cost?
3. Consider whether a change in one of your school's policies (for example, dropping all distribution requirements) would have overall benefic al or harmful effects.

4. Suppose you had a theory that eating an apple a day kept the doctor away. How would you go about testing this theory?

5. In this chapter, we will examine descriptions and explanations for the mental work you have just done. How did you accomplish the tasks? What processes did you use?

Thinking is a broad term. Psychologists who study thinking often study what look like very different tasks. Defini g *thinking* turns out to be a tough job, and one that itself requires thought. **Thinking** has been defi ed as "going beyond the information given" (Bruner, 1957); as "a complex and high-level skill" that "fill[s] up gaps in the evidence" (Bartlett, 1958, p. 20); as a process of searching through a problem space (Newell & Simon, 1972); and as what we do "when we are in doubt about how to act, what to believe, or what to desire" (Baron, 1994, p. 3).

Clearly, the term *thinking* is used to refer to more than one specific activity. Th s suggests there may be different types of thinking. One distinction that may prove useful is between *focused* and *unfocused* thinking. Focused thinking begins with a clear starting point and has a specific goal. (We will see examples of focused thinking in this chapter, as well as in much of the material in Chapter 11 on decision making.) Unfocused thinking has the character of daydreaming, or unintentionally calling to mind a number of different and loosely related ideas. We will primarily explore focused thinking, especially in the fi st section of the chapter, in the discussion on problem solving. We will discuss creative thinking, which some have described as including aspects of unfocused thinking. We will then turn our attention to more formal *reasoning*, which encompasses the cognitive processes we use when we draw inferences from information given to us. When cognitive psychologists speak of reasoning, they typically mean a specific kind of thinking: the kind done in solving certain kinds of puzzles or mysteries. As is probably obvious from these opening paragraphs, thinking, problem solving, and reasoning are all highly related!

You may wonder why psychologists study thinking through the use of problems and puzzles that appear *not* to mirror the kind of thinking that occurs in everyday life (such as when you think about what shirt to wear, what to order in a restaurant, or what route to take to get to work). One reason stems from the intuition that everyday thinking often occurs so rapidly and automatically that it would be hard to study. Moreover, people likely bring much of their background knowledge to bear in their everyday thinking. You presumably choose what to wear for the day on the basis of what you expect to be doing, the weather, and perhaps on external standards or expectations regarding dress. Because people have varying background knowledge and goals, then, it would be nearly impossible to devise a problem that is equal in difficulty for different individuals. By presenting standardized sets of problems, investigators have more control over the information participants have available and how it is given to them.

Various problems are presented throughout the chapter as opportunities to work with the phenomena of thinking. We suggest that to maximize the value of these undertakings you rely on a time-honoured method of observation in experimental psychology while working through the problems: introspection. **Introspection** is the detailed, concurrent, and nonjudgmental observation of the contents of your consciousness as you work on a problem. Although introspection has problems and critics (see Ericsson & Simon, 1984, for a detailed summary), it can at the very least provide the basis for hypotheses and tests using more objective measures. The key to proper use of this technique is to avoid doing more than is asked for: Don't explain or justify what you're thinking about, just report it. Box 10-1 provides instructions on how to introspect.

The problems presented throughout this chapter are similar in at least one respect: They fall into the class of problems called *well defined*. **Well-defined problems** have a clear goal (you know immediately if you've reached the solution), present a small set of information to start from, and often (but not always) present a set of rules or guidelines to abide by while you are working toward a solution. In contrast, **ill-defined problems** don't have their goals, starting information, or steps clearly spelled out.

The difference between well- and ill-defined problems can be illustrated as follows. Consider the problem of figuring the sales tax on a purchase, given that you know the price of the item you are buying, whether it is taxable, the rate of taxation, and basic rules of multiplication. If you are armed with this background information, it should be relatively easy for you, a university student, to arrive at the tax. Contrast this with another problem often encountered: composing a letter that articulately and sensitively conveys a difficult message (for example, a "Dear John" or "Dear Jane" letter to someone you're still fond of, or a letter to your boss asking for a promotion). It's not clear in any of these cases of ill-defined problems what information you should start from (how much of your education and how many of your qualifications and past year's accomplishments do you tell your boss about?). It's not clear when you've reached the goal (is the current draft good enough, or can it be made better?), or what rules (if any) apply.

Box 10-1 Instructions for Introspecting

1. Say whatever's on your mind. Don't hold back hunches, guesses, wild ideas, images, intentions.
2. Speak as continuously as possible. Say something at least once every 5 seconds, even if only "I'm drawing a blank."
3. Speak audibly. Watch out for your voice dropping as you become involved.
4. Speak as telegraphically as you please. Don't worry about complete sentences and eloquence.
5. Don't overexplain or justify. Analyze no more than you would normally.
6. Don't elaborate past events. Get into the pattern of saying what you're thinking now, not of thinking for a while and then describing your thoughts.

Source: Perkins (1981, p. 33).

New York Times Co./Contributor/Getty

Bobby Fisher. Psychologists studying problem solving typically focus on well-defined problems, such as those encountered in playing chess. This photo shows Bobby Fisher, perhaps the greatest chess player of all time, and expert problem solver.

Psychologists have focused on well-defi ed problems for several reasons: They are easy to present, they don't take weeks or months to solve, they are easy to score, and they are easy to change. It is assumed that problem solving for ill-defi ed problems works in similar ways to problem solving for well-defi ed problems, although the assumption has not been extensively tested (Galotti, 1989). In one study, Schraw, Dunkle, and Bendixen (1995) demonstrated that performance on well-defi ed problems was not correlated with performance on an ill-defi ed one.

CLASSIC PROBLEMS AND GENERAL METHODS OF SOLUTION

The way to solve a problem depends, to a great extent, on the problem. For instance, if your problem is to fly to Vancouver from Toronto, you might call various airlines or travel agents or even surf the web pages of relevant airlines or general travel websites such as Expedia or Travelocity. In contrast, if your problem is to manage your fi ances, you normally would not ask for assistance from a travel agent, but you might from a banker. These are *domain-specifi* problem-solving approaches—they work for only a limited class of problems. Here, we will be reviewing only a certain class of general, domain-independent techniques. These methods are stated at a general enough level that, in principle, they can be used with a wide variety of problems, not just with problems of a certain type or domain.

Generate-and-Test Technique

Here is the fi st problem for you to try. Thi k of 10 words beginning with the letter *c* that are things to eat or drink. Write down all the words that occur to you, even if they end

How many foods can you think of that begin with C? Here are some examples: cream cheese, candy, cookies, celery, carrots, cantaloupe, cheese, cocoa, cereal (Cheerios), and crackers (Cheese Nips).

up not meeting the criteria. How are you solving this problem? The process you used to solve this problem was probably the **generate-and-test technique**. As the name suggests, it consists of generating possible solutions and then testing them. When you worked on this problem, some names may have come to mind that sound as though they started with *c* but didn't (for example, *ketchup* [unless you spell it *catsup]* and *sarsaparilla)*, and some that start with *c* but aren't edible or drinkable *(cable, canoe, cat)*. Again, the process used was thinking of possible solutions (generating) and then seeing if those possibilities met all the criteria (testing).

Generate-and-test is a technique that loses its effectiveness very rapidly when there are many possibilities and when there is no particular guidance for the generation process. If you forget the combination to your locker, for instance, the technique may eventually work if given enough time, but your frustration level by that time might exceed your willingness to persevere with the task. Moreover, if you don't have a way to keep track of the possibilities you have tried, along with the ones you have yet to try, you might be in real trouble. Generate-and-test can be useful, however, when there aren't a lot of possibilities to keep track of. If you've lost your keys somewhere between the cafeteria and your room and you made intermediate stops in a classroom, a coffee shop, and the bookstore, you can use this technique to help you search.

Means-Ends Analysis

Suppose you want to visit a friend who lives in Saskatoon, and you are currently residing in Toronto. There are several possible means of transportation: walking, bicycling, taking a taxi, taking a bus, taking a train, driving a car, or taking a plane or helicopter. The most practical means might be to fly on a commercial airline; it's the fastest and fits your budget. However, to board your fli ht you have to get to the nearest airport, which is 20 km west of your residence. Again, you could walk, bicycle, take a taxi, and so on. The most effici t and cost-effective means is to drive your car. However, the car is parked in the garage, not where you are sitting when you are ready to depart for the airport. So, you have to get to the car. You would probably choose to walk there (as opposed to, say, calling a cab).

The technique of problem solving described here is called **means–ends analysis**. It involves comparing the goal (Saskatoon) with the starting point (Toronto), thinking of possible ways of overcoming the difference (walking, bicycling, taking a taxi, and so on), and choosing the best one. The selected option (taking a plane) may have certain prerequisite conditions (for example, being at the airport, with a ticket). If the preconditions aren't met, then a *sub-goal* is created (for example, "How can you get to the airport?"). Th ough the creation of subgoals, the task is broken down into manageable steps that allow a full solution to be constructed.

Newell and Simon (1972) and their associates studied means–ends analysis while solving certain arithmetic problems, such as the following:

DONALD

+ GERALD

ROBERT

Given that D = 5, determine the values for the other letters. (Problems in which letters stand for digits are known as *crypt arithmetic* problems.)

The researchers created a computer program, called GPS, or General Problem Solver, that solves problems in crypt arithmetic and in logic using means–ends analysis. GPS uses the following basic strategy. First, it looks at the object it is given (such as the preceding crypt arithmetic problem with letters) and compares it with the desired object (an arithmetic problem with numbers in place of all letters, in which the solution is actually the addition of the two numbers above the line). By doing so, GPS detects any differences between the actual and the desired object.

Next, GPS considers the operations available to change objects. Here, the available operations include those that replace certain letters with certain digits, for example, D = 5. The operations used are chosen with the aim of reducing differences between actual and desired objects. In cases where none of the available operations applies to the actual object, GPS tries to modify the actual object so that operations can apply. GPS also tries to keep track of various kinds of differences between desired and actual objects and to work on the most difficult differences fi st. Thus, if several possible operations are found, all of which could apply to an actual object, GPS has some means of ranking the different operations such that certain ones are used fi st.

Newell and Simon (1972) gave several problems in logic and in crypt arithmetic to both human participants and GPS and compared the "thinking" of both. Human participants generated verbal protocols, much like the ones you have been asked to generate as you have read this chapter; GPS produced a printout of its goals, its subgoals, and the operations it applied as it worked.

Comparing the protocols generated, Newell and Simon concluded that there were many similarities between the performance of GPS and the performance of the Yale students who served as participants. Notice that means–ends analysis, the general heuristic, or shortcut strategy, used by GPS, is a more focused method of solution than generate-and-test: It guides the problem solver more in choosing what step to take next. Means–ends analysis also forces the problem solver to analyze aspects of the problem before starting to work on it and to generate a plan to solve it. Often this requires establishing subgoals. Notice here that the problem solver is acting less "blindly" and only after some thought.

Means–ends analysis is not always the optimal way to reach a solution, however, because sometimes the optimal way involves taking a temporary step backward or further from the goal. For example, imagine you live in a western suburb of Calgary (note that the airport is in the northeast part of the city) but want to take a fli ht from Calgary to Vancouver. To do so, you have to move, temporarily, a greater distance (farther east) from your goal than your current distance. Means–ends analysis can make it more difficult to see that the most effici t path toward a goal isn't always the most direct one.

Working Backward

Another general problem-solving technique is called **working backward**. Its user analyzes the goal to determine the last step needed to achieve it, then the next-to-last step, and so on. Working backward, like means-ends analysis, often involves establishing subgoals.

Working backward is a very important technique for solving many problems, including the famous Towers of Hanoi problem depicted in Figure 10-1. A successful episode of problem solving might be something like the following: "First I have to get the bottom disk moved over. But to do that I have to move the top two disks. I can do that if I move the second disk to the spare peg, but to do that I have to move the top disk out of the way. I could do that by temporarily moving it to the goal peg, then moving the second disk to the spare peg, then moving the top disk back to the spare peg, then moving the bottom disk over." Notice that the solution process usually does not start with the problem solver making a move and seeing what happens. Instead, even after only a little practice, the usual pattern is to plan moves in advance, setting up many intermediate goals along the way (Egan & Greeno, 1974). Of course, it takes a few trials before the problem solver adopts the correct solution; if the puzzle consists of more than three disks, the participants are unlikely to solve it with the minimum number of moves on the fi st few trials (Xu & Corkin, 2001).

Working backward is most effective when the backward path is unique, which makes the process more effici t than working forward. And, as you may have noticed, working backward shares with means–ends analysis the technique of reducing differences between the current state and the goal state.

FIGURE 10-1 The Towers of Hanoi problem. Determine a sequence of moves to transfer the three disks from the first to the third peg, moving only one disk at a time and never placing a bigger disk on top of a smaller one.

Reasoning by Analogy

The next problem is famous in the literature and is known as "the tumour problem":

Given a human being with an inoperable stomach tumour and rays that destroy organic tissue at suffi ent intensity, by what procedure can one free him of the tumour by these rays and at the same time avoid destroying the healthy tissue that surrounds it?

Originally posed to participants by Duncker (1945, p. 1), the problem is often a difficult challenge. Duncker argued from studying the performance of several participants that problem solving is not a matter of blind trial and error; rather, it involves a deep understanding of the elements of the problem and their relationships. To fi d a solution, the solver must grasp the "principle, the functional value of the solution," fi st and then arrange the specific details. The solution to the tumour problem is to send weak rays of radiation (weak enough so that no individual ray will infli t damage) from several angles, such that all rays converge at the site of the tumour. Although the radiation from any one ray will not be strong enough to destroy the tumour (or the healthy tissue in its path), the convergence of rays will be strong enough. Incidentally, this technique is commonly used today to treat tumours (see Box 10-2).

Box 10-2 Analogy in the Real World

The Alberta Radiosurgery Centre is currently the only centre in Canada using a groundbreaking new technology that allows doctors to create multiple beams of radiation that precisely conform to the dimensions of a brain tumour, while leaving the surrounding tissue unaffected.

Gick and Holyoak (1980) presented participants with Duncker's tumour problem after each person had read a story such as the one in Box 10-3. Although the story appeared very dissimilar to the tumour problem, the underlying method of solution was the same. Gick and Holyoak found that participants who had read the story of the general *and* were told that it contained a relevant hint were more likely to solve the tumour problem than were

---

Box 10-3 The Story of the General

A small country was ruled from a strong fortress by a dictator. The fortress was situated in the middle of the country surrounded by farms and villages. Many roads led to the fortress through the countryside. A rebel general vowed to capture the fortress. The general knew that an attack by his entire army would capture the fortress. He gathered his army at the head of one of the roads, ready to launch a full-scale direct attack.

---

participants who simply read the general story but did not have the analogy between the problems explicitly pointed out. The former group of participants were said to be using the problem-solving technique of **reasoning by analogy**. Th s involves using knowledge from one relatively known domain and applying it to another domain.

However, the general then learned that the dictator had planted mines on each of the roads. The mines were set so that small bodies of men could pass over them safely, since the dictator needed to move his troops and workers to and from the fortress. However, any large force would detonate the mines. Not only would this blow up the road, but it would also destroy many neighboring villages. It therefore seemed impossible to capture the fortress.

However, the general devised a simple plan. He divided his army into small groups and dispatched each group to the head of a different road. When all was ready he gave the signal and each group marched down a different road. Each group continued down its road to the fortress so that the entire army arrived together at the fortress at the same time. In this way, the general captured the fortress and overthrew the dictator.

The tumour problem and the problem of the general differ in their surface features but share an underlying structure. The components of one correspond at least roughly with the components of the other: The army is analogous to the rays; the capturing of enemy forces to the destruction of the tumour; the convergence of soldiers at the fortress to the convergence of rays at the site of the tumour. To use the analogy participants must engage in the "principle-fi ding" analysis described by Duncker, moving beyond the details and focusing on the relevant structures of the problem. Gick and Holyoak (1980) referred to this process as the induction of an abstract *schema* (using the term in the ways defi ed in Chapters 6 and 7). They presented evidence that participants who construct such a representation are more likely to benefit from work on analogous problems. Another famous analogy is that of the relationship between the structure of the hydrogen atom and the solar system depicted in Figure 10-2.

It is interesting that participants often had to be explicitly told to use the story of the general to solve the tumour problem. Only 30% of participants spontaneously noticed the analogy although 75% solved the problem if told that the story of the general would be useful in constructing the solution (for comparison, only about 10% solved the problem without the story). Th s is similar to a fi ding reported by Reed, Ernst, and Banerji (1974): Participants' performance was facilitated by their previous work on an analogous problem, but only if the analogy was pointed out to them.

In later work, Gick and Holyoak (1983) found that they could do away with explicit hints if they gave two analogous stories rather than one. Participants
read the story of the general and a story about a fi e chief putting out a fi e by having a circle of fi efi hters surround it, each one throwing buckets of water at once. Participants were told the experiment was about story comprehension and were asked to write summaries of each story and a comparison of the two before being given the tumour problem to solve. The authors proposed that providing multiple examples helps participants to form an abstract

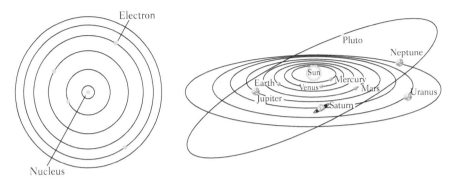

FIGURE 10-2 "The atom is like the solar system." Many of us who have taken an introductory course in physics may have learned the structure of the atom by comparing it to our solar system. In fact, this is much like how the structure of the atom was originally formulated by Niels Bohr in the early 20th century. In this analogy, the sun and planet in the solar-system domain are analogous to the nucleus and electron in the atom domain.

schema (in this case, what the authors called a "convergence" schema), which they later apply to new, analogous problems. Catrambone and Holyoak (1989) further suggested that unless participants were explicitly asked to compare stories, they did not form the necessary schema with which to solve the problem.

Kevin Dunbar, a professor at the University of Toronto, has done extensive work looking at the way scientists and politicians use analogies in the real world. First, looking at scientists, he interviewed the scientists, attended the laboratory meetings, and read grant proposals and drafts of papers. He found that scientists would spontaneously use between 3 and 15 analogies in a single one-hour lab meeting (Dunbar & Blanchette, 2001)! They used these analogies to understand unexpected experimental fi dings, fix experimental problems, and formulate new hypotheses. To look at the use of analogy in another real-world context, Dunbar and Blanchette (2001) turned their focus to the use of analogy in politics. Many of you may remember the referendum on independence that took place in 1995 in Quebec. The electorate was presented with the choice of voting to keep Quebec within the country of Canada or voting to make Quebec a new country. They analyzed the use of analogy by politicians and journalists in newspaper articles during the fi al week of the referendum. To do this, they took every newspaper story that appeared in three major Montreal newspapers and searched for all uses of analogy. They found over 400 articles on the referendum, which used over 200 analogies. Their analyses revealed that politicians and journalists used sources from very distant domains other than politics around 75% of the time. They extended the research to analyze political meetings and live rallies. Again, they found that over 70% of the analogies used were from non-political domains. Politicians were basing their analogies not on superfic al features but rather on structural similarities, showing that people effectively use analogy on a daily basis.

As can be seen in the example above, analogies can be useful in that they allow one to understand a new domain (which might be difficult to comprehend) by comparing it to something that is already known and understood. In this way, analogies are often used as a teaching device in that they provide a helpful tool to explain complex concepts to others. One potential risk of analogies though, is that they can be taken too far, in that one might assume that the links map on too directly between the two domains. For example, when considering the "*Th atom is like the solar system*", one might falsely assume that electrons and planets behave in identical manners, which they do not as electrons do not actually orbit around the nucleus.

BLOCKS TO PROBLEM SOLVING

A problem, by defin tion, is something that can't be solved in a single, obvious step. For instance, we don't count combing our hair as an instance of problem solving because the step of using a comb does not require much thought and no particular obstacles need to be overcome.

Problem solving, in contrast, carries the meaning of a goal with some barriers or constraints. Sometimes the barriers and constraints are so strong that they prevent, or at least seriously interfere with, coming up with a successful solution. In this section, we will review some factors that apparently hinder problem solving on a variety of problems.

Mental Set

Figure 10-3 presents a number of problems on the same theme: obtaining an exact amount of water given three different-size measuring jars. Before reading on, work on each problem in the order given, and write down the time it takes you to complete each one. Also, record any thoughts about the relative difficulty of the problems.

If you actually worked on the problems, you probably found that the fi st one took a relatively long time, but you were faster and faster at solving the subsequent problems given the number of problems you had previously worked. You probably also noticed a common pattern to the problems: All could be solved by the formula $B - A - 2C$. Did you use this formula to solve the second-to-last problem? If you did, that is interesting because an apparently more direct solution would be $A + C$. The very last problem is also interesting in that it does not fit the fi st formula at all but is quickly solved with a very easy formula, $A - C$. Did it take you some time to realize this? If so, your performance might be characterized as being constrained by *mental set*.

Mental set is the tendency to adopt a certain framework, strategy, or procedure—or, more generally, to see things in a certain way instead of in other equally plausible ways. Mental set is analogous to **perceptual set**, the tendency to perceive an object or pattern in a certain way on the basis of your immediate perceptual experience. Like perceptual set, mental set seems to be induced by even short amounts of practice. Working on several water jar problems in a row that follow a common pattern makes it easy to apply the formula but harder to see new relationships among the three terms.

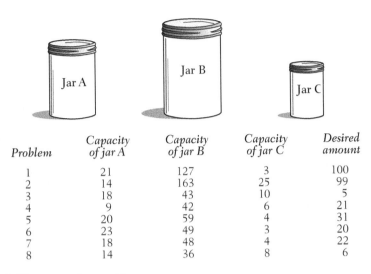

Problem	Capacity of jar A	Capacity of jar B	Capacity of jar C	Desired amount
1	21	127	3	100
2	14	163	25	99
3	18	43	10	5
4	9	42	6	21
5	20	59	4	31
6	23	49	3	20
7	18	48	4	22
8	14	36	8	6

FIGURE 10-3 The water jar problem.

Source: Luchins, A.S. (1942). Mechanization in Problem Solving. The Effect of Einstellung. *Psychological Monographs*, 54, Page 1.

Luchins (1942) reported on experiments in which problems such as those in Figure 10-3 were given to university students. After solving the fi st four problems using the formula $B - A - 2C$, all the students solved the fi h problem using this method, instead of the more direct $A + C$ method available. Even more striking, when the $B - A - 2C$ solution wouldn't work, students suffering from mental set were unable to even see the more obvious $A + C$ solution, which would have worked!

Mental set often causes people to make certain unwarranted assumptions without being aware of making them. Th s is depicted in a problem famous in literature, known as the two-string problem (Maier, 1930, 1931). A person is shown to a room that has two strings attached to the ceiling. The strings are spaced so far apart the person can't hold on to both at the same time. His task is to tie these strings together somehow. All he has in the room with him are a table, a book of matches, a screwdriver, and a few pieces of cotton. What can he do?

The solution, which many people have difficulty discovering, is to use the screwdriver as a weight to make one of the strings into a pendulum. Swing this string, walk to the other string and grab it, wait for the pendulum to swing toward you, grab it, and tie the two strings together. Fewer than 40% of the participants in Maier's experiment solved this without a hint. One source of difficulty seemed to be their unwillingness to think of other functions for a screwdriver; they failed to notice that the screwdriver could be used as a weight as well as for its intended function. Th s phenomenon is called **functional fixedness**. It appears to be an instance of mental set, in that a person subject to functional fi edness has apparently adopted a rigid mental set toward an object.

Lack of Problem-Specific Knowledge or Expertise

Until now, we have been discussing general problem-solving abilities with problems that have a puzzlelike character. The assumption is that most of these problems are equally unfamiliar to everyone and that people go about solving them in basically the same way. Other kinds of problems—for example, those in chess or other skilled games; textbook problems in physics, geometry, or electronics; computer programming; and problems in diagnosis—seem to be different in kind from the puzzles we have been talking about. In particular, experts and novices approach most such problems differently (Chi, Glaser, & Farr, 1988).

We saw in Chapter 7 that experts and novices differ in their perceptual abilities, with experts able to "pick up on" more perceptual information than a novice would. Effects of expertise are not limited to perceptual abilities, however. Familiarity with a domain of knowledge seems to change the way one solves problems within that frame of reference. A good example is to compare the ability of undergraduate psychology majors and their professors to design experiments. Typically, professors are much better at solving the problems connected to the task. Their experience in designing experiments lets them sort out the relevant from the irrelevant information and call to mind various situations that need to be noticed. It also provides a number of shortcut rules to use in estimating the number of participants to be used, the kinds of statistical analyses that can be performed, the duration of the experiment, and so on. Problem solvers who come to a problem with a limited knowledge base are clearly at a disadvantage.

A classic study of expert–novice differences was carried out by de Groot (1965). He examined the thinking processes of both chess masters and weaker players, finding that the master players considered about the same number of possibilities but somehow chose the best move more easily. Chase and Simon (1973), in a replication study, found that the more expertise a chess player had, the more information he extracted even from brief exposures to chessboards set up to reflect an ongoing chess game. That is, when a chess master and chess beginner are both shown a chessboard for 5 seconds, the chess master will remember more about where the pieces are placed—but only if the pieces are configured to depict a possible chess game.

Gobet and Simon (1996) examined the sophistication of play of Gary Kasparov, a Professional Chess Association world champion, as he played simultaneous games against four to eight opponents who were all chess masters. His opponents were each allowed 3 minutes per move (on average); Kasparov, one-fourth to one-eighth that amount of time for each game (because he was playing multiple games simultaneously). Despite the tremendous time constraints, Kasparov played almost as well as he did under tournament conditions, when facing only one opponent and having four to eight times as much time to think through and plan his moves. Gobet and Simon concluded that Kasparov's superiority came from his ability to recognize patterns more than from his ability to plan future moves. They based this conclusion on the fact that the time pressure of simultaneous games would severely hamper Kasparov's ability to think ahead, yet the overall quality of his play did not suffer.

Lesgold and colleagues (1988) compared the performance of five expert radiologists with that of fi st-, second-, third-, and fourth-year medical residents as they diagnosed X-ray pictures. They found the experts noted more specific properties of the X-ray films, hypothesized more causes and more effects, and clustered more symptoms together than did any of the nonexpert groups of medical residents.

Glaser and Chi (1988), reviewing this and other studies of expert–novice differences, described several qualitative distinctions between the two groups. First, experts excel in their own domains; that is, their knowledge is domain-specific. A grand master chess player, for example, would not be expected to solve chemistry problems as well as a chemist would. We noted in Chapter 7 that experts perceive larger meaningful patterns in their domain of expertise than novices do. Experts are faster than novices at performing skills in their domain of expertise, and they show greater memorial abilities for information within that domain.

In problem solving, experts see and represent a problem in their domain at a deeper and more principled level than do novices, who tend to represent information superfic ally (Chi, Feltovich, & Glaser, 1981). For example, when solving physics problems, experts tend to organize the problems in terms of physics principles, such as Newton's fi st law of motion; novices instead tend to focus on the objects mentioned in the problem, such as an inclined plane or a frictionless surface. Experts also spend proportionately more time qualitatively analyzing a problem, trying to grasp or understand it, relative to novices, who are more likely to plunge in and start looking for solutions. Finally, throughout the process of problem solving, experts are more likely to check for errors in their thinking.

Expertise by itself is not always enough for problem solving, as shown dramatically in a case study of an experienced architect with a lesion to the right prefrontal cortex (Goel & Grafman, 2000). Patient P.F was a 57-year-old architect who suffered a grand mal seizure and was treated for a stroke. Subsequent MRI scans showed a predominantly right-hemisphere lesion to the prefrontal cortex, a part of the brain previously implicated in defic ts in the ability to plan and solve problems. Goel and Grafman asked P.F. (and a control architect, matched for age and education) to come to the lab to develop a new design for their lab space. Both P.F. and the control participant regarded this task as relatively easy.

P.F. was observed to have "his sophisticated architectural knowledge base . . . intact, and he used it quite skillfully during the problem structuring phase" (p. 415). However, P.F. was unable to move from this phase to the problem-solving phase, was unable to generate a preliminary design until two-thirds of the way through the two-hour session, and created an erratic and minimal preliminary design that was never developed or detailed. These authors concluded that preliminary designs represent ill-structured problem solving (of the type described at the beginning of the chapter), and that P.F.'s lesion "has resulted in a selective impairment of the neural system that supports ill-structured representations and computations" (p. 433).

Finding Creative Solutions

Many of the problems psychologists ask people to solve require *insight*, a change in frame of reference or in the way elements of the problem are interpreted and organized. The process by which insight occurs is not well understood. Many scientists and artists have reported working on a problem for months or years, making no progress; then, when they are relaxing or their attention is elsewhere, they suddenly arrive at the solution. Insight problems are often used in problem solving research; anagrams and riddles are examples of insight problems. For example, by moving only three dots, try to invert the following triangle:

Whatever it is, it appears to play a vital role in what is commonly called **creativity**. Although the term is difficult to defi e precisely, many psychologists agree that creativity has to do with appropriate novelty—that is, originality that suits some purpose (Hennessey & Amabile, 1988; Runco, 2004). Appropriate ideas that lack novelty are mundane; conversely, original ideas that do not address some problem in a useful way are bizarre. Other cognitive scientists talk of creativity as consisting of a combination, or recombination, of knowledge, information, or mental representations—things the creator "already has," knows of, or has depicted (Dartnall, 2002).

so it looks like this:

Great artistic, musical, scientific, or other discoveries often seem to share a critical moment, a mental "Eureka" experience when the proverbial lightbulb goes on. Many biographies of composers, artists, scientists, and other eminent experts begin with "Eureka" stories (Perkins, 1981, presented a review of some of these). Such stories lead to the notion that creative people have something that less creative people don't have or that their cognitive processes work in very different ways (at least while they are being creative) from those of less creative people.

In this section, we will focus on two types of explanations for creative insight: one that describes creativity as special cognitive processing and one that describes it as the result of normal, everyday cognition.

Unconscious Processing and Incubation

You probably have had the experience where you are completely stuck on a problem, fi d-ing it absolutely unworkable. In frustration, you put the problem aside and move on to other things only to fi d that the solution—apparently randomly—pops into your head.

Suddenly, you see the problem in a whole new light. The experience we are describing is a textbook case of **unconscious processing**, or **incubation**. The idea is that while your mind was actively running other cognitive processes, some other sort of processing was happening in the background. (Those of you who like computer metaphors might describe this as "batch processing" as opposed to "interactive processing.") The unconscious processing churned away until the answer was found. Those who believe in incubation typically believe in the existence of an unconscious layer of the mind that can process information without giving rise to conscious awareness.

Smith and Blakenship (1989) offered one empirical demonstration of incubation effects by means of picture–word puzzles called *rebuses*. After the participants had solved 15 rebuses, they were presented with a 16th, which had a misleading cue that induced fix tion on an incorrect interpretation. They were later given this critical rebus a second time, without the cue, and were again asked to solve the puzzle and also to recall the cue. Control participants saw the second presentation of the rebus immediately, but experimental participants received either a 5- or 15-minute "break" from the puzzle, during which they either did nothing or were asked to complete a demanding music perception task (to prevent them from continuing to work on the rebus surreptitiously). The authors predicted that those who were given longer "filled" intervals (during which the music task was presented) would be more likely to forget the misleading cue and thus to solve the rebus. In fact, this pattern of results is exactly the one they report.

Most empirical studies, however, fail to fi d positive effects of incubation: Participants who take physical and mental breaks during problem solving, and who therefore have more opportunity for incubation, rarely show increased ability to solve problems more thoroughly or more quickly than participants who work steadily at the problem (Olton, 1979). Moreover, participants in another study on incubation effects reported that during the "break" periods they surreptitiously thought aloud about the problem. In fact, participants in another experimental condition who during the break were prevented from this covert thinking about the problem (by having them memorize a text passage) showed very few effects of incubation (Browne & Cruse, 1988).

Designing critical tests of the incubation hypothesis is very difficult: Experimenters must make sure participants really do cease thinking about the problem during the incubation interval, a challenging task for experimenters who cannot read minds!

Everyday Mechanisms

Does creative insight depend on special cognitive processes, such as incubation? An alternative view asserts that it results from ordinary cognitive processes that virtually every person uses in the normal course of life (Perkins, 1981). Perkins's ideas provide a coherent overview of this approach to the study of creativity and will be reviewed in detail here. Other authors offer slightly different proposals but share Perkins's idea that the processes leading to creativity are not extraordinary (Langley & Jones, 1988; Sternberg, 1988; Ward, Smith, & Finke, 1999; Weisberg, 1988).

Perkins (1981) described examples of cognitive processes that underlie normal everyday functioning as well as creative invention. One such process is *directed remembering*. Th s is the ability to channel your memory in order to make conscious some past experience or knowledge that meets various constraints. The fi st task in this chapter, asking you to think of foods and drinks whose names begin with *c*, is a directed-remembering task. Perkins argued that the same process goes on in creative invention. Darwin's construction of evolution theory, for instance, had to provide an explanation consistent with existing scientific knowledge. That knowledge constrained the types of explanations he could invent.

A second relevant cognitive process is *noticing*. An important part of creation, artists and scientists assert, is revising drafts. In revising, one needs to notice where the problems are. Noticing also plays a role in many "Eureka!" or "Aha!" experiences, according to Perkins, when creators notice a similarity between one problem and another.

Contrary recognition, or the ability to recognize objects not for what they are but as something else, is another important creative process. Seeing a cloud as a castle is a familiar example. Th s ability obviously relates to analogical thinking in that it requires the creator to move beyond the bounds of reality, of what is, and to imagine reality in other ways.

Th s approach to creativity, then, assumes that creative individuals use the same cognitive processes that so-called noncreative people use. Its proponents argue that "flashes of insight" actually

Everett Historical/Shutterstock.com

Leonardo da Vinci was perhaps the most creative inventor-scientist of recorded history. He was an internationally renowned inventor, scientist, engineer, architect, painter, sculptor, musician, mathematician, anatomist, astronomer, geologist, biologist, and philosopher in his time. His inventive designs included flying machines, parachutes, submarines, and underwater breathing devices. He was the quintessential Renaissance man.

occur in a progressive, step-by-step fashion. Incubation, following this line of argument, has to do with making a fresh start on the solution process, forgetting old approaches that did not work. Note that this description is quite similar to descriptions of what it means to break a mental set.

Indeed, the relationship between problem solving and the contrary recognition approach to creativity is strong. Both include the idea of a mental search for possibilities that are novel and that meet various requirements or constraints. A person's creativity has to do with her willingness to search harder and longer for solutions that meet multiple constraints. What makes for creativity, then, are a creator's own values for original, useful results; her ability to withstand potentially long periods without success; and her plans and abilities. Consistent with this idea, Barr, Pennycook, Stolz, and Fugelsang (2015) found that one's willingness to think analytically (i.e., think hard about a problem) predicted one's success in a creative thinking task. These ideas challenge the notion that creative solutions only arise from unconscious intuitive processes.

Many proposed accounts of creativity remain, for the most part, untested empirically. Thus, the question of whether acts of creativity use special-purpose or regular cognitive processes remains open, as researchers struggle to develop appropriate empirical methods to investigate creativity (Runco & Sakamoto, 1999). The proposals just described, then, should be seen as ideas that can guide future investigations rather than as well-developed theories that have survived rigorous testing.

REASONING

The term *reasoning* is often used interchangeably with the term *thinking*, and you may therefore notice a great deal of overlap between the topics covered in this section with those of the former sections. When reasoning, we typically have one or more particular goals in mind—our thinking is focused. Reasoning involves inferences or conclusions drawn from other information. Some of the conclusions we draw involve new information; however, many are so mundane we may not even notice we have done any mental work to draw them. For instance, a friend says to you, "Last night at soft all, I managed to catch a pop fly" From this, you almost automatically infer that your friend in fact tried to catch that ball. Her word *managed* presupposes effort on her part, and this presupposition cues your inference. All this happens so quickly and automatically that you would probably not even notice you had drawn an inference. In fact, you took your friend's statement (the **premise**) and drew the conclusion you did on the basis of your understanding of the words in the premise and their presuppositions.

We will examine a variety of reasoning tasks in the upcoming sections. To describe people's performance, you will fi st need to understand something about logical principles and arguments and kinds of reasoning tasks. These will be reviewed in the next section. We will also examine some factors that seem to hinder reasoning performance and cause people either to draw erroneous conclusions or to overlook counterexamples and exceptions to the conclusions they draw. Finally, we will examine two general frameworks that attempt to explain the mental processes we use when we draw inferences and conclusions.

Cognitive psychologists, along with philosophers, draw many distinctions between kinds of reasoning. One common distinction divides reasoning into two types: deductive and inductive. There are several ways to explain this distinction. One way of thinking about the difference is to say that **deductive reasoning** goes from the general to the specific or particular (for example,

"All university students like pizza; Terry is a university student; therefore, Terry likes pizza"). **Inductive reasoning** goes from the specific to the general (for example, "Brian is a university student; Brian lives in a dormitory; therefore, all university students live in dormitories").

Another way to describe the difference between the two types of reasoning is to say that in deductive reasoning, no new information is added; any conclusion drawn represents information that was already implicit in the premises. Inductive reasoning, in contrast, can result in conclusions that contain new information.

A third, related way of talking about the differences between deductive and inductive reasoning has to do with the claims that can be made for the kinds of conclusions drawn. Deductive reasoning, if performed correctly, results in conclusions that are said to have **deductive validity** (Skyrms, 1975). An argument is deductively valid if and only if it is impossible for the premises to be true and the conclusion (or conclusions) to be false. Deductive validity thus provides the reasoner with a nice guarantee: Start with true premises and reason according to logical principles, and the conclusion you come to cannot be false. The argument about Terry and the pizza is a deductive argument: If it is true that all university students like pizza and that Terry is a university student, then we know, with absolute certainty, that Terry likes pizza.

It would be very nice, in many ways, if all kinds of reasoning resulted in guaranteed conclusions. However, deductive validity is a property that holds only for deductive reasoning. Many kinds of reasoning are inductive rather than deductive, and in these cases we cannot be certain of our conclusions; we can have only stronger or weaker confide ce in them. Take the argument about Brian's living in a dormitory Even if Brian is a university student and lives in a dormitory, that does not in any way guarantee the conclusion that all university students live in dormitories.

In general, inductive reasoning deals with probable truth, not guaranteed truth. Assuming that inductive reasoning has begun with true premises and followed acceptable principles, it has the property of **inductive strength**. An argument has inductive strength if it is improbable (but not impossible) for the premises to be true and the conclusion false (Skyrms, 1975).

In the next two sections, we will review examples of specific deductive and inductive reasoning tasks. These examples should help clarify the distinction between the two types of reasoning, which many argue call upon different modes of evaluation (Rips, 2001).

Deductive Reasoning

Deductive reasoning has been of interest to psychologists, philosophers, and logicians since at least the time of Aristotle (Adams, 1984). Various systems of logic were devised to set a standard to evaluate human reasoning. Although there are several kinds of deductive reasoning, we will examine only two:

propositional and syllogistic reasoning. Before examining people's performance on these reasoning tasks, fi st we need to review the tasks themselves. To do so, let's briefly review some logical terms.

Propositional Reasoning

Propositional reasoning involves drawing conclusions from premises that are in the form of propositions. A *proposition* can be thought of as an assertion—for example, "John likes chocolate cake," "The population of Waterloo, Ontario is around 100,000," "Today is Friday." Propositions are either true or false. For the sake of convenience, they may be abbreviated to single letters—for example, letting p stand for the proposition "Mary is a philosophy major."

Simple propositions, such as the one just given, can be hooked together into more complicated (compound) propositions by using certain **logical connectives**. These connectives include & (ampersand), which functions somewhat as the English word *and* does (for example, "John likes chocolate cake, and Mary likes root beer"); **v**, which functions somewhat as the English word *or* does, only less so (for example, "George lives in Calgary, or my skirt is made of cotton"); , the negation operator, akin to *not* (for example, "It is not true that the moon is made of green cheese"); and →, called the material implication connective, which works roughly like the English construction "If . . . , then . . ." (for example, "If it is after five o'clock, then I should go home").

Evaluating the truth status of such compound propositions can be a difficult task. The fi al truth values of any compound expression depend only on the truth values of the individual propositions. Logicians have often used truth tables as a systematic way to consider all possible combinations of truth values of individual propositions. In a **truth table**, every possible combination of truth values of individual propositions is listed, and the defin tions of the connectives are used to fill in the overall truth value of the fi al expression. Th s method of solution is algorithmic, in the sense that it's guaranteed to reveal whether a compound proposition is always true (in which case it's called a **tautology**), sometimes true, or always false (in which case it's called a **contradiction**).

One big problem with truth tables, however, is that they grow at a very fast rate as the number of individual propositions increases. If there are n simple propositions in an expression, the truth table for that expression will be 2^n lines long. Various "shortcut" methods have therefore been developed, many of them in the form of rules of inference. Two well-known rules are *modus ponens* and *modus tollens*. Box 10-4 presents examples of valid rules

---

Box 10-4 Examples of Inferences Rules and Fallacies

Symbols above the lines are premises; symbols below the lines are conclusions.

		Denying the	Affi ming the
Modus Ponens	*Modus Tollens*	Antecedent	Consequent
(valid)	*(valid)*	*(fallacy)*	*(fallacy)*
$p \rightarrow q$	$p \rightarrow q$	$p \rightarrow q$	$p \rightarrow q$
P	$\neg q$	$\neg p$	q
q	$\neg p$	$\neg q$	p

The second fallacy, *denying the antecedent*, is exemplifi d in the argument "$p \rightarrow q$; $\neg p$, therefore $\neg q$." Using the example, these propositions would be instantiated as "If a man wears a tie, then he's a Liberal. John does not wear a tie. Therefore, he is not a Liberal." For the reason just given (namely, the possible existence of a T-shirt-wearing Liberal), this argument is also false.

---

of inference. To say that a rule is valid is to say that if the premises are true and the rules are followed, the conclusion will also be true.

Also shown in Box 10-4 are two other "rules" that turn out not to be valid; that is, they can produce conclusions that are false even if the premises are true. "Rules" of this sort are called **fallacies**. Let's work through examples of why these rules are fallacies. Consider *affirming the consequent* as it applies to the following example: "If a man wears a tie, then he's a Liberal. John is a Liberal. Therefore, he wears a tie." Notice that the fi st premise ("If a man wears a tie, then he's a Liberal") is *not* equivalent to the converse ("If a man is a Liberal, then he wears a tie"). In fact, the fi st premise allows for the possibility of a T-shirt-clad Liberal, which contradicts the conclusion.

Now that we have discussed the nature of propositional reasoning, it is time to examine psychological investigations of how people actually perform on such tasks. Wason (1968, 1969, 1983; Wason & Johnson-Laird, 1970) studied people's propositional reasoning in a task he invented called the selection task, or the four-card task. Figure 10-4 presents an example. Participants see four cards, two with a letter and two with a digit. They are told that all four cards have a letter on one side and a digit on the other. They are given a rule such as "If a card has a vowel on one side, then it has an even number on the other side." We can restate this rule in propositional terms by letting p equal "A card has a vowel on one side" and q equal "A card has an even number on the other side." Then the rule can be written as "$p \rightarrow q$." The four cards presented to participants might be something like "A" (exemplifying p), "D" (exemplifying p), "4"

FIGURE 10-4 The nine-dot and the six-matches problems.

(exemplifying ¬q), and "7" (exemplifying ¬q). The person is asked to turn over all the cards, and only those cards, that would allow her to see if the rule is true. Before reading on, write down the one or more cards you would turn over. Also write down the reasons for your selections.

Th s is a task on which people make many errors. The correct answer is to select "A" and "7." To see why, refer to Box 10-4. Card "A" is relevant because, together with the rule ("If a card has a vowel on one side, then it has an even number on the other side"), it forms an instance of *modus ponens:* "$p \rightarrow q$, and p." Card "7" is similarly relevant because, together with the rule, it forms an instance of *modus tollens*. The "D" card is irrelevant because it exemplifies ¬p and thus is an instance of denying the antecedent. And choosing the "4" card is equivalent to committing the fallacy of affirming the consequent. Generally, most people know to select "A" but neglect to select "7" or mistakenly select "4." However, when versions of the task with real-world scenarios and combinations are presented (e.g., "If you borrow my car, then you have to fill up the tank with gas"), performance considerably improves. We will discuss some general explanations for this pattern of performance later.

Syllogistic Reasoning

Another type of puzzle or problem commonly used to study reasoning is called a *syllogism*. The reasoning done with this kind of problem is called **syllogistic reasoning**. Th s type of problem presents two or more premises and asks the reasoner either to draw a conclusion or to evaluate a conclusion that the problem supplies, to see if the conclusion must be true whenever the premises are true. Although logicians recognize different types of syllogisms, we'll deal only with what are called *categorical syllogisms*. Box 10-5 presents some examples. As you look at these try to solve them, making notes on which ones are hard, which ones are easy, and why.

Categorical syllogisms present premises that deal with classes of entities. As a result, the premises have words called *quantifi rs* in them. Quantifie s provide information about how many members of a class are under consideration: all, none, or some. All the following are examples of quantifi d premises: "All Gordon setters are dogs," "No polar bears are inanimate objects," "Some fl wers are blue," and "Some ballerinas are not tall." As you might expect by now, the words *all* and *some* are being used in ways that differ slightly from normal English usage. Here, *all* means "every single"; *some* means "at least one, and perhaps all." (It is

---

Box 10-5 Examples of Categorical Syllogisms

Premises are above the lines; valid conclusions, if they exist, are below the lines.

All red books are astronomy books.
All astronomy books are large.

All red books are large.

Some pilots are magicians.
All magicians are Pisces.

Some pilots are Pisces.

No liberals are vegetarians.
Some wealthy people are not vegetarians.

Nothing follows.

Some documents are not paper.
Some documents are not legal.

Nothing follows.

All psychology majors are curious.
No tennis players are curious.

No tennis players are psychology majors.

No union members are fearful.
No children are fearful.

Nothing follows.

---

important to note that, logically speaking, the proposition "Some X are Y" does not mean that "Some X are not Y," even though this inference might seem natural.)
Certain rules can be used to draw valid conclusions from categorical syllogisms (Damer, 1980). For example, a categorical syllogism with two negative premises (such as "No X are Y" or "Some X are not Y") has no conclusion that necessarily follows. Similarly, a categorical syllogism in which both premises are quantifi d by "some" has no valid conclusion. In fact, the majority of categorical syllogisms do not have valid (always true in every case) conclusions.

With practice, people seem to develop their own "shortcut rules" for solving syllogisms. A research participant in a syllogistic reasoning study articulated such a rule after working on several syllogisms: "I thought about it a lot . . . and I realized that, when there's a *some* and a *some*, nothing ever follows" (Galotti, Baron, & Sabini, 1986, p. 19). Performance on many categorical syllogisms is error-prone (Ceraso & Provitera, 1971; Woodworth & Sells, 1935). In general, people tend to be slower and make more errors when one or more premises are quantifi d by *some* or when one or more premises are negative. So, for example, when presented with syllogisms such as "Some businessmen are Conservatives. Some Conservatives are avid movie goers," most people erroneously conclude it must be true that "Some businessmen are avid movie goers." (To see why this is not the case, notice that the fi st premise allows for the possibility that some Conservatives may exist who are not businessmen. Maybe they are all lawyers. Perhaps only these Conservative lawyers are avid movie goers.)

Inductive Reasoning

Inductive reasoning, or reasoning about conclusions that are likely (but not guaranteed) to be true, probably occurs in everyone's thinking several times in the course of an ordinary day. Although inductive conclusions aren't guaranteed true, they may be more useful, because they actually add new information to our thinking. In general, it is easier to think of real-life examples of inductive reasoning than to think of real-life examples of deductive reasoning. Holyoak and Nisbett (1988) provided several examples of ordinary induction:

A child who has never heard verbs rendered incorrectly into the past tense exclaims, "I goed to bed." A stock analyst, observing that for several years market prices for petroleum stocks have risen steadily in the final two months of the year and then dropped in January, urges her clients to buy petroleum stocks this year at the end of October and sell in late December. A physicist, observing the patterns formed by light as it undergoes refraction and diffraction, hypothesizes that light is propagated as waves. (p. 50)

Holyoak and Nisbett (1988) defi ed *induction* as "inferential processes that expand knowledge in the face of uncertainty" (p. 1). They noted that induction often involves categorization and the formation of rules or hypotheses. Thus, you'll probably observe a great deal of overlap between induction and categorization (discussed in Chapter 7). There are a number of different inductive reasoning tasks, but we'll focus here on hypothesis testing. An example of an inductive reasoning task that involves hypothesis testing was developed by Peter Wason (1960, 1977). The task is as follows: You are given the numbers 2, 4, and 6 and are told that this triplet of numbers follows a rule. Your job is to determine what the rule is, but to do so you need to observe certain guidelines. You may not ask direct questions about the rule. Instead, you have to offer your own examples of triplets, and for each one you give you'll be told whether it follows the rule. Also, you should try not to guess; announce a rule only when you are confide t you know what it is.

Of the 29 original participants, only 6 discovered the correct rule without fi st making incorrect guesses. Thi teen others made one wrong guess, 9 reached two or more incorrect conclusions, and 1 reached no conclusion at all (Wason, 1960). These results suggest, fi st of all, that this task is deceptively difficult. The manner in which most people go wrong seems to be as follows: They develop a general idea of the rule, then construct examples that follow the rule. What they fail to do is to test their rule by constructing a counterexample—a triplet that, if their rule is correct, *won't* receive a yes answer from the experimenter. Wason called this approach **confirmation bias**, because the participants seem to be trying to confi m that their rule is true, rather than trying to test their rule.

To explain why this approach is problematic, Wason pointed out a feature of the task that mirrors the situation facing any scientist testing other scientific hypotheses: An infin te number of hypotheses can be constructed consistent with any set of data (in this case, the triplets judged by the experimenter to follow the rule). For instance, suppose at a certain point in the experiment, you've found out that all the following triplets follow the rule (whatever it is): 2, 4, 6; 8, 10, 12; 20, 22, 24; 100, 102, 104. What rules are consistent with this set?

Here are just a few: "Any three even numbers that increase by 2"; "Any three even numbers that increase by 2, but the last number is not greater than 500"; "Any three even numbers where the second is the arithmetic average of the fi st and third"; "Any three even numbers where the second is the arithmetic average of the fi st and third, but the last number is not greater than 500"; "Any three even numbers that increase"; "Any three increasing numbers"; "Any three numbers"; "Any three things." Th s list suggests it's very easy, with a little thought, to generate hundreds of rules for any given set of numbers.

Th s means that no rule can be "proven" true, just as no scientific hypothesis can be proven true. To see this latter point, pretend you are a scientist with a hypothesis that predicts certain experimental results. You think, "If my hypothesis is true *[p]*, then I'll obtain this pattern of results *[q]*." You then run the experiment, and, as luck or nature would have it, you do in fact obtain that pattern of results. Can you, on the basis of your rule $(p \rightarrow q)$ and your obtained pattern of results (q), conclude that your hypothesis is proven true $(p)\sim$? No, because if you did you would be committing the fallacy of affirming the consequent.

There simply is no pattern of results (even from hundreds of experiments) that can prove a theory true, just as no rule about three numbers can be proven true, even by a large number of examples that apparently follow it. Instead, the best one can do is to try to disprove as many incorrect rules (or, if you are a scientist, as many alternative hypotheses) as possible. So, if you think the correct rule is "any three increasing even numbers," you are better off testing the rule with a triplet that is a *counterexample* to the rule (for example, 3, 5, 7). Why? If this triplet *follows* the rule, then you know immediately that your hypothesis is wrong. Suppose you instead generate another example of the rule (such as 14, 16, 18). If you're told it does follow the rule, you won't be able to use it to prove your hypothesis true (because no hypothesis can ever be proven true), and you haven't managed to rule anything out.

Patterns of Reasoning Performance

We have just reviewed examples of different reasoning tasks. We have seen that all of them can be quite demanding and that people who are untrained in logic often struggle with them. We have also seen that people can draw erroneous conclusions and be quite confide t about them (even though they are wrong!). In this section, we will look at some patterns of performance across these different reasoning tasks, trying to identify some reasons why people's reasoning can sometimes go astray. We will also review explanations that psychologists have offered for the mental processes people use in reasoning.

Two people reasoning with exactly the same kind of premises will perform differently, depending on what the premises are "about." Th s is called a **content effect**. Recall the Wason four-card task, in which four cards are laid in front of you, labelled "A," "D," "4," and "7." Your task is to turn over all and only the cards that could test the rule "If a card has a vowel on one side, it has an even number on the other side." It turns out that performance improves dramatically if the four cards contain different information: on one side, a person's age; on the other, what the person is drinking. Then the four cards shown say "drinking a beer," "drinking a Coke," "16 years of age," and "22 years of age." The rule to be investigated is "If a person is drinking a beer, then the person must be over 19 years of age." Th s experiment was conducted by Griggs and Cox (1982, Experiment 3), who found that about 75% of their college student participants solved the problem correctly when it was about drinking age but that none could solve the equivalent problem about letters and numbers.

What explains this effect? Griggs (1983) offered what he calls a "memory cueing" explanation. The idea is that certain contents of the problem cue, or call to mind, personal experiences that are relevant to the rule. College student participants in Griggs and Cox's (1982) experiment did well on the drinking-age version of the problem, it is argued, because their own experience with drinking-age laws (and perhaps with violations of those laws) let them think of what combinations of ages and beverages would violate the rule. The same participants had no comparable relevant experience to draw on when they reasoned about vowels and numbers in the other version of the task.

Related to content effects are **believability effects**. People are likely to judge as valid any conclusion that reinforces their initial assumptions, regardless of whether the conclusion follows from the premises (Evans, Barston, & Pollard, 1983; Thompson, 1996; Torrens, Thompson, & Cramer, 1999). Consider this syllogism: "Some university professors are intellectuals. Some intellectuals are liberals." The correct response to this syllogism (as you now know) is that no particular conclusion follows from it. Generally, though, most people (who haven't just read a chapter on thinking and reasoning) tend to conclude that these premises lead inevitably to the conclusion "Some university professors are liberals." Th s conclusion agrees with their previous beliefs and stereotypes about college professors: Professors are absent-minded and theoretical, they are intelligent but sometimes impractical, they are unconcerned about money but are concerned about social justice. Notice that a change in this syllogism's content makes it much clearer why this conclusion isn't always true: "Some men are teachers. Some teachers are women." Th s syllogism calls to mind a different mental picture. Our world knowledge lets us filter out the suggested conclusion, "Some men are women," because we know this to be false in the world. You might also notice that this error could be described in terms of limited search within the problem space hypothesis.

Why does this happen? Perhaps the most commonly held explanation is termed the *disconfirmation hypothesis*. Th s view states that people are more critical of conclusions they do not believe and are thus more likely to search for reasons to refute or disconfi m an unbelievable conclusion than a believable one (Edwards & Smith, 1996; Koehler, 1993). If this hypothesis is true, people should take longer to reason about unbelievable conclusions than

Flamingo Images/Shutterstock.com

Griggs and Cox's (1982) work shows that people's reasoning about possible drinking age violations is far better than their performance on identically structured abstract reasoning tasks.

believable conclusions because the unbelievable conclusions contradict their beliefs. Valerie Thompson and her colleagues (Thompson, Striemer, Reikoff, Gunter, & Campbell, 2003) at the University of Saskatchewan tested this hypothesis by measuring participants' reaction time as they reasoned with a series of categorical syllogisms containing believable and unbelievable conclusions. They hypothesized that if the disconfi mation hypothesis is correct, reasoners should take longer to reason about unbelievable conclusions. Surprisingly, they found that reasoners took signifi antly longer to reason with believable than about unbelievable conclusions. We won't go into the specifics of Thompson et al.'s model here. One of their key arguments, however, is that people reason longer with believable conclusions because they try harder to justify their acceptance. Th s idea is similar to the confi mation bias we discussed earlier, and underscores the dramatic effect our beliefs have on our reasoning.

Two Theoretical Approaches to the Study of Reasoning

So far, we've looked at a number of different reasoning tasks and offered several descriptions of the way people approach these tasks. In this section, we'll outline two major approaches to the study of reasoning—theoretical frameworks that attempt to explain a wide variety of reasoning, not just the reasoning that occurs on a specific task. We will label these frameworks the *rules approach* and the *mental models approach*. After we discuss each approach, we will turn our attention to some recent functional brain imaging work that has provided added evidence to this debate.

The Rules Approach

Some philosophers and psychologists have seen reasoning as a special mental process, one for which people rely on special-purpose mental rules to draw conclusions. That is, using the terminology of Chapter 9, they see reasoning as a modular process.

One idea is that the rules of logic are the same rules we use to draw conclusions (this position was articulated by the philosophers Kant and Mill; see Henle, 1971, for details). Most modern psychologists reject the strong version of this idea but agree that people use "mental logics" or systems of inference rules to draw conclusions (Braine, 1978, 1990; Braine, Reiser, & Rumain, 1984; Osherson, 1975; Rips, 1984, 1988, 1990). Using this **rules approach**, these researchers make an analogy between mental logics and grammars: Both are systems of rules to which we have only implicit access. So, you can't be expected to state all the rules you follow to draw conclusions—you may not even know you follow rules! However, the researchers argue that if we carefully observe your behaviour while you reason, we will fi d regularities in the way you draw conclusions that are most easily explained by assuming you have followed—probably without being conscious of doing so—a set of rules. (You might review our discussion in Chapter 9 of people's implicit awareness of grammatical rules to get a better idea of how this might work.)

Different researchers describe slightly different sets of inference rules. Generally, rules take the form "(premises) → (conclusion)." Here's a specific example (from Braine, 1978): "$p \lor q$; p therefore q." The idea is that when given information, people try to match it to one of these rules and use the rules to draw appropriate conclusions. Imagine being told, for instance, that either *Game of Thrones* or *Homeland* won an award for best television drama, and that *Game of Thrones* did not win. You match this information to the rule just given and easily conclude that the victor must have been *Homeland*. Braine considered the use of inference rules as automatic and, typically, errorless.

The key issue for the rules explanation of reasoning is how people figu e out when and what rules apply. Braine (1990) proposed the existence of abstract rules that we use in all situations. Patricia Cheng and her colleagues (Cheng & Holyoak, 1985; Cheng, Holyoak, Nisbett, & Oliver, 1986; Nisbett, Fong, Lehman, & Cheng, 1987) rejected the idea of abstract rules, instead proposing sets of rules that are sensitive to the context. The idea here is that different rules are called to mind in different situations.

One example is the permission schema, made up of four rules:

Rule 1. If the action is to be taken, then the precondition must be satisfi d.

Rule 2. If the action is not to be taken, then the precondition need not be satisfi d.

Rule 3. If the precondition is satisfi d, then the action may be taken.

Rule 4. If the precondition is not satisfi d, then the action must not be taken.

The permission schema would be activated in certain contexts but not others. For instance, the problem "One may consume alcoholic beverages only if born before June 3, 1986. Beth's birthday is July 31, 1996. May Beth drink a beer?" would evoke the permission schema. Presumably people's familiarity with age restrictions on drinking helps them construe the problem in terms of permission: Does Beth, given her age, have legal permission to consume an alcoholic beverage? A problem similar in abstract form—"All employees use WestJet whenever they travel to Edmonton. Sara, an executive, is flying to Montreal. Will Sara necessarily fly WestJet?"—would not necessarily evoke the permission schema because nothing in the problem makes the reasoner construe it as a problem about permission.

Notice the difference between the proposals of Braine (1990) and Cheng (Cheng et al., 1986). Cheng's idea is that in reasoning, people interpret problems in terms of what they are about (for example, drinking) and, on the basis of this analysis, use different schemata. In her view, two problems that have the same abstract logical structure (that is, can be expressed the same way symbolically) may be treated very differently, depending on how people interpret the problems. Braine, instead, argued that people can and do use the same set of abstract rules in all situations.

Leda Cosmides and her colleagues (Cosmides, 1989; Cosmides & Tooby, 2002; Fiddick, Cosmides, & Tooby, 2000) offer an evolutionary account of reasoning rules. Her argument is based on the idea that people (as well as all other organisms) have been shaped by evolutionary forces.

Even if they have not paid much attention to the fact, cognitive psychologists have always known that the human mind is not merely a computational system with the design features of a modern computer, but a biological system "designed" by the organizing forces of evolution. This means that the innate information-processing mechanisms that comprise the human mind were not designed to solve arbitrary tasks, but are, instead, adaptations: mechanisms designed to solve the specific biological problems posed by the physical, ecological, and social environments encountered by our ancestors during the course of human evolution. However, most cognitive psychologists are not fully aware of just how useful these simple facts can be in the experimental investigation of human information-processing mechanisms. (Cosmides, 1989, p. 188)

Cosmides goes on to argue that much of cognition is not supported by domain-general or independent mechanisms, rules, or algorithms, but instead by many, very specific mechanisms, adapted evolutionarily to solve very specific problems. For example, she believes that evolution has pressured humans to become very adept at reasoning about social contracts and social exchange.

Social exchange—cooperation between two or more individuals for mutual benefit—is biologically rare: few of the many species on earth have evolved the specialized capacities necessary to engage in it. . . . Humans, however, are one of these species, and social exchange is a pervasive aspect of all human cultures.

The ecological and life-historical conditions necessary for the evolution of social exchange were manifest during hominid evolution. Pleistocene small group living and the advantages of cooperation in hunting and gathering afforded many opportunities for individuals to increase their fitness through the exchange of goods, services, and privileges over the course of a lifetime. (1989, pp. 195–196)

Cosmides (1989) asserts that any evolutionarily adaptive mechanism for reasoning about social exchange must fulfill two criteria: (a) It must concern itself with costs and benefits of social exchanges, and (b) it must be able to detect cheating in social exchanges. A person who was not able to think in terms of costs and benefits would not be able to reason successfully about the worthiness of a proposed social exchange, and a person unable to detect cheating would presumably be at a big disadvantage in any society.

Cosmides (1989) predicted that people would be especially adept at the Wason selection task when the content of the task could be construed in terms of social costs and benefits. So, she reasoned, people do well on the underage drinking version of the task because this version causes people to invoke their special-purpose reasoning mechanism about social exchange. The drinking problem version of the Wason selection task asks reasoners to look for violations (cheating) of a social contract: that only those who have attained legal majority (thus paying a kind of "cost") are authorized to partake of a "benefit" (consuming alcoholic beverages). Reviewing the literature on content effects in reasoning, Cosmides concluded that unless the content had an implicit or explicit cost–benefit structure, people's reasoning was not enhanced.

According to the rules approach, a common source of error in reasoning is the failure to interpret a problem in terms of the appropriate rules—in other words, a failure to see which rules are relevant in a particular instance. People may fail to make any mental match to an appropriate rule or may use inference rules that do not apply to a given situation. It may also be that inference rules do not exist for many kinds of reasoning; in such cases, people are assumed to use some other kinds of strategies, and these may be prone to error.

The rules approach to reasoning is particularly effective at explaining content effects in reasoning, as we have seen. The explanation goes as follows: Presumably, different contents "cue" different sets of rules, although exactly how this process works is not well understood. It may be that personal experience facilitates this cueing, so that people are more likely to reason correctly with premises about drinking ages simply because their own experiences cause them to interpret the situation in terms of a permission rule.

Cheng and colleagues (1986) have reported success in teaching people to recognize and use pragmatic reasoning rules correctly after only brief periods of practice. Th s suggests that people quickly learn to use inference rules as a guide to processing information on certain tasks. Similarly, the existence of logic courses in colleges and universities suggests that rules of logic can be taught. The hope is, of course, that people who learn to use a set of inference rules in one situation will transfer their understanding of the rules to new circumstances.

The Mental Models Approach

Proponents of the **mental models approach** deny that reasoning consists of using special-purpose rules of inference and that reasoning involves special-purpose cognitive processes. Philip Johnson-Laird (1982, 1983), a major spokesperson for the models approach, argued that the processes we use to draw conclusions are also the ones we use to comprehend language.

Reasoning, for Johnson-Laird, consists of constructing mental models to depict the premises. Effective reasoning occurs when the reasoner checks to be sure his or her fi st idea of what the conclusion might be is assessed by an attempt to construct alternative models consistent with the premises but inconsistent with the hypothesized conclusion.

To explore Johnson-Laird's approach, consider the following syllogism: "Some of the scientists are parents. All of the parents are drivers." Figure 10-5 offers one interpretation of how these premises might be mentally modelled for this relatively easy-to-solve reasoning problem. Scientists are depicted as people holding a flask; drivers, as people standing next to a car; and parents, as people holding a child. The diagram indicates that some scientists are drivers but (possibly) some other scientists aren't drivers (those shown in faded lines) and,

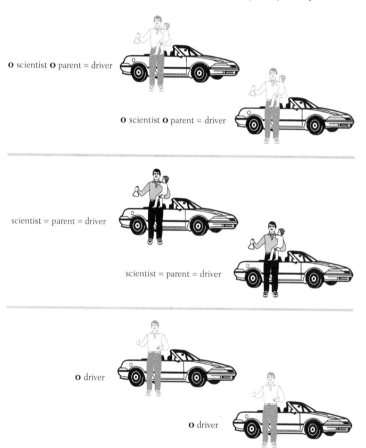

The **o** before the elements indicates optional individuals who may or may not be present.

o scientist o parent = driver

o scientist o parent = driver

scientist = parent = driver

scientist = parent = driver

o driver

o driver

Syllogism depicted: Some of the scientists are parents. All of the parents are drivers.

FIGURE 10-5 Model representation of an easy categorical syllogism.

Reprinted from *Cognition*, vol. 31, issue 2, Jane Oakhill, P.N. Johnson-Laird, Alan Garnham, Believability and Syllogistic Reasoning, pp. 117-140, Copyright © 1989, with permission from Elsevier.

also possibly, some drivers aren't parents (also rendered in faded lines). Notice that the two scientists in the middle of the diagram (the ones who aren't "optional") are drivers, leading to the necessarily true conclusion, "Some of the scientists are drivers."

How do people construct these mental models? The fact that people understand stories or conversations, Johnson-Laird argued, makes them expert constructors of mental models. Whenever we read a story, for instance, we build some sort of mental picture of the text in order to comprehend it. Similar mental processes occur when we take part in or even observe a conversation.

These processes are also the ones we use when we encode a premise such as "Some of the scientists are parents." What, then, distinguishes language comprehension from reasoning? In the case of language comprehension, we usually stop constructing models once we construct one that both represents the essential information and makes sense. Reasoning requires one more thing: the ability and willingness to try to construct alternative models that represent all the possibilities.

Consider another of Johnson-Laird's syllogisms, this one more difficult to work with: "All of the beekeepers are artists. None of the chemists are beekeepers." You might try this one yourself before reading on. Figure 10-6(A) depicts the model most people generate fi st. Notice that no individual is both a chemist and a beekeeper nor both a chemist and an artist. Th s depiction would lead one to conclude, "None of the chemists are artists." However, if they keep at it, people may discover other possible depictions, such as the one shown in Figure 10-6(B), where one artist is a chemist. Th s depiction means the preceding conclusion cannot be true. At this point, a reasoner who had constructed both models might conclude, "Some of the chemists are not artists." Again, however, another possibility exists, the one depicted in Figure 10-6(C). Here, all the chemists are artists, so the last conclusion cannot be valid, either. Is there no valid conclusion, then? In fact, there is. The one statement true of all three models is "Some of the artists are not chemists." In particular, the beekeeper/artists, necessarily depicted in each model, are not chemists.

One problem with the mental models framework is specifying what information models contain and what information is omitted. Notice, for instance, that in Figures 10-7 and 10-8 we did not specify any physical, ethnic, or philosophical information about the people depicted. How much information the reasoner chooses to represent and how this decision affects performance are issues that remain to be investigated.

The construction of a mental model can be considered a creative act. Perkins (1985) argued that—contrary to stereotype—model building (and therefore good reasoning) relies on imagination. The more imaginative the process, the more likely a reasoner is to generate potential counterexamples and avoid drawing hasty conclusions. Interestingly, this view links reasoning with other kinds of thinking, helping to explain the apparent links among reasoning, problem solving, and decision making.

In the mental models approach, errors in reasoning derive from several possible sources. One is the failure to construct relevant models. If the premises are not presented in an optimal

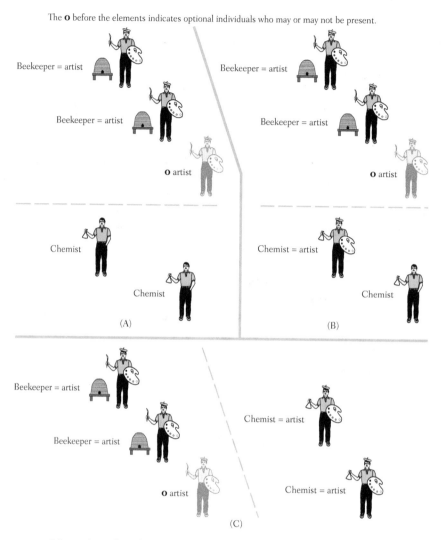

The **o** before the elements indicates optional individuals who may or may not be present.

(A)

(B)

(C)

Syllogism depicted: All of the beekeepers are artists. None of the chemists are beekeepers.

FIGURE 10-6 Model representation of a harder categorical syllogism.

Source: Oakhill, J., Johnson-Laird, P.N., & Garnham, A. (1989). Believability and syllogistic reasoning. *Cognition*, 3. Copyright © 1989. Reprinted with permission from Elsevier.

order (for example, in a syllogism, in the order A-B, B-C), it is harder to construct an integrated representation of both premises that accurately depicts all the relevant information. If there is a great deal of extraneous information in the premises, mental resources may be diverted from the processes needed to selectively represent the essential information.

A second source of error is the failure to assess the implications of all the models found. For instance, in the previous example, someone might have decided that no conclusion relating artists and chemists was valid, overlooking the one relation shown in all three models. A final and important source of error is the failure to search for and construct enough models. This accounts for the findings described earlier—namely, that people often fail to consider enough of the possibilities allowed by any set of premises.

Dual Process Models of Reasoning

Parallel to the Rules and Mental Models approaches to reasoning, researchers have also examined the phenomenological nature of the processes that underlie reasoning. Here, some researchers have advocated for a Dual Process model of reasoning. These dual process models divide thinking into, (1) *Type 1* processes that are more autonomous, intuitive, and do not require working memory, and (2) *Type 2* processes that are more deliberative, analytic, and require working memory (Evans & Stanovich, 2013). In colloquial terms, you can think of Type 1 processes as thinking with your "Gut" or your "Heart", and Type 2 processes as thinking with your "Brain". When presented with a reasoning problem, people are thought to invoke both Type 1 and Type 2 processes (in either a serial or parallel fashion). Specifically, a particular response to a reasoning problem may come quickly and effortlessly to mind. This would likely be the result of Type 1 processes. You may also decide that a particular reasoning problem might need further deliberation. This further deliberation would require the engagement of working memory intensive Type 2 processes. Here, many biases observed in reasoning tasks (e.g., the content effects discussed early in this chapter) are thought to be the result of the failure to adequately engage analytic thinking (i.e., Type 2 thinking).

Much research has recently focused on the cognitive mechanisms that determine one's willingness to engage Type 2 processes – put simply – what will make someone realize that they should not trust their initial response, but instead engage more deliberative Type 2 thinking. One interesting proposal that has received empirical support, is that one's willingness to engage Type 2 processes when reasoning depends on the efficiency of the metacognitive monitoring of Type 1 outputs (Thompson, Prowse-Turner, & Pennycook, 2011). Here, one's confidence (or in Thompson et al's terms – Feeling of Rightness) in an initial Type 1 response will determine the likelihood that one will engage in Type 2 processes, with lower confidence resulting in greater odds of Type 2 engagement. In related work, others have focused on manipulations to increase the reliance on Type 2 thinking. For example, researchers have found that providing explicit instructions to think using logic (e.g., Evans, Allen, Newstead, & Pollard, 1994) can facilitate performance in deductive reasoning.

Neuropsychological Evidence on Deductive Reasoning

Some neuropsychological work has begun to try to distinguish between the rules and the mental models approaches to explaining reasoning performance. Vinod Goel from York University (see Box 10-6) and his colleagues (Goel, Buchel, Frith, & Dolan, 2000; Goel & Dolan, 2001; Goel,

---

Box 10-6 Canadian Research Highlight

Dr. Vinod Goel (http://www.yorku.ca/vgoel/) is a Professor of psychology at York University in Toronto. He is best known for his work on functional neuroanatomical foundations of complex reasoning, where he has provided key neuroimaging data that has helped adjudicate between rule-based and mental model theories of reasoning. He has also made major contributions in the areas of cognitive and emotional interactions in rational thought, the processing of humour, creativity, and the differential roles of the prefrontal cortex in real-world problem solving.

Source: http://www.yorku.ca/vgoel/

Gold, Kapur, & Houle, 1998) have conducted numerous studies of adults performing various reasoning tasks, including categorical syllogisms and three-term series problems (for example, "Karen is in front of Larry. Larry is in front of Jane. Is Karen in front of Jane?"). Research participants worked on problems while undergoing an fMRI or PET scan.

These studies found that different areas of the brain are activated for different tasks, and depending on whether the premises are concrete, as in the Karen-Larry-Jane example, or abstract ("K is in front of L. L is in front of J. Is K in front of J?"). Goel and associates interpreted their results as being more in line with the mental models approach, as they found signifi ant involvement of areas of the brain having to do with visual and spatial perception. However, much work remains to be done to assess the generality of these results across various reasoning tasks.

Waltz and colleagues (1999) found that patients with prefrontal cortex damage were catastrophically hampered in their ability to reason with problems requiring the integration of multiple propositions (e.g., Beth is taller than Tina, Amy is taller than Beth) when the premises were not in a direct order permitting easy integration (Amy is taller than Beth, Beth is taller than Tina). Interestingly, patients with prefrontal cortex damage did not show defic ts in their IQs or in their semantic memories. The defic t persisted on inductive reasoning tasks that required integration of different relations as well. The authors believe that the prefrontal cortex, shown to be important in many complex cognitive tasks, might be specialized for the integration of relations—that is, putting together different pieces of information into a uni-fi d mental representation.

SUMMARY

1. Thi king, the manipulation of information, occurs for a wide range of what appear to be very different tasks. Psychologists draw distinctions among types of problems (for example, between well-defi ed and ill-defi ed ones) and among types of thinking (for

example, focused versus unfocused). It is not yet clear, however, whether the cognitive processes used for different tasks are themselves really different in kind. An alternative possibility is that what look like different kinds of thinking really stem from different combinations of the same cognitive processes.

2. Some psychologists studying problem solving have discovered general strategies (for example, generate-and-test, means–ends analysis, reasoning by analogy) that they believe people use in a wide variety of situations and have explored different blocks to problem solving (mental set, functional fi edness, incorrect or incomplete problem representations).

3. Other psychologists argue for the importance of domain-specific knowledge and strategies as a better predictor of whether a given person will have success solving a given problem. These investigators point out that problem-solving strategies often vary with the expertise, or background knowledge, of the problem solver.

4. Psychologists studying creativity differ over whether there is one general creativity, independent of domain, or whether creativity, like expertise, is specifi
to a domain. Some argue for special-purpose creative cognitive processes, such as incubation and unconscious processing; others believe that creativity makes use of everyday, ordinary cognitive processes such as directed remembering and contrary recognition.

5. There are a variety of types of reasoning. Deductive reasoning involves conclusions that are logically necessary, or valid. Examples include propositional or syllogistic reasoning. Inductive reasoning can lead only to conclusions that possess some degree of inductive strength. Examples here include analogies and hypothesis testing.

6. Formal reasoning includes tasks in which all the premises are supplied and the problems are self-contained; they usually have one correct, unambiguous answer and often contain content of limited interest. Everyday reasoning tasks often involve implicit premises, are typically not self-contained, and are often of personal relevance.

7. Theoretical approaches to the study of reasoning vary and depend heavily on whether reasoning is considered a separate process from other kinds of mental activity. Those who consider reasoning to be very distinct focus on self-contained problems, often emphasizing special-purpose rules of inference as the mechanism for drawing conclusions. Others see reasoning as an extension of other aspects of mental life, such as language comprehension or thinking. In this view, the way to understand reasoning is not to search for special-purpose cognitive processes or rules but to examine general aspects of mental performance—why people fail to consider enough of the relevant evidence or to imagine enough of the possibilities.

8. The prefrontal cortex has been implicated as playing a very important role in a person's ability to integrate relations—that is, to build a mental representation that incorporates multiple propositions or relationships.

REVIEW QUESTIONS

1. Do well-defi ed and ill-defi ed processes make use of the same cognitive processes? How might psychologists go about trying to answer this question?
2. Compare and contrast the generate-and-test, the means–ends analysis, and the reasoning-by-analogy approaches to problem solving.
3. What might the Gick and Holyoak results on reasoning by analogy suggest about people applying theoretical principles in real-world situations? Explain.
4. What kinds of cognitive processes have been proposed to account for creativity? How can an experimental psychologist test the role of any one of these processes?
5. Describe the similarities and differences between inductive and deductive reasoning.
6. Describe and contrast two methods by which people can derive conclusions in propositional reasoning tasks.
7. (*Challenging*) Consider factors that hinder people's reasoning. In what ways are these factors present for other kinds of thinking and problem-solving tasks? What does your answer imply about the relationship between thinking and reasoning?
8. Describe and give a new example of confi mation bias.
9. Describe the rules and mental models approaches to studying reasoning. What are the differences and similarities between them?
10. What are the key factors that distinguish Type 1 and Type 2 processes?

KEY TERMS

believability effects
confi mation bias
content effect
contradiction
creativity
deductive reasoning
deductive validity
fallacy
functional fi edness
generate-and-test technique
ill-defi ed problem
incubation

inductive reasoning
inductive strength
introspection
logical connectives
means-ends analysis
mental models approach
mental set
perceptual set
premise
problem solving
propositional reasoning
reasoning by analogy

rules approach
syllogistic reasoning
tautology
thinking
Type 1 processes
Type 2 processes
truth table
unconscious processing
well-defi ed problem
working backward

Making Decisions

You've arrived for your first year of university and realize you must soon declare a major. What cognitive processes do you use to consider the options, evaluate your priorities, and make a choice?

Cognitive psychologists use the term *decision making* to refer to the mental activities that take place in choosing among alternatives. In the instance just given, the decision about an undergraduate major often is part of a larger set of decisions about a career and future life. Typically, decisions are made in the face of some amount of *uncertainty*. It is not 100% certain, say, how well you will do in the courses required for various majors, or how well you will like them, or how much various majors will help you obtain a good job after graduation. You will not know for sure if you will enjoy the professors who teach the courses you have not yet taken, or if the topics will be interesting or useful, or if they will be relevant to your long-term goals and aspirations. You know you need to decide but you may not know how. You may be aware that a lot of information relevant to the decision exists but don't know quite how to collect, organize, and use it all in the time allotted.

The dilemma is familiar to anyone who has had to make a significant and difficult life choice. The degree of uncertainty can be vexing. So, too, is the number of conflicting goals and objectives. The first-year university student typically wants a major that not only is interesting but also is one in which she shows some aptitude, enjoys the professors and other students who are majoring in the same field, and sees some relevance to a future job and some flexibility for future career paths.

The number of options available also comes into play. Many schools have dozens of majors available (some have many more). There are also options to double-major, declare minors, participate in co-op programs, and so on, adding complications. The amount of information that is potentially relevant can quickly grow to be staggering, in which case the decision maker needs some help in organizing it all.

Because decisions are often made under conditions of uncertainty, some don't yield the hoped-for results, even if made carefully and after thorough, unbiased consideration of the evidence. Psychologists generally argue that the "goodness" of decision making cannot be measured by the success of individual decisions—luck, for instance, often plays too big a role. Instead, the yardstick of success is often taken to be the **rationality** of the decision. Various people define this term differently, but a typical definition comes from von Winterfeldt and Edwards (1986a): Rational decision making "has to do with selecting ways of thinking and acting to serve your ends or goals or moral imperatives, whatever they may be, as well as the environment permits" (p. 2). In other words, to be rational means to consider all your relevant goals and principles, not just the first ones that come to mind. If you go to buy a new car, and choose one because you like the colour, but neglect other goals—fuel economy, performance, reliability, comfort, for example—you are undercutting your own decision making. Rational decision making also involves gathering information as painstakingly and fairly as possible under the circumstances. It requires you to examine not only evidence that supports your initial inclinations but also evidence that does not.

We will look at descriptions of how people gather and use information in making decisions. Many of these descriptions will show how decision making falls short of optimality. Psychologists have argued that the lack of optimality stems, in large part, from **cognitive overload**—when the information available overwhelms the cognitive processing available. Strategies for coping with information overload, though often useful, can lead to error and irrationality. Next, we will examine what people do after they have gathered the evidence, how all the pieces are put together. Finally, we will look briefly at ways of improving real-world decision making.

PHASES OF DECISION MAKING

We can divide decision making tasks into five different categories (Galotti, 2002).

- Set or revise goals
- Make plans
- Gather information
- Structure the decision
- Make a final selection

These tasks often occur in a particular order, but there may be "cycles" to an order, in which certain tasks are revisited and redone.

We use the term *phases* of decision making to convey the ideas that there may or may not be a set order to the tasks, that the performance of one task can overlap with the performance of another, that some tasks can be skipped, and that tasks can be done in different orders.

Setting Goals

When we try to understand why a person makes one decision rather than another, it often turns out that the reasons have to do with the decision maker's *goals* for the decision (Bandura, 2001; Galotti, 2005). Students may state that they plan to declare a biology major, because their goal is to go into medical school. Others may think about majoring in economics, because they want to get into a competitive corporate training program.

The idea in setting goals is that the decision maker takes stock of his or her plans for the future, his or her principles and values, and his or her priorities. That is, the decision maker needs to develop answers to the question "What am I trying to accomplish?" Those answers are the decision maker's goals, and they influence decision making in various ways.

Gathering Information

Before making a decision, the decision maker needs information. Specifically, she or he needs to know what the various options are. For example, what are the likely consequences of each option, both short- and long-term? Who is affected in each option, and how? Do the effects change over time? Will taking or not taking a particular course of action obligate the decision maker to other decisions or plans in the future? In other words, does each option open or close off other options?

In addition to information about options, decision makers may need or want to gather information about possible criteria to use in making their choice. If you've never bought a car before, you might talk with knowledgeable friends to get information and advice from them. Or you might try to develop your own "wish list" of features that an ideal car for you would have, based on your goals.

Structuring the Decision

For complex decisions, decision makers need a way of organizing all their information. This is especially true when there are a great number of options, and when there are lots of considerations to be used in making the decision. Consider again the example of choosing a university major. Galotti (1999) surveyed first-year university students over a period of a year as they thought about this decision. Many of the students surveyed listed a wide variety of criteria they considered in making this decision. Among these criteria were considerations such as "Do I enjoy the material?" "Will it lead to a career I am interested in?" "Does it have a lot of requirements?" "Do I like the professors who teach the classes?" In the study, students listed about seven different criteria and about four different options, or possible majors. To really consider all these criteria and options, a typical decision maker will need to think about 28 different pieces of information (for example, "Is biology a subject I enjoy?" "Is chemistry a subject I enjoy?" "Is psychology a subject I enjoy?").

Twenty-eight different things to think about is quite a lot. Somehow the decision maker needs to determine or invent a way of managing this information. The way she or he does this is called **decision structuring.**

Making a Final Choice

After gathering all the information he or she is going to gather, the decision maker needs to select from among the final set of options. This may involve a procedure as simple as flipping

Real-life decisions, like buying a car, are often difficult because of the number of criteria and alternatives available.

MAD_Production / Shutterstock.com

a coin or throwing a dart at a wall, or it may be considerably more complex. This process may involve other decisions—such as deciding when to cease the "information-gathering" phase of the main decision or deciding which information is more relevant or reliable.

Evaluating

A helpful (and often omitted) last phase of decision making is an evaluation of the entire process. What went well? What didn't go so well? The aim here is to reflect on the process and identify those aspects that could be improved, as well as those that ought to be used again for similar decisions in the future.

With this overview, let's take a more detailed look at some of the processes involved in decision making. We're going to concentrate on the middle three— gathering information, structuring the decision, and making a final choice— largely because these are the processes most studied so far by cognitive psychologists.

Many decisions require people to assess the probability of certain events' happening or not. We'll begin our discussion of how people gather information, therefore, with a brief look at concepts of probability, and how well nonexperts use and understand them. Refer to Box 11-1 for an example of decision-making research being conducted in the real world.

Box 11-1 Decision Making Research in the Real World

People working for the Canadian forces are faced with a multitude of tasks that require decision making under conditions of stress and uncertainty. Researchers at the Defence Research and Development Canada (DRDC) centre in Toronto are studying individual and team decision making in a number of domains. For example, they have been examining how fatigue due to sleep loss affects decision-making performance, decision making under stress, and decision making using ambiguous information in both military and civilian situations.

BASIC CONCEPTS OF PROBABILITY

As already mentioned, most difficult decisions and plans are made under conditions of uncertainty. After all, it would be no problem to decide which major to declare if you knew how your life would turn out in consequence of each available option. In this ideal case, you would simply look over all the outcomes and choose the option that led to the outcome you most preferred. Because people are rarely, if ever, in these circumstances, most real-life decisions involve estimating the chances or odds of different outcomes and events. To understand how people do this, it is necessary first to understand some concepts relevant to probability and uncertainty.

Although there are other competing interpretations (see Baron, 2000), **probability** can generally be thought of as a measurement of a degree of uncertainty (von Winterfeldt & Edwards, 1986a). Probabilities are numbers between 0 and 1, where 0 represents complete certainty that an event will not happen, and 1 represents complete certainty that it will. Intermediate values can be thought of as corresponding to intermediate levels of confidence that an event will occur. Someone who asserts the probability of an event to be .90 is saying he is very sure (though not certain) the event will take place.

Generally, people untrained in probability theory have little trouble with probabilities of either 0 or 1; they are less adept at using intermediate values of probability in a coherent way. Their use of intermediate numbers departs in significant ways from probability theory, and it is not hard to see why. What does it mean to say you are 30% sure of something, and how does that differ from 40% sure? What these numbers "mean" in the context of a real-life decision is not at all intuitive.

Probability theory treats differences in intermediate values of probability as corresponding to different gambles or lotteries. Consider a lottery in which there are 10 tickets and you have purchased 3. If the winning ticket is *randomly selected* (meaning that each of the 10 tickets has a completely equal chance to be chosen), then the probability of your winning is .3. If you were to buy another of the remaining 7 tickets, the probability would rise to .4. The difference between the probabilities of .4 and .3 corresponds to one lottery ticket in this example.

People's intuitions regarding the rules of probability theory are often "way off the mark." Baron (1988) offered the following example (do it intuitively first, then compare it to the calculations): A 30-year-old woman discovers a lump in her breast and goes to her physician. The physician knows that only about 5 in 100 women of the patient's age and health have breast cancer. A mammogram (breast X-ray) is taken. It indicates cancer 80% of the time in women who have breast cancer but falsely indicates cancer in healthy patients 20% of the time. The mammogram comes out positive. What is the probability that the patient has cancer? (Stop here and give your estimate.)

Although your intuitive estimate may be as high as 50% or even 80%, calculation of the correct answer results in an answer of .17. How could this *be*? Most people find their own intuitive estimates are much higher (sometimes four or five times higher) than the actual value. The calculation uses a formula known as Bayes's theorem, a thorough treatment of which can be found in Baron (1988).

For present purposes, the point we want to make does not require a detailed examination of the formula and its derivation. Here's an informal way to explain how to get to the value of .17. Take a random sample of 100 women of this age and health status. Of these, 5 should be expected to have cancer. Of those 5, 4 should be expected to show a positive test. That leaves 95 women who should be expected not to have cancer, of whom 19 should be expected to have a positive test result. So, 4 of the 23 people with a positive test result actually have cancer. Dividing 23 into 4 yields .17.

Of course, probability estimates can differ from one person to the next, or from one time to the next. For example, if you're in a bad mood, your estimates of the likelihood of success in one of your ventures may be much lower than when you're happier. If you're more optimistic you may predict successful outcomes to be more probable than your pessimistic friends. For these and similar reasons, psychologists often distinguish between **subjective probabilities,** which are influenced by characteristics of the probability estimator, and *objective* probabilities, which are not. Of course, in many real-life circumstances there may be no objective probabilities available.

COGNITIVE ILLUSIONS IN DECISION MAKING

How do people gather the information they will use to make a decision? Often the information comes from their own memories. Students choosing a major, for instance, may think back to their experiences in different courses or to things they have heard older students say about their experiences in different majors. Once information is gathered, the decision maker must decide on the importance and/or relevance of each piece of information. If you don't care about becoming a biologist, for instance, the information on the biology department's course offerings may not seem very important to you. The way people gather and assess the relevance of different pieces of information is the topic of this section.

Research on people's decision-making skills and styles has consistently demonstrated the existence of certain systematic and common **biases,** ways of thinking that lead to systematic errors. Typically, the biases are understandable and often justifiable ways of thinking under most conditions but can lead to error when misapplied. These systematic biases have been labelled **cognitive illusions** (von Winterfeldt & Edwards, 1986b). The term itself is meant to invoke the analogy to perceptual illusions (recall Chapter 3): errors of cognition that come about for understandable reasons and that provide information relevant to understanding normal functioning. We can and do consider these illusions "errors," in the sense that one's percept does not correspond with what's really there. However, these illusions are not used as evidence that the whole perceptual system is faulty and unreliable. Rather, illusions (perceptions under certain specific conditions) tell us something about the way the perceptual system works generally—what cues are attended to, how they are interpreted, and so forth.

In a similar way, errors in decision making tell us something about the ways people gather, sort, and integrate the information they use for making a choice. The cognitive illusions described next also give us information on when unaided human decision making is likely to be optimal and when it is not. Finally, these descriptions can help us design and implement educational programs or interventions to improve the quality of decisions and plans people make.

Just what is a cognitive illusion? Von Winterfeldt and Edwards (1986b) specified that something counts as a cognitive illusion only if there is a "correct" way of answering a question or making a decision, there is also an intuitive estimate or decision, and there is a discrepancy between the two that always goes in the same direction. Answers that randomly fluctuate around the correct value, then, do not count as illusions.

Availability

Consider the problems in Box 11-2, and give your first intuitive response to each before reading further. Tversky and Kahneman (1973) presented problems such as these to undergraduate students. The general findings were that people's intuitions were systematically wrong. In Problem 1, for instance, the letter *L* occurs more frequently in the third position than in the initial position.

Box 11-2 Problems Demonstrating Availability

1. Consider the letter *L*. In the English language, is this letter more likely to appear in the first position of a word or the third position of a word? Give your intuition or "gut reaction."
2. Ten students from a nearby university have indicated a willingness to serve on a curriculum committee. Their names are Ann, Bob, Dan, Elizabeth, Gary Heidi, Jennifer, Laura, Terri, and Valerie.
   a. The dean wants to form a two-person committee. What is your estimate of the number of distinct committees that could be formed? (Don't use formulas; just respond intuitively.)
   b. The dean wants to form an eight-person committee. What is your estimate of the number of distinct committees that could be formed? (Don't use formulas; just respond intuitively.)
3. Consider the two structures shown below:

A	B
XX	XXXXXXX
XX	XXXXXXX
XX	XXXXXXX
XX	
XX	
XX	
XX	
XX	
XX	

A *path* in a structure is a line that connects one "x" from each row, starting with the top row and finishing at the bottom row. How many paths do you think each structure has? (Again, give an intuitive estimate.)

In Problems 2 and 3, the A and B options have the same number (of committees in the former case, and of paths in the latter).

What accounts for the errors? Tversky and Kahneman (1973) argued that when faced with the task of estimating probability, frequency, or numerosity people rely on shortcuts or rules of thumb, known as **heuristics,** to help make these judgments easier. One such heuristic is known as the **availability heuristic**—"assessing the ease with which the relevant mental operation of retrieval, construction, or association can be carried out" (p. 208). In other words, instances (for example, particular words, particular committees, or particular paths) that are more easily thought of, remembered, or computed stand out more in one's mind. Those instances are particularly salient and hence are deemed to be more frequent or probable.

In problem 1, it turns out to be easier to think of words that begin with *l* (such as *lawn, leftover,* and *licorice)* than to think of words that have *l* as the third letter *(bell, wall, ill)*. The reason for this may stem from the way our lexicons, or "mental dictionaries," are organized or with how we learn or practice words—alphabetically by the first letter. As with paper or electronic dictionaries, it's relatively easier to search for words by initial letter than by "interior" letters.

In problem 2, the appropriate formula for determining the number of distinct committees that can be formed is $10!/\{(x!)([10-x]!)\}$, where x is the size of the committee. Notice that for $x = 2$, $10 - x = 8$, and that for $x = 8$, $[10 - x] = 2$, implying there should be an equal number of two-person committees and eight-person committees (namely, 45). Tversky and Kahneman (1973) argued that two-person committees are more distinct. There are five two-person committees with no overlap in membership, but any two eight-person committees will have at least some overlap. Distinctiveness makes different committees easier to think of. Therefore, two-person committees are more available (because they are more distinctive) and hence deemed more numerous. You can easily see, however, that two-person and eight-person committees must be equally numerous. Consider that every two-person committee defines an eight-person noncommittee, and vice versa.

The same kind of analysis applies to problem 3. The number of paths in either structure is given by the formula xy, where x is the number of x's in a row and y is the number of rows. The number of paths in structure A, then, is $2^9 = 512$. The number of paths in structure B is 8^3, also equal to 512. Again, though, it is easier to see more non-overlapping paths in A than in B; different paths in A are less confusable than different paths in B. Paths in A are shorter and therefore easier to visualize than those in B. The ease of visualization makes paths more available and hence deemed more numerous in A than in B.

Everyday analogues that involve the use of the availability heuristic have also been reported. Ross and Sicoly (1979), for instance, surveyed 37 married couples (husbands and wives separately and independently) about the estimated extent of their responsibility for various household activities, such as making breakfast, shopping for groceries, and caring for children. Husbands and wives both were more likely to say they had greater responsibility than did their spouse for 16 of the 20 activities. Moreover, when asked to give examples of their own and their spouse's contributions to each activity, each spouse listed more of her or his own activities than activities of her or his spouse.

Ross and Sicoly (1979) explained these findings in terms of the availability heuristic. Our own efforts and behaviours are more apparent and available to us than are the efforts and behaviours of others. After all, we are certain to be present when we perform an action, but we may or may not be when a friend or spouse does. Our own thoughts and plans are important to us, and we may be formulating them just at the time when other people do or say something, thus distracting us from their contributions. In general, what we do, think, say, or intend is more accessible to us than to anyone else and also more accessible than anyone else's deeds, thoughts, words, or intentions. Small wonder, then, that in joint ventures each partner often feels she or he shoulders a greater share of the burden.

Availability can be both an efficient and effective heuristic. If we can be sure that ease of constructing or calling instances to mind is unbiased, then it may be the best, or even only, tool to use when judging frequency or probability. If you are trying to decide which course you typically do more papers for, psychology or philosophy, it probably is fair to judge the frequency of papers by trying to recall specific paper assignments for each course. In this case, there is probably no particular reason to believe psychology papers are more memorable than philosophy papers. If there is (for example, you took philosophy three years ago but psychology this semester), then the comparison is probably not fair.

However, if you are trying to decide which occurs more often, hours you spend working on a group project or hours someone else spends working on the same project, using availability to judge may be unfair. You have been there whenever you have worked, but you may not have been there all the times when other group members have worked. And even if you had been there, you probably would have been paying more attention to your own work and planning than to your partners' work and planning. Thus, examples of your own work are likely to be more memorable and more available to you than examples of anyone else's work.

The point of demonstrating the availability heuristic, then, is not to warn you away from its use. Instead, as with all other heuristics, the idea is to suggest you think carefully first about whether the range of examples you are drawing from is equally accessible.

Representativeness

Two students, Linda and Joe, are having a boring Saturday afternoon in the student union. For lack of something better to do, they each begin flipping a coin, keeping track of the way it lands over time. Then they compare results. Linda reports that her sequence of coin flips was heads, heads, heads, tails, tails, tails. Joe gets the following results: tails, tails, heads, tails, heads, heads. Which student has obtained a more statistically probable series of results?

Most people who respond to this question intuitively believe Joe did. After all, his sequence of responses is less patterned and more "random looking." In fact, however, both outcomes are equally likely. The problem is that people generally expect that a random *process,* such as a coin flip, will always produce results that are random looking. That is, they expect the results to be representative of the process that generated them. People who make judgments this way are said to be using the **representativeness heuristic.**

Kahneman and Tversky (1973) demonstrated people's use of the representativeness heuristic in a series of studies. In one study, undergraduate participants were assigned to three conditions. Those in the *base rate* condition were told, "Consider all first-year graduate students in the United States today. Please write down your best guesses about the percentage now enrolled in each of the following nine fields of specialization." The nine fields are shown in Box 11-3. Those in the *similarity* condition were presented with the personality sketch shown in Box 11-3(A) and were asked to rank the nine fields in terms of "how similar Tom W. is to the typical graduate student in each of the following nine fields of graduate specialization." Participants in the *prediction* condition were also given the personality sketch but were told it was written several years ago, during Tom W.'s senior year of high school, based on his response to projective tests (such as the Rorschach test). They were then asked to predict for each field the likelihood that Tom W. was currently a graduate student in it.

Box 11-3(B) shows that the mean similarity rankings are very similar to the mean likelihood rankings, and independent of the mean judged base rate, again suggesting use of the representativeness heuristic. Participants who had been asked to estimate the likelihood that Tom W. is a graduate student in field X do so, apparently, by comparing his personality description to their beliefs about what typical graduate students in field X are like, ignoring base rates. Base rates are important information, however. Just as in the mammogram example given earlier, the failure to include base rate information in your estimates of probability can lead to answers that are in error, often by an order of magnitude or more.

A related error in judgment is called the **gambler's fallacy.** Imagine yourself standing beside a roulette wheel in Atlantic City. You watch the wheel come up red on eight successive trials. Assuming you are still willing to believe the wheel is equally likely to come up black as it is to come up red, where would you place a bet for the next spin? Many people would bet on black, reasoning that if black and red are equally likely, then the previous outcomes have skewed the process a bit and it is now "blacks turn." However, on the next trial the chances of black are exactly the same as the chances of red. The wheel is not "keeping track" in any way of past results, so it is not going to "correct" or "make up for" past results. Although *in the long run* the number of times black comes up should equal the number of times red comes up, this does not mean that in the short run the proportions will be even. This explanation applies also to the coin-flipping example given earlier. A random process (such as a coin flip or a roulette wheel spin) will not always produce results that look random, especially in the short run.

Tversky and Kahneman (1971) described people's (mistaken) belief in the *law of small numbers.* The idea is that people expect small samples (of people, of coin flips, of trials in an experiment) to resemble in every respect the populations from which they are drawn. In

Box 11-3 Data from a Prediction Study

A. *Personality sketch of Tom W.*

Tom W. is of high intelligence, although lacking in true creativity. He has a need for order and clarity, and for neat and tidy systems in which every detail finds its appropriate place. His writing is rather dull and mechanical, occasionally enlivened by somewhat corny puns and by flashes of imagination of the sci-fi type. He has a strong drive for competence. He seems to have little feel and little sympathy for other people and does not enjoy interacting with others. Self-centred, he nonetheless has a deep moral sense.

B. *Estimated base rates of nine areas of graduate specialization, and summary of similarity and prediction data for Tom W.*

Graduate Specialization Area	Mean Judged Base Rate (in %)	Mean Similarity Rank	Mean Likelihood Rank
Business administration	15	3.9	4.3
Computer science	7	2.1	2.5
Engineering	9	2.9	2.6
Humanities and education	20	7.2	7.6
Law	9	5.9	5.2
Library science	3	4.2	4.7
Medicine	8	5.9	5.8
Physical and life sciences	12	4.5	4.3
Social science and social work	17	8.2	8.0

actuality, small samples are much more likely to deviate from the population and are therefore a less reliable basis on which to build a conclusion than are larger samples. The gambler's fallacy problem can be thought of as an instance of belief in the law of small numbers.

People expect that a small sample of roulette wheel spins (such as 8) will show the same proportion of reds as will a very large sample (such as 100,000). However, the chances of finding large deviations from the expected proportion are much greater with a small N

sample. Said another way, only very large samples can be expected to be representative of the population from which they come. Sedlmeier and Gigerenzer (2000) explored the issue of people's intuitions about sample size in greater depth, arguing that people sometimes do have correct intuitions about sample size, but often don't.

"Man who" arguments are another example of the misuse of the representativeness heuristic. The term was coined by Nisbett and Ross (1980). A "man who" argument is usually advanced by someone who has just confronted, for instance, a statistical summary of a number of cases reporting that lung cancer rates are significantly higher among smokers than nonsmokers. The reply "I know a *man who* smoked three packs a day and lived to be 110" is a particularly vivid example of ignoring base rate information and instead paying as much attention to small sample sizes (the individual man who was known, $N = 1$) as to large ones (those cases summarized, where N may be 10,000 or more).

Gambler's fallacy can cause people to make biased decisions.

Framing Effects

Driving down the road, you notice your car is running low on gasoline, and you see two service stations, both advertising gasoline. Station A's price is $1.00 per litre; station B's, $0.95 per litre. Station A's sign also announces, "5 cents/litre discount for cash!" Station B's sign announces, "5 cents/litre surcharge for credit cards." All other factors being equal (for example, cleanliness of the stations, whether you like the brand of gasoline carried, number of cars waiting at each), to which station would you choose to go? Many people report a preference for Station A, the one that offers a cash discount (Thaler, 1980).

It is interesting that people have this preference, because both stations are actually offering the same deal: a price of $0.95 per litre if you use cash and $1.00 per litre if you use a credit card. Tversky and Kahneman (1981) explained this phenomenon in terms of **framing effects:** People evaluate outcomes as changes from a reference point, their current state. Depending on how their current state is described, they perceive certain outcomes as gains or losses. The description is therefore said to "frame" the decision, or to provide a certain context for it. We have already seen with previous cognitive topics (such as perception, thinking, reasoning) that context effects can play a large role in affecting cognitive performance. Framing effects, in essence, can be thought of as context effects in decision making.

Here's what appears to be going on in the gas station example. Described as a "cash discount," the price seems a bargain—you assume you are starting from a reference point of $1.00 a litre and then saving or gaining a nickel. In the case of station B, however, you describe the situation to yourself as follows: "OK, so they're charging $0.95. Sounds good. But hey, wait a minute. If I want to use my card, they'll jack up the price to $1.00. Hey, I'd lose a nickel a litre that way. What rip-off artists they are! Heck, I'll just go to station A." Kahneman and Tversky (1979) argued that we treat losses more seriously than we treat gains of an equivalent amount (whether of money or of some other measure of satisfaction). That is, we care more about losing a dollar than we do about gaining a dollar, or more about losing a nickel than gaining a nickel.

The problem is that simply changing the *description* of a situation can lead us to adopt different reference points and therefore to see the same outcome as a gain in one situation and a loss in the other. That in turn may lead us to change our decision, not because anything in the problem has changed but simply because the way we describe the situation to ourselves has changed.

Anchoring

Suppose we ask you to answer a numerical question with an estimate (assuming you don't know the exactly correct value): As of 2016, what was the population of Toronto? (We'll provide you with the correct answer later.) Imagine we give two people, call them Tim and Kim, this question, but give each one a "starting value," obtained by spinning a roulette wheel. Now, Kim and Tim watch us spin the wheel, and they know that it operates (and stops) purely by chance and that the "starting value" is arbitrary. Kim's starting value is 2 million; Tim's, 3 million. If they are like most research participants in Tversky and Kahneman's (1973) study, Kim will arrive at an estimate of around 2.25 million; Tim, around 2.75 million. In other words, their initial starting point will have a huge effect on their final estimates, showing evidence of the phenomenon known as **anchoring.** (The correct value is 2,731,571, according to the 2016 Canadian Census.)

Likewise, consider two groups of high school students, each given five seconds to estimate a complex expression. Group 1 estimates $8 \times 7 \times 6 \times 5 \times 4 \times 3 \times 2 \times 1$, and reports a mean estimate of 2,250; Group 2 estimates $1 \times 2 \times 3 \times 4 \times 5 \times 6 \times 7 \times 8$, and reports the answer to be (on average) 512. As you can tell, both problems are identical. You probably are not able to tell this quickly, but both estimates are too small: The correct value is 40,320.

Tversky and Kahneman (2000) explain these results this way: People tend to perform the first few steps of multiplication, then extrapolate. The extrapolation tends to be too little rather than too much. That explains the fact that both groups of participants underestimated the answer. In addition, those who started with $1 \times 2 \times 3$ began with a smaller value than did those who began with $8 \times 7 \times 6$, so the first group more severely underestimated the result.

Sunk Cost Effects

A major educational initiative is begun in your hometown; $3 million is invested to help students stay away from cigarettes, liquor, and other drugs. In the third of four years, evidence begins to accumulate that the program is not working. A local legislator proposes ending funding to the program before the scheduled date. Howls of protest go up from some individuals, who claim that to stop a program after a large expenditure of funds would be a waste. These individuals are falling prey to what Arkes and Blumer (1985) have dubbed the **sunk cost effect:** "[the] greater tendency to continue an endeavor once an investment in money, effort, or time has been made" (p. 124).

Why is this an error? The explanation goes something like this: Money spent is already gone. Whether or not a great deal of money (or time, or energy, or emotion) has been spent does not affect the likelihood of future success. Those resources have been used, regardless of which option is chosen. All that should affect a decision, therefore, are the expected future benefits and costs of each option (Arkes & Hutzel, 2000). Try to remember this phenomenon the next time you contemplate spending large sums of money to repair an old car just because you have already spent a great deal on it.

Illusory Correlation

You and a friend, both students of psychology, observe fellow students around campus and discover a behavioural pattern you call "hair twisting": The person pinches a strand of hair between thumb and forefinger and proceeds to twist it around the forefinger. You believe this behaviour is especially likely in people undergoing a great deal of stress. Needing a research paper for your psychology class, you undertake a study with your friend. You observe a random sample of 150 students for a day, categorizing them as hair twisters or not hair twisters. (Assume that you and your friend make your observations independently and that your interrater reliability, the agreement of categorization between you two, is high.) Later, each participant is given a battery of psychological tests to decide whether he or she is under significant amounts of stress.

The results are shown in Box 11-4. Given these data, give your intuitive estimate of the relationship between stress and hair twisting. If you have had a course in statistics, you can

---

Box 11-4 Example of Illusory Correlation

	Under Stress	**Not Under Stress**
Hair twister	20	10
Not a hair twister	80	40

Given the data above, give your intuitive estimate of the correlation between the two variables (from 0 to 1).

---

try estimating the correlation coefficient or chi square test of contingency statistic; if not, try to put into words your belief about how strong the relationship is.

This question was posed to 30 students, not unlike yourselves, taking a cognitive psychology course. Most believed there was at least a weak relationship between the two variables. In fact, there is absolutely no relationship. Notice that the proportion of hair twisters is .20 (20/100 and 10/50) for both the participants under stress and the participants not under stress. Nevertheless, the students' intuitions are typical: People report seeing data associations that seem plausible even when associations are not present. In this example, hair twisting and stress are plausibly related because hair twisting sounds like a nervous behaviour and because nervous behaviours are likely to be produced under conditions of anxiety.

The phenomenon of seeing nonexistent relationships is called **illusory correlation.** Notice that in the example given, it occurs even under ideal conditions (all the data are summarized and presented in a table, so you do not need to recall all the relevant cases from memory). There is no ambiguity over where individual cases fall (everyone is classified as a hair twister or not, and under stress or not), and there is no reason to expect personal biases on your part to interfere with your estimate. The data are dichotomous (that is, yes or no) for both variables and therefore easy to work with.

A compelling example of illusory correlation was observed by Derek Koehler (see Box 11-5) and one of his students at the University of Waterloo (King & Koehler, 2000). They were interested in the degree to which findings of graphologists, individuals who make inferences about personality based on handwriting samples, could be accounted for by illusory correlations. They collected 40 handwriting samples from university students whose task was to simply copy a 143-word cooking recipe in their usual writing. The handwriting samples were rated by 10 independent judges on the same dimensions that professional graphologists use (size, speed, rhythm, shape, spacing, and slope). The handwriting samples were then paired with fabricated personality profiles and presented to undergraduates who knew nothing about graphology. Surprisingly students tended to "discover" the same relationships between handwriting features and personality

Box 11-5 Canadian Research Highlight

Dr. Derek Koehler (https://uwaterloo.ca/psychology/people-profiles/derek-j-koehler) is a professor of psychology at the University of Waterloo. He is probably best known for his work on the intuitive assessment of uncertainty involved in everyday planning, prediction, and decision making. This research includes the study of how people evaluate evidence when estimating the probability of uncertain events, how generating hypotheses, scenarios, or explanations influences the perceived likelihood of future events, and how current intentions influence self-predictions of future behaviour. In the course of this research, he has asked basketball fans to predict the outcomes of upcoming NBA games, physicians to judge the probability that a patient is suffering from a particular illness, homeowners to predict when they will complete a household project, and students to estimate the probability that they will donate blood at an upcoming donation clinic. More recently, he has been examining the degree to which intuitive and analytic thinking contribute to real world reasoning and decision making.

traits that trained graphologists do. For example, a large font was judged to correspond to egotism, and perceived fast writing was associated with impulsiveness. What explanation can we derive for these findings? Think back to Chapter 6 when we covered semantic memory. The word "fast" and the word "impulsive" are likely strongly associated in memory. This may lead people to see fast handwriting and an impulsive personality as being associated in the world. That is, variables that tend to be falsely associated typically seem to have some prior association in people's minds. The point here is that the associations we bring to a situation often colour our judgment to such an extent that we see them even if they are not there.

Hindsight Bias

Consider the following decision: You need to choose between declaring a psychology major and an economics major. You consult your own performance, goals, likes, and dislikes and have long discussions with professors in both departments, majors in both departments, friends, parents, and relevant others. You finally decide to become an economics major, primarily because of your interest in the topics in your classes and also because you like the economics professors so much.

A few months later you start to discover you like your economics classes less and less, and you find your psychology courses more interesting than you previously had. You reopen the decision about your major, spend another couple of weeks rethinking your goals and interests, and decide to switch majors to psychology. When you announce this decision to your best friend, she says, "Well, I knew this was going to happen. It was pretty much inevitable. You don't seem the type to fit in with the other majors in that department, and also, given the stuff you said about last term's assignments, I knew you wouldn't like it for long." Other friends of yours also express little surprise at your latest decision, confiding that they "knew all along" that you would change your major.

How is it that you yourself didn't foresee this inevitable change in majors? How is it that your friends could see into your future and you could not? In fact, one likely answer is that your friends are in error and that they are suffering from something called **hindsight bias.** Fischhoff (1982b) described this bias as a tendency to "consistently exaggerate what could have been anticipated in foresight" when looking back (in hindsight) on an event (p. 341). The idea is that once you know how a decision has turned out, you look back on the events leading up to the outcome as being more inevitable than they really were.

Fischhoff (1975) demonstrated hindsight bias experimentally in the following way. Participants were asked to read a passage similar to the one shown in Box 11-6. Passages described either historical events (as does the one in Box 11-6) or clinical case descriptions of people. All participants were asked to rate the likelihood of a number of possible outcomes of the event. Some were additionally told which one of the outcomes had actually occurred and were asked to estimate (in hindsight) the probabilities of all the possible outcomes.

Results showed that participants who were told what the outcome actually was gave higher estimates of the probability that it would have happened, given the description in the passage, than did those who were not told what outcome had occurred. Surprisingly, participants saw as inevitable the outcome that they were told had happened, regardless of which outcome it was. Participants who were told that the British won saw British victory "all along" in the passage; those who were told that the Gurkas won saw that outcome as inevitable. Those who were told that the clash ended in a military stalemate also said that they saw that outcome coming.

How does hindsight bias apply to your friends in the hypothetical situation just described? Recall that they told you they "knew all along" that your decision to major in economics would not turn out well. It is likely, however, that your friends are looking back in hindsight, knowing how your original decision turned out, and are therefore more able to think of reasons why your decision turned out this way. Their ability to predict, in foresight, how your decision would turn out is probably far weaker. In short, to quote an old maxim, "Hindsight is always 20/20." Other investigations have demonstrated the occurrence of hindsight bias in real-life contexts, with participants' (mis)recollections of such events as the economic effects of the introduction of the euro (Hoelzl, Kirchler, & Rodler, 2002), the outcome of the O. J. Simpson trial (Demakis, 2002), and the 9/11 attacks (Villejoubert, 2005).

Box 11-6 Example of Hindsight Bias

Read the following passage, then answer the question below:

[1] For some years after the arrival of Hastings as governor-general of India, the consolidation of British power involved serious war. [2] The first of these wars took place on the northern frontier of Bengal where the British were faced by the plundering raids of the Gurkas of Nepal. [3] Attempts had been made to stop the raids by an exchange of lands, but the Gurkas would not give up their claims to country under British control, [4] and Hastings decided to deal with them once and for all. [5] The campaign began in November 1814. It was not glorious. [6] The Gurkas were only some 12,000 strong; [7] but they were brave fighters, fighting in territory well suited to their raiding tactics. [8] The older British commanders were used to war in the plains where the enemy ran away from a resolute attack. [9] In the mountains of Nepal it was not easy even to find the enemy. [10] The troops and transport animals suffered from the extremes of heat and cold, [11] and the officers learned caution only after sharp reverses. [12] Major-General Sir D. Octerlony was the one commander to escape from these minor defeats.

In light of the information appearing in the passage, what was the probability of occurrence of each of the four possible outcomes listed below? (The probabilities should sum to 100%.)

———British victory
———Gurka victory
———Military stalemate with no peace settlement
———Military stalemate with a peace settlement

Confirmation Bias

In most school districts, parents can place their public school children in one of several options for grade one. Parents of kindergartners, therefore, spend a lot of time and energy trying to find the "best" option for their child. Some parents do this by talking to other parents. For example, parents interested in the French immersion option may seek out other parents who have children enrolled in the immersion program, and ask if they like it. After a prospective parent has talked to, say, five happy French immersion parents, their own sense grows that the immersion program is right for their child.

What's wrong with that, you may ask? Who better to tell a parent what the experience is like than another parent? Well, the name for the way in which the prospective parent is gathering information is called **confirmation bias,** discussed in Chapter 10. This is the tendency to search only for information that will confirm one's initial hunch or hypothesis, and to overlook or ignore other information.

Parents go wrong if they *only* seek information that would potentially confirm their hunch that a particular option is the best. If they only talk to parents of children in the program, they talk to parents most likely to be happy customers of the program. (If they weren't happy with the program, then presumably those parents would have placed their children in other programs.) The most rational decision, then, would be made by talking to a randomly selected set of parents, or to parents who have transferred out of a particular option, as well as to parents with children still in that option.

Overconfidence

Consider the questions in Box 11-7, and choose from the two possible answers. After answering, give a rating of your confidence. If you have absolutely no idea of what the answer is, choose the value .5, to indicate that you think the odds you are right are 50–50. (Any number lower than .5 would indicate you think you are more likely to be wrong than right, so you should have chosen the other answer.) A rating of 1.00 means you are 100% certain your answer is correct. Values between .5 and 1.00 indicate intermediate levels of confidence, with higher numbers reflecting higher confidence.

Box 11-7 Some Trivia Questions

Choose one answer for each question, and rate your confidence in your answer on a scale from .5 (just guessing) to 1.0 (completely certain).

Which magazine had the largest circulation in 1978?
a. *Time*   **b.** *Reader's Digest*

Which city had the larger population in 1960?
a. Vancouver   **b.** Montreal

Who was the 14th Prime Minister of Canada?
a. Diefenbaker   **b.** Pearson

Which Union ironclad ship fought the Confederate ironclad ship Merrimack?
a. *Monitor*   **b.** *Andover*

Who began the profession of nursing?
a. Nightingale   **b.** Barton

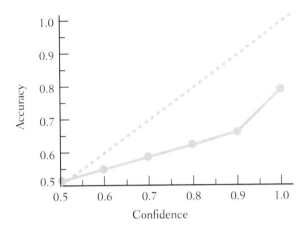

FIGURE 11-1 Example of a calibration curve. (The dotted line indicates perfect calibration.)

For the purposes of this discussion, it matters very little how accurate your answers are. (If you simply *must* have the correct answers, they are b, b, a, a, a.) What matters here is the relationship between your accuracy and your confidence rating. In several studies (reviewed by Lichtenstein, Fischhoff, & Phillips, 1982), participants were given a long list of questions similar to those in Box 11-7. After they answered all the questions and gave confidence ratings, their accuracy was plotted as a function of their confidence ratings. For example, the experimenters looked at all the questions for which a participant rated his confidence as .6 and calculated the proportion of those questions he answered correctly.

Typical findings are shown in Figure 11-1. Notice that the 45-degree line would indicate that confidence and accuracy were perfectly synchronized: questions for which a participant had a confidence rating of .6 would actually be answered accurately 60% of the time. This kind of finding is rarely, if ever, found. Instead, typical curves are "bowed" out from the 45-degree line, as shown in the figure.

This kind of curve—plotting confidence against accuracy—is called a **calibration curve.** The closer the curve is to the 45-degree line, the better the calibration, or "fit," between confidence and accuracy. Deviations from the curve below this line are said to indicate **overconfidence,** where confidence ratings are higher than actual accuracy. Deviations above the line would indicate *under-confidence,* a phenomenon that rarely occurs. The general idea is this: For all the questions to which participants give a .8 confidence rating (meaning they estimate the probability of their answering correctly as 80%), they are correct only about 60% of the time. Further, when participants say they are 100% certain of the answer, they are correct only about 75% to 80% of the time.

Said another way, people's impressions of their own accuracy are typically inflated. Overconfidence is a real impediment to good decision making. If your confidence in your judgment is inappropriately high, you probably will spurn any offers of help in making decisions because you will fail to see the need for it. Even when good decision aids are available to help you overcome other biases and errors of judgment, overconfidence will make you weight your own intuitions more heavily than any objective information that might be available. Overconfidence, then, can be thought of as arrogance in decision making. In related work, Pennycook, Ross, Koehler, and Fugelsang (2017) found that those individuals who were most biased in their responses to a numerical reasoning task showed the largest accuracy/confidence miscalibration. They interpreted these data as suggesting that one of the main reasons people are biased, is because they lack the accurate metacognitive awareness of their performance.

These findings covered above should be qualified, however, by research by Brenner, Griffin, and Koehler (2005), who have found that people's confidence by accuracy confidence calibration depends on the diagnosticity (or quality) of the evidence available. They argue that people's judgments rely primarily on evidence regarding the particular case at hand and tend to neglect relevant aggregate properties associated with the class of instances to which the case belongs. For example, when a physician assesses a patient's risk of a disease, they may invoke case-based features of the patient, such as their diet and family history. In so doing, they may ignore important base-rate features that are characteristic of the larger class of instances. Ignoring the base rate in this instance typically results in overconfidence. If, however, the physician effectively incorporates the relevant aggregate properties to the interpretation of the specific case, they are typically more accurate, and the confidence by accuracy calibration reveals underconfidence.

So far, we have reviewed a (very incomplete) list of heuristics and biases in decision making and planning. Again, the point here is not that these ways of gathering and assessing information are always wrong or bad. Instead, the examples point out places where decision making does not go as smoothly as it could. The existence of these biases also tells us something about how human beings "naturally" cope with information, particularly when information is in abundance. Documenting such errors can be the first step to setting up effective remedial programs.

UTILITY MODELS OF DECISION MAKING

The previous section described errors and patterns of thinking that people use when gathering information. Another issue, though, is how people sift through all the gathered information to reach a decision. In this section, we will review models that describe, or purport to describe, exactly what people are doing when they structure a decision and choose from alternatives.

It will be useful first to describe in a more general way the kinds of models of decision making (and thinking) that exist. **Normative models** define ideal performance under ideal circumstances. **Prescriptive models** tell us how we "ought" to make decisions. They take into account the fact that circumstances in which decisions are made are rarely ideal, and they provide guidance about how to do the best we can. Teachers try to get students to follow prescriptive models. **Descriptive models,** in contrast, simply detail what people actually do when they make decisions. These are not necessarily endorsements of good ways of thinking; rather, they describe actual performance. The distinctions among normative, prescriptive, and descriptive models are important as we consider various specific theories.

Expected Utility Theory

Making a decision such as choosing a major can be compared to a gamble. In most gambles, you win (or lose) particular amounts of money depending on certain outcomes. Probability theory tells us (assuming fair coins, decks of cards, and the like) what the odds are of any outcome. The dollar amount won or lost tells us the monetary worth of each outcome.

It would be nice if we could somehow combine information about probabilities and amounts that can be won or lost. In fact, one way is to calculate the *expected value* of each outcome. By multiplying the probability of each outcome by the amount of money won or lost for that outcome and summing these values over all possible outcomes, we can determine the expected value of the gamble. Presumably, then, if we were offered a choice between two gambles, we could choose the better one by calculating the expected value of each and choosing the gamble with the higher value.

This idea of expected value can be expressed in the form of an equation,

$$(1) \quad EV = \Sigma(pi \times vi)$$

where *EV* stands for "expected value" of the gamble, *pi* is the probability of the *i*th outcome, and *vi* is the monetary value of that outcome. For example, imagine a lottery with ten tickets numbered 1 through 10. If the ticket drawn is numbered 1, you win $10. If the ticket drawn is numbered 2, 3, or 4, you win $5. Any other numbers drawn are worth nothing. The *EV* of this lottery, then, is

$$(.1 \times \$10) + (.3 \times \$5) + (.6 \times \$0) = \$1.60$$

What good does it do you to calculate the expected value? For one thing, it provides you with a guide to how much money (if any) you should be willing to spend to buy a lottery ticket. If you are making rational decisions, you should not spend more for the ticket than the expected value of the lottery. (In some lotteries for charity, of course, you may want to donate more money simply to support the cause. In that case, you would need to add the expected value of the lottery and the amount of money you are willing to donate.)

Not every decision involves monetary outcomes. We often care about other aspects of possible outcomes: our chances for happiness, success, or fulfillment of goals. Psychologists, economists, and others use the term **utility** to capture ideas of happiness, pleasure, and the satisfaction that comes from achieving one or more personal goals. A choice that fulfills one goal has less utility than a choice that fulfills that same goal plus another. For these decisions, we can use the kind of equation just given, using utility instead of monetary value. Equation 1 now becomes

$$(2) \quad EU = \Sigma(pi \times u_i)$$

where *EU* stands for the "expected utility" of a decision and u_i is the utility of the *i*th outcome. The summation is again over all the possible outcomes.

Let's translate our original example of choosing a major into the *EU* model. Imagine that you have listed all possible majors, estimated the probability of success in each, and determined your overall utility for success or failure. Table 11-1 provides an example. You estimate you have a good chance of success in some majors (such as sociology). You do not think you have much chance of success in others (perhaps physics). At the same time, you place different values on success in various majors. In this example, you value psychology the most, followed by chemistry and biology. Your utility for failure also differs among the possible majors. For some, your overall utility even for failure is positive (such as biology, mathematics). For others, your overall utility for failure is strongly negative (such as psychology, sociology). The last column gives the overall expected utility for each major. It suggests that the best decision, given the estimates of probability and utility, is a chemistry major, with psychology and biology as second and third choices, respectively.

You may be wondering how utility is measured in this example. The measurement of utilities turns out to be fairly straightforward. If you select one outcome and assign it the value of 0, then you can assign other values using this as the reference point. It does not matter which outcome is chosen as the zero point, because the final decision depends on differences in *EUs,* not on the absolute value of the utilities (see Baron, 1994, for more on this process).

Many see **expected utility theory** as a normative model of decision making. It can be shown (see Baron, 2000) that if you always choose so as to maximize expected utility, then over a sufficiently large number of decisions your own satisfaction will be highest. In other words, there is no better way of choosing among options that in the long run will increase overall satisfaction than using EU.

As we implied earlier, not all investigators regard EU theory as normative. Frisch and Clemen (1994) offered several shortcomings of EU theory. The first is that EU theory provides an account only of making the final selection from a set of alternatives, not of making decisions in which one faces a "status quo" versus "make a change" option. Moreover, EU theory does not describe the process(es) by which people *structure* a decision—that is, gather information and lay out the possibilities and parameters.

Table 11-1 An Example of Expected Utility Calculations for the Decision to Major in Selected Subjects

Major	Probability of Success	Utility For Success	For Failure	Expected Utility
Art	.75	10	0	7.50
Asian studies	.50	0	−5	−2.50
Biology	.30	25	5	11.00
Chemistry	.45	30	4	15.70
Economics	.15	5	−10	−7.75
English	.25	5	0	1.25
French	.60	0	−5	−2.00
German	.50	0	−5	−2.50
History	.25	8	0	2.00
Mathematics	.05	10	5	5.25
Philosophy	.10	0	−5	−4.50
Physics	.01	0	0	0.00
Psychology	.60	35	−20	13.00
Religion	.50	5	−5	0.00
Sociology	.80	5	−25	−1.00

Note: The probability of each outcome (success and failure) is multiplied by the utility for each outcome, and summed across both, giving the overall expected utility of choosing that major. Probabilities and utilities come from the individual making the decision and are subjective estimates.

Image Theory

A more recently proposed descriptive model of decision making, quite different from EU models, is that of **image theory** (Beach, 1993; Beach & Mitchell, 1987; Mitchell & Beach, 1990). The fundamental assumption of this theory is that in making real-life decisions, people rarely go through a formal structuring process in which they lay out all their options and criteria and then weigh and integrate various pieces of information, as EU models predict. Instead, most of the decision-making work is done during a phase known as the "prechoice screening of options." In this phase, decision makers typically winnow the number of options under active consideration to a small number, sometimes one or two. They do this by asking themselves whether a new goal, plan, or alternative is compatible with three images: the *value image* (containing the decision maker's values, morals, and principles), the *trajectory image* (containing the decision maker's goals and aspirations for the future), and the *strategic image* (the way in which the decision maker plans to attain his or her goals).

To return to our example of choosing a major, image theory might describe the university student as "trying on for size" various majors. That student might quickly reject certain majors because they aren't perceived as fitting well with the student's values or principles (e.g., what they value as important). Alternatively, options might be dropped from further exploration if they don't fit well with the student's view of his or her own future (e.g., their career aspirations) or the path a student plans to take to achieve his or her future vision (e.g., getting into medical or law school).

According to image theory, options judged incompatible with one or more of these three images (value, trajectory, strategic) are dropped from further consideration. This prechoice screening process is noncompensatory: Violations of any image are enough to rule out that option, and no tradeoffs are made. Screening may result in a single option remaining active; in this case the decision maker's final choice is simply whether to accept the option. If there is more than one survivor of the prechoice screening phase, then the decision maker may go on to use a compensatory (i.e., making tradeoffs) or other decision strategy to make the final choice. If there are no survivors, decision makers presumably attempt to discover new options.

Image theory offers some intriguing ideas to researchers studying real-life decision making. Some preliminary work supports it, but more studies are needed to fully assess how well it captures the early processes of decision making.

Recognition-Primed Decision Making

Researcher Gary Klein (1998) studied experts making time-pressured, high-stakes (often life-or-death) decisions: firefighters, intensive care pediatric nurses, military officers. What he found was that few of their decision processes were captured by utility-like models, with the listing and evaluating of several options simultaneously. Instead, he argues, experts are most likely to rely on intuition, mental simulation, making metaphors or analogies, and recalling or creating stories. Klein and his associates expanded these studies into a series of investigations they dub "naturalistic decision making" (Lipshitz, Klein, Orasanu, & Salas, 2001), and the model they created is called **recognition-primed decision making.**

Much of the work in expert decision making is done, Klein argues, as the experts "size up" a situation. As they take stock of a new situation, they compare it to other situations they've previously encountered, calling to mind narrative stories about what happened in those situations and why. Typically, Klein found, experts consider one option at a time, mentally simulating the likely effect of a particular decision. If that simulation fits the scenario, the decision

Box 11-8 Example of Real-Life Expert Decision Making

It is a simple house fire in a one-story house in a residential neighborhood. The fire is in the back, in the kitchen area. The lieutenant leads his hose crew into the building, to the back, to spray water on the fire, but the fire just roars back at them.

"Odd," he thinks. The water should have more of an impact. They try dousing it again, and get the same results. They retreat a few steps to regroup.

Then the lieutenant starts to feel as if something is not right. He doesn't have any clues; he just doesn't feel right about being in that house, so he orders his men out of the building—a perfectly standard building with nothing out of the ordinary.

As soon as his men leave the building, the floor where they had been standing collapses. Had they still been inside, they would have plunged into the fire below.

maker implements it; if not, she tries to find either another option or another metaphor for the situation. Box 11-8 provides an example in which a firefighter describes a sort of "sixth sense" he had in arriving at a decision.

DECISION MAKING, EMOTIONS, AND THE BRAIN

So far in this chapter, we have covered a number of phenomena that affect how people make decisions. Research on the brain mechanisms subserving decision making has experienced a dramatic increase in popularity over the years. This has been fuelled in part by the burgeoning field of **neuroeconomics.** This field examines how the brain interacts with the environment to enable us to make complex decisions. Although we can't begin to do justice to the growing number of studies in this field in this chapter, we will provide a small sampling of some of the developments.

What brain regions subserve complex decision making? It will not be surprising to you, based on what we have covered in previous chapters, that the frontal lobes play a large role in decision making. Some of the first evidence to suggest that damage to the frontal lobes could alter aspects of decision making came from the case of Phineas Gage. While working on a railway project in 1848, he experienced a severe brain injury when a three-foot-long tamping iron accidentally exploded and was propelled through the prefrontal cortex of his brain. Astonishingly, he lived to tell about it—however, not without noticeable deficits in decision making.

Since that time, numerous studies have examined the brain regions that underlie decision making. Perhaps the most interesting advances that the study of the brain has provided us is that it has underscored the complex interplay between emotion and cognition in making decisions. That is, decision making can be highly emotional! One task that has informed

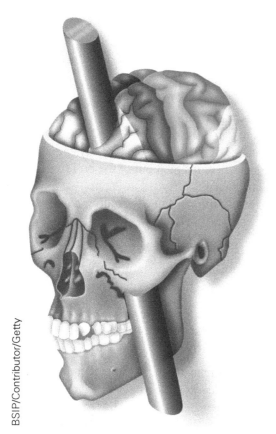

BSIP/Contributor/Getty

Artistic Drawing of Skull of Phineas Gage

our understanding of the brain mechanisms underlying decision making is the **ultimatum game.** Imagine the situation where you have the opportunity to split $10 with someone. You will receive a one-time offer from your partner, and then you have the opportunity to either accept or reject this offer. If the offer is accepted, you split the money as determined; if it is rejected you both go home with nothing. What would you do if your partner offered you 5 dollars? How about if she offered you 1 dollar? The standard "rational" choice would be to accept all offers as any money is better than no money. However, if you behave like most participants in this task, you would likely accept the offer of 5 dollars, and reject the offer of 1 dollar. Why is this so? Sanfey, Rilling, Aronson, Nystrom, and Cohen (2003) looked at fair versus unfair offers in the ultimatum game while being scanned in an fMRI experiment. They found that unfair offers received during the ultimatum game were followed by activations in the insula, and the dorsolateral prefrontal cortex. We know that the prefrontal cortex is involved in a whole host of cognitive tasks such as working memory and executive processes, but what about the insula? Interestingly, the insula has been predominantly implicated in response to negative emotional states such as anger and disgust. These findings suggest a complex interplay between cognition and emotion. The degree to which the negative emotional reaction *caused* the offer rejection or was a byproduct of the decision is open for debate.

We just considered how negative emotions can influence cognitive processes in a two-person decision-making exchange. How do cognitive and emotional processes influence making simple purchase decisions? Knutson, Rick, Wimmer, Prelec, and Loewenstein (2007) showed experimental subjects a series of routine consumer products (such as a box of Godiva chocolates) and the prices at which they could buy those items from the researchers. All participants were given a fixed amount of money they could spend to purchase products during the experiment. The prices of the items had been discounted approximately 70% from their retail prices to promote spending. Knutson and colleagues found that activity in three brain regions predicted purchasing decisions. First, activity in the nucleuas accumbens (NAcc) and medial prefrontal cortex (MPFC) was associated with a preference for a product (a desire to possess it), and predicted that the participant would buy the item. The insula, on the other hand, was activated in accordance with high prices and negatively associated with purchasing behaviour. Taken together, these studies suggest that emotional processes contribute to and may help determine the type of decision a person might make. In addition, by understanding the brain mechanisms that underlie complex decision making we can increase the precision with which the behaviours can be understood and modelled.

IMPROVING DECISION MAKING

We have reviewed evidence suggesting that two major components of decision making—the gathering and integration of information—are typically performed less than optimally (Tetlock, 2002). These studies therefore raise the question "How can these activities be improved?" In this section, we will look at some of the major reasons why decision making goes awry and suggest some ways of eliminating the problems—or at least reducing their impact.

One of the major obstacles to improving the ways in which people gather and integrate information is overconfidence. People who believe their decision making is already close to optimal simply will not see the need for any assistance, even if it is available and offered. Such people may not even seek or look at evidence regarding their performance. Overconfidence, then, is a twofold problem because of its effects in particular decisions and because it inflates people's view of their own decision-making and planning capabilities.

In general, simply telling people about biases in decision making and planning (including overconfidence) results in little or no improvement (Arkes, 1986; Fischhoff, 1982a). Real improvement in reducing bias seems to require extensive practice with the task, individual feedback about one's performance, and some means of making the statistical and/or probabilistic aspects of the decisions clearer. Under some of these conditions, substantial reductions in bias have been reported (Arkes, 1986; Nisbett, Krantz, Jepson, & Kunda, 1983). For example, Nisbett and his collaborators (reviewed by Nisbett et al., 1987) found that even relatively brief, 30-minute training sessions in statistical reasoning could improve people's ability to apply statistical principles to everyday life. Apparently, then, certain kinds of training can improve at least some aspects of decision making.

A second obstacle to improving decision making has to do with people's feelings and expectations about how decisions ought to be made. Cultural expectations lead many of us to trust our intuitions (or at least the intuitions of experts) over any kind of judgment made with equations, computer programs, mathematical models, or the like. This preference is especially evident with very important decisions. We want to be sure that decisions concerning, say, job or graduate school applicants, medical diagnoses and treatments, or even mortgage loans, are made humanely—taking all relevant evidence into account and not looking just at numbers.

Meehl (1954, 1965) confronted this issue some years ago. He examined the relative effectiveness of holistic, clinical impressions with judgments made by statistical models of data. A good example would be to compare an admissions counsellor's prediction of an applicant's chances for success at a given university with the prediction of a statistical model that weighted SAT scores, high school GPA, degree of involvement in extracurricular activities, strength of letters of recommendation (however measured), and whatever other variables were established to be relevant to predicting success at that college. Numerous studies of this kind overwhelmingly support use of the nonhuman model (Dawes, 1982; Dawes & Corrigan, 1974). Thus, contrary to our (strong) intuitions, it *is* often better, fairer, more rational, and in the long run more humane to use decision aids than to rely exclusively on human impressions or intuitions (Kleinmuntz, 1990).

Does this mean that all decisions should be made by computer? On the contrary, people will always be needed to select and judge the relevance of the information to be used in a decision. Dawes (1982) argued that people are quite proficient at figuring out *which* variables are good predictors. Human shortcomings show up when people try to integrate all the information relevant to a decision. Linear models, in contrast, are good at integrating information that human judges have selected as relevant. **Decision analysis** (Keeney 1982; von Winterfeldt & Edwards, 1986b) is an emerging technology that helps people gather and integrate information by using human judges' feelings, beliefs, and judgments of relevance but helps ensure that integration of information is carried out in an unbiased way.

Based on the findings of several studies conducted by a multidisciplinary team of researchers at McMaster University led by cognitive psychologist Lee Brooks, improving some types of real-world decision making may require a more novel approach. By studying the cognitive processes underlying medical diagnosis, they have found that much of clinical diagnosis contributing to decision making is done on a *non-analytic* and *unconscious* basis. For example, by examining the diagnosis of dermatological conditions (Brooks, Norman, & Allen, 1991), and electrocardiograms (Hatala, Norman, & Brooks, 1999), they found that the diagnostic decisions that clinicians made were based predominantly by referencing stored *exemplars* in memory (recall Chapter 7 when we covered the exemplar model of categorization). Specifically, they posit that clinicians make many of their diagnoses through an *effortless* and *unconscious* match between the current case with a particular prior example stored in memory. This unconscious reasoning has a couple of important and perhaps counterintuitive consequences that the researchers have highlighted in a recent review article (see Norman, Young, & Brooks, 2007). First, expert decision making may be associated with *less* rather than *more* decision making time. Why is this the case? If the process of making a diagnosis by mapping the current case to stored examples is effortless and unconscious, then that process is going to be fast. If, however, no stored example is easily accessible in memory, the clinicians will have to slow down and start deliberately searching through long-term memory for an example. This process is slow and potentially error prone. Second, expert clinicians cannot easily predict the errors of other experts. This is due to the fact that no two experts will have had the same experience, and thus the same stored exemplars in memory. Third, ambiguous features can easily be misinterpreted. These three consequences have been supported by numerous experiments conducted by their research team. This being the case, what can be done to reduce biases and improve medical diagnosis? The authors argue that the current training offered to clinicians underestimates the importance of clinical experience with specific case examples in developing expertise. Therefore, presenting future medical practitioners with more examples will give them the necessary exemplars in memory to refer to. In addition, they note that more effort should be placed on assessing the type and the sequence of clinical experiences needed for diagnostic mastery.

The popular television show *House* depicted a team of diagnosticians faced with the complex task of diagnosing patients revealing a wide array of symptoms. How do clinicians make such medical diagnoses in the real world, and how can diagnoses be improved? Lee Brooks and his team of collaborators at McMaster University have been examining this issue with experts and novices in a variety of domains.

Despite all the literature documenting people's errors in judgment and decision making, people do make decisions every day. It is therefore worth remembering that any good theory of decision making must explain how people have survived thus far and where the sources of people's competence lie. At the same time, it is probably safe to conclude that complex and important decisions can usually be made more carefully.

Decision making is a relatively new topic for cognitive psychology. Therefore, we can expect to learn a great deal more about it in the years to come. This kind of research will not only produce better models of the ways in which people process and use information but, it is hoped, help in the long run to improve these skills.

SUMMARY

1. Decision making requires setting goals; gathering information; organizing, combining, and evaluating information; and making a final selection.
2. Because real-life decisions are often made under conditions of uncertainty, many decisions require some sort of probability estimates, even if only vague and intuitive ones. Research reviewed in the chapter suggests that people's understanding of concepts relating to probability theory is often vague or weak, especially for probabilities that are not exactly equal to either .00 or 1.00.
3. Because the process can be so complex, it is perhaps not surprising that decision making can go wrong or be suboptimal in a number of ways. People's intuitions about uncertainty and probability, their activities to acquire or remember relevant information, and the processes they use to integrate different pieces of information can easily be shown to be error prone. You can think of at least some biases and errors in decision making

as cognitive illusions: They arise for understandable reasons and may actually be quite useful in some circumstances. For example, using availability to estimate the relative frequency of something may work perfectly well as long as you can be sure that examples have been collected in an unbiased fashion.

4. The existence of framing effects suggests that the way people evaluate options often is inappropriately coloured by the way they describe (or "frame") those options. If the description frames the status quo in a positive light, then people see changes as more risky and shy away from those options; the converse is true if the status quo is defined in more negative terms.

5. One of the most general biases that people typically exhibit is overconfidence in their own judgment. Several demonstrations make the point that people often feel much more sure of their thinking and their predictions for the future than is justified (on the basis of their track records, for instance). Overconfidence can also play a role in more specific biases, such as hindsight bias and illusory correlation. In general, overconfidence can prevent people from critically examining their own thinking or from admitting of possibilities other than their favoured one.

6. Some normative models of decision making purport to show how people *should* make decisions under ideal circumstances (e.g., expected utility theory). Other, descriptive models describe how people *actually* make decisions. One such model, image theory, places more emphasis on the initial phases of decision making, the screening of options, than on the later stages of decision making, in which one option is selected. Recognition-primed decision making, a model developed from studies of experts, suggests that much of the work of decision making is done when an expert "sizes up" a decision situation.

7. The field of neuroeconomics has recently emerged as a discipline that examines how emotions and cognition jointly contribute to real-life decisions.

8. Decision analysis, a collection of techniques to help people consider all relevant options and tradeoffs, can improve the quality of decision making.

REVIEW QUESTIONS

1. What are the major phases of decision making?
2. Why do some psychologists regard heuristics and biases in decision making as "cognitive illusions"?
3. Give two examples of the use of the availability heuristic in everyday life—one example where it would be appropriate and another example where it might not. Show why your examples are illustrative of availability.
4. Give an explanation for the illusory correlation phenomenon. Discuss the implications of your explanation.

5. Discuss the relationship between hindsight bias and overconfidence.
6. What is a calibration curve? Illustrate your answer with a diagram and text explaining the relevant features.
7. Explain the distinctions among normative models, prescriptive models, and descriptive models of thinking.
8. What is expected utility theory, and how does it relate to decision making?
9. Describe image theory, and contrast it with EU theory.
10. What are the major similarities and differences between image theory and the recognition-primed model of decision making?
11. What do fMRI studies of decision making reveal about the role of emotion in making purchases?
12. What do studies of clinical impressions and intuitions imply about decision making? Do you accept these implications? Why, or why not?

KEY TERMS

anchoring
availability heuristic
bias
calibration curve
cognitive illusions
cognitive overload
confirmation bias
decision analysis
decision structuring
descriptive model of decision
    making

expected utility (EU) theory
framing effect
gambler's fallacy
heuristic
hindsight
illusory correlation
image theory
neuroeconomics
normative model of decision
    making
overconfidence

prescriptive model of
    decision making
probability
rationality
recognition-primed decision
    making
representativeness heuristic
subjective probability
sunk cost effect
ultimatum game
utility

CHAPTER 12

Individual, Aging, and Gender Differences in Cognition

So far, we have been assuming that cognitive development proceeds in pretty much the same way for everyone. In effect, we've been ignoring what psychologists call **individual differences,** stable patterns of performance that differ qualitatively and/or quantitatively across individuals. Here, we will consider some other sources of individual differences—intelligence, expertise, and bilingualism. Normal aging is also associated with large changes in cognition, and understanding the relationship between the aging brain and behavioural measures of cognitive performance has led to the development of a new domain of research: the cognitive neuroscience of aging. Finally, we will also consider gender differences in cognition, and how one's biological sex changes cerebral organization and performance on cognitive tasks.

Why are cognitive psychologists interested in individual or gender differences in cognition? Simply stated, if people vary systematically in the way they approach cognitive tasks, then psychologists cannot speak of "the" way cognition works. To present only one approach, if in fact there are several, is to ignore human diversity and to assume that only one way exists for carrying out a task. Researchers interested in individual and gender differences try to explain why some people seem to consistently outperform others on cognitive tasks and how different strategies or approaches to tasks likely underlie these effects.

INDIVIDUAL DIFFERENCES IN COGNITION

Intelligence

Many psychologists equate cognitive abilities with **intelligence.** Hunt (1986), for example, has stated that "'intelligence' is solely a shorthand term for the variation in competence on cognitive tasks that is statistically associated with personal variables. . . . Intelligence is used as a collective term for 'demonstrated individual differences in mental competence'" (p. 102). Most psychologists agree that people vary in their intellectual (as well as several other important) abilities. Psychologists disagree over whether the best way to describe this variation is in terms of one general mental ability (called intelligence) or in terms of more numerous and varied intellectual abilities (Sternberg & Detterman, 1986).

Even psychologists who accept the idea of a general mental ability called intelligence debate just what the ability is. Some see it in terms of a capacity to learn efficiently; others, in terms of a capacity to adapt to the environment. Other conceptions of intelligence include viewing it as mental speed, mental energy, or mental organization (Gardner, 1983, 1999; 2011; Sternberg, 1986a). Many psychologists who study intelligence have looked at stable individual differences among various cognitive capacities to describe more general differences in people's performance on broader intellectual tasks.

A study by Keating and Bobbitt (1978) illustrates this point. These investigators conducted three experiments with both high-mental-ability (as assessed by a nonverbal intelligence test) and average-mental-ability third-, seventh-, and eleventh-graders. The experiments were all based on cognitive tasks previously used with adults. The authors found that when they controlled for the effects of age (and presumably, therefore, for developmental level), ability differences were still apparent, especially on the more complicated cognitive tasks. Figure 12-1, for instance, shows results of the memory-scanning task (from Chapter 5) as a function of set size, age, and ability level. Note that older children had faster reaction times than younger children and that within each age group high-ability students were faster than average-ability students.

Keating and Bobbitt (1978) believed that both age and ability differences result from the efficiency with which basic cognitive processes (such as encoding and memory scanning) are carried out. They asserted that high-ability children (and adults) simply acquire, store, and manipulate basic information more rapidly and efficiently than do their same-age, normal-ability peers.

The same kinds of speed and efficiency differences also occur between older and younger children.

Psychologists and educators debate fiercely the issue of whether intelligence is one thing or several. A controversial popular book, *The Bell Curve* (Herrnstein & Murray 1994), stirred a simmering pot of contention when it appeared, making (among others) the following strong assertions:

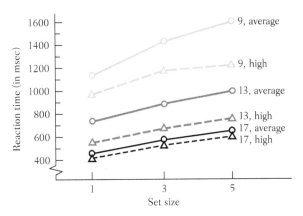

FIGURE 12-1 Mean reaction time (RT) in a memory-scanning task, for children of different ages and abilities.

Source: Republished with permission of Blackwell Publishing, Inc., from *Child Development*, Daniel P. Keating, Bruce L. Bobbitt, vol. 49, issue 1, © 1978; permission conveyed through Copyright Clearance Center, Inc.

Here are six conclusions regarding tests of cognitive ability, drawn from the classical tradition, that are by now beyond significant technical dispute:

1. There is such a thing as a general factor of cognitive ability on which human beings differ.
2. All standardized tests of academic aptitude or achievement measure this general factor to some degree, but IQ tests expressly designed for that purpose measure it most accurately.
3. IQ scores match, to a first degree, whatever it is that people mean when they use the word *intelligent* or *smart* in ordinary language.
4. IQ scores are stable, although not perfectly so, over much of a person's life.
5. Properly administered IQ tests are not demonstrably biased against social, economic, ethnic, or racial groups.
6. Cognitive ability is substantially heritable, apparently no less than 40 percent and no more than 80 percent. (Herrnstein & Murray, 1994, pp. 22–23)

A large part of the reaction to this work stemmed from what critics took to be the authors' refusal to present other points of view in a balanced or responsible way (Gould, 1995; Kamin, 1995). Many critics in particular decried the idea that there is one basic cognitive ability, called intelligence, that is accurately measured by IQ (intelligence quotient) tests. Many others complained about the assumption that intelligence (whatever it is) is fixed and heritable.

One theorist, Howard Gardner (1983, 1993, 1999, 2011), had previously offered a theory directly contradicting the claims of Herrnstein and Murray. Gardner (1993) offered what he

sattva78/Shutterstock.com

IQ testing in children.

called a "pluralistic" theory of mind. He began by questioning what "an intelligence" is and offered this definition: "the ability to solve problems, or to fashion products, that are valued in one or more cultural or community settings" (p. 7). On the basis of a review of clinical data with brain-damaged individuals, studies of prodigies and gifted individuals, and experts in various domains from various cultures, Gardner (1983) proposed the existence of (at least) seven distinct, independent "human intellectual competences, abbreviated hereafter as 'human intelligences'" (p. 8). These intelligences, with two others added in Gardner's 1999 work, are listed in Table 12-1. Gardner (1983, 1993, 1999, 2011) argued that our Western culture places certain kinds of intelligence, specifically linguistic and logical-mathematical, on a pedestal. At the same time our culture gives short shrift to the other intelligences, especially bodily-kinesthetic and interpersonal. We regard skilled athletes or politicians as people with talents, but not as people who have a different sort of intelligence, like famous scientists or great poets. We make a distinction between talents and intelligence, Gardner believes, only so that we can hold on to the concept that there is only one mental ability. Gardner calls for a broader view of people's mental and cognitive abilities. He argues for a different kind of schooling that, instead of focusing only on linguistics and logic, also trains students as carefully in music, self-awareness, group processes, dance, and the performing arts. See Figure 12-2 for examples of multiple intelligences.

Gardner's theory has captured the attention and enthusiasm of many psychologists and educators, some of whom are trying to implement the previously described **multiple intelligences (MI) theory** in their classes (see Gardner, 1993 and 1999, for some descriptions). There exist proposals for multiple creativities as well as intelligences, and educators have adopted these ideas enthusiastically (Han & Marvin, 2002). However, Gardner's theory awaits the development of assessment tools for each intelligence.

Researchers and educators who hold to the concept of IQ as measuring the one true mental ability called intelligence have sophisticated tests that generally predict school performance adequately Those interested in the idea of multiple intelligences have a great deal of work ahead of them to define the parameters of all the intelligences, to create valid measures of each, and to describe the interrelationships among different kinds of intelligences.

Table 12-1 Multiple Intelligences

Linguistic intelligence	The capacity to use language to communicate and to accomplish other goals; sensitivity to subtleties in both written and spoken language; the ability to learn foreign languages.
Logical-mathematical intelligence	The ability to solve problems, design and conduct experiments, draw inferences; the capacity to analyze situations.
Musical intelligence	The ability to analyze and respond to musical patterns; to compose or perform music.
Bodily-kinesthetic intelligence	The ability to use one's body to perform artistically or athletically; to create physical products; to use either the whole body or parts of the body skillfully.
Spatial intelligence	The ability to navigate skillfully through both wide and confined spaces; to visualize spatial scenes; to create products with spatial properties.
Interpersonal intelligence	The capacity to understand other people's emotions, motivations, intentions, and desires; the ability to work effectively with others.
Intrapersonal intelligence	The ability to understand one's own emotions, motivations, intentions, and desires, and to use the information for self-regulation.
Naturalist intelligence	The ability to recognize flora and fauna of one's environment; to skillfully classify organisms with respect to species and to chart the relationships among different species.
Existential intelligence	The capacity to see one's place in the cosmos, especially in light of such issues as the nature of the human condition, the significance of life, the meaning of death, the ultimate fate of the world, both physical and psychological. *(Note:* Gardner is still evaluating whether this capacity fully merits the label "intelligence.")

Note: The first seven items were presented in Gardner (1983); the last two come from Gardner (1999).

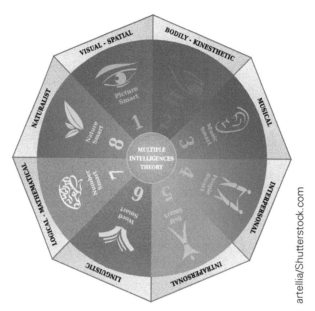

artellia/Shutterstock.com

FIGURE 12-2 Examples of multiple intelligences.

Experts versus Novices

Throughout earlier chapters, we have seen that people with expertise in a certain realm often approach a cognitive task differently from novices. We first encountered this topic in Chapter 3 when we discussed perceptual learning. If you recall, the point was made there that experts and novices, given equal exposure to information, acquire or "pick up on" different amounts of it. For example, anecdotal accounts from spectators watching a hockey game (a frequent Canadian pastime), live or on TV, suggest that experts (those who have been watching hockey since childhood) have no problem locating the puck when it is in play; novices, however, complain that the puck is difficult to see because of its size. In general, experts will perceive more distinctions, especially subtle ones, than novices do. This point is illustrated in an example of an art historian and a layperson unfamiliar with art standing before a Picasso painting. The layperson (novice) "sees" less information than the art historian (expert), who may be rather effortlessly picking up information about brushstrokes or composition that the novice simply cannot perceive.

We saw next in Chapter 7 that experts and novices differ in their conceptual representations of information. Novices in a given domain, for example, tend to classify objects or instances together on the basis of superficial or perceptual similarities; experts often use their knowledge to form deeper principles with which to classify. For example, if given a number of paintings, a novice might categorize on the basis of the subject of the picture (landscapes, still lifes, portraits). An art expert would be far more likely to categorize on the basis of artist, historical period, composition, and other aspects of a painting that require a certain degree of knowledge.

Work by de Groot (1965) and Chase and Simon (1973) on chess experts and chess novices has suggested other relevant cognitive-processing differences between the two groups. For example, when shown a chessboard arranged in a midgame configuration (that is, the pieces arranged in such a way as to represent a game in process), an expert chess player could reconstruct the positions of approximately 16 (out of 25) pieces after only a 5-second glance. A chess beginner, given the same board and the same exposure, could reconstruct the positions of only about 5 pieces.

Interestingly, the authors showed it was not simply that the experts had better memories. Indeed, when shown chessboards with 25 chess pieces randomly arranged on them, the expert and the beginner showed equivalent performance, being able to reconstruct the positions of only 2 or 3 pieces. Instead, Chase and Simon (1973) argued that the chess expert used chess knowledge to group or "chunk" chess pieces into meaningful configurations; as such they are able to encode structures, but not random, chess configurations more quickly and accurately. As Chapter 5 suggests, the chunking process can increase the amount of information held in working memory.

London, Great Britain, England - 08/11/2017: Madame Tussaud Museum, wax figure of Pablo Picasso, world-renowned Spanish painter, sculptor and lithographer.

Editorial credit: Marco Tiberio / Shutterstock.com

Recent work by Eyal Reingold at the University of Toronto, and his colleagues, has gone on to show that early perceptual encoding is what differentiates expert from intermediate chess players, rather than an enhanced memory for chess pieces, or ability to think ahead to the next move. In their work (Reingold, et al., 2001; Charness et al., 2001), expert and intermediate players attempted to choose the best move in each of five different positions, while their eye movements were monitored with specialized recording equipment. As expected, experts were both faster and more accurate in choosing the best move, but what differed between the

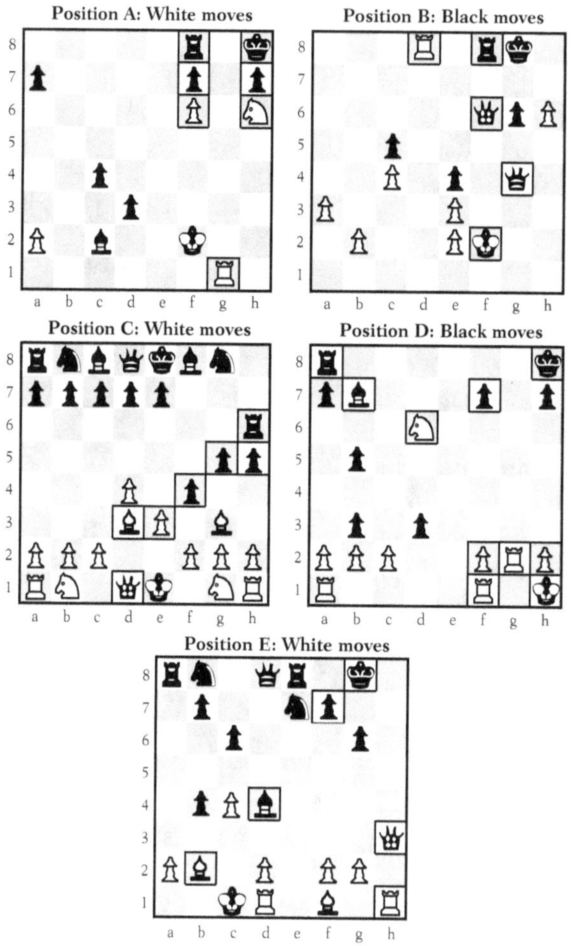

FIGURE 12-3 Example of chess positions.

groups was the spatial distribution of their eye fixations: experts produced more fixations on empty squares than intermediates. As well, they made fewer fixations on each trial than did the novices, and when they did fixate actual chess pieces, these were more likely to be on ones directly relevant to the next move. They concluded that experts perceptually encode chess configurations rather than individual chess pieces. See Figure 12-3 for examples of chess positions.

Reingold and colleagues (2001) also showed that the visual span was significantly larger for experts while they processed structured, but not random, chess positions. That is, experts made greater use of parafoveal processing to extract information from a larger portion of a chessboard than did intermediates (see Figure 12-4). This suggests an early perceptual processing advantage is what distinguishes experts from intermediate players.

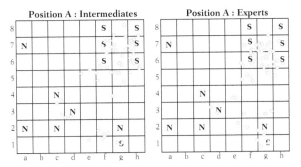

FIGURE 12-4 Scattergrams of eye-gaze positions in intermediate and expert chess players.

Bilingualism

Thus far we have seen that knowledge in a certain domain affects how one approaches cognitive tasks within that domain. In this next section we consider how early and lifelong training in one domain can lead to measurable changes on a host of cognitive tasks. Most research in cognitive psychology involves English-speaking participants, and conclusions are based with little regard for the fact that many participants speak more than one language. In Canada, the 2011 Census data showed that 17.5% of the Canadian population, or 5.8 million persons, reported speaking at least two languages at home. In 2006, 14.2% did so (nearly 4.5 million persons), so the number of bilingual individuals is growing. . Importantly, existing evidence from psychological studies strongly suggests that bilingualism affects cognitive processing (de Groot & Kroll, 1997).

People who are **bilingual** are regularly faced with the task of attending to one set of labels for objects, or methods of expression, while simultaneously ignoring labels from their other known language, depending on the language in which they are trying to communicate. Given that bilinguals have had massive practice throughout their lives in exercising such control processes, they may experience a boost in such functions that generalizes

Bilingual children are regularly faced with the task of attending to one set of labels while ignoring labels from their other known language; In this example, a child learns two languages at the same time, English from his mother, German from his father.

Sangoiri/Shutterstock.com

across tasks. It has been found that the ability to attend selectively to relevant information, and ignore competing distracting information, develops earlier in bilingual than monolingual children (Bialystok, 2001).

Recent studies have shown that bilingual children and lifelong bilingual adults who use both languages in their daily lives show an advantage on tasks involving attentional control. Specifically, when the task requires inhibiting salient but misleading perceptual information, or response conflict, bilinguals are faster and more accurate than monolinguals (Bialystok, 2001; Bialystok et al., 2004), but perform similarly to monolinguals when the task does not contain misleading cues. The bilingual processing advantage is not confined to tasks involving language processing, but has been found in a variety of simple experimental tasks (Bialystok & Martin, 2004) such as the ability to see the alternate image in a reversible ambiguous figure (Bialystok & Shapero, 2005; see Figure 12-5), and the Simon task (Bialystok et al., 2004).

In a typical Simon task, a more controlled cognitive task than the ambiguous figures one, coloured patches are presented to the right or left of a screen, above right and left response keys. The experimental rule may be "if the patch is red press left, if green press right," and the stimulus patch is then presented above either the appropriate key (congruent response) or the inappropriate key (incongruent response). The general finding is that incongruent stimulus– response pairs are associated with longer response times than congruent pairs (the "Simon effect"), and it is argued that smaller Simon effect values indicate better cognitive control (Lu & Proctor, 1995). The finding that bilingual children and adults (Bialystok et al., 2004) have smaller Simon effects than their monolingual peers suggests that bilingualism leads to the development and maintenance of more efficient attentional control.

The exact nature of this superior control, however, is still under investigation (see Kroll et al. 2010 for a review). Green (1998) proposes a model of cognitive functioning in bilingual individuals in which the language that is not in current use is suppressed by the same executive functions used generally to control attention and inhibition. One further set of findings shows that the bilingual advantage is strong in children, declines to a relatively small effect in older children and young adults, but then reappears strongly in older adults (Bialystok, 2001; Bialystok et al., 2004; Bialystok, Craik, & Ryan, 2006). Other studies have noted a negative

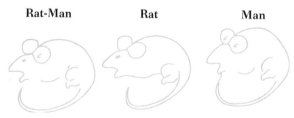

FIGURE 12-5 Example of ambiguous figure used in Bialystok & Shapero, 2005. Bilingual children are more successful than monolinguals in seeing the other image in the images.

side effect of bilingualism: they perform poorly than monolinguals on tasks involving lexical access (Gollan et al., 2002; Ransdell & Fischler, 1989; Rosselli et al., 2000), and more recent work suggests a bilingual disadvantage in memory retrieval of verbal information (Fernandes et al., 2007). These deficits have been attributed to the need to maintain a vocabulary base that is about twice as large as that of a monolingual speaker, and the reduced frequency with which bilinguals access any given word (Michael & Gollan, 2005). The common thread in studies of individual differences in ability, intelligence, expertise, and bilingualism is that patterns of cognitive performance can differ across individuals, and a challenge for cognitive psychologists is to characterize how these differences affect both the quantitative and qualitative nature of task performance.

THE EFFECTS OF AGING ON COGNITION

Patterns of Preserved and Declining Functions

A common complaint among older adults is a perceived decline in memory functions with increasing age. The new phrase "a senior's moment" has been coined to capture those situations in which the older adult fails to recall a name, source of information, or intention to do something. These examples reflect what cognitive researchers call episodic, source, and prospective memory. Numerous studies of normally aging (non-demented) adults show that significant **age differences** in memory exist for lists of words (Smith, 1977) or text (Dixon et al., 1982), and details about the context in which items were initially experienced (source memory; Park & Puglisi, 1985; Park, Puglisi, & Lutz, 1982). These deficits are not limited to verbal material, as declines are also seen in memory for faces (Bartlett et al, 1989) and abstract visual material (Smith et al., 1990).

Research demonstrates that performance on short-term and episodic memory tasks shows a marked decline with age. These age-related impairments appear to depend on the amount of executive control or attentional demands of the task. For example, older adults show better performance on short-term memory tasks that require the simple maintenance of information. For example, repeating a list of numbers in the order they were presented is preserved in old age, though repeating those same numbers in the reverse order of presentation is impaired (Bopp & Verhaeghen, 2005). Similarly, on episodic memory tests that provide a retrieval cue, such as on a recognition test, in which the previously presented item is re-presented, leaving the senior only to discriminate old from new, age differences in performance are rarely seen (Craik, 1986). In these cases seniors can rely on **environmental support**— external aids, hints, category headings—to help structure their search through memory for the correct response. It is when seniors must re-construct the episode, or when they must re-order or organize information on-line, that larger memory deficits are seen, as on tests of free recall or when source judgments about where or when information was initially acquired is needed (Craik, 1986; Craik & McIntryre, 1987).

Box 12-1 Exercise Helps Sustain Mental Activity as We Age

A review of the research on the effects of exercise on brain functioning supports the view that physical exercise helps people maintain cognitive abilities, including memory, well into old age. In a few of the studies that examined men and women over 65 years old, the findings showed that those who exercised for at least 15 to 30 minutes at a time three times a week were less likely to develop Alzheimer's disease, even if they were genetically predisposed to the disease. There's also evidence that fitness training may improve some mental processes even

Exercise helps maintain cognitive abilities in old age.

more than moderate activity. Aerobic training has been shown to increase brain volume in aging humans. (See Kramer and Colcombe, 2018 for a review.)

There are, of course, individual differences in the extent of memory change that seniors can expect to experience, and variables such as cardiovascular health (see Box 12-1). As well, research from the Victoria Longitudinal Study in British Columbia suggests that people differ in their use of memory strategies and memory aids, and this factor alone can predict memory decline over a five-year period (Dixon & de Frias, 2007)

Despite declines in these sorts of memory functions, others remain intact or even increase with advancing age. Semantic memory for names and labels of objects (Park, Polk, Mikels, Taylor, & Marshuetz, 2001; Salthouse, 1982, 1991), vocabulary levels (Park et al., 2001; Salthouse, 1991), and general word knowledge (Salthouse, 1982) remain intact, and continue to increase over the lifespan. As well, older adults have relatively preserved performance on tests of non-declarative memory, in which memory is assessed indirectly as

Famed pianist Arthur Rubinstein maintained his expert level of performance by adopting specific strategies as he got older.

an increase in processing efficiency upon encountering an item a second time (Light & Singh, 1987), as in the case of preserved repetition priming in old age (Fleischman et al., 2004).

Baltes, Staudinger, and Lindenberger (1999), in a review of the literature, concluded that a general decline in the speed of processing of elementary cognitive operations occurs with age, perhaps accounting for the pattern of findings just reviewed. Paul Baltes and Margaret Baltes have argued, however, that older adults often can strategically compensate for such declines by using selective optimization with compensation:

When the concert pianist Arthur Rubinstein, as an 80-year-old, was asked in a television interview how he managed to maintain such a high level of expert piano playing, he hinted at the coordination of three strategies. First, he played fewer pieces (selection); he practiced these pieces more often (optimization); and to counteract his loss in mechanical speed he now used a kind of impression management, such as playing more slowly before fast segments to make the latter appear faster (compensation). (Baltes et al., 1999, pp. 483–484)

Models of Age-Related Changes in Cognition

Multiple theories have been proposed to explain the memory deficits observed with age. These deficits have been framed in terms of a general slowing in processing speed (Salthouse, 1996), less effective inhibition processes (Hasher & Zacks, 1988), or reduced attentional resources (Craik, 1986). Although no one single framework has been able to adequately describe all of the data on memory and aging, most theories converge on the idea that changes in brain function, particularly in the frontal lobe, underlie these deficits.

During aging, the brain undergoes many changes, including reductions in brain volume stemming from grey and white matter atrophy (shrinkage), synaptic degeneration that impairs communication between neurons, and reductions in regional cerebral blood flow (rCBF) to the brain (Cabeza et al., 2016; Raz et al., 2005. Examination of the brains of seniors who have donated their brains to science show that the weight and volume of the brain shrinks at a persistent rate of 2% per decade (Kemper, 1994), and that brain volume decreases with increasing age (Raz et al, 2005). The largest decrease in volume is found in the frontal cortex (front of the brain), with smaller correlations in other brain regions such as the temporal lobes (sides of brain overtop the ears), parietal cortex (top of brain), the hippocampus (a structure known to be involved in memory), and the cerebellum (involved in fine and gross motor control).

Studies of living seniors have examined rCBF over the cortex, and throughout the entire brain, and found that aging is associated with a decrease over the entire brain (Madden & Hoffman, 1997). Interestingly, there is a shift in distribution of rCBF with advancing age: middle-age adults show more rCBF in anterior (frontal) than posterior brain regions, whereas older adults show more rCBF in posterior than anterior regions (West, 1996). These changes undoubtedly are responsible for most of the observed age-related changes in cognitive function reported in many studies of aging. Identifying precisely how these brain changes impact cognition is a formidable challenge, though new testing methodologies and advances in neuroimaging analysis techniques have led to testable hypotheses and models of the link between brain and behaviour. Understanding the relationship between the aging brain and behavioural measures of cognitive performance has led to the development of a new domain of research: the **cognitive neuroscience of aging.**

In cognitive psychology, the effects of aging on task performance are measured in accuracy and/or response time, whereas the effects on the brain are measured as changes in blood flow and metabolism (with PET), changes in electrical activity (with EEG), and changes in blood-oxygen-level-dependent (BOLD) signal (with fMRI) within the brains of older compared to younger adults during a cognitive task. Recent advances in neuroimaging have allowed an exploration of the brain basis of age-related declines in memory function, and changes in basic sensory processing. These studies suggest that a combination of differential recruitment of brain regions and strategies applied to solve tasks accounts for the observed differences in cognitive performance across younger and older adults.

More recently, neuroimaging studies have begun exploring how an aging brain manages to perform well on a given task. Some studies report no differences in overt cognitive task performance across age groups, but striking differences in how the brains of young and old achieve performance. Adaptive versus maladaptive modes of processing are now being explored among groups of seniors. It is this aspect of neuroimaging that we will focus on, as it highlights how seniors, despite many neural structural differences relative to younger adults, make use of these to achieve their cognitive goals. Allowing examination of how the brains of older adults find alternate routes to achieving performance is the real strength of neuroimaging research of aging, and also highlights the superb adaptability of the human brain when faced with less than optimal hardware.

According to the reduced resource view of cognitive aging, seniors have less efficient cognitive resources available to perform a cognitive task, due to neural changes in the frontal lobe of the aging brain (Craik, 1983, 1986; Craik & Byrd, 1982). According to this view, to perform a given cognitive task older adults must engage additional neural regions than younger adults. Similarly, in Morris Moscovitch's component-process model of memory (1989), if the memory task is one that requires significant frontal-lobe resource requirements, such as organization, response monitoring, or attentional control (selection) functions, this loss in available resources with advancing age begins to affect behavioural performance unless additional resources can be recruited.

This pattern has been found using neuroimaging techniques: older adults show more brain activity in the frontal lobes compared to younger adults during episodic encoding, episodic memory retrieval, working memory, perception, and inhibitory control. In her seminal neuroimaging study of aging, Cheryl Grady—who works at the Rotman Research Institute, affiliated with the University of Toronto—and her colleagues (1997) performed PET scans on younger and older adults while encoding faces for a later memory test. They

Box 12-2 Canadian Research Highlight

Dr. Fergus Craik is a professor of psychology at the University of Toronto, holds the Dr. Max and Gianna Glassman Chair in Neuropsychology and works at the Rotman Research Institute of Baycrest Hospital in Toronto (http://research.baycrest.org/fcraik). He was elected a Fellow of the Royal Society in 2008. He is best known for his work on levels of processing effects in memory. He has also made major contributions in the areas of encoding and retrieval and models of age-related cognitive decline and prospective memory and conducts research using neuroimaging techniques.

Source: http://rotman-baycrest.on.ca/index.php?section=205

showed that during encoding younger adults activated the left side of the frontal cortex to a greater degree than did older adults, and also showed greater activation of temporal lobe areas. Interestingly, the correlation between brain activity in left-frontal and hippocampal structures in the temporal lobes was .94 in young and .02 in older adults. These results suggest that older adults are characterized by both a change in activity and in connectivity of brain structures during encoding. Similar results were reported by Cabeza, Grady, and colleagues (1997) in addition to an observed bilateral activation of frontal cortex in older adults but unilateral left activation in young.

From these data came the first suggestion that older adults may adapt to the decline in neural structures by increasing activation in other, homologous parts of the brain. That is, the compensatory recruitment theory was born. Since then we have seen the rapid development of a new field of research: cognitive neuroscience of aging, devoted to understanding the relationship between changing brain structures associated with normal aging, and performance on cognitive tasks.

Cognitive Neuroscience of Aging

Studies of Basic Sensory Functions

Neuroimaging studies of cortical regions required for early stages of perceptual analysis have consistently shown an age-related decline in activation of these regions. For example, Ross and colleagues (1997) showed a decreased brain activity in occipital regions (at the back of the brain) in older relative to younger adults, in response to a visually presented red flash. Other studies involving more complex materials led to the same finding. rCBF measures are reduced during a face matching and location judgment task in older compared to younger adults (Grady et al., 1992, 1994, 2000), during the processing of verbal material in a lexical decision task (Madden et al., 1996), a word-pair encoding task (Cabeza et al., 1997), and during retrieval (Anderson et al., 2000). The consistent finding of reduced occipital activation in aging has been interpreted as reflecting an age-related decline in the quality of bottom-up sensory input (Madden, 2007).

Another consistent finding in the neuroimaging literature is that activation in frontal regions tends to increase on cognitive tasks, in older relative to younger adults. These will be reviewed shortly, and have been interpreted as reflecting a heavier reliance on top-down attentional control processes in older adults (Cabeza et al., 2002; McIntosh et al., 1999) to compensate for deficits in bottom-up processing. In line with this suggestion, Madden and colleagues (2007) recently showed that during a letter search task older adults showed activation in frontal and parietal regions that was correlated with search performance, but in younger adults performance correlated with activation in occipital lobes (see Figure 12-6). Notably, these patterns were observed only in the more difficult search task, and not in the neutral control condition. This suggests that older adults may cope with increased task

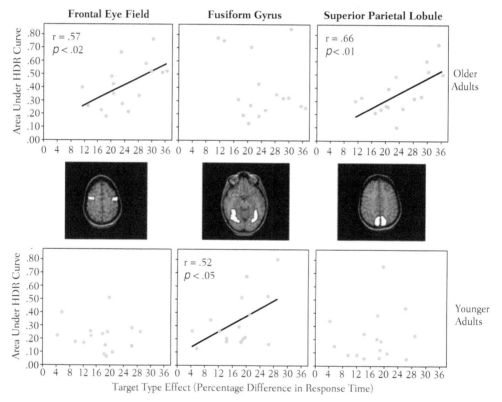

FIGURE 12-6 Areas shown in white depict three brain regions showing increased activation during top-down visual search. Older adults are shown in the top panel and younger adult in the bottom panel. The figure illustrates the finding that, when search involves top-down attention (i.e., the observer's expectation regarding the probability of the target's colour), activation of the frontal and parietal regions was correlated with search performance for older adults but not for younger adults. In younger adults, performance correlated instead with activation in the fusiform region (occipital lobe; from Madden, 2007).

demands in a visual search task by placing a greater reliance on top-down (frontal) than bottom-up (occipital) processing strategies.

Thus, older adults engage frontal functions at task difficulty levels for which young adults do not, as young can still rely on their intact sensory function to guide performance. As we shall see, this is a theme that resonates throughout the literature, whether the task in question taps sensory functions, working memory, encoding, or episodic retrieval.

Studies of Working Memory

The concept of working memory, first proposed by Baddeley & Hitch in 1974, and discussed in Chapter 5, has been the basis of a tremendous amount of research over the past few decades. There is a large literature examining how aging affects working memory capacities, and these all generally show age-related declines in both the maintenance of information in working memory and in ability to manipulate its contents (Belleville, Rouleau, & Caza, 1998; Hartman et al, 2001; Van der Linden, Bredart, & Beerten, 1994). Age deficits in executive, inhibitory, and cognitive flexibility are found in many studies, and this forms the basis of several theories of aging and decline in function (Engle, 2002; Hasher & Zacks, 1988; McDowd, & Shaw, 2000).

In their influential theory of normal cognitive aging, Hasher and Zacks (1988) suggested that older adults have trouble ignoring distracting information—a deficit in selective attention. Irrelevant background information enters working memory, thereby slowing information processing, which leads to difficulties in processing, or retrieving, task-relevant information. Neuroimaging studies of working memory function have shown that aging is associated with an overactivation of brain regions supporting executive functions in the frontal lobes. That is, older adults activated both sides of the frontal lobes during a working memory task, while younger adults activated only one side (Reuter-Lorenz et al, 2000).

As we shall see, this bilateral recruitment of brain regions in older adults is one of the most pervasive findings in the cognitive neuroscience of aging, and has led to the development of the influential hemispheric asymmetry reduction in older adults (HAROLD) model (Cabeza, 2002). In support of this claim, a meta-analysis in which perception of faces, working memory, and episodic memory was compared across age groups showed increased bilateral frontal activity on all tasks in older adults (Grady, 2002). Grady suggests that this increase in frontal involvement reflects an increased reliance on executive-type resources on lower-level or easier tasks that is not necessary for young. We will first discuss advances in neuroimaging research in the area of long-term memory, and then consider this model more fully.

Studies of Encoding and Retrieval for Long-Term Memory

As we learned in Chapter 6, "deep" processing at encoding involves semantic processing of an item usually in terms of its meaning or relation to oneself, in contrast to "shallow" processing in which surface characteristics such as font, number of syllables, or colour are processed.

Deep encoding leads to better memory (Craik & Lockhart, 1972). Recent neuroimaging work has shown that relative to younger adults, old show a decrease in left frontal cortex activation during deep encoding conditions, and a corresponding decrease in later memory performance (Daselaar et al., 2003; Grady et al., 1999; Grady et al., 2002; Stebbins et al., 2002). These results suggest that one reason why older adults may have poorer memories than younger adults is an inability to recruit brain regions involved in semantic processing in the left frontal cortex, which young use to more richly encode items, leading to improved memory.

What is missing from these studies, however, is a consideration of how these reported changes in brain activation directly relate to memory performance in older adults. If bilateral involvement in old adults is compensatory (Cabeza et al., 1997), it should be possible to take advantage of the variability in memory performance inherent in group studies and split up data depending on level of performance, to compare the brain activation patterns in high versus low performers. If bilateral activation reflects compensatory recruitment for declines in other brain regions, then it should be evident in high-performing relative to low-performing seniors.

To test this claim, Cabeza et al. (2002) grouped seniors into high and low performers before scanning, according to performance on a battery of neuropsychological tests that assess memory functions. During scanning, a group of young adults and the two groups of older adults performed a source memory retrieval task, known to produce right frontal activity in young. Results offered clear support for the compensation view. High-performing older adults showed bilateral frontal activation, whereas young adults and low-performing seniors showed unilateral right activation (see Figure 12-7).

While the Cabeza study concerned activation patterns during retrieval, similar results are reported in an episodic encoding task. Rosen et al. (2002) scanned young adults and old adults split into high and low performers based on neuropsychological testing during deep and shallow encoding of verbal material. High-performing seniors and young recruited similar left frontal regions as well as a homologous region in right frontal regions, whereas low-performing seniors showed lower left and right frontal activation.

While the field of cognitive neuroscience of aging suggests some common patterns that characterize cognitive performance and brain activation, it is important to keep in mind that these are likely also influenced by individual differences from other sources. Such factors as intelligence, health, years of formal education, expertise, and cognitive style all continue to play important roles. The topic of the effects of aging on cognition, still in its relative scholarly infancy, will no doubt continue to support the idea that any individual's level of cognitive functioning depends on many factors, including factors specific to the individual such as those just described as well as those of the task and the overall context (Lerner, 1990).

One example comes from work on the interaction of bilingualism and aging. As mentioned previously, lifelong bilinguals show an advantage of a variety of tasks involving attentional control. Continued use of more than one language provides continual practice with executive functions such as selection and inhibition. Bilingualism may therefore serve as a protective

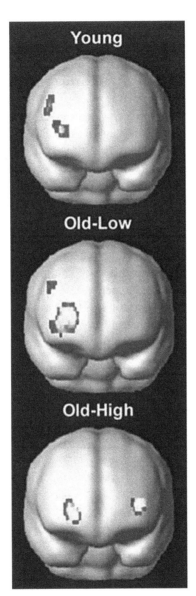

FIGURE 12-7 Brain activity in frontal cortex during a source memory task was lateralized to the right in young and in old low-performing senior participants, but bilateral in old high-performing senior participants.

Source: Reprinted from *NeuroImage*, Vol. 17, issue 3, Roberto Cabeza, Nicole D. Anderson, Jill K. Locantore, Anthony R. McIntosh, Title of article, pp. 1394-1402, Copyright © 2002, with permission from Elsevier.

factor against the usual decline in such functions that characterizes normal aging (Bialystok et al., 2004). Ellen Bialystok, from York University in Toronto, and her colleagues have shown just that: bilingualism is associated with smaller Simon effect costs (described earlier)—they respond more rapidly than monolinguals on task conditions that place a load on working memory. Thus, controlled processing is carried out more effectively by bilinguals and offsets normal age-related losses in executive functions. Bialystok has recently expanded her research to examine whether bilingualism might also protect against or delay the onset of dementia. In a sample of almost 200 patients diagnosed with dementia, those who were bilingual showed symptoms of onset four years later than monolinguals (Bialystok et al., 2007). Thus cognitive ability, and cognitive decline, can vary drastically depending on individual differences.

This brief look at individual differences in cognitive abilities was intended to stress an important point: *Not all people approach cognitive tasks in exactly the same way.* Age, ability, expertise, and bilingualism can differ among people and can affect their efficiency in acquiring or processing information, leading to differences in how much information is picked up or how thoroughly it is processed. These differences, in turn, could have great effects on how well a complicated cognitive task is performed.

In the last four decades, some psychologists have also wondered about the existence of gender as a source of individual differences in cognition. In the next section, we will examine whether men and women show differences in cognition, and the basis for these effects.

GENDER DIFFERENCES IN COGNITION

The possible existence of gender differences can be fascinating. This fascination is especially pronounced in our culture, as psychologist Carol Nagy Jacklin (1989) noted:

> *Speculation about differences between females and males is a national preoccupation. In our culture, people care whether there are fundamental differences between girls and boys, and we place more emphasis on the possibility of such differences than on other kinds of distinctions that could be made. For example, we rarely wonder whether blue-eyed and brown-eyed or short and tall children differ from one another in intellectual abilities or personality. (p. 127)*

Some cautions are in order before we examine the evidence regarding gender differences in cognition, especially because of the sensitive nature of the topic. One of the most important cautions regards the term **gender difference.**

To say there is a gender difference in performance on Task X can mean a number of very different things, as illustrated in Figure 12-8. One possible meaning is that the scores from members of one sex are higher than the scores from members of another sex, a possibility illustrated in Figure 12-8(A). Notice that the lowest-scoring member of one sex (the distribution to the right) still outperforms the very best member of the lower-scoring sex.

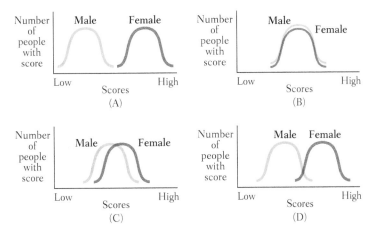

FIGURE 12-8 Examples of hypothetical gender distributions. Each curve depicts a hypothetical distribution of scores on some test for persons of one gender.

Although many people interpret statements about gender (or other group) differences in these terms, reality is almost never this simple.

More realistic depictions of gender differences in performance are given in Figures 12-8(B), 12-8(C), and 12-8(D). Figure B illustrates no gender difference. Figures C and D illustrate real gender differences in the mean level of performance, with different degrees of overlap in scores between people of different genders. In each case, although females on average score higher than males, some males score higher than some females. In both cases, then, it is impossible to predict how any individual (Michael, Joshua, Emily, or Abigail) would score. All we can say is that given large numbers of men and women, the average score for women will be higher than the average score for men.

A more powerful technique for combining results from different studies is called **meta-analysis.** It involves the use of statistical methods in integrating the findings from different studies. This approach is gaining widespread popularity among psychologists. It allows the investigator to compare different studies quantitatively. A measure commonly used in meta-analysis is **d,** defined as the difference in mean scores between two groups, divided by the average standard deviation for the two groups. This measure is known as the **effect size.**

To take a concrete example of effect size, consider the following example: Suppose women outperform men on a specific verbal task. If the mean score for women is 100 and the mean score for men is 50 but if, on average, the standard deviation for the two groups is 75, the effect size of the study would be [100 – 50]/75, or .67. Essentially, an effect size tells us how much standardized difference lies between two (or more) means. Cohen (1969) provided rules of thumb for interpreting this value: Effect sizes of .20 are considered small; of .50, medium; and of .80, large. So our hypothesized value of .67 would count as a medium-to-large effect.

Verbal Abilities

What kinds of abilities count as "verbal abilities"? Different authors provide different definitions, of course, but a typical description includes breadth of vocabulary, speech fluency, grammar, spelling, reading comprehension, oral comprehension, and the ability to solve language puzzles such as verbal analogies or anagrams (Halpern, 1992; Williams, 1983).

The common finding is that women outperform men on tasks involving receptive and productive language, and on high-level verbal tasks such as analogies, comprehension of prose, and episodic memory tasks, whereas men outperform women on tasks assessing visuospatial ability (Herlitz et al., 1997; Voyer et al., 1995). An example of a verbal task that shows a female advantage is presented in Figure 12-9. Here the first letter of each of 4 different words is given, and the task is to fill in missing letters to make a meaningful sentence. Female are better and faster than males on this task, in the range of one-quarter of a standard deviation (from Kolb & Whishaw, 2003).

To get an idea of the consistency in the finding of a female advantage across multiple studies, Hyde and Linn (1988) conducted a meta-analysis of 165 studies (both published and unpublished) that met the following criteria: Participants were from the United States and Canada, were more than 3 years old, and lacked language deficits (such as dyslexia); the studies reported original data; and the authors provided enough information for the calculation of effect sizes. The types of verbal abilities examined included vocabulary, analogies, reading comprehension, oral communication, essay writing, general ability (a mixture of other measures), anagrams, and verbal scores from standardized tests such as the Scholastic Aptitude Test in the United States and the Graduate Record Examination used for admission to graduate schools in the United States and Canada.

Of the studies surveyed, roughly three-quarters showed superior female performance. However, when data were assessed in terms of statistical significance, only 27% of the studies found statistically significant higher female performance, 66% found no statistically significant gender differences, and 7% found statistically significant higher male performance. When the types of verbal tasks were taken into account, the only tasks to show reliable female superiority were those for anagrams, speech production, and general ability. The average d measures for these tasks were .22, .20, and .33, respectively, suggesting that these gender differences existed, but were small. Analyzing gender differences as a function of age, the authors also found little

1. M ————————— F ——————————— L ——————————— C —————

2. P ——————————— E ——————————— Y ——————————— V —————

3. S ——————————— M——————————— T ——————————— M—————

FIGURE 12-9 Verbal fluency-type task.

variation in *d* measures according to whether the participants were preschoolers, children of elementary school age, adolescents, or adults. In a more recent study, de Frias and her colleagues (2006) showed that women performed at a higher level than men on episodic recall, face and verbal recognition, and tests of verbal semantic fluency, and these gender differences in cognitive function are stable over a 10-year period and from ages 35 to 90 years.

One variable that can modify the strength of the female advantage on verbal tests is the levels of ovarian hormones in circulation. Performance of women changes throughout the menstrual cycle as estrogen levels go up and down. Recent work from the University of Western Ontario in London shows that high levels of estrogen are associated with lower performance on some spatial tasks but higher performance on verbal and working memory tasks (Duff & Hampson, 2000; Hampson, 2004).

Visuospatial Abilities

The term *visuospatial abilities* is awkward and hard to define, as previous authors have noted (Halpern, 1992; McGee, 1979; Williams, 1983). Typically, it refers to performance on tasks such as the mental rotation or mental transformation of different objects, shapes, or drawings, maze learning, map reading, throwing accuracy, and even geographical knowledge, in which males outperform females (Kimura, 2002). One task that shows the largest gender difference is mental rotation, shown in Figure 12-10. Over the past 25 years, researchers have reported consistently large (*d* = .90) gender effects on mental rotation tasks (Loring-Meier & Halpern, 1999). On average, males perform better than females, although many individual females can outperform many individual males, even on this task. Work has also shown that performance on mental rotation tests is highly correlated with tests of navigation in both simulated and real-world environments (Galea & Kimura, 1993; Moffat et al, 1998; Saucier et al, 2002).

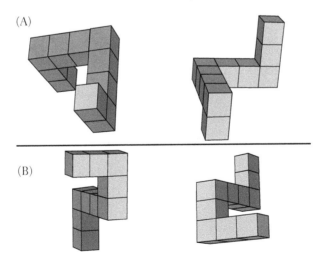

(A)

(B)

FIGURE 12-10 Example of a mental rotation task.

Another test that shows gender differences in children and university-age students is the water-level task, first introduced by Thomas and colleagues (1973). Here, participants are shown a tipped flask, as shown in the illustration in Figure 12-11, and are asked to draw in the waterline. In men the estimation of the angle of the water was about 2% off the horizontal; in women, 69% showed an error of 15% to 20% in their estimations, and failed to note that the waterline would remain horizontal.

Linn and Petersen (1985), who conducted a meta-analysis of gender differences in spatial ability, concluded that the size of the gender difference in mental rotation differs as a function of the specific task. Generally speaking, the more rapid processing of symbolic information required, the larger the gender difference. Mental rotation tasks that involved complex three-dimensional items generally showed larger gender differences than did mental rotation tasks with simpler, two-dimensional items. Linn and Petersen (1985) offered a number of possible reasons for the gender difference; for example, females may rotate items more slowly or may use different strategies in approaching the task.

Male advantage
Spatial relation–type task

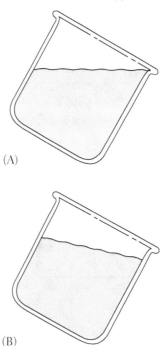

(A)

(B)

FIGURE 12-11 Spatial relation task.

Source: Kolb, B. & Whishaw, I.Q. (1980). *Fundamentals of Human Neurophychology.* © 1980, 1985, 1990, 1996, 2003 by Worth Publishers.

Ultimately, the reasons for a gender difference in spatial ability may be found in biological factors, such as lateralization; socialization factors, such as access to puzzles and video games; or some combination.

Cerebral Organization in Males and Females

Another reason for gender differences may have to do with **neurological differences** in male and female brains. In a review, Levy and Heller (1992) noted that, in general, females tend to have cerebral hemispheres that are less lateralized, or specialized in function, than are the cerebral hemispheres of males. It has long been known in psychology, as we discussed in Chapter 2, that the cerebral hemispheres have slightly different roles to play in our cognitive lives. For most of us (especially right-handed people), verbal fluency, verbal reasoning, and other types of analytical reasoning seem to be governed by left-hemisphere functioning. The right hemisphere, in contrast, seems specialized for understanding spatial relations, art, and music, as well as for interpreting emotional information and carrying out holistic processing. These differing functions across the hemispheres are illustrated in Figure 12-12.

To say that males are more lateralized than females is to say that males show greater asymmetries in the functioning of their two cerebral hemispheres. Females, for example, appear to have language functions represented in both hemispheres, at least to some degree. Related to this, women who suffer left-hemisphere damage often show better recovery of language

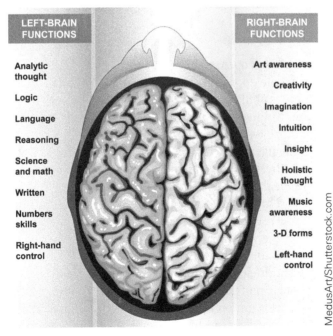

FIGURE 12-12 Brain hemisphere function.

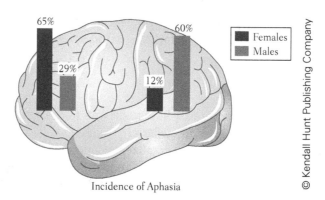

FIGURE 12-13 Aphasias occur more often in females when damage is near the front of the brain. In males, they occur more often when damage is in more posterior regions of the brain (after Kimura, 1992).

functioning than do men with the same type of damage (Levy & Heller, 1992). As well, Kimura has shown that the pattern of cerebral organization within each hemisphere may differ across gender. Aphasia is a speech disorder that occurs following left-hemisphere damage or stroke. As shown in Figure 12-13, aphasia in females occurs most often when damage is near the front of the brain, but in males aphasia is more common when damage is in the posterior, or toward the back of the brain (Kimura, 1992).

SUMMARY

1. Cognition may not always operate the same way for all people. Potential sources of variation in the way people approach the cognitive tasks in their lives include individual differences in cognitive abilities, expertise, bilingualism, as well as age and gender.

2. Individuals apparently differ in their cognitive abilities, especially in such things as mental speed, storage capacity, and attention span. Some psychologists equate these cognitive abilities with intelligence. Other cognitive psychologists do not make this equation but see cognitive abilities as a part of intelligence. Still other psychologists reject the idea that there is one single thing called intelligence.

3. People's expertise can affect the ways in which they approach a cognitive task within their domain of expertise. Experts perceive more distinctions and categorize information differently from the way novices do. Experts can use their domain-related knowledge to chunk information so as to use their memories more effectively

4. Bilingual children and lifelong bilingual adults who use both languages in their daily lives show an advantage on tasks involving attentional control.

5. Age-related deficits in cognition are found on tests of episodic memory, and on short-term or working memory tasks in which information must be re-ordered or manipulated

on-line. Despite declines in these sorts of memory functions, semantic memory, vocabulary levels, and general world knowledge remain intact, and continue to increase over the lifespan.

6. Neuroimaging studies show striking differences in how the brains of young and old achieve performance on cognitive tasks. Older adults show more bilateral brain activation in the frontal lobes, and less activation in occipital lobes; these differences are interpreted as reflecting a heavier reliance on top-down attentional control processes in older adults, to compensate for deficits in bottom-up processing.

7. The common finding is that women outperform men on tasks involving receptive and productive language, and on high-level verbal tasks such as analogies, comprehension of prose, and episodic memory tasks, whereas men outperform women on tasks assessing visuospatial ability. One variable that can modify the strength of the female advantage on verbal tests is the levels of ovarian hormones in circulation, which fluctuate with the menstrual cycle. Gender differences in visuospatial task performance have been shown to vary as a function of children's socioeconomic status.

8. Another reason for gender differences may have to do with neurological differences in male and female brains. Females tend to have cerebral hemispheres that are less lateralized, or specialized in function, than are the cerebral hemispheres of males.

REVIEW QUESTIONS

1. Discuss the reasons why cognitive psychologists need to know about stable individual and/or gender differences in cognition.
2. What cautions must be given in interpreting findings on individual differences in cognition?
3. Explain the logic of a meta-analysis.
4. What are the pros and cons of being a lifelong bilingual person?
5. Discuss age-related changes in brain and cognitive functions. How does brain activity differ during performance of memory tasks between younger and older adults?
6. What is the effect of a head injury to the brain, on language function, in males and females?

KEY TERMS

age differences
bilingual
cognitive neuroscience of
   aging
effect size *(d)*

environmental support
gender differences
individual differences
intelligence
meta-analysis

multiple intelligences (MI)
   theory
neurological differences

Glossary

ablation Removal of cells or tissues, often through surgical means.

affordance A perceptual property of objects, places, and events that makes clear what actions or behaviours on the part of the perceiver are permitted in interaction with the object, place, or event.

age differences A possible reason for differences in performance.

amnesia Profound impairments in the long-term memory

amygdala An area of brain tissue with extensive connections to the olfactory system and hypothalamus, thought to be involved in mood, feeling, instinct, and short-term memory.

anchoring A decision-making heuristic in which final estimates are heavily influenced by initial value estimates.

anterograde amnesia Lack of memory for events that occur after a brain injury.

aphasia A disorder of language, thought to have neurological causes, in which either language production, language reception, or both are disrupted.

artifact Concept pertaining to manufactured or human-designed objects.

artificial intelligence A branch of computer science concerned with creating computers that mimic human performance on cognitive tasks.

association A connection or link between two units or elements.

attention Cognitive resources, mental effort, or concentration devoted to a cognitive process.

attention hypothesis of automatization The proposal that attention is needed during a learning phase of a new task.

attenuation theory A model of attention in which unattended perceptual events are transmitted in weakened form but not blocked completely before being processed for meaning.

autobiographical memory Memory for events and other information from ones own life.

automatic processing The carrying out of a cognitive task with minimal resources. Typically, automatic processing occurs without intention, interferes minimally with other cognitive tasks, and may not involve conscious awareness.

availability heuristic A strategy in which one estimates the frequency or probability of an event by the ease with which mental operations, such as retrieval of examples or construction of examples, can be carried out.

basic level of categories A hypothesized type of concept thought to be at a psychologically fundamental level of abstraction.

behaviourism A school of psychology that seeks to define psychological research in terms of observable measures, emphasizing the scientific study of behaviour.

believability effect The tendency to draw or accept conclusions from premises when the content of the conclusion makes intuitive sense, regardless of the logical necessity.

between-subjects design A research paradigm in which different experimental subjects participate in different experimental conditions.

bias A tendency to think in a certain way or to follow certain procedures regardless of the facts of the matter.

bilingual Describes people who are regularly faced with the task of attending to one set of labels for objects or methods of expression while simultaneously ignoring labels from their other known language depending on the language in which they are trying to communicate.

bottom-up process Cognitive (usually perceptual) process guided by environmental input. Also called "data-driven" process.

brain imaging The construction of pictures of the anatomy and functioning of intact brains through such techniques as computerized axial tomography (CAT, or CT), positron emission tomography (PET), magnetic resonance imaging (MRI), or functional magnetic resonance imaging (fMRI).

Broca's aphasia Also called *expressive* or *motor aphasia*; symptoms of this organic disorder include difficulty in speaking, using grammar, and finding appropriate words.

calibration curve A plot of accuracy against confidence judgments. The more the curve approaches a 45-degree line, the better the "calibration" or "fit" between the two.

capacity The sum total of cognitive resources available at any given time.

CAT scan *See* computerized axial tomography scan.

categorization The organization of information into coherent, meaningful groups.

category A grouping of items sharing one or more similarities.

central executive The proposed component of working memory responsible for directing the flow of information and selecting what information to work with.

cerebellum Part of the brain that controls balance and muscular coordination.

cerebral cortex The surface of the cerebrum, the largest structure of the brain, containing both sensory and motor nerve cell bodies.

change blindness The inability to detect changes to an object or scene, especially when given different views of that object or scene.

chunking The formation of individual units of information into larger units; often used as a means of overcoming short-term-memory limitations.

classical view of concepts The idea that all examples or instances of a concept share fundamental characteristics or features.

clinical interview A research paradigm in which an investigator begins by asking participants a series of open-ended questions but follows up on the responses with specific questions that have been prepared in advance.

coding The form in which information is mentally or internally represented.

cognitive economy A principle of hierarchical semantic networks such that properties and facts about a node are stored at the highest level possible. For example, the fact "is alive" would be stored with the node for "animal" rather than stored with each node under animal, such as "dog," "cat," and the like.

cognitive illusions The systematic biases and errors in human decision making.

cognitive neuropsychology A school of psychology that investigates the cognitive abilities and deficits of people with damaged or otherwise unusual brain structures.

cognitive neuroscience of aging A new domain of research on the relationship between the aging brain and behavioural measures of cognitive performance.

cognitive overload Breakdown of cognitive processing that occurs when the available information exceeds processing capacity

cognitive revolution A movement in psychology that culminated after World War II, characterized by a belief in the empirical accessibility of mental states and events.

cognitive science An interdisciplinary field drawing on research from cognitive psychology, computer science, philosophy, linguistics, neuroscience, and anthropology. The central issues addressed involve the nature of mind and cognition and how information is acquired, stored, and represented.

computer metaphor The basis for the information-processing view of the brain. Different types of psychological processes are thought to be analogous to the workings of a computer processor.

computerized axial tomography (CAT, or CT) scan An imaging technique in which a highly focused beam of X-rays is passed through the body from many different angles. Differing density of the organs of the body result in different deflections of the X-rays, which allows visualization of the organ.

concept A mental representation of a category.

confirmation bias A tendency to seek only information consistent with ones hypothesis.

connectionism An approach to cognition emphasizing parallel processing of information through immense networks of interconnected nodes. Models developed in the connectionist tradition are sometimes declared to share certain similarities with the way collections of neurons operate in the brain; hence, some connectionist models are referred to as *neural networks.*

constructivist approach to perception An understanding of perception as a process requiring the active construction of subjective mental representations not only from perceptual information, but from long-term memory as well.

content effect Performance variability on reasoning tasks that require identical kinds of formal reasoning but are dissimilar in superficial content.

context effect The effect on a cognitive process (for example, perception) of the information surrounding the target object or event. Sometimes called "expectation effect" because the context is thought to set up certain expectations in the mind of the cognitive processor.

contradiction A statement that is false by definition of its form (for example, "A and not-A are both true").

controlled observation A research paradigm in which an observer standardizes the conditions of observation for all participants, often introducing specific manipulations and recording responses.

controlled processing The carrying out of a cognitive task with a deliberate allocation of cognitive resources. Typically, controlled processing occurs on difficult and/or unfamiliar tasks requiring attention and is under conscious control.

corpus callosum The large neural structure containing fibres that connect the right and left cerebral hemispheres.

creativity Cognitive processes that employ appropriate novelty; originality that suits some purpose.

decay A hypothesized process of forgetting in which material is thought to erode, break apart, or otherwise disintegrate or fade.

decision analysis A technology that helps people gather and integrate information in an optimal way.

decision making The process(es) by which an individual selects one course of action from among alternatives.

decision structuring The process(es) by which an individual establishes the criteria and options for consideration.

deductive reasoning Drawing conclusions from only the given premises.

deductive validity A property of some logical arguments such that it is impossible for the premises to be true and the conclusion(s) to be false.

demand characteristic A property of certain tasks such that an experimental subjects behaviour or responses are "cued" by the task itself.

descriptive models of thinking Models that depict the processes people actually use in making decisions or solving problems.

dichotic listening task A task in which a person hears two or more different, specially recorded messages over earphones and is asked to attend to one of them.

direct perception A theory of perception, proposed by James J. Gibson, holding that information in the world is "picked up on" by the cognitive processor without much construction of internal representations or inferences. The emphasis is on direct acquisition of information.

distal stimulus An object, event, or pattern as it exists in the world. Contrast with **proximal stimulus.**

divided attention The ways in which a cognitive processor allocates cognitive resources to two or more tasks that are carried out simultaneously

dual-coding hypothesis Paivios assertion that long-term memory can code information in two distinct ways, verbally and visually, and that items coded both ways (for example, pictures or concrete words) are more easily recalled than items coded in only one way (for example, abstract words).

dual-task performance An experimental paradigm involving presentation of two tasks for a person to work on simultaneously.

echo A sensory memory for auditory stimuli.

ecological approach An approach to the study of cognition emphasizing the natural contexts or settings in which cognitive activities occur, and the influences such settings have in the ways in which cognitive activities are acquired, practised, and executed.

ecological validity A property of research such that the focus of study is something that occurs naturally outside an experimental laboratory.

EEG *See* electroencephalography

effect size *(d)* A measure used in meta-analysis, defined as the difference in mean scores between two groups, divided by the average standard deviation for the two groups.

elaboration A technique to enhance recall.

electroencephalography (EEG) A technique to measure brain activity, specifically, to detect different states of consciousness. Metal electrodes are positioned all over the scalp. The waveforms that are recorded change in predictable ways when the person being recorded is awake and alert, drowsy, asleep, or in a coma.

empiricism A philosophical doctrine emphasizing the role of experience in the acquisition of knowledge.

encoding The cognitive process(es) by which information is translated into a mental or internal representation and stored.

encoding specificity A principle of retrieval asserted by Tulving: At the time material is first put into long-term memory, it is encoded in a particular way, depending on the context present at the time; at the time of recall, the person is at a great advantage if the same information available at encoding is once again available.

environmental support External aids, hints, category headings to help seniors structure their search through memory for the correct response.

episodic memory A memory system proposed by Tulving that is thought to hold memories of specific events with which the cognitive processor had direct experience.

event-related potential (ERP) An electrical recording technique to measure the response of the brain to various stimulus events.

executive functioning Cognitive processes including planning, making decisions, implementing strategies, inhibiting inappropriate behaviours, and using working memory to process information.

exemplar view of concepts The idea that a concept consists of mental representations of actual instances or examples.

exhaustive search A search for information in which each item in a set is examined, even after the target is found.

expected utility theory A normative model of decision making in which the decision maker weights the personal importance and the probabilities of different outcomes in choosing among alternatives in order to maximize overall satisfaction of personal goals.

experiment A test of a scientific theory in which the researcher manipulates the independent variable.

experimental control A property of research such that the causes of different behaviours or other phenomenon can be isolated and tested. Typically, this involves manipulating independent variables and holding constant all factors but the one(s) of interest.

experimenter expectancy effect The influence on the performance of experimental participants generated by an experimenters beliefs or hypotheses, which somehow get subtly transmitted to the participants.

explicit memory Consciously recalled or recollected memory.

expressive aphasia *See* Broca's aphasia.

eyewitness memory A narrative memory of a personally witnessed event.

faculty psychology The theory that different mental abilities, such as reading or computation, are independent and autonomous functions, carried out in different parts of the brain.

fallacy An erroneous argument.

false memory "Recollections" of "events" that never in fact occurred. *See also* **recovered memory.**

family resemblance A structure of categories in which each member shares different features with different members. Few, if any, features are shared by every single member of the category.

fan effect The phenomenon whereby retrieval time to retrieve a particular fact about a concept increases as more facts are known about that concept.

feature A component, or part, of an object, event, or representation.

feature comparison model of semantic memory A model of semantic memory positing that words or concepts are mentally represented in terms of a set of elements called *features.*

feature integration theory A proposal that perception of familiar stimuli occurs in two stages. The first, automatic, stage involves the perception of object features. The second, attentional, stage involves the integration and unification of those features.

filter theory A theory of attention proposing that information that exceeds the capacity of a processor to process at any given time is blocked from further processing.

flashbulb memory A phenomenon in which people recall their personal circumstances (for example, where they were, whom they were with, what they were doing) at the time they heard of or witnessed an unexpected and very significant event (for example, an assassination, a natural disaster).

fMRI *See* functional magnetic resonance imaging.

forebrain The part of the brain containing the thalamus, hypothalamus, hippocampus, amygdala, and the cerebral cortex.

forgetting The processes that prevent information from being retrieved from a memory store.

form perception The process by which the brain differentiates objects from their backgrounds.

framing effect Decision-making bias caused by a propensity to evaluate outcomes as positive or negative changes from their current state.

frontal lobe A division of the cerebral cortex located just beneath the forehead containing the motor cortex, premotor cortex, and the prefrontal cortex.

functional fixedness A problem-solving phenomenon in which people have difficulty seeing alternate uses for common objects.

functional magnetic resonance imaging (fMRI) An imaging technique that uses MRI equipment to examine blood flow in a noninvasive, nonradioactive manner.

functionalism A school of psychology emphasizing questions such as why the mind or a particular cognitive process works the way(s) it does.

gambler's fallacy An erroneous belief that a random process (for example, a coin flip or a spin of a roulette wheel) will automatically keep track of the outcomes in order to make the overall rate of an outcome in the short run equal to the overall rate of that outcome in the long run.

generate-and-test technique A problem-solving strategy in which the solver enumerates (generates) possible solutions and then tries each to see if it constitutes a solution.

gender differences A possible reason for differences in performance.

Gestalt principles of perceptual organization Laws that explain the regularities in the way people come to the perceptual interpretations of stimuli. The emphasis is on the apprehension of whole structures rather on than the detection and assembly of parts of structures.

Gestalt psychology A school of psychology emphasizing the study of whole entities rather than simple elements. Gestalt psychologists concentrate on problems of perception and problem solving and argue that peoples cognitive experience is not reducible to their experience of simple elements (for example, sensations) but, rather, to the overall structure(s) of their experience.

grammar A system of rules that produces well-formed, or "legal," entities, such as sentences of a language.

Gricean maxims of cooperative conversation Pragmatic rules of conversation, including moderation of quantity, quality, relevance, and clarity

heuristic A rule of thumb, or shortcut method, used in thinking, reasoning, and/or decision making.

hindbrain The part of the brain, containing some of the most evolutionarily primitive structures, that is responsible for transmitting information from the spinal cord to the brain, regulating life support functions, and helping to maintain balance.

hindsight bias A tendency to exaggerate the certainty of what could have been anticipated ahead of time.

hippocampus A structure of the brain in the medial temporal lobe; damage or removal can result in amnesia.

human factors engineering An applied area of research that focuses on the design of equipment and technology that is well suited to peoples cognitive capabilities.

hypothalamus A structure in the forebrain that controls the pituitary gland and so-called homeostatic behaviours, such as eating, drinking, temperature control, sleeping, sexual behaviours, and emotional reactions.

icon A sensory memory for visual stimuli.

ill-defined problem A problem that does not have the goals, starting information, and/or legal steps stated explicitly

illusory correlation An association between factors that is not supported by data but seems plausible.

image theory A descriptive theory of decision making that posits that the process consists of two stages: (1) a noncompensatory screening of options against the decision makers image of values and future, in which the number of options is reduced to a very small set, and (2) if necessary, a compensatory choice process.

imaginal scanning A task in which a participant is asked to form a mental image and to scan over it from one point to another.

implicit encoding A principle of imagery that holds mental imagery is used in retrieving information about physical properties of objects, or of physical relationships among objects, that may not have been explicitly encoded.

implicit learning Learning that occurs without explicit awareness of what has been learned.

implicit memory Memory that is not deliberate or conscious but exhibits evidence of prior experience.

inattentional blindness The phenomenon of not perceiving a stimulus that might be literally right in front of you, unless you are paying attention to it.

incidental learning The retention of information even when it is not required of, or even intended by, the processor.

incubation Unconscious processing that works on a specific problem while the mind is otherwise occupied.

individual differences Stable patterns of performance that differ qualitatively and/or quantitatively across individuals.

inductive reasoning Reasoning that involves drawing conclusions that are suggested, but not necessarily true.

inductive strength A property of some logical arguments such that it is improbable (but not impossible) for the premises to be true and the conclusion false.

information processing approach An approach to cognition that uses a computer metaphor in its explanations. Information processing equates cognition with the acquisition, storage, and manipulation of information (for example, what we see, hear, read about, think about) through a system consisting of various storage places and systems of exchange.

informationally encapsulated process A process with the property of informational encapsulation.

intelligence Postulated by some psychologists to represent the sum total of a persons cognitive abilities and resources.

interference A hypothesized process of forgetting in which material is thought to be buried or otherwise displaced by other information but still exists somewhere in a memory store.

introspection A methodological technique in which trained observers are asked to reflect on, and report on, their conscious experience while performing cognitive tasks.

knowledge representation The mental depiction, storage, and organization of information.

knowledge-based view of concepts The idea that concepts function in relation to their instances as a scientific theory does to data supporting it.

language A system of communication that is governed by a system of rules (a grammar) and can express an infinite number of propositions.

lateralization Specialization of function of the two cerebral hemispheres.

late-selection theory A model of attention in which all perceptual messages, whether attended or not, are processed for some meaning.

levels-of-processing theory of memory An alternative to the modal view of memory, proposed by Craik and Lockhart, that postulates that memory depends not on a particular memory store but on the initial processing done to the information at the time of acquisition. "Shallow" or superficial levels of processing (for example, processing at the level of visual shape or acoustic sound) are thought to lead to less retention than "deeper" levels of processing (for example, processing done on the meaning of the information).

lexical ambiguity The idea that some words have different meanings; for example, *bank* can refer to the side of a river or to a financial institution.

lexical decision task A task in which an experimental subject is presented with letter strings and asked to judge, as quickly as possible, if the strings form words.

limited-capacity processor A system that acquires, stores, manipulates, and/or transmits information but has fixed limits on the amount or rate of processing that it can accomplish.

linguistic competence Underlying knowledge that allows a cognitive processor to engage in a particular cognitive activity involving language, independent of behaviour expressing that knowledge. Contrast with **linguistic performance.**

linguistic performance The behaviour or responses actually produced by a cognitive processor engaged in a particular cognitive activity involving language. Contrast with **linguistic competence.**

linguistics A field of study focusing on the structure, use, and acquisition of language.

localization of function The "mapping" of brain areas to different cognitive or motor functions; identifying which neural regions control or are active when different activities take place.

logical connectives Symbols used in logic arguments to form compound propositions. Examples: &, v.

long-term memory (LTM) A memory store thought to have a large, possibly infinite capacity that holds on to incoming information for long periods of time, perhaps permanently. Also called *secondary memory.*

long-term potentiation A process, hypothesized to be a mechanism for long-term learning, in which neural circuits in the hippocampus are subjected to repeated and intense electrical stimulation, resulting in hippocampal cells that are more sensitive to stimuli than they were previously.

magnetic resonance imaging (MRI) A body-imaging technique in which a person is surrounded with a strong magnetic field. Radio waves are directed at a particular part of the body, causing the centres of hydrogen atoms in those structures to align themselves in predictable ways. Computers collate information about how the atoms are aligning and produce a composite three-dimensional image.

means–ends analysis A problem-solving strategy in which the solver compares the goal to the current state, then chooses a step to reduce maximally the difference between them.

medulla oblongata A structure in the hindbrain that transmits information from the spinal cord to the brain and regulates life support functions such as respiration, blood pressure, coughing, sneezing, vomiting, and heart rate.

memory The cognitive processes underlying the storage, retention, and retrieval of information.

memory consolidation The biochemical processes) by which neural synaptic connections are strengthened or weakened.

memory system A kind of memory (for example, episodic memory, semantic memory) that operates on distinct principles and stores a distinct kind of information.

memory trace The mental representation of stored information.

mental models approach to the study of reasoning The idea that reasoning proceeds with general-purpose cognitive processes used in the construction of mental representations.

mental representation An internal depiction of information.

mental rotation A type of visual imagery task in which subjects are asked to form an image of a stimulus and then to imagine how it would look as it rotates around a horizontal or vertical axis.

mental set The tendency to adopt a certain framework, strategy, or procedure based on immediate experience or context.

meta-analysis A technique to review findings in the literature involving the use of specific statistical methods in integrating the findings from different empirical studies.

method of loci A memorization method that requires the learner to visualize an ordered series of physical locations as mnemonic cues for a list of information.

midbrain The part of the brain containing structures that are involved in relaying information between other brain regions, or in regulating levels of alertness.

mnemonics Strategies to facilitate retention and later retrieval of information.

modal model of memory A theoretical approach to the study of memory that emphasizes the existence of different memory stores (for example, sensory memory, short-term memory, long-term memory).

modularity hypothesis Fodor's proposal that some cognitive processes, in particular language and perception, operate on only certain kinds of inputs and operate independent of the beliefs and other information available to the cognitive processor or other cognitive processes.

morpheme The smallest meaningful unit of language.

motor cortex A structure in the frontal lobe that controls fine motor movement in the body.

MRI *See* magnetic resonance imaging.

multiattribute utility theory (MAUT) A normative model of decision making that provides a means of integrating different dimensions and goals of a complex decision. It involves six steps: (a) breaking a decision down into independent dimensions, (b) determining the relative weights of each of those dimensions, (c) listing all the alternatives, (d) ranking all the alternatives along the dimensions, (e) multiplying the rankings by the weightings to determine a final value for each alternative, and (f) choosing the alternative with the highest value.

multiple intelligences (MI) theory Howard Gardners theory that intelligence can be divided into distinct types, including musical, bodily-kinesthetic, logical-mathematical, linguistic, spatial, interpersonal, and intrapersonal intelligences.

nativism A philosophical doctrine emphasizing the role of innate factors in the acquisition of knowledge.

naturalistic observation A research paradigm in which an observer observes participants in familiar, everyday contexts while ideally remaining as unobtrusive as possible.

natural-kind concept Concepts pertaining to naturally occurring substances.

neural network *See* connectionism.

neuroeconomics A new field that examines how the brain interacts with the environment to enable us to make complex decisions.

neurological differences A possible reason for gender differences.

nominal-kind concept Concepts pertaining to ideas or objects that have well-delimited definitions.

nonanalytic concept formation Cognitive processes that implicitly acquire knowledge of a complex structure during the memorization of examples.

normative models of thinking Models that define ideal performance under ideal circumstances in making decisions or solving problems.

occipital lobe A division of the cerebral cortex located at the back of the head that is involved in the processing of visual information.

overconfidence An overly positive judgment of ones own decision-making abilities and performance.

paired associates learning A memory task in which experimental subjects are first presented with a list of pairs of words (for example, *flag-spoon*) and later asked to recall the second word in a pair (for example, *spoon*) when presented with the first (for example, *flag*).

Pandemonium model A model of letter perception based on a bottom-up hierarchy of feature detectors.

paradigm A body of knowledge that selects and highlights certain issues for study. It includes assumptions about how a particular phenomenon ought to be studied and the kinds of experimental methods and measures that are appropriate to use.

parallel search A search for information in which several stores or slots of information are simultaneously examined to match to the target.

parietal lobe A division of the cerebral cortex located at the top rear part of the head; contains the primary somatosensory cortex.

pattern recognition The classification of a stimulus into a category.

percept The outcome of a perceptual process; the meaningful interpretation of incoming information.

perception The interpretation of sensory information to yield a meaningful description or understanding.

perceptual set The tendency to perceive an object or pattern in a certain way, based on ones immediate perceptual experience.

person–machine system The idea that machinery operated by a person must be designed to interact with the operators physical, cognitive, and motivational capacities and limitations.

PET scan *See* positron emission tomography.

phoneme The smallest unit of sound that makes a meaningful difference in a given language.

phonetics The study of speech sounds.

phonological loop The proposed component of working memory responsible for subvocally rehearsing auditory information.

phonology The study of the ways in which speech sounds are combined and altered in language.

phrenology The idea (now discredited) that psychological strengths and weaknesses could be precisely correlated to the relative sizes of different brain areas.

plasticity The ability of some brain regions to "take over" functions of damaged regions.

pons A structure in the hindbrain that acts as a neural relay centre, facilitating the "crossover" of information between the left side of the body and the right side of the brain and vice versa. It is also involved in balance and in the processing of both visual and auditory information.

positron emission tomography (PET) A brain-imaging technique that shows which areas of the brain are most active at a given point in time.

pragmatics The rules governing the social aspects of language.

prefrontal cortex A region in the frontal lobe that is involved with executive functioning.

premise A statement, from which others are inferred, that helps establish what is already known about a problem.

prescriptive models of thinking Models that tell us how we "ought" to make decisions or solve problems but that take into account actual circumstances.

primacy effect The improvement in retention of information learned at the beginning of a task.

primary somatosensory cortex A region in the parietal lobe involved in the processing of sensory information from the body—for example, sensations of pain, pressure, touch, or temperature.

priming The facilitation in responding to one stimulus as a function of prior exposure to another stimulus.

proactive interference A phenomenon in which earlier learned material disrupts the learning of subsequent material.

probability Measurement of a degree of uncertainty, expressed as a number between 0 and 1.

problem solving The cognitive process(es) used in transforming starting information into a goal state, using specified means of solution.

process dissociation framework The idea that memory tasks typically call on a mixture of automatic and intentional cognitive processes.

propositional reasoning Drawing conclusions from premises that are in the form of true or false assertions.

propositional complexity of a sentence The number of underlying distinct ideas in a sentence.

prosopagnosia A specific inability to recognize faces, even very familiar ones, with intact recognition of other objects.

prototype An abstract representation of an idealized member of a class of objects or events.

prototype view of concepts The idea that all concepts are organized around idealized mental representations of examples.

proximal stimulus Reception of information and its registration by a sense organ—for example, retinal images in the case of vision.

psychological essentialism The idea that people possess implicit theories about fundamental characteristics that all instances of a concept contain or embody.

psychological refractory period (PRP) An interval of time following presentation of a first stimulus during which a person cannot respond to a second stimulus, presumably because of a central bottleneck in attentional processing.

quasi-experiment An empirical study that appears to involve some, but incomplete, experimental control—for example, through nonrandom assignment of subjects to conditions.

rationality A property of thinking or decision making such that the processes used are selected with the processor's overall goals and principles in mind.

reasoning Cognitive process(es) used in transforming given information, called *premises*, into conclusions. Reasoning is often seen as a special kind of thinking.

reasoning by analogy Problem solving that employs an analogy between the current problem and another problem that has already been solved.

recall The retrieval of information in which the processor must generate most of the information without aids. *See also* **recognition.**

recency effect The improvement in retention of information learned at the end of a task.

receptive aphasia *See* Wernickes aphasia.

recognition The retrieval of information in which the processor must decide whether the information presented has been previously presented. *See also* **recall.**

recognition-primed decision making A theory of expert decision making that holds that decision makers choose options based on analogy of a given situation with previously encountered situations.

recovered memory Autobiographical memories, usually of traumatic events, that are not accessible for some period of time but later become able to be retrieved. *See also* **false memory.**

rehearsal A mnemonic strategy of repeating information (either aloud or silently) to facilitate retention and later retrieval.

relational-organizational hypothesis The idea that visual imagery aids memory by producing a greater number of associations.

repetition priming Priming that facilitates the cognitive processing of information after a recent exposure to that same information.

representativeness heuristic A belief that outcomes will always reflect characteristics of the process that generated them—for example, an expectation that the outcome of a series of coin flips will always look random.

repressed memory A controversial explanation of amnesia for traumatic events. *See also* **false memory, recovered memory.**

retention duration The amount of time a memory trace remains available for retrieval.

retina A layer of visual receptor cells at the rear of the eyeball.

retinal image A proximal stimulus for vision, consisting of the projection of light waves reflected from stimuli and projected to a surface at the back of the eye.

retrieval The processes by which stored information is brought back to conscious awareness.

retrieval cue A stimulus that helps a person recall or recognize stored information.

retroactive interference A phenomenon in which subsequently learned material lowers the probability of recalling earlier learned material.

retrograde amnesia Amnesia concerning old events.

rules/heuristics approach to the study of reasoning The idea that reasoning proceeds through the application of rules or heuristics, either general or domain specific.

schema An organized framework for representing knowledge that typically includes characters, plots, and settings, and incorporates both general knowledge about the world and information about particular events.

schemata Frameworks for organizing and representing knowledge that contain roles, variables, and fixed parts.

schemata/scripts view of concepts The idea that all concepts are schemata.

selective attention The focusing of cognitive resources on one or a small number of tasks to the exclusion of others.

self-terminating search A search for information that stops when a target is found.

semantic memory A memory system proposed by Tulving that is thought to hold memories of general knowledge.

semantic priming A phenomenon in which exposure to one word (e.g., *nurse*) facilitates the recognition of semantically related words (e.g., *doctor*).

semantics The study of meaning.

sensory memory A memory store thought to hold on to incoming sensory information for very brief periods of time. A different sensory memory store is hypothesized for each sensory system.

serial position effect The phenomenon that items at the beginning or end of a list of items are more easily recalled than are items from the middle of the list.

serial search A search for information in which several stores or slots of information are sequentially examined to match to the target.

short-term memory (STM) A memory store thought to hold on to incoming information for up to 20–30 seconds. Also called "primary memory." It is thought to have a small capacity (up to 7 plus or minus 2 "slots").

size constancy The phenomenon that ones perception of an object remains constant even as the retinal image of the object changes size (for example, because the object has moved closer or farther away from the perceiver).

space around the body The area immediately around a persons body, in which the person can easily perceive and act on objects.

space of navigation Large spaces that people walk through, explore, or travel to and through.

space of the body Awareness of where the different parts of ones body are located at any given moment and what other objects different body parts are interacting with; used, along with internal sensations, to direct different parts of the body spatially

spatial cognition How people represent and navigate in and through space.

spatial cue A cue that directs attention to a particular area in space.

spreading activation The excitation of one node in a semantic network by the excitation of another node to which it is connected; the excitation is said to flow across the connections.

state-dependent learning The phenomenon that recall is easier when the pharmacological state of the person at recall matches his or her pharmacological state during encoding.

state-dependent memory The phenomenon that material is easier to retrieve when the learner is experiencing the same state or context (for example, physical location, physiological state) that she or he was experiencing at the time of encoding. *See also* **encoding specificity.**

storage The mental "holding on" to information between the time it is encoded and the time it is retrieved.

Stroop effect A task invented by J. R. Stroop in which a subject sees a list of words (colour terms) printed in an ink colour that differs from the word named (for example, *green* printed in blue ink). The subject is asked to name the ink colours of the words in the list and demonstrates great difficulty in doing so, relative to a condition in which non-colour words form the stimuli.

structuralism One of the earliest schools of cognitive psychology. It focused on the search for the simplest possible mental elements and the laws governing the ways in which they could be combined.

subjective contour Illusory outline created by certain visual cues that lead to erroneous form perception. The existence of this phenomenon suggests that perception is an active constructive process.

subjective probability An intuitive estimate of the likelihood of occurrence of an event.

subordinate level of categories A hypothesized type of concept thought to make fewer distinctions than does a basic level concept.

subtraction technique The idea that the relative amount of activation in a particular brain region needed for a given cognitive task can be measured by subtracting a control state (responding to a light) from a task state (discriminating colour).

sunk cost effect A bias in decision making in which already "spent" costs unduly influence decisions on whether to continue.

superordinate level of categories A level of categorization broader than the basic level, including exemplars that can be quite dissimilar from one another.

syllogistic reasoning Reasoning with problems concerning relationships among categories; for example, "All A are B; Some B are C; therefore, Some A are C."

syntax The arrangement of words within sentences; the structure of sentences.

tacit knowledge Peoples underlying and implicit beliefs about a task or event.

tautology A statement that is true by definition of its form (for example, "A is either true or it is false").

template A stored pattern or model to which incoming information is matched in order to be recognized and classified.

temporal lobe A division of the cerebral cortex located on the side of the head, involved in the processing of auditory information and in some aspects of memory

thalamus A structure in the forebrain involved in relaying information, especially to the cerebral cortex.

thinking A cognitive process used to transform or manipulate information that may be either focused (that is, solving problems with clear goals) or unfocused (that is, invoking loosely related ideas without clear purpose).

top-down process Cognitive (usually perceptual) process directed by expectations (derived from context, past learning, or both) to form a larger percept, concept, or interpretation. Also called *conceptually driven* or *theory-driven process.*

truth table A method of showing when compound logical expressions are true and when they are false by considering every possible assignment of truth values to propositions.

ultimatum game A task that has informed our understanding of the brain mechanisms underlying decision making.

unconscious processing *See* incubation.

utility A measure of a persons happiness, pleasure, or satisfaction with a particular outcome.

visual agnosia An impairment in the ability to interpret (but not to see) visual information.

visual image A mental representation of a stimulus thought to share at least some properties with a pictorial or spatial depiction of the stimulus.

visual search task A task in which subjects are asked to detect the presence of a particular target against an array of similar stimuli.

visuospatial sketch pad The proposed component of working memory that maintains visual or spatial information.

well-defined problem A problem whose goals, starting information, and legal steps are stated explicitly.

Wernicke's aphasia Also called *receptive* or *sensory aphasia*; symptoms of this organic disorder include difficulty in understanding speech and producing intelligible speech, although speech remains fluent and articulate.

Whorfian hypothesis of linguistic relativity The idea that language constrains thought and perception, so that cultural differences in cognition could be explained at least partially by differences in language.

within-subjects design A research paradigm in which the same experimental subjects participate in different experimental conditions.

word superiority effect The phenomenon that single letters are more quickly identified in the context of words than they are when presented alone or in the context of random letters.

working backward A problem-solving technique that identifies the final goal and the steps, in reverse order, that are necessary to reach the goal.

working memory (WM) A memory structure proposed by Baddeley described as consisting of a limited-capacity work space that can be allocated, somewhat flexibly, into storage space and control processing. It is thought to consist of three components: a central executive, a phonological loop, and a visuospatial sketch pad.

References

Adams, M. J. (1984). Aristotle's logic. In G. H. Bower (Ed.), *The psychology of learning and motivation* (Vol. 18, pp. 255–311). Orlando, FL: Academic Press.

Aginsky, V., & Tarr, M. J. (2002). How are different properties of a scene encoded in visual memory? *Visual Cognition, 7,* 147–162.

Akshoomoff, N. A., & Courchesne, E. (1994). ERP evidence for a shifting attention deficit in patients with damage to the cerebellum. *Journal of Cognitive Neuroscience, 6,* 388–399.

Allen, S., & Brooks, L. (1991). Specializing the operation of an explicit rule. *Journal of Experimental Psychology: General, 120,* 3–19.

Altmann, E. M., & Gray, W. D. (2002). Forgetting to remember: The functional relationship of decay and interference. *Psychological Science, 13,* 27–33.

Altmann, G (1987). Modularity and interaction in sentence processing. In J. L. Garfield (Ed.), *Modularity in knowledge representation and natural language understanding* (pp. 249–257). Cambridge, MA: MIT Press.

Amsel, A. (1989). Behaviorism, neobehaviorism, and cognitivism in learning theory: Historical and contemporary perspectives. Hillsdale, NJ: Erlbaum.

Anderson, J. R., & Bower, G H. (1973). *Human associative memory.* New York: Wiley.

Anderson, J. R., & Reder, L. M. (1999). The Fan Effect: New results and new theories. *Journal of Experimental Psychology: General, 128,* 186–197.

Anderson, M. C, & Neely J. H. (1996). Interference and inhibition in memory retrieval. In E. L. Bjork & R. A. Bjork (Eds.), *Memory* (pp. 237–313). San Diego, CA: Academic Press.

Anderson, N. D., Iidaka, T., Cabeza, R., Kapur, S., McIntosh, A. R., & Craik, F. I. M. (2000). The effects of divided attention on encoding- and retrieval-related brain activity: A PET study of younger and older adults. *Journal of Cognitive Neuroscience, 12,* 775–792.

Arbuthnott, K. D. (2005). The effect of repeated imagery on memory. *Applied Cognitive Psychology, 19,* 843–866.

Arbuthnott, K. D., Arbuthnott, D. W., & Rossiter, L. (2001). Guided imagery and memory: Implications for psychotherapists. *Journal of Counselling Psychology, 48,* 123–132.

Arbuthnott, K. D., Geelen, C, & Kealy K. L. (2002). Phenomenal characteristics of guided imagery, natural imagery, and autobiographical memories. *Memory & Cognition, 30,* 519–528.

Arkes, H. R. (1986). Impediments to accurate clinical judgment and possible ways to minimize their impact. In H. R. Arkes & K. R. Hammond (Eds.), *Judgment and decision making* (pp. 582–592). Cambridge, UK: Cambridge University Press.

Arkes, H. R., & Blumer, C. (1985). The psychology of sunk cost. *Organizational Behavior and Human Decision Processes, 35,* 124–140.

Arkes, H. R., & Hutzel, L. (2000). The role of probability of success estimates in the sunk cost effect. *Journal of Behavioral Decision Making, 13,* 295–306.

Armstrong, S. L., Gleitman, L. R., & Gleitman, H. (1983). What some concepts might not be. *Cognition, 13,* 263–308.

Ashcraft, M. H. (1978). Property norms for typical and atypical items from 17 categories: A description and discussion. *Memory and Cognition, 6,* 227–232.

Atkinson, R. C, & Shiffrin, R. M. (1968). Human memory: A proposed system and its control processes. InK. W. Spence & J. T. Spence (Eds.), *The psychology of learning and motivation: Advances in research and theory* (Vol. 2, pp. 89–195). New York: Academic Press.

Averbach, E., & Coriell, A. S. (1961). Short-term memory in vision. *Bell System Technical Journal, 40,* 309–328.

Ayduk, O., Mischel, W., & Downey, G. (2002). Attentional mechanisms linking rejection to hostile reactivity: The role of "hot" versus "cool" focus. *Psychological Science, 13,* 443–448.

Baddeley, A. D. (1966a). The influence of acoustic and semantic similarity on long-term memory for word sequences. *Quarterly Journal of Experimental Psychology, 18,* 302–309.

Baddeley A. D. (1966b). Short-term memory for word sequences as a function of acoustic, semantic, and formal similarity. *Quarterly Journal of Experimental Psychology, 18,* 362–365.

Baddeley, A. D. (1976). *The psychology of memory.* New York: Basic Books.

Baddeley, A. D. (1978). The trouble with levels: A re-examination of Craik and Lockharts framework for memory research. *Psychological Review, 85,* 139–152.

Baddeley, A. D. (1981). The concept of working memory: A view of its current state and probable future development. *Cognition, 10,* 17–23.

Baddeley, A.D. (1984). Neuropsychological evidence and the semantic/episodic distinction. *Behavioral and Brain Sciences, 7,* 238–239.

Baddeley, A. D. (1986). *Working memory.* New York: Oxford University Press.

Baddeley, A. D. (1990). *Human memory: Theory and practice.* Boston: Allyn & Bacon.

Baddeley, A. [D.] (1992). Is working memory working? *Quarterly Journal of Experimental Psychology, 44A,* 1–31.

Baddeley, A. [D.] (1993a). Working memory and conscious awareness. In A. F. Collins, S. E. Gathercole, M. A. Conway & P. E. Morris (Eds.), *Theories of memory* (pp. 11–28). Hove, UK: Erlbaum.

Baddeley, A. [D.] (1993b). *Your memory: A user's guide.* London: Multimedia Books.

Baddeley, A. (2000). *The episodic buffer: a new component of working memory?* Trends in cognitive sciences, 4(11), 417–423.

Baddeley, A. D. (2002). *Human Memory: Theory and Practice, Revised Edition.* East Sussex, UK: Psychology Press Ltd.

Baddeley, A. (2012). *Working Memory: Theories, Models, and Controversies,* Annual Review of Psychology 63:1, 1–29

Baddeley, A. D., & Hitch, G. J. (1974). Working memory. In G A. Bower (Ed.), *The psychology of learning and motivation* (Vol. 8, pp. 47–90). New York: Academic Press.

Baddeley, A. D., & Wilson, B. A. (2002). Prose recall and amnesia: Implications for the structure of working memory. *Neuropsychologia, 40,* 1737–1743.

Bahrick, H. P. (1983). The cognitive map of a city: Fifty years of learning and memory. In G. H. Bower (Ed.), *The psychology of learning and motivation* (Vol. 17, pp. 125–163). New York: Academic Press.

Bahrick, H. P. (1984). Semantic memory content in perma-store: Fifty years of memory for Spanish learned in school. *Journal of Experimental Psychology: General, 113,* 1–29.

Baldwin, J. M. (1895). *Mental Development in the Child and the Race: Methods and Processes.* New York: Macmillan & Co.

Baltes, P. B., Staudinger, U. M., & Lindenberger, U. (1999). Lifespan psychology: Theory and application to intellectual functioning. *Annual review of psychology, 50,* 471–507.

Bandura, A. (2001). Social cognitive theory: An agentic perspective. *Annual Review of Psychology, 52,* 1–26.

Banich, M. T. (1997). Neuropsychology: The neural base of mental function. New York: Houghton Mifflin.

Banich, M. T. (2004). *Cognitive neuroscience and neuropsychology* (2nd ed.). Boston: Houghton Mifflin.

Barkley R. A. (1998). Attention-deficit hyperactivity disorder: A handbook for diagnosis and treatment (2nd ed.). New York: Guilford.

Barnes, J. M., & Underwood, B. J. (1959). "Fate" of first-list associations in transfer theory. *Journal of Experimental Psychology, 58,* 97–105.

Baron, J. (1988). *Thinking and deciding.* Cambridge, UK: Cambridge University Press.

Baron, J. (1994). *Thinking and deciding* (2nd ed.). Cambridge, UK: Cambridge University Press.

Baron, J. (2000). *Thinking and deciding* (3rd ed.). Cambridge: Cambridge University Press.

Barr, N., Pennycook, G., Stolz, J.A., & Fugelsang, J.A. (2015). Reasoned connections: A dual-process perspective on the role of analytic processing in creative thought. *Thinking & Reasoning (Special Issue: Creativity and Insight Problem Solving), 21,* 61–75.

Barsalou, L. W. (1983). Ad hoc categories. *Memory and Cognition, 11,* 211–227.

Barsalou, L. W. (1985). Ideals, central tendency, and frequency of instantiation as determinants of graded structure in categories. *Journal of Experimental Psychology: Learning, Memory, and Cognition, 11,* 629–654.

Barsalou, L. W. (1987). The instability of graded structure: Implications for the nature of concepts. In U. Neisser (Ed.), *Concepts and conceptual development* (pp. 101–140). New York: Cambridge University Press.

Bartlett, F C. (1932). *Remembering: A study in experimental and social psychology.* Cambridge, UK: Cambridge University Press.

Bartlett, F [C] (1958). *Thinking: An experimental and social study.* New York: Basic Books.

Bartlett, J. C, Leslie, J. E., Tubbs, A., & Fulton, A. (1989). Aging and memory for pictures of faces. *Psychology and Aging, 109,* 4(3), 276–283.

Barton, M. E., & Komatsu, L. K. (1989). Defining features of natural kinds and artifacts. *Journal of Psycholinguistic Research, 18,* 433–447.

Bass, E., & Davis, L. (1988). The courage to heal: A guide for women survivors of child sexual abuse. New York: Harper & Row.

Bates, E., Devescovi, A., & Wulfeck, B. (2001). Psycholinguistics: A cross-language perspective. *Annual Review of Psychology, 52,* 639–696.

Beach, L. R. (1993). Broadening the definition of decision-making: The role of prechoice screening of options. *Psychological Science, 4,* 215–220.

Beach, L. R., & Mitchell, T. R. (1987). Image theory: Principles, goals, and plans in decision-making. *Acta Psychologica, 66,* 201–220.

Beirness, D. J., Simpson, H. M., & Desmond, K. (2002). *Risky Driving: Road Safety Monitor 2002.* Traffic Injury Research Foundation (TIRF), Ottawa.

Bekoff, M., & Allen, C. (2002). The evolution of social play: Interdisciplinary analyses of cognitive processes. In M. Bekoff, C. Allen, & G. M. Burghardt (Eds.), *The cognitive animal: Empirical and theoretical perspectives on animal cognition* (pp. 429–436). Cambridge, MA: MIT Press.

Belleville, S., Rouleau, N., & Caza, N. (1998). Effect of normal aging on the manipulation of information in working memory. *Memory & Cognition, 26*(3), 572–583.

Besner, D., & Stolz, J. A. (1999). Unconsciously controlled processing: The Stroop effect reconsidered. *Psychonomic Bulletin & Review,* 449–455.

Bialystok, E., Craik, F. I. M., & Ryan, J. (2006). Executive control in a modified antisaccade task: Effects of aging and bilingualism. *Journal of Experimental Psychology: Learning Memory and Cognition, 32,* 1341–1354.

Bialystok, E. (2001). *Bilingualism in development: Language, literacy, & cognition.* Cambridge: Cambridge University Press.

Bialystok, E., & Martin, M. M. (2004). Attention and inhibition in bilingual children: Evidence from the dimensional change card sort task. *Developmental Science, 7,* 325–339.

Bialystok, E., & Shapero, D. (2005). Ambiguous benefits: The effect of bilingualism on reversing ambiguous figures. *Developmental Science, 8,* 595–604.

Bialystok, E., Craik, F. I. M., Klein, R., & Viswanathan, M. (2004). Bilingualism, aging, and cognitive control: Evidence from the Simon Task. *Psychology and Aging, 19,* 290–303.

Bialystok, E., Craik, F. I. M., & Freedman, M. (2007). Bilingualism as a protection against the onset of symptoms of dementia. *Neuropsychologia, 45,* 459–464.

Biederman, I., & Gerhardstein, P. C. (1993). Recognizing depth-rotated objects: Evidence and conditions for three-dimensional viewpoint invariance. *Journal of Experimental Psychology: Human Perception and Performance, 19,* 1162–1182.

Biederman, I., Glass, A. L., & Stacy, E. W., Jr. (1973). Searching for objects in real-world scenes. *Journal of Experimental Psychology, 97,* 22–27'.

Bierwisch, M. (1970). Semantics. In J. Lyons (Ed.), *New horizons in linguistics* (pp. 166–184). Baltimore: Penguin Books.

Black, I. B. (2004). Plasticity: Introduction. In M. S. Gazzaniga (Ed.), *The cognitive neurosciences* (3rd ed., pp. 107–109). Cambridge, MA: MIT Press.

Blair, M., & Homa, D. (2001). Expanding the search for a linear separability constraint on category learning. *Memory & Cognition, 29,* 1153–1164.

Bloom, A. H. (1981). *The linguistic shaping of thought: A study in the impact of language on thinking in China and the West.* Hillsdale, NJ: Erlbaum.

Bopp, K. L., & Verhaeghen, P. (2005). Aging and verbal memory span: A meta-analysis. *Journal of Gerontology: Series B: Psychological Sciences and Social Sciences, 60B*(5), 223–P233.

Borowsky R., Loehr, J., Friesen, C. K., Kraushaar, G, Kingstone, A., & Sarty G. E. (2005). Modularity and intersection of What', Where', and How' processing of visual stimuli: A new method of fMRI localization. *Brain Topography: Journal of Functional Neurophysiology, 18,* 67–75.

Bousfield, W. A. (1953). The occurrence of clustering in recall of randomly arranged associates. *Journal of General Psychology, 49,* 229–240.

Bower, G H. (1970a). Analysis of a mnemonic device. *American Scientist, 58,* 496–510.

Bower, G H. (1970b). Imagery as a relational organizer in associative learning. *Journal of Verbal Learning and Verbal Behavior, 9,* 529–533.

Bower, G H., Black, J. B., & Turner, T. J. (1979). Scripts in memory for text. *Cognitive Psychology, 11,* 177–220.

Bower, G. H., & Karlin, M. B. (1974). Depth of processing pictures of faces and recognition memory. *Journal of Experimental Psychology, 103,* 751–757.

Braine, M. D. S. (1978). On the relation between the natural logic of reasoning and standard logic. *Psychological Review, 85,* 1–21.

Braine, M. D. S. (1990). The "natural logic" approach to reasoning. In W. F. Overton (Ed.), *Reasoning, necessity, and logic: Developmental perspectives* (pp. 133–157). Hillsdale, NJ: Erlbaum.

Braine, M. D. S., Reiser, B., & Rumain, B. (1984). Some empirical justification for a theory of natural propositional logic. In G. H. Bower (Ed.), *The psychology of learning and motivation* (Vol. 18, pp. 313–371). Orlando, FL: Academic Press.

Bransford, J. D., & Franks, J. J. (1971). Sentence memory: A constructive versus interpretive approach. *Cognitive Psychology, 3,* 331–350.

Bransford, J. D., & Johnson, M. K. (1972). Contextual prerequisites for understanding: Some investigations of comprehension and recall. *Journal of Verbal Learning and Verbal Behavior, 11,* 717–726.

Brenner, L., Griffin, D., & Koehler, D. J. (2005). Modeling patterns of probability calibration with Random Support Theory: Diagnosing case-based judgment. *Organizational Behavior and Human Decision Processes, 97,* 64–81.

Brewer, W. L. (1988). Memory for randomly sampledautobiographical events. In U. Neisser & E. Winograd (Eds.), *Remembering reconsidered: Ecological and traditional approaches to the study of memory* (pp. 21–90). New York: Cambridge University Press.

Briand, K. A., & Klein, R. M. (1989). Has feature integration theory come unglued? A reply to Tsal. *Journal of Experimental Psychology: Human Perception and Performance, 15,* 401–406.

Briggs, G. E. (1954). Acquisition, extinction, and recovery functions in retroactive inhibition. *Journal of Experimental Psychology, 47,* 285–293.

Broadbent, D. E. (1958). *Perception and communication.* New York: Pergamon Press.

Brooks, L. R. (1968). Spatial and verbal components of the act of recall. *Canadian Journal of Psychology, 22,* 349–368.

Brooks, L. R. (1978). Nonanalytic concept formation and memory for instances. In E. Rosch & B. B. Lloyd (Eds.), *Cognition and categorization* (pp. 169–211). Hillsdale, NJ: Erlbaum.

Brooks, L. R. (1987). Decentralized control of categorization: The role of prior processing episodes. In U. Neisser (Ed.), *Concepts and conceptual development: Ecological and intellectual factors in categorization* (pp. 141–174). Cambridge, UK: Cambridge University Press.

Brooks, L., & Vokey J. (1991). Abstract analogies and abstracted grammars: Comments on Reber (1989) and Mathews et al. (1989). *Journal of Experimental Psychology: General, 120,* 316–323.

Brown, E. L., & Deffenbacher, K (1979). *Perception and the senses.* New York: Oxford University Press.

Brown, J. (1958). Some tests of the decay theory of immediate memory. *Quarterly Journal of Experimental Psychology, 10,* 12–21.

Brown, R., & Hanlon, C. (1970). Derivational complexity and order of acquisition in child speech. In J. R. Hayes (Ed.), *Cognition and the development of language* (pp. 11–53). New York: Wiley.

Brown, R., & Kulik, J. (1977). Flashbulb memories. *Cognition, 5,* 73–99.

Browne, B. A., & Cruse, D. F. (1988). The incubation effect: Illusion or illumination? *Human Performance, 1,* 177–185.

Bruner, J. S. (1957). Going beyond the information given. In Colorado University Psychology Department (Eds.), *Contemporary approaches to cognition* (pp. 41–69). Cambridge, MA: Harvard University Press.

Bruner, J. S., Goodnow, J. J., & Austin, G. A. (1956). *A study of thinking.* New York: Wiley.

Bub, D. N. (2000). Methodological issues confronting PET and fMRI studies of cognitive function. *Cognitive Neuropsychology, 17,* 467–484.

Bugelski, B. R., Kidd, E., & Segmen, J. (1968). Image as a mediator in one-trial paired associate learning. *Journal of Experimental Psychology, 76,* 69–73.

Cabeza, R., Bruce, V., Kato, T, & Oda, M. (1999). The prototype effect in face recognition: Extensions and limits. *Memory & Cognition, 27,* 139–151.

Cabeza, R., & Nyberg, L. (2000). Imaging cognition II: An empirical review of 275 PET and fMRI studies. *Journal of Cognitive Neuroscience, 12,* 1–47.

Cabeza, R., Nyberg, L., & Park, D. C. (Eds.). (2016). Cognitive neuroscience of aging: Linking cognitive and cerebral aging. Oxford University Press.

Cabeza, R., Anderson, N., Locantore, J. K, & McIntosh, A. R. (2002). Aging gracefully: Compensatory brain activity in high-performing older adults. *NeuroImage, 17,* 1394–1402.

Cabeza, R., Grady C. L., Nyberg, L., McIntosh, A. R., Tulving, E., Kapur, S., Jennings, J. M., Houle, S., & Craik, F. I. M. (1997). Age-related differences in neural activity during memory encoding and retrieval: A positron emission tomography study. *Journal of Neuroscience, 17,* 391–400.

Cabeza, R., Rao, S. M., Wagner, A. D., Mayer, A. M., & Schacter, D. L. (2001). Can medial temporal lobe regions distinguish true from false? An event related functional MRI study of veridical and illusory recognition memory. *Proceedings of the National Academy of Sciences, 98,* 4805–4810.

Cahill, L., & McGaugh, J. L. (1995). A novel demonstration of enhanced memory associated with emotional arousal. *Consciousness & Cognition, 4,* 410–421.

Campbell, D. T., & Stanley, J. C. (1963). *Experimental and quasi-experimental designs for research.* Chicago: Rand McNally

Caplan, D. (1994). Language and the brain. In M. A. Gernsbacher (Ed.), *Handbook of psycholinguistics* (pp. 1023–1053). San Diego, CA: Academic Press.

Carlson, L., Zimmer, J. W., & Glover, J. A. (1981). First-letter mnemonics: DAM (Don't Aid Memory). *Journal of General Psychology, 104,* 287–292.

Carlson, N. R. (1994). *Physiology of behavior* (5th ed.). Boston: Allyn & Bacon.

Carlson, N. R. (2004). *Physiology and behavior* (8th ed.). Boston: Allyn & Bacon.

Carmichael, L., Hogan, H. P., & Walter, A. A. (1932). An experimental study of the effect of language on the reproduction of visually perceived form. *Journal of Experimental Psychology, 15,* 73–86.

Casat, C. D., Pearson, D. A., & Casat, J. P. (2001). Attention-deficit/hyperactivity disorder. In H. B. Vance & A. Pumariega (Eds.), *Clinical assessment of child and adolescent behavior* (pp. 263–306). New York: Wiley

Casey, B. J., Giedd, J. N., & Thomas, K. M. (2000). Structural and functional brain development and its relation to cognitive development. *Biological Psychology, 54,* 241–257.

Catani, M., Jones, D. K., & Ffytche, D. H. (2005). Perisylvian language networks of the human brain. *Annuals of Neurology, 57,* 8–16.

Catrambone, R., & Holyoak, K. J. (1989). Overcoming contextual limitations on problem-solving transfer. *Journal of Experimental Psychology: Learning, Memory, and Cognition, 15,* 1147–1156.

Ceraso, J., & Provitera, A. (1971). Sources of error in syllogistic reasoning. *Cognitive Psychology, 2,* 400–410.

Cermak, L. S. (2014). Memory as a processing continuum. In New Directions in Memory and Aging (PLE: Memory): Proceedings of the George A. Talland Memorial Conference (Vol. 22, p. 261). Psychology Press.

Chambers, D., & Reisberg, D. (1992). What an image depicts depends on what an image means. *Cognitive Psychology, 24,* 145–174.

Charness, N., Reingold, E. M., Pomplun, M., & Stampe, D. M. (2001). The perceptual aspect of skilled performance in chess: Evidence from eye movements. *Memory and Cognition, 29,* 1146–1152.

Chase, W. G, & Simon, H. A. (1973). Perception in chess. *Cognitive Psychology, 4,* 55–81.

Cheng, P. W., & Holyoak, K. J. (1985). Pragmatic reasoning schemas. *Cognitive Psychology, 17,* 391–416.

Cheng, P. W., Holyoak, K. J., Nisbett, R. E., & Oliver, L. M. (1986). Pragmatic versus syntactic approaches to training deductive reasoning. *Cognitive Psychology, 18,* 293–328.

Cherry, E. C. (1953). Some experiments on the recognition of speech, with one and two ears. *Journal of the Acoustical Society of America, 25,* 975–979.

Chi, M. T. H., Feltovich, P. J., & Glaser, R. (1981). Categorization and representation of physics problems by experts and novices. *Cognitive Science, 5,* 121–125.

Chi, M. T. H., Glaser, R., & Farr, M. (Eds.). (1988). *The nature of expertise.* Hillsdale, NJ: Erlbaum.

Chomsky, N. (1957). *Syntactic structures.* The Hague: Mouton.

Chomsky, N. (1959). A review of Skinners *Verbal Behavior. Language, 35,* 26–58.

Chomsky, N. (1965). *Aspects of the theory of syntax.* Cambridge, MA: MIT Press.

Christiansen, M. H., & Chater, N. (Eds.) (2001). *Connectionist psycholinguistics.* Westport, CT Ablex.

Christianson, S. A. (1992). Emotional stress and eyewitness memory: A critical review. *Psychological Bulletin, 112,* 284–309.

Clark, H. H., & Clark, E. V. (1977). *Psychology and language.* New York: Harcourt Brace Jovanovich.

Clark, H. H., & Van Der Wege, M. M. (2002). Psycholinguistics. In H. Pashler (Series Ed.) & D. Medin (Vol. Ed.), *Stevens' handbook of experimental psychology* (3rd ed.): *Vol. 2. Memory and cognitive processes* (pp. 209–259). New York: Wiley.

Cohen, J. (1969). *Statistical power analysis for the behavioral sciences.* New York: Academic Press.

Cohen, N. J. (1997). Memory. In M. T. Banich (Ed.), *Neuropsychology: The neural base of mental function* (pp. 314–367). New York: Houghton Mifflin.

Cohen, N. J., & Eichenbaum, H. (1993). *Memory, amnesia, and the hippocampal system.* Cambridge, MA: MIT Press.

Colcombe S. J., Erickson, K. I., Scalf, P. E., Kim, J. S., Prakash, R., McAuley E., Elavsky S., Marquez,

D. X., Hu, L., Kramer, A. F. (2006). Aerobic exercise training increases brain volume in aging humans. *J Gerontol A Biol Sci Med Sci., 61*(11), 1166–70.

Collins, A. M., & Quillian, M. R. (1969). Retrieval time from semantic memory. *Journal of Verbal Learning and Verbal Behavior, 8,* 240–247.

Coltheart, M. (1980). Iconic memory and visible persistence. *Perception and Psychophysics, 27,* 183–228.

Conrad, R. (1964). Acoustic confusion in immediate memory. *British Journal of Psychology, 55,* 75–84.

Conway A. R. A., Cowan, N., & Bunting, M. F. (2001). The cocktail party phenomenon revisited: The importance of working memory capacity. *Psychonomic Bulletin and Review, 8,* 331–335.

Conway, M. A., Anderson, S. J., Larsen, S. F., Donnelly, C. M., McDaniel, M. A., McClelland, A. G. R., Rawls, R. E., & Logie, R. H. (1994). The formation of flash bulb memories. *Memory and Cognition, 22,* 326–343.

Cooper, L. A. (1975). Mental rotation of random twodimensional shapes. *Cognitive Psychology, 7,* 20–43.

Cooper, L. A. (1976). Demonstration of a mental analog of an external rotation. *Perception and Psychophysics, 19,* 296–302.

Cooper, L. A., & Shepard, R. N. (1973). The time required to prepare for a rotated stimulus. *Memory and Cognition, 1,* 246–250.

Cooper, L. A., & Shepard, R. N. (1975). Mental transformations in the identification of left and right hands. *Journal of Experimental Psychology: Human Perception and Performance, 1,* 48–56.

Cosmides, L. (1989). The logic of social exchange: Has natural selection shaped how humans reason? Studies with the Wason selection task. *Cognition, 31,* 187–276.

Cosmides, L., & Tooby J. (2000). The cognitive neuroscience of social reasoning. In M. S. Gazzaniga (Ed.), *The new cognitive neurosciences* (pp. 1259–1270). Cambridge, MA: MIT Press.

Cosmides, L., & Tooby, J. (2002). Unraveling the enigma of human intelligence: Evolutionary psychology and the multimodular mind. In R. J. Stern-berg & J. C. Kaufman (Eds.), *The evolution ofintelligence* (pp. 145–198). Mahwah, NJ: Erlbaum.

Cowper, E. A. (1992). A concise introduction to syntactic theory: The government binding approach. Chicago: University of Chicago Press.

Craik, F. I. M. (1986). A functional account of age differences in memory. In F. Klix & H. Hagendorf (Eds.). *Human memory and cognitive abilities, mechanisms and performances* (pp. 409–422). Amsterdam: Elsevier

Craik, F. I. M., & Byrd, M. (1982). Aging and cognitive deficits: The role of attentional resources. In F. I. M. Craik & S. Trehub (Eds.), *Aging and cognitive processes* (pp. 191–211). New York: Plenum.

Craik, F. I. M., & Lockhart, R. S. (1972). Levels of processing: A framework for memory research. *Journal of Verbal Learning and Verbal Behavior, 11,* 671–684.

Craik, F. I. M., & McIntyre, J. S. (1987). Age differences for item and source information. *Canadian Journal of Psychology. Special Issue: Aging and Cognition, 41*(2), 175–192.

Craik, F. I. M., & Tulving, E. (1975). Depth of processing and retention of words in episodic memory. *Journal of Experimental Psychology: General, 104,* 268–294.

Crowder, R. G. (1976). *Principles of learning and memory.* Hillsdale, NJ: Erlbaum.

Cuenod, C. A., Bookheimer, S. Y, Hertz-Pannier, L., Zeffiro, T. A., Theodore, W. H., & LeBihan, D. (1995). Functional MRI during word generation, using conventional equipment: A potential tool for language localization in the clinical environment. *Neurology, 45,* 1821–1827.

Damer, T. E. (1980). *Attacking faulty reasoning* (2nd ed.). Belmont, CA: Wadsworth.

Daneman, M., & Carpenter, P. A. (1980). Individual differences in working memory and reading. *Journal of Verbal Learning and Verbal Behavior, 19,* 450–466.

Daneman, M., & Hannon, B. (2001). Using working memory theory to investigate the construct validity of multiple-choice reading comprehension tests such as the SAT. *Journal of Experimental Psychology: General, 130,* 208–223.

Dartnall, T. (2002) (Ed.), *Creativity, cognition, and knowledge: An interaction.* Westport, CT Praeger

Daselaar, S. M., Veltman, D. J., Rombout, S. A., Raaijmakers, J. G, & Jonker, C. (2003). Deep processing activates the medial temporal lobe in young but not in old adults. *Neurobiology & Aging, 24,* 1005–1011.

Dawes, R. M. (1982). The robust beauty of improper linear models in decision making. In D. Kahneman, P. Slovic, & A. Tversky (Eds.), *Judgment under uncertainty: Heuristics and biases* (pp. 391–407). Cambridge, UK: Cambridge University Press.

Dawes, R. M., & Corrigan, B. (1974). Linear models in decision making. *Psychological Bulletin, 81,* 95–106.

Dawson, M. R. W. (1998). *Understanding cognitive science.* Malden, MA: Blackwell.

de Frias, C. M., Nilsson L. G., Herlitz, A. (2006). Sex differences in cognition are stable over a 10-year period in adulthood and old age. *Neuropsychol Dev Cogn B Aging Neuropsychol Cogn., 13*(3–4), 574–87.

De Groot, A. D. (1965). *Thought and choice in chess.* The Hague: Mouton.

De Groot, A. M. B., & Kroll, J. F. (Eds.). (1997). *Tutorials in bilingualism: Psycholinguistic perspectives.* Mahwah, NJ: Erlbaum.

Demakis, G J. (2002). Hindsight bias and the Simpson trial: Use in introductory psychology. In R. A. Griggs (Ed.), *Handbook for teaching introductory psychology: Vol. 3: With an emphasis on assessment* (pp. 242–243). Mahwah, NJ: Erlbaum.

Demers, R. A. (1988). Linguistics and animal communication. In F. J. Newmeyer (Ed.), *Linguistics: The Cambridge survey: Vol. 3. Language: Psychological and biological aspects* (pp. 314–335). Cambridge, UK: Cambridge University Press.

Demetriou, A., Christou, C, Spanoudis, G, & Platsi-dou, M. (2002). The development of mental processing: Efficiency, working memory, and thinking. *Mongraphs of the Society for Research in Child Development, 67,* 1–169.

Deutsch, J. A., & Deutsch, D. (1963). Attention: Some theoretical considerations. *Psychological Re-view, 70,* 80–90.

Di Lollo, V., Enns, J. T, & Rensink, R. A. (2000). Competition for consciousness among visual events: The psychophysics of reentrant visual pathways. *Journal of Experimental Psychology: General, 129,* 481–507.

Dixon, M., Bub, D. N., & Arguin, M. (1997). The interaction of object form and object meaning in the identification performance of a patient with category-specific visual agnosia. *Cognitive Neuropsychology, 14,* 1085–1130.

Dixon, M. J. (2000). A new paradigm for investigating category-specific agnosia in the new millennium. *Brain and Cognition, 42,* 142–145.

Dixon, M. J., Smilek, D., & Merikle, P. M. (2004). Not all synaesthetes are created equal: Projector versus associator synaesthetes. *Cognitive, Affective & Behavioral Neuroscience, 4*(3), 335–343.

Dixon, R. A., & de Frias, C. M. (2007). Mild memory deficits differentially affect 6-year changes in compensatory strategy use. *Psychology & Aging, 22,* 632–638.

Dixon, R. A., Simon, E. W., Nowak, C. A., & Hultsch, D. F. (1982). Text recall in adulthood as a function of level of information, input modality, and delay interval. *Journal of Gerontology, 37,* 358–364.

Donders, F. C. (1868; 1969). On the speed of mental processes. *Acta Psychologica, 30,* 412–431.

Dunbar, K., & Blanchette, I. (2001). The invivo/invitro approach to cognition: The case of analogy. *Trends in Cognitive Sciences, 5,* 334–339.

Duncker, K. (1945). On problem-solving. *Psychological Monographs, 58*(Whole No. 270).

Duff, S. J., & Hampson, E. (2000). A beneficial effect of estrogen on working memory in postmenopausal women taking hormone replacement therapy. *Hormones and Behavior, 38,* 262–276.

Ebbinghaus, H. (1913). *Memory: A contribution to experimental psychology* (H. A. Ruger & C. E. Bussenius, Trans.). New York: Columbia University, Teachers College. (Original work published 1885)

Edwards, K., & Smith, E. E. (1996). A disconfirmation bias in the evaluation of arguments. *Journal of Personality and Social Psychology, 71,* 5–24.

Egan, D. E., & Greeno, J. G. (1974). Theory of rule induction: Knowledge acquired in concept learning, serial pattern learning, and problem solving. In L. W. Gregg (Ed.), *Knowledge and cognition* (pp. 43–103). Potomac, MD: Erlbaum.

Eich, J. E. (1980). The cue-dependent nature of state-dependent retention. *Memory and Cognition, 8,* 157–173.

Eimas, P. D. (1985). The perception of speech in early infancy. *Scientific American, 204,* 66–72.

Ellard, C. G., & Shaughnessy S. C. (2003). A comparison of visual and nonvisual sensory inputs to walked distance in a blind-walking task. *Perception, 32,* 567–578.

Ellis, A. W., & Young, A. W. (1988). *Human cognitive neuropsychology.* Hillsdale, NJ: Erlbaum.

Engle, R. (2002). Working memory capacity as executive attention. *Current Directions in Psychological Science, 11*(1), 19–23.

Ericsson, K. A., & Simon, H. A. (1984). *Protocol analysis: Verbal reports as data.* Cambridge, MA: MIT Press/Bradford.

Evans, J. St. B. T., Allen, J. L., Newstead, S. E., & Pollard, P. (1994). Debiasing by instruction: The case of belief bias. *European Journal of Cognitive Psychology, 6,* 263–285.

Evans, J. St. B. T, Barston, J., & Pollard, P. (1983). On the conflict between logic and belief in syllogistic reasoning. *Memory and Cognition, 11,* 295–306.

Evans, J. St. B. T., & Stanovich, K. E. (2013). Dual-process theories of higher cognition: Advancing the debate. *Perspectives on Psychological Science, 8,* 223–241.

Fan, J., McCandliss, B. D., Sommer, T., Raz, A., & Posner, M. I. (2002). Testing the efficiency and independence of attentional networks. *Journal of Cognitive Neuroscience, 14,* 340–347.

Fancher, R. E. (1979). *Pioneers of psychology.* New York: Norton.

Farah, M. J. (1985). Psychophysical evidence for a shared representational medium for mental images and percepts. *Journal of Experimental Psychology: General, 114,* 91–103.

Farah, M. J. (1988). Is visual imagery really visual? Overlooked evidence from neuropsychology *Psychological Review, 95,* 307–317.

Farah, M. J. (1990). Visual agnosia: Disorders of object recognition and what they tell us about normal vision. Cambridge, MA: MIT Press.

Farah, M. J., Péronnet, F., Gonon, M. A., & Giard, M. H. (1988). Electrophysiological evidence for a shared representational medium for visual images and visual percepts. *Journal of Experimental Psychology: General, 117,* 248–257.

Feldman, J. (1999). The role of objects in perceptual grouping. *Acta Psychologica, 102,* 137–163.

Feldman, J. A., & Ballard, D. H. (1982). Connectionist models and their properties. *Cognitive Science, 6,* 205–254.

Fernandes, M. A., Craik, F. I. M., Bialystok, E., & Kreuger, S. (2007). Effect of bilingualism, aging, and semantic relatedness on memory under divided attention. *Canadian Journal of Experimental Psychology, 61,* 128–141.

Fiddick, L., Cosmides, L., & Tooby J. (2000). No interpretation without representation: The role of domain-specific representations and inferences in the Wason selection task. *Cognition, 77,* 1–79.

Finke, R. A. (1989). *Principles of mental imagery.* Cambridge, MA: MIT Press.

Fischhoff, B. (1975). Hindsightfiforesight: The effect of outcome knowledge on judgment under uncertainty. *Journal of Experimental Psychology: Human Perception and Performance, 1,* 288–299.

Fischhoff, B. (1982a). Debiasing. In D. Kahneman, P. Slovic, & A. Tversky (Eds.), *Judgment under uncertainty: Heuristics and biases* (pp. 422–444). Cambridge, UK: Cambridge University Press.

Fischhoff, B. (1982b). For those condemned to study the past: Heuristics and biases in hindsight. In D.Kahneman, P. Slovic, & A. Tversky (Eds.), *Judgment under uncertainty: Heuristics and biases* (pp. 335–351). Cambridge, UK: Cambridge University Press.

Fleischman, D. A., Wilson, R. S., Gabrieli, J. D. E., Bienias, J. L., & Bennett, D. A. (2004). A longitudinal study of implicit and explicit memory in old persons. *Psychology and Aging, 19*(4), 617–625.

Fodor, J. A. (1983). The modularity of mind: An essay on faulty psychology. Cambridge, MA: MIT Press.

Fodor, J. A. (1985). Précis of The modularity of mind. Behavioral and Brain Sciences, 8, 1–42.

Fodor, J. A., & Pylyshyn, Z. W. (1981). How direct is visual perception? Some reflections on Gibsons "ecological approach." *Cognition, 2,* 139–196.

Frisch, D., & Clemen, R. T. (1994). Beyond expected utility: Rethinking behavioral decision research. *Psychological Bulletin, 116,* 46–54.

Frith, C. D. (1991a). A PET study of word finding. *Neuropsychologia, 29,* 1137–1148.

Frith, C. D., & Friston, K J. (1997). Studying brain function with neuroimaging. In M. D. Rugg (Ed.), *Cognitive neuroscience* (pp. 169–196). Cambridge, MA: MIT Press.

Fromkin, V, & Rodman, R. (1974). *An introduction to language.* New York: Holt, Rinehart & Winston.

Fugelsang, J., & Dunbar, K (2005). Brain-based mechanisms underlying complex causal thinking. *Neuropsychologia, 43,* 1204–1213.

Galea, L. A. M., & Kimura, D. (1993). Sex differences in route-learning. *Personality and Individual Differences, 14,* 53–65.

Galotti, K. M. (1989). Approaches to studying formal and everyday reasoning. *Psychological Bulletin, 105,* 331–351.

Galotti, K. M. (1999). Making a "major" real-life decision: College students choosing an academic major. *Journal of Educational Psychology, 91,* 379–387.

Galotti, K M. (2002). Making decisions that matter: How people face important life choices. Mahwah, NJ: Erlbaum.

Galotti, K M. (2005). Setting goals and making plans: How children and adolescents frame their decisions. In J. E. Jacobs & P. A. Klaczynski (Eds.), *The development of judgment and decision making in children and adolescents* (pp. 303–326). Mahwah, NJ: Erlbaum.

Galotti, K. M., Baron, J., & Sabini, J. P. (1986). Individual differences in syllogistic reasoning: Deduction rules or mental models? *Journal of Experimental Psychology: General, 115,* 16–25.

Galotti, K. M., Clinchy, B. McV, Ainsworth, K. H., Lavin, B., & Mansfield, A. F. (1999). A new way of assessing ways of knowing: The Attitudes Toward Thinking and Learning Survey (ATTLS). *Sex Roles, 40,* 745–766.

Galotti, K. M., & Ganong, W. F., III. (1985). What non-programmers know about programming: Natural language procedure specification. *International Journal of Man–Machine Studies, 22,* 1–10.

Galotti, K. M., & Komatsu, L. K. (1993). Why study *deduction? Behavioral and Brain Sciences, 16,* 350.

Galotti, K. M., Komatsu, L. K., & Voelz, S. (1997). Children's differential performance on deductive and inductive syllogisms. *Developmental Psychology, 33,* 70–78.

Galotti, K. M., & Kozberg, S. F. (1987). Older adolescents' thinking about academic/vocational and interpersonal commitments. *Journal of Youth and Adolescence, 16,* 313–330.

Galotti, K. M., Reimer, R. L., & Drebus, D. W. (2001). Ways of knowing as learning styles: Learning MAGIC with a partner. *Sex Roles, 44,* 419–436.

Galton, F (1907). *Inquiries into human faculty and its development.* London: J. M. Dent & Sons. (Original work published 1883)

Gardner, B. T, & Gardner, R. A. (1971). Two-way communication with an infant chimpanzee. In A. M. Schrier & F. Stollnitz (Eds.), *Behavior of nonhuman primates* (Vol. 4, pp. 117–184). New York: Academic Press.

Gardner, H. (1983). Frames of mind: The theory of multiple intelligences. New York: Basic Books.

Gardner, H. (1985). The mind's new science: A history of the cognitive revolution. New York: Basic Books.

Gardner, H. (1993). Multiple intelligences: The theory in practice. New York: Basic Books.

Gardner, H. (1999). Intelligence reframed: Multiple intelligences for the 21st century. New York: Basic Books.

Gardner, H. (2011). Frames of mind: The theory of multiple intelligences. Basic books.

Garrett, M. F. (1988). Processes in language production In F. J. Newmeyer (Ed.), *Linguistics: The Cambridge survey: Vol. 3. Language: Psychological and biological aspects* (pp. 69–96). Cambridge, UK: Cambridge University Press.

Garrett, M. F. (1990). Sentence processing. In D. N. Osherson & H. Lasnik (Eds.), *An invitation to cognitive science: Vol. 1. Language* (pp. 133–175). Cambridge, MA: MIT Press.

Garry, M., & Wade, K. A. (2005). Actually, a picture is worth less than 45 words: Narratives produce more false memories than photographs do. *Psychological Bulletin and Review, 12,* 359–366.

Gathercole, S. E. (1994). Neuropsychology and working memory: A review. *Neuropsychology, 8,* 494–505.

Gauthier, I., & Tarr, M. J. (1997a). Becoming a "greeble" expert: Exploring mechanisms for face recognition. *Vision Research, 37,* 1673–1682.

Gauthier, I., & Tarr, M. J. (1997b). Orientation priming of novel shapes in the context of viewpoint- dependent recognition. *Perception, 26,* 51–73.

Gazzaniga, M. S. (Ed.). (2004). *The cognitive neurosciences* (3rd ed.). Cambridge, MA: MIT Press.

Gernsbacher, M. A. (1993). Less skilled readers have less efficient suppression mechanisms. *Psychological Science, 3,* 294–298.

Gernsbacher, M. A., & Kaschak, M. P. (2004). Neuroimaging studies of language production and comprehension. *Annual Review of Psychology, 54,* 91–114.

Gibson, E. J. (1969). Principles of perceptual learning and development. New York: Meredith.

Gibson, J. J. (1950). *The perception of the visual world.* Boston: Houghton Mifflin.

Gibson, J. J. (1979). *The ecological approach to visual perception.* Boston: Houghton Mifflin.

Gick, M. L., & Holyoak, K. J. (1980). Analogical problem solving. *Cognitive Psychology, 12,* 306–355.

Gick, M. L., & Holyoak, K J. (1983). Schema induction and analogical transfer. *Cognitive Psychology, 15,* 1–38.

Glaser, R., & Chi, M. T. H. (1988). Overview. In M. T. H. Chi, R. Glaser, & M. J. Farr (Eds.), *The nature of expertise* (pp. xv–xxviii). Hillsdale, NJ: Erlbaum.

Gobet, F., & Simon, H. A. (1996). The roles of recognition processes and look-ahead search in time constrained expert problem solving: Evidence from grand-master-level chess. *Psychological Science, 7,* 52–55.

Godden, D. R., & Baddeley A. D. (1975). Context dependent memory in two natural environments: On land and underwater. *British Journal of Psychology, 66,* 325–332.

Godden, D. R., & Baddeley, A. D. (1980). When does context influence recognition memory? *British Journal of Psychology, 71,* 99–104.

Goel, V, Buchel, C, Frith, C, & Dolan, R. J. (2000). Dissociation of mechanisms underlying syllogistic reasoning. *NeuroImage, 12,* 504–514.

Goel, V, & Dolan, R. J. (2001). Functional neuroanatomy of three-term relational reasoning. *Neuropsychologia, 39,* 901–909.

Goel, V, Gold, B., Kapur, S., & Houle, S. (1998). Neuroanatomical correlates of human reasoning. *Journal of Cognitive Neuroscience, 10,* 293–302.

Goel, V, & Grafman, J. (2000). Role of the prefrontal cortex in ill-structured planning. *Cognitive Neuropsychology, 17,* 415–436.

Goldman, S. R., & Varnhagen, C. K. (1986). Memory for embedded and sequential story structures. *Journal of Memory and Language, 25,* 401–418.

Goldstein, E. B. (1994). *Psychology.* Pacific Grove, CA: Brooks/Cole.

Gollan, T. H., Montoya, R. I., & Werner, G. A. (2002). Semantic and letter fluency in Spanish-English bilinguals. *Neuropsychology, 16,* 562–576.

Goodman, N. (1972). *Problems and projects.* Indianapolis, IN: Bobbs-Merrill.

Gould, S. J. (1995). Mismeasure by any measure. In R. Jaccoby & N. Glauberman (Eds.), *The bell curve debate: History, documents, opinions* (pp. 3–13). New York: Times Books.

Grady C. L. (2002). Age-related differences in face processing: A meta-analysis of three functional neuroimaging experiments. *Canadian Journal of Experimental Psychology, 50,* 208–220.

Grady, C. L., Bernstein, L. J., Beig, S., & Siegenthaler, A. L. (2002). The effects of encoding strategy on age-related changes in the functional neuroanatomy of face memory. *Psychology & Aging, 17,* 7–23.

Grady, C. L., Haxby J. V, Horwitz, B., Schapiro, M. B., Rapoport, S. I., Ungerleider, L. G., Mishkin, M., Carson, R. E., & Herscovitch, P. (1992). Dissociation of object and spatial vision in human extrastriate cortex: Age-related changes in activation of regional, cerebral blood flow measured with [15O] water and positron emission tomography. *Journal of Cognitive Neuroscience, 4,* 23–34.

Grady, C. L., McIntosh, A. R., Horwitz, B., & Rapoport, S. I. (2000). Age-related changes in the neural correlates of degraded and nondegraded face processing. *Cognitive Neuropsychology, 217,* 165–186.

Grady, C. L., McIntosh, A. R., Rajah, M. N., Beig, S., & Craik, F. I. M. (1999). The effects of age on the neural correlates of episodic encoding. *Cerebral Cortex, 9*(8), 805–814.

Grady, C. L., Maisog, J. M., Horwitz, B., Ungerleider, L. G., Mentis, M. J., Salerno, J. A., Pietrini, P., Wagner, E., & Haxby, J. V (1994). Age-related changes in cortical blood flow activation during visual processing of faces and location. *Journal of Neuroscience, 14,* 1450–1462.

Graesser, A. C, & Clark, L. F. (1985). *The structures and procedures of implicit knowledge.* Norwood, NJ: Ablex.

Green, D. W. (1998). Mental control of the bilingual lexicosemantic system. *Bilingualism: Language and Cognition, 1,* 67–81.

Greenberg, S. N., Healy A. F., Koriat, A., & Kreiner, H. (2004). The GO model: A reconsideration of the role of structural units in guiding and organizing text online. *Psychonomic Bulletin and Review, 11,* 428–433.

Gregory, R. L. (1972). Cognitive contours. *Nature, 238,* 51–52.

Grice, H. P. (1975). Logic and conversation. In P. Cole & J. L. Morgan (Eds.), *Syntax and semantics: Vol. 3. Speech acts* (pp. 41–58). New York: Seminar Press.

Griggs, R. A. (1983). The role of problem content in the selection task and in the THOG problem. In J. St. B. T. Evans (Ed.), *Thinking and reasoning: Psychological approaches* (pp. 16–43). London: Rout-ledge & Kegan Paul.

Griggs, R. A., & Cox, J. R. (1982). The elusive thematic- materials effect in Wason's selection task. *British Journal of Psychology, 73,* 407–420.

Hahn, U., & Chater, N. (1997). Concepts and similarity. In K. Lamberts & D. Shanks (Eds.), *Knowledge, concepts, and categories* (pp. 43–92). Cambridge, MA: MIT Press.

Halle, M. (1990). Phonology. In D. N. Osherson & H. Lasnik (Eds.), *An invitation to cognitive science: Vol. 1. Language* (pp. 43–68). Cambridge, MA: MIT Press.

Halpern, D. F (1992). *Sex differences in cognitive abilities* (2nd ed.). Hillsdale, NJ: Erlbaum.

Hamann, S. B. (2001). Cognitive and neural mechanisms of emotional memory. *Trends in Cognitive Sciences, 5,* 394–400.

Hampson, E. (2004). Cognitive function: Sex differences and hormonal influences. In G. Adel-man & B. H. Smith (Eds.), *Encyclopedia of Neuroscience* (3rd ed.) [CD-ROM]. New York: Elsevier Science B.V.

Han, K., & Marvin, C. (2002). Multiple creativities? Investigating domain-specificity of creativity inyoung children. *Gifted Child Quarterly, 46,* 98–109.

Harley, T. A. (1995). The psychology of language: From data to theory. Hillsdale, NJ: Erlbaum.

Harnad, S. (Ed.). (1987). *Categorical perception.* Cambridge, UK: Cambridge University Press.

Harris, R. J. (1977). Comprehension of pragmatic implications in advertising. *Journal of Applied Psychology, 62,* 603–608.

Hartman, M., Dumas, J., & Nielsen, C. (2001). Age differences in updating working memory: Evidence from the Delayed-Matching-to-Sample Test. *Aging, Neuropsychology and Cognition, 8*(1), 14–35.

Hasher, L., & Zacks, R. T. (1984). Automatic processing of fundamental information. *American Psychologist, 39,* 1372–1388.

Hasher, L., & Zacks, R. T. (1988). Working memory, comprehension, and aging: A review and a new view. In G. H. Bower (Ed.), *The psychology of learning and motivation: Vol. 22. Advances in research and theory* (pp. 193–225). San Diego, CA: Academic Press.

Hatala, R., Norman, G., & Brooks, L. (1999). Influence of a single example on subsequent electrocardiogram interpretation. *Teaching and Learning in Medicine, 11,* 110–117.

Hauser, M. D. (2000). *Wild minds: What animals really think.* New York: Henry Holt.

Haviland, S. E., & Clark, H. H. (1974). What's new? Acquiring new information as a process in comprehension. *Journal of Verbal Learning and Verbal Behavior, 13,* 512–521.

Hay, J. F., & Jacoby L. L. (1996). Separating habit and recollection: Memory slips, process dissociations, and probability matching. *Journal of Experimental Psychology: Learning, Memory, and Cognition, 22,* 1323–1335.

Hedges, L. V., & Olkin, I. (1985). *Statistical methods for meta-analysis.* New York: Academic Press.

Heider, E. R. (1972). Universals in color naming and memory. *Journal of Experimental Psychology, 93,* 10–20.

Heit, E. (1997). Knowledge and concept learning. In K. Lamberts & D. Shanks (Eds.), *Knowledge, concepts, and categories* (pp. 7–41). Cambridge, MA: MIT Press.

Henle, M. (1971). Of the scholler of nature. *Social Research, 38,* 93–107.

Hennessey, B. A., & Amabile, T. M. (1988). The conditions of creativity. In R. J. Sternberg (Ed.), *The nature of creativity* (pp. 11–35). Cambridge, UK: Cambridge University Press.

Hergenhahn, B. R. (1986). *An introduction to the history of psychology.* Belmont, CA: Wadsworth.

Herlitz, A., Nilsson, L. G., & Bäckman, L. (1997). Gender differences in episodic memory. *Memory and Cognition, 25*(6), 801–811.

Herrnstein, R. J., & Murray, C. (1994). The bell curve: Intelligence and class structure in American life. New York: Free Press.

Hillner, K P. (1984). History and systems of modern psychology: A conceptual approach. New York: Gardner Press.

Hirst, W., Phelps, E. A., Meksin, R., Vaidya, C. J., Johnson, M. K., Mitchell, K. J., ... & Mather, M. (2015). A ten-year follow-up of a study of memory for the attack of September 11, 2001: Flashbulb memories and memories for flashbulb events. *Journal of Experimental Psychology: General, 144*(3), 604.

Hirst, W., Spelke, E. S., Reaves, C. C, Caharack, G, & Neisser, U. (1980). Dividing attention without alternation or automaticity *Journal of Experimental Psychology: General, 109,* 98–117.

Hochberg, J. E. (1978). *Perception* (2nd ed.). Engle-wood Cliffs, NJ: Prentice Hall.

Hockett, C. F. (1960). The origin of speech. *Scientific American, 203*(3), 88–96.

Hoelzl, E., Kirchler, E., & Rodler, C. (2002). Hindsight bias in economic expectations: I knew all along what I want to hear. *Journal of Applied Psychology, 87,* 437–443.

Hoffman, R. R., Bamberg, M., Bringmann, W., & Klein, R. (1987). Some historical observations on Ebbinghaus. In D. S. Gorfein & R. R. Hoffman (Eds.), *Memory and learning: The Ebbinghaus Centennial Conference* (pp. 57–76). Hillsdale, NJ: Erlbaum.

Holyoak, K. J., & Nisbett, R. E. (1988). Induction. In R. J. Sternberg & E. E. Smith (Eds.), *The psychology of human thought* (pp. 50–91). Cambridge, UK: Cambridge University Press.

Horton, D. L., & Mills, C. B. (1984). Human learning and memory. *Annual Review of Psychology, 35,* 361–394.

Hubel, D. H., & Wiesel, T. N. (1962). Receptive fields, binocular interaction, and functional architecture in the cats visual cortex. *Journal of Physiology, 166,* 106–154.

Hubel, D. H., & Wiesel, T. N. (1968). Receptive fields and functional architecture of the monkey striate cortex. *Journal of Physiology, 195,* 215–243.

Hultsch, D. F. (1975). Adult age differences in retrieval: Trace-dependent and cue-dependent forgetting. *Developmental Psychology, 11,* 197–201.

Hunt, E. (1978). Mechanics of verbal ability. *Psychological Review, 85,* 109–130.

Hunt, E. (1986). The heffalump of intelligence. In R. J. Sternberg & D. K Detterman (Eds.), *What is intelligence? Contemporary viewpoints on its nature and definition* (pp. 101–107). Norwood, NJ: Ablex.

Hyde, J. S., & Linn, M. C. (1988). Gender differences in verbal ability: A meta-analysis. *Psychological Bulletin, 104,* 53–69.

Hyman, I. E., Jr., Husband, T. H., & Billings, F. J. (1995). False memories of childhood experiences. *Applied Cognitive Psychology, 9,* 181–198.

Incisa della Rocchetta, A., & Milner, B. (1993). Strategic search and retrieval inhibition: The role of the frontal lobes. *Neuropsychologia, 31,* 503–524.

Intons-Peterson, M. J. (1983). Imagery paradigms: How vulnerable are they to experimenters' expectations? *Journal of Experimental Psychology: Human Perception and Performance, 9,* 394–412.

Jacklin, C. N. (1989). Female and male: Issues of gender. *American Psychologist, 44,* 127–133.

Jacoby L. L. (1991). A process dissociation framework: Separating automatic from intentional uses of memory. *Journal of Memory and Language, 30,* 513–541.

Jacoby, L. L. (1998). Invariance in automatic influences of memory: Toward a users guide for the process-dissociation procedure. *Journal of Experimental Psychology: Learning, Memory and Cognition, 24,* 3–26.

Jacoby, L. L., Woloshyn, V., & Kelley C. M. (1989). Becoming famous without being recognized: Unconscious influences of memory produced by dividing attention. *Journal of Experimental Psychology: General, 118,* 115–125.

James, W. (1983). *The principles of psychology.* Cambridge, MA: Harvard University Press. (Original work published 1890)

Johansson, G. (1973). Visual perception of biological motion and a model for its analysis. *Perception and Psychophysics, 14,* 201–211.

Johnson, M. H., Munakata, Y, & Gilmore, R. O. (Eds.). (2002). *Brain development and cognition: A reader* (2nd ed.). Oxford, UK: Blackwell.

Johnson-Laird, P. N. (1982). Ninth Bartlett memorial lecture: Thinking as a skill. *Quarterly Journal of Experimental Psychology, 34A,* 1–29.

Johnson-Laird, P. N. (1983). *Mental models.* Cambridge, MA: Harvard University Press.

Johnston, J. C, McCann, R. S., & Remington, R. W. (1995). Chronometric evidence for two types of attention. *Psychological Science, 6,* 365–369.

Just, M. A., & Carpenter, P. A. (1980). A theory of reading: From eye fixations to comprehension. *Psychological Review, 87,* 329–354.

Just, M. A., & Carpenter, P. A. (1987). *The psychology of reading and language comprehension.* Boston: Allyn & Bacon.

Kahneman, D. (1973). *Attention and effort.* Engle-wood Cliffs, NJ: Prentice Hall.

Kahneman, D., & Tversky A. (1973). On the psychology of prediction. *Psychological Review, 80,* 237–251.

Kahneman, D., & Tversky, A. (1979). Prospect theory: An analysis of decisions under risk. *Econometrica, 47,* 263–291.

Kalat, J. W. (1995). *Biological psychology* (5th ed.). Pacific Grove, CA: Brooks/Cole.

Kamin, L. J. (1995). Lies, damned lies, and statistics. In R. Jaccoby & N. Glauberman (Eds.), *The bell curve debate: History, documents, opinions* (pp. 81–105). New York: Times Books.

Keating, D. P., & Bobbitt, B. L. (1978). Individual and developmental differences in cognitive-processing components of mental ability. *Child Development, 49,* 155–167.

Keeney R. L. (1982). Decision analysis: An overview. *Operations Research, 30,* 803–838.

Keil, F C. (1989). *Concepts, kinds, and cognitive development.* Cambridge, MA: MIT Press.

Kemler Nelson, D. K (1984). The effect of intention on what concepts are acquired. *Journal of Verbal Learning and Verbal Behavior, 23,* 734–759.

Kemper, T. L. (1994). Neuroanatomical and neuropathological changes during aging and dementia. In M. L. Albert & J. E. Knoefel (Eds.), *Clinical neuropsychology of aging.* (2nd ed., pp. 3–67). New York, NY: Oxford University Press.

Kempler, D., Metter, E. J., Riege, W. H., Jackson, C.A., Benson, D. F., & Hanson, W. R. (1990). Slowly progressive aphasia: Three cases with language, memory, CT and PET data. *Journal of Neurology, Neurosurgery, and Psychiatry, 53,* 987–993.

Kensinger, E. A., Choi, H. Y., Murray, B. D., & Rajaram, S. (2016). How social interactions affect emotional memory accuracy: Evidence from collaborative retrieval and social contagion paradigms. Memory & cognition, 44(5), 706–716.

Keppel, G., & Underwood, B. J. (1962). Proactive inhibition in short-term retention of single items. *Journal of Verbal Learning and Verbal Behavior, 1,* 153–161.

Kerr, N. H. (1983). The role of vision in "visual imagery" experiments: Evidence from the congenitally blind. *Journal of Experimental Psychology: General, 112,* 265–277.

Kim, N. S., & Ahn, W. (2002). The influence of naïve causal theories on lay concepts of mental illness. *American Journal of Psychology, 115,* 33–65.

Kimura, D. (1961). Cerebral dominance and the perception of verbal stimuli. *Canadian Journal of Psychology, 15,* 166–171.

Kimura, D. (1963). Speech lateralization in young children as determined by an auditory test. *Journal of Comparative and Physiological Psychology, 56,* 899–902.

Kimura, D. (1992). Sex differences in the brain. *Scientific American, 267,* 118–125.

Kimura, D. (2002). Sex hormones influence human cognitive pattern. *Neuroendocrinology Letters, Special issue, Supplement 4, 23,* 67–77.

King, R. N., & Koehler, D. J. (2000). Illusory correlations in graphological inference. *Journal of Experimental Psychology: Applied, 6,* 336–348.

Kingstone, A., Smilek, D., & Ristic, J., (2003). Attention, researchers! It is time to take a look at the real world. *Current Directions in Psychological Science, 12,* 176–180.

Kintsch, W., & Keenan, J. (1973). Reading rate and retention as a function of the number of propositions in the base structure of sentences. *Cognitive Psychology, 5,* 257–274.

Kirkpatrick, E. A. (1894). An experimental study of memory. *Psychological Review, 1,* 602–609.

Kitchin, R. M. (1994). Cognitive maps: What are they and why study them? *Journal of Environmental Psychology, 14,* 1–19.

Klatzky, R. L. (1980). *Human memory: Structures and processes* (2nd ed.). San Francisco: W. H. Freeman.

Klein, G. (1998). Sources of power: How people make decisions. Cambridge, MA: MIT Press.

Klein, R. (1988). Inhibitory tagging system facilitates visual search. *Nature, 334,* 430–431.

Kleinmuntz, B. (1990). Why we still use our heads instead of formulas: Toward an integrative approach. *Psychological Bulletin, 107,* 296–310.

Knauff, M., & Johnson-Laird, P. N. (2002). Visual imagery can impede reasoning. *Memory & Cognition, 30,* 363–371.

Knutson, B., Rick, S., Wimmer, G. E., Prelec, D., & Loewenstein, G. (2007). Neural predictors of purchases. *Neuron, 53,* 147–156.

Koehler, J. J. (1993). The influence of prior beliefs on scientific judgments of evidence quality. *Organizational Behavior and Human Decision Processes, 56,* 28–55.

Koffka, K. (1935). *Principles of Gestalt psychology.* New York: Harcourt Brace & Company

Kolb, B. (1995). *Brain plasticity and behaviour.* Laurence Erlbaum: Toronto.

Kolb, B., & Gibb, R. (2007). Brain plasticity and recovery from early cortical injury. *Developmental Psychobiology, 49,* 107–118.

Kolb, B., & Whishaw, I. Q. (2003). *Fundamentals of human neuropsychology,* 5th ed. New York: W. H. Freeman.

Komatsu, L. K (1992). Recent views of conceptual structure. *Psychological Bulletin, 112,* 500–526.

Komatsu, L. K. (1995). *Antecedents of cognitive psychology.* Unpublished table, Carleton College, Northfield, MN.

Koslowski, L. T, & Cutting, J. E. (1977). Recognizing the sex of a walker from a dynamic point-light display. *Perception and Psychophysics, 21,* 575–580.

Kosslyn, S. M. (1973). Scanning visual images: Some structural implications. *Perception and Psychophysics, 14,* 90–94.

Kosslyn, S. M. (1976). Can imagery be distinguished from other forms of internal representation? Evidence from studies of information retrieval times. *Memory and Cognition, 4,* 291–297.

Kosslyn, S. M., Ball, T. M., & Reiser, B. J. (1978). Visual images preserve metric spatial information: Evidence from studies of image scanning. *Journal of Experimental Psychology: Human Perception and Performance, 4,* 47–60.

Kosslyn, S. M., & Ochsner, K. N. (1994). In search of occipital activation during visual mental imagery. *Trends in Neuroscience, 17,* 290–292.

Kosslyn, S. M., Reiser, B. J., Farah, M. J., & Fliegel, S. L. (1983). Generating visual images: Units and relations. *Journal of Experimental Psychology: General, 112,* 278–303.

Kosslyn, S. M., Thompson, W. L., Kim, I. J., & Alpert, N. M. (1995). Topographical representations of mental images in primary visual cortex. *Nature, 378,* 496–498.

Kramer, A. F., Erickson, K I., Colcombe, S. J. (2006). Exercise, cognition, and the aging brain. *J Appl Physiol. 101*(4), 1237–42.

Kramer, A. F., & Colcombe, S. (2018). Fitness effects on the cognitive function of older adults: A meta-analytic study—revisited. Perspectives on Psychological Science, 13(2), 213–217.

Krebs, D. L. (2007). Understanding evolutionary approaches to human behavior. *Human Development, 50,* 286–291.

Kroll, J. F., Van Hell, J. G., Tokowicz, N., & Green, D. W. (2010). The Revised Hierarchical Model: A critical review and assessment. Bilingualism: Language and Cognition, 13(3), 373-381.

Kulatunga-Moruzi, C, Brooks, L., & Norman, G. R. (2004). Using comprehensive feature lists to bias medical diagnosis. *Journal of Experimental Psychology: Learning, Memory, and Cognition, 30,* 563–572.

Kung, H. F. (1993). SPECT and PET ligands for CNS imaging. *Neurotransmissions, 9*(4), 1–6.

LaBerge, D. (1995). *Attentional processing: The brain's art of mindfulness.* Cambridge, MA: Harvard University Press.

Lachman, R., Lachman, J. L., & Butterfield, E. C. (1979). *Cognitive psychology and information processing: An introduction.* Hillsdale, NJ: Erlbaum.

Lamberts, K., & Shanks, D. (Eds.). (1997). *Knowledge, concepts, and categories.* Cambridge, MA: MIT Press.

Landauer, T. K. (1986). How much do people remember? Some estimates of the quantity of learned information in long-term memory. *Cognitive Science, 10,* 477–493.

Lane, S. M., Mather, M., Villa, D., & Morita, S. K. (2001). How events are reviewed matters: Effects of varied focus on eyewitness suggestibility. *Memory & Cognition, 29,* 940–947.

Langley P., & Jones, R. (1988). A computational model of scientific insight. In R. J. Sternberg (Ed.), *The nature of creativity: Contemporary psychological perspectives* (pp. 177–201). Cambridge, UK: Cambridge University Press.

Lashley K. S. (1929). *Brain mechanisms and intelligence.* Chicago: University of Chicago Press.

Laughlin, P. R., Lange, R., & Adamopoulos, J. (1982). Selection strategies for "Mastermind" problems. *Journal of Experimental Psychology: Learning, Memory, and Cognition, 8,* 475–483.

Lave, J. (1988). *Cognition in practice.* Cambridge, UK: Cambridge University Press.

Lave, J., Murtaugh, M., & de la Rocha, O. (1984). The dialectic of arithmetic in grocery shopping. In B. Rogoff & J. Lave (Eds.), *Everyday cognition: Its development in social context* (pp. 67–94). Cambridge, MA: Harvard University Press.

Lea, G. (1975). Chronometric analysis of the method of loci. Journal of Experimental Psychology: Human Perception and Performance, 1, 95–104.

LeDoux, J. E. (1996). *The emotional brain.* New York: Simon & Schuster.

Lerner, R. M. (1990). Plasticity, person–context relations, and cognitive training in the aged years: A developmental contextual perspective. *Developmental Psychology, 26,* 911–915.

Lesgold, A., Rubinson, H., Feltovich, P., Glaser, R., Klopfer, K, & Wang, Y. (1988). Expertise in a complex skill: Diagnosing x-ray pictures. In M. T. H. Chi, R. Glaser, & M. J. Farr (Eds.), *The nature of expertise* (pp. 311–342). Hillsdale, NJ: Erlbaum.

Lettvin, J. Y, Maturana, H. R., McCullogh, W. S., & Pitts, W. H. (1959). What the frogs eye tells the frog's brain. *Proceedings of the Institute of Radio Engineering, 47,* 1940–1941.

Levine, S. C, Vasilyeva, M., Lourenco, S. F., Newcombe, N. S., & Huttenlocher, J. (2005). Socio-economic status modifies the sex difference in spatial skill. *Psychological Science, 16,* 841–845.

Levinson, S. C. (2000). *Presumptive meanings.* Cambridge, MA: MIT Press.

Levinson, S. C, Kita, S., Haun, D. B. M., & Rasch, B. H. (2002). Returning the tables: language affects spatial reasoning. *Cognition, 83,* 265–294.

Levy, J., & Heller, W. (1992). Gender differences in human neuropsychological function. In A. A. Gerall, H. Moltz, & I. L. Ward (Eds.), *Handbook of behavioral neurobiology* (Vol. 11, pp. 245–274). New York: Plenum Press.

Li, P., & Gleitman, L. (2002). Turning the tables: language and spatial reasoning. *Cognition, 83,* 265–294.

Lichtenstein, S., Fischhoff, B., & Phillips, D. (1982). Calibration of probabilities: The state of the art to 1980. In D. Kahneman, P. Slovic, & A. Tversky (Eds.), *Judgment under uncertainty: Heuristics and biases* (pp. 306–334). Cambridge, UK: Cambridge University Press.

Light, L. L., & Singh, A. (1987). Implicit and explicit memory in young and older adults. *Journal of Experimental Psychology: Learning, Memory, and Cognition, 13*(4), 531–541.

Lin, E. L., & Murphy, G L. (2001). Thematic relations in adults' concepts. *Journal of Experimental Psychology: General, 130,* 3–28.

Linn, M. C, & Petersen, A. C. (1985). Emergence and characterization of sex differences in spatial ability: A meta-analysis. *Child Development, 56,* 1479–1498.

Lindsay, D. S., & Read, J. D. (1994). Psychotherapy and memories of childhood sexual abuse: A cognitive perspective. *Applied Cognitive Psychology, 8,* 281–338.

Linton, M. (1975). Memory for real-world events. In D. A. Norman & D. E. Rumelhart (Eds.), *Explorations in cognition* (pp. 376–404). San Francisco: W. H. Freeman.

Linton, M. (1982). Transformations of memory in everyday life. In U. Neisser (Ed.), *Memory observed: Remembering in natural contexts* (pp. 77–91). San Francisco: W. H. Freeman.

Lipshitz, R., Klein, G., Orasanu, J., & Salas, E. (2001). Taking stock of naturalistic decision making. *Journal of Behavioral Decision Making, 14,* 331–352.

Lisker, L., & Abramson, A. (1970). The voicing dimension: Some experiments in comparative phonetics. *Proceedings of the Sixth International Congress of Phonetic Sciences,* Prague, 1967 (pp. 563–567). Prague, Czechoslovakia: Academia.

Liu, L. G. (1985). Reasoning counterfactually in Chinese: Are there any obstacles? *Cognition, 21,* 239–270.

Locke, J. (1964). *An essay concerning human understanding* (A. D. Woozley, Ed.). New York: New American Library. (Original work published 1690)

Loftus, E. F. (1975). Leading questions and the eyewitness report. *Cognitive Psychology, 7,* 560–572.

Loftus, E. F. (1979). *Eyewitness testimony.* Cambridge, MA: Harvard University Press.

Loftus, E. F. (2000). Remembering what never happened. In E. Tulving (Ed.), *Memory, consciousness, and the brain* (pp. 106–118). Philadelphia: Psychology Press.

Loftus, E. F., & Ketcham, K. (1994). *The myth of repressed memory.* New York: St. Martins Press.

Loftus, E. F., & Pickrell, J. E. (1995). The formation of false memories. *Psychiatric Annals, 25,* 720–725.

Logan, G. D., & Etherton, J. L. (1994). What is learned during automatization? The role of attention in constructing an instance. *Journal of Experimental Psychology: Learning, Memory, and Cognition, 20,* 1022–1050.

Logan, G. D., Schachar, R. J., & Tannock, R. (2000). Executive control problems in childhood psychopathology: Stop signal studies of attention deficit hyperactivity disorder. In S. Monsell & J. Driver (Eds.), *Control of cognitive processes: Attention and performance XVIII* (pp. 653–677). Cambridge, MA: Bradford.

Logan, G D., Taylor, S. E., & Etherton, J. L. (1996). Attention in the acquisition and expression of automaticity *Journal of Experimental Psychology: Learning, Memory, and Cognition, 22,* 620–638.

Loring-Meier, S., & Halpern, D. F. (1999). Sex differences in visuospatial working memory: Components of cognitive processing. *Psychonomic Bulletin and Review, 6,* 464–471.

Lu, C.-H., & Proctor, R. W. (1995). The influence of irrelevant location information on performance: A review of the Simon and spatial Stroop effects. *Psychonomic Bulletin & Review, 2,* 174–207.

Luchins, A. S. (1942). Mechanization in problem solving: The effect of *Einstellung. Psychological Monographs, 54*(Whole No. 248).

Mack, A. (2003). Inattentional blindness: Looking without seeing. *Current Directions in Psychological Science, 12,* 180–184.

MacLeod, C. M. (1991). Half a century of research on the Stroop effect: An integrative review. *Psychological Bulletin, 109,* 163–203.

Madden, D. J. (2007). Aging and visual attention. *Current Directions in Psychological Science, 16*(2), 70–74.

Madden, D. J., & Hoffman., J. M. (1997). Application of positron emission tomography to age-related cognitive changes. In K. R. R. Krishman & P. M. Doraiswamy (Eds.), *Brain imaging in clinical psychiatry* (pp. 575–613). New York: Marcel Dekker.

Madden, D. J., Spaniol, J., Whiting, W. L., Bucur, B., Provenzale, J. M., Cabeza, R., White, L. E., & Huettel, S. A. (2007). Adult age differences in the functional neuroanatomy of visual attention: A combined fMRI and DTI study. *Neurobiology of Aging, 28,* 459–476.

Madden, D. J., Turkington, T. G, Coleman, R. E., Provenzale, J. M., DeGrado, T. R., Hoffman, J. M. (1996). Adult age differences in regional cerebral blood flow during visual word identification: Evidence from H2150 PET. *Neuroimage, 3,* 127–142.

Maier, N. R. F. (1930). Reasoning in humans: I. On direction. *Journal of Comparative Physiological Psychology, 10,* 115–143.

Maier, N. R. F. (1931). Reasoning in humans: II. The solution of a problem and its appearance in consciousness. *Journal of Comparative Physiological Psychology, 12,* 181–194.

Mandler, G. (1967). Organization and memory. In K. W. Spence & J. T. Spence (Eds.), *The psychology of learning and motivation (Vol.* 1, pp. 327–372). New York: Academic Press.

Marr, D. (1982). Vision: A computational investigation into the human representation and processing of visual information. San Francisco: W. H. Freeman.

Marslen-Wilson, W., & Welsh, A. (1978). Processing interactions and lexical access during word recognition in continuous speech. *Cognitive Psychology, 10,* 29–63.

Martin, C. D., Nazir, T, Thierry, G, Paulignan, Y, & Demont, J-F. (2006). Perceptual and lexical effects in letter identification: An event-related potential study of the word superiority effect. *Brain Re-search, 1098,* 153–160.

Martin, K. A., Moritz, S. E., & Hall, C. R. (1999). Imagery use in sport: A literature review and applied model. *Sport Psychologist, 13,* 245–268.

Martindale, C. (1991). *Cognitive psychology: A neural network approach.* Pacific Grove, CA: Brooks/Cole.

Massaro, D. W. (1979). Letter information and orthographic context in word perception. *Journal of Experimental Psychology: Human Perception and Performance, 5,* 595–609.

Massaro, D. W., & Cohen, M. M. (1983). Evaluation and integration of visual and auditory information in speech perception. *Journal of Experimental Psychology: Human Perception and Performance, 9,* 753–771.

Matlin, M. W. (1988). *Sensation and perception* (2nd ed.). Boston: Allyn & Bacon.

McClelland, J. L. (1988). Connectionist models and psychological evidence. *Journal of Memory and Language, 27,* 107–123.

McClelland, J. L. (2000). Connectionist models of memory. In E. Tulving & F. I. M. Craik (Eds.), *The Oxford handbook of memory* (pp. 583–596). New York: Oxford University Press.

McClelland, J. L., & Rumelhart, D. E. (1981). An interactive activation model of context effects in letter perception: Part 1. An account of basic findings. *Psychological Review, 88,* 375–407.

McCloskey M. E., & Glucksberg, S. (1978). Natural categories: Well defined or fuzzy sets? *Memory and Cognition, 6,* 462–472.

McDowd, J. M., & Shaw, R. J. (2000). Attention and aging: A functional perspective. In F. I. M. Craik & T. A. Salthouse (Eds.), *The handbook of aging and cognition,* 2nd ed. (pp. 221–292). Mahwah, NJ: Lawrence Erlbaum Associates Publishers.

McGaugh, J. L. (2000). Memory—A century of consolidation. *Science, 287,* 248–251.

McGee, M. G. (1979). Human spatial abilities: Psychometric studies and environmental, genetic, hormonal, and neurological influences. *Psychological Bulletin, 86,* 889–918.

McGeoch, J. A. (1932). Forgetting and the law of disuse. *Psychological Review, 39,* 352–370.

McIntosh, A. R., Bookstein, F. L., Haxby J. V., & Grady C. L. (1996). Spatial pattern analysis of functional brain images using Partial Least Square. *NeuroImage, 3,* 143–157.

McIntosh, A. R., Sekuler, A. B., Panpeci, C, Rajah, M. N., Grady, C. L. Sekuler, R., & Bennett, P. J. (1999). Recruitment of unique neural systems to support visual memory in normal aging. *Current Biology, 9*(21), 1275–1278.

McKoon, G, Ratcliff, R., & Dell, G. S. (1986). A critical evaluation of the semantic-episodic distinction. *Journal of Experimental Psychology: Learning, Memory, and Cognition, 12,* 295–306.

McNeill, D. (1966). Developmental psycholinguistics. In F. Smith & G. A. Miller (Eds.), *The genesis of language: A psycholinguistic approach* (pp. 15–84). Cambridge, MA: MIT Press.

Medin, D. L. (1989). Concepts and conceptual structure. *American Psychologist, 44,* 1469–1481.

Medin, D. L., Lynch, E. B., & Solomon, K. O. (2000). Are there kinds of concepts? *Annual Review of Psychology, 51,* 121–147.

Medin, D. L., & Smith, E. E. (1984). Concepts and concept formation. *Annual Review of Psychology, 35,* 113–138.

Meehl, P. E. (1954). Clinical versus statistical prediction: A theoretical analysis and a review of the evidence. Minneapolis: University of Minnesota Press.

Meehl, P. E. (1965). Seer over sign: The first good example. *Journal of Experimental Research in Personality, 1,* 27–32.

Melton, A. W. (1963). Implications of short-term memory for a general theory of memory. *Journal of Verbal Learning and Verbal Behavior, 2,* 1–21.

Menon, R. S., Ogawa, S., Tank, D. W., & Ugurbil, K. (1993). 4 tesla gradient-recalled echo-time dependence of photic stimulation induced signal changes in the human primary visual cortex. *Magnetic Resonance Medicine, 30,* 380.

Mervis, C. B. (1980). Category structure and the development of categorization. In R. Spiro, B. C. Bruce, & W. F Brewer (Eds.), *Theoretical issues in reading comprehension* (pp. 279–307). Hillsdale, NJ: Erlbaum.

Mervis, C. B., Catlin, J., & Rosch, E. (1976). Relationships among goodness-of-example, category norms, and word frequency. *Bulletin of the Psycho-nomic Society, 7,* 283–284.

Meyer, D. E., & Schvaneveldt, R. W. (1971). Facilitation in recognizing pairs of words: Evidence of a dependence between retrieval operations. *Journal of Experimental Psychology, 90,* 227–234.

Michael, E. B., & Gollan, T. H. (2005). Being bilingual and becoming bilingual: Individual differences and consequences for language production. In J. F. Kroll and A. M. B. de Groot (Eds.). *Handbook of bilingualism: Psycholinguistic approaches* (pp. 389–407). New York, NY: Oxford University Press.

Michaels, C. F., & Carello, C. (1981). *Direct perception.* Englewood Cliffs, NJ: Prentice Hall.

Milham, M. P., Banich, M. T., Webb, A., Barad, V., Cohen, N. J., Wszalek, T., & Kramer, A. F. (2001). The relative involvement of anterior cingulate and prefrontal cortex in attentional control depends on nature of conflict. *Cognitive Brain Research, 12,* 467–473.

Miller, G. A. (1956). The magical number seven, plus or minus two: Some limits on our capacity for processing information. *Psychological Review, 63,* 81–97.

Miller, G. A., & Glucksberg, S. (1988). Psycholinguistic aspects of pragmatics and semantics. In R. C. Atkinson (Ed.), *Stevens' handbook of experimental psychology: Vol. 2. Learning and cognition* (2nd ed., pp. 417–472). New York: Wiley.

Miller, G. A., & Johnson-Laird, P. N. (1976). *Language and perception.* Cambridge, MA: Harvard University Press.

Miller, G. A., & Nicely, P. (1955). An analysis of perceptual confusions among some English consonants. *Journal of the Acoustical Society of America, 27,* 338–352.

Miller, J. L. (1990). Speech perception. In D. N. Osherson & H. Lasnik (Eds.), *An invitation to cognitive science: Vol. 1. Language* (pp. 69–93). Cambridge, MA: MIT Press.

Milner. D. A., & Goodale, M. A. (1995). *The visual brain in action.* (Oxford Psychology Series, No. 27). Oxford: Oxford University Press.

Minda, J. P., & Smith, D. J. (2001). Prototypes in category learning: The effects of category size, category structure, and stimulus complexity. *Journal of Experimental Psychology: Learning, Memory, and Cognition, 27,* 775–799.

Mitchell, T. R., & Beach, L. R. (1990). "... Do I love thee? Let me count ...": Toward an understanding of intuitive and automatic decision-making. *Organizational Behavior and Human Decision Processes, 47,* 1–20.

Miyake, A. (2001). Individual differences in working memory: Introduction to the special section. *Journal of Experimental Psychology: General, 130,* 163–168.

Miyashita, Y. (1995). How the brain creates imagery: Projection to primary visual cortex. *Science, 268,* 1719–1720.

Moates, D. R., & Schumacher, G. M. (1980). *An introduction to cognitive psychology.* Belmont, CA: Wadsworth.

Moffat, S. D., Hampson, E., & Hatzipentalis, M. (1998). Navigation in a virtual maze: Sex differences and correlation with psychometric measures of spatial ability in humans. *Evolution and Human Behavior, 19,* 73–87.

Montello, D. R. (2005). Navigation. In P. Shah & A. Miyake (Eds.), *The Cambridge handbook of visuospatial thinking* (pp. 257–294). New York: Cambridge University Press.

Moray, N. (1959). Attention in dichotic listening: Affective cues and the influence of instructions. *Quarterly Journal of Experimental Psychology, 11,* 56–60.

Moray, N., Bates, A., & Barnett, T. (1965). Experiments on the four-eared man. *Journal of the Acoustical Society of America, 38,* 196–201.

Moscovitch, M. (1989). Confabulation and the frontal system: Strategic vs. associative retrieval in neuropsychological theories of memory. In H. L. Roediger III & F I. M. Craik (Eds.), *Varieties of memory and consciousness: Essays in honour of Endel Tulving* (pp. 133–160). Hillsdale, NJ: Erlbaum.

Moyer, R. S. (1973). Comparing objects in memory: Evidence suggesting an internal psychophysics. *Perception and Psychophysics, 13,* 180–184.

Mozer, M. C. (2002). Frames of reference in unilateral neglect and visual perception: A computational perspective. *Psychological Bulletin, 109,* 156–185.

Murdock, B. B. (1962). The serial position effect of free recall. *Journal of Experimental Psychology, 62,* 482–488.

Murphy, G L. (2005). The study of concepts inside and outside the laboratory: Medin versus Medin. In W. Ahn, R. L. Goldstone, B. C. Love, A. B. Mark-man, & P. Wolff (Eds.), *Categorization inside and outside the laboratory: Essays in honor of Douglas L. Medin* (pp. 179–196). Washington DC: American Psychological Association.

Murphy, G. L., & Medin, D. L. (1985). The role of theories in conceptual coherence. *Psychological Review, 92,* 289–316.

Murray, D. J. (1988). *A history of Western psychology* (2nd ed.). Englewood Cliffs, NJ: Prentice Hall.

Murtaugh, M. (1985). The practice of arithmetic by American grocery shoppers. *Anthropology and Education Quarterly, 16,* 186–192.

Nadel, L., Hupbach, A., Gomez, R., & Newman-Smith, K. (2012). Memory formation, consolidation and transformation. Neuroscience & Biobehavioral Reviews, 36(7), 1640-1645.

Nadel, L., & Moscovitch, M. (1997). Memory consolidation, retrograde amnesia and the hippocampal complex. *Current Opinions in Neurobiology, 2,* 217–227.

Nairne, J. S. (1997). *Psychology: The adaptive mind.* Pacific Grove, CA: Brooks/Cole.

Neath, I. (1998). Human memory: An introduction to research, data, and theory. Pacific Grove, CA: Brooks/Cole.

Neath, I., & Surprenant, A. (2003). *Human memory* (2nd ed.). Belmont, CA: Wadsworth.

Neely J. H. (1977). Semantic priming and retrieval from lexical memory: Roles of inhibitionless spreading activation and limited-capacity attention. *Journal of Experimental Psychology: General, 106,* 226–254.

Neely, J. H. (1990). Semantic priming effects in visual word recognition: A selective review of current findings and theories. In D. Besner & G Humphreys (Eds.), *Basic processes in reading: Visual word recognition.* Hillsdale, NJ: Erlbaum.

Neisser, U. (1963). Decision-time without reaction-time: Experiments in visual scanning. *American Journal of Psychology, 76,* 376–385.

Neisser, U. (1967). *Cognitive psychology.* New York: Appleton-Century-Crofts.

Neisser, U. (1976). Cognition and reality: Principles and implications of cognitive psychology. San Francisco: W. H. Freeman.

Neisser, U. (1982a). Memory: What are the important questions? In U. Neisser (Ed.), *Memory observed: Remembering in natural contexts* (pp. 3–19). San Francisco: W. H. Freeman.

Neisser, U. (1982b). Snapshots or benchmarks? In U. Neisser (Ed.), *Memory observed: Remembering in natural contexts* (pp. 43–48). San Francisco: W. H. Freeman.

Neisser, U. (1987). Introduction: The ecological and intellectual bases of categorization. In U. Neisser (Ed.), *Concepts and conceptual development: Ecological and intellectual factors in categorization* (pp. 1–10). Cambridge, UK: Cambridge University Press.

Newell, A., & Simon, H. A. (1972). *Human problem-solving.* Englewood Cliffs, NJ: Prentice Hall.

Newman E.J., Frenda S.J., Loftus E.F. (2014) False Memories. In: Bruinsma G., Weisburd D. (eds) Encyclopedia of Criminology and Criminal Justice. Springer, New York, NY

Nickerson, R. S., & Adams, M. J. (1979). Long-term memory for a common object. *Cognitive Psychology, 11,* 287–307.

Nisbett, R. E., Fong, G. T., Lehman, D. R., & Cheng, P. W. (1987). Teaching reasoning. *Science, 238,* 625–631.

Nisbett, R. E., Krantz, D. H., Jepson, C, & Kunda, Z. (1983). The use of statistical heuristics in everyday inductive reasoning. *Psychological Review, 90,* 339–363.

Nisbett, R., & Ross, L. (1980). *Human inference: Strategies and shortcomings.* Englewood Cliffs, NJ: Prentice Hall.

Norman, D. A. (1968). Toward a theory of memory and attention. *Psychological Review, 75,* 522–536.

Norman, D. A., & Bobrow, D. G (1975). On data-limited and resource-limited processes. *Cognitive Psychology, 7,* 44–64.

Norman, G., Young, M., & Brooks, L. (2007). Non-analytic models of clinical reasoning: The role of experience. *Medical Education, 41,* 1140–1145.

Nowakowski, R. S. (1987). Basic concepts of CNS development. *Child Development, 58,* 568–595.

Oakhill, J., Johnson-Laird, P. N., & Garnham, A. (1989). Believability and syllogistic reasoning. *Cognition, 31,* 117–140.

O'Craven, K. M., & Kanwisher, N. (2000). Mental imagery of faces and places activates corresponding stimulus-specific brain regions. *Journal of Cognitive Neuroscience, 12,* 1013–1023.

Olton, R. M. (1979). Experimental studies of incubation: Searching for the elusive. *Journal of Creative Behavior, 13,* 9–22.

Orne, M. T. (1962). On the social psychology of the psychology experiment: With particular reference to demand characteristics and their implication. *American Psychologist, 17,* 776–783.

Osherson, D. (1975). Logic and models of logical thinking. In R. J. Falmagne (Ed.), *Reasoning: Representation and process* (pp. 81–91). Hillsdale, NJ: Erlbaum.

Paivio, A. (1965). Abstractness, imagery, and meaningfulness in paired-associate learning. *Journal of Verbal Learning and Verbal Behavior, 4,* 32–38.

Paivio, A. (1969). Mental imagery in associative learning and memory. *Psychological Review, 76,* 241–263.

Paivio, A. (1971). *Imagery and verbal processes.* New York: Holt, Rinehart & Winston.

Paivio, A. (1975). Perceptual comparisons through the mind's eye. *Memory and Cognition, 3,* 635–647.

Paivio, A. (1983). The empirical case for dual coding. In J. C. Yuille (Ed.), *Imagery, memory and cognition* (pp. 307–332). Hillsdale, NJ: Erlbaum.

Palmer, S. E. (1975). The effects of contextual scenes on the identification of objects. *Memory and Cognition, 3,* 519–526.

Papp, K. R., Newsome, S. L., McDonald, J. E., & Schvaneveldt, R. W. (1982). An activation-verification model for letter and word recognition: The word-superiority effect. *Psychological Review, 89,* 573–594.

Park, D. C, & Puglisi, J. T. (1985). Older adults' memory for the color of pictures and words. *Journal of Gerontology, 40*(2), 198–204.

Park, D. C, Polk, T. A., Mikels, J. A., Taylor, S. F., & Marshuetz, C. (2001). Cerebral aging: Integration of brain and behavioural models of cognitive function. *Dialogues in Clinical Neuroscience: Cerebral Aging, 3,* 151–165.

Park, D. C, Puglisi, J., & Lutz, J. T. (1982). Spatial memory in older adults: Effects of intentionality *Journal of Gerontology, 37*(3), 330–335.

Pashler, H. E. (1993). Doing two things at the same time. *American Scientist, 81,* 48–55.

Pashler, H. E. (1998). *The psychology of attention.* Cambridge, MA: MIT Press.

Pashler, H., Johnston, J. C, & Ruthruff, E. (2001). Attention and performance. *Annual Review of Psychology, 52,* 629–651.

Pennycook, G., Ross, R.M., Koehler, D.J., & Fugelsang, J. (2017). Dunning-Kruger effects in reasoning: Theoretical implications of the failure to recognize incompetence. *Psychonomic Bulletin & Review, 24,* 1774–1784.

Perkins, D. N. (1981). *The mind's best work.* Cambridge, MA: Harvard University Press.

Perkins, D. N. (1985). Reasoning as imagination. *Interchange, 16,* 14–26.

Perky, C. W. (1910). An experimental study of imagination. *American Journal of Psychology, 21,* 422–452.

Petersen, S. E., Fox, P. T, Posner, M. I., Mintun, M. A., & Raichle, M. E. (1988). Positron emission tomographic studies of the cortical anatomy of single word processing. *Nature, 331,* 585–589.

Petersen, S. E., Fox, P. T., Snyder, A. Z., & Raichle, M. E. (1990). Activation of extrastriate and frontal cortical areas by visual words and word-like stimuli. *Science, 249,* 1041–1044.

Peterson, L. R., & Peterson, M. J. (1959). Short-term retention of individual items. *Journal of Experimental Psychology, 58,* 193–198.

Pexman, P. M. (in press). It's fascination research: The cognition of verbal irony. To appear in *Current Directions in Psychological Science.*

Pexman, P. M., Ferretti, T. R., & Katz, A. N. (2000). Discourse factors that influence on-line reading of metaphor and irony. *Discourse Processes, 29,* 201–222.

Pexman, P. M., Glenwright, M., Hala, S., Kowbel, S., & Jungen, S. (2006). Children's use of trait information in understanding verbal irony. *Metaphor & Symbol, 21,* 39–60.

Pinker, S. (1980). Mental imagery and the third dimension. *Journal of Experimental Psychology: General, 109,* 354–371.

Pinker, S. (2002). *The blank slate: The modern denial of human nature.* New York: Viking Press.

Plaut, D. C, McClelland, J. L., Seidenberg, M S., & Patterson, K. (1996). Understanding normal and impaired word reading: Computational principles in quasi-regular domains. *Psychological Review, 103,* 56–115.

Pomerantz, J. R., & Kubovy M. (1981). Perceptual organization: An overview. In M. Kubovy & J. R. Pomerantz (Eds.), *Perceptual organization* (pp. 423–456). Hillsdale, NJ: Erlbaum.

Posner, M. I., & Cohen, Y. (1984). Components of visual orienting. In H. Bouma, & D. G. Bouwhuis (Eds.), *Attention and performance X* (pp. 531–556). Hillsdale, NJ: Erlbaum.

Posner, M. I., & Fan, J. (2001, March). *Attention as an organ system.* Paper presented at Neurobiology of Perception and Communication: From Synapse to Society. De Lange Conference IV, Houston, Texas.

Posner, M. I., & Raichle, M. E. (1994). *Images of mind.* New York: Scientific American Library.

Posner, M. I., & Snyder, C. R. R. (1975). Attention and cognitive control. In R. L. Solso (Ed.), *Information processing and cognition: The Loyola Symposium* (pp. 55–85). Hillsdale, NJ: Erlbaum.

Posner, M. I., Nissen, M. J., & Ogden, W. C. (1978). Attended and unattended processing modes. The role of set for spatial location. In H. L. Pick & I. J. Saltzman (Eds.), *Modes of perceiving and processing information* (pp. 137–157). Hillsdale, NJ: Erlbaum.

Posner, M. I., Snyder, C. R. R., & Davidson, B. J. (1980). Attention and the detection of signals. *Journal of Experimental Psychology: General, 109,* 160–174.

Postman, L., & Phillips, L. (1965). Short-term temporal changes in free recall. *Quarterly Journal of Experimental Psychology, 17,* 132–138.

Postman, L., & Stark, K. (1969). Role of response availability in transfer and interference. *Journal of Experimental Psychology, 79,* 168–177.

Premack, D. (1976). *Language and intelligence in ape and man.* Hillsdale, NJ: Erlbaum.

Price, C. J., Moore, C. J., & Friston, K. J. (1997). Subtractions, conjunctions, and interactions in experimental design of activation studies. *Human Brain Mapping, 5,* 264–272.

Price, C. J., Wise, R. J. S., & Frackowiak, R. J. S. (1996). Demonstrating the implicit processing of visually presented words and pseudowords. *Cerebral Cortex, 6,* 62–70.

Pritchard, T. C, & Alloway, K. D. (1999). *Medical neuroscience.* Madison, CT: Fence Creek.

Pullum, G. K. (1991). *The great Eskimo vocabulary hoax and other irreverent essays on the study of language.* Chicago: University of Chicago Press.

Putnam, H. (1975). The meaning of "meaning." In H. Putnam (Ed.), *Philosophical papers: Vol. 2. Mind, language and reality* (pp. 215–271). New York: Cambridge University Press.

Pylyshyn, Z. W. (1973). What the minds eye tells the minds brain: A critique of mental imagery. *Psychological Bulletin, 80,* 1–24.

Pylyshyn, Z. W. (1981). The imagery debate: Analogue media versus tacit knowledge. *Psychological Review, 88,* 16–45.

Quinlan, P. T. (2003). Visual feature integration theory: Past, present, and future. *Psychological Bulletin, 129,* 643–673.

Quinn, P. C, Bhatt, R. S., Brush, D., Grimes, A., & Sharpnack, H. (2002). Development of form similarity as a Gestalt grouping principle in infancy. *Psychological Science, 13,* 320–328.

Radford, A. (1988). *Transformational grammar* Cambridge, UK: Cambridge University Press.

Ransdell, S.E., & Fischler, I. (1989). Effects of concreteness and task context on recall of prose among biligual and monolingual speakers. *Journal of Memory and Language, 28,* 278–291.

Rayner, K., & Sereno, S. C. (1994). Eye movements in reading. In M. A. Gernsbacher (Ed.), *Handbook of psycholinguistics* (pp. 57–81). San Diego, CA: Academic Press.

Raz, A., Shapiro, T, Fan, J., & Posner, M. I. (2002). Hypnotic suggestion and the modulation of Stroop interference. *Archives of General Psychiatry, 59,* 1155–1161.

Raz, N., Gunning, F. M., Head, D., Dupuis, J. H., McQuain, J., Briggs, S. D., Loken, W. J., Thornton, A. E., & Acker, J. D. (1997). Selective aging of the human cerebral cortex observed in vivo: Differential vulnerability of the prefrontal gray matter. *Cerebral Cortex, 7,* 268–282.

Raz, N., Lindenberger, U., Rodrigue, K. M., Kennedy, K. M., Head, D., Williamson, A., ... & Acker, J. D. (2005). Regional brain changes in aging healthy adults: general trends, individual differences and modifiers. Cerebral cortex, 15(11), 1676–1689.

Reber, A. S. (1967). Implicit learning of artificial grammars. *Journal of Verbal Learning and Verbal Behavior, 6,* 855–863.

Reber, A. S. (1976). Implicit learning of synthetic languages: The role of instructional set. *Journal of Experimental Psychology: Human Learning and Memory, 2,* 88–94.

Reed, S. K., Ernst, G. W., & Banerji, R. (1974). The role of analogy in transfer between similar problem states. *Cognitive Psychology, 6,* 436–450.

Reicher, G. M. (1969). Perceptual recognition as a function of meaningfulness of stimulus material. *Journal of Experimental Psychology, 81,* 275–280.

Reingold, E. M., Charness, N., Pomplun, M., & Stampe, D. M. (2001). Visual span in expert chess players: Evidence from eye movements. *Psychological Science, 12,* 49–56.

Rensink, R. A. (2002). Change detection. *Annual Review of Psychology, 53,* 245–277.

Reuter-Lorenz, P. A., Jonides, J., Smith, E. S., Hartley, A., Miller, A., Marshuetz, C, & Koeppe, R. A. (2000). Age differences in the frontal lateraliza-tion of verbal and spatial working memory revealed by PET. *Journal of Cognitive Neuroscience, 12,* 174–187.

Riby L. M., Perfect, T. J., & Stollery B. T. (2004). Evidence for disproportionate dual-task costs in older adults for episodic but not semantic memory. *Quarterly Journal of Experimental Psychology, 57A,* 241–267.

Rips, J. (1984). Reasoning as a central intellective ability. In R. J. Sternberg (Ed.), *Advances in the psychology of human intelligence* (Vol. 2, pp. 105–147). Hillsdale, NJ: Erlbaum.

Rips, L. J. (1988). Deduction. In R. J. Sternberg & E. E. Smith (Eds.), *The psychology of human thought* (pp. 116–152). Cambridge, UK: Cambridge University Press.

Rips, L. J. (1990). Reasoning. *Annual Review of Psychology, 41,* 321–353.

Rips, L. J. (2001). Two kinds of reasoning. *Psychological Science, 12,* 129–134.

Risko, E. F., Stolz, J. A., & Besner, D. (2005). Basic processes in reading: Is visual word recognition obligatory? *Psychonomic Bulletin & Review, 12,* 119–124.

Rizzella, M. L., & O'Brien, E. J. (2002). Retrieval of concepts in script-based texts and narratives: The influence of general world knowledge. *Journal of Experimental Psychology: Learning, Memory, and Cognition, 28,* 780–790.

Roediger, H. L., III. (1990). Implicit memory: Retention without remembering. *American Psychologist, 45,* 1043–1056.

Roediger, H. L., III, & Guynn, M. J. (1996). Retrieval processes. In E. L. Bjork & R. A. Bjork (Eds.), *Memory* (pp. 197–236). San Diego, CA: Academic Press.

Roland, P. E., & Friberg, L. (1985). Localization of cortical areas activated by thinking. *Journal of Neurophysiology, 53,* 1219–1243.

Rosch, E. (1973). On the internal structure of perceptual and semantic categories. In T. E. Moore (Ed.), *Cognitive development and the acquisition of language* (pp. 111–144). New York: Academic Press.

Rosch, E., & Mervis, C. B. (1975). Family resemblances: Studies in the internal structure of categories. *Cognitive Psychology, 7,* 573–605.

Rosch, E., Mervis, C. B., Gray, W. D., Johnson, D. M., & Boyes-Braem, P. (1976). Basic objects in natural categories. *Cognitive Psychology, 8,* 382–439.

Rosch, E., Simpson, C, & Miller, R. S. (1976). Structural bases of typicality effects. *Journal of Experimental Psychology: Human Perception and Performance, 2,* 491–502.

Rosen, A. C, Prull, M. W., O'Hara, R., Race, E. A., Desmond, J. E., Glover, G. H., Yesavag, J. A., & Gabrieli, J. D. E. (2002). Variable effects of aging on frontal lobe contributions to memory. *Neuroreport: For Rapid Communication of Neuroscience Research, 13*(18), 2425–2428.

Rosenbaum, R.S., Gilboa, A., Levine, B., Winocur, G., & Moscovitch, M. (2009). Amnesia as an impairment of detail generation and binding: Evidence from personal, fictional, and semantic narratives in K.C. Neuropsychologia, 47, 2181–2187.

Rosenbaum, R. S., Köhler, S., Schacter, D. L., Moscovitch, M., Westmacott, R., Black, S. E., Gao, F, & Tulving, E. (2005). The case of K.C.: Contributions of a memory-impaired person to memory theory. *Neuropsychologia, 43,* 989–1021.

Rosenbaum, R. S., Priselac, S., Köhler, S., Black, S. E., Gao, F. Q., Nadel, L., & Moscovitch, M. (2000). Studies of remote spatial memory in an amnesic person with extensive bilateral hippocampal lesions. *Nature Neuroscience, 3,* 1044–1048.

Ross, J., & Lawrence, K. A. (1968). Some observations on memory artifice. *Psychonomic Science, 13,* 107–108.

Ross, M., & Sicoly F. (1979). Egocentric biases in availability and attribution. *Journal of Personality and Social Psychology, 37,* 322–336.

Ross, M. H., Yurgelun-Todd, D. A., Renshaw, P. F., Maas, L. C, Mendelson, J. H., & Mello, N. K. (1997). Age-related reduction in functional MRI response to photic stimulation. *Neurology, 48,* 173–176.

Rosselli, M., Ardila, A., Araujo, K., Weekes, V. A., Caracciolo, V., Padilla, M., & Ostrosky-Solis, F. (2000). Verbal fluency and repetition skills in healthy older Spanish-English bilinguals. *Applied Neuropsychology, 7,* 17–24.

Roth, E. M., & Shoben, E. J. (1983). The effect of context on the structure of categories. *Cognitive Psychology, 15,* 346–378.

Rubens, A. B., & Benson, D. F. (1971). Associative visual agnosia. *Archives of Neurology, 24,* 305–316.

Rubia, K., & Smith, A. (2001). Attention deficit-hyperactivity disorder: Current findings and treatment. *Current Opinion in Psychiatry, 14,* 309–316.

Rugg, M. D. (1997). Introduction. In M. D. Rugg (Ed.), *Cognitive neuroscience* (pp. 1–10). Cambridge, MA: MIT Press.

Rumelhart, D. E. (1989). The architecture of mind: A connectionist approach. In M. I. Posner (Ed), *Foundations of cognitive science* (pp. 133–159). Cambridge, MA: Bradford Books.

Rumelhart, D. E., & McClelland, J. L. (1982). An interactive activation model of context effects in letter perception: Part 2. The contextual enhancement effect and some tests and extensions of the model. *Psychological Review, 89,* 60–94.

Rumelhart, D. E., & Norman, D. A. (1988). Representation in memory. In R. C. Atkinson (Ed), *Stevens' handbook of experimental psychology: Vol. 2. Learning and cognition* (2nd ed., pp. 511–587). New York: Wiley

Rumelhart, D. E., & Todd, P. M. (1993). Learning and connectionist representations. In D. E. Meyer & S. Kornblum (Eds), *Attention and performance XIV* (pp. 3–30). Cambridge, MA: MIT Press/ Bradford Books.

Runco, M. A. (2004). Creativity. *Annual Review of Psychology, 55,* 657–687.

Runco, M. A., & Sakamoto, S. O. (1999). Experimental studies of creativity. In R. J. Sternberg (Ed), *Handbook of creativity* (pp. 62–92). Cambridge, UK: Cambridge University Press.

Ryan, L., Nadel, L., Keil, K, Putnam, K, Schnyer, D., Trouard, T, Moscovitch, M. (2000). Hippocampal complex and retrieval of recent and very remote autobiographical memories: Evidence from functional magnetic resonance imaging in neurologically intact people. *Hippocampus, 11*(6), 707–14.

Sacks, O. (1985). The man who mistook his wife for a hat, and other clinical tales. New York: Summit Books.

Salthouse, T. A. (1982). *Adult cognition.* New York: Springer-Verlag.

Salthouse, T. A. (1991). *Theoretical perspectives in cognitive aging.* Hillside, NJ: Erlbaum.

Salthouse, T. A. (1996). The processing speed theory of adult age differences in cognition. *Psychology Review, 103,* 403–428.

Sanfey, A. G., Rilling, J. K., Aronson, J. A., Nystrom, L. E., & Cohen, J. D. (2003). The neural basis of economic decision-making in the ultimatum game. *Science, 300,* 1755–1758.

Saucier, D. M., Green, S. M., Leason, J., MacFadden, A., Bell, S., Elias, L. J. (2002). Are sex differences in navigation caused by sexually dimorphic strategies or by differences in the ability to use the strategies? *Behavioral Neuroscience, 116,* 403–410.

Savage-Rumbaugh, S., McDonald, K., Sevcik, R. A., Hopkins, W. D., & Rubert, E. (1986). Spontaneous symbol acquisition and communicative use by pygmy chimpanzees *(Pan paniscus). Journal of Experimental Psychology: General, 115,* 211–235.

Schacter, D. L. (1987). Implicit memory: History and current status. *Journal of Experimental Psychology: Learning, Memory and Cognition, 13,* 501–518.

Schacter, D. L. (1989). On the relation between memory and consciousness: Dissociable interactions and conscious experience. In H. L. Roediger III & F. I. M. Craik (Eds.), *Varieties of memory and consciousness* (pp. 355–389). Hillsdale, NJ: Erlbaum.

Schacter, D. L. (1996). Searching for memory: The brain, the mind, and the past. New York: Basic Books.

Schneider, W., & Shiffrin, R. M. (1977). Controlled and automatic human information processing: I. Detection, search, and attention. *Psychological Re-view, 84,* 1–66.

Schraw, G., Dunkle, M. E., & Bendixen, L. D. (1995). Cognitive processes in well-defined and ill-defined problem solving. *Applied Cognitive Psychology, 9,* 523–538.

Schwartz, S. P. (1978). Putnam on artifacts. *Philosophical Review, 87,* 566–574.

Schwartz, S. P. (1979). Natural kind terms. *Cognition, 7,* 301–315.

Schwartz, S. P. (1980). Natural kinds and nominal kinds. *Mind, 89,* 182–195.

Scoville, W. B., & Milner, B. (1957). Loss of recent memory after bilateral hippocampal lesions. *Journal of Neurology, Neurosurgery, & Psychiatry, 20,* 11–21.

Searle, J. R. (1979). *Expression and meaning: Studies in the theory of speech acts.* Cambridge, UK: Cambridge University Press.

Sedlmeier, P., & Gigerenzer, G (2000). Was Bernoulli wrong? On intuitions about sample size. *Journal of Behavioral Decision Making, 13,* 133–139.

Seger, C. A. (2008). How do the basal ganglia contribute to categorization? Their roles in generalization, response selection, and learning via feedback. *Neuroscience and Biobehavioral Reviews, 32,* 265–278.

Seger, C. A., Poldrack, R. A., Prabhakaran, V., Zhao, M., Glover, G H., & Gabrieli, J. D. E. (2000). Hemispheric asymmetries and individual differences in visual concept learning as measured by functional MRI. *Neuropsychology, 14, 361–369.*

Sekuler, A. B., & Bennett, P. J. (2001). Generalized common fate: Grouping by common luminance change. *Psychological Science, 12,* 437–444.

Selfridge, O. G (1959). Pandemonium: A paradigm for learning. In *Symposium on the mechanization of thought processes* (pp. 513–526). London: HM Stationery Office.

Shepard, R. N. (1966). Learning and recall as organization and search. *Journal of Verbal Learning and Verbal Behavior, 5,* 201–204.

Shepard, R. N. (1967). Recognition memory for words, sentences, and pictures. *Journal of Verbal Learning and Verbal Behavior, 6,* 156–163.

Shepard, R. N., & Metzler, J. (1971). Mental rotation of three-dimensional objects. *Science, 171,* 701–703.

Shiffrin, R. M. (1988). Attention. In R. C. Atkinson, R. J. Herrnstein, G. Lindzey & R. D. Luce (Eds.), *Stevens' handbook of experimental psychology: Vol. 2. Learning and cognition* (2nd ed., pp. 739–811). New York: Wiley

Shimura, A. P. (1986). Priming effects in amnesia: Evidence for a dissociable memory function. *Quarterly Journal of Experimental Psychology, 38A,* 619–644.

Shimura, A. P. (1995). Memory and frontal lobe function. In M. S. Gazzaniga (Ed.), *The cognitive neurosciences* (pp. 803–813). Cambridge, MA: Bradford.

Simons, D. J., & Ambinder, M. S. (2005). Change blindness: Theory and consequences. *Current Directions in Psychological Science, 14,* 44–48.

Simons, D. J. & Chabris, C. F. (1999). Gorillas in our midst: Sustained inattentional blindness for dynamic events. *Perception, 28,* 1059–1074.

Simons, D. J., & Levin, D. T. (1997). Change blindness. *Trends in Cognitive Sciences, 1,* 261–267.

Simons, D. J., Nevarez, G., & Boot, W. R. (2005). Visual sensing *is* seeing: Why mindsight' in hindsight, is blind. *Psychological Science, 16,* 520–524.

Singer, M., & Rembillard, G. (2004). Retrieving text inferences: Controlled and automatic influences. *Memory & Cognition, 21,* 1223–1237.

Skinner, B. F. (1984). Behaviorism at fifty. *Behavioral and Brain Sciences, 7,* 615–667. (Original work published 1963)

Skyrms, B. (1975). Choice and chance: An introduction to inductive logic (2nd ed.). Encino, CA: Dickenson.

Smilek, D., Birmingham, E., Cameron, D., Bischof, W., & Kingstone, A. Cognitive Ethology and exploring attention in real-world scenes. *Brain Re-search, 1080,* 101–119.

Smith, A. D. (1977). Adult age differences in cued recall. *Developmental Psychology, 13*(4), 326–331.

Smith, A. D., Park, D. C, Cherry, K., Berkovsky K. (1990). Age differences in memory for concrete and abstract pictures. *Journal of Gerontology, 45*(5), 205–209.

Smith, E. E., & Medin, D. L. (1981). *Categories and concepts.* Cambridge, MA: Harvard University Press.

Smith, E. E., Shoben, E. J., & Rips, L. J. (1974). Structure and process in semantic memory: A featural model for semantic decisions. *Psychological Review, 81,* 214–241.

Smith, J. D., & Kemler, D. G (1984). Overall similarity in adults' classification: The child in all of us. *Journal of Experimental Psychology: General, 113,* 137–159.

Smith, M. C. (1979). Contextual facilitation in a letter search task depends on how the prime is processed. *Journal of Experimental Psychology: Human Perception and Performance, 5,* 239–251.

Smith, M. C, Besner, D., & Miyoshi, H. (1994). New limits to automaticity: Context modulates semantic priming. *Journal of Experimental Psychology: Learning, Memory, and Cognition, 20,* 104–115.

Smith, Stephen. (2016). Linking cognition to brain connectivity. Nature neuroscience, 19, 1, 7-9.

Smith, S. M., & Blakenship, S. E. (1989). Incubation effects. *Bulletin of the Psychonomic Society, 27,* 311–314.

Smith, S. M., Brown, H. O., Toman, J. E. P., & Goodman, L. S. (1947). The lack of cerebral effects of d-tubercurarine. *Anesthesiology, 8,* 1–14.

Spelke, E., Hirst, W., & Neisser, U. (1976). Skills of divided attention. *Cognition, 4,* 215–230.

Sperling, G (1960). The information available in brief visual presentations. *Psychological Monographs, 74* (Whole No. 498).

Springer, S. P., & Deutsch, G. (1998). *Left brain, right brain: Perspectives from cognitive neuroscience* (5th ed.). New York: W. H. Freeman.

Squire, L. R., Cohen, N. J., & Nadel, L. The medial temporal region and memory consolidation: A new hypothesis. In H. Weingartner and E. Parker (Eds.), *Memory Consolidation,* Hillsdale, NJ: Lawrence Erlbaum Associates, 1984, 185–210.

Stebbins, G. T., Carrillo, M. C, Dorman, J., Dirksen, C, Desond, J., Turner, D. A., Bennett, D. A., Wilson, R. S., Glover, G, & Gabrieli, D. E. (2002). Aging effects on memory encoding in the frontal lobes. *Psychology & Aging, 17,* 44–55.

Stein, B. S., & Bransford, J. D. (1979). Constraints on effective elaboration: Effects of precision and subject generation. *Journal of Verbal Learning and Verbal Behavior, 18,* 769–777.

Sternberg, R. J. (1986a). Intelligence applied: Understanding and increasing your intellectual skills. San Diego: Harcourt Brace Jovanovich.

Sternberg, R. J. (1986b). Toward a unified theory of human reasoning. *Intelligence, 10,* 281–314.

Sternberg, R. J. (1988). A three-facet model of creativity. In R. J. Sternberg (Ed.), *The nature of creativity: Contemporary psychological perspectives* (pp. 125–147). Cambridge, UK: Cambridge University Press.

Sternberg, R. J. (2006). *Cognitive psychology.* California, USA: Thomson Wadsworth.

Sternberg, R. J., & Detterman, D. K. (Eds.). (1986). What is intelligence? Contemporary viewpoints on its nature and definition. Norwood, NJ: Ablex.

Sternberg, S. (1966). High-speed scanning in human memory. *Science, 153,* 652–654.

Sternberg, S. (1969). Memory-scanning: Mental processes revealed by reaction-time experiments. *American Scientist, 57,* 421–457.

Strayer, D. L., & Johnston, W. A. (2001). Driven to distraction: Dual-task studies of simulated driving and conversing on a cellular telephone. *Psychological Science, 12,* 462–466.

Stolz, J. A., & Besner, D. (1996). The role of set in visual word recognition: Activation and activation blocking as non-automatic processes. *Journal of Experimental Psychology: Human Perception and Performance, 22,* 1166–1177.

Stolz, J. A., & Besner, D. (1998). Levels of representation in visual word recognition: A dissociation between morphological and semantic processing. *Journal of Experimental Psychology: Human Perception and Performance, 24,* 1642–1655.

Strategies for Reducing Driver Distraction from In-Vehicle Telematics Devices: A Discussion Document. (2003). TP14133E. Prepared by: Standards Research and Development Branch: Road Safety and Motor Vehicle Regulations Directorate. Government of Canada.

Streimer, C, & Danckert, J. (2007). Prism adaptation reduces the disengage deficit in right brain damage patients. *Neuroreport, 18*, 99–103.

Stroop, J. R. (1935). Studies of interferences in serial verbal reactions. *Journal of Experimental Psychology, 18*, 643–662.

Stuss, D. T. (1986). Language functioning after bilateral prefrontal leucotomy *Brain & Language, 28*, 66–70.

Stuss, D. T. (1992). Biological and psychological development of executive functions. *Brain and Cognition, 20*, 8–23.

Stuss, D. T., Alexander, M. P., Palumbo, C. L., Buckle, L., Sayer, L., & Pogue, J. (1994). Organizational strategies of patients with unilateral or bilateral frontal lobe injury in word list learning tasks. *Neuropsychology, 8*, 355–373.

Stuss, D. T., Alexander, M. P., Hamer, L., Palumbo, C., Dempster, R., Binns, M., & Izukawa, D. (1998). The effects of focal anterior and posterior brain lesions on verbal fluency. *Journal of the International Neuropsychological Society, 4*(3), 265–278.

Suess, H., Oberauere, K., Wittman, W. W., Wilhelm, O., & Schulze, R. (2002). Working-memory capacity explains reasoning ability—and a little bit more. *Intelligence, 30*, 261–288.

Swinney D. A. (1979). Lexical access during sentence comprehension: (Re)consideration of context effects. *Journal of Verbal Learning and Verbal Behavior, 18*, 645–659.

Tanenhaus, M. K., Magnuson, J. S. , Dahan, D. , & Chambers, C. (2000). Eye movements and lexical access in spoken-language comprehension: Evaluating a linking hypothesis between fixations and linguistic processing. *Journal of Psycholinguistic Research, 29*, 557–580.

Tarr, M. J. (2000). Visual pattern recognition. In A.E. Kazdin, (Ed.), *Encyclopedia of psychology* (pp.1–4). Washington, DC: American Psychological Association.

Tarr, M. J., & Pinker, S. (1989). Mental rotation and orientation-dependence in shape recognition. *Cognitive Psychology, 21*, 233–282.

Terrace, H. S. (1979). *Nim.* New York: Knopf.

Tetlock, P. E. (2002). The virtues of cognitive humility: For us as well as them. In R. Gowda & J. C. Fox (Eds.), *Judgments, decisions, and public policy* (pp. 355–368). New York: Cambridge University Press.

Thaler, R. H. (1980). Toward a positive theory of consumer choice. *Journal of Economic Behavior and Organization, 1*, 39–60.

Thomas, H., Jamison, W., & Hummel, D. D. (1973). Observation is insufficient for discovering that the surface of still water is invariantly horizontal. *Science, 181*, 173–174.

Thomson, D. M., & Tulving, E. (1970). Associative encoding and retrieval: Weak and strong cues. *Journal of Experimental Psychology, 86*, 255–262.

Thompson, V. (1996). Reasoning from false premises: The role of soundness in making logical deductions. *Canadian Journal of Experimental Psychology, 50,* 315–319.

Thompson, V. A. Prowse-Turner, J., & Pennycook, G. (2011). Intuition, reason, and metacognition. *Cognitive Psychology, 63,* 107–140.

Thompson, V, Striemer C, Rielkoff R., Gunter R., & Campbell, J. (2003). Syllogistic reasoning time: Disconfirmation disconfirmed. *Psychonomic Bulletin & Review, 10*(1), 184–189.

Torrens, D., Thompson, VA., & Cramer, K. (1999). Individual differences and the belief-bias effect: Mental models, logical necessity, and abstract reasoning. *Thinking and Reasoning, 5,* 1–28.

Toth, J. P., Lindsay, D. S., & Jacoby L. L. (1992). Awareness, automaticity and memory dissociations. In L. R. Squire & N. Butters (Eds.), *Neuropsychology of memory* (2nd ed., pp. 46–71). New York: Guilford Press.

Toth, J. P., Reingold, E. M., & Jacoby, L. L. (1994). Toward a redefinition of implicit memory: Process dissociations following elaborative processing andself-generation. *Journal of Experimental Psychology: Learning, Memory, and Cognition, 20,* 290–303.

Trabasso, T, Secco, T, & van den Broek, P. W. (1984). Causal cohesion and story coherence. In H. Mandl, N. L. Stein, & T. Trabasso (Eds.), *Learning and comprehension of text* (pp. 83–111). Hillsdale, NJ: Erlbaum.

Trabasso, T, & van den Broek, P. W. (1985). Causal thinking and the representation of narrative events. *Journal of Memory and Language, 24,* 612–630.

Treisman, A. M. (1960). Contextual cues in selective listening. *Quarterly Journal of Experimental Psychology, 12,* 242–248.

Treisman, A. M. (1964). Verbal cues, language, and meaning in selective attention. *American Journal of Psychology, 77,* 206–219.

Treisman, A. M., & Gelade, G. (1980). A feature integration theory of attention. *Cognitive Psychology, 12,* 97–136.

Treisman, A. M., & Schmidt, H. (1982). Illusory conjunctions in the perception of objects. *Cognitive Psychology, 14,* 107–141.

Tsal, Y. (1989a). Do illusory conjunctions support the feature integration theory? A critical review of theory and findings. *Journal of Experimental Psychology: Human Perception and Performance, 15,* 394–400.

Tsal, Y. (1989b). Further comments on feature integration: A reply to Briand and Klein. *Journal of Experimental Psychology: Human Perception and Performance, 15,* 407–410.

Tulving, E. (1972). Episodic and semantic memory. In E. Tulving & W. Donaldson (Eds.), *Organization of memory* (pp. 381–403). New York: Academic Press.

Tulving, E. (1983). *Elements of episodic memory.* New York: Oxford University Press.

Tulving, E. (1989). Remembering and knowing the past. *American Scientist, 77,* 361–367.

Tulving, E. (1995). Introduction to Section IV: Memory. In M. S. Gazzaniga (Ed.), *The cognitive neurosciences* (pp. 751–753). Cambridge, MA: Bradford.

Tulving, E., & Thomson, D. M. (1973). Encoding specificity and retrieval processes in episodic memory. *Psychological Review, 80,* 352–373.

Tulving, E., Hayman, C. A. G, & MacDonald, C. A. (1991). Long-lasting perceptual priming and semantic learning in amnesia—A case experiment. *Journal of Experimental Psychology: Learning, Memory & Cognition, 17,* 595–617.

Turvey M. T, Shaw, R. E., Reed, E. S., & Mace, W. M. (1981). Ecological laws of perceiving and acting: In reply to Fodor and Pylyshyn (1981). *Cognition, 9,* 237–304.

Tversky A., & Kahneman, D. (1971). Belief in the law of small numbers. *Psychological Bulletin, 2,* 105–110.

Tversky, A., & Kahneman, D. (1973). Availability: A heuristic for judging frequency and probability. *Cognitive Psychology, 4,* 207–232.

Tversky, A., & Kahneman, D. (1981). The framing of decisions and the psychology of choice. *Science, 211,* 453–458.

Tversky, A., & Kahneman, D. (2000). Judgment under uncertainty: Heuristics and biases. In T. Connolly, H. R. Arkes, & K. R. Hammond *(Eds.), Judgment and decision making* (2nd ed., pp. 35–52). New York: Cambridge University Press.

Tversky, B. (1981). Distortions in memory for maps. *Cognitive Psychology, 13,* 407–433.

Tversky, B. (2005). Functional significance of visuospatial representations. In P. Shah & A. Miyake (Eds.), *The Cambridge handbook of visuospatial thinking* (pp. 1–34). New York: Cambridge University Press.

Underwood, B. J. (1957). Interference and forgetting. *Psychological Review, 64,* 49–60.

van den Broek, P., & Gustafson, M. (1999). Comprehension and memory for texts: Three generations of reading research. In S. R. Goldman, A. C. Graesser, & P. van den Broek (Eds.), *Narrative comprehension, causality, and coherence: Essays in honor of Tom Trabasso* (pp. 15–34). Mahwah, NJ: Erlbaum.

Van der Linden, M., Brédart, S., & Beerten, A. (1994). Age-related differences in updating working memory. *British Journal of Psychology, 85*(1), 145–152.

Villejoubert, G. (2005). Could they have known better? Review of the special issue of Memory on the Hindsight Bias. *Applied Cognitive Psychology, 19,* 140–143.

von Winterfeldt, D., & Edwards, W. (1986a). *Decision analysis and behavioral research.* Cambridge, UK: Cambridge University Press.

von Winterfeldt, D., & Edwards, W. (1986b). On cognitive illusions and their implications. In H. R. Arkes & K. R. Hammond (Eds.), *Judgment and decision making: An interdisciplinary reader* (pp.642–679). Cambridge, UK: Cambridge University Press.

Voyer, D., Voyer, S., & Bryden, M. P. (1995). Magnitude of sex differences in spatial abilities: A meta-analysis. *Psychological Bulletin, 117,* 250–270.

Waltz, J. A., Knowlton, B. J., Holyoak, K. J., Boone, K. B., Maishkin, F. S., de Menezes Santos, M., Thomas, C. R., & Miller, B. L. (1999). A system for relational reasoning in human prefrontal cortex. *Psychological Science, 10,* 119–125.

Wang, D., Buckner, R.L., & Liu, H. (2014). Functional Specialization in the Human Brain Estimated By Intrinsic Hemispheric Interaction Journal of Neuroscience, 34 (37) 12341-12352; DOI: 10.1523/JNEUROSCI.0787-14.2014

Ward, J. (2015). The student's guide to cognitive neuroscience New York, New York : Psychology Press

Ward, T. B., Smith, S. M., & Finke, R. A. (1999). Creative cognition. In R. J. Sternberg (Ed.), *Handbook of creativity* (pp. 189–212). Cambridge, UK: Cambridge University Press.

Warren, R. M. (1970). Perceptual restoration of missing speech sounds. *Science, 167,* 392–393.

Warren, R. M., & Obusek, C. J. (1971). Speech perception and phonemic restorations. *Perception and Psychophysics, 9,* 358–362.

Warrington, E. K., & Shallice, T. (1984). Category specific semantic impairments. *Brain, 107,* 829–854.

Warrington, E. K., & Weiskrantz, L. (1970). Amnesic syndrome: Consolidation or retrieval? *Nature, 228,* 628–630.

Wason, P. C. (1960). On the failure to eliminate hypotheses in a conceptual task. *Quarterly Journal of Experimental Psychology, 12,* 129–140.

Wason, P. C. (1968). Reasoning about a rule. *Quarterly Journal of Experimental Psychology, 20,* 273–281.

Wason, P. C. (1969). Regression in reasoning? *British Journal of Psychology, 60,* 471–480.

Wason, P. C. (1977). "On the failure to eliminate hypotheses . . ."—a second look. In P. N. Johnson-Laird & P. C. Wason (Eds.), *Thinking: Readings in cognitive science* (pp. 307–314). Cambridge, UK: Cambridge University Press.

Wason, P. C. (1983). Realism and rationality in the selection task. In J. St. B. T. Evans (Ed.), *Thinking and reasoning: Psychological approaches* (pp. 44–75). Boston: Routledge & Kegan Paul.

Wason, P. C, & Johnson-Laird, P. N. (1970). A conflict between selecting and evaluating information in an inferential task. *British Journal of Psychology, 61,* 509–515.

Watkins, O. C, & Watkins, M. J. (1980). The modality effect and visual persistence. *Journal of Experimental Psychology: General, 109,* 251–278.

Watson, J. B. (1930). *Behaviorism.* New York: Norton.

Waugh, N. C, & Norman, D. A. (1965). Primary memory. *Psychological Review, 72,* 89–104.

Weisberg, R. W (1988). Problem solving and creativity. In R. J. Sternberg (Ed.), *The nature of creativity* (pp. 148–176). Cambridge, UK: Cambridge University Press.

Welford, A. T. (1952). The "psychological refractory period" and the timing of high speed performance: A review and a theory. *British Journal of Psychology, 43,* 2–19.

Wells, G. L., & Hasel, L. E. (2007). Facial composite production by eyewitnesses. *Current Directions in Psychological Science, 16,* 6–10.

West, R. L. (1996). An application of prefrontal cortex function theory to cognitive aging. *Psychology Bulletin, 120,* 272–292.

Whittlesea, B. W A., & Price, J. R. (2001). Implicit/ explicit memory versus analytic/nonana-lytic processing: Rethinking the mere exposure effect. *Memory & Cognition, 29,* 234–246.

Whorf, B. L. (1956). *Language, thought, and reality.* Cambridge, MA: MIT Press.

Wickens, D. D., Born, D. G., & Allen, C. K. (1963). Proactive inhibition and item similarity in short-term memory. *Journal of Verbal Learning and Verbal Behavior, 2,* 440–445.

Williams, J. H. (1983). *Psychology of women: Behavior in a biosocial context,* 2nd ed. New York: Norton.

Wilson, J. F. (2003). *Biological foundations of human behavior.* Belmont, CA: Thomson.

Wingfield, A. (2016). Evolution of models of working memory and cognitive resources. *Ear and hearing,* 37, 35S–43S.

Winston, P. H. (1992). *Artificial intelligence* (3rd ed.). Boston: Addison-Wesley

Wittgenstein, L. (1953). *Philosophical investigations.* New York: Macmillan.

Wood, N. L., & Cowan, N. (1995). The cocktail party phenomenon revisited: Attention and memory in the classic selective listening procedure of Cherry (1953). *Journal of Experimental Psychology: General, 124,* 243–262.

Woods, S. K, & Ploof, W. H. (1997). Understanding ADHD: Attention deficit hyperactivity disorder and the feeling brain. Thousand Oaks, CA: Sage.

Woodworth, R. S., & Sells, S. B. (1935). An atmosphere effect in formal syllogistic reasoning. *Journal of Experimental Psychology, 18,* 451–460.

Xu, Y, & Corkin, S. (2001). H.M. revisits the Tower of Hanoi puzzle. *Neuropsychology, 15,* 69–79.

Yuille, J. C. (Ed.). (1983). *Imagery, memory and cognition.* Hillsdale, NJ: Erlbaum.

Zatorre, R. J., Halpern, A. R., Perry, D. W, Meyer, E., & Evans, A. C. (1996). Hearing in the minds ear: A PET investigation of musical imagery and perception. *Journal of Cognitive Neuroscience, 8,* 29–46.

Zillmer, E. A., & Spiers, M. V. (2001). *Principles of neuropsychology.* Belmont, CA: Wadsworth.